THE Whisk(e)y
TREASURY

THE WORLD'S MOST COMPLETE WHISK(E)Y A TO Z
WALTER SCHOBERT

The Whisk(e)y Treasury

www.angelshare.co.uk

The Angels' Share is an imprint of
Neil Wilson Publishing Ltd
303a The Pentagon Centre
36 Washington Street
GLASGOW
G3 8AZ

Tel: 0141-221-1117
Fax: 0141-221-5363
E-mail: info@nwp.sol.co.uk
www.nwp.co.uk

Originally published in German by Wolfgang Krüger Verlag GmbH, 1999.
Original edition © Wolfgang Krüger Verlag GmbH, Frankurt am main 1999.

This English language edition published in 2002 © Walter Schobert, 2002.

The author has asserted his moral right under the
Design, Patents and Copyright Act, 1988, to be identified
as the Author of this Work.

A catalogue record for this book is available from the British Library.

ISBN 1-903238-01-3
Typeset in Bodoni
Designed by Belstane
Printed by WS Bookwell, Finland

Contents

Foreword by James McEwan,
Master Distiller, Bruichladdich Distillery   vii

Preface   ix

A to Z of references   1

Bibliography   367

Foreword

I first met Walter Schobert some years ago when I collected him from Glasgow Airport and took him and a number of other journalists over to Islay via Oban. Our route took us down through rural Argyll in order to make the ferry at Kennacraig on West Loch Tarbert. As we headed south Walter began to point out many of the remote kirks which we passed along the way and then started to tell me the history of each one. I was flabbergasted. 'How on earth do you know so much about these kirks?' I asked.

'It helps if you are a minister!' he replied and then revealed that he was not just a noted whisky writer, but had also been a minister in the German Lutheran Church, the director of the German Filmmuseum and a professor at Heidelberg University!

In a sense Walter's love of whisky – the spirit of Scotland – is reflected in this marvellous book. It is truly a bible for anyone with a love for the subject and I believe it will become the standard reference work on the subject. His gospel betrays his outstanding knowledge of whisky on a worldwide basis, one that has earned him respect and admiration – particularly in his native Germany where his efforts in raising the profile of Scotch are legendary.

Establishing a second home on Islay has brought Walter even closer to his favourite subject and he hopes to retire permanently there. Such commitment is to be valued because the Scotch industry needs people like Walter who works tirelessly for it for little or no return.

The Whisk(e)y Treasury is Walter's magnum opus and if you have the least bit of interest in Scotch you should value this book.

by **James McEwan**
Master Distiller, Bruichladdich Distillery

Preface

The original German-language edition of this book accompanied me during three years of my life – three long years. It took another two years to complete the work for the English edition, thus making a grand total of five years, in which it was continually necessary to add new entries and revise old ones. New brands came onto the market, venerable old companies disappeared, there were mergers and takeovers – both friendly and hostile: all processes which many regard as quite modern events in today's world, but which, until recently, were not so usual in the whisk(e)y industry, with its long tradition and roots going back into the past two centuries. Of course the merry-go-round has never before turned as quickly as it does today.

Just four years ago Guinness and GrandMetropolitan merged to form Diageo, the world's largest drinks company. The consequences can still be felt today and have not only affected many spheres in many countries – the effects reach into this book as well. In the spring of 2000 the news broke that Seagram was to be sold to the French company Vivendi. The wine and spirits portfolio was to go to a consortium made up of Groupe Pernod-Ricard and Diageo. The deal is now completed and I have tried to take this into account in this book. The French company are going to take over Seagram's Scottish activities which were run by the Chivas & Glenlivet Group with its flagships Chivas Regal and Glenlivet.

Such developments made it necessary to amend many entries. And the changes will continue. It is in the nature of a book like this that it is no longer totally up-to-date on the day that it goes to press and new information up to May of 2002 has been incorporated. After that date the first gaps will begin to appear. Perhaps it will be possible to keep readers informed via the Internet in the future ... we shall see.

It is also inevitable that such a book is incomplete – and contains mistakes – just like every other book since cuneiform characters were first chiselled into stone. I am grateful when they are pointed out to me so that they can be eliminated in later editions. As for trying to achieve a fully comprehensive book ... well, there are more than 4,000 Scotch whisky blends; they come and they go. Even in the case of malt whisky, which until a few years ago was relatively easy to keep tabs on, it has now become almost impossible to maintain an overview. More and more bottlings are coming onto the market from proprietors and ever increasingly from independent bottlers. Some of these are only available in certain countries, or are reserved for a particularly active dealer.

Of course this book concentrates on the classical whisk(e)y countries of Scotland, Ireland, Canada and the USA, but they are no longer alone. India has more distilleries than the United States, and Japan produces more whisky than Scotland. It's fun tracking down these exotic whiskies, but at the same time there is the risk that it will not be possible to find them all. I would be grateful for tips and information. Otherwise I have tried to make this book as user-friendly as possible. The strength of any given whisky is rendered as a percentage of alcohol by volume but without repeating the letters 'abv' after each figure. Thus a whisky with a strength of forty per cent abv is rendered as 40% throughout. All cross references are prefixed with a →.

A book like this would not be possible without the assistance of the many people who have been willing to help with information, answer questions so patiently or give me tips. In fact I have had a great many such helpers. In my *Single Malt Note Book*, I needed two whole pages for acknowledgments. For this book even that would not have been enough. There were many company employees in Scotland, Ireland and the USA who never tired of answering my questions. They are too numerous to mention, but they all know how grateful I am. Many friends in both Germany and Scotland, the two countries where I live, have stood by me with help and advice and have given me the necessary support to carry on. I am very happy and thankful to have such friends.

They are also too innumerable to name them all, but nevertheless I would like to mention some of them. In alphabetical order my thanks go to: Michael Aschke, Claudio Bernasconi, Bettina Bohl, Angela Borowski, David Boyle, Grant Carmichael, May Cleland, Jim McEwan, Dieter Gräf, David Grant, Alan S Gray, Larry Hutchison, David F Hynes, Werner Hertwig, Lyndsay and Richard Joynson, Eily Kilgannon, Dieter Kirsch, Horst Kroll and my friends at the Whisky Club Kyrburg, Dr. Bill Lumsden, André Leonhards, Stephan Macha, Bill and Maggie Miller, Eckehard Nau, Bärbel and Lutz Reifferscheidt, David Robertson, Bernd Schäfer and the other members of the Franconian Highland Circle, Henrike von Schau, Lilly and Dietrich Scheunemann, Günter Schöneis, David Stewart, Otto Steudel, Andrew Symington, John Thorne, Ian Urquhart, Claive Vidiz, Wulf Weißbach and Jürgen Zichnowitz. There are many, many more – I haven't forgotten them, and they all know that it is just not possible to mention them, but I am full of gratitude.

My thanks go to my long-suffering publishers in Germany and Scotland, to my proof readers in Frankfurt who were really put to the test, Gavin Smith, and, above all, also to my brave translator, Sally Pegrum. They all believed, despite everything, that this book would indeed be finished one day. A very heartfelt thanks goes to my family and, especially, to my wife, for the love, patience and willingness to accompany me through the many years. I dedicate this book to her.

Walter Schobert
Nerabus, Isle of Islay, May 2002

A

Abbott's Choice Scotch blend. Today one of the numerous (small) labels from the large portfolio of → GuinnessUDV. Formerly owned by → DCL, via its subsidiary John McEwan & Co, who established the brand in the mid- to late-19th century. As the → Linkwood Distillery was also owned by the same company for a time, it can be assumed that this malt played a large part, at least in earlier times, in the composition of the blend.

Aberdeen Angus Argentinian blend. A *whisky nacionale* produced in → Argentina. It consists of malts imported from Scotland and grains which are distilled in Argentina.

Aberfeldy Scottish malt distillery. Situated on the River Tay near the village of the same name, it belongs to the southern → Highlands. Founded between 1896-8 by the whisky merchants John → Dewar & Sons, Perth. This firm gave up its independence in 1925 and merged with → DCL, having previously amalgamated with James Buchanan and Co. A new → stillhouse was built in 1972 and the capacity was increased to four → stills, but the maltings were given up to make way for a dark grains plant. With the takeover of → DCL by → Guinness, Aberfeldy passed into the ownership of → UD, who had the licence transferred to the old name of John Dewar & Sons. After the merger of Guinness with → Grand Metropolitan, the new drinks giant → Diageo had to sell the brand because of injunctions imposed by the Monopolies Commission in the USA (where the blend Dewar's → White Label is the best-selling Scotch) and Brussels. The buyers were the rum giants → Bacardi who, as a dowry, gained possession of the Aberfeldy Distillery, as well as three other Scottish distilleries. In the spring of 2000 an excellently equipped visitor centre called 'Dewar's World of Whisky' was opened by the new owners of the distillery.

The malt from Aberfeldy has always been used for Dewar's blends, particularly → White Label and → Ancestor. It became more widely available as a single malt in a distillery bottling when, in 1992, → UD included a 15-year-old Aberfeldy in its 'Flora & Fauna' series. It was also included in its → cask strength version, distilled in 1980 with a strength of 62%. A 25-year-old is now available at the distillery, while a 12-year-old is also on sale elsewhere.

Aberfoyle Scotch vatted malt from → Robertson & Baxter. Named after the town in the Trossachs just a few miles away from → Glengoyne, the company's own distillery. Their malts very likely make up an important part of this 8-year-old whisky, along with others such as → Tamdhu, → Glen Rothes and → Highland Park, which the producers have access to via their connections with → Highland Distillers which are owned by the → Edrington Group.

Aberlour Scottish malt distillery. Its name (pronounced Aber-lower – as in 'power') means 'mouth of the Lour'. It lies directly on the A95, at the foot of Ben Rinnes and thus in the heart of → Speyside. The waterfall Lyne of Ruthrie is nearby. Here there is a spring whose water was valued by the Druids and later used by St. Dunstan for baptisms: welcome motifs for advertising and marketing. The official name of the distillery – which since 1974 has belonged to the French company → Groupe Pernod-Ricard and is managed by its Scottish subsidiary → Campbell Distillers – is still Aberlour- → Glenlivet. The year 1879 appears on the labels as the date of founding. This was when James Fleming re-established the distillery; however there was already a distillery with the same name in 1826. The present plant was rebuilt in 1898 after a fire. In

1973 four → stills were added. Although it is so easily accessible by road, the distillery is not open to the public.

The malt from Aberlour is an ingredient in the → Clan Campbell blends. Aberlour has been available as a single malt for a relatively long time; at one time in a bottle with a square base, then in the seventies with the mark VOHM (Very Old Highland Malt) in a classical cognac bottle, and as a 5-year-old in Italy. The standard → distillery bottling, which has received many distinctions and prizes, is 10 years old. It is 40%, while the 12-year-old is 43%. There are also vintage versions: from 1969, 1970, 1971 and 1976. In the last few years there have also been numerous new → expressions, partly restricted to individual markets. The 100° proof (57%), as well as the Antique (43%), is only available at duty-free outlets. While the 15-year-old Cuvée Marie d'Ecosse is only officially sold in France, it is also available in Germany.

The 15-year-old → Sherry Wood Finish has contributed to the trend towards → finishings. In contrast, the 18-year-old is matured completely in old sherry casks. The a'bunadh (pronounced 'a-buhn-a', Gaelic for 'original') which was initially only available on the duty-free market is 59.6%, (→ cask strength). It bears the signature of James Fleming and the label specifies that it is 'unfiltered'. At the millennium there was a special limited edition of it with 2,000 bottles from 'the best sherry casks'. The labels are made of pure sterling silver. For the same occasion casks which Campbell Distillers had already offered for sale in 1989 were bottled, and 364 buyers were each able to acquire 360 bottles of their own malt. The Aberlour Special Reserve, composed from 40 (→ First and → Second Fill) sherry casks and bottled at 45%, was initially only obtainable in France and was then on offer through the Internet.

Adam's Choice (Presumably) Indian whisky sold by the African branch of → Mohan Meakin in Nairobi. The form of the bottle could be called a 'motif carafe', such as those offered by other firms (e.g. → Whyte & Mackay or Jim → Beam), except that this one is in the form of a naked woman and is in particularly bad taste.

Adams Canadian blend from → Seagram. This brand was created by Samuel → Bronfman after he had bought United Distillers Ltd in 1953 and changed its name to Thomas Adams Distillery. The new name was a reminder of a whisky pioneer whose distillery was licensed in 1802. There are several versions: Adams Double Distilled contains at least 5-year-old rye whiskeys, Adams Private Stock six-year-olds, and Adams Antique 12-year-olds. There is also a → Four Roses, which shouldn't be mistaken for the bourbon which, confusingly, is also from the house of Seagram. The Adams whiskeys are rarely available outside Canada.

Adelphi Distillery Scottish whisky company founded in 1993 by James Walker and named after a distillery which had once belonged to his great-grandfather. The old distillery, which at times was also called 'Loch Katrine Adelphi' and 'Gorbals', was in Glasgow and so belonged to the → Lowlands region. It is said to have already been in operation in 1825, and from 1880 was owned by A Walker & Sons, who were already active in Liverpool and Limerick in Ireland. Adelphi produced grain as well as → malt whisky. In 1902 it was sold to → DCL which closed it, although the → warehouses were in existence until 1960.

The company is one of the numerous recently established → independent bottlers such as → Glenhaven, → Blackadder and → Murray McDavid. The standards set by the older competitors such as → Cadenhead and → Gordon & MacPhail have been maintained in their single malts. The bottlings are without any → colouring and without the → chill filtering which impairs the aroma of a whisky. In addition, James Walker only bottles at → cask strength. He has, however, a very decent blend made with 20 malts from 'private stock', called The Adelphi Director's Reserve, in his range. → Breath of Angels, another blend, was, unfortunately, only available for a short time.

ADP (Amalgamated Distilled Products) Scottish whisky company. Founded in 1969 as a subsidiary of the Argyll Group and given a sound base by the acquisition of A → Gillies & Co and its → Glen Scotia Distillery. The financially strong parent company promoted quick growth by acquiring many rights to names and brands. At the beginning of the eighties, the company had a portfolio of more than 20 blends, which were produced in the firm's own bottling plant at Grangemouth. Here more than a million → cases per year could be filled. ADP also acquired the American company → Barton Brands, together with its Scottish subsidiary Barton Distilling (Scotland), which at the time owned the Barton Distillery in → Bardstown, Kentucky, and the Scottish distilleries → Littlemill and → Loch Lomond (which was first sold in 1985 to → Inver House and then to → Glen Catrine Bonded Warehouse Ltd). The company quickly folded. Initially it was acquired in a management buy-out by executives, with the participation of → Schenley (Canada), and continued as → Gibson International, though this firm was soon to disappear from the Register of Companies under circumstances which remain a mystery to this day.

Affinity Whisky drink. A type of → Manhattan made with Scotch instead of bourbon. Orange bitters replace the usual angostura bitters.

African Safari (Presumably) Indian whisky sold in a bottle shaped like the African continent. Produced by → Mohan Meakin whose headquarters are in → India, but who also have a branch in Nairobi.

Against the Grain Scotch single malt. Only to be found in selected branches of the British wine and spirits chain → Oddbins. The well-known caricaturist, Ralph Steadman, was responsible for the charmingly eccentric label. It tells us which distillery the 10-year-old → 'Campbeltown Malt' comes from: → Springbank and it has the typical Springbank (and → Cadenhead) strength of 46%.

Age In the majority of whisk(e)y-producing countries there are legal requirements which regulate how long a whisky must be stored before it can be sold. In Scotland, Ireland, Canada and Japan the laws prescribe three years, in the USA two years. The → Bottled in Bond whiskeys are an exception and must mature for at least four years. The minimum age should not be confused with the age at which the producers bring their whiskies onto the market. It is only sub-standard blends that are bottled at three years. As quality improves with longer maturation, whiskies are usually left in their casks for much longer. They are bottled when their producers think they are mature. A statement of age is not prescribed for this. In the case of Scotch blends, the price gives a clue to the age. If an age is, however, printed on the label, it refers to the youngest whisky contained in the blend, i.e. '8 years old' means that all whiskies are at least 8 years old, but some of them may, of course, be much older. Malt whisky is usually bottled at 10 or 12 years, but those bottled for the Italian market are often younger. In the USA, where the bourbons are usually very young when they are bottled, a trend towards older bottlings, with → small batch and → single barrel whiskeys coming into fashion, has been noticeable in the last few years. Whether ageing really suits bourbons is a controversial point. In any case, at the end of 1988, the owners of → Maker's Mark published a witty advertisement, in which easily identifiable bottles from their competitors were shown and mocked as 'overproofed, overpriced, overaged'.

Age of Sail Scotch blend from → Lombard Scotch Whisky, based on the Isle of Man.

Ageing Japanese blend from → Suntory. Still appearing on the product list of 1992, its production has, in the meantime, ceased. It consisted of → malt and → grain whiskies that had matured for at least 15 years, and thus belonged to the → premium category.

A H Hirsch straight bourbon, gives its place of origin as → Lawrenceburg in Kentucky, but certainly isn't distilled there. In fact it originates from → Michter's Distillery in Scheaferstown, Pennsylvania. It offers the last chance to try a whiskey from this distillery, which finally had to shut down in 1988. The large stocks still stored there had to be burned by judges' order, because every now and then they would attract burglars – a really sad and paradoxical decision, as the law sought to fight vandalism with vandalism.

Adolf Hirsch, a former executive at → Schenley, acquired several barrels from 1974, before this barbaric act. He had them bottled under his name, but later sold his supply to the Hue family who owned the liquor store 'Cork 'n' Bottle' in Covington, Kentucky. To prevent any further ageing of the whiskey, they emptied the barrels into steel tanks. This explains the mystery as to why all bottlings give 1974 as the year of distilling, but show different ages. The 20-year-old at 91.6° (45.8%) still comes from the barrels which have not been transferred to the steel tanks, as does the 19-year-old at 93° (46.5%), but very few bottles of the latter remain. The 16-year-old at 91.6° (45.8%), which is identical to → Boone's Knoll, and the 13-year-old which is a private bottling for a Californian whiskey-lover and is, in fact, a Van Winkle Rye, are not from the original supplies.

It's a shame that the bottles don't give any indication of their noble origins and that neither Pennsylvania, with its great whiskey tradition, nor the venerable Mitcher's Distillery which enjoys protected monument status, is mentioned. This is quite amazing considering the loquaciousness of most other American labels. At least they managed to mention the → pot stills which were used at Michter's for the second distillation.

Ainslie & Heilbron Scottish whisky company. The first part of its name goes back to the company James Ainslie & Co which was founded in 1868. The second part is even older and dates from 1827. It provides a good example of how complicated the history of Scotch whisky has sometimes been; how companies were formed and then dissolved, how takeovers alternated with mergers and new alliances were constantly being formed. The name Ainslie is, above all, linked with the → Clynelish Distillery. Ainslie & Co, initially survived the whisky crisis linked to the name of → Pattison at the turn of the century unscathed, only to be forced to sell in 1912.

The survival of the names Ainslie and Heilbron was due to the merger of the two companies by the businessman James Calder, who also bought the company Colville Greenlees, situated in → Campbeltown. In 1926 → DCL took over and restructuring resulted in subsidiaries; on the one hand → Macdonald Greenlees (which owned Glendullan), and on the other, Ainslie & Heilbron. The latter was charged with the management of → Clynelish. The result was that the name Ainslie & Heilbron still appeared on bottles of the single malt from this distillery. These were not filled by the proprietor, but by → Gordon & MacPhail. After the takeover of → DCL by → Guinness, Ainslie and Heilbron was responsible for various blends, which were only of local importance. Ainsley's, which was particularly popular in Greece, was one of those which UD had to give up after the merger of its parent company Guinness with → Grand Metropolitan to form → Diageo. The name and the brand were acquired by the Belgian company Bruggemann in 1998, and they added a Pure Malt to their portfolio in 2000.

Alberta Canadian whiskey company based in Vancouver and with two production sites: in Burlington, Ontario and in Calgary, Alberta. The Alberta Distillery was built in 1946 in an area that is especially suited to whiskey production. There is good water from the Rocky Mountains and the best rye from Canada's largest grain region. Today the distillery is owned by → Jim Beam Brands, the spirits subsidiary of → American Brands/ → Fortune Brands. Luckily this time the change in ownership didn't result in a change in methods and production style. Alberta is the only distillery in Canada which distils both its whiskeys exclusively from rye. It is also unusual in that even the base whisky that, as elsewhere, is distilled up to 95%, is made from rye. Together with the second whiskey, also produced solely from rye (and at 65%, a much weaker distillation and therefore much more aromatic), the blends have a very individual character. Storage in new or → ex-bourbon barrels contributes to their character.

Alberta produces whiskeys of different ages

using the company's own name: (Carrington is 3-years-old, Windsor 4 and Tanglerridge 10-years-old). In addition there are whiskeys which are sold in the USA in → bulk and distributed from there by the parent company Jim Beam, such as → Autumn Gold, → Canadian Gold and → Canada House. The company's name is borne by the 5-year-old Alberta Premium, a 'Special Mild Canadian Rye Whisky' and by Alberta Springs which is available as a Canadian whiskey at 45%, and as a 10-year-old rye at 40%. Its label states that it is refined by → charcoal mellowing. This isn't the → leaching method used in Tennessee, but the usual filtering through charcoal.

Albion's Scotch blend with the suffix Finest Old. It is produced by the Scottish Albion Blending Co, a subsidiary of → Kinross Whisky Company.

Alcopops The name for drinks containing alcohol that have been brought onto the market in the past few years. The target market for alcopops is, above all, young people. In fact this drink plays a large part in the products which are offered ready-mixed in either cans or bottles. The pioneers in this field were the owners of → Jim Beam and → Jack Daniel's, who have for some time offered 'Coke with a kick'. Scottish whisky firms have tried to exploit the trend as well. For example, → UD mixed their blend Bell's with Coke, lemonade and the Scottish cult drink 'Irn Bru', as well as with chilli to produce → Red Devil, though all the brands were discontinued after a comparatively short time. It is not only those who think it is a shame to mix whisk(e)y with anything but clear springwater who criticise alcopops. Many people believe them to be dangerous or even damaging, because young consumers in particular aren't, as a rule, aware of how much alcohol they are drinking in this form.

Ale This word is commonly used to describe certain beers and sometimes in connection with whisky production. There are parallels, of course, between the production of both, especially between beer and → malt whisky, as well as other whiskies. According to German *Reinheitsgebot* (quality control) laws, → beer may only be made out of pure malt barley, just like malt whisky in Scotland, whereas in the USA only a 51% portion of malted barley is legally required. Another common factor is the sugaring of the starches contained in the grains through grinding and → mashing, as well as the processing of the → wort by adding yeast to produce an alcoholic liquid. This is then usually referred to as the → wash in the case of whisky, or sometimes (in the USA) → beer, or (in Scotland) → ale. The required alcoholic strength is then achieved during the next stage by distilling in → stills. In this process a residue is left at the bottom of the stills which is called → stillage in America, and → pot ale (or sometimes → burnt ale) in Scotland. This is then removed and may be used as animal feed in Scotland, whilst across the ocean they use it as the base for the → sour mash process.

Alexander Dunn Scotch blend. Produced by the Surrey-based company Alexander → Dunn, who have several versions on offer; as 3, 5 and 12-year-old blends and as a 12-year-old vatted malt. The main markets are in France and Japan.

Alcohol Term for a product which is initially formed when a solution containing sugar is made to ferment by adding yeast to it. Simplified, the sugar is split into alcohol and carbon dioxide. In the case of whisk(e)y, grain is the basis for the solution and the end-product of the fermentation is a kind of beer, called → wash in Scotland and → beer in the USA. Distillation, by heating the → stills, can further increase the alcohol content. Nowadays this is measured in volume percentage; earlier the measure was → °proof, which was defined differently in the UK and the USA. The word itself is of Arabic origin. *Al kuhl* or *al-koh'l* was originally the name for a black powder used to decorate the eyes. This led the author Ambrose Pierce to call alcohol 'the liquid that can get a man black eyes'. The chemical formula for the alcohol present in whisky is C_2H_5-OH.

All Malt Japanese vatted malt. Introduced by → Nikka in 1992, it was the first vatted malt to contain malts from two distilleries each using different distilling processes. In one the malted grain is distilled in a → pot still in classic fashion. The second malt is also exclusively based on malt barley, but it is distilled in a → Coffey still in Nikka's distillery in → Nichinomiya. The whisky is the product of a company that is happy to acknowledge its debt to the Scottish tradition which its founder, Masatake → Taketsuru, got to know and love (as well as his Scottish wife, Rita) during his studies in Glasgow. In 1995 a further version of the product joined the first one, with the established name in small print on the label and → Malt Club in larger print below.

All Saint's American company with a small series of Scotch single malts in its range. These are called the → 'Highland Collection' because the labels on the bottles show pictures by the British artist Albany Wiseman. They also have an 8-year-old malt with the attractive name → Ulle bé Naomh and the single malt → Orach Dram. → Loch Morar is another single malt which is on offer at three ages, 8, 12 and 18-year-old.

Allan's Scotch blend from → Eaglesome in → Campbeltown. The firm belongs to → J & A Mitchell & Co, whose flagship is the → Springbank Distillery, also located in the town.

Allied Distillers Ltd Bristol-based subsidiary of → Allied Domecq PLC. It is responsible for is responsible for the soon-to-be mothballed Dumbarton grain distillery, which for a time also produced Inverleven and Lomond malts in pot stills. The company used to own 11 other malt distilleries, but of these → Balblair and → Pulteney were sold in 1995/6, and the famous Islay distillery → Ardbeg was sold in 1997. → Glendronach, → Imperial and → Scapa were temporarily closed in 1998 but while Scapa wasn't sold, it was handed over into the care of → Highland Distillers, whose → Highland Park Distillery is situated nearby Scapa on Orkney. In the year 2000 it was finally the turn of Glencadam to close. At present only → Laphroaig, → Miltonduff and → Tormore are operational. Glendronach reopened in Spring 2002.

One of the most important activities of the company was the beer business, to which it really owes its creation. Its 'ovum' was the UK beer giant Allied Breweries, which initially incorporated several renowned whisky companies, such as → Stewart & Son of Dundee and Wm → Teacher & Sons of Glasgow. In 1987 the brewers completely took over the Canadian company Hiram → Walker, having owned nearly half its shares previously. This brought several distilleries and a whole range of brands into the Allied fold (e.g. → Canadian Club, → Ballantine's). An attempt to take over → DCL failed and instead the wine and spirits sector of another UK brewery giant Whitbread was taken over, meaning that the blends → Long John and → Black Bottle and the gin brand 'Beefeater' became part of the portfolio, as well as other distilleries, including the Islay jewel Laphroaig.

The alliance with Domecq, which brought its Spanish whisky subsidiary → DYC with it, as well as its Scottish distillery → Lochside showed the limits of growth. Apart from the distilleries already named, several brands were also disposed of, and in 1996 the shares in the brewery subsidiary Carlsberg-Tetley were sold. They also parted with the large Scottish maltings, Robert Kilgours in Kirkcaldy, and with a chain of 2,700 pubs. In January 1999, the Irish subsidiary → Cantrell & Cochrane was sold with its liqueur → Cochrans and → Tullamore Dew, which is particularly successful in Germany. An attempt was also made to establish a presence in India by means of engagements and joint ventures; initially with a share in → Jagatijt Industries and then with partnerships with → Clan Morgan of Delhi and → Tilaknagar. A small part of the near £1 billion raised by the sale of the pubs flowed into the acquisition of a 70% share in the company Jinro, which controls nearly half the spirits market in Korea, a country which, after Russia, has the largest consumption of spirits in the world.

Allied Domecq PLC International company which was created in 1955 from union of Allied Lyons with the Spanish sherry and brandy company Pedro Domecq. In the world rankings of drinks companies it takes second place behind the giant → Diageo, formed in 1997. The headquarters of the company are in Bristol. It is particularly active in the spirits sector and owns distilleries in Canada (→ Walkerville), in the USA (→ Maker's Mark) and in Scotland.

The North American whisk(e)y interests are gathered together in the Hiram Walker subsidiary, and the Scottish ones in Allied Distillers Ltd. In terms of Scotch whisky sales, Allied occupies third place behind → GuinnessUDV and is ahead of → Groupe Pernod-Ricard's whisky subsidiary, → Chivas-Glenlivet Group. Famous brands belonging to the company include the sherries La Ina and Harvey's Bristol Cream → Cockburn's port, the cognac Courvoisier, the brandies Carlos and Fundador, Lamb's Rum and Beefeater gin.

Allied series Scotch single malts. They all come from distilleries owned by Allied Distillers Ltd or their parent company → Allied Domecq PLC, but are bottled by → Gordon & MacPhail, the → independent bottler from Elgin. They bear a label which, along with the name of the distillery, shows the name of the company holding the licence. → Ardmore, → Balblair, → Glenburgie, → Imperial, → Inverleven, → Old Pulteney and → Scapa belong to the series.

Allt A' Bhainne Scottish malt distillery. Sometimes also written as Alt-à-Bhaine or Allt-à-Bhaine, the name is pronounced 'olt-a-vane' and means 'burn of milk'. It is situated on the southern side of Ben Rinnes, to the south-west of → Dufftown, and was owned by → Seagram until 2002, when Groupe Pernod-Ricard took it over. Seagram's Scottish subsidiary, → Chivas Bros, built the distillery in 1975, two years after → Braes of Glenlivet, as part of an ambitious programme which originally envisaged five new distilleries. Although there are only two → stills, it was designed for large output and could produce five million litres annually. The distillery is very modern, with computer controlled production. The architecture takes some getting used to and is not exactly romantic but, nevertheless, it fits quite well in the landscape. The pagoda roofs over the modern buildings are pretty, but fulfil no function whatsoever. The → new spirit is not stored on site but is taken to → bonds at Keith by road tanker.

Allt A'Bhainne has, up to now, never been bottled by the → proprietor, but there have been various → independent bottlings including → Signatory and → Cadenhead. Gordon Currie, had an impressive selection of malt whiskies in the Whisky Castle in nearby Tomintoul, including two malt whiskies from Allt A'Bhainne in his 'Castle Collection'.

Ambassador Scotch blend. Originally launched on the market by the small company → Taylor and Ferguson. After they were taken over in the 1930s by Hiram → Walker, its new owners sold Ambassador successfully, particularly in the USA. Of several versions previously available, only the 12-year-old → de luxe blend is still obtainable today. One of the malts used undoubtedly comes from the → Scapa Distillery, whose licence was registered with Taylor & Ferguson until 1995, which then became part of → Allied Domecq PLC in 1987.

American Biker Kentucky straight bourbon from → Twelve Stone Flagons, a firm which has become well-known for its → Usquaebach bottlings, which are excellent. Its American product doesn't fit the picture at all, perhaps because it is aimed at a different target group: Harley Davidson lovers, who otherwise would probably rather reach for a Budweiser. The company launched the brand in 1996, getting the whiskey from → Heaven Hill and reducing it to 80° (40%).

American Brands An American company with mixed interests in numerous fields of business. After selling Gallaher, the largest cigarette company in the UK, in 1996, and having thus totally withdrawn from the tobacco business, golf and whisk(e)y have become its main interests. It also owns Master Lock (locksmiths) and the well-known detective agency, Pinkerton. Cobra Clubs (golfclubs), Footjoy (golf shoes and gloves) and Titleist (golfballs and other accessories) also belong to it. It entered the whisky market in 1967 when it acquired the brand → Jim Beam, as well as both the distilleries of the same name in Boston and Clermont. National Distillers, bought in 1987, were the owners of the → Old Crow, → Old Taylor and → Grand Old-Dad distilleries near Frankfort, Kentucky, as well as several local brands. The three distilleries were closed down immediately, but the whiskeys of the same name still exist. Today, however, they are all produced at Jim Beam. In 1990 the company acquired the → Whyte & Mackay company through what was at the time its UK cigarette subsidiary. In their turn the Scots then acquired the independent → Invergordon Distillers for their American parent company.

In order to free itself completely from its tobacco past, it was renamed → Fortune Brands, and the worldwide whisk(e)y interests were reorganised. There are now three subsidiaries under the umbrella of → JBB Worldwide (Jim Beam Brands): JBB (The Americas) is responsible for North and South America, JBB (Pacific) for the rest of the world excluding Europe and Africa, which are included under JBB (Greater Europe).

This latter subsidiary was criticised for not developing the → Whyte & Mackay brand and underperformed commercially until the directors decided on a management buy out which was completed in October 2001. The new company which was formed, called → Kyndal, took over JBB's whisky portfolio in an effort to re-energise the company's brands.

One of the most regrettable consequences of JBB's ownership had been the surrender of the name Whyte & Mackay as a company in its own right. It may have been shrewd, in the face of globalisation, to have brought the most important brand to the fore in the company name, but it did show a lack of sensitivity and respect for European, and especially Scottish, traditions and feelings, let alone those of Africa, which simply had to step back behind Europe. The fact that the company had continued with the time-honoured bourbon brands connected with Frankfort, Kentucky, showed that they did have respect for history.

Amrut Indian distillery in Bangalore which produces → malt whisky as well as grain spirit and is thus one of 15 malt whisky distilleries on the subcontinent. It belongs to Amrut Distilleries which mainly makes the blend Maqintosh (sic).

An Cnoc Scotch single malt. This is a → proprietor's bottling of a malt produced at the → Knockdhu Distillery. It originally bore the name of its distillery, as a Scotch malt really should, and was launched in 1990 as Knockdhu. In 1993 it came onto the market as a 12-year-old under its new name In 2001 a 12year-old was launched from 1983. The change in name was due to an agreement with → Justerini & Brooks, in order to avoid confusion with its → malt whisky → Knockando. For a 21 and 23 year-old bottling the original name was reverted to.

Analyser Term for the first of two columns used in the production of whisky in → patent stills or → column stills. The second column is the → rectifier. They both contain perforated plates of copper or stainless steel, layered on top of each other, acting like small stills. Hot steam and the cold wash meet in the columns. The columns are thus named because in them the components containing alcohol in the wash are separated from the water. For this reason they are also known as separating columns.

Ancestor Scotch blend, also sometimes called Dewar's Ancestor. It is the → de luxe version of the classic → White Label from the house of John → Dewar & Sons. It was not, and is not, available in the UK home trade. This fact has led to malicious tongues maintaining that the sales of the company's leading brand would be threatened if its fans could only get a taste of Ancestor. The → malt from the company's own distillery, → Aberfeldy traditionally played an important part in it. The producers were → UD, the successors of → DCL, who have owned Dewar & Sons since 1925. The brand changed owners, following the alliance of UD and → IDV to form → UDV (now → GuinnessUDV), as a result of a directive from the American Federal Trade Commission and now belongs to → Bacardi. As the rum giants would hardly have been in a position to produce the brand themselves, they have contractually ensured delivery of the finished product from → GuinnessUDV.

Ancestral Scotch single malt from The → Inverarity Vaults of Biggar, near Edinburgh. The company was founded by the former → UD director of production, Professor Ronnie Martin and his son Hamish. It offers the blend → Inverarity and a → Speyside single salt of the same name. This formerly came from → Aultmore, was 8 years old and matured in → bourbon casks, whilst the Ancestral was 14 years old and, unusually for Aultmore, matured in → sherry casks. → Bacardi, the new owners of Aultmore, have unfortunately terminated their contract with Inverarity, and the whisky now comes from → Balmenach distillery.

Anchor American distillery, with a single small copper → pot still. Uniquely it produces a single malt rye whiskey, the very first of its kind, and, to my knowledge, the first malt that is not made from malted barley but from malted rye. The expression 'malt' may have to be redefined in future.

The distillery is in Potrero, a district of San Francisco, and is California's first distillery. Anchor is also probably the first micro-distillery, and as revolutionary as the Anchor Brewery which, with its 'Steam Beer', 'Liberty Ale', 'Porter' and its Christmas beer, sparked off the trend for micro-breweries and the establishment of an increasing number of new small breweries. With a wide variety of beers they are competing against the brewery giants and their 'test-tube brews'. The Anchor Brewery was founded by one man, who also set up the distillery. He had already made a name for himself as a successful wine-grower and producer of York Creek wines, and has, in any case, one of the most famous names in America: Fritz Maytag. His great-grandfather invented the Maytag washing machine (the brand is now owned by Hoover), and America has his father to thank for 'Maytag Blue', one of the country's best cheeses.

Owing to his threefold occupation, Maytag is probably the only man in the world who has simultaneously distinguished himself as a wine-grower, brewer and distiller – and already it is clear that there will soon be other micro-distilleries which will produce small quantities of extraordinary whiskey. Maytag doesn't reveal much about his production. He doesn't disclose where the rye comes from and who malts it. What is known is that his 'distillery' is a screened-off room in his brewery, where there is a steel tank in which mashing and fermentation takes place before the → beer is distilled twice in the still. It was Maytag's notion to make his rye in the same way as the Irish and Scottish settlers in America had once done. He allows his → Old Potrero to mature a little longer than its predecessors did: the first batch of just 1,448 bottles was filled at 13 months and at the → cask strength of a strapping 124° (62%). It is not sold to the trade, and collectors will have a difficult job getting hold of a bottle, as it only goes to a handful of selected restaurants in San Francisco, California, Maryland and Washington DC.

Ancient Age American whiskey distillery. It is situated in Leestown on the edge of Kentucky's capital, Frankfort. It was sometimes also known as → Leestown Distillery and has recently been renamed → Buffalo Trace. In the course of its history it has changed its name almost more often than it has changed its owner, and its present ownership is almost as obscure as its beginnings. It is sure that one Benjamin Harrison Blanton settled at → Rock Hill Farm in Leestown in 1865 after the Civil War and began to produce whiskey. He might have been the son of the quarry owner who, in 1830, supplied the stones for the construction of the government building in Frankfort, and who had made a fortune in the Californian gold rush.

In 1869 the O C F (Old Copper Fire) Distillery was set up on the land of Blanton Jr. Edmund Haynes Taylor, who later built the → Old Taylor Distillery had a share in it and renovated it in 1873 together with George T Stagg, who later took over the distillery and gave it his name. In 1897 he employed Blanton's son as an office clerk. This Blanton was to remain for over half a century and shape the distillery; a statue commemorates him to this day as does the Kentucky straight bourbon → Blanton's which was launched onto the market in 1984 as the first American → single barrel. Colonel Albert B Blanton was manager from 1912, and survived → prohibition, during which he couldn't carry on distilling, but was allowed to bottle whiskey from existing stocks for medicinal purposes. At this time → Schenley took over the plant. In

Ancient Privilege

1953 Blanton retired and the distillery bore his name until 1969, when it was renamed Ancient Age Distillery, after its most famous brand, which utilsed the water tower (which rises over the distillery and is visible for some distance) in its advertisements.

At this time → Elmer T Lee was already master distiller, having trained at Blanton and still today, in his retirement, keeps an eye on things and chooses the barrels for the whiskey bearing his name. Gary Gayheart is responsible for production today. In 1982 Ferdie Falk and Robert Baranaskas, the founders of the company → Sazerac in New Orleans, became the new owners and introduced a new name: Ancient Age Distilling Company. It can still be seen on many bottles produced at the distillery. Ten years later however there was a new restructuring when Sazerac sold the Ancient Age Distilling Company to the Japanese syndicate → Takara Shuzo & Okura. This syndicate had distinguished itself as owners of the Scottish → Tomatin Distillery, though the smaller partner, Okura, went bankrupt in 1998. Sazerac itself kept the distillery and founded the Leestown Distilling Company as a new subsidiary.

Ancient Age is produced in Leestown, though the brand was first made in Canada in 1936, and has only has been produced in the USA as a genuine Kentucky straight bourbon since 1946. The formula used for it is 80% corn to 10% rye and 10% malted barley. In the USA there is a 38-month-old, but the normal versions are 4 years old and there are three different strengths of 80°/40%, 90°/45% and (as → Bottled in Bond) at 100°/50%. The 80° and the 100° are meant to be identical to the → Bulleit. The 10 Star is 6 years old. Ancient Ancient Age (also known as Triple A, 86°(43%) or 90°(45%) → and Barrel 107, named after its strength of 107° (53.5%) are 10 years old. One blend has the adjunct Preferred. Leestown is the name of another blend.

The company also produces → Benchmark, → Eagle Rare, and → Kentucky Dale and the company's single barrels: Blanton's, Elmer T Lee, → Hancock's Reserve and → Rock Hill Farms. They are not only excellent bourbons, but also serve as a good example of how difficult it can be for the uninitiated to decode labels. For example, Hancock's Distillery, the producer named on the label, doesn't actually exist. The name is a trademark belonging to Sazerac and the alleged distillery is a small room in which this whiskey is bottled. At the same time as the new name, a Buffalo Trace came onto the market at 90° (45%) and a Buffalo Trace rye Whiskey, distilled in 1981 and discovered in the warehouses in 1997 (and thus an 18-year-old), appeared in a limited edition of 3,600 bottles (110°/55%). Since 1999 the → Old Charter and the → W L Weller whiskeys have come from Leestown, after Sazerac acquired the brands from → UDV.

Ancient Privilege Scotch blend from W → Brown & Sons in Glasgow. In contrast to what its name implies, it is a young 5-year-old → standard blend.

Angels' share The term given to the portion of alcohol which evaporates from stocks of maturing spirits. How large this angels' share is, depends on various factors: on the length of maturation, the temperature and the micro-climate in which the cask is stored, and also on the character and the quality of the cask itself. The British Customs and Excise has always been very strict, and has tried to track down any abuse, beginning to get suspicious when more than 2% a year of the contents of any cask is lost. Furthermore, in Scotland, the whisky loses in strength as well as volume, while in the USA, where there are often high temperatures in the warehouses it may increase in strength during maturation.

Angus Dundee UK whisky company based in London which is also said to have been founded there in 1950, but names Glasgow as its company base on its labels, and, not the Scottish city included in its name. It is also possible that it was named after a person. The little-known company belonging to the Hillman family caused a stir in 2000 when it bought → Tomintoul Distillery from → Whyte & Mackay. The owners of the company make every effort to market both parts of the name in their products: they have a Scotch blend The → Dundee, and one that has been christened → Forfar, after another town in the area. Apart from these the company also has the blends →

Cattle Pride, Clan Ben, → Highland Legend, → Piper's Clan and → Scottish Royal in its range. There is a vatted malt named → Auchterar. The whisky named Angus Dundee is a vatted malt, and the name Montgomery is used for a series of single malts.

Angus McKay Scotch vatted malt from → Burn Stewart. In Italy it used to be available as a 5-year-old, but at present it is only obtainable in France aged 8 and 12 years.

Ankara Turkish whisky, available in two versions: as a blend calling itself *Türk Visiki* and as *Malt Viski* without the second 'i'. Both are 43%. They are distributed by the Turkish state enterprise Tekel and actually contain whiskies distilled in → Turkey at the Ankara Brewery where some students of agriculture began production on a very small scale on an experimental basis for study purposes. There are several versions as to the exact date of these experiments. On the bottles of the malt whisky, it says that whisky has been made in the alcohol factory in Ankara since 1963, that it is matured in special casks and sold after 5 years, and that all this, of course, happens in accordance with Turkish law.

Antiquary, The Scotch blend. It formerly used the suffix 'De Luxe Old Scotch Whisky' and is named after the novel by Walter → Scott. The owner of the brand was the → DCL subsidiary J & W Hardie, and through them it had a particularly close connection to → Benromach Distillery. Hardie introduced it in the 19th century but sold it in 1917 to J & G → Stewart, who soon after merged with → DCL. Later Hardie came to DCL as a subsidiary of Wm. → Sanderson and the blend was sold, again bearing the name of its inventor. Both the brand and the company name were sold in 1996 by → UD to the → Tomatin Distillery Co. The new Japanese owners will continue to offer it as a 12-year-old blend, but will obtain it finished, at least until 2008, from → GuinnessUDV. Sufficient casks have already been put aside so that the whisky, which is particularly successful in the USA, Portugal and South America, can still be composed and sold according to the same recipe.

Antiquity Indian whisky. Its producers call the blend a 'Rare Premium'. It is sold at 42.8% which is usual in India, and comes from → Shaw Wallace, who are best-known for their → Moghul Monarch.

Apology Scotch whisky cocktail consisting in equal parts of Grand Marnier and a good blend.

Ardbeg Scottish malt distillery. Its name means 'small hillock'. It lies on the south-east coast of of → Islay on the road leading from the harbour village of → Port Ellen to Kildalton in the east, where the visitor can find a famous and very beautiful Celtic cross. Together with the distillery in Port Ellen which bears the name of the village → Laphroaig and → Lagavulin, Ardbeg forms part of an imposing chain of distilleries, which not only lie close together, but also produce a style of malt whisky synonyomus with Islay. It is smoky, peaty, salty and has a definite medicinal touch, showing strong phenol tones reminiscent of seaweed. It evokes as much enthusiastic assent from its lovers as fierce rejection from its despisers. Ardbeg is considered the most bullish of the four malts. It is produced in a distillery which has worked in a traditional way for a very long time and until 1980 produced a part of its → malt requirement in its own → floor maltings. Ardbeg was closed first in 1989 and then again in July 1996.

Ardbeg's remote location was popular with illicit distillers until one Alexander Stewart began to work there legally in 1794, followed by John McDougall in 1815. The distillery remained in McDougall family ownership until 1973. Then the Ardbeg Distillery Trust, → DCL and Hiram → Walker (Scotland) formed a new company, which was finally taken over by the Canadian company in 1977. It later came under the influence of the spirits and brewery giants → Allied Lyons, who merged with Pedro Domecq to form → Allied Domecq PLC. They also owned the Laphroaig Distillery and decided to concentrate on that malt as their main brand, Ardbeg was then placed on a care and maintenance programme with very limited distilling outout.

Ardmore

Deliverance came in spring 1997 when → Glenmorangie plc bought Ardbeg and its stock in bond for £7 million, and since then have invested a large amount in extensive renovation which has also included the setting up of a visitor centre. A resurrection of the maltings is being considered and all the characteristic features of the distillery have been left unchanged – especially the peculiar 'purifier' on the lyne arm of the → spirit still which allows a part of the distillate to reflux. Directly after the takeover production on a small scale was recommenced and is now running at 800,000 litres per annum.

As a single malt Ardbeg was more commonly available from → independent bottlers than from the proprietors, but this is changing. The old official → distillery bottling, a 10-year-old Ardbeg, with its black label, is still mourned by many. There was a very limited 'guaranteed over 15 years old' in 1996 with the old label, and a 30-year-old malt that continued to be sold by the new owners. They celebrated their new child with a very expensive Provenance, a malt distilled in 1974, and six months after the purchase of the distillery, brought out a 17-year-old and a → vintage from 1978. Some bottles contained only 42.8% instead of the customary 43% and are thus sought after by collectors. Both were sweeter and not nearly as heavy as a traditional Ardbeg, and most expectations were better fulfilled by the vintage 1975, and 1977 brought out in 1998 and in 2001 respectively.

The new 10-year-old has been greeted with general acclaim, with a fresh and sweet taste at the front before the old Ardbeg character breaks through. This was the first → proprietor's bottling whose label clearly specified that it had not been → chill filtered. A 1976 bottling of a 23-year-old sherry cask was only available to visitors to the distillery and its 497 bottles bore labels which Stuart Thomson had signed by hand. Such labels are also borne by the 248 and 266 bottles from two ex-sherry-casks nos. 4702 and 4718 (one of which was intended for the Italian, the other for the French market): the whisky was distilled on 28th December 1975 and bottled on 20th October 1999. Two further casks (whose contents were distilled on 24th November 1974) were reserved for members of the Ardbeg Committee, which can be joined via the internet (www.ardbeg.com). 528 bottles (55%) were filled from cask no. 2392 on 17th July 2000 and 466 bottles (53.2%) were filled a day later from cask no. 2394. Since July 2000 there has been a further 21-year-old expression for the Ardbeg Committee, a cask bottling for Japan and the introduction of the 25-year-old Lord of the Isles bottling at 46%.

Ardmore Scottish malt distillery. Its name is pronounced 'ard-moor', and the distillery lies to the south of Huntly, in the village of Kennethmont. It stands next to the railway line from Aberdeen to Inverness, and is sometimes counted as a → Speyside and sometimes as belonging to the eastern → Highlands. It was built during 1898/9 by Wm → Teacher & Sons. The distillery has had a relatively uneventful history and remained in the ownership of its founder for a long time. In 1955, two → stills were added to the existing pair and that number was doubled to eight in 1974. The founding company still holds the licence, but today it belongs via → Allied Distillers Ltd to → Allied Domecq PLC. A steam engine remains from the original equipment and coal is still used, partly at least, for heating the stills. The lion's share of Ardmore, like its sister → Glendronach, goes into the blend Teacher's → Highland Cream. There is no distillery bottling of Ardmore as a single malt, though one could consider → Gordon & MacPhail's 1977 bottling in their → Allied series as a 'semi-official bottling'. The 100th anniversary of the distillery was the occasion of the very first → proprietor's bottling: the 21-year-old Centenary, distilled in 1977 and bottled in 1997, bearing the signature of the manager and really only intended for workers at Allied.

Argentina It is a country with a great whisky culture, where it is still a part of daily life and it is considered good form to drink whisky in a smart bar between 5pm and 10pm accompanied by a dish of *ingredientes* – olives, ham and cubed cheese. There is a choice between the (expensive) *whiskies importades*, mostly Scotch blends, and a *whisky nacionale*, a blend that is made in Argentina from Scotch malts and locally distilled grains. There are several distilleries for such grain distillates, owned, amongst others, by → Seagram. There are a lot of these local whiskies, the following of which are widely available → Aberdeen Angus, → Best Seller, → Black Jack, → Blender's Pride and The → Breeder's Choice.

Argyll Scottish county comprising the middle west of the country and the islands off the coast. The Argyll of today is still largely identical to the old territory of the clan Campbell, whose chief, the Duke of Argyll, maintains the ancestral home of the clan at Inveraray Castle on → Loch Fyne.

Apart from his extensive estates, the last duke (who died in 2001) also had wide commercial interests; amongst other things he was engaged in the whisky business and was on the board of → Campbell Distillers, the subsidiary of → Groupe Pernod-Ricard, and he profited from the sale of the whiskies whose black jugs are decorated with his coat of arms and his signature. These were commissioned by him from his Beinn Bhuidhe Holdings and filled as a blend and as a 12, 15 or 17 -year-old single malt. Whilst Argyll's colleague, the chief of the clan → MacLeod from Dunvegan Castle on Skye, really only sells his single malt to visitors to his castle, the whisky from His Grace, The Duke, is not only available in Inveraray, but elsewhere as well.

Aristocrat Indian Whisky. Its producers call it 'Malted', which is often doubted, at least by those who have actually drunk the brand that is so popular in → India and who, above all, know about the somewhat cavalier Indian manner with definitions. There they like to write the mythical word 'malt' on the label, even if the bottles only contain a distillate from molasses, something similar to rum, with just a small amount of whisky as well, or perhaps just malt extract. The producer is the → Jagatjit company who own the Jagatjit Nagar Distillery in Hanira to the north of Delhi in the Punjab. There, in the largest distillery in the country, malt whisky is produced, but there is no concrete proof that it plays a part in the Aristocrat.

Armorik Single malt from Brittany. The Waremghem Distillery in Lannion call their product 'old' and says that it is distilled twice in traditional → stills..

As we get it Term used by Scottish distillery workers for whisky that is direct from the cask – or even, as → new spirit, from the still. At this stage, however, it is not yet allowed to be called Scotch whisky, because that presupposes at least three years in the cask. In any case it refers to a very special substance: one that is not diluted with water, thinned or even → chill-filtered or treated in any way. Thus the expression is the popular phrase for what is officially termed original → cask strength and/or sometimes → high °proof.

As We Get It Cask strength Scotch malt whisky bottled by the J G → Thomson company, belonging to the brewery giant Bass. It supplies pubs belonging to the parent company, along with their blend, → Old Inverness (formally a brand from HD Wines in Inverness), a single malt at cask strength, between 55% and 60%. Earlier, the range included a → Balvenie, a now much sought- after → Macallan, and an → Aberlour. Basically these are a special kind of single-cask bottling, which are not always regarded very kindly by the distillery owners, a situation that led to the bottling launched in 1998 at 60.3%, which bore no distillery name.

Asama Japanese blend from → Sanraku-Ocean. It is named after a mountain near the company's malt distillery. It is their leading brand and a Japanese → super–premium blend.

Asda UK supermarket chain, which has belonged to the American giant Wal-Mart since 1988. Like all their competitors, Asda has whiskies produced exclusively for them which they then sell as their own brand or with the company's name. Apart from the blends → Oak Cask Matured and → Old Scotch Whisky they have a vatted Highland Malt in their range. Asda gets four malts from → Glenmorangie plc which are sold under the name → Old Glenn (sic). They are proud to have been the first to offer their customers an alphabetical system which describes the

Atholl Brose

character of the whisky, from 'A' meaning light, to 'J' meaning heavy, strong and smoky.

Atholl Brose Scotch → whisky liqueur from → Gordon & MacPhail. The full name is → Dunkeld Atholl Brose.

Auchentoshan Scottish malt distillery. Its name comes from the Gaelic for 'corner of the field'. It lies on the western outskirts of → Glasgow, near the Clyde and close to the A82. Although it uses water that comes from the Kilpatrick Hills, which are in the → Highlands → whisky region, Auchentoshan is ascribed to the → Lowlands. It is the only remaining distillery which, with its three → stills, uses → triple distillation, a method that used to be customary for this region, producing a clean and fragrant whisky. Only lightly-peated malt is used. Allegedly founded in 1800, Auchentoshan has had a very changeable and complicated history, experiencing , even by Scottish standards, many changes of ownership and interruptions in production. Only in the last few decades has it become quieter: Eadie Cairns, who bought the distillery from Bass Charrington in 1969, sold it to the whisky broker Stanley P → Morrison. With it he was able to add a Lowland to the range of malts from his → Highland distillery → Glen Garioch, and his Islay distillery → Bowmore. Stanley P → Morrison Ltd was acquired by the Japanese distilling giant Suntory in 1987. The new company, Morrison-Bowmore Ltd completely renovated Auchentoshan and invested a lot of money in order to make its malt a well-known brand.

Whisky from Auchentoshan is used in the company blend → Rob Roy, but is also readily available as a single malt in several distillery bottlings. There is a Select, without a statement of age, and bottlings aged 10 and 21 years (a → vintage from 1972). The 22, 25 and 31-year-old malts came in ceramic containers. In 1997 several old casks from 1975 and one from 1965 were discovered in the 'Official Distillery Archive'. They were bottled at → cask strength, the 21-year-old at 55.4%, the 31-year-old at 48.9%. Another 31-year-old followed at 45.6% and a 30-year-old at 47.5%. The Three Wood, launched in 1998, was not so exclusive, and with it → Morrison Bowmore bowed to the new trend of → finishings. There is no statement of age and it is a composition of malts that matured in casks previously containing bourbon, Oloroso and Pedro Ximenez Sherry.

Auchroisk Scottish malt distillery. Its name, pronounced 'othrusk', means 'ford over the red stream'. It is situated close to Mulben, near → Keith, and therefore belongs to → the Speyside region. It was only opened in 1974 and so is one of the youngest and most modern distilleries in Scotland. Its buildings fit very harmoniously into the landscape. Via → IDV it belonged to → Grand Metropolitan and was managed by → Justerini & Brooks (Scotland), but following the merger of Grand Met and Guinness it is now one of → UDV's Scottish distilleries.

It was a manager of Justerini & Brooks who discovered a hidden spring, and was so enthusiastic about the quality of the water, that he persuaded his bosses to buy the land for several million pounds. With its eight → stills, Auchroisk can produce 7 million litres of alcohol per year. The malt is unpeated, as the whisky was destined from the very beginning to be used in the → J & B blends. For this reason mainly → bourbon casks are used with a portion of → sherry as 'polish'.

Under IDV's ownership a bottling called → Singleton of Auchroisk was first marketed. It had no age statement but indicated the year of distillation on the label and this was between 10 and 12 years before bottling. The Singleton Particular 1980 was also bottled exclusively for Japan. A 10-year-old is available in the 'Flora & Fauna' series.

Auchterar Scottish vatted malt from the Glaswegian firm → Angus Dundee.

Auld Acquaintance Scotch single malt from an unknown distillery. It comes from the → independent bottler James → MacArthur and its label is decorated with a portrait of Scotland's national poet Robert → Burns. The name is a reminder of the poem *Auld Lang Syne*. There is also a blend of the same name.

This used to be supplied by a company that was known for its → McCallum's Perfection and which, at one time, had shares in the → Cragganmore Distillery. The brand, later owned by → DCL, was one of those that → Guinness had to sell after the merger with Grand Metropolitan.

Auld Lang Syne Scotch blend from → Lang Brothers. It is named after the famous poem by Robert → Burns whose portrait decorates the packaging. When this was introduced in October 1997 it was only available at branches of the UK supermarket chain → Safeway. Now it is also well represented in other markets, including the USA.

Auld Sandy Scotch blend produced by the wine merchants → Balls Brothers, who have been in existence since 1854. They still have a shop in London, but mainly run several 'Wine Bars with Restaurant'. The brand is only available in the UK.

Aultmore Scottish malt distillery. Its name, pronounced 'oltmoor', means 'large stream'. It lies to the north of → Keith and therefore belongs to → Speyside. It was built in 1896 by Alexander Edward, who already owned → Benrinnes Distillery, inherited from his father, and who was founder of → Craigellachie Distillery. Two years after the opening of Aultmore, he also bought → Oban, but had to sell to John → Dewar & Sons in 1923. Two years later they joined → DCL and the new owners of Aultmore increased the number of → stills from two to four. Aultmore went to the → Guinness subsidiary → UD in 1987 and it was then one of the four distilleries which → Diageo, formed after the merger of → Guinness and → Grand Metropolitan, sold to → Bacardi, when it had to part with → Dewar's White Label, as a result of directives from the Federal Trade Commission and the European Commission. Aultmore is one of White Label's principal consituent malts.

Aultmore was bottled in small quantities as a single malt by DCL (with John & Robert Harvey as distillers on the label). Afterwards UD, who transferred the licence to → UMGD/Wm. → Sanderson & Sons, included a 12-year-old Aultmore as a distillery bottling in its → 'Flora & Fauna' series. When it was supplemented with a → cask strength series, an Aultmore from 1983 at 58.8% was included again – just as the series 'Rare Malts' included a 21-year-old malt from 1974 at 60.9%. The old owners celebrated the 100th anniversary of the distillery in 1997 with a 16-year-old malt whisky with the cask strength of 63%. How long the new masters of the distillery will allow the previous owners to carry on selling a whisky from Aultmore is a matter for speculation (they have already withdrawn the allowance from → Inverarity Vaults Ltd, who had an 8-year-old Inverarity and a 14-year-old → Ancestral in their range, both of which were produced at Aultmore.

Austin, Nichols Distilling Co American whisky company. It is, confusingly, sometimes written without the comma. Their products proudly – and justifiably – bear the date 1855. In that year a Mr Fitts used the money that he had made in the Californian gold rush to found a business in New York that dealt with importing foodstuffs. After prohibition, the chairman of the time decided to start trading in wines and spirits as well, to give the company its present name, and to begin with the production of gin and blended and straight bourbon.

One of his brands found such favour with friends on a hunting trip that he decided to name it after the bird that they had been pursuing: in 1942 the brand Wild Turkey was created and since then has become one of the biggest brands being produced in a range of expressions as a Kentucky straight bourbon and as a straight rye. Originally the required whiskeys were obtained from other distilleries, but in 1970 it was decided to become independent. The choice fell upon the → Boulevard Distillery near Lawrenceburg, which had long been a supplier. Since then all the company's bourbons have been produced there. Since the 1980s, the rye whiskey which had previously been bought from → Michter's, has also been produced at Boulevard.

Today the firm (which gives its address on the bottles as Lawrenceburg, but actually has its headquarters in Manhattan) belongs to the French company → Groupe Pernod-Ricard. The only person to survive all the changes of ownership of the last decades, is the master distiller, Jimmy Russell, who has been there since 1955. For several years now, he has not only been concerned with the quality of the general whiskeys, but also personally chooses the barrels for the → single barrel bottlings → Kentucky Legend and →Kentucky Spirit, along with the → small batch bourbon → Rare Breed, that comes in → barrel °proof and which many think is one of the best of its kind. A further task of Russell's is to look after the blended → Nichols and the whisky liqueurs of his employers.

Australia It is amazing that a country that has all the prerequisites has not made whisky history, or even developed its own style of whisky, and doesn't even have any large-scale whisky production. There is good grain, there is good water and, even more importantly, there is the human factor: immigrants from England, Scotland, Ireland and, not to be forgotten, America, who brought with them, not only the knowledge of how to make whisk(e)y, but also the need to drink it. Perhaps they preferred to drink the originals, which were readily available. In any case the Australians have never put nearly as much effort into whisky production as they have into wine-growing.

Of course there were illicit stills, the spirit → Tom Cobb refers as openly to this tradition as does the youngest distillery in the country, which quotes the date 1822 on the bottles of its → Sullivans. However, the official beginnings of Australian whisky history date from 1866, when the Myers Distillery was set up in Ballarat, Victoria. It had a tough fight against the imported Scotch blends though, as the large Scottish companies had recognised the potential market of the continent, and had set up their own branches or had named agents. By the 1880s, Australia was the most important market in the world for several of them, including Johnnie Walker. Myers only became more successful when customs duties were raised and they had a fast-selling brand in Old Court.

It was also the customs duties which led the Scottish → DCL (under whose umbrella most of these Scottish trading houses, such as → Walker, → Haig and → Buchanan had joined together) to produce in Australia itself. With several smaller producers, they founded United Distillers, not to be confused with the successor to DCL and the new company built the → Corio Distillery in Victoria and named its brands after it. Another was → Four Seasons. Other foreign firms also did business in Australia. For example, → Gilbey, later a subsidiary of → IDV/→ Grand Metropolitan, produced a blend called → Bond 7. → Seagram sold the 5-year-old Marksman, which contained a very modest share of 10% Scotch malts and 90% Australian → grain whisky. That didn't quite concur with the legal requirements, which stipulated that malt whisky should be made from barley and that blends must contain 25% malt whiskies. The minimum maturation time is still only two years and the minimum strength was 37% until 1966, when it was raised to the customary 40%. A year before, Corio, the last Australian distillery, stopped working and distilled its stocks for gin, because the public demand was increasing for Scotch blends, and, more than anything, for bourbon. It is unfortunately not known from which stocks the → Great Outback stemmed. Produced in the 1980s, it sufaced in 1999, with some bottles as a blend and some as a single malt.

For a long time it seemed that the continent had disappeared from the whisky map. Then it became known that, since 1993, a tiny malt distillery had been in production on Tasmania. It is run by the → Small Concern Whisky Co, and since 1998 has been selling its 'Pure Tasmanian Malt' under the name of → Cradle Mountain. A year previously, however, there had been the first bottling of an Australian single malt, namely Sullivans Cove. It came from the → Tasmania Distillery, which began to operate in 1995 and has proved to be very aware of tradition.

Autumn Gold Canadian whisky. Produced by → Alberta Distillers in Ontario, Canada, but brought in road tankers to the USA and sold there by Alberta's parent company, → Jim

Beam. It is one of the fashionable lights that only contains 35% alcohol.

Avery's of Bristol English company that is one of the old wine houses of the UK. It was established in Bristol in 1793, still has an excellent name and is one of the leading businesses in the country. It specialises in clarets, and port. It was especially important to old-established merchants to offer their customers their own brands and, where possible, their own bottlings of wine and spirits. One or two of their own blends, and possibly a vatted or even a single malt was listed in their range. Avery's, who since 1994 have been under the umbrella of the → Hallgarten Group, have three blends: → Bristol Vat, Highland Blend and the → Queen Elizabeth.

Avoca Irish whiskey from the → Cooley Distillery. This company first began production in 1987, and has ensured that its main competitor, → IDG, no longer has a monopoly in Ireland, and that Irish whiskey production is not in foreign (French) hands. A part of its successful strategy has been to create brands, named after defunct Irish companies which, in history-conscious Ireland, still have kudos or derive their names from Irish geography. This blend is named after a small river to the south of Dublin. It is bottled at 40%, and was originally produced for Dunne's, the department store chain.

Avonside Scotch blend. Named after the river that rises near → Tomintoul Distillery and flows into the → Spey near → Cragganmore. It comes from the house of → Gordon & MacPhail via the subsidiary Avonside Whisky Ltd, and has a high malt content giving it a typically Speyside character. There is an 8-year-old at 40% and 57%.

Award Scotch blend from William → Lundie & Co in Glasgow. A simple → standard blend without an age statement.

B

Baby whisky Term for the freshly distilled spirit that, strictly speaking, shouldn't be called whisky at all, because the law in Scotland as well as in Ireland, the USA and Canada, prescribe a certain minimum maturing period before the liquid may be called whisk(e)y. In Scotland and Ireland the minimum period is three years, and in America a bourbon which doesn't declare its age must be four years old. In America the fresh distillate is called → white dog, whilst in Scotland and Ireland they speak of spirit, → new make, or sometimes of → clearic spike or → fillings.

Bacardi A company which produces the most successful spirit brand in the world. More than 20 million → cases of Bacardi white rum are sold each year. Bacardi is also the largest drinks company in private ownership. The reason that this company, founded by Don Facundo Bacardi y Masó in Santiago de Cuba and operating from Nassau in the Bahamas since its expropriation by Castro in 1960, appears in a whisky book is that it went into the whisky business in 1995, when it bought General Beverages, and expanded its interests in 1998 with the purchase of the brand Dewar's → White Label. The Luxembourg holding was the parent company of the Italian Vermouth dynasty Martini & Rossi which, in its turn, has been linked with the Scottish company William → Lawson since the 1970s. Apart from plants in Coatbridge and in Glasgow, it owns the → Macduff Distillery; selling their malt whisky under the name → Glen Deveron, and it also has several blends. In some countries Bacardi owns the distribution rights to brands that they do not produce themselves. For example in Germany it was not the German subsidiary of the producer → UDV which was responsible until 1999 for → Johnnie Walker, but Bacardi. When UD's parent company → Guinness merged with → Grand Metropolitan to form → Diageo, and its spirits subsidiary UD merged with → IDV to form → UDV, the trade regulatory bodies in Washington and Brussels required the sale of the brand Dewar's. Bacardi paid £1.15 billion for it, ensured long-term supply in its contract, and at the same time, also took over four Scottish distilleries: → Aberfeldy, → Aultmore, → Craigellachie and → Royal Brackla. In order to present a unified front in future, the rum kings also decided to drop the name William Lawson and run their Scottish activities under the name of John → Dewar & Sons.

Backset A term for a process customary in whiskey production in the USA. It is used by all the distilleries in Kentucky and is even legally prescribed in Tennessee. It utilises the → sour mash or → thin stillage, the part of the residue left over after distillation in the → wash or → beer still. After separation from the solid grain components, it is used for the preparation of the next → mash or for the next → fermentation, and has two functions: firstly, it kills certain unwanted bacteria and secondly, it helps the whiskey to maintain its character from distillation to distillation.

Bagpiper Indian whisky. The standard bottling, which sells more than 3 million → cases, annually (36 million bottles), is by far the best-selling brand in this country – and is number five in terms of worldwide sales. The fact that it uses the popularity of famous (male) Indian filmstars in its advertising, undoubtedly helps account for its success at home. Here two very influential branches of the Indian economy have come together, and their sheer size and financial might are not easily understood by anyone from outside India. India's film production is the largest in the world and exceeds that of Hollywood. The whisky industry is experiencing the greatest expansion rates in the world and is bigger than that of Japan. It has more distilleries than any other country, except Scotland. Herbertsons, a subsidiary of → United Brewers of India, broadcast a weekly 'Bagpiper' show on television. There are talent-spotting shows, where the winners can take part in an aptitude test and have the chance of becoming stars themselves.

Bagpiper's Melody Scotch whisky cocktail. Equal parts of crème de menthe and a good blend are shaken with ice and served in a cocktail glass.

Bailey's Irish cream liqueur. It is the most successful, and according to connoisseurs of the genre, incomparably the best. The fact that it was the first, is emphasised by the word 'original' appearing twice on the label. It has become so well established that you could be forgiven for thinking that it has been around for a long time. But it was first launched onto the market in 1974 by → Gilbey of Ireland. In those days the company belonged to → IDV, today → GuinnessUDV, whose parent company → Diageo profits from the immense success of the liqueur. Since its introduction, it has developed into a great Irish success story: the brand makes up 47% of all exported drinks and 1% of all Irish exports. It can be bought in more than 160 countries and occupies 15th position among the best-selling spirits worldwide. The statistics are even more impressive with regard to the quantities of milk used for the liqueur: 40 million gallons are needed per year, exactly one third of all Irish milk production.

Success did not come without effort: Gilbey had numerous difficulties to overcome in order to achieve greater shelf life. This was a prerequisite for a product made out of fresh cream, which might sit in a shop or in a consumer's home for some time. The conserving properties of → Irish whiskey alone are not enough to guarantee this. Eventually the problem was solved and Bailey's now possesses an 18-month shelf life. Apart from Irish cream and whiskey (from → IDG), and cocoa, its composition is kept secret. Jim Murray calls Bailey's 'the sexiest, most complex of all Ireland's cream liqueurs'. There are two versions; the original at 17% and a lighter one, produced mainly for the USA, with as much alcohol but 50% less fat content.

Bailie Nicol Jarvie, The Scotch blend. It was launched on the market at the beginning of the twentieth century by Nicol Anderson, and today belongs to → Macdonald & Muir who now trade as → Glenmorangie plc. It is not named after its creator, but a character in Walter Scott's *Rob Roy*. For a long time this blend from the → premium sector with a Victorian label was not strongly marketed, but in recent times its owners have been working to raise its profile.

Baird-Taylor Scotch whisky company founded in Glasgow in 1838. In 1935 it passed to → DCL, so that its name today belongs to their successors, → GuinnessUDV. Baird-Taylor had several blends, of which only the → standard *Baird-Taylor's Selected* has survived. Today it is made by the Ardross Blending Company for the French firm Sipiec. The brand's registered owner is → John Begg.

Baker's Kentucky straight bourbon. It is one of four in the → small batch series from → the Fortune Brands subsidiary → JBB. The others are → Basil Hayden's, → Booker's and → Knob Creek. The name comes from Baker Beam, a grand nephew of James → 'Jim' Beam, after whose death Baker worked as master distiller at both the distilleries in Boston and Clermont for many years, and was responsible for production. The label notes proudly that Baker was a sixth-generation whiskey maker and that there is a 'Beam family tradition of putting our best secrets inside the bottle, not here on the label'. It also recommends drinking Baker's with ice or a measure of water – which is probably a good idea considering the strength of 107° (53.5%). It is 7 years old, and the bottles bear a batch number.

Balblair Scottish malt distillery. Its name comes from the Gaelic for 'settlement on the plane'. It lies on the old A9 between the Dornoch Firth and the village of Edderton, not far from → Glenmorangie and, like this distillery, belongs to the northern → Highlands. The author → Alfred Barnard, in his famous book of 1887, quotes 1790 as the year of foundation, but the present plant dates back to 1871/2. Several buildings from this time are still standing and, together with the old, attractive brick chimney, contribute to the impression Balblair makes of a small, Victorian distillery. Via the Cummings company it passed to the Canadian Hiram → Walker company, who also owned → Ballantine & Son and both today are a part of → Allied Domecq PLC. In the summer of 1996 their subsidiary Allied Distillers Ltd sold Balblair to → Inver House Distillers Ltd, having already sold → Pulteney and closed → Glendronach.

Balblair was (and is) an important component of the → Ballantine's blend, which is reflected in the Ballantine-style bottles in which it was launched on the Italian and German markets. It is a relatively light and mildy peaty single malt, and the → distillery bottling is 5-years-old. → Gordon & MacPhail still supply a 10-year-old in its → Allied series (also at 57%). In the autumn of 1998, the new owners kept their promise and brought out two → proprietor's bottlings in tastefully designed bottles: a 16-year-old and a malt with no age statement, which was named Elements because, as the label says, it was 'a creation of the elements'. Both also bear the slogan 'A Spirit of the Air' because they were distilled where 'the air is said to be the purest in Scotland'. These permanent bottlings were joined in the spring of 2000 by a 33-year-old Balblair, at 45%, presented in an attractive wooden box together with a glass.

Ball of malt The customary expression for a glass of whiskey in Ireland. It doesn't have to be a malt.

Ballantine & Son, George Scotch whisky company. Its origins go back to a grocer's store established by George Ballantine in Edinburgh in 1827. Although he soon began to sell whisky, it was not the Edinburgh branch of the family, but the Glaswegian one, which created the basis for an enterprise which, although in other hands since 1919, is still present in name, through the giant distillery complex in → Dumbarton on the banks of the rivers Clyde and Leven, and through the blend → Ballantine's which is one of the best-selling brands in the world.

James Barclay took over the company after the First World War, and by diligenty cultivating contacts in prohibition America (where the actor David Niven was in his sales force), he made sure there was a market for the brand when prohibition ended in 1933. It was also Barclay who sold Ballantine & Son (and the → Stoddart company) to Hiram → Walker, thus facilitating access to Scotland for the Canadians. They set up the Dumbarton Distillery in 1938, bought → Miltonduff and → Glencadam distilleries, and had great success with their various Scotches (including → Old Smugglers) in North America and Europe. Ballantine's also managed to break into the market of the state-run stores of the former Eastern bloc countries. Today the rights to the name and brands belong to → Allied Domecq PLC and its European subsidiary, Allied Distillers Ltd.

Ballantine's Scotch blend. It was brought onto the market by George → Ballantine & Son in the 19th century and from 1895 was allowed to bear Queen Victoria's royal warrant on its label. Success accompanied the brand throughout the years and through all its changes of ownership, from the founding company through → Stoddart and → Hiram Walker to → Allied Domecq PLC. The company can be proud of the fact that it owns one of the best-selling brands in the world: in 1997 it was number one in Europe, and occupied fourth place worldwide.

The → standard blend Ballantine's Finest, is now accompanied by a 12-year-old → de luxe blend called Gold Seal. The duty-free business is particularly active: there is a 15-year-old and a 19-year-old available in East Asia, a 17-year-old all over the world, and an 18-year-old in South America. The 21-year-old comes in a decanter, and the rare 30-year-old is one of the most expensive whiskies of all. Ballantine's Founder's Reserve 1827 and Royal Blue, only available in Japan, are recent additions to the range.

Malts for the blends come from the company's own distilleries, → Miltonduff, → Glenburgie and → Scapa and undoubtedly from → Balblair and → Pulteney as well, even though Allied sold both these distilleries to → Inver House Distillers Ltd some time ago. Like → GuinnessUDV with → Johnnie Walker, Allied Distillers Ltd have added a vatted malt to their range of blends. The Ballantine's Pure Malt launched in 2000 was aimed at maintaining the interest of fans of the traditional brand in a market which is becoming smaller for blends whilst sales of malt whiskies continue to grow. Purity, which contains 20-year-old malts, caused a sensation, partly because of the stylish drop-shaped form of the bottle, and because of its volume (50cl). The blend Ballantine's Serenity and the → grain whisky Ballantine's Vitality are just as 'economical'. All three are only available in Japan and at Asian duty-free shops.

Balls Brothers Old established English wine merchants, founded in London in 1854. The company was known for its own two whiskies, the Scotch → Auld Sandy and its Irish 'brother' → Ould Paddy. Whilst the latter is no longer produced, the Scotch is still in their range. Bottles can only be bought in the company's London shop. It is available by the glass at the establishments that now represent Balls Brothers' main activity, which are wine bars with restaurants.

Ballygeary Irish whiskey. A blend of malt and → grain whiskeys, both distilled by → Cooley in Riverstown near the Ulster border and also bottled by them. It is mainly sold in the UK as the house brand of Malt House Vintners, the spirits subsidiary of the cash and carry chain, Bookers.

Balmenach Scottish malt distillery founded in 1824. Its name, with the emphasis on the second syllable, is from the Gaelic for 'settlement in the middle'. It lies in the heart of → Speyside near Cromdale off the A95, between Grantown-on-Spey and Bridge of Avon. It was founded by the MacGregor family of whom two famous Scottish authors are members: Sir Robert Bruce Lockart and Sir Compton Mackenzie. In his book *Scotch*, Lockart affectionately describes life at the distillery where he spent many of his boyhood holiays. Mackenzies's best-known book is the bestseller → *Whisky Galore*. As a → DCL distillery, Balmenach passed to → UD in 1987, and they closed it in 1993, having transferred the licence a year before from John → Crabbie & Co to its subsidiary → UMGD. In December 1997 the distillery was sold to → Inver House Distillers Ltd, who started up production again in 1998.

For a long time the whisky was only available as a single malt from → independent bottlers like → Cadenhead and → Gordon & MacPhail. A → distillery bottling aged 12 years was then included in the → 'Flora & Fauna' series. The → Deerstalker of the same age is also said to be a Balmenach. Now that → Inver House Distillers Ltd have launched → proprietor's bottlings from their newly acquired distilleries → Pulteney and → Balblair, we can surely hope for a new Balmenach. In 2001, a 28-year-old Balmenach was launched.

Balvenie Scottish malt distillery. Its name comes from nearby Balvenie Castle, meaning 'town or settlement of fortune' with the emphasis on the second syllable, but sometimes on the first. It is one of the many distilleries in → Dufftown in the → Speyside region and stands near the → Glenfiddich Distillery, only being separated from it by a railway line. Like Glenfiddich, it belongs to William → Grant & Sons which remains an independent company.

The founder and his sons contructed it almost entirely with their own hands, using building materials from the remains of the ruined estate house named New Balvenie Castle. The first → stills were bought second-hand from → Lagavulin and → Glen Albyn. Today distilling takes place in eight stills which are larger than those at Glenfiddich. The waste heat is also recycled. They have a peculiar shape with a kind of balloon between the still body and the swan's neck. This feature can be found in other distilleries and is called a 'Balvenie' still. The water for both distilleries comes from → the Robbie Dubh springs. Balvenie still has its own → floor maltings, producing about 15% of the → malt required for distillation.

There used to be a 10-year-old Founder's Reserve as a → distillery bottling and an approximately 18-year-old Classic. In its place, for Balvenie's 100th anniversary in 1992, a series of three new malts was created in a specially developed style of bottle. They are also available as a set with an attractive wooden 'tantalus'. It includes a 10-year-old Founder's Reserve, a 15-year-old → cask strength Single Barrel and the 12-year-old → Double Wood. This one, in particular, demonstrates the significance of finishing a single malt in a different cask: whilst the younger malt was matured in oak casks which previously contained → bourbon, the 12-year-old was transferred into → sherry casks to finish maturing. David Stewart, Master Blender and chief noser of the company, thus invented the first → finishing and set off a trend that has often been imitated, though not always so successfully.

At the end of 2000 a 25-year-old Single Barrel was added to the series, but in 1997 Stewart again chose the right kind of wood and the right time for the → second maturing by complementing the first three malts with a sensational 21-year-old, which he had allowed to finish for a few months in → port casks. There is only a small quantity, but nevertheless more than the → vintages, (such as 1968, 1966, 1964, 1961 and even 1951 of which there was enough to fill just 90 bottles at 51.9%). As only one cask was filled their availability is limited, and they are prized by collectors. Now and then very small quantities, or even single bottles, are issued: for the 25th anniversary of the German *Playboy*, magazine readers entered a draw for 25 bottles of a 25-year-old Balvenie.

Banff Defunct Scottish malt distillery. Formerly also known locally as Inverboyndie, it was named after the town of Banff which lies to its east. It belonged to the → Highlands region and was built in 1863. The distillery experienced two catastrophes during its history: a fire in 1877 and on 16 August 1941 it was bombed by a lone Luftwaffe aircraft. The distillery was closed in 1983, when in the ownership of DCL, having passed to SMD in 1932. It was subsequently demolished.

The former licence holder, Slater Roger & Co, did not have a → proprietor's bottling, so Banff is only available as a single malt in → independent bottlings: Cadenhead had several versions, including some at → cask strength, and one from 1974 belongs to the Connoisseur's Choice series from → Gordon & MacPhail. The → Scotch Malt Whisky Society has also offered its members several expressions at various times. A → cask strength at 58.8% was included in the → Silent Stills series from → Signatory.

Banoch Brae Scotch blend from Cellars International.

Barclay's Kentucky straight bourbon from → Barton. The producers can't, or won't, say where the whiskey got its name (but they can't say where their own name came from either). The label claims that the 80° (40%) drink has 'Quality, Character, Value'.

Bardstown Small town to the south of Louisville on the Blue Grass Parkway. Its greatest tourist attraction is still the *Old Kentucky Home*, that the songwriter → Stephen Foster, who later died of alcohol poisoning, sang about. A straight rye whiskey from the → Heaven Hill Distillery in Bardstown was also named after him. This isn't the only distillery in town, there are also the → Willett and → Barton Distilleries. But even that is not all, as one should really also count both → Jim Beam distilleries as belonging to Bardstown. Although their owners always give the addresses of their Clermont and Boston/Beam distilleries as Frankfort, Kentucky, Clermont and Boston lie four times closer to Bardstown than to Frankfort. With a total of five distilleries still in existence, the small community of fewer than 10,000 inhabitants puts all other whisky-making centres in Kentucky into the shade. In addition, it also has the splendid → Oscar Getz Museum of Whiskey History. There is no worthier location for the Bourbon Festival each September. This makes it the whiskey capital of America.

Barley The essential cereal grain used for whisk(e)y production. In the case of malt whisky it is, along with water and yeast, the only natural ingredient allowed. In Scotland malted barley *must* be used to make malt whisky. It does not matter where the barley comes from when making Scotch whisky, as it is the quality that counts, not the source. Barley has always been used for malt whisky until Fritz Maytag made his → Old Potrero out of malted rye.

Barley is also used in other countries and for other types of whisk(e)y: in Ireland → pot still whiskey is made from a mash consisting of malted and unmalted barley. In the USA bourbon whiskey must be made out of at least 51% corn, and rye whiskey from at least 51% rye. However a quantity of malted barley, varying from distillery to distillery, is also added to the mash. Without some malted barley → fermentation would not occur.

In Scotland the choice of malted barley varies according to the suitability of each strain. The criteria for usage includes a high starch content and low protein and nitrogen contents. Varieties which → germinate readily are also preferred; they must be ripe and very dry. Although there is enough barley in the country itself to cover the needs of the distilleries, → local barley is not used exclusively – although some distilleries, such as Springbank, occasionally claim to do so. Today the grain also comes from England and central Europe, the preferred sorts being 'Camargue' and 'Chariot', whilst the formerly very popular and almost exclusively-used 'Golden Promise' is now difficult to obtain. The barley only influences the whisky in respect of the quantity of alcohol it yields.

Barnard, Alfred English author of *The Whisky Distilleries of the United Kingdom*, published in 1887. The book is a complete inventory of all the distilleries in operation in the UK and Ireland at that time. Barnard visited them on a journey which took up the whole of 1886 and noted every detail of their location, financial situation, technical equipment and characteristics. He detailed 129 distilleries in Scotland, of which all but nine produced malt whisky, 28 distilleries in Ireland and four in England. The book was published by the trade journal *Harper's Weekly Gazette*, which is still in existence today under the title *Harper's – the Wine and Spirit Weekly*. It is probably the oldest surviving specialist journal of its kind.

The book became the bible of whisky historians. The first edition is very scarce and reprints are much sought-after today. The first appeared in 1969 from David & Charles of Newton Abbot, and in 1987 the 'Centenary Edition' was published by Mainstream of Edinburgh and Lochar of Moffat with a foreword by David Daiches and an introduction by Michael Moss. In 2000 two German enthusiasts arranged a new reprint. The monumental work, in which engravings of the distilleries are also reproduced, was not the author's only book. He also wrote the multi-volume *Noted Breweries of Great Britain & Ireland*. It is also not well-known that he wrote a second whisky book: in 1893 he published *A Visit to Pattison & Elder & Cos, Leith, and Glenfarclas-Glenlivet Distillery*, a work for the → Pattison company, the collpase of which threw the Scotch whisky industry into its biggest crisis, at the end of the 19th century.

Barrel A synonym for → cask. In whisky industry usage it refers to a certain size. A barrel contains approximately 185 litres, and so lies between the → quarter and the → hogshead. When speaking about a barrel, it is always an 'American barrel', made from American oak. When it arrives in Scotland from the USA, usually dismantled but sometimes whole, the barrel has usually already been used for maturing bourbon.

Barrel proof Term used for the whiskeys in America which are bottled at → barrel strength. In Scotland and Ireland they use the term → cask strength.

Barton American distillery in → Bardstown. It is owned by the company Barton Brands, which since the beginning of the 1990s has belonged to the → Canandaigua Wine Company. The distillery has only borne its present name since 1944, and to this day no-one can explain where it got it from. The distillery dates back to 1889 when it was built by → Tom Moore, who had previously owned another distillery in partnership with Ben Mattingly. Today there is still a Barton's brand named after him (whilst the → Mattingly & Moore now comes from the nearby → Heaven Hill Distillery).

Moore's distillery was a victim of → prohibition, but in 1934 it was reopened by a businessman called Henry Teur. Ten years later, a man named Oscar Getz appeared on the scene. He is not only famous for having built up the distillery and the company, but has also been immortalised by his fantastic whiskey museum and the book *Whiskey. An American Pictorial History* (1978). Until Getz left the company, the museum was located in the distillery, and today is one of the attractions of Kentucky's whisky capital, Bardstown. Getz was also the creator of → Kentucky Gentlemen and many other brands. He was the driving force, too, behind the expansion of the business to Scotland, which

Basil Hayden's

began in 1959 with a share in the → Littlemill Distillery and continued with the construction of the → Loch Lomond Distillery six years later.

Littlemill was taken over completely in 1971, which led to the formation of a Scottish subsidiary called Barton Distilling (Scotland), and to one of the most obscure chapters in the history of Scotch whisky and American whiskey. In 1982 the American parent company and its Scottish subsidiary were bought up by → ADP, which soon after parted with Loch Lomond. In 1989 ADP was sold by its owners, the Argyll Group, to → Gibson International, backed by → Schenley (Canada) and several managers from ADP, who declared themselves bankrupt at the beginning of the 1990s. Since then, the Scottish assets were sold to → Glen Catrine Bonded Warehouse Ltd, while the American parts business is called Barton Brands again and belongs to the wine company that profited by selling cheap supermarket wine.

Perhaps the recent muddled history has made them so reserved at Barton where they refuse, for example, to reveal the → mash bill or provide information about how many brands they now own. This policy hasn't exactly helped improve the image of the whiskeys, which have always been deemed rather mediocre (and too young). Nevertheless it is known that there are 13 fermenting tubs in the distillery, a large steel → beer still and a copper → doubler, that several different mashing formulas are probably used and that the barrels are stored in 30 seven-storey warehouses. The company is successful and it has expanded further to move up from 8th to 4th place in the list of the largest spirits companies in the USA.

In two further distilleries (in Atlanta and in California), Barton also produces gin, tequila, rum and vodka. Barton still owns the US rights to several brands of Scotch such as → Inver House, → House of Stuart and → Highland Mist. The range was substantially increased again in 1995, when they not only bought the two (closed down) distilleries → Medley and → Glenmore from → UD, but also a whole series of brands such as → Fleischmann's, The Glenmore, → Kentucky Tavern and → Old Thompson. They had previously acquired the widely available → Ten High from → Hiram Walker. The house brand, so to speak, is the Very Old Barton. Other straight whiskeys include → Barclay's, → Clementine's and (Colonel Lee, which is also available as a → light whiskey. A further 'light' is Barton's QT Barton's Premium, Barton's Reserve, → Corby's, (Fleischmann's and → Imperial are blended. → Cabin Hollow, → Corn Chip, → Golden Grain and → Old Dispensary are straight corn whiskeys.

Basil Hayden's Kentucky straight bourbon. Like → Baker's, → Booker's and → Knob Creek, it belongs to the → small batch series from → the JBB subsidiary of → American Brands. It gets its name from one of the pioneers of American whiskey. In 1785 Basil Hayden founded a Catholic settlement in Kentucky and is said to have already begun distilling by 1796, at the same time as the bottle label notes, that George Washington was President and the state of Kentucky was just four years old. Hayden is the man after whom his successors named a distillery and a great brand: → Old Grand-Dad.

The distillery is no longer in operation but the whiskey is still available, being made in both the → Jim Beam distilleries in Boston and Clermont, but in contrast to their most well-known product, it has a much higher rye content. It is also responsible for the character of the → small batch, which is first bottled at 8 years at 80° (40%). The bottle is supposed to be a replica of one from the 1920s, decorated with a label that is draped over it like a poncho, which tells the story of Hayden. It also has a very distinctive metal wrapper around its middle.

Baxter's Barley Bree Scotch blend. Nowadays it is a brand from → GuinnessUDV and is mainly sold in South Africa and South America. Why it bears the name Baxter is not known, as it used to come from James Watson & Company, who were formerly based in Dundee were founded in 1815. They were said to have had great quantities of whisky at their disposal, as well as the three distilleries → Ord, → Parkmore and → Pulteney, when they were bought by → Buchanan, → Dewar and John → Walker in 1923. When, shortly afterwards, they merged with → DCL, the whisky stocks were divided and the distilleries went to John Dewar & Son. As the blend → Watson's No 10 no longer exists, Barley Bree is the only one that is left over from the old company. Its name means 'barley juice' or 'barley brew' and used to be a popular Scottish expression for whisky.

Beam Important American whiskey dynasty. It has made a greater impact in the history of American whiskey than any other family. Its roots lie in Germany, the name being changed from Böhm once the family had arrived in the USA. Jacob was the ancestor of today's Beams. He was the son of a man who had arrived in his new homeland in 1752, living originally in Maryland and then Pennsylvania, before crossing the Appalachian Mountains through the Cumberland Gap in 1788, and settling in Kentucky. There he not only worked as a farmer, but also distilled whiskey on a small scale.

Jacob was born in 1770, and at first helped his father with his work before building his own distillery in 1788. 1795 is said to have been the year in which he sold his first barrel of whiskey and when he decided to distil on a commercial basis: at least this is the year quoted by the → James B Beam Distilling Company today as the official beginning of their history. From these small beginnings, it has developed into one of the largest American whiskey producers.

Jacob's son David and his grandson David M, carried the company on, but it was the great grandson, James Beauregard Beam, who laid the foundation of the company of today; he was the legendary 'Jim' after whom the most successful of all bourbons is named. He took over the management of the company in 1892 and still held it in 1920 when he was forced to cease distilling because of → prohibition. He was 55 years old at the time and was 68 when prohibition ended and he started up again, forming a new company in 1933.

One of its shareholders was Harry Blum, to whom Jim sold his shares in 1945, two years before his death and three years after the famous brand had first come onto the market. The family still remained active in the business even after the change in ownership and the death of Jim – and it is still active, even though the company and its two distilleries in Clermont and Boston have belonged to the conglomerate → American Brands/→ Fortune Brands since 1967.

Jim's son T Jeremiah is employed in a managing position as well as his nephew Carl, who for a while was master distiller. His son → Baker Beam, on the other hand, gave his name to one of the → small batch bourbons. Grandson → Booker Noe II, master distiller for many years and officially long since retired, is still the figurehead of the company and its ambassador. Beams are to be encountered whenever one studies the history of American whiskey companies.

A descendant of Jacob (and uncle of Jim) founded the → Early Times Distillery, and the → Samuel's family were helped by Elmo Beam when they founded the → Maker's Mark Distillery. At → Heaven Hill something like a new dynasty has been formed, with Parker Beam succeeding his father Earl Beam as master distiller, while his son Craig is already preparing to take over from him one day.

Beam's 8 Star American blended whiskey from → Jim Beam. It is supposed to contain a high proportion of → straight bourbon.

Beatlestone Scottish whisky cocktail. Equal parts of a good blend and dry vermouth are mixed with a lot of ice, stirred well and served in a cocktail glass.

Beer Term that is sometimes used in whisk(e)y production instead of the otherwise customary → wash. It refers to the alcoholic liquid that is produced when the → wort has yeast added to it in the → washbacks and → fermentation occurs. The process lasts 40 to 72 hours and leaves behind a sour bitter liquid of 7% to 9%.

Beer still Term used especially in Canada and the USA to indicate the still in which the → wash is distilled. In these countries → pot stills are only rarely used. Instead, production is based on a type of still invented by Robert → Stein and Aeneas → Coffey; the → patent, known as → continuous or → column still. In Canada the beer still consists of two columns, to which an analagous pair is joined in order to produce an even purer, cleaner whiskey, which is also quite neutral in taste, after a second distillation. In the USA the beer still consists of a single column and the result of this distillation is sent through a → doubler or → thumper to increase the strength of the spirit.

Begg, John Important figure in the history of Scotch whisky. Begg was an early proprietor of the → Lochnagar Distillery and was famous for his good nose for publicity. After a visit to the distillery from neighbouring Balmoral Castle Queen Victoria appointed him supplier of whisky to the Queen's Cellar and allowed him to change the name of the distillery from 'New Lochnagar' to 'Royal Lochnagar'. He also created a range of blends, of which → John Begg Blue Cap was the most successful. The slogan 'Take a peg of John Begg' was created for it and became so famous that there was even a Yiddish translation. Begg's company, carried on by his son, later became a subsidiary of → DCL and is therefore today a part of → GunnessUDV.

Bell's Islander Standard Scotch blend. It was introduced at the end of the 1980s by the → UD subsidiary Arthur → Bell & Sons. Its name refers to the fact that it contains a large proportion of → island whiskies from → Islay, → Skye and → Orkney.

Bell & Sons, Arthur Scottish whisky company able to maintain its independence, though only as a joint-stock company, from 1949 until they were taken over by → Guinness in 1985. This was the first takeover of a Scotch Whisky company by the Irish beer brewers. Two years later, in controversial circumstances Guinness then took over → DCL, the firm which consisted of many of the great Scottish family companies, such as John → Walker, John → Dewar and → Buchanan.

The founder of the company, who in 1976 was celebrated in a book by Jack House as the *Pride of Perth*, was Arthur Bell. In 1840 he joined the wine and spirits business of his relative Thomas Sandeman (who, in turn, was related to the famous Sandeman family of Oporto) in Perth. the gateway to the → Highlands. Eleven years later he set up a flourishing business, the expansion of which was so successful that in 1863 he became the first Scottish whisky dealer to be appointed a London agent and he went on to develop a retail network in many other countries. He also supported compulsory quality standards and was one of the pioneers who introduced standard bottle sizes.

But it was his sons who first created the Bell's brand, after Arthur's death in 1900. They expanded their activities to all areas of the whisky business by taking over the company P → Mackenzie which owned the → Blair Athol and → Dufftown distilleries. In 1936 they also took over the → Inchgower Distillery. The last brother died in 1942; the business was then managed by W G Farquharson, who turned it into a joint-stock company. In 1974 the new → Pittyvaich Distillery was built next to the Dufftown Distillery. At this time the company was strong, particularly in the home market in the UK and especially in Scotland, where it occupied a dominant position. They also achieved great success in the export market, and became an attractive candidate for a takeover. Shortly after acquiring → Bladnoch Distillery from → Inver House Distillers Ltd, in 1983, Guinness struck.

The most important brand of the company has always been the blend → Bell's, and they have also sold it in decanters, which are bell-shaped and are very popular. Decorated with colourful pictures celebrating many possible royal occasions and with a special Christmas edition each year, they achieve good prices at auctions.

→ UD, the spirits subsidiary of Guinness, was responsible for a relaunch in which they substituted the old blend with a new 8 year old in 1994. → Bell's Islander was also brought onto the market. The Bell's brand played an important part in the development of fashionable new drinks like → Red Devil and alcopops like Bell's with Irn Bru or Coke, aimed at new, mainly young, buyers.

Bellows Kentucky Whiskey. Bellows Club is a Kentucky straight bourbon and Bellows Partner's Choice is blended. There used to be far more versions and the bottles announced that Bellows & Company had been 'an esteemed brand since 1830'. Today both brands come from

→ JBB, whose parent company → American Brands acquired it when they bought National Distillers in 1987, along with their distilleries in Frankfort, → Old Crow, → Old Taylor and → Grand Old-Dad. None of these distilleries are in operation today, the whiskeys bearing their names are produced in Boston and Clermont at the two → Jim Beam distilleries.

Bell's Scotch blend from the house of Arthur → Bell & Sons, a → GuinnessUDV subsidiary since 1985. The previous successful → standard blend did not have an age statement and probably contained malt whiskies from the company's own distilleries → Blair Athol, → Dufftown, → Inchgower and → Pittyvaich. It was replaced in 1994 by the 8-year-old Bell's which was marketed intensively, particularly with expensive TV campaigns. It was the first → standard blend to carry an age statement.

The brand is also available aged 12 and 21 years and as → Bell's Islander, with a high proportion of island malts.

In order to win new, and particularly, younger customers, → alcopops were also introduced to the market: ready-mixed Bell's Cola, Bell's Lemonade and Bell's IrnBru, the latter being a soft drink produced in Scotland that enjoys almost cult status. These were not a commercial success and were withdrawn as was the 'Red Hot Spirit' named → Red Devil which contained 8-year-old Bell's and red chili peppers.

Beltane Scotch blend from The Beltane Whisky Co. Behind it stands none other than the famous Phillip 'Pip' Hills, founder of the → Scotch Malt Whisky Society.

Beltane an uncoloured, and therefore very pale blend, that is very young and should be drunk cold or used for mixing. Whether it represents a return to basics, making a blend in the same way as before the turn of the 19th century, as Hills claims, is a matter for dispute.

The old Celtic festival of Beltane, that the whisky is named after, is celebrated on 1st May by lighting a fire to greet the new life beginning in the spring. Traditionally, by the light of the warming and purifying fire, a new partner was sought.

Beltline Cocktail Scottish whisky cocktail. A third of Scotch and a sixth each of lemon juice, red vermouth, 'Bénédictine' and rum are shaken with a lot of ice.

Ben Aigen Scotch blend. It is a simple → standard blend from a subsidiary of → Gordon & MacPhail. It is named after the mountain that lies between Rothes and → Craigellachie, right next to the Elgin company.

Ben Alder Scotch blend. It originates from the house of → Gordon & MacPhail, who introduced it in 1900 with the name Dew of Ben Alder. The majestic mountain is part of the high plateau between Ben Nevis and Shiehallion, which can best be seen by looking in a southerly direction from the → Dalwhinnie Distillery.

Ben Nevis Scottish malt distillery. It belongs to the western → Highlands and lies on the northern perimeter of Fort William on the A82 at the foot of Scotland's highest mountain, from which it gets its name. Its foundation in 1825 is attributed to John Macdonald.

Because of his unusual size John Macdonald was nicknamed → 'Long John'. A blend still bears this name today, but it no longer has anything to do with the clan. The brands were sold, along with the distillery, between 1910 and 1920, and later each went to separate owners. It was 1981 before they were brought back together (for a short time only) in one company. The owners of the time, the brewers and distillers → Seager Evans, added a → patent still (which was later dismantled), to the four → pot stills of Ben Nevis and produced the blend → Dew of Ben Nevis. For a while the distillery was owned by the Canadian Jo Hobbs, who also set up the 'Great Glen Cattle Ranch'.

Three years later the distillery was sold to the Japanese company → Nikka who invested a lot of money and made a showpiece of it after its reopening. They set up an attractive visitor centre; the video shown there entertains the visitor with its robust humour and is certainly one of the best of its kind.

Nikka now markets another blend bearing the old name Dew of Ben Nevis and has also sold the brand → Glencoe. Several → independent

Ben Roland

bottlings of the single malt have been brought out. Up to now there have been (at least) eight → vintage bottlings: a 25-year-old from 1966 (59%) in a valuable crystal decanter, a 26-year-old from the years 1969 (55.4%), 1970 (52.7%), also from 1970 with 53.7%, from 1971 (54.5%) and from 1973 (50.8%). There are 19-year-old bottlings from 1972 (56.8%) and from 1976 (58.3%). A very small quantity of 10-year-old malt came onto the market in 1996 and 1997, each at 46%. → Independent bottlers such as Cadenhead or → MacArthur also have it from time to time. → Signatory was even able to hunt down a cask from 1963 from the → patent still and bottle it at 54%.

Ben Roland Scotch blend. Offered exclusively by branches of → Unwins, a chain of High Street wine-supermarkets in competition with → Oddbins and → Victoria Wine. On the bottle the producer is named as Phillips Newman & Co, who own the chain. The grandfather of the present director launched the brand onto the market in 1924.

Ben Wyvis Scottish malt distillery. It gets its name from the highest mountain on the East Coast of the UK. The first Ben Wyvis distillery was in Dingwall at the end of the Cromarty Firth right the famous → Ferintosh Distillery. For some time Ben Wyvis, built in 1879, was also called Ferintosh. It was very large for its time, but not very successful, and after several changes of ownership passed to → DCL. Although they transferred the licence to John → Begg, they finally closed the distillery two years later. The warehouses continued to be used for a long time and are still to be seen next to the Inverness–Wick railway line.

In 1965 the name Ben Wyvis reappeared on the Scottish whisky map when → Invergordon Distillers decided to set up a new malt distillery with two → stills in the middle of their huge grain complex in Invergordon, which lies on the northern banks of the Cromarty Firth, not very far from the mountain. Like the original Ben Wyvis, however, it didn't have a very long life. It was dismantled in 1977 and has been forgotten to such an extent that today even most of the workers at Invergordon can't remember it.

Despite assertions to the contrary by its owners, the malt was available at least once as a single malt in a → proprietor's bottling, if apparently only in Canada, and there was also a bottling from Robert Dunbar & Co, London & Glasgow. In the spring of 2000 → Signatory announced that they had acquired five casks from the legacy of an American investor, two of which, however, were empty. The other three were each bottled at → cask strength. Cask no. 685 produced 191 bottles (51%), cask no. 686 84 (50.1%) and cask no. 687 151 (50.6%). They were presented in a wooden box accompanied by a certificate and a miniature. Invergordon also discovered in a further three casks of a Ben Wyvis distilled in 1973. Unfortunately they were not bottled separately and the total of 471 bottles, which were 27 years old and diluted to 43%, bore labels stating that they were the last ones from the distillery.

Ben y Vraichie 30% Scotch whisky liqueur. Named after a mountain in Perthshire and produced by G & U Liqueurs in Pitlochry.

Benchmark Kentucky straight bourbon. The brand was originally launched onto the market by → Seagram in 1967, but then sold to → Sazerac in 1989. Nowadays it is produced at the → Ancient Age Distillery in → Leestown (which was renamed → Buffalo Trace in 2000). Since the introduction of → Blanton's, the owners have been pioneers of → single barrel bourbons and, as a logical consequence, in 1995 added to the first version, the Premium at 80° (40%), the Benchmark XO. Its barrels are chosen by master distiller Gary Gayheart and bottled with the somewhat higher strength of 94° (47%). Sazerac is based in New Orleans, not Kentucky, and this is stated on the label.

Beneagles Scotch blend. It was created in 1922 by the family firm of Peter Thomson, based in Perth, and inspired by the luxury hotel that had just been built in the area: → Gleneagles. That means 'valley of the eagles', whilst Beneagles is the 'eagle mountain'.

The company achieved international success after the war when it was decided to bottle the whisky in original china containers that are, for example, in the shape of a curling stone. They were especially popular in the USA where → Jim Beam in a Cadillac or in the head of John Wayne attracts collectors. There was also a series with chess pieces called 'The Thistle and the Rose' and one with birds of prey, whose star was, of course, a golden eagle (→ Whyte & Mackay also had a series with birds of prey and one with owls, sometimes even filled with a single malt; and of course there is the → Famous Grouse in a grouse-shaped container).

At the beginning of the 1980s Thomson was taken over, first by the hotel chain Stakis and then by the brewing company → Scottish & Newcastle who operated it through their → Waverley Vintners subsidiary. They have the blend made in normal containers by → Invergordon and sell them in the company's own chain of pubs. The birds and the other figures, often quaint miniatures, have been continued by → Lombard. Thomson had a further brand, → Huntingtower, which is still supplied by Waverley.

Benmore Scotch blend, from the Gaelic for 'Big Mountain'. This small brand, which is mainly sold in Belgium and Australia, is part of the huge range from → GuinnessUDV. Its name is the last reminder of the old company, Benmore Distilleries, who owned four distilleries, of which Benmore and Lochhead (both in → Campbeltown) and Lochindaal on Islay have long since disappeared. The → Dallas Dhu Distillery has survived as a museum.

Benachie/Bennachie Scottish malt distillery. It was founded between 1822 and 1824 and was called Jericho at first – it got its water from the River Jordan. In the early 1880s it was renamed Benachie, after the nearby mountain Bennachie, that lies next to Inverurie, but was closed in 1913. A new whisky company has emerged in Inverurie and has named itself after this old distillery, although this time with a double 'n'. Their leading product is The Bennachie: a vatted malt that is marketed aged 10, 17 and 21 years. It also sells a series of blends. → Union Glen, → The Formidable Jock Bennachie, → Don's Dram and → Manchester United are in the → standard blend category, and → Murrayfield (10 and 12 years) and The → Scottish National Tartan which comes in two versions aged 21 and 30 years and in crystal decanters, belong to the → premium blend sector. A further blend, → Pot Lid, is no longer being produced at present.

Benriach Scottish malt distillery. Its name is emphasised on the second syllable and comes from the Gaelic for 'dreary mountain'. It lies to the south of Elgin, next to → Longmorn, and belongs to the → Speyside region. It was taken over by its neighbour's owners in 1898, the year of its foundation. It was closed down just two years later, as a result of the collapse of the whisky boom following the → Pattison brothers' bankruptcy. It was rebuilt in 1965 by → Glenlivet Distillers and from 1977 to 2000, belonged via The → Chivas & Glenlivet Group, to the Canadian distillery giant → Seagram. In 2000 a joint venture between → Diageo and → Groupe Pernod-Ricard acquired → Seagram's wine and spirits operations for £5.5 billion. Benriach still has its own → floor maltings and works with eight → stills.

Benriach's whisky was only available as a single malt from → independent bottlers. Since the purchase of the Edinburgh-based → Hill Thomson & Company, the production of the distillery has gone almost entirely into the blend → Queen Anne, which is bottled at Benriach. To the surprise and joy of malt whisky lovers, Seagram decided to include this malt as a → proprietor's bottling in their → 'Heritage Selection'.

Benrinnes Scottish malt distillery. Which it lies in the centre of → Speyside, at the foot of the hill from which it takes its name. At its foundation in 1835 it was christened Lyne of Ruthrie, after the farmstead on which it was based. In 1838 the distillery was taken over by William Smith & Co and renamed. In 1922 it passed to John → Dewar & Sons, who merged with → DCL three years later. When UD was formed in 1987 the new parent company transferred the licence from Crawford & Co to → UMGD. For a long time Benrinnes whisky was only available from → independent bottlers (who still offer many versions). UD also made a → proprietor's bottling available as a 15-year-old single malt in their → 'Flora & Fauna' series. Benrinnes also came out as a → 'Rare Malt': distilled in 1974, 21 years old, and bottled at 60.4%.

Benromach

Benromach Scottish malt distillery. Its name, emphasised on the second syllable, is from the Gaelic for 'shaggy, thorny mountain'. It lies beyond the railway line on the northern perimeter of Forres, and thus belongs to the → Highlands region. It was founded during the whisky boom at the end of the 19th century and, like so many other distilleries, closed down almost immediately after it was built. In the course of time it underwent several changes of name and owner. For a time it bore the name of the town and first belonged to D & J McCallum and later to the American → National Distillers.

The distillery endured several periods of silence in strange contrast to the excellence of the reputation it had, and still has, in the whisky industry. In 1983, the owners at that time, → DCL, were responsible for the last closure. The distillery was sold to → Gordon & MacPhail in 1992. The company, who up to that date had been known only as → independent bottlers, and repeatedly featured the malt from Benromach in their → 'Connoisseurs Choice' series, and had a bottling in honour of their 100th anniversary. After extensive renovation and the installation of new mash and fermenting vessels and, above all, new → pot stills, production began again. On 15th October 1998 it was inaugurated by Prince Charles – 100 years to the day after its foundation.

One of its licence holders was J & W Hardie, with whom the blend The → Antiquary is associated. UD did not include the whisky from Benromach in any of its series although in 1998 they brought out a 1978 'Rare Malt' with 63.8%. In 1966, the owners had launched a 12-year-old as a single malt in a → proprietor's bottling onto the market, which was replaced at the beginning of 1999 by a 15-year-old. They also celebrated the reopening with a Benromach Centenary, which originated from three very old sherry casks which had first been used in 1886, 1895 and 1901. They were refilled into these casks at 15 years and then bottled two years later as a 17-year-old.

Benson Indian whisky, that describes itself as 'malted' on the label. This means that it either contains a proportion of real malt or perhaps malt extract. It is one of the four brands of the → Haryana Distillery, which belongs to Modi enterprises.

Benveg Scottish blend. A simple, inexpensive → standard blend that the → independent bottlers → Signatory from Edinburgh use to round off their range, which is otherwise known for its high-class single malts.

Berghoff Kentucky straight bourbon from the Berghoff Distilling Company in Lawrenceburg. The company do not say where product originates from. The whiskey is 10 years old and 90° (45%).

Bernheim American distillery in Louisville, Kentucky. It has existed in its present form since 1992. In 1987, the old distillery and both its brands → I W Harper and → Old Charter, were acquired by → UD, who, as successors to → DCL still owned the → Stitzel-Weller Distillery just six kilometres away and who also purchased the → Glenmore Distillery in 1991. Afterwards UD decided to close down all its distilleries, except George → Dickel's → Cascade Hollow in Tennessee, and to build a new building in Kentucky where all its bourbon brands were to be produced. In March 1999 the ownership arrangements changed again. The new distillery was one of a number that the company, which in the meantime had become → UDV, had sold to a syndicate for $171 million. The syndicate consisted of → Sazerac, David → Sherman and → Heaven Hill and it also acquired, along with the distillery that was finally taken over by Heaven Hill, the brands → Old Charter and → W L Weller.

The plant is able to produce two entirely different varieties of whiskey: the normal type with a → mash bill of corn, rye and malt barley, and the so-called 'wheated whiskeys' in which the rye is replaced with wheat. Stitzel-Weller were known for its wheated whiskeys Old Fitzgerald, Rebel Yell and W L Weller, all of which were produced in the new plant. The master distiller, Edwin S Foote, has a special copper → beer still for them, whilst the still for the Bernheim brands is of stainless steel. The → mash tuns for both series are the same, but different yeasts are used and a different formula: for the Bernheim whiskeys 86% corn to 6% rye and 8% malt barley, for the Stitzel-Weller bourbons 75% corn, 20% wheat and only 5% malted barley. They are all specially made with a very low grade of alcohol, so that certain aromatic substances are not lost in distillation, and are filled into barrels for maturation at an unusually low 56%. Different kinds of warehousing are also used for each type. The 'Bernheims' are stored in huge brick buildings in which there are great differences in temperature, whilst the 'Stitzel-Wellers' rest in traditional iron-clad → warehouses.

The name of this vast new distillery goes back to one of the greatest pioneers of American whiskey: Isaac Wolfe Bernheim who emigrated to the USA from southern Germany. He is regarded as the inventor of the hip flask, although his fortune came from one of the first brands of whiskey that he had already registered as a trademark in 1879. He didn't give it his own name, but the initials of his first names, as it is probable that he feared sales would be affected by prejudice (he was Jewish). He borrowed the surname from a friend. With his brother, he made such a great fortune that he became a philanthropist. Amongst other things he left behind the great Bernheim Forest which includes parts of Bullitt County and Nelson County.

In 1888 the brothers had shares in a distillery that they completely rebuilt after a fire in 1897, and it was from here that their whiskey which continued to be sold as 'medicinal alcohol' during → prohibition. After the dry years were over the company acquired the rights and the stocks of Old Charter which had been stored at Stitzel-Weller. Their own brand went to two whiskey brokers in Chicago who sold them to → Schenley in 1937, who ultimately passed to UD. At that time the company held the rights to more than 90 different brands, and although many of which they sold, they still actively manage a few. Apart from the brands already mentioned, → James E Pepper is also produced by Bernheim, whilst → Kentucky Tavern has been sold to → Barton.

Berry Bros & Rudd Long-established company based in London, and is as well-known by both wine and whisky lovers. The shop, at 3, St James's Street, is probably the oldest wine shop in the world, and the furnishings appear to have remained unchanged since 1731. The company itself dates back to the 17th century, and it celebrated its 300th anniversary in 1998. Members of the Berry and Rudd families remain active in the company. The firm has mainly made a name for itself with bottlings of port, sherry, claret and other French wines, in its own name and label. This tradition came to an end as the EU only allows the bottling of wine and other drinks at their place of origin.

Amongst the specialities from Berry Bros, apart from the vatted Berry's All Malt are some very rare single malts from well-disposed distilleries, which until recently displayed labels showing the time-honoured shop. The good relationship with distilleries is, above all, due to the product which has made the company famous all over the world: Cutty Sark. It is made by → Robertson & Baxter and is certainly by far the most well-known, but by no means the only blend of the company: they also have Berry's Best, → Blue Hanger and St. James's. Additionally they own the worldwide distribution rights to the single malt → Glenrothes, which again demonstrates the bond with Robertson & Baxter → Highland Distillers.

Best Seller Blend produced in Argentina. It is one of the many *whiskies nacionales* in South America. They are mixed from Scotch malt whiskies and Argentinian grain distillates and are much cheaper than the originals imported from Scotland, called *importades*.

Betty Boothroyd Scotch single malt. It was, and still is, made by → UD/ → GuinnessUDV in honour of the former speaker of the British House of Commons after who it is named. It is a 12-year-old malt from → Glendullan, and is only available in the → House of Commons.

Big Five Term for the five large enterprises which have played the most prominent and decisive part in the evolution of Scottish whisky from a local speciality to a drink of worldwide significance and corresponding economic importance. They are James → Buchanan & Co, John → Dewar & Sons, John → Haig & Co, John → Walker & Sons and → White Horse Distillers. They were all founded in the 19th century, starting off as whisky dealers or distillers, but their owners led their businesses from these small beginnings to a great future. Initially expansion was mainly to England, and from London they built up a national and then worldwide distribution network. Together they suffered from the consequences of World War I, and even more from → prohibition in the USA. All five, sooner or later, lost their independence and found themselves under the umbrella of their former competitor, the vast → DCL. The Big Five had already experienced the way in which success in business led to social recognition: they were knighted and became the proverbial → 'whisky barons', some pursued a career in politics or contributed to the glamour of British society in the inter-war years as philanthropists or racehorse owners. Arthur → Bell & Sons, who were not swallowed up by the DCL successor Guinness until 1985, and William → Grant & Sons, who were the only large Scottish company to remain independent and in family ownership, did not belong to the Big Five.

Big T Scotch blend. It is produced by the → Tomatin Distillery which belongs to the Japanese syndicate → Takara Shuzo & Marubeni. In Japan the brand is sold as 'Tomatin Big T'. There the → standard blend is labelled as a 5-year-old, whilst its age is not indicated on the European bottling. The better quality version contains at least 12-year-old grains and malts, of which the lion's share come from Tomatin distillery.

Bisset's Scotch blend. It used to come from John Bisset & Co in two versions: Finest Old and Gold Label. Bisset founded his business in 1828. From 1926 to 1992 the enterprise was responsible for the → Royal Brackla Distillery, whose malts were undoubtedly used for the blends. Today the whisky is one of many small brands owned by UDV.

B J Holladay Kentucky straight bourbon. Its producer is the → McCormick Distilling Co, resident in → Weston.

BL Gold Label Scotch blend which today comes from → UDV, but was originally produced by → Bulloch Lade & Co. At the time that they were taken over in 1927 by DCL, the company also owned → Caol Ila Distillery, whose malt constituted a large part in the blend. It was so successful that for a time its distribution had to be allocated. Today it is only a small brand, but still a great whisky.

Black & White Scotch blend and one of the great old brands. It was introduced by the → 'Whisky Baron' James → Buchanan in the 1880s, but was called The Buchanan Blend. When he managed to get a contract with the bar of the House of Commons he renamed the whisky → House of Commons. Because of its striking and easily identifiable black bottle with a white label, everybody ordered the 'black and white' and Buchanan, a brilliant salesman and marketeer decided to rename this leading brand Black & White.

The famous little terriers that advertise it are Buchanan's own invention. Two of the malts used came from the company distilleries → Glentauchers and → Dalwhinnie. → DCL, who took over Buchanan's company in 1925, had to take the brand off the UK market at the end of the 1970s by order of the authorities in Brussels and replaced it with a → Buchanan's. It is now available again under Black & White, but nowadays it comes from the DCL successor → UDV and is said to be different, somehow lighter, than before. Besides the → standard blend, there is also a Black & White Select which is sold only in Japan.

Black Barrel Scotch blend from the → Premier Scotch Whisky Co. Like all blends from this house, it is available aged 3, 5, 8, 10 and 12 years.

Black Barrel Single Grain Scotch Single Grain. It has been available since 1995 in the UK and since 1996 elsewhere. It represents new territory for the house of William → Grant & Sons, a name that has long been associated with innovation (→ Glenfiddich). Apart from → Cameron Brig, which is hardly of more than local importance, and The → Invergordon, where the marketing attempt was only half-hearted, Black Barrel is the first of its genre to be consistently sold worldwide. It is aimed at a new, mainly young consumer group who have not yet had any experience of whisky, and is meant as an introduction to the spirit. Soft and clean in taste, it can be enjoyed pure or with ice, or mixed with a soft drink. It is produced in →

Girvan, is continuously distilled and matured for at least four years in selected → bourbon casks, which have, in the customary way, been charred over an open fire.

Black Bottle Scotch blend. It is very popular in Scotland, but has yet to gain international appeal. It was created in 1897 by the tea blending Graham brothers of Aberdeen. It was originally for their own use, but was then marketed at the wish of friends. Its bottle is in the shape of a → pot still. Via → Long John Distillers the brand passed to → Allied Distillers Ltd, who sold it to → Highland Distillers in 1995. At the beginning of 1998 the new owners brought out the brand in two versions, the bottles and labels being a more modern design. The first is a → premium blend with no age statement and the second, which for the present is only available in a few countries such as Holland, Sweden and New Zealand, carries an age statement that guarantees that the whiskies used are at least 10 years old. A big advertising campaign was launched, emphasing that it is the only blend in which malts from all the → Islay distilleries are united. This gives a character and a power that make it a great blended whisky.

Black Bush Irish whiskey from → Bushmills. It has an unusually high proportion (80%) of malts in its make-up. They are mainly matured in casks which previously contained Oloroso Sherry. Its → grain whiskeys used to come from the Bushmills distillery, but now come from → Midleton and are specially distilled there for the brand. Originally named Bushmills Liqueur Whiskey and conceived as a counterpart with a lot of character to the light → White Bush (today Bushmills Original), it was given the name Black Bush by its admirers before the producers followed suit. It has considered by many to be the most complex and expressive of all Irish whiskeys (malts included).

Black Castle Indian whisky produced by → Haryana Distillery and bottled by Ajanta Chemicals, both enterprises belonging to one of the largest industrial groups in India. It is a 'Malted Whisky', which might indicate a normal blend, but in India it could also mean malt extract or a sugar-molasses distillate is used rather than real malt.

Black Cock Scotch blend from → Burn Stewart. There are two versions, the → standard with the absolute minimum age prescribed for whisky of three years, and the 12-year-old→ de luxe blend.

Black Dog Scotch standard blend formerly from → Whyte & Mackay / → JBB (Greater Europe) plc. A black dog is a type of fly used in fly-fishing to catch salmon and trout. It is also a term used by some Scots to describe the kind of depressing hangover that follows a night of heavy whisky drinking: 'a black dog on your shoulder'.

Black Douglas Scotch blend from → The → Chivas & Glenlivet Group. → Hart Brothers also produced a whisky by this name. It is Black Douglas 'The Good Sir James' (1286-1330), the thane of Robert the Bruce who was knighted after Bannockburn and fell in battle in Spain.

Black Jack Blend that is produced in → Argentina formerly for Seagrams, and one of the popular *whiskies nacionales*. The → grain whisky used for it is distilled in Argentina and blended with malts imported from Scotland. The brand is now also available in Brazil and Venezuela.

Black Knight Indian whisky from → Mohan Meakin. It consists of a mixture of a small amount of malt whisky and a much larger quantity of a distillate from molasses. The malt comes from the → Mohan Nagar Distillery.

Black Memorial Japanese blend. It is a brand from the house of → Nikka and a 'special'. According to Japanese criteria this means that it contains a malt share of more than 30%. It hasn't been produced for some time, but can still be found.

Black Nikka Japanese blend from → Nikka that has no malt share, consisting entirely of different grains and has no malt share. It has been produced since 1964/7. Nikka's founder, Masataka → Taketsuru, the 'father of Japanese whisky', brought a → Coffey still from Scotland, and installed it in → Nishinomiya. The company also owns another in Tochigi. Since 1995 there has been a second version of the brand.

Black Prince Scotch blend. Today it comes from

→ Burn Stewart, but was originally the product of Henkes United Distillers Group of Holland. It was then sold to a London company but returned to Holland when Bols bought it. Burn Stewart took it over in 1991 and have developed it considerably. It has been a → standard blend Select, a 12-year-old → de luxe blend and a 17-year-old version in a china decanter. Besides the → Burberry, and Scottish Leader, Black Prince is the company's most successful product. The Black Prince, named after the colour of his armour, was the eldest son of King Edward III.

Black Rooster Scotch blend from the house of Peter J → Russell & Co in Broxburn, near Edinburgh. It hasn't been produced for some time. The company, which owns → MacLeod's → Isle of Skye, also does bottlings for other firms such as → Sainsbury. There is also → Red Rooster.

Black Shield A → standard Scotch blend from the Broxburn firm Peter J → Russell & Co.

Black Stag A → standard Scotch blend from W → Brown & Sons in Glasgow, aged 5 years.

Blackthorn Whisky cocktail. It is a variation of the Manhattan, and is mixed with equal parts of Irish whiskey and dry vermouth, rounded off with a dash of angostura and anisette.

Black Top Scotch blend from Aberfoyle & Knight in Glasgow, an → independent company, which works together with Peter → Russell & Co. The brand has been in existence since 1996. The → standard 12, 15 and 18-year-old versions were originally intended for export, especially to → Venezuela, Italy and Denmark. Since 1998 they have also been available in the UK.

Black Velvet Canadian whisky. It was the leading brand of → Gilbey Canada, which later became a subsidiary of → IDV and today belongs to UDV. Since February 1999 Black Velvet has been owned by → Canandaigua. According to information from its producer, it is No. 4 of its kind in the world. In the 1950s it was brought onto the market as Black Label. The name was quickly changed as it became better known. Its success was so great, that Gilbey built a new distillery for it, the → Palliser Distillery in Alberta. Connoisseurs who can remember the 'old' Black Velvet from the former distillery in Toronto, swear that the new one hasn't an intense a taste.

A Red Velvet, a Golden Velvet, a Regal Velvet and a Royal Velvet were brought out. They were aimed at various regional markets and belong as → premiums or even super-premiums, to various price categories. The Black Velvet is also to be had in several expressions (and age groups), so it may taste differently fin different countries. The 50th anniversary of the brand was celebrated with 3,600 → cases of a 20-year-old 50th Anniversary Reserve.

Black Watch, The Scotch blend formerly from the house of → Seagram, who took over the brand with the purchase of → Hill Thomson & Company. It gets its name from a famous Scottish regiment based in Perth.

Black-50 Japanese blend from → Nikka. It is one light whiskies, a category that hopes to make the 'right' whiskies accessible to a younger public.

Blackadder International → Independent bottler. The company was founded in 1995 by John Lamond and Robin Tucek after they had both left The Malt Whisky Association (not to be confused with the → Scotch Whisky Association), the business that they had established at the end of the 1980s. The Malt Whisky Association only sells its whiskies to members, whilst Blackadder is on offer to all. The two proprietors are also the authors of the popular *Malt Whisky File*. Blackadder supplies malts which, although reduced to 43%, are always bottled without → chill filtering and without → colouring. Undiluted malts come in cask strength→ with the description → 'Limited Edition' or 'Raw Cask'.

Because not all distillery owners appreciate their whisky being bottled by someone else, the name of the distillery of origin is not always specified, but is broadly hinted at. For example Loch Indaal is a → Bruichladdich while Blairfindy is a → Glenlivet, (who went to court in the USA to prevent another independent bottler from using its name). → The Legendary is the → single cask bottling of an inexpensive → Speyside, that is offered as a 10-year-old. Mostly younger, and thus cheaper malts, are offered with the description 'Clydesdale', all at 43%, but many without an age statement. Another of the company's labels is → 'Celtic Connections'; the contents of a cask are sometimes bottled as 'Blackadder' and as 'Celtic Connections', for different markets. The main markets are in Sweden, Germany and Japan.

Blackstone Canadian malt whisky, which in itself makes it very special. Apart from → Glen Ogopolo, no other bottled malt whisky is known to have come from Canada (→ Glenora is still awaited). It is supposed to be made from 'malted grain', so not specifically from barley, which is an absolute prerequisite for Scotch malts. It is also not clear whether it has ever seen a → pot still. Its age – 8 years – is all that is stated.

Blackwood Canadian whisky whose origins cannot be ascertained. It is distributed by the French company CMI in Charantes, at 40%, and is advertised as being 'Fully Matured In Oak Casks'.

Bladnoch Scottish malt distillery. Its name means 'place of small splinters'. It lies a mile from Wigtown in Dumfries and Galloway, on the banks of the River Bladnoch, belongs to the → Lowlands region, and is the most southernmost Scottish distillery of all. It was founded in 1817 (or 1814 according to some sources) and for more than a century was associated with the name McClelland. It was closed in 1938 and went temporarily into Northern Irish ownership (→ Royal Irish) and later, – via → Inver House Distillers Ltd – into American hands. In 1983 it was bought by Arthur → Bell & Sons, who a short time later were taken over themselves by → UD. They transferred the licence to → UMGD in 1992, but a year later decided to close the distillery, the last one in an area which had once had more than a dozen.

In 1993 the Northern Irish investor Raymond Armstrong bought Bladnoch. He planned to build holiday homes and run a distillery heritage centre, but ultimately came to believe that Bladnoch should distil whisky again. In autumn 1997 → UD gave permission for the resumption of small-scale production: during the summer months, in order to ensure future stocks of Bladnoch single malt. Distillation began during 2000.

Bladnoch had already been brought onto the market as a → distillery bottling by Arthur → Bell, and at present is still available as a 12-year-old in the → 'Flora & Fauna' series. It is also available from a number of independent bottlers.

Blair Athol Scottish malt distillery. Its name, pronounced with the emphasis on the 'A', means 'plain (or moor) of Atholl'. It stands beside the (old) A9 at the southern end of Pitlochry and belongs to the → Highlands region. There was a distillery on this site in the late 1790s, and the current buildings give the impression of solid age with their dark grey colour. Many of them are relatively young, however: Arthur → Bell & Son, the blender from nearby Perth, who took over the plant in 1933 (together with → Dufftown) rebuilt it in 1949. Today the distillery is a pretty sight, particularly in summer, and with its visitor centre is one of the main attractions in the small but busy tourist town.

It has nothing to do with the nearby castle of Blair Atholl (to the north of Pitlochry) or with the whisky liqueur → Atholl Brose (which are both spelt with a double 'l') from the house of → Gordon & MacPhail. But it is connected with the blend → Bell's. Its producer has also brought it out as an 8 year old single malt in a → distillery bottling. After Arthur Bell & Son had been bought by → Guinness, a 12-year-old Blair Athol became part of the → 'Flora & Fauna' series. It was also represented in its → cask strength version, distilled in 1981 at 55.5%.

A 1981 → 'Rare Malt' was also at cask strength (55.5%). The 18-year-old Bicentenary 1798 – 1998 (56.7.%) celebrated the foundation of the first distillery at this location and the label on the back of the bottle bore the names of the distillery workers.

Blairmhor Scotch whisky from the → Inver House Distillers Ltd subsidiary R C Carmichael & Sons. It used to be sold as a blend with the description 'Old' and today is a vatted malt, at 8 years old.

Blanton's

Blanton's Kentucky straight bourbon. It can really claim to have profoundly changed the world of American whiskey, setting new quality standards for the whole genre: just like → Glenfiddich once did for Scotch malts, it was the first of the → single barrel bourbons. Behind the decision to launch such a product lay the unconditional belief, as in the case of its Scottish role-model, in first-rate quality and in a solid marketing stategy. Although it now has many competitors (three in its own company alone), it is still, not only in terms of sales figures, but also in terms of the number of prizes and distinctions that it has won.

Its spiritual father is → Elmer T Lee, who for many years was responsible for production at the → Ancient Age Distillery in Leestown. Although the distillery has frequently changed hands, there have only been four Master Distillers since 1912. The longest-serving was Colonel Albert B Blanton, whose father had already played a part in its foundation. He began work as an office clerk in the 19th century and managed the distillery between 1912 and 1953 – certainly the right man to name a bourbon. Lee, after whom a → single barrel is named today, learned his craft with the old Colonel Blanton (so called because he was a member of the Honorable Order of Kentucky Colonels) and today still personally chooses every single barrel which is to be used for Blanton's.

On the bottle they proudly announce: 'We believe this is the finest bottle of whiskey ever produced, affording you extra flavour, bouquet and character.' The bottle is octagonal in shape and looks like a decanter. It is fitted with a cork that is decorated with a horse and rider. Everything, from the bottling and the corking, the labelling and the packing of the bottle in a cloth bag, is done by hand – including the writing of the labels which name the bottling, the number of the bottle and the cask, and even the shelf in the → warehouse where it matured. A dark horse means that the bottle is intended for the USA, whilst a light one is destined for export. It is bottled at 93° (47.5%). The new 1997 Gold Edition is considerably stronger at 115° (57.5%).

Blend, blended Term for whiskies that are not bottled as an individual whisky type, such as a straight in the USA or a single malt in Scotland, but as a mixture of differing types. The word itself derives from the Old English 'blandan' and from the Old Norse 'blanda', which means 'to mix'. Blended whisky represents the greatest share of whisky production world-wide.

In Canada, apart from a few exceptions, there are only blends. The Canadians have always set great store by the fact that their whiskys are less the products of distilleries than of master blenders. The pioneer Samuel Bronfman, the founder of Seagram, said 'distilling is a science and blending an art'. Canadian whiskys consist, as a rule, of a high percentage of distilled basic whisky with which other distillates, with lower alcohol volumes, are blended. The addition of → flavourings is also allowed.

In Ireland the former exclusively → pot still whiskey has long since been replaced by blends. There is the classical Scottish form, a mixture of grain and malt distillates that is used, for example, in → Black Bush or in some brands from → Cooley. In the case of the brands from IDG, which today are all produced in Midleton, the process is not quite clear. It is said that whiskey-making in Ireland is the art of the distiller. They are able to produce quite different whiskeys from various mashes and with the combination of pot stills and → column stills in place at Midleton. Whether they are used singly or 'married' to each other, is open to conjecture.

In the USA the blended Americans are not as important as they were in the 1950s or 1960s. In those days Seagrams 7 Crowns was very successful, a relatively light whiskey, whose relationship to Canadian products is clear. After prohibition, especially the Americans preferred the products of their northern neighbour to their ownt. The American variety is lighter and, above all, cheaper than the straights, but must have at least a 20% share of them. The rest may then be neutral spirit distilled from grain. A small amount of sherry is allowed in order to improve the colour.

Blends are of greatest importance in Scotland, in fact for many people they are a synonym for

Scottish whisky or Scotch. Indeed, of Scotch whiskies sold, more than 90% are blends. Most consumers still expect a blend when they order a Scotch somewhere, and not a malt, although the market share for malts has been steadily rising in recent years. Many companies only see this as compensation for overall fall in sales of blends, a fact which malt lovers find difficult to accept.

It is true to say that malt was the original Scotch whisky although up to the 19th century, it wasn't a drink with more than local importance. What stood in its way, is the very fact that has made it successful today: that each malt has its own, individual character – each cask of malt is different to the next. The fact that Scotch whisky has become popular outside of Scotland is due to two things: continuous distillation and the creation of blends. By means of the new distilling methods, it was possible to produce a lighter (some say characterless) whisky, that was also cheaper to make because the raw material did not have to be expensive malted barley, but could be any type of grain whatsoever.

However, it was the discovery of how to blend this grain with the distinctive malts that led to the breakthrough. Andrew Usher is considered to have been the man who thought of the idea of blending malts with grains. It was his aim to produce a new type of whisky which, regarding aroma, taste and also colour (which was improved by adding caramel), could be produced consistently again and again. Usher's invention laid the foundation stone for the development of whisky-making into a great industry and for Scotch to become one of the most succesful international drinks.

Usher's recipe soon found imitators. Many of them were local grocers or wine merchants. They bore names like Chivas, Ballantine, Walker or Dewar. To begin with they made their own blend known in local circles, but at the beginning of the 1870s their activities spread southwards, conquering London and finally the whole world. Many of the great brands can be traced back to these pioneers, who from humble beginnings developed mighty firms, whose owners acquired great fortunes and soon assumed important positions in public life.

Bronfman was right: it is an art to produce blends. It is practised by highly trained specialists, the master blenders, who again and again must produce a product which is consistent in its appearance and its taste. They often use a formula for this, but it is subject to change because, for example, a certain malt may no longer available. They must be able to rely completely upon their sensory memory and on their nose. The quality of their blends can be measured by the share of malts used, which can be between 5% and 60%, by the age of the original whiskies chosen, and, not least, by how the whiskies harmonise with each other, particularly by the 'marriage' between the grains and malts.

There are different methods of bringing them together. It is more expensive to first mix the malts and the grains separately, and then marry them, subsequently allowing to mature, possibly for several months, in large wooden casks before adding water to reduce them to a normal strength of 40%-43% and bottling them. The legislators also have an input: they demand that where an age is given, it must be that of the youngest whisky used. Blends are divided into → standard, → premium and → de luxe categories. Prices are calculated according to the age and the malt content.

Blend of Nikka, The Japanese blend, launched onto the market by its producer → Nikka in 1986. Like many other brands from this company, it comes in a glass carafe which suggests quality. It distinguishes itself with a very high malt share of more than 50%, which is stressed on the label by the reference 'Maltbase' and which is evident in its taste. In 1989 its success led to it being complemented with a → de luxe version named The Blend of Nikka Selection, followed by another version containing whiskies aged at least 17 years.

Blender's Pride Argentinian blend formerly from → Seagram. A *whisky nacionale*, made from grains distilled in Argentina and malts imported from Scotland. It is also popular and widely available in neighbouring Brazil and in Venezuela, the country with the highest per capita whisky consumption in the world.

Blood and Sand Scotch whisky cocktail. Shake equal parts of Scotch, red vermouth, orange juice and cherry brandy together with ice. Those who prefer a lighter drink can add more orange juice and reduce the amount of cherry brandy.

Blood Tub Term for a → cask containing 30-40 litres. In the 19th century, before whisky was sold in bottles but was dispersed 'loose' or in stoneware jugs, many private households had their own little whisky cask in the cellar known as the blood tub. This was then kept full by a trusted dealer. The London wine and whisky house La → Réserve have latched onto this custom and offer their customers malts in blood tubs. Richard Joynson of → Loch Fyne Whiskies, has installed such a cask so that he could offer his customers a vatted malt from his → living cask.

Bloody Macallan Whisky cocktail created by Gary Regan and Mardee Haidin Regan, the authors of *The Book of Bourbon*: two parts Macallan and five parts tomato juice are poured into an ice-filled glass. A slice of cucumber and a piece of ginger round off the drink.

Blue Hanger Scotch blend from the renowned house of → Berry Bros and Rudd. They have named the whisky, bottled at a solid 45.6% abv, after a former customer. William 'Blue' Hanger was a regular visitor to the legendary shop at 3 St. James's Street, London, that is also pictured on the label. Hanger was considered to be one of the best-dressed men of his day.

Blue Ribbon Scotch whisky liqueur from the house of → Drambuie. Like the original liqueur, it consists of a secret mixture of herbs, heather honey and whiskies. This more expensive version, which at present is only available in duty-free outlets contains malts which are all at least 15 years old.

Bobby Burns Whisky cocktail. A variety of Manhattan, but made with Scotch. The dash of angostura is replaced by 'Bénédictine'.

Body Term which does not, as is sometimes assumed, describe the strength or alcohol content of a whisk(e)y, but which is a description of its character and its structure. Even a very strong whisky at, for example, 60% can be light, and conversely a malt whisky which has been diluted to 40% can have a full body. The word serves to describe an optical impression as well as the taste. Body is classified as full, medium or light. It is shown by swilling the whisky in the glass and watching how it flows back down the sides. Shapes are formed which look like church windows and are called legs. If they run quickly and close together they are the sign of a light body, if they flow slowly at a wider distance from each other, are thick and oily, then a full body with an intense taste can be expected. In the mouth body is determined by the viscosity and creaminess of the spirit.

Bond Term which is used for whiskies (and other goods) for which neither tax nor customs duty has yet been paid. They are stored in special secure bonded warehouses, i.e. storehouses that are customs sealed or in bond. This method is very popular with whisk(e)y producers and dealers throughout the world, because, in the first place, it saves them money which they can invest elsewhere. For this reason especially, the distillery owners have lobbied for laws that allow the storage of newly distilled whisk(e)y, → new spirit in bond. The taxes and the customs duties are first due when a cask is sold or bottled. One disadvantage is that the duties may have increased considerably in the meantime. Whisky lovers become conscious of this fact when they buy a new cask and let it lie in the distillery, only to be confronted with a rather large bill after 10 years maturation. A special form are the → Bottled in Bond whiskeys in the USA.

Bond 7 Australian blend, it was once made by → Gilbey, the → IDV/ → Grand Metropolitan subsidiary in Australia and exported to Latin America. It was one of the country's last whiskies before small-scale whisky distilling began in Tasmania in the mid-1990s. Production has been discontinued.

Bonnie Scot Indian whisky. It calls itself a 'Special Malted Whisky', so doesn't claim to be a real malt. It tastes like one, but connoisseurs of Indian whisky attribute this to the added malt extract rather than to the distillate. The brand belongs to → Jagatjit, who with their Jagatjit

Nagar Distillery in Hanira in the Punjab, own the largest distillery in India.

Booker's Kentucky straight bourbon. It belongs to the → small batch series (→ Baker's, → Basil Hayden's, → Knob Creek) from → the JBB subsidiary of → Fortune Brands, and was the very first of this new type of bourbon. It bears the name of the man, who, as the grandson of → 'Jim' Beam and as master distiller for many years, is a great ambassador for the firm, although he has retired, and a walking encyclopaedia of whisky production. It was Booker Noe who had the idea for the 'new' bourbons. They established, like the → single barrel bourbons which were created almost simultaneously, a completely new genre which radically changed the world of bourbon and proved that American whiskey can be just as full of character and individuality as Scotch malt whisky – provided it is left to mature for a long enough period and that special attention is paid to the choice of barrel.

Mr. Noe Jr was particularly thorough with the bourbon that is named after him and insisted that, for example, only → single barrels should be used for 'his' bourbon and that they should be bottled at → barrel °proof, that is → cask strength, and (an exception in the case of bourbon) they should be unfiltered. Foregoing → chill filtering may result in slight clouding – which is proof that the whiskey has been left in its natural state. The bottled whiskeys are between 6 and 8 years old, their strength is between 120° (60%) and 127° (63.5%) on average. They come from the middle of the warehouse, where the best conditions for maturation are said to be. The label looks as though it was written by Noe himself and notes the lot-number. A new version is the 8-year-old Booker's True Barrel Bourbon that again has 127° and is somewhat more expensive than the original.

Boone's Knoll Kentucky straight bourbon from Boone's Knoll Distillery, based in → Lawrenceburg, Kentucky. It is named after Daniel Boone, the great American pioneer and scout. The company is backed by the Hue family's spirits store 'Cork 'n' Bottle' in Covington, Kentucky. They own the last remaining stocks of → Michter's Distillery in Pennsylvania. Adolf Hirsch was able to acquire part of them before a court ordered all the other barrels to be destroyed. The Hues have bottling done for them under the name → A H Hirsch at → Van Winkle. Boone's Knoll is identical to the 16-year-old Hirsch bourbon and also is 91.6° (45.8%).

Boston Club Japanese blend from → Kirin-Seagram. Like all brands from the Canadian-Japanese joint venture, it is a composition of Japanese grains and malts, which may not only come from Japan but may also be imported from Scotland.

Boswell's Reserve Scotch blend from the house of Brodie Crawford & Co, whose flagship is → Brodie's Supreme. This blend, brought out on the 200th anniversary of his birth, commemorates James Boswell who is best known for the biography of his colleague, the author and lexicographer Dr. Samuel Johnson, and for the diary of their journey together through Scotland and to the Hebrides.

Bottled in Bond Term for American whiskeys that has come to imply a certain quality. It was originally used to describe the process where the owners would not pay tax immediately after distillation, but when they were bottled. Under certain conditions they were allowed to be stored duty-free and tax-free in bond. In 1897 a law to this effect was passed by the American government. In return the distillers had to pledge that they would allow their whiskey to mature for at least four years. It also had to be 100°(50%) alcohol and come from one distilling period, mostly from one single year. The long storage period was unusual for those times and meant that the consumer expected a particular quality from a 'BiB'. Today such whisky still arouses special expectations. It is no longer the age that makes such a whiskey attractive, especially because there are so many relatively old bourbons, but it is the fascination of the fact that it is a → vintage, the distillate of one year.

Bottlers, The Scottish whisky company, one of the increasing number of → independent bottlers to have appeared in recent years. Founded in 1996, it is a subsidiary of the wine

Boulevard

dealers Raeburn Fine Wine, renowned in Scotland and belonging to Zubair Mohamed. The company has a cellar in a building that has played a part of the history of wine and whisky: 'The Vaults' in Giles Street in Edinburgh's port of Leith was used for wine storage 800 years ago, and today the → Scotch Malt Whisky Society also resides there. The bottlings are of a very high quality, with a great deal of information on their labels. The month of distillation and bottling is always quoted, as well as the age and the number of the cask. The bottlings are nearly all → cask strength, and up to now have included two casks of a 30-year-old → Dalmore, a 31-year-old → Springbank, a 21-year-old Craigellachie, a 25-year-old Highland Park and, a special rarity, a 30-year-old → Inverleven, which was of sensational quality.

Boulevard American distillery which has only recently changed its name from the → Wild Turkey Distillery. It lies half an hour's drive to the south of Kentucky's capital, Frankfort, in Anderson County near Lawrenceburg, close to the Kentucky River. Before it was bought by → Austin Nichols it belonged to the Ripy family, one of the great whiskey clans of Kentucky.

The Ripy brothers acquired their first distillery in 1869. It was situated near Lawrenceburg in a small place called Tyrone (named after their father who had immigrated there from Ireland). Through the course of the years the brothers owned several distilleries in the area, including the → Old Joe Distillery, where → Seagram today produce → Four Roses and where, in the → warehouses, some of the Wild Turkey barrels mature. In 1905 they bought the plant which in those days was called the D L Moore Distillery, and started running it again after the end of → prohibition.

After that the distillery changed hands several times, although when the present master distiller Jimmy Russell began work there, a Ripy was still manager. The changes of ownership (today it is owned by the French company → Groupe Pernod-Ricard) continued, but Russell has been there to ensure continuity. He makes sure that the old mash bills are heeded and that the old yeast is cared for. There are still nine fermenting vessels made of cypress wood in use. The warehouses are ventilated naturally and the position of the barrels in them continually changed. It is also thanks to Russell that the old buildings on the quirky railway bridge over the river have maintained their charm.

Bourbon Type of American whiskey. It takes its name from a county in Kentucky which was named after a French aristocratic family. Today's Bourbon County lies to the north east of Lexington and to the east of Frankfort. It was much larger than it is today. Of the 2,000 distilleries in Kentucky, only a handful still exist. Curiously none of them are to be found in the modern County, so that the most famous of all American whiskeys bears the name of an area with which it no longer has a connection. Bourbon is not a term that describes origin, but type. As long as they obey the exact legal requirements set down in 1964, any producer in the USA may call their grain distillate 'bourbon', wherever their → stills may be located.

If it wishes to call itself 'straight', i.e. Kentucky straight bourbon, then the American Bureau of Alcohol, Tobacco and Firearms insists that it must be made from a mash that consists of at least 51% corn, i.e. maize. In practise it is normally much more: each distillery has its own recipe, the mash bill. If it exceeds 80% then it is called 'corn whiskey'. Rye, or in some brands e.g. from Stitzel or for Maker's Mark, wheat is also used 5% to 15% always consists of malt barley, without which fermentation would be difficult.

Further legal requirements state that in the distilling process the volume of alcohol may not exceed 80% or 160°, but this is seldom achieved 65% being customary. Water must be added to the distillate before filling in new barrels. The barrels must be made of American oak, may not be used for anything else, and must be charred before filling. They must be stored for at least two years, and four years in the case of the → bottled in bond whiskeys. This is also the age at which most, if not all, bourbons are bottled. They need less time to mature than Scotch whiskies because the new oak wood has a considerable and quickly noticeable impact. It gives them vanilla and caramel tones.

If a bourbon does not bear an age, it is at least four years old. The number of older bourbons has grown as, along with the standard bottlings, it is also worth producing whiskeys from specially selected barrels in → small batch or even → single barrel bottlings. Not everyone is convinced that they can cope with these high ages; the producers of Maker's Mark recently published a witty advertisement which makes fun of 'overaged' whiskeys. The fact that several age groups of one whiskey may bear different names also leads to confusion.

Bourbon Crusta Whiskey cocktail. Mix 4cl bourbon with 2cl each of triple sec, Maraschino and fresh lemon juice, and add a lot of ice. Two dashes of homemade orange bitter would be ideal. If unavailable, then add a piece of orange peel. Shake well and serve in a cocktail glass.

Bourbon Deluxe Kentucky whiskey, existing in two varieties: as a Kentucky straight and as a blend. The brand formerly came from National Distillers and now belongs via → JBB to their parent company → Fortune Brands.

Bourbon Heritage Collection, The Series of five Kentucky straight bourbons. They have modelled themselves on the six famous → 'Classic Malts of Scotland', with which → UD wrote a new chapter in the history of malt whisky in 1992. After the firm had become more deeply involved in the USA by acquiring other companies, their brands and their distilleries, it seemed appropriate to use the ideas that had been tried out and proved so successful in Scotland, and to put forward some of its most important American whiskeys in an equally prominent fashion, by marketing them as a collection.

UD, now → UDV, owned several distilleries in the USA but ran only two: George → Dickel's → Cascade Hollow Distillery in Tullahoma, Tennessee and the → Bernheim Distillery in Louisville, Kentucky. The Special Barrel Reserve came from the former and the other four whiskeys come from Bernheim: the → I W Harper Gold Medal, the → Old Charter Proprietor's Reserve and also the two wheated whiskeys → Old Fitzgerald Very Special and → W L Weller Centennial, which until 1993 was produced by → Stitzel-Weller. Three of these brands, the Old Charter, the Old Fitzgerald and the Weller were sold, together with the Bernheim Distillery in March 1999 to a syndicate consisting of → Heaven Hill, → Sazerac and David Sherman.

Bourbon Highball Whiskey cocktail. In the classical version a generous portion of bourbon is filled into a long glass with a lot of ginger ale, but lemonade or Sprite may also be used. It should be accompanied by a twist of lemon peel.

Bourbon Milk Punch Whiskey cocktail. In a cocktail shaker mix one part bourbon and two parts milk with a teaspoon of very fine sugar, and the tip of a teaspoon each of vanilla extract, nutmeg and cinnamon and shake together with ice. Serve in a long-drink glass.

Bourbon Slushie Whiskey cocktail. Shake 4cl bourbon and a teaspoon of sugar with ice until frothy. Garnish with lemon or cherries.

Bourbon Supreme Kentucky straight bourbon from the David → Sherman Company of St. Louis.

Bourbontown Club Kentucky straight bourbon of uncertain origin. It is bottled by the company → Kentucky Bourbon Distillers who also own the → Willett Distillery in → Bardstown, which was shut down in the early 1980s. It is not far from → Heaven Hill and there is some reason to believe that it is made there.

Bow Street Street in Dublin where the old distillery of John → Jameson used to be situated. Since extensive renovation in 1998 it has been given a new lease of life. When Jameson merged with → Power and with the → Cork Distillery in 1966 it existed as a brand under the umbrella of the newly formed → IDG, and the decision was made to move the entire production to → Midleton. None of the old Dublin distilleries were used again.

The remains of the old building became increasingly delapidated Around the corner lies the new building of the administrative branch of the IDG which belongs to → Groupe Pernod-

Bowmore

Ricard who have decided to close down the 'Whiskey Corner' and set up a new museum in the old buildings. It offers a successful glimpse into the history and production methods, has a lovely sampling room and a restaurant which is well frequented by locals.

The name Bow Street has always been mentioned on every bottle of Jameson, but the whiskey actually comes from Midleton. Only once since the end of Jameson's distillery in Dublin has there been a bottling with the name of Bow Street on its label. It came from the Scottish company → Cadenhead, who insisted on celebrating their own 150th anniversary with a series of old Irish whiskeys. One of these was the Bow Street, distilled in 1963, yet with a strength of 68.1% at bottling.

Bowmore Scottish malt distillery. Its name comes from the Gaelic for 'big house', 'large reef' or 'sea rock'. It lies directly on the shores of Loch Indaal in the capital of the whisky island of Islay, after which it is named. A further tourist attraction in this little place, apart from the distillery, is the Round Church whose circular walls are supposed to prevent the devil from hiding in corners.

Bowmore still has its own → floor maltings, which supply 50% of the required malt. It is even cheaper than that from the large maltings in → Port Ellen, who supply the remainder of the Islay distilleries, thanks to an energy-saving system of heat recovery which is even used to heat the community swimming pool, situated in an old → warehouse. The distillery location, in the middle of the island, is reflected in its whisky, which displays all the characteristics of → Islay. It is not nearly as extreme as the malts from the distilleries on the southern edge, but is much smokier, peatier and more 'medicinal' than , for example → Bunnahabhain or → Bruichladdich. It is not surprising that a Bowmore displays salty tones as well, the warehouses are not only situated at the water's edge, but some are also partly below sea-level.

With a foundation date of 1779, Bowmore is one of the oldest distilleries in Scotland. The earlier owners, Sherrif & Co offered a single malt in a → distillery bottling, and the bottle with a sailing ship on its label is much sought-after. Since Stanley P → Morrison took over the distillery in 1963, there have been an immense number of bottlings: there is currently the Legend with no age statement (8-years-old in Italy), which is made for Japan as Select. The 10, 12 and 17-year-old expressions come in transparent bottles with a similarly transparent and elegant label. It shows one of the barnacle geese that visit the island in winter. The 21-year-old is decorated with a paper label. The Surf is only available at duty-free outlets, and the Mariner is a 15-year-old.

For the 200th anniversary there were two versions of the Bicentenary, and for the 30th anniversary of the takeover by Morrison, several casks of their first distillate were bottled. Of the Black Bowmore, which was distilled in 1964 and which is named after its dark colour, there were about 1,800 bottles each of a 1993, 1994 and, as a final edition, 1995; they now enjoy cult status and achieve record collectors' prices. Motivated by the success that certainly also owes something to its extremely dark colour, there followed a Bowmore Darkest at 43% (from → sherry casks), that expressly emulates the Black Bowmore. The Bowmore Cask Strength comes at 56%. Since 1994 Bowmore's parent company has been the Japanese distilling giant Suntory, which also own the Chateau Lagrange in France. The caused a revival the old Scottish custom of maturing whisky in red wine casks, resulting in the Bowmore Claret (56%), in an edition limited worldwide to 12,000 bottles, now a sought-after rarity. It was followed in 2000 by an unlimited Bowmore Dusk Bordeaux Wine Casked (50%), which also received a → finishing in red wine barrels. At the same time Bowmore Voyage Port Casked (56%) was released, again in a limited edition of 12,000 bottles.

There have always been → vintage malts, and at present the company, is finding customers by using continually changing motifs on the packaging and with valuable ceramic bottles (e.g. for a 22-year-old Moonlight and a 30-year-old Sea Dragon). Anyone wishing to own one of the rare bottles of a 40-year-old Bowmore will have to invest more than four thousand pounds; the key that comes with it not only opens the case in which the bottle is presented, but also the door to the distillery's cottage, in which the lucky owner is allowed to spend a weekend. In comparison the 38-year-old Bowmore 1957 is almost a bargain at a price of approx. £1,000. The 861 bottles had to be filled in 1996 as otherwise the minimum strength of 40%. would no longer have been achieved. A similar price was asked for the 35-year-old Bowmore 1964 Distillation. There was only a → hogshead left for this, which produced 99 bottles.

A cheaper version is the → McClelland Islay, which is actually a (5-year-old) Bowmore. There has also been a Bowmore Blend, which contained 21-year-old whiskies. With it Morrison Bowmore took part in the International Wine & Spirit Competition for the 500th anniversary of Scotch whisky in 1994, (with the motto 'The → Spirit of Scotland'), in which the large companies fought to create the best blend for the festive occasion. There are also Bowmores from the → independent bottlers. The 31-year-old Bowmore from the Hart Brothers, also to be found in their → Dynasty Decanter, was of excellent quality.

Brackla Scottish malt distillery in the → Highlands near Cawdor Castle. Its 'proper' name is → Royal Brackla. Founded in 1812, latterly owned by UD it was one of four sold to Bacardi as part of the Dewar's deal in 1998. There is no distillery bottling yet, but UD released a Flora & Fauna bottling in 1993/4 and a 20-year-old (59.8%) in its rare malts range in 1998.

Braemar Scotch blend named after the small town on the River Dee that is best known for its Highland Games. Nowadays it bears the information that its producer is Grant, MacDonald & Co which belongs to → Allied Domecq PLC, and it is sold in branches of its former subsidiary → Victoria Wine. Originally it was one of the blends that Stowells of Chelsea had in their range – the only one still existing when the company, whose boxed wines can be found on every UK supermarket shelf, were sold to the brewery giant Whitbread, who soon resold it.

Braemar Cocktail Whisky cocktail. Mix equal parts of a red vermouth with a good blend. Round it off with a splash of lemon.

Braes of Glenlivet Scottish malt distillery. Its name means 'banks of the Glenlivet'. It lies in a very remote spot on a small road that can be reached via the B9008 leading from → Dufftown to the village of → Tomintoul (but not to the distillery of the same name). It is located on the borders of the → Speyside region and is one of Scotland's youngest distilleries, having been set up in 1973/4 by the → Seagram subsidiary → Chivas Brothers shortly before the nearby → Allt A'Bhainne Distillery, as part of an ambitious programme. They both share modern, highly-automated plants and pretty pagoda roofs..

The malt from the six → stills was never really meant to be marketed in → proprietor's bottlings, but → Signatory, as well as → Cadenhead and the → Scotch Malt Whisky Society, have brought out → independent bottlings. A real speciality is the 20-year-old from → Hart Brothers: which spent its entire maturation time in a madeira cask, not just a → finishing like, for example, the → Glenmorangie Madeira.

In 1994 Seagram brought out a → Benriach and a → Glen Keith, although they don't have a Braes of Glenlivet and haven't included it in their → 'Heritage Selection'. This was because they were afraid of confusion with The → Glenlivet, which also belongs to the company. The distillery name was changed to → Braeval. The company now belongs to the Diageo/Groupe Pernod-Ricard partnership. There have been Cadenhead and Signatory bottlings of Braes of Glenlivet.

Braeval Scottish malt distillery previously known as → Braes of Glenlivet.

Brandy Cask Scotch single malts from → Speyside, with which the → independent bottler → Gordon & MacPhail broke new ground in 1993: for the first time two malts appeared on the market which had been matured in an oak cask that had contained cognac. Simultaneously, two bottlings of single malts from former → port casks appeared (→ Cadenhead had, at about the same time, two bottlings from rum casks). This method is very different from → finishing which was used for the first time by William → Grant & Sons in their → Balvenie Double Wood where malts are refilled from their original cask to mature in a second, often unusual, cask. This has now quite fashionable (→ Glenmorangie, Balvenie, Distillers Edition). The bottling of malts that have spent their whole lives, so to speak, in an atypical and unusual cask, has, in contrast, remained an exception. No other bottlings from brandy casks have appeared so far. Gordon & MacPhail do not tell us which whiskies are involved, but they do state the exact day of distillation and bottling, as well as the cask number. Cask 3241 was distilled on 6th June 1963 and bottled on 19th May 1993, cask 7293 comes from 7th DEecember 70 and was bottled a few days earlier, on 9th May 1993.

Brazil This huge country only produces grain distillates, or → grain whiskies, itself. They are processed with malts imported from Scotland to produce their own *nacionale* blends, which are very popular in South America, owing to the fact that they represent a very reasonably priced alternative to the *importades*, which have heavy tax and customs duty imposed on them by the government, and which are unaffordable for many people. → IDV/→ UDV and → Seagram produce special brands for the Brazilian market (which are also sold in other countries on the continent): → Drury's, → Gregson's, → Natu Nobilis and → Old Eight.

Breath of Angels Scotch blend brought out by the → independent bottler → Adelphi, whose name was taken from an old distillery in Glasgow. The desired outcome was to achieve something that would be a reminder of 'the time of the Adelphi Distillery of about a 100 years ago'.

Breeder's Choice, The Argentinian blend, that is widely popular in its home country. It belongs to the reasonably priced whiskies *nacionale*. They consist of locally distilled grains blended with malts that are imported from Scotland.

Breton's Hand and Seal Canadian whisky, which → IDV brought out in the USA. It is a blend of whiskeys distilled in the company's own → Palliser Distillery, and of single malts from → Glenora. This is the only distillery in Canada which works in the Scottish style. The bottles are sealed by hand and bear batch numbers.

Brewing Term for an important stage in the production of whisk(e)y that is not much different to beer brewing. It begins when the grain used as raw material is either malted or boiled so the starches are converted into sugar. This happens during mashing. The resulting → worts are then fermented in hot water together with yeast, at the end of which an alcoholic liquid is obtained called → wash in Scotland, and → beer in the USA. During the next stage of production, heating in the stills, it becomes whisk(e)y. In distilleries every employee is proud of their work and each one knows that without them, their knowledge and care, no whisk(e)y could be produced.

Brig O'Perth Scotch blend. The brand was introduced by Matthew → Gloag & Son, the old trading firm in Perth that was taken over by → Highland Distillers. The whisky has always existed in the shadow of → Famous Grouse, the company's much bigger brand. Its label, with the old bridge over the River Tay has changed little over the hundred years of its existence.

Bristol Vat Scotch blend. It is the house brand of → Avery's of Bristol which today belongs to the → Hallgarten Group. They also produce two other higher class blends: the → Highland Blend and the → Queen Elizabeth.

Brodie's Supreme Scotch blend from Brodie Crawford & Co. The company is based in Guildford, Surrey, and mainly deals with the export of spirits. They also have several imported brands, such as a Canadian → rye named → Royal Lord. The name is used for a Scotch blend as well as other spirits. Apart from their leading brand, which is named after the 800-year-old Brodie family and their castle, the blends → Boswell's Reserve, → Commander-in-Chief, → Forth House, → McDowall and the vatted malt → Glenmoy belong to their range.

Broker A particularly important profession in the Scottish malt whisky industry, as the main product is not the single malts but the blend. Each producer is dependent on other distilleries for the ingredients of their blends, and each distillery has casks maturing that, immediately after bottling, will be bought by other companies.

Brokers act as agents for the casks of young distillate, (the spirit cannot be called whisky until it is three years old), as well as buying on their own accord and allowing casks to mature.

A successful broker will have casks of mature whisky at his disposal that can be used for blends or bottled as single malts, perhaps bought by independent bottlers. Some brokers, like the → Hart brothers, have become independent bottlers themselves.

Broking may become a dying trade as many large companies prefer to buy and sell direct.

Bronfman Canadian whisky and spirits dynasty. It was founded by Samuel Bronfman and produced the men who made → Seagram into one of the largest drinks companies in the world. In 1889, Bronfman, together with his parents and his three brothers, arrived as a Jewish immigrant in Manitoba, after fleeing from Tsarist Russia. The family bought a hotel, and when new laws forced them to close the bars, they went into whisky dealing then blending with great success. In 1924 they created the Distillers Corporation Limited and built their own distillery in LaSalle in the French-speaking province of Quebec.

In 1928 they acquired Joseph Emm Seagram's company and traded as DC-SL (Distillers Corporation – Seagrams Limited). The company was managed by Samuel Bronfman who forecast, for instance, the imminent end of prohibition, and accordingly stocked up with whisky. He also made sure that his business constantly grew by taking over other companies. He was created new brands such as → 7 Crown and → Crown Royal and was clever at marketing: using the back of the bottles to publicise the 10 Canadian provinces.

Bronfman enforced strict controls to maintain the quality of his products, and insisted on overseeing the blending himself. Despite all his efforts to sell as much alcohol as possible, he also publicly supported its moderate consumption and even financed an advertising campaign for this purpose. After his death the family maintained considerable influence in the → Seagram company, the only one still in Canadian hands. Edgar Bronfman purchased MCA, the parent company of Universal Studios in Hollywood, and in 1998 acquired Polygram. In 2000 he sold the company to the French telecommunications giant → Vivendi, who were mostly interested in Seagram's media holdings and put up the spirits section for auction. It was subsequently purchased by a partnership between UDV and Groupe Pernod-Ricard. Bronfman Jr is politically active and occupies a prominent position as President of the Jewish World Congress.

Brooklyn Whiskey cocktail. Stir equal parts of rye whiskey and red vermouth and a small shot of maraschino together with ice, strain and serve in a cocktail glass.

Brookstone American blend. It comes from the New Orleans based → Sazerac Company and is produced in its → Ancient Age Distillery in → Leestown.

Brora Scottish malt distillery which was called → Clynelish until 1969. It is several miles north of Dunrobin Castle, near the A9, not far from the North Sea, and belongs to the → whisky region of the northern → Highlands. The former owner of the castle, the Duke of Sutherland, built the distillery in 1819 to provide an outlet for grain grown by his tenants.

→ Ainslie & Heilbron held the licence to the distillery, but from 1930 it belonged to → DCL, and therefore ultimately to → UD. The fact that a new distillery, also called Clynelish, was erected on the same site in 1967/68 led to some confusion. For a short time both plants operated under the same name, but then the old distillery was renamed 'Brora'. It was closed down for a short time in 1968, though it reopened soon after. For a short time both malts, from the old and the new distilleries, were also called Clynelish. It is possible to distinguish between them: according to the workers who were employed there at the time, the malt from the old distillery was peatier and heavier, and was similar to an → Islay whisky. Its production was interrupted from time to time and finally ceased in 1983. The buildings still stand, but UDV has no intention of distilling in them again.

The name Brora is seldom found on a bottle. It appeared on → independent bottlings from → Gordon & MacPhail, which first had a Brora 1972 in its → 'Connoisseurs Choice' series and then a 1982. Two → cask strength bottlings from → Cadenhead come from the same year. The → Scotch Malt Whisky Society was able to offer its members cask number 61. In the → 'Rare Malts Selection' from UD there was a → distillery bottling of Brora from 1972 in cask strength at 58.7% and 60.02%, one from 1975 with 59.1% and one from 1977 at 56.9%. There were possibly more bottlings in this series that were only for sale in certain countries.

Brown & Sons, W Scottish whisky company. It was founded in 1976 in Glasgow, and since then has brought out a whole series of brands: the → Glen Stuart, available as a blend and as a vatted malt, and the blends → Ancient Privilege, → Black Stag, → Cairndew Mist and → Diplomatic Privilege. The company also exports old malts which are not bottled under their own name. It offers 30-year-old single malts under the label → 'Sennachie', which come from various distilleries, but which are not named, although it does state that they are from the → Speyside region.

Brown-Forman Corporation American company with worldwide activities. It owns several distilleries and, since 2000, a 10% share in → Glenmorangie plc. It is also involved in the wine business and holds the US distribution rights to various important wine and whisky brands. It has also diversified into other areas such as porcelain. It is unique amongst modern American whisk(e)y companies in that it goes back to the 19th century and has members of the founding family who, as majority shareholders, play a leading part in running the business: Owsley Brown II, the present Chairman and Chief Executive, is a direct descendant of the man who, in 1870, laid the foundations of the company.

George Garvin Brown was of Scottish descent; his grandfather emigrated to the New World in 1750 and his father was one of Daniel → Boone's scouts. Together with his half-brother → J T S Brown, he founded a company which in 1872 brought out → Old Forester, on the label of which the whisky was spelt without the American 'e'. It was supplied in bottles to protect it from being tampered with, and is said to have been the first → original bottling in the country. Since then its bottles have borne Brown's signature and the quality seal 'There is nothing better in the market'.

The Brown's partnership didn't last long; J T S believed cheaper whiskeys could have more success. After his departure, a former boss of Brown's began working at the company and was later joined by George Forman. He acquired a share in the company, which was bought back by Brown after Forman's death – along with the right to continue use of the Forman name. George Garvin Brown saw the dangers of → prohibition which had already begun in Tennessee in 1910. The company was one of the 10 to receive a licence to sell alcohol during the dry years – strictly for medicinal purposes.

The company's expanded and acquired importance by acquiring the brand → Early Times, and with it the distillery on the Dixie Highway, the 'Distillery Row', in Louisville, Kentucky. These buildings now serve as the company's headquarters. The old Early Times bottle has in the meantime given way to an Old Forester bottle. In 1940, Brown-Forman acquired the Shivley distillery somewhat further nort – this now bears the name 'Early Times' and both brands are produced there. In 1940 they also bought the oldest existing distillery in the United States, founded in 1838 by Oscar Pepper and which has been called → Labrot & Graham since 1878. It was shut down in 1971, but was rebuilt in the mid 1990s and now produces a particularly high-grade bourbon → Woodford Reserve came onto the market in 1997 to publicise the name.

The most important acquisition in the history of the company was the 1956 purchase of the distillery and the brand → Jack Daniel. In 1971 they bought → Canadian Mist with its distillery in Canada. Further important expansion occurred with the acquisition of the popular liqueur Southern Comfort. Today, the Californian wine-growing estates Fetzer, Korbel and, Sonoma-Cutrer Vineyards, also belong to Brown-Forman, as well as Bolla in Italy. The company has also moved into quite different fields of business, with the acquisition of the porcelain companies Lenox, Dansk Contemporary Tabletop and Gorham Silver and the leather manufacturer Hartmann.

The company now also owns the Bluegrass Cooperage near Louisville, where barrels for their own use and for other distilleries are made on a large scale.

Brown-Forman is the American distributor of → Bushmills, → Glenmorangie and → Usher's, as well as of 'Finlandia Wodka'. They also produce the premixed drinks: Southern Comfort and Cola and Jack Daniel's & Cola. At the other end of the market is The → President's Choice for a Distinguished Gentleman, of which precisely 24 barrels were bottled.

Brown Fox Whiskey cocktail. Take two parts bourbon to one part 'Bénédictine' and serve in a tumbler with ice.

Bruichladdich Scotch malt distillery. Its name, pronounced 'broo-ich-lad-ee' with the emphasis on the penultimate syllable, comes from the Gaelic for 'brae (bank or slope) on the shore'. It is an → Islay distillery situated on the western banks of Loch Indaal, opposite → Bowmore. Since the closure of the Loch Indaal Distillery in Port Charlotte, it is the most westerly distillery in Scotland. Its whisky is lighter and finer than the more extreme malts on the southern side of the island, which is due in part to the fact that on this side of the island, known as the Rhinns, the water is not notably peaty. In addition, very little peat has been used to dry the malt which comes from the maltings in → Port Ellen.

Those who have an eye for such details will enjoy the sight of several old pieces of equipment from the 19th century that were possibly installed in 1881 when the distillery was built by the Harvey family. It was in American hands (National Distillers) for a time. In 1968 it was taken over by → Invergordon Distillers and the number of → stills was increased to four. Shortly after this company was taken over by → Whyte & Mackay / → JBB(Greater Europe) plc and the new owners ordered its closure – a fate which Bruichladdich shared with its 'sisters' → Tamnavulin and → Tullibardine. It was meant to be short term, but the speed at which even transient closures can lead to serious damage was demonstrated in the summer of 1998 when production was supposed to start again for two months. This proved to be impossible as the spring had dried up.

However, this was not the end for Bruichladdich. An announcement in December 2000, to the effect that the distillery would soon be operational again was the best Christmas present for the inhabitants of Islay (where Bruichladdich is allegedly the most popular malt of all) and for every lover of whisky. The distillery was bought by → Murray McDavid and its new director and shareholder is Jim McEwan of Bowmore fame.

Its whisky is available as a single malt in a → proprietor's bottling aged 10, 15 and 21 years. A 17-year-old is available in the typical duty-free litre bottles. The Centenary in a glass decanter is 15-years-old. From earlier Invergordon times there is a 25-year-old and a 26-year-old, each at 45%, in the → 'Stillman's Dram' series. A → single cask from the only cask that was ever bottled by the distillery itself is a much sought-after rarity. At the beginning of 1998 a 10-year-old → Sherry Wood was brought out especially for the French market. A 10-year-old malt, which Invergordon produced in the autumn of 1987 in the series 'The → Malts of Scotland', bearing the pseudonym → Druichan Islay was probably also a Bruichladdich. In future Bruichladdich is to be made both as a lightly-peated single malt, and as a much more heavily-peated whisky, according to the distillery's new proprietors.

Brusna Irish distillery in County Westmeath. It is named after the river beside which it lies, but is much better known by the name of → Kilbeggan. It used to belong to J Locke and today it is used by the → Cooley Distillery for warehousing and maturing its whiskeys. Their → Locke's Irish Whiskey shows the lovely old buildings on its label with the original name.

Buchanan & Co, James Scottish whisky company. Its name is much less well-known than its product, the blend → Black & White, which, in turn, owes its fame to two little dogs, a black Scottish Terrier and a white West Highland Terrier. This pair of dogs, who made advertising history, were the invention of the company's founder, Lord Woolavington.

Woolavington was born James Buchanan in 1849 and was the first of the great → 'whisky barons'. The success of his enterprise was not only due to his unfailing perseverance regarding the quality of his product, but also to his brilliant salesmanship. The son of Scottish parents, he was born in Canada, grew up in Northern Ireland, and gained his first work experience in Glasgow as an office clerk. His first job with the whisky trade came when he went to London as an agent for Charles → Mackinlay. Five years later, in 1884, he became self-employed – and quickly became successful when he realised that it was better to sell Scotch in bottle than casks. He created the clearly identifiable black bottle with a white label, and did not rest until he had obtained contracts to become the sole supplier to the London music halls. His whisky was also the 'house blend' in the bar of the House of Commons.

Buchanan then proudly changed the name of his brand from The Buchanan Blend to → House of Commons, but when everybody there kept asking for the black bottle with the white label, he gave it the name by which it is known today. He was a pioneer in marketing and paid attention to corporate identity long before this expression was recognised. Until the 1930s his black and white horse-drawn carriages with their liveried drivers were part of the London scene.

He purchased the blending company → Lowrie and together they built the → Glentauchers Distillery and acquired → Convalmore, thus increasing his independence. Like his peer and competitor Tommy → Dewar, he insisted on travelling all over the world to set up branches. When these two then joined together to form a single enterprise in 1915, it was the alliance of two marketing geniuses. Together they hoped to be able to resist the increasingly powerful → DCL, but the large competitor swallowed them up a decade later. DCL sold Glentauchers to → Allied Distillers Ltd and transferred the licence of the → Dalwhinnie Distillery to its subsidiary James Buchanan & Co. This name reappeared on a bottle again in the 1970s when DCL was forced by the EU to withdraw Black & White from the UK market and replace it with → Buchanan's. It has long since returned, though, and the name James Buchanan & Co is also to be seen on the label of → Royal Household and the vatted malt → Strathconan.

Buchanan's Scotch blend, that paradoxically is one of the oldest, and at the same time, one of the youngest brands. The original name reappeared in the 1970s when → DCL, which had taken over Buchanan's company, was forced by the European Union to withdraw several large brands from the UK market; these included → Johnnie Walker, which was replaced by → John Barr, as well as Black & White, in whose place Buchanan's Blend was brought out again. Even long after they were allowed to sell Black & White again, → UD, the successors of DCL, kept the 'substitute' in their range. The Buchanan's Blend is 8 years old and is available as Buchanan's Special Reserve in South America, and as Buchanan's De luxe elsewhere. When → Guinness took over → DCL in 1986, the Monopolies and Mergers Commission required them to give up several brands and so the brand was sold to → Whyte & Mackay, now part of → Kyndal.

Bucktrout's Scotch blend with the suffix Gold Label. It is only available in Guernsey. The origins of the Bucktrout Company go back to the activities of a French shopkeeper, who opened a store in 1830. Bucktrout still trade on the island today with wine and tobacco products. They had their own bottlings, among which was a Scotch, which they originally bottled in their own cellars. EU regulations, which only permit bottling at the place of production, make this impossible today, but the house brand still exists.

Buena Vista Irish whiskey. It is produced by → IDG in → Midleton exclusively for the restaurant of the same name in Hyde Street, Fisherman's Wharf, San Francisco and thus, like → Tullamore Dew, is an Irish whiskey that is rarely available in its home country. It is 40%, is light in character, and serves just one purpose – to disappear into the famous → Irish Coffee at the Buena Vista. It is drunk in such quantities that they require 3,000 cases of whiskey a year. It was, incidentally, the American journalist Stan Dalaplane who introduced it there. Before it was possible to fly the Atlantic non-stop, he had to make a stop-over landing at Shannon airport, and was so impressed by the concoction of coffee, whiskey and cream that the barman mixed for him on a cold, wet day, he wanted to be able to drink it at home as well. He recommended it to his favourite café and began a tradition.

Buffalo Trace American distillery, which has been called Buffalo Trace since 2000. It was previously known, among other names, as → Ancient Age or → Leestown. The official reason for the new name was that research showed that the buildings were located on an old trail (and a ford over the Kentucky River) used by buffaloes. The company and its brands belonged to a syndicate formed by → Sazerac and the Japanese → Takara Shuzo & Okura, which in 1998 acquired from → UDV the brands → Old Charter and → W L Weller. In the same year Okura went bankrupt and was replaced by Marubeni. The new name of the distillery was introduced by a sensational bottling: a rye whiskey, distilled in 1981, which in 1997 had been rediscovered in the warehouses, which are racked up to 12 storeys high and are heated in winter. 3,600 bottles at 110° proof/55% were launched onto the market. This was followed by a standard bottling of a 90° proof/45% Buffalo Trace.

Bully Whisky cocktail used as a hangover cure: a good measure of Scotch is served in a wineglass with the yolk of an egg and drunk in one go.

Bulk Term for whiskies that are not filled in bottles but are sold 'loose' in bulk. The word is also used for large purchases. The practice of selling in bulk rather than in bottles is customary in all countries where whisk(e)y is produced. It is used for various reasons, although it sometimes arouses controversy in the industry: it makes it more difficult for the producers to control the quality of their product, something which is easier to do (except in the case of criminal forgery) when selling whiskey in bottled format.

Delivery in bulk is mainly of importance for exports. Individual distillates, as well as ready made blends, are dispatched and shipped in broad tankers or containers. They are used for filling liqueur chocolates and for other foods that require a whisk(e)y aroma, but are mainly used for the production of whiskies that are to be bottled in the country of receipt. Malts from Scotland are often blended with domestic grains – a typical example was the German whisky → Racke rauchzart. The largest amount of malt in bulk goes to Japan. In many countries e.g. in South America, they differentiate between the *nacionale* blends which they produce themselves (and which are, of course, cheaper) and the *importades* blends; sometimes the same brand is available in both versions. There are no figures available for any other whisk(e)y producing country apart from Scotland: in 1997, according to Alan S Gray (in his → Whisky Newsletter) the share of blends in bulk was 14.9% of all exports, with malts making up 3.69%.

Bulleit Kentucky straight bourbon. Nowadays it is produced by the → Sazerac Company in → Leestown and comes from the Ancient Age Distillery. There are two kinds, the first at 80° (40%), the second, named Thoroughbred, achieves 100° (50%). Both are said to be 5 or 6 years old. It is named after the lawyer Tony B Bulleit, who was born in → Louisville and later moved to Lexington. He had it privately bottled in small quantities for himself. Today there are only about 300 cases produced and they are marketed by → Seagram. Earlier the name of Owensboro, the site of → Glenmore and → Medley, appeared on the label as well as Frankfort, of a version at 80° (40%).

Bulloch Lade & Co Scottish whisky company. Established in the 1730s in Glasgow, it was able to maintain independence until 1927, when it was swallowed up by → DCL. It was famous for its blend → BL Gold Label and the vatted malt → Glen Ila. From 1880 to 1922 the company owned the → Caol Ila Distillery and also, for a time, via a subsidiary, → Dallas Dhu and the blend → Roderick Dhu. The vatted malt has been discontinued by the DCL successor → UD, but the licence for Caol Ila has been transferred back to Bulloch Lade

Bunnahabhain

again. The blend BL, which was previously very successful, is also available again: it is bottled in Scotland for Canada, and it is exported in → bulk to the USA and New Zealand. Bulloch Lade are also named as the producers on the label of → King Arthur.

Bunnahabhain Scottish malt distillery. Its name, pronounced 'boo-na-ha-ven' is emphasised on the penultimate syllable, and comes from the Gaelic from mouth of the river. It lies beside the Sound of → Islay, in the north eastern corner of the island, in such a remote spot that in 1881 road had to be built down to the sea before erecting houses for the workers, a shop and even a school for children of distillery workers. Nowadays several of the old houses can be rented as comfortable holiday cottages. Built in 1881 by The Islay Distillery Company Litd, who amalgamated in 1887 with Glenrothes-Glenlivet Distillery to form Highland Distilleries Ltd: → They, however, lost their independence to the Edrington Group. They operate with four → stills, and the → malt comes from the large maltings in → Port Ellen.

Bunnahabhain is a significant component of the blend → Black Bottle, and is available as a 12 year-old single malt in a → distillery bottling. Its label shows a saluting helmsman and relates to the song *Westering Home*, which is the island's anthem. Homecoming seafarers sing about Islay being a place where they can 'say goodbye to care'. The whisky proves that belonging to a certain → whisky region does not automatically produce a particular style. Bunnahabhain is atypical for Islay, being soft, smooth, fruity and light.

One reason for this is the water, which is relatively hard (as in the case of → Glenmorangie) and only slighty peated. The malt is also only very lightly peated. Apart from that the owners also place importance on using a large proportion of → sherry casks for maturation, and the location by the sea imports a delicate salt tone. There are a lot of old casks with malt distilled in 1963 maturing at the distillery. A small amount appeared on the market in 1997 as a sought-after (and expensive) → vintage bottling. A

Bunnahabhain was brought out in 1968 under the name 'The → Family Silver'.

Bunny Hug Whisky cocktail. Take equal parts of a blend, gin and Pernod, shake them with ice and serve in a cocktail glass.

Bunratty Potcheen Irish spirit. The fact that it is not intended for the Irish is evident from the name, which is the English translation from the Irish Gaelic, poitín, illicitly-distilled alcohol. Real poitín is always illegal. Of course the Bunratty Mead & Liqueur Co, who market the drink at 40%. in a simple bottle, a clay jug, in a ceramic bottle, do so legally. They wisely forgo selling this in Ireland. But it is available in the duty-free shops at Irish airports. It has nevertheless been successful enough to produce imitators: → UD reintroduced the discontinued → Hackler onto the market and Vins Francais brought out a 'poteen' named → Knockeen.

Burberry Scotch blend. The company that are famous for trenchcoats, worn by English soldiers in the colonies and by Humphrey Bogart in Hollywood, has followed the example of many other clothes and fashion companies, who have expanded their traditional products in the lifestyle direction, by supplementing them with perfume, cosmetics. The Burberry whisky is produced by → Burn Stewart. The Burberry is available in several expressions and price bands, as a blend, a vatted or a single malt. The basic blend is called Premium, the higher grades are available at 12, 15, 20, 23 (duty-free only) and 25 years old. The vatted and the single malt are 15 years old. In 1994 Burn Stewart created a Burberry blend as their contribution to the 'The → Spirit of Scotland' competition.

Burke & Barry Blended American Whiskey produced by a 'Distilling Company' of the same name in Owensboro, Kentucky and Lawrenceville, New Jersey. It has a strength of 86°(43%) and its label describes it as 'charcoal filtered'. There is a Scotch blend of the same name whose label also mentions a 'Distilling Company'. Although it is also obtainable in the UK, it appears mainly to be sold in Germany by the company Dethleffsen,

International Drinks, in Flensburg. The label describes its character as 'distinctive' and its style has 'a touch of class'.

Burn McKenzie Scotch blend. Nowadays it comes from → Burn Stewart, one of whose subsidiaries was Burn McKenzie & Co who had a → de luxe version of the blend with no age statement. It is now available aged 3 years (the minimum age for a whisky) and 12 years.

Burn Stewart Scottish whisky company. It first appeared in its present form in 1988, resulting from a management buy out. It is a joint-stock company whose full name is Burn Stewart Distillers plc. A London-based company with several subsidiaries and some well-established brands, which operated as a → broker in the UK and was also active as an exporter, also bore this name.

Today Burn Stewart is based in East Kilbride. In 1991 the company bought the → Deanston Distillery from → Invergordon and two years later the → Tobermory/Ledaig Distillery on the island of Mull. Both whiskies are available as single malts. There is also a malt named → Glen Ardoch, which is bottled as a single and as a vatted malt, and three vatted malts, → Angus McKay, → Glen Blair and → Glen Elg. → Scottish Leader is the most important brand and is one of the most succesful blends of all.

The Burn Stewart is available as a → standard blend without an age statement and as a 12-year-old → de luxe blend. Further brands are: → Black Cock, → Black Prince, → Burn McKenzie, → Burberry, → Glen Rowan, → Highland Rose, → Old Argyll, → Old House, → Old Royal and → Scottish Castle. Whilst the cream liqueur → Drumgray has been around for some time, in 1997 the company took advantage of the 700th anniversary of the victory of William Wallace over the English at Stirling Bridge (and of the newly-won, worldwide popularity of the Scottish hero through Mel Gibson's movie *Braveheart*) to launch a new whisky liqueur named → Wallace. Using the name 'The → Select Hogshead', the company supplies single malts for The Whisky Shop chain, as it has large stocks of malts for its blends these have

inluded a 14-year-old → Glenlochy at 50% from a → sherry cask and an equally strong → Port Ellen.

Burns, Robert Scottish poet, honoured and loved as the 'national bard', not least of all because he was a voice of the people and wrote in style which is accessible to all.

He immortalised whisky as John Barleycorn. He mourned the passing of the → Ferintosh, and he forged the immortal words 'Freedom and Whisky gang thegither'.

In honour of Burns, friends of Scotland and whisky meet together on January 25th every year to celebrate with 'Burns Supper', at which there are numerous toasts, including one to the lassies, and his 'Immortal Memory' is honoured. Haggis is served and there is much singing and even more drinking, until they part from each other with the song → 'Auld Lang Syne'. Although there is a blend called Robbie Burns and a cocktail called Bobbie Burns, there is no great whisky in his honour.

Burn's Heritage Scotch blend. It comes from → Morrison Bowmore, the Glaswegian company which is owned by the Japanese drinks giants → Suntory. Its name is, of course, a reference to Robert Burns, the national bard of Scotland.

Burnside Scottish malt distillery. It was located in → Campbeltown, the capital of Kintyre, and was founded in 1825 by McMurchy, Ralston & Co, ceasing operation 99 years later. It shared the fate of so many distilleries in the Campbeltown → whisky region and didn't survive prohibition in America. The fact that its name has not been completely forgotten is due to a single malt of the same name that was brought out by J & A → Mitchell. The company run → Springbank in Campbeltown, one of the two distilleries still existing in the area. Springbank issues miniature bottlings from time to time bearing the names of bygone distillates.

At Springbank a second malt is produced named after → Longrow distillery, and

Burnt ale

recently there has been a third malt, named after → Hazelburn. They both use varyingly peated malt and a different → separation is used in the distilling process.

It is not known where the 15-year-old Burnside comes from. Though it may well be a Springbank, it certainly has nothing to do with the Burnside that William → Grant & Sons supply to other companies for blending. That is a vatted and not a single malt, with distillates from the → Glenfiddich Distillery and a small share from → Balvenie. By mixing the two they are able to prevent casks of their own whiskies being brought onto the market as single malts by any → independent bottlers.

Burnt ale Term for the residue containing yeast, with liquid and solid components, which remains after the first distillation at the bottom of the → beer or wash still. It is also called → stillage in the USA and, when separated from the solid parts, is known as→ sour mash. In Scotland the liquid, also known as pot ale, is not simply disposed of in the environment, but is mostly converted to high-protein cattle feed (→ dark grains). However at → Lagavulin and at → Laphroaig it is drained off into the sea – with the wonderful effect that the scallops 'harvested' there are particularly large and tasty which, according to the distillery manager, is a result of the nutritious food that they get.

Bush Pilot's Canadian whisky. This is a speciality because it is an unblended → single cask bottling, probably the only one of its kind in the country. At 13 years the 'Private Reserve' is relatively old for a Canadian whisky. The brand was the idea of Frederick H Johnson Jr, who wanted to commemorate 'my father's Great Northern Skyways to the wilderness of Canada'. He has it exclusively bottled by the American company Robert Denton in Bloomfield Hills (Michigan), who buy the barrels from → Potter in British Columbia. Although Potter own the tiny → Cascadia Distillery, it is unlikely that the whisky is distilled there. It is more likely that it comes from the → Okanaga Distillery of Hiram → Walker, built in 1971 but since closed down, which is just a few miles from Cascadia.

Bushmills Irish malt distillery. It lies on the River Bush in County Antrim in Northern Ireland and since 1896 has borne the official name The → Old Bushmills. Its history is related under that heading. Bushmills whiskeys still bear the old name on their labels. It has produced malt for over 100 years and is therefore an exception in Ireland. The single malt has been available as a → distillery bottling for a long time, and is traditionally a 10-year-old. The Italians are able to enjoy a 5-year-old.

Two blends also have a long tradition: the powerful → Black Bush and the Bushmills Original, that used to be called → White Bush after the colour of its label. In contrast Bushmills 1608 is a recent addition. This date refers to the year in which, according to company history, Bushmills Distillery was founded. It is a fact that the blend contains a very high malt share of 90%.

A 16-year-old malt, the so-called → Threewood, is another recent addition to the range. It consists of whiskeys of which one half were matured in ex-sherry casks and the other half in ex- → bourbon casks. They are then married and allowed to mature further in casks which contained port (from Sandeman). A malt which underwent a second maturation (in a Madeira cask) was the 21-year-old brought out at the end of 2000 in numbered bottles. The Distillery Reserve is a 12-year-old malt that is only available at the distillery visitor centre. It should not be confused with the Distiller's Reserve. This term is used by Bushmills for casks which are filled for individual customers. Five bottlings with the dark green label giving precise information regarding the cask number, strength, day of distillation and bottling are known, two of which were for 'World of Whiskies' at Heathrow Airport in London, and one for the customers of Otto Steudel from Celtic in Nuremberg, Germany. With a degree of foresight, 350 'millennium' casks were put aside in 1975, which were bottled for their subscribers in time for 31st December 1999.

Butt Term for a cask size. Like 'bottle', it is derived from the Latin word *butta*. It has been used since the Middle Ages, but for varying cask sizes. In the modern whisky industry a butt contains about 500 litres and is thus double the size of a → hogshead. It is the second largest cask after the → puncheon. It is normally made of Spanish oak and has often already contained → sherry before being used for Scotch → malt spirit.

C

Cabin Hollow Kentucky straight corn whiskey. It comes from Barton and is bottled at 100°(50%). Today the company belongs to → Canandaigua, and the whisky is produced at the Barton Distillery in → Bardstown.

Cabin Still Kentucky straight bourbon. It used to be made by → Stitzel-Weller and was sold in various strengths, mainly to local markets in the southern states of the USA. In 1954 a Cabin Still Hillbilly in porcelain was brought out. It is said to have been the first motif carafe of all; it has had a large number of imitators such as Jim Beam. After Stitzel-Weller was swallowed up by → DCL in 1984, its successor → UD sold the brand, together with the remaining barrels, to → Heaven Hill. These old whisky stocks are still bottled and marketed in three versions at 80°(40%), 86° (43%) and 90° (45%).

Cadenhead, William Scottish whisky company. The mere mention of the name Cadenhead brings a sparkle to the eyes of malt whisky lovers. Thirty years ago, when there were few single malts on the market apart from → Glenfiddich, → Glen Grant (that was only 5-years-old) and in Scotland → Glenmorangie, it was these stocky bottles with their black labels and white writing that represented an oasis in the desert for the lover of malts. Cadenhead have always been precise in stating the origins of the whiskies, which at that time were still described as → pure malt and bottled at 46%. These were identified as being bottled by William Cadenhead, 18 Golden Square, Aberdeen.

In 1842 William Cadenhead founded his wine and spirits shop in Netherkirkgate, Aberdeen, but the present address is 30 Union Square, → Campbeltown. Along with → Eaglesome, Cadenhead is now a subsidiary of J & A → Mitchell who also own the → Springbank distilleries and Glengyle. The address and the owners have changed, but Cadenhead can be proud that together with → Gordon & MacPhail, they are the oldest and still among the most important → independent bottlers. The company has profited from the malt boom of recent years – and has made use of it to expand their activities. In the process they have extended their practice of offering their customers single malts in as pure a form as possible: they have long done without → chill filtering and any → colouring, and since the introduction of the 'Authentic Collection', have bottled at → cask strength. The previously square bottles have now been replaced by more standard-shaped ones.

The abundance of bottlings makes it impossible to even attempt listing which single malts from which distilleries were and are available from Cadenhead. It may be a coincidence, but on the occasion of its 150th anniversary the Scottish company issued a glorious series of single malts – from of all places, Irish distilleries. Most of these no longer exist: → Bow Street, → John's Lane, → Jones Road, Old → Bushmills, → Royal Irish and → Tullamore. There have often been great rarities (such as → Ladyburn) and there are often very old malts such as the series of five which were brought onto the market in 2000 for the millennium: a 1963 → Benrinnes (26 years old, 52%), a 1962 → Caperdonich (37 years, 48%), a 1964 → Glen Grant (36 years, 53%), a 1962 → Glenburgie (37 years, 51%) and a 1962 → Glenlossie (37 years, 54%).

It is easier to say what has not been available: even Cadenhead has not yet been able to offer a → Glenmorangie. But on the other hand they have good stocks of demerara rum, as two Springbanks have been available from ex-rum casks. There also appear to be one or two bourbon barrels in store in Campbeltown: in the

'Authentic Collection' there was a 6-year-old at 66.3% and a 9-year-old American at 64.2%, each bearing 'Distilled at Frankfort, Kentucky' on the label.

The company also carries the blends → Hielanman, → Moidart and → Putachieside. It has a subsidiary by the name of → Duthie, who are also independent bottlers. The → Triple S is a curiosity: a crystal-clear, fresh distillate, bottled in 50cl bottles, a single Scottish spirit which is probably a Springbank. Cadenhead owns a shop in London's Covent Garden and for many years has had a small shop on Edinburgh's Royal Mile, which has all the current bottlings in stock. This includes a bottle of Springbank from 1919.

Cairnbaan Scotch blend from → Eaglesome. The company based in → Campbeltown is a subsidiary of → J & A Mitchell, who also own the → Springbank Distilleries and Glengyle. Some of their malt must surely be contained in this blend. It is not known where the other malts come from, but as Mitchells also own → Cadenhead, one of the great → independent bottlers, they have large stocks of malts from other distilleries at their disposal.

Cairndew Mist Scotch blend. It comes from W Brown & Sons in Glasgow and, like most of their brands, is a → standard, aged 5 years.

Calchou → Independent bottler, which has adopted the old name for the Borders town of Kelso as its trademark. The driving force behind the enterprise is John McDougall, who was formerly distillery manager at → Balvenie, → Laphroaig, and → Springbank Distillery and now also works as an independent consultant. For his first bottling he chose a malt from → Orkney. That much is stated on the label though the fact that it is a 9-year-old single malt from Highland Park is not revealed.

Caledonian Scottish grain distillery. It lies almost in the heart of Edinburgh, right next to Haymarket Station, having been built in 1855 and for many years it was the largest distillery in the country. In 1884 it was acquired by → DCL, which from 1966 ran it via its subsidiary Scottish Grain Distillers. From the outside it still looks very old-fashioned and unchanged. It was twice badly damaged by fire, and during the Second World War more than a million gallons of whisky went up in flames. It was closed down in 1987, and much of the site has been cleared and redeveloped, though the landmark distillery chimney is a listed structure and remains in place.

Every now and then a cask of whisky from the distillery turns up. → Signatory were able to locate a grain distilled in 1958 and bottle it in 1996 at 44.2%.

Calvert American blend. It calls itself Extra and uses the description 'Soft Whiskey'. The producer named on the label is the Calvert Distilling Co in Baltimore, but the brand today belongs to → JBB. They acquired it when their parent company → Fortune Brands, bought out → National Distillers in 1987. It should not be confused with the Canadian blend → Lord Calvert which is from → Seagram.

Cambus Scottish grain distillery. It gets its name from the village where it is located on the banks of the River Devon near Alloa in Clackmannanshire. The area was very well-known for its whisky activities at the beginning of the 19th century. The → Steins and the → Haigs worked there and → Carsebridge Distillery and → Cameronbridge Distillery are not far away. This site was originally occupied by a mill. Cambus first gained some significance in 1836 when a → → patent still was installed and it began to distill → grain whisky. The owners were among the founders of → DCL and Cambus remained part of the company until it was taken over by → GuinnessUDV. Although the whisky was always very much in demand from blenders, the distillery was closed in 1993.

Several casks of grain from Cambus were located by → Cadenhead (31 years old, 53.2%) and → Signatory (1964, 43%). But there is every reason to believe it was this distillery that was the first to sell its whisky as Single Grain, even earlier than Cameronbridge, and certainly much earlier than → Invergordon and → Girvan. In 1906, in the London borough of Islington, the → 'What is Whiskey' case went to court, concerning what could legally be named whisky. At the time DCL triumphantly brought a 7-year-old Cambus onto

Cameronbridge

the market, and advertised cheekily that it contained 'Not a Headache in a Gallon'. It is not known whether the judges tried it but a short time later they passed judgement to the effect that malt is not the only real whisky, grains and blends may also call be called whisky – a momentous decision.

Cameronbridge Scottish grain distillery, sometimes also known as Cameron Bridge. It lies in Windygates in Fife and was built by John Haig in 1824. It can claim to be one of the first distilleries which, alongside the traditional methods of distilling malted barley in → pot stills, installed → continuous stills for making → grain whisky. The inventor of this method, Robert → Stein, was a cousin of John Haig, who had encountered his uncle's experiments at the nearby Kilbagie Distillery and put them into practise in Cameronbridge in 1827. When Aeneas → Coffey perfected the method in 1831 two Coffey-stills were installed alongside the two Stein stills, which were in use until 1929.

At the turn of the 19th century, Cameronbridge was able to produce malt as well as various → grain whiskies, and therefore also a similar variety of different whisky types, as is today possible at → Midleton in Ireland. For a long time only → grain whiskies have been produced there. Since 1987 it has been owned by UD/UDV, who installed → column stills in which gin can be made. Although a single grain from Cameronbridge, called Cameron Brig Old Choice, was not the first of single grain market, it was, for a long time, the only one available. Now that → Invergordon and William → Grant & Sons with their → Black Barrel also offer single grains, the rather old-fashioned label has been exchanged for a more modern one. The whisky in these bottles is 12 years old.

Campbell & Clark Scottish whisky company founded in 1934, and from 1970 was half-owned by the American company → Sazerac. They had close connections with the → Speyside Distillery Co, to whom it now belongs. They sold several blends under their own name, which still exist, such as → Murdoch's Perfection and → Old Monarch. They sold → King's Crest and → Scottish Prince under the name of the company's subsidiary Colin Forbes Ross & Co, and these are again on the market. Speyside Distillery Co also uses the name for single malt bottlings such as one from the → Glen Mhor Distillery.

Campbell Distillers Scottish whisky company which can trace its beginnings back to 1879 and the firm S Campbell & Sons. Until 1945 they were only concerned with the production of blends, but then they bought the → Aberlour Distillery. In 1974 both the company and the distillery were taken over by the French Groupe Pernod-Ricard, who transferred the base of their Scottish subsidiary from Glasgow to nearby Kilwinning. They acquired two further distilleries, the small but fine → Edradour and → Glenallachie, which lies close to Aberlour. Whilst Glenallachie maintains a low profile and a single malt in a → proprietor's bottling is no longer available, the other two distilleries (and their malts) enjoy greater exposure and their owners are rewarded by the fact that Edradour continues to be considered the most beautiful distillery in Scotland. Aberlour is a very successful brand which recently replaced → Glenfiddich as France's no. 1 brand. The company's most successful product is the blend → Clan Campbell, which at present is rated the fastest growing Scotch of all, with a reported 800,000 cases sold annually. Other brands are: → House of Campbell, → House of Lords and → White Heather.

Campbeltown Scottish → whisky region. It gets its name from the most important town in Kintyre and includes all the distilleries on the peninsula. During the 19th century and up to the 1920s, there were many distilleries in the town and its surroundings, some say there were as many as 30. Good shipping connections existed here and the casks could be easily exported – even to America. This ceased being an advantage when → prohibition arrived in the USA and the whisky from Kintyre was no longer needed. During and after → prohibition one distillery after another was forced to close down. Today there are only two distilleries left, → Glen Scotia and → Springbank, the latter producing three different malts: one with its own name, → Longrow and since 1997 → Hazelburn. Both names are a reminder of two of the distilleries which were closed down.

Because of the small number of distilleries, some authors no longer recognise Campbeltown as a separate region, but include it either with the → Lowlands or the western → Highlands.

Campbeltown Loch Scotch blend. The label names the producer as the Campbeltown Loch Whisky Co, 30, Union Square, Campbeltown. That tells us who is behind the company: the → Eaglesome shop can be found at this address, a subsidiary of J & A Mitchell, who also own the → Springbank Distillery, which is just a few minutes away, and the important → independent bottlers → Cadenhead. The blend is bottled at 40% and includes whiskies that are at least 10 years old. It therefore lies between the → premium and the → de luxe sectors of the market.

Canada One of the four great whisky producers of the world, with its own type of whisky. Nature provides everything necessary for whisky production: a wealth of grains and good water. The first spirit made in Canada was gin or geneva, which immigrants from France or Holland (→ Melcher) had brought with them. They mainly settled in Quebec whilst those from the UK settled in Upper Canada as Ontario was then called. This is where the history of whisky in Canada began – with millers who converted their surplus grains into spirit. Except for the Molsons, who began as brewers and remained such, all the important whisky pioneers of the mid 19th century began with this dual occupation: → Gooderham and Worts, J P → Wiser, Joseph Emm → Seagram, Henry → Corby and Hiram → Walker. Their distilleries soon became flourishing businesses, sometimes constituting proper communities, such as Corbyville and → Walkerville.

However, the pioneers were also confronted with difficulties. The law repeatedly forbade the sale of alcohol and like all countries with a Puritan influence, there was a strong temperance movement. Canada also suffered under → prohibition, and its effects have still not been overcome everywhere. In some places sales are still government controlled, each province has its own alcohol laws and taxes can be extremely high. Paradoxically, it was prohibition in the neighbouring USA that allowed Canadian whisky to flourish.

Canadian whisky producers left the distribution to smugglers and gangsters – and watched with satisfaction as their good and pure whisky became more and more popular. Indeed this laid the foundations of the current popularity of Canadian whisky in the USA (where they still drink more of it than their own whiskey).

In those years the ascent of Canada to become one of the greatest whisky producers in the world began with personalities such as Samuel → Bronfman and Harry → Hatch – as well as the rise of their firms, Hiram Walker and Seagram, to become international companies. Seagram was in Canadian hands until the autumn of 2000, Walker is now a subsidiary of → Allied and both compete with → UDV, which in 1999 sold all its Canadian business, except for one brand, to Canandaigua and → Jim Beam, who also operate in Canada. The rationalisation in the Canadian spirits market has been quite dramatic. Of more than 200 distilleries that were in existence in 1840, many closed in the following twenty years, and today only 10 still remain: the tiny → Highwood and → Kittling Ridge, → Cascadia from → Potter, which only distils sporadically and → Glenora, which is not only the youngest distillery in Canada but as a → malt distillery is unique in Canada. The others, → Alberta, → Canadian Mist, → Gimli, → Palliser, → Valleyfield and Walkerville belong to large companies, Walkerville is the only distillery that is still left from the pioneering days.

Canada House Canadian whisky. It is produced by → Alberta Distillers and although it is made in Canada, the parent company → Jim Beam Brands imports it to the USA in → bulk, and bottle it there exclusively for the American market.

Canadian Age American blend. Its name is somewhat misleading: it is produced in the USA by → Sazerac at their → Ancient Age Distillery in → Leestown. It is only sold in Canada. It is more usual for Canadian-made whiskies to be sold as American company own-brands in the US market.

Canadian Club Canadian whisky. It is one of the really big brands and for many people is the

Canadian Company

embodiment of its type. It was the creation of the Canadian pioneer Hiram → Walker, who first produced it in 1884. Thus it was one of the very first worldwide whisky brands. Originally it was just called Club, and was meant to be a demanding whisky for a demanding public – club members. In order to guarantee its quality, Walker only supplied it in bottles. He was so successful with this method that many imitators followed suit, and called their whiskies by the same name. Walker's American competitors soon insisted that he should clearly mark the Canadian origin on his bottles. This ensured that the new name, Canadian Club, was easier to identify. Even after Walker's death the company had to warn against copies in advertisements..

Its admirers call the brand CC. It is special among Canadian whiskeys in that its individual whiskeys are not blended in the barrel after maturation, but are first mixed and then filled into barrels to mature for varying periods. The standard version matures for 6 years, the Classic for 12. The 8-year-old Black is only available in Japan and a 20-year-old (which in Canadian terms is positively ancient) only in the USA and Asia. There is also a Premium 100 in the range, which is named after its 100° strength. The CC Citrus is only 35% and is aimed at a young public interested in a light and fresh spirit. In 1998 the present owners of the brand, → Allied Domecq PLC, broadened the spectrum and brought out the Canadian Club Reserve, which is 10 years old. 'Aged at least 8 years', the Canadian Club Sherry Cask at 41.33% is obviously a result of the trend for → finishings which was triggered off by → Balvenie and, particularly, → Glenmorangie, but was a new departure for Canada.

Canadian Company Canadian whisky that for the time being is only available in its home country and in Taiwan, where it is the best-selling Canadian whisky. It has been distinguished with several gold medals at international spirits competitions. It was launched onto the market by the Rieder company, which was founded in 1970. They also owned the → Kittling Ridge Distillery in Grimsby, Ontario, where only fruit distillates were produced. Although whisky is now also made there, the distillates used for this blend are from other distilleries. There are two versions, that are 4 and 10 years old.

Canadian De Luxe Canadian whisky. It is the houseblend of the David → Sherman Company in St. Louis, produced in Canada, and only on sale in the USA.

Canadian Gold Canadian whisky. It is 3 years old and is produced by → Alberta Distillers. Halewood Vintners, a subsidiary of Halewood International, import it exclusively into the UK, where Canadian whiskeys are seldom found.

Canadian Host Canadian whisky. Although produced in Canada, it is taken in → bulk to the USA and bottled and marketed there by → Barton.

Canadian Hunter Canadian whisky. It is 4 years old and is one of the Canadians sold solely in the USA. It has been produced by → Seagram, which has had great success with it. Its name certainly plays a part in this.

Canadian Ltd Canadian whisky. One of → Barton's own brands. The whisky is produced in Canada then bottled in the USA. Barton took over the brand together with the company from → Glenmore.

Canadian Mist Canadian distillery. It lies in the small town of Collingwood, about 60 miles from Toronto. Curiously the brand name is two years older than the distillery in Ontario. It was created by → Barton in 1965, and the whisky used for it came from → Melcher in Canada. The brand quickly became a success, and its owners decided to build it a distillery of its own. It was completed in 1967, in only four months, and is unique in several respects: it is the only one in the country that uses a mixture of corn and malted barley, its distillates never come into contact with copper, and it does not distil the rye share itself but obtains it from the → Early Times Distillery in Louisville, Kentucky. This curious fact is easy to explain: both the distillery and the brand have belonged to → Brown-Forman since 1971, and they are the owners of Early Times (and, amongst others, of the → Jack Daniel Distillery). Nearly the entire production is sent from Collingwood in tankers in → bulk to Kentucky, where it is blended (with a small share of bourbon) and from there marketed in the USA with great success. There Canadian Mist is the number 1 Canadian whisky, which with its 3 million cases sold even beats → Seagrams VO and → Canadian Club by a million each. The whisky sold in the USA is 3 years old and the small amount that sold in Canada is 4 years old. A second version, The → 1885 Special Reserve, has been brought out.

Canadian O F C Canadian whisky. It is also sometimes called → Schenley O F C, as it originally came from Schenley. In 1987 it was taken over, together with → Valleyfield distillery, by → UD. The abbreviation means 'Original Fine Canadian'. The 6-year-old is for the home market, the export version is 8 years old; both are 40%. The latter is considered to be the best of the Valleyfield whiskeys and the masterpiece of Luc Madore, the Master Blender for many years.

Canadian Springs Canadian whisky, which comes from the David → Sherman Company of St. Louis. It bottles the whiskeys which it has bought and imported in → bulk, and sells them as their own brand on the home market.

Canadian Supreme Canadian whisky. The blend is one of → Barton's own brands and is only available in the USA. The whiskeys used for it originate in Canada and are bottled in the States.

Canadian Whisky Canadian is an independent whisky style, which as well as being defined by its origin, is principally defined by its method of production. Canadian whiskeys are considered to be not so much the product of distillers, but rather of virtuoso master blenders. Apart from the malts which will soon be available from → Glenora and which will be an absolute exception, and the obscure → Blackstone, all Canadian whiskeys are blends, even when the bottle says 'rye' (which in the USA means that it is a distillate whose mash consists of at least 51% rye). → Bush Pilot's alone is a real → straight, like the American bourbons and Tennessees. The share of real straight in Canadian blends is mostly about 5%, and seldom 10%.

Every distillery produces a basis whisky, a clean → grain whisky which is slowly distilled until it achieves about 95%. This basis is really nothing other than neutral spirit. It provides the base, so to speak, for the blends, which require many other much weaker distilled and thus more aromatic, whiskeys. It is these which give the end product its various nuances of taste. In addition, and this is something unique to Canada, up to 9.09% 'non-Canadian whiskeys' may be used, the so-called → flavourings.

Nearly all Canadian whiskeys are the product of continuous distillation. Their differences result from the composition of the → mash, the various yeasts and → stills. Practically every kind of still is in use in Canada, and they are often used in combination with each other in order to determine the character of the brand. The mash may consist of → rye, which may be malted or unmalted, of → corn, or of malted or unmalted → barley, or of a combination of grain types. In this way individual distilleries are able to produce a large number of different individual brands (for example → Seagram has about 50). Sometimes (as with → Canadian Club), the young whisky is first blended and then matured. In other places the individual whiskeys are blended and married after maturing in casks. Casks made of new oak are used, or ex-bourbon or ex-sherry casks. Canadians are bottled young, often at the minimum legal age of three years, the better ones at six years and only very few at over 10 years. The alcohol strength is mostly 40%, but spirits with less may also call themselves whisky (→ Silk Tassel, → Northern Light, → VO).

Canadian Whisky Guild, The The name of a small series (consisting so far of three versions) with which the Canadians are now also trying to achieve the success which the Scots (with their → single casks) and the Americans (with their (small batches) have been able to celebrate. The creators of the series are → Allied Domecq respectively their Canadian subsidiary (Hiram Walker, who went back to their roots and even named one of the three whiskeys after the company who was present at the birth of Canadian whisky, → Gooderham & Worts. The two others are → Lot No. 40 and → Pike Creek.

Canandaigua Wine Company American wine and spirits company. Founded in 1945 in New York and, mainly as a result of selling cheap supermarket wine, it has made so much money that it is now among the third most successful wine producers in the country. At the beginning of the 1990s, it acquired → Barton Brands and their distillery in → Bardstown. In 1993 Canandaigua added Vintners International to its portfolio, and in 1994 → they bought Almaden and Inglenook Wine, also large and renowned wine firms, from IDV. In 1995 they acquired a whole range of brands from → UD's subsidiary → Glenmore, such as those products associated with → Schenley, the → Glenmore whiskies, → 'Fleischmann's Gin' and 'Vodka', the Kentucky straight bourbon → Kentucky Tavern and the blended → Old Thompson. At the end of 1998, the company (dominated by the Sands family) ventured into Europe and bought the UK group Matthew Clark for £215 million. Clark are dealers in cider, wine, spirits and mineral water, wines and → 'Strathmore' water. It also owns the blends → Moorland, → Old St. Andrews and → Queen's Own. In February 1999 Canandaigna bought the → UDV production sites in → Alberta and Quebec from → Diageo as well as the brands → Black Velvet, → Golden Wedding, → MacNaughton's, → McMasters and → Triple Crown. This took them to 10th position in the international rankings.

C & J Fine Old Scotch blend which used to be made by C & J → McDonald. The company was a subsidiary of Arthur → Bell & Sons and is now owned by → UDV.

Cantrell & Cochrane Irish whiskey company based in Dublin. They own the mineral water brand 'Ballygowan'. In Italy they produce the successful liqueur 'Fangelico' and in Ireland the whiskey liqueurs → Carolans and → Irish Mist. But their most successful product is → Tullamore Dew, which is distilled at → Midleton by → IDG. In 1993 this brand, which is particularly successful in Germany and Denmark, passed from → Groupe Pernod-Ricard subsidiary IDG, to Cantrell & Cochrane, who at the time were a mutual subsidiary of → Guinness and → Allied Domecq PLC. It is still not certain whether this sale was voluntary, or whether it was the result of pressure from the Irish Monopolies Commission, who had previously prevented IDG from buying competitors John J → Teeling and the → Cooley Distillery. Teeling's company had ended IDG's monopoly as sole owners of the Irish whiskey industry. As a result of an agreement with the Irish Monopolies Commission → Diageo, parted with the Irish company and sold its shares to its partner Allied. Cantrell & Cochrane were in considerable financial difficulties, and in January 1999 decided to sell their Irish subsidiary to BC Partners, which had arisen out of the collapse of Barings Bank and which had previously only been involved in publishing and poultry-breeding.

Caol Ila Scottish malt distillery. Its name, pronounced 'kaal-eela' with the emphasis on the long 'i', means 'Sound of → Islay', comes from the location of the distillery which overlooks the stretch of water which separates Islay from the neighbouring Jura. On a map it can be found to the north of Port Askaig. It is not accessible from the port, however, but via a minor-road leading down to the sea, off the Bridgend to Port Askaig road. From the → stillhouse, which was completely rebuilt in 1974 and enlarged to six stills, one gets perhaps the best view of the famous Paps of the → Isle of Jura. It was built in 1846, and from 1863 belonged to → Bulloch, Lade &Co, whose blends always contained a generous share of Caol Ila. The distillery passed to DCL in 1927, and is now in the ownership of UDV. Its malt, a medium Islay in style, was always coveted by blenders, and was also highly regarded by whisky connoisseurs. But they could only get it, if at all, from → independent bottlers.

For a long time it was only available as a single malt in a → distillery bottling to visitors to the distillery and in Italy, where there were two versions aged 12 and 15 years. It became more readily available when UD included a 15-year-old in the → 'Flora & Fauna' series. It was only slightly smoky and peaty but nevertheless powerful, and was a good representative of its island home. At least four 'Rare Malts' bottlings were available, of which the two from 1975 were 20 and 21 years old, the former at 61.12% and the latter at 61.3%. They were a surprise as they showed no traces of smoke: in 1975 unpeated malt was used – a sign that a distillery such as Caol Ila, whose whisky was not only intended for bottling as single malt, always had to produce quite different malts, according to demand, which were required by its proprietors for its own and other blends.

A much sought-after rarity is an anniversary bottling, for the 150th birthday of Caol Ila in 1996. The 20-year-old malt, bottled at → cask strength of 57.86%, was presented to the guests at the anniversary celebrations and to the employees, whose names appear on the label on the back of the bottle. Among the numerous → independent bottlings were three interesting versions brought out by → Gordon & MacPhail in their → 'Private Collection': three casks of 1988 Caol Ila which were taken to Elgin in 1994 and later transferred to new barrels, which had previously contained calvados, claret and cognac, for → finishing.

Cape Breton Silver Canadian spirit, at 50%. Its label bears an exact note of its ingredients in two English and French: malted barley and the water from MacLellan's Brook – all that is needed to make a classic malt whisky. But the distillate is not allowed to be called whisky, because it is too young. It comes from → Glenora Distillers. Glenora is a very young distillery that has been built in traditional Scottish style. It was opened in 1990 and lies on Cape Breton in Nova Scotia. The nickname for the illicit distillate in this area was 'Cape Breton Silver'. The clear distillate is thus linked to an old tradition.

Caperdonich Scottish malt distillery. Its name, emphasised on the penultimate syllable, comes from the Gaelic for 'secret source'. The distillery is situated in the small town of → Rothes, which has no fewer than five distilleries, and belongs to the → Speyside → whisky region. It was built by J & J → Grant, the owners of → Glen Grant, in 1897/8. This was at the time of the whisky boom, and because it was located opposite its elder sister, they simply named it 'Glen Grant No. 2'. They were connected to each other by a pipeline over the road. Caperdonich was the last of the five distilleries to be built in Rothes, while Glen Grant, established in 1840, was the first. Three years after opening Caperdonich had to be closed again, because the boom was followed by a devastating recession resulting from the → Pattison brothers' bankruptcy. Caperdonich was silent until 1965, when it was revitalised and modernised. It now has four → stills and is able to operate almost fully automatically.

Its malts are used almost exclusively for the making of blends. It is only occasionally available as an → independent bottling, mostly from → Gordon & MacPhail, who are based in Elgin, just a few miles north of Rothes and who regularly include it in their → 'Connoisseurs Choice Series'. → Cadenhead and → Signatory (in the series → 'Sailing Ships' and → 'Dun Eidean') have also each bottled a cask. The only known → distillery bottling was available in Italy many years ago. The takeover of the distillery and its owners by → Seagram in 1977 has, unfortunately, not changed the situation. The licence for Caperdonich was registered with → Chivas Brothers, who belong to the → Chivas & Glenlivet Group, the Scottish subsidiary of Seagram, though it has now passed to a Diageo/Groupe Pernod-Ricard partnership along with the rest of Seagram's spirits assets.

Captain Collins Whisky cocktail. It is a variety of Collins, made with Canadian whisky.

Captain's Table Canadian whisky. It comes from → McGuinness, a company which owned several distilleries, including one in Bridgetown. It was later in the hands of → Heublein, and as a subsidiary of → Corby today belongs to the empire of Hiram → Walker/→ Allied Domecq PLC.

Cardhu Scottish malt distillery. Its name, pronounced 'cardú', comes from the Gaelic for 'black rock'. Until 1975 it was named after the place where it is located: Cardow. Then it was officially given the name of its whisky. Only → independent bottlers such as → Cadenhead will sometimes call it Cardow (which is pronounced cardú). The distillery lies between Upper Knockando and Cardow, on the northern banks of the Spey, near the B9102 which runs from → Craigellachie to Grantown-on-Spey. It therefore belongs to the → Speyside → whisky region.

The first century of its history was marked by two women who have achieved legendary status. In 1811 Helen Cummings and her husband began to distill whisky illicitly at their farm in Cardow, before obtaining a licence in 1824. People still tell a lot of stories about her to this day, most of which concern the imaginative ways in which she played tricks on the excisemen. Her daughter-in-law, Elizabeth, erected a new building on the present site in 1885. She is one of the few women to have played a leading part in the history of Scottish whisky.

Since 1893 Cardhu has been associated with John → Walker & Sons and their world-famous brand → Johnnie Walker. That hasn't changed to this day, although the distillery, the company and the brand now belong to → UDV. During the DCL era, Cardhu was already being marketed as a single malt in a → distillery bottling. The 12-year-old was presented in a bottle whose design has been thinned down in recent years. There was also a 5-year-old for the Italian market. Cardhu has played a prominent part in the marketing strategy of UD/UDV along with → Glen Ord, → Royal Lochnagar, and to a lesser degree→ Mortlach and → Royal Brackla. These are the only single malts of the company to assume such an important position; the other UDV malts are only available in series such as → 'Classic Malts' or → 'Flora & Fauna' and → 'Rare Malts', which also includes a 27-years-old Cardhu (60.02%), distilled in 1973.

Carlton Scotch blend. It is produced by the London-based company Charles H → Julian in two versions, a → standard blend and a → premium blend.

Carlton Club Scotch blend produced by Douglas MacKay (not to be confused with → Whyte & Mackay) in Glasgow and mainly exported to Europe.

Carolans Irish cream liqueur. It is the number two of its kind after Bailey's, the unchallenged market leader, and is bottled at 17%. It was launched onto the market in 1978. Its producers are T J Carolan & Sons, who in the meantime have become a subsidiary of → Cantrell & Cochrane who have → Tullamore Dew, which is particularly successful in Germany and Denmark, and → Irish Mist in their range. The company was owned by → Allied Domecq PLC and → UDV. The latter had to part with its share for reasons associated with the monopolies laws, and sold it to Allied, which in 1999 resold it to an enterprise named BC Partners. The liqueur contains matured Irish whiskey, neutral spirit, cream and honey. In 1994 it was joined by Carolans Irish Coffee Cream.

Carrington Canadian whisky. It claims '35 years Distilling Excellence' for itself on the label, but that refers to the producer not the whisky. The whisky is three years old and it is said to taste intensely of rye – which is the only raw material used at its home distillery → Alberta. This new brand belongs to Alberta Distillers, the Canadian subsidiary of → Jim Beam.

Carsebridge Scottish grain distillery. It lies, like → Cambus, near Alloa and the Firth of Forth. Like other grain distilleries in the → Lowlands, it predates the invention of copper or → patent stills, having begun its life in 1799 as a malt distillery. It was finally equipped with → a copper still in 1851/52, and greatly expanded in subsequent years. The founding company, John Bald & Co, ran it themselves until 1877, when it joined → DCL, in whose foundation they were active. Carsebridge failed to survive the whisky crisis of 1983, when DCL had to shut many of its distilleries because of over-capacity. It had vast warehouses that are still used by the DCL successors → UD/ → GuinnessUDV. → Signatory found an old cask from 1965 and bottled it as a Single Grain at 57.8%. → MacArthur also had a Carsebridge in their range.

Carstairs White Seal American blended whiskey. It comes from the → Sazerac Company in New Orleans, but is produced in → Leestown. There Sazerac, together with the Japanese syndicate → Takara Shuzo & Okura, run the → Ancient Age Distillery.

Cascade Hollow American distillery which is sometimes just called Cascade. It lies near Tullahoma in Tennessee, which was known mainly as an important railroad town. The present distillery was built in 1958 by →

Schenley, who held the rights to the name Cascade at the time. They chose a site for rebuilding that was barely half a mile away from where John F Brown and F E Cunningham had built a distillery in 1877. It was located near Cascade Falls and Cascade Springs, where the water comes from today.

In the 1880s→ George Dickel was getting his entire stocks from Cascade, which already spelt whisky without the 'e' usual in America. In 1888, Dickel and his brother-in-law Victor Schwab, bought the distillery. Dickel retired that year, and died in 1894.

Schwab and his son enlarged the distillery and made it into the biggest in Tennessee. The Schwabs, too, became victims of prohibition, which had began in their state in 1910, and which forced them to shut the distillery. Both the company and the brand changed owners several times. The whisky was initially produced at → Stitzel in Kentucky, where prohibition began later, and at the end of the dry period it was produced in → Leestown. The rights to the brand eventually passed to Schenley.

The new owners employed the old master distiller Ralph Dubbs, who planned the rebuilding and whose successor, Jennings 'Dave' Backus, still uses the yeast that Dubbs developed. The mash at Cascade consists of 80% corn, 12% rye and 8% malted barley. They work very traditionally – and on a very small scale, at least compared to their great neighbours, the → Jack Daniel Distillery.

At Dickel's the famous Tennessee Sour Mash method is used. In 1941 this became recognised by the American government as an individual whisk(e)y type. However, the process is a little different to that used at Jack Daniel: both use charcoal for → charcoal mellowing or → leaching. That is obtained from sugar maple and is filled in large, 10-foot high tubs. At Dickel's the charcoal is covered with a woollen blanket and the fresh distillate doesn't drip out of the holes of copper pipes, but out of a perforated steel disc. Unlike their neighbours, they wait until the whole tub is filled with whiskey before beginning to draw it off and filling it into

barrels. Since 1987 → UD, (later → UDV) have been the owners of this little jewel, which they bought from Schenley, and it is pleasing that the new bosses haven't changed anything in Tullahoma, but have left everything as it was – apart from small changes to the label which gives Cascade Hollow as the address.

So the George Dickel No. 8 Brand and the somewhat older George Dickel Superior No. 12 Brand still exist. It was one of the 10 world whiskeys recommended by Jim Murray. A 10-year-old version has also been on the market for several years. In 1994 a Special Reserve Barrel came out, that is also included in the series the → 'Bourbon Heritage Collection'. That is slightly strange as the Dickel is really a Tennessee – one which is always, and quite unjustly, put in the shade by the mighty Jack Daniel's, and is one of only two of its kind in the whole world.

Cascadia Canadian distillery. It lies in Kelowna, British Columbia and was founded in the 1960s by the International Potter Distilling Company, Vancouver. There is also a brewery on the same site, called the Granville Island Brewery. The company is one of the few in Canada that has managed to maintain its independence. They produce the blends → Potter's Special Old and → Royal Canadian as well as → Bush Pilot's, which they make exclusively for an American company. Almost none of the whiskeys that Potter uses for these brands comes from Cascadia. The distillery only works for one week a year, just long enough to prevent the licence expiring.

Case, cases Term which is used in the international whisk(e)y and spirits trade to describe a unit of measurement. It is used for statistics which show the amount of whisk(e)y that an individual company, or the whole industry in one country, has sold. The position of a brand in the rankings of the best-selling whiskies in a country, in terms of exports, internationally or world wide, is measured in cases. A case, formerly made of wood but today usually of cardboard, always contains 12 bottles. A case with 75cl bottles contains exactly 9 litres, with 70cl bottles, 8.4 litres. If the litres of pure alcohol (lpa) are to be measured, then the volume of alcohol must be taken into consideration. The larger bottles contain 3.6 litres at 40% and 3.87 litres at 43%. The smaller bottles contain 3.36 litres at 40% and 3.61 litres at 43%.

Casino A well-represented supermarket chain, particularly in France, which includes whisky in its range. It imports a blend at 40% from Ireland with the plain name Irish Whiskey, and this is made by → Cooley. → Glenmorangie produces the vatted malts → Glen Vegan and → Dalvegan exclusively for Casino.

Casks In nearly every country where whisky is made it is a legal requirement that maturation should take place in wooden casks, usually made of → oak. There are, however, quite different regulations concerning the length of maturation and character of the casks. In America it is stipulated that bourbon may only mature in absolutely new barrels made of American oak (quercus alba), and it must remain there for at least two years. If it is bottled before it is four years old, then its age must be noted on the label (so that any bourbon without an age is always at least 4 years old). Should the barrels be used again, then the name 'bourbon' may not be used. There are very few such American whiskeys, but the Americans need not worry that they will be left sitting on a mountain of barrels: the Scots and the Irish are grateful recipients. In both countries the law stipulates three years minimum maturation before the grain distillate can call itself whisk(e)y, but there are no rules that state that the casks must be new. In fact such → new casks made of European oak (quercus robur) are rarely, if ever, used. That is because the fresh wood is seen as impairing quality.

At one point there were a lot of used casks in Scotland and Ireland and, once the beneficial effects of wooden casks had been discovered in the 19th century, it was no problem for the distillers to get a new batch. Until that time whisk(e)y had mainly been stored (if at all) in clay jugs or glass vessels. Casks were used for nearly everything, for butter and salt, and above all wine was imported by the cask. Until recently any self-respecting wine merchant had his own bottlings of claret, sherry or port. Sherry casks in particular have always been coveted in the whisky industry.

There is now a shortage of them and they have become expensive, costing up to £400– and distilleries like → Macallan, which exclusively use sherry butts for their → proprietor's bottlings of malts, have long since begun to have their casks made in Spain, renting them out, so to speak, to sherry producers and then bringing them over to Scotland. Other distilleries consider sherry to be too dominant and use a mixture of various kinds of cask.

Some swear by ex-bourbon barrels; one example of this is the 10-year-old → Glenmorangie. At the Glenmorangie Distillery they have been experimenting with other cask types for many years, and have made a significant contribution to the new → finishings fashion. So nowadays not only casks that have previously contained the light Fino or the dark Oloroso are used, but also Pedro Ximenez casks (for example at → Lagavulin or → Auchentoshan). There have also been malt whiskies from Madeira casks on the market, while port pipes are particularly popular. There have even been one or two malts from wine casks, such as → Glenmorangie, and → Glen Moray.

Ex-bourbon barrels are the most popular, they are also considerably cheaper at about £25 each. They either arrive in Scotland as dismantled → hogsheads and are then fitted together again complete with a new lid, or they are shipped whole. American barrels are slightly smaller than British hogsheads, and so are often re-built with additional staves to increase their capacity. Five American Barrels may be re-made into four hogdheads. Either way, they undergo a process which they have already undergone in the USA; they are burnt for a short time before being charred again for about a minute. This charcoal layer lends the whisky just as intensive aromatic substances as the wood itself does, as well as the aromas which the wood has absorbed from the bourbon or sherry. A slightly nutty tone often hints at sherry, a vanilla one at bourbon. Cellulose gives off caramel, sweetness and colour, tannin lends the whisky a slightly astringent dryness, and oak wood makes the whisky more mellow and complex.

The cask has a considerable influence on maturation and on the character of the whisk(e)y, perhaps more than the shape of the stills or the → water. Apart from the wood, the size is also important. Even if they contain the same whisky and lie side by side, no two casks develop in an absolutely identical way. It is these differences that the master blender tries to smooth out, but which also makes malt whisky from → single casks so attractive. Casks are valuable and, accordingly, are carefully looked after, they are also used more than once in Scotland. A good first → refill sherry cask is even sometimes preferable to a new one.

Cask strength A way of bottling whisky, and particularly single malts, that is becoming increasingly popular with whisky lovers (in America they use the term → barrel °proof). Water is not used to reduce the alcohol content of a whisky to an artificial or legally prescribed level of, for example, 40% or 43%, but it is bottled at the volume that has been achieved naturally during maturation. In this process alcohol evaporates and is lost into the atmosphere as the → angels' share. The amount lost is dependent on many factors, such as the warmth, or the humidity that the cask is subject to. The quality of the cask itself plays a great part, as does the length of maturation. For this reason it is by no means certain that casks, even those laying next to each other, will contain the same amount of alcohol after a given period of time.

The → Scotch Malt Whisky Society was a pioneer in bottling at cask strength, and many → proprietors and especially → independents have followed suit. In America there are also more and more → barrel °proof bottlings. When → single casks are bottled in this way new labels must be printed for a relatively small number of bottles, as the exact volume must be stated on them. This was a particularly expensive enterprise for → UD, who had already printed labels for its cask strength edition → 'Flora & Fauna' series, only to find out that the alcohol content had slightly decreased between printing and bottling. The labels had to be printed again. Some companies try to make do by not taking the term quite so literally and using a set, but distinctly higher, volume. Thus → Glenfarclas and → Macallan have versions at 57% and William → Grant & Sons use 51% for the 15-year-old versions of their → Balvenie and → Glenfiddich.

Cassidy's Irish whiskey, which comes from the → Cooley Distillery, but is produced exclusively for the UK supermarket chain → Marks & Spencer as Distillers Reserve. The producers and the sellers proudly claim to be competing with → Black Bush, and aim to achieve this with a good share of whiskeys which have matured in → sherry casks. It is higher than other blends from Cooley, but is still 40%.

Castle, The Scotch single malt. The castle in question is pictured on the label: Edinburgh Castle. The whisky is sold in the Castle's Historic Scotland shop, together with other malts that are also named after castles administered by the authority; St. Andrew's Castle and Stirling Castle. They all contain 46% alcohol, which is an indication that they have been bottled at Springbank – but which doesn't mean that the whisky comes from this distillery. The fourth of the castle malts is dedicated to Urquhart Castle, and is only 40%, this is from Gordon & MacPhail, whose present owners are the Urquharts.

Castle Collection A small series of → independently bottled single malts. Gordon Currie, who formerly ran the 'Whisky Castle' in Tomintoul, is behind the series. The castle is in fact a whisky shop with a large range of → distillery and independent bottlings, as well as a rarity or two. The first malt that Currie bottled under his own label came from a neighbouring distillery and was previously almost unobtainable: it was an → Allt-à-Bhainne. The 'Castle Collection No. 2' was a → Glenturret, and No. 3 was a → Glenallachie, a rarity seldom found in a bottle. For No. 4 Gordon Currie returned 'home' and filled a second cask from Allt A'Bhainne in bottles. Its label shows a guarded castle gate. Each of the malts in the series so far has been bottled at 43%.

Castle Pride Scotch blend. It is a brand from the Glaswegian company → Angus Dundee.

Catto's Scotch blend. Its name commemorates

James Catto & Co of Aberdeen, founded in 1861. They were particularly successful in exporting whiskies to countries where a lot of Scottish immigrants lived. Initially → Gilbey, best known for their gin, only took over a share of the company, but then bought it entirely in 1945. The brand eventually passed to → IDV, who resold it to → Inver House Distillers Ltd in 1990. There is a → standard blend Rare Old Scottish Highland aged 12, 21 and 25 years.

Celtic Irish whiskey from the Cooley Distillery. It refers to two traditions with Celtic roots: whisk(e)y and football. The Scottish Premier League football team sell it as their own brand.

Celtic Connections Series of Scotch single malts from the → independent bottlers → Blackadder International. The Celtic Connections is used for specific markets, although the same whiskies are sold elsewhere as → Blackadder International. The company has many → cask strength malts, but these are reduced to 43%.

Celtic Crossing Irish whiskey liqueur. Its name is a reminder of the saddest chapter in Irish history: the Great Famine.

The label remembers those 'who left our shores never again to see their homeland'. The Gaelic Heritage Corporation Ltd from Bailieboro in County Cavan brought out the liqueur 'to celebrate 150 years of Irish heritage and achievements around the world.' This is also where the Emmet company is based with its two products → Dubliner and → Emmets. From 1991 they belonged to → IDV / → Grand Metropolitan and are therefore now part of → UDV. The liqueur is 30% and is available in a normal bottle as well as in a ceramic jug.

Centenary Reserve Series of Scotch single malts produced by → Gordon & MacPhail to celebrate their 100th anniversary in 1995. Malts were chosen from distilleries which were already well-represented in the 'Conoisseurs Choice' range of the large → independent bottlers from Elgin and with whom they traditionally have had particularly good relations: a → Balblair from 1973, a → Benrinnes from 1978, a → Caol Ila from 1966, a → Glenburgie from 1948, a → Glenrothes from 1978, a → Highland Park from 1970, a → Mortlach from 1984 and a → St. Magdalene from 1980. The Caol Ila in particular was something of a sensation. It was quickly snapped up, and now fetches top prices. Even on this occasion the bottling was not at → cask strength, but reduced to 40%, the company's standard percentage.

Centennial Canadian whisky. It comes from the independent → Highwood Distillers Company. They are based in → Alberta and do not run a distillery of their own, but buy from other producers. It could be that they buy from the local distillery, which belongs to → Jim Beam / → American Brands.

Century Scotch vatted malt. Its full name is The Century of Malts and it comes from the → former Seagram subsidiary → Chivas Brothers. It was launched on the market in 1996 and is the result of a union of 100 single malts. However, the Century is not unique, and certainly not the first of its kind, as is stated on the label. It is the third time that this number of whiskies have been 'married', the first being the → Ultima from J&B, which is a blend, followed by the Centenary in the blue ceramic bottle which → Gordon & MacPhail brought out for the 100th anniversary of their company in 1995 and which also contained 100 single malts. Signatory, the → independent bottlers from Edinburgh, brought a further one onto the market with their → Signatory Supreme which contained 104 malts. But the Century does bring together some real rarities: the → Craigduff being one, and the → Glenisla, which uses the old name → Strathmill.

Chairman's Scotch blend. It was made for the pubs owned by → Eldridge, Pope & Co In 1996 this independent brewery, founded in 1837, discontinued their brewing activities, and handed them over to Thomas Hardy. Since that time they have only been involved in the management of their pubs, which are mainly in the Dorset area around Dorchester. They still have stocks of this blend.

Chairman's Reserve Scotch blend from the former → Seagram's subsidiary The → Chivas & Glenlivet Group. According to the prevailing laws regarding whisky, its whiskies are 50 years old and thus it obviously belongs to the highest → de luxe category. It is an absolute rarity.

Champion Indian whisky from the → Haryana Distillery, who also use the name for a gin and a rum. It is a → standard blend.

Charcoal mellowing Term which is mainly used, along with → leaching and the (correct) expression → Lincoln County Process, for a very special method that is only practised in the two → Tennessee distilleries of → Jack Daniel and → George Dickel. It was a major factor in these whiskeys, whose production doesn't otherwise differ from those in neighbouring Kentucky, being granted the status of an independent whisk(e)y type by the American government in 1941. The process is particularly emphasised in Jack Daniel's advertising, and it is extremely impressive when great trunks of sugar maple are sawed into large planks and carefully layered in stacks, to be finally set alight and turned into charcoal by the blazing flames. The charred pieces are then filled into great wooden vats, which at Jack Daniel's are a good two metres in diameter and three and a half metres high. The distillery has 25 such tubs. At the top there are perforated pipes, and from these the newly produced → white dog drips, and spreads over the charcoal, very slowly trickling to the ground, where it is collected for storage and maturation in the barrels made of new American oak. It takes about 7 to 10 days for the substance to reach the bottom.

This method costs money, and time, and as those black and white advertising photos from Lynchburg show us, time is just what they have a lot of: time to make the whiskey especially smooth and easily digestible, because that is the real aim: to remove certain unwanted flavour components. Sometimes the whiskey is even treated a second time, directly before bottling. Daniel's competitor at the nearby → Cascade Hollow Distillery, doesn't advertise so much, but treats their George Dickel with just as much care, although with a few variations. The whisky (with no 'e') doesn't flow from pipes but from perforated discs, and the charcoal is covered with woollen blankets. Both help it run more evenly through the charcoal layer. Both Daniel and Dickel sell the washed-out charcoal.

Charlie Richards Scotch blends. It is a brand from the company of the same name, a subsidiary of → Halewood International Ltd.

Chequer's Scotch blend. Along with → Abbot's Choice, it used to be the main brand of John McEwan & Co. They were formerly a subsidiary of → DCL and then of → UD, and held the licence for the → Linkwood Distillery until 1992. The whisky is 12 years old and is sold mainly in South America.

Chicken Cock American whiskey. Its label doesn't say who actually produces it, just states that it is 100° (50%) and comes from a certain Kentucky Distilleries and Warehouse Company in Louisville, Kentucky. Apart from that there is a printed triangle with the words: 'Aged in Wood for Medicinal Use'.

Chieftan's Choice Series of Scotch whiskies from Peter J → Russell & Co, Edinburgh, who use the name of their subsidiary company → MacLeod. It includes blends as well as single and vatted malts. The blends are 8, 12 and 18 years old. A 32-year-old blend in a black decanter is also available although only in Taiwan. In the case of the vatted malt only the area of origin is stated, which isn't unusual – for a long time the single malts didn't disclose their origin either. Perhaps it was feared that it would put the good relationships with the distilleries' proprietors at risk, as they don't appreciate → independent bottlers using the names of their distilleries. But perhaps the reason was simply that different malts were always used for the various names in the series. The age of each bottling, which is often very high, is mentioned. There was a 30-year-old → Lowland, two from → Speyside aged 21 and 32 years and a → Highland aged 26 years. They were followed by a further single malt aged 29 years and then by one aged 32 years. Probably encouraged by the success of other → independent bottlers, they have now recently begun to market malts which are precisely defined, like the two 15-year-olds → Banff and → Convalmore and a 19-year-old → Teaninich. They are all bottled at 43%.

Chill-Filtering Term for a process that is used in bottling whiskies. It should not be confused with other methods of filtering, particularly not with → leaching, which is practised in Tennessee. Whiskies contain congeners, substances, which under certain circumstances make them cloudy and opaque, especially if they are served cold or diluted with chilled water. The producers of blends, and particularly those who offer single malts in → proprietor's bottlings, believe that customers find this unacceptable. For this reason they cool the whiskies to 5°, a temperature at which these allegedly undesirable substances solidify and can be removed by filtering.

The problem is that these substances also affect the taste. For this reason other bottlers, mostly the → independents, insist on leaving their whiskies in a natural state, without chilling and filtering them. Pioneers of this attitude and practice were the → Scotch Malt Whisky Society. Their insistence on the right of the whisky lover to the full taste has now become accepted practise. It is no longer just the independent bottlers, but also some of the large companies, who have given up the practice of chill filtering. For example → UD pointed out on the bottles of their → 'Rare Malts' series, that they may become cloudy if the recommendation to dilute these → cask strength whiskies with water before drinking is followed. This is in fact a guarantee that the whiskies have been bottled in the natural state achieved after maturing in casks. The label of the recent proprietor's botting of a 10-year-old → Ardbeg states that is not chill filtered.

China The People's Republic is still terra incognita for almost all western drinks producers, although the consumption of western spirits has continually risen in recent years among those who could afford them. This has had two consequences: on the one hand, the Chinese have tried to imitate the western-style drinks and produce them themselves. → Sunflower is an example of such a Chinese whisky.

The large international drinks companies have been getting into position, ready for the opening of the Chinese market. South East Asia had been the source of immense growth for these companies until the end of the economic boom in 1998. They were nearly all without exception represented in Hong Kong, at the gateway, so to speak, of the great country. The number of people potentially interested in Scotch in China is estimated to be almost one thousand million. The opening up of this market could easily compensate for the losses that Scotch blends have suffered elsewhere.

The first of the giants to get a foot in the door, was → Seagram. In 1988 the Canadians managed to set up a joint venture with Shanghai Distilleries. One of the first results was a whisky called Seagram's 7 Star, which is no longer included in the company's lists. Instead there is now → D'Accord, as a whisky as well as a gin, vodka and brandy. → Groupe Pernod-Ricard is represented in Taiwan and Hong Kong and has a share in the company Dragon Seal in the People's Republic. → Allied Domecq PLC and → GuinnessUDV, whose → Johnnie Walker is the most popular whisky, are also active, but at present have no subsidiaries or joint ventures. These would make distribution easier to organise, as well as making in → bulk imports possible, so that bottling could take place in the country itself, or, as in many other countries, blends could be produced using Scotch malts and domestically distilled → grain whisky. → Glenmorangie plc occupy a special position: they are the only company that are allowed to export their ready-bottled products to China. Just how valuable this privilege is was shown at the beginning of 1999, when the luxury brand group → LVMH paid a million pounds for a share in it. They hope that it will open up better sales opportunities for their cognacs and champagnes.

Chivas & Glenlivet Group, The Scottish whisky company, a subsidiary of the Canadian → Seagram, which drew together its nine Scottish malt distilleriesas well as several whisky companies and their brands under this name. The name reflects a whole chain of mergers. They include the takeover of the old blends and export company → Chivas Brothers, together with their top product → Chivas Regal, as well as the purchase of a small conglomerate that resulted from the alliance of → Glen Grant and → Glenlivet in 1953 and their merger with → Longmorn in 1970. In the same year they took over → Hill Thomson & Company with their brands, some of which were well-known, such as

→ Queen Anne and → Something Special. Seven years later in 1977, the Scottish company had become so attractive that it caught the attention of the Canadians. They reorganised their Scottish businesses and gave their subsidiary the Chivas and Glenlivet Group name.

Apart from those already named, the company also owned the malt distilleries → Allt A'Bhainne, → Benriach, → Braeval, → Caperdonich, → Glen Keith and → Strathisla. Apart from Allt A'Bhainne and Braeval, all their malts are available in → distillery bottlings. The best known blend is still Chivas Regal, which has been complemented by new expressions and products in recent years including the → Chivas Imperial, the → Chivas Brothers 1801 and the Chivas → De Danu. The following also belong to the range, with no guarantee that the list is complete: → 100 Pipers, → Passport, → Royal Citation, → Royal Salute and → Royal Strathyclan. → Black Watch, Queen Anne and → Something Special are still bottled with the name Hill Thomson. Further small brands include → Black Douglas, → Chairman's Reserve, → Highland Clan, → Prince Charlie, → St. Leger and → Treasury. There is also a → whisky liqueur, the → Lochan Ora. The vatted malt → Century is a new creation.

Chivas Brothers Scottish company based in Paisley near Glasgow. Its history began in 1801, when William Edward founded his grocer's store in Aberdeen. James Chivas joined the business in 1837 and in 1858 took on his brother John as a business partner, with the firm becoming Chivas brothers. The company earned great respect for its first-class products, and even became suppliers to the royal court when Queen Victoria bought Balmoral Castle, on Dee Side, not far from Aberdeen. The company became so successful and acquired such a good reputation that after the death of the last of the Chivas the new owners kept the name. Their best-known product was the blend → Chivas Regal. Its success aroused the interest of the Canadian company → Seagram acquired Chivas Brothers in 1949, running it as their Scottish subsidiary.

After acquiring the Milton Distillery, which was later renamed → Strathisla, → Glen Keith was built. In the 1970s → Allt A'Bhainne and → Braeval, two completely new distilleries, were founded. In 1977 Seagram bought Glenlivet Distillers, which had arisen from a whole series of mergers, and so came into the possession of → Glen Grant, → Glenlivet, → Caperdonich, Benriach and → Longmorn distilleries. The Scottish activities of Seagram came under the collective name The → Chivas & Glenlivet Group, which ran distilleries as well as having a whole collection of single malts and blends in their range. Today, the operation is simply known as Chivas Brothers, and belong to a Diageo/ Groupe Pernod-Ricard partnership. The name Chivas Brothers can still be found on the bottles of the nobler brands such as → Chivas Regal, → Chivas Imperial and → Chivas Brothers 1801, which came out in 1997. The name also appears on Chivas → De Danu, the → Royal Salute, → Royal Citation and Chivas Oldest & Finest. Their old shop in Aberdeen still exists.

Chivas Imperial Scotch blend. It comes from → Chivas Brothers and is, so to speak, the luxury version of the → de luxe blend → Chivas Regal. The whiskies contained in it are at least 18 years old.

Chivas Regal Scotch blend. It is among the top sellers of its kind, with over 3 million → cases sold per year, and is no 1 in its category of top → de luxe blends. It was created by Chivas Brothers in 1891, and shortly afterwards began to be exported to North America. It was so popular and successful that both the company and the brand were bought by → Seagram in 1949. They subsequntly acquired Milton Distillery in → Keith. Now known as → Strathisla, its malts are at the heart of Chivas Regal.

Its producers have also had access to malts from the other distilleries in the Seagram empire, such as → Glen Grant, → Glenlivet and → Longmorn. It is said to contain more than 30 whiskies. For a long time it was only available in two versions, aged 12 and 15 years. In December 1997 the company brought out an 18-year-old Imperial Premium, as well as a new version without the name 'Regal' called Chivas Brothers 1801, referring to the beginnings of the famous brothers company. It is 50% and comes in a bottle modelled on one from the 19th century. The 18-year-old is also available as Rare Old on some markets. The latest addition is the Oldest & Finest which is presented in an elegant wooden case. The Chivas → De Danu, named after a Celtic goddess, is only available in Italy and the USA, and came onto the market at the end of 1998.

Choice Japanese blend. It comes from → Nikka and like all the firm's blends, is only available in Japan.

Christopher's Scotch blend. It used to be sold in many versions by Christopher & Co. They were a subsidiary of → Waverley Vintners and sold Christopher's Finest Old in both → standard and → de luxe expressions. There was also a Christopher's Four Lions and an 8-year-old vatted malt. The brand, which isn't actively sold today, was taken over a few years ago by → Invergordon Distillers, which since October 2001 has been a subsidiary of → Kyndal, the company formed from → JBB (Greater Europe) plc.

Chwisgi Cymreig The term is Welsh for 'Welsh whisky'. It is used by The → Welsh Whisky Co, whose activities are closely bound to the traditions of the country. In 1784 a small whisky industry was established in Wales. They called what they produced *whisci*. In his book *An A–Z of Whisky*, Gavin D Smith has gone into the matter, and was told by Professor Derec Lywyd Morgan of Old College, University of Wales in Aberystwyth: 'Welsh developed chw- from the wh (hw) of English; ... but in South Wales dialects the chw- becomes hw-, invariably spelt wh-. That is why you have chwisgi and whisgi.' Got that?

Clan Ardroch Scotch blend. It comes from the Liverpool trading house → Hall & Bramley Ltd, who mainly sell wine. The meaning of its name is not clear, as no such clan actually exists in Scotland. On the other hand 'Ardrach' comes from the Gaelic and means ferry or boat. It is claimed that the brand is in memory of the many Irish who had to leave their country. When emigrating to the alleged promised land of America, they first had to stop off in Liverpool. A museum is situated in one of the old harbour buildings which commemorates them and their fate.

Clan Ben Scotch blend. It comes from the Glasgow-based company → Angus Dundee.

Clan Campbell Scotch blend. It comes from → Campbell Distillers, whose origins as a blending company go back to 1879, and who today belong to the French company → Groupe Pernod-Ricard.

The blend was already in existence before the Duke of → Argyll, the clan chief of the Campbells, joined the management of the company. He helped to make it successful, especially in the UK and → France, and it became a brand with one of the highest growth rates of all. It now ranks among the top 15 best-selling Scotch blends. Over a million → cases of it have been sold. It is available as standard blend and as a → de luxe blend. It has been repackaged since 1996 is called 'The Noble Scotch Whisky' and is decorated with the coat of arms and a small history of the clan. At present there is a blend with no age statement, a Highlander which was earlier available aged 12 years and now aged 8 years, an 18-year-old Legendary and a 21-year-old with no additional name. A vatted malt is a recent addition to the range.

Clan MacGregor Scotch blend from William → Grant & Sons, who originally only produced it for the North American market, but now also sell it elsewhere. It is one of the most successful new introductions of recent times: more than a million → cases of it are sold annually. The clan which gave it its name were outlawed in 1603. Anyone who could hand over a dead MacGregor was rewarded by the English – this was only repealed by Parliament in 1774.

Clan Morgan of Delhi Indian company. It entered into a joint venture with → Allied Domecq PLC in 1997, which included a jointly-run bottling plant in Rajasthan. Here the imported blends → Old Smuggler and → Teacher's are bottled and distributed on the Indian subcontinent by another partner, → Tikinagar.

Clan Munro Scotch blend from the whisky company of the same name. This is backed by William → Lawson Distillers, who, with Martini & Rossi, are a subsidiary of → Bacardi. They gave up the name Lawson in 1998 when they bought the brand and the rights to the name Dewar from → UDV.

Clan Murdock Scotch blend. It was originally created by Murdock McLellan, who not only dealt in whisky, but was also well-known for his agricultural experiments. He earned a lot of respect from his colleagues in the whisky industry with his research into the most fertile kinds of barley. Today the brand belongs to → Glenmorangie plc.

Clan Roy Scotch blend that comes from → Morrison Bowmore, who market it under the name of their subsidiary T & A → McClelland. There is a 3-year-old → standard version and one aged 25 years which is sold in a ceramic container in duty-free shops in France and Russia.

Clancey's Irish whiskey. It is a 40% blend and is produced by the → Cooley Distillery. It is supplied exclusively to the supermarket chain Wm Morrison, whose headquarters are in Bradford in the north of England, and who only sell the brand in their own shops.

Clansman Scotch blend. It comes from → Glen Catrine Bonded Warehouse Ltd and is a → standard blend which is mainly sold in South America.

Clarion No 7 Standard Scotch blend, formerly called Clarendon No 7. It was produced for the Flagman company in London and, whilst it is not mentioned in the 1998 edition of *Harpers Wine and Spirit Directory*, it is still available in some overseas outlets.

Clarke's American whiskey. Its producer, or at least its bottler, is the Clarke's Distillery Company in → Lawrenceburg, → Kentucky. The year 1866 appears on the label this is probably the date of foundation of this otherwise little-known company. It is also unusual in that it does not bear the description 'Kentucky Straight Bourbon', but is called 'Kentucky Straight Sour Mash'. The fact that it matures in barrels made of oak (*quercus sessiliflora*) is emphasised. It has a bottle strength of 80°(40%), is imported in Germany by the Lobuschkellerei Hamburg and sold exclusively at ALDI, also being available at the branches of this discount chain in the UK.

Classic Cask, The American whiskeys bottled by the company of the same name in → Bardstown. The label describes them as hand crafted Single Batch. There are two versions to date: a 15-year-old Kentucky straight rye distilled in 1984 and bottled in 1999 and a 17-year-old Kentucky straight bourbon from 1982 (both 90°(45%)).

Classic Malts of Scotland Series of six malt whiskies from Scottish distilleries. It was launched onto the market in 1991 by → UD, and was the first serious attempt by the group. At the time UD owned nearly 40%. Some of the malts had never previously been available as → proprietor's bottlings. Selling them in a series rather than singly was a brilliant marketing concept: the classic six represent the six → whisky regions of Scotland, and how different their malts are: → Glenkinchie stands for the Lowlands, → Dalwhinnie for the → Highlands, → Cragganmore for → Speyside, Oban for the western → Highlands, → Talisker from Skye for the → Islands and → Lagavulin for → Islay.

Each does represent a certain style and that are all excellent representatives of Scotch malt. It is doubtful however, whether the style is really representative of the whole region. A welcome side-effect of the series was that consumers, who are often confused by the variety of malts and their sometimes rather complicated names, were given an aid to orientation and an initial introduction.

Considerable advertising efforts and campaigns have helped this concept to blossom and make the series a winner. The consumers also have their its favourites from the series: the most popular is Lagavulin. The 'Classic Malts' are also presented in a video. They can be bought as a miniature set, and together with a plinth, as a box of six. Customer relations are promoted by free membership of the 'Friends of the Classic

Malts' (previously 'Classic Malt Society').

In December 1997 the first series of 'normal' classics was supplemented with a second, the → 'Distillers Edition'. It includes malts from the same six distilleries but each has had a → finishing, a second maturing period in carefully selected casks, which are judged to be appropriate for the character of the individual malts: for Glenkinchie Amontillado Sherry wood was chosen, for Dalwhinnie Oloroso Sherry, for Cragganmore port casks, for Oban Montilla Fino Sherry, for Talisker Amoroso Sherry wood and for Lagavulin the heavy, sweet Pedro Ximenez Sherry. The labels bear the crest and the year of foundation of each distillery, the desciption of the cask type and the signature of the distillery manager. Initially the bottles were only sold at duty-free outlets with members of the 'Friends' able to get single bottles from the series of six. The edition is now generally available, although still in small quantities.

Classic of Schenley Canadian whisky. Which has extremely limited distribution: there are just 300 crystal carafes of it. It was bottled by the Canadian branch of → Schenley in 1983 in commemoration of their first Canadian whisky, which had been launched on the market 35 years before. Only the oldest and the finest whiskeys of the company were chosen for this collector's item, all between 17 and 20 years old.

Claymore, The Scotch blend. It is named after the Scottish broadsword and was introduced during the 1890s by A Ferguson & Co, who were later absorbed by DCL. During the 1970s, DCL relaunched Claymore, as a cheap brand to use up surplus stocks of mature malts. The Brussels injunction to stop sales of → Johnnie Walker in the UK also played its part; DCL needed a substitute for this classic. In 1986 further requirements from the Monopolies and Mergers Commission led to the sale of Claymore, which by then had become very successful, to → Whyte & Mackay. The new owners managed to establish the → standard blend among the top 10 in the UK. On some markets it is also available aged 12 and 21 years and as a 31-year-old → de luxe blend.

Clearic spike Very old term which is seldom used today. It refers to the new spirit, the fresh distillate that leaves the → spirit safe after the last run for filling into casks for maturing. It was customary in Scotland for workers to be 'drammed', for example at the beginning and at the end of a shift, by being given a shot of freshly distilled spirit. The practice no longer occurs.

Clementine's Kentucky straight bourbon. This is one of the many small brands from → Barton, which are often only sold to individual markets. This one is made exclusively for Japan.

Club Scotch blend, it was the first brand from → Justerini & Brooks, introduced in 1880, and was very successful at the time. It was the period when Londoners used to drinking brandy had to look round for a new drink, because the *phylloxera vastatrix* (vine louse) catastrophe in France had denied them their usual favourite drink. Later it was overshadowed by J & B, which became the leading brand of the company worldwide. It is still produced in small quantities as a nostalgic gesture, and is reserved exclusively for the customers of Justerini and Brooks shops in London and Edinburgh. Only time will tell whether this gesture will be continued, and whether the brand will be able to resist the pressures of rationalisation kindled by the merger of → Guinness and Justerini's parent company.

Clubhouse Scotch blend. It is produced by → Old St. Andrews Ltd, who have become known for the original packaging of their leading brand. It bears the same name as the company and comes in bottles in golfbags or shaped like golfballs. Many golfers appreciate the '19th hole', because then they can drink a whisky in the clubhouse, either in celebration or to ease their frustration.

Cluny Scotch blend. The brand has existed for a long time: it was introduced in 1857 by John E MacPherson & Sons, which was founded seven years earlier in Newcastle. After several changes in ownership they now belong to → Invergordon Distillers. The whisky is named after an episode in the history of the MacPherson clan, whose chiefs, Cluny had to flee with Prince Charlie after the Battle of Culloden, and was kept hidden by relatives for nine long years in a cave known as 'Cluny's Cage'. The MacPherson who created the brand was his cousin. Previously available as a → standard, the whisky is now only available in → de luxe form at 12, 17 and 21 years -old.

Clydesdale Series of Scotch single malts from the → independent bottlers → Blackadder International. It uses this name for younger whiskies which have not matured for more than eight years in their → single cask, or which have been bottled with no age statement. They are relatively reasonable in price because of their youth and because they are reduced to 43%.

Clynelish Scottish malt distillery. Its name, pronounced 'clein-liesch', comes from the Gaelic for 'slope of the garden'. It lies several miles to the north of Dunrobin Castle near → Brora on the A9, and belongs to the → whisky region of the northern → Highlands. There are actually two distilleries here, one which is constructed of stone and looks very traditional, and one which is much more modern in style. For a time they both even bore the same name. The new distillery was built in 1967/8, beside the older one built by → DCL, respectively its subsidiary → SMD. After they had both been in operation for a while with the names Clyenlish A and Clynelish B, it was decided to do something about the confusing situation, and the first and older one was called → Brora from then on. It was later closed down. The licence for both had been registered with the old company → Ainslie & Heilbron. In 1992 it was transferred to the → UD subsidiary → UMGD, and is now part of UDV.

There was not a → proprietor's bottling of Clynelish as a single malt from either Ainslie or DCL. Two versions of Clynelish are available, at 40% and 57%, from → Gordon & MacPhail. It is certain that the 14-year-old malt in the → 'Flora & Fauna' series from UD, comes from the six → stills of the new distillery, as does the 22-year-old at 58.64%, and the 24-year-old at 61.3% and the 22-year-old (58.95%) in the → 'Rare Malts Selection'. When the → independents like → Cadenhead and → Signatory write Clynelish on the bottles it is the whisky produced in the old distillery.

Cock o' the North Scotch whisky liqueur. It was launched onto the market in 1998 by the Cock o' the North Whisky Liqueur Co. Lord Huntly and his son Alistair Granville Gordon, Earl of Aboyne are behind this company. Both are members of the Gordon clan. 'Cock o' the North' has been the title of the Gordon's clan chief since the 16th century, and the 5th Duke of Gordon played a part in passing the legislation to legalise whisky making.

As in the case of other whisky liqueurs, the recipe is kept secret. The 'extras' are what makes it different to others, and especially to → Drambuie. The accent is not on honey and herbs but on fruits, especially the blaeberry, a Scottish form of bilberry. The whisky used is a single malt from → Speyside.

Cock of the Walk Kentucky straight bourbon. It is 12 years old and 114° (57%). The label names the distillery as Cock of the Wall, Bardstown, although this has never existed. The → Kentucky Bourbon Distillers are behind this company.

Cockburn Scotch single malt, that was launched onto the market by → Cockburns of Leith. According to reports it is a → Tamdhu. Its label bears James Hogg's great words that have been translated into Italian: 'If a body could just find oot the exact' proportion and quantity that ought to be drank every day and keep to that, I verily trow that he might leeve for ever without dying at a', and doctors and kirkyards would go oot o' fashion.' On the bottle the quotation is attributed to Walter → Scott – perhaps because he is better known, or because he was a customer of the old company in Leith.

Cockburn & Campbell Scottish wine and whisky company. They began doing business more than 150 years ago in Edinburgh, and maintained their independence for a long time. In 1972, however, they were bought by the brewery Young & Co, at this time as the old → warehouse in Duke Street, famous for its extremely high humidity, was also given up. To the astonishment of the sceptical excisemen almost no alcohol evaporated in the warehouse, so that there was hardly any → angels' share. The company used to have eight brands, four of

Cockburn & Murray

which were simply numbered, Cockburn's No. 1 – 4. The No. 4 was later rechristened The → Royal and Ancient. This, and the vatted → Special Malt, are the only brands that survive today. A further blend, Loch Troon, was a reminder of another famous golf course. The London-based Young & Co are one of the larger independent breweries in the UK, with 500 pubs of their own, in addition to which they supply a further 180. The whisky is available in all of them.

Cockburn & Murray Scottish whisky company. It has been owned by Peter J → Russell & Co since 1953. Even after the takeover the old name decorated the labels of an 8-year-old blend which was made mainly for the Italian market for quite some time. Although it is not being bottled at present, it can still be found in Italy.

Cockburn's of Leith Scottish company with such a great tradition that it is a true embodiment of the trading aristocracy of the town. It began trading as Cockburn (pronounced Coburn) & Company (Leith). It is known as a trader of wine and whisky, and is well known for port. It was founded in 1796 by the brothers Robert and John Cockburn; Henry, the third brother, was a judge who became Lord Cockburn and was famous for his book *Memorials of My Time*.

The company still proudly displays its account books in which, apart from the royal household and many aristocrats, Walter → Scott and even Charles Dickens are mentioned. One of the Cockburn brothers went to Portugal and established the port trading company. The company remained independent until 1981, when it was taken over by → Drambuie. In 1993 they resold Cockburn to the Wine Company, who were then taken over by the Wine Emporium, founded in Edinburghin 1986.

The new owners closed the lovely shop on Southbridge, but decided to give up their own name and adopt that of the older company. At the end of 1997 they took over another old Edinburgh wine company, J E Hogg. Cockburn's oldest brand was → V O 8. They had a vatted malt bearing their name and the blends The → Dominie , → Imperial Gold Medal and → Old Decanter. According to reports they will all be revamped, but will nevertheless be continued. In 1995 a 6-year-old single malt called → Cockburn came onto the market.

Cocktails Mixed drinks based on spirits.

Coffey, Aeneas This Irishman, born around 1780, is still famous today, not because he went from being a simple gauger or excisemen, the occupation so hated by the distillers, to become Inspector-General of Excise in Ireland, but because in the end he became a whisky-maker himself – and developed a method which revolutionised production by making it easier, cheaper and more rational. Ironically it was mainly Scottish whisky that profited from this method – at the expense of the Irish distillers. In 1824 Coffey acquired the Dock Distillery in Dublin and began to experiment there (and later at → Port Ellen on → Islay), no longer distilling his whiskey big batch in the traditional pot stills, but continually in column-shaped stills – following on from experiments which had already been carried out in Fife, by Robert → Stein.

From the very beginning Coffey worked with separating plates in both columns, this was more effective than Stein's process, because it produced a cleaner spirit. His colleague's ideas were particularly welcomed in the Scottish → Lowlands, and were also greeted enthusiastically by the gin-makers of London. This invention enabled production at much higher speeds, so that a considerably higher quantity was produced, which became much more economical as most grains could be used and not just expensive → malted barley. The Coffey still or, as it is also known, → patent, → continuous or → column still, produced a completely new type of whisky, → grain whisky. This made the development of blends possible – with all its consequences, as it was this Scotch that permitted the creation of brands in the modern sense. Coffey who died in England in November 1852, is gratefully remembered by the large whisky companies, who owe their success and perhaps even their existence, to his pioneering work.

Coffey Grain Japanese → grain whisky, produced by → Nikka. Their founder, Masataka → Taketsuru, had a → coffey still imported from Scotland in 1962 and installed it at → Nichinomiya. Here several types of whisky are produced, including one from 100% malted barley (also to be found in Nikka's → All Malt). Nikka Coffey Grain Whisky is very special: it must be the only → grain whisky on the market which is unequivocally produced by this special form of continuous distillation. For this reason alone it is worth trying, although it is also ideal for creating a blend of one's own, mixing it with the three versions of Nikka's → Pure Malt.

Coldstream Guard Scotch blend. → Inver House Distillers Ltd already had this brand in their range when they belonged to the American company Publicker Industries Inc. A straightforward → standard blend with no age statement.

Coleburn Scottish malt distillery. Its name comes from the Gaelic for 'stream on the corner'. It lies between Elgin and Rothes, near the A941 and belongs, or rather belonged, to → the Speyside region. Although the little distillery looks much as it did when it was founded in 1897, its two → stills have long been out of operation. It was built by John Robertson & Son, who were known for their → Yellow Label. Although initially it survived the great culling of distilleries in 1983, it was closed two years later by → DCL, which had owned it since 1930. Their successors, → UD, dissolved the licence which had been registered under J & G Stewart, which produced the famous → Usher blends. The malt from Coleburn also disappeared from these whiskies. It had never been available as a single malt in a → distillery bottling until UDV decided in 2000 to bring out a 21-year-old, distilled in 1979 (59.4%) in their → 'Rare Malts Selection'. It is only very seldom that → independent bottlers manage to get hold of a cask. Anyone who can get a → 'Connoisseurs Choice' bottling from → Gordon & MacPhail, the 12-year-old from → MacArthur, the → cask strength 1978 bottle at 59.1% from Cadenhead or the → Signatory Coleburn from 1983, can consider themselves very lucky, and should maybe think twice about whether to drink or save it.

Colonel Collins Whiskey cocktail. Another version of Collins, this time prepared on a bourbon basis. In the USA it is also called John Collins.

Colonel Lee Kentucky straight bourbon. It can be confused with the 'light whiskey' with exactly the same that is made by the same producer, → Barton. The straight is → bottled in bond and has a bottle strength of 100° (50%).

Colonel's Special Indian whisky from → Mohan Meakin. It wouldn't traditionally be defined as a whisky because it consists mainly of a molasses distillate, and so is a blend of malt whiskies (or malt extract) and a kind of rum. This method is widespread in India, where it is nevertheless called 'whisky'. The malt share of the product is said to come from the → Mohan Nagar Distillery.

Coleraine Irish whisky distillery, whose glorious past is now commemorated by just one blend. It comes from → Bushmills. Coleraine (who spell whisky without the 'e') could claim to be the oldest distillery in the world. The licence granted by the English king to Thomas Phillips, which Bushmills refer to, was not for a specific distillery but was bestowed on an area in County Antrim in Northern Ireland. Both Coleraine and Bushmills are situated in this area – and Coleraine is actually named in this precious document.

The distillery was actually founded in 1820, although a number of distilleries were in operation in and around the town during the mid-18th century. Its malt whisky was so successful that it was soon served in the bars of the House of Commons in London. After the death of its founder, James Moore, it was taken over by Robert Taylor. His business bloomed and his whisky was considered to be among the best. His successors were not so fortunate, however, being troubled with both World Wars, and especially by prohibition in the USA. The distillery had to be closed down at the beginning of the 1920s. It was 1938 before it could be reopened – and shortly after it had to close down again, because of the shortage of barley during the Second World War.

Later, when blended whisky was produced in Ireland, a → patent still was installed. The last malt whisky flowed in 1964, and grain spirit production ceased in 1978. It was cheaper for the new owners to get their grain from the modern complex in → Midleton.

What was lost with the malt from Coleraine, can only be judged by those able to sample one of the 396 bottles of a 34-year-old single malt distilled in 1959. It was bottled by IDG in 1993. This time the whiskey was spelt with an 'e' and the Coleraine Distillery Ltd was named on the label. Even after such a long time the contents still had the stately strength of 57.1%. It was highly praised by all those who opened their bottles. Those less privileged can now get the blend called → Coleraine. It is a → standard blend and is mainly sold on the local market in Northern Ireland.

Collins Whisk(e)y cocktails with many variations. They are determined by the type of whisk(e)y used as a basis. The proportions are always three parts of whisk(e)y stirred with one part lemon juice and a teaspoon of sugar, filled with lots of soda or mineral water. Serve with plenty ice and a maraschino cherry and a slice of orange. The Scotch version is called 'Sandy Collins', the Irish 'Mike Collins', the Canadian 'Captain Collins' and the one with bourbon, 'Colonel' or 'John Collins'.

Colouring Process widely used in the production of Scotch blends and other whiskies, although it was thought that it wasn't used for Scotch single malts. Colouring involves the addition of caramel, the purpose of which is to give the whisky a consistent colour. This effect was virtually a prerequisite for the creation of Scotch blends and their establishment as international drink brands: once a customer had decided on a certain brand they want to always have the same aroma and taste, and also the same colour. From the beginning of blend production sugar colouring or caramel was added to compensate for colour differences. The taste is not affected as only a minute amount is needed to achieve the required effect.

It was, however, a different matter with single malt whisky, where individuality is expressed, amongst other ways, in its colour – a natural result of maturation in various types of → cask. There has been great surprise, and disappointment among many malt lovers on discovering in recent years that more and more bottles have a label, in Dutch or Greek, stating that food colouring has been used to 'adjust' the colour. More and more of these malts are being produced.

Some → independent bottlers are making it clear that their malts are bottled completely naturally, without colouring and without → chill filtering.

For some time now the → Scotch Whisky Association has been making sure that a directive from the European Commission to declare all use of colouring is adhered to. Gradually all labels are beginning to include a statement about colouring. Only absolutely natural food colours are used for colouring both blends and malts.

Column still A type of still, the use of which began in the 1820s. Until that time→ pot stills had been used exclusively. It was invented by the Scot Robert → Stein and Aeneas → Coffey, who worked as a tax official in Dublin. The equipment is usually called a → patent still, or, because it enables uninterrupted production, a → continuous still. It usually consists of two columns made of copper or stainless steel, up to 15 metres high, in which perforated plates also made of copper or steel are layered on top of each other, working like small stills. The cold → wash, which is fed into the top of the second column, runs down to meet the steam coming up from below. A continuously running process finally condenses very pure ethyl-alcohol at approximately 95%. In Scotland → grain whisky is produced in → column stills. At → Midleton in Ireland, column stills are used along with pot stills, and in line with the practice of triple-distillation, three columns are combined. In Canada a second pair of columns is used so that they can produce an even 'cleaner' whiskey. In the USA practically all whiskeys are distilled in columns to which a → doubler or a → thumper has been attached.

Comander-in-Chief Scotch blend with no age statement. It is one of the less well-known brands from Brodie Crawford & Co, whose best-known product is → Brodie's Supreme.

Condenser During distillation in → pot stills, the steam is cooled to become liquid again in the condenser. In the → wash still the → wash, and in the → spirit still the → low wines, are converted to steam by heating, which then rises and at the head of the still is led, via the → lyne arm, to the condensers. They are cooled by water. An older form is the → worm, which is connected to the lyne arm and runs in a spiral through a wooden tub. Distilleries that still use 'worms' swear by them. They were often set up in the open air outside the → stillhouse. They can be seen at → Edradour, Dalwhinnie → Glenkinchie, → Knockdhu, → Mortloch or → Talisker. Most have been replaced by modern equipment.

Connemara Irish single malt. Since its foundation in 1987 the young Irish company → Cooley Distillery has sprung a few surprises. They have broken with some Irish whisky-making principles and have tended to orientate towards Scottish traditions. They not only brought equipment from Scotland, but also got the help of Scottish experts. Billy Walker from → Burn Stewart and Jimmy Lang from → Chivas worked in Riverstown. Cooley also began to work with peated malt.

That was not only a break with Irish tradition but it gave them the chance to produce several differing single malts. Their declared intention was to make a whiskey which could compete with the heavy → Islays. After Cooley had first successfully introduced the unpeated → Tyrconnell, they followed it with Connemara, named after that beautiful part of the west of Ireland. It is bottled in two versions: at 40% and since 1997 as a → cask strength, which differs from bottling to bottling. After one at 60.9%, came a second at 60.2%.

Connexion Japanese blend. It comes from → Nikka and is only available in Japan. The firm also supplies a spirit made of rum and rye with the same name, a rye distillate which comes in Tetrapacks as well as bottles.

Connoisseurs Choice The name used by the independent bottlers → Gordon & MacPhail for malt whiskies from distilleries which have either long since closed down or have been demolished. They also bottle whisky from distilleries who don't do proprietor's bottlings, which is why they are so coveted by collectors. The bottlings are always at 40% and the year of distillation is always shown on the label although it is rare to see the date of bottling.

Consulate Scotch blend. It is produced exclusively for the American market by → QSI, a subsidiary of William → Grant & Sons, as a 'value for money' product.

Continuous still Another name for a → column still, → or patent still

Convalmore Scottish malt distillery. Its name, emphasised on the penultimate syllable, comes from the Gaelic for 'great Conval'. The Convall Hills are situated to the west and south-west of Dufftown, and Convalmore distillery lies on the northern outskirts of → the town and therefore belongs to the → Speyside region. The distillery, founded in 1894, went on fire in 1909. It was then owned by → James Buchanan and Co, and became part of → DCL in 1925. They closed it down in 1985, and their successors → UD sold the completely empty plant to William → Grant & Sons, who already owned → Glenfiddich, → Balvenie and → Kininvie, in the same town. They only use the → warehouses of Convalmore for maturing their own malts. The whisky has never existed as a single malt in a → proprietor's bottling. → Independent bottlers such as → Cadenhead or → Gordon & MacPhail in the 'Connoisseurs Choice' series, have included it in their ranges from time to time. In their → 'Silent Stills' series (no. 4) → Signatory had a 23-year-old Convalmore from 1976, bottled at 60.8%.

Cooley Distillery Irish whiskey company founded in 1987. During the short period of its existence has caused a stir in the world of Irish whiskey. The number of Irish whiskeys available has almost doubled in this time. Cooley has also produced new products such as peated single malts.

John J → Teeling bought the Ceimici Teo Distillery

in → Riverstown, Dundalh, near the border with Northern Ireland, from the Irish state for £120,000.

Teeling and his fellow investors had to spend a further three million pounds to convert the plant from the production of industrial alcohol to both malt and → grain whiskeys. They were able to acquire the old → pot stills of the long defunct → Comber Distillery, and from → Inver House Distillers Ltd they bought a → mash tun from → Moffat Distillery which had also been closed down. Experts, like the Master Blender Billy Walker, were brought over from Scotland. Unlike all other Irish distilleries, Cooley only distils twice – as is the rule in Scotland, and this illustrates the Scottish influences at work. Teeling's named the distillery after the nearby Cooley Mountains, acquired the → Kilbeggan Distillery (which only survived in museum form) for the use of the → warehouses, and bought the rights to the names of venerable companies and fondly-remembered brands, such as → Locke, → Millar, → Watt, → Tyrconnell and → Inishowen.

The young company, launched → The Tyrconnell, a very young malt, onto the market in 1992. A threatened takeover by IDG was prevented by the Irish Monopolies Commission. Teeling was successful in finding partners with the necessary money to carry on. He concluded contracts for distribution with → UD, → Heaven Hill and, perhaps more importantly with the Scottish company → Invergordon, which had passed into American ownership. They bought whiskey from Cooley to make a number of → blends that are mostly exclusively sold in supermarkets such as → Sainsbury, → Marks & Spencer and → Tesco. The contract with Invergordon has now been dissolved.

It is hard to encompass all of Cooley's brands: along with Tyrconnell and the revolutionary Connemara (made with peated malt), → Shanagarry and → Slieve Na gCloc (exclusive to Oddbins) which are all single malts, there is the → blend → Kilbeggan and Locke's, which comes as both a blend and a malt. From → Avoca to → Ballygeary, to → Cassidy's, to a brand for → Waitrose, there is hardly a single letter of the alphabet without a Cooley's whiskey.→ Dunlow alone is obtainable in five different versions for five French supermarket chains. There is even a → Celtic, bottled in honour of Celtic FC, founded in 1888.

Cooper's Choice, The The → Vintage Malt Whisky Company in Glasgow, one of the youngest → independent bottlers, established in 1992, use this name for their → single cask bottlings from selected Scotch malt distilleries. As their range, by its nature, is constantly changing and bottlings which have been sold out are continually being replaced with new ones, the following is just a sample of what was available in 1998: → Aberfeldy 1982, → Aultmore 1983, → Balmenach 1978, → Benrinnes 1981, → Caol Ila 1982, → Clynelish 1982, → Convalmore 1981, → Dailuaine 1981, → Glendullan 1978, → Macduff 1978, → Port Ellen 1983, → Royal Brackla 1979, → Teaninich 1983, → Tomatin 1977. A special series presents → sherry cask bottlings, all bottled at 50%: Aultmore, → Imperial and → Linkwood, all from 1983. This list alone demonstrates that the range from Glasgow deserves special attention: some of these malts are very difficult to come by. A Convalmore or an Imperial has always been a rarity, and Port Ellen is on the way to becoming one.

Cor, John Scottish monk who was a member of the Benedictine order and lived at Lindores Abbey, near Newburgh in Fife. John Cor was the first named maker of malt, and has become immortal because it was he was mentioned in the oldest known document concerning whisky. The document, part of the Scottish Exchequer Rolls for 1494, which today are preserved by the Keeper of the Records in Edinburgh, is written in Latin and states 'eight bolls of malt to Friar John Cor wherewith to make aquavitae'. The whisky was destined for King James IV. To commemorate John Cor, and the beginning of the history of whisky, the → Scotch Whisky Association ran a competition in 1994 with the motto 'The Spirit of Scotland', where whisky companies were invited to enter a blend specially made for the event. Amongst the entrants were → UD, who named their whisky Friar John Cor Quincentenary.

Corby Canadian whiskey company based in Agincourt, Ontario who can trace their origins back to Henry Corby, who emigrated from England in 1857 and built a mill, and a distillery, near Belleville. Corbyville lay on the River Moira, not far from where it flows into Lake Ontario. After a fire in 1907 it was rebuilt in traditional style, and must have been an architectural jewel although this building has long since been closed down. In the 1920s Harry Hatch, was responsible for a renaissance: the man who a short time later bought → Gooderham and Worts, and then Hiram → Walker, laid the foundations for one of the two great companies that today dominate Canadian whiskey. → Hiram Walker, itself owned by → Allied Domecq PLC, holds a majority share in Corby. Nowadays their whiskeys come from → Walkerville, the company's only distillery. The most important brands are a reminder of another long gone Canadian distillery → McGuinness, → Meagher's, → Royal Reserve, → Silk Tassel and → Wiser's.

The Canadians thought the names Corbyville and Corby Distillers were appropriate names for one of the country's more unique whiskeys, → Lot No. 40. This has now been followed by two further specialities, the → Gooderham & Worts and the → Pike Creek. The → Canadian Whisky Guild was credited as 'editor' of all three.

Corio Australian blend. The bottles still in existence are the last remnants after its producers, United Distillers, ceased production at the Corio Distillery in Melbourne and redistilled all the bottled stocks to gin. There are still two very small, quite new distilleries on the island of Tasmania.

Cork Town in the south-west of the Republic of Ireland, once a centre for Irish whiskey. Of the many distilleries that used to exist in the town and its surroundings, → Hewitt's Watercourse Distillery, North Mall, Daly's of John Street and The Green are still known today, at least among historians. They later joined the nearby → Midleton Distillery, where apart from → Cooley, the entire whisky production in the Republic is concentrated. The original → Paddy came from Cork, and still bears the name of the old company on its label. Hewitts are a reminder of the importance of Cork.

Corn Type of American whiskey. It differs from the others in that 80% corn must be used for its mash. This very high share makes it cheap, but also one-dimensional in taste. If this is combined with high alcohol content, then the result is sweet and sharp, reminiscent of the freshly distilled illicit spirit moonshine. Just like bourbon and rye, corn is not allowed to be at more than 160° (80%) when it comes from the stills. Another difference is that it may be matured in new or old barrels; only a straight corn, of which no known examples exist anymore, would have to be matured exclusively in new barrels. There is no legally prescribed minimum maturing period for corn. Georgia Moon is no older than 30 or 50 days old when it is bottled, or filled in preserving jars. Only a few corns are generally available, such as Cabin Hollow, Corn Crib, Golden Grain, J W Corn, Mellow Corn, Old Dispensary and McCormicks Platte Valley, which are all only of limited local importance.

Corn Base Japanese blend, that tries to imitate → bourbon: it consists of a corn distillate produced in the USA and imported to Japan. This distillate is 'married' to whiskies produced in Japan by → Nikka, all of which have a minimum age of eight years.

Corn Crib A Kentucky corn. It is one of only a handful left of its kind and comes from → Barton Brands and their distillery in → Bardstown.

Corner Creek Reserve Kentucky straight bourbon. It comes from an otherwise unknown company that bears the name of its brand. It is bottled at 88° (44%). This is rather special: whilst other bourbons use either rye or wheat for their mash, along with the legally prescribed corn and the malt barley required for fermentation, both grain sorts are used for Corner Creek Reserve.

Corney & Barrow A company established in 1780, which earned its reputation as a wine merchant with branches in London, Edinburgh and Newmarket but which, as co-owners of James → Catto & Co, was also intensively involved in the whisky business. The blend Corney & Barrow was produced by Catto. The blend was then passed to Peter J → Russell, and although they no longer produce it, the blend can still be found today. In 1994 Corney and Barrow merged with another very old wine dealer, Whighams of Ayr, who brought their own blend → Duart Castle with them.

Country Gentlemen's, The Scotch blend that is made exclusively for the Country Gentlemen's Association by a company called Hedley Wright & Co in Bishop's Stortford. Its owner is a member of the famous → Mitchell family, and the present owner of → Springbank Distillery.

County American blended whiskey from the David → Sherman Company of St. Louis.

Cousin Elvis Kentucky straight bourbon aged 12 years at 101° (0.5%) The C E Distilling Company, who are named as bottlers, are one of the many companies whose names are used by the → Kentucky Bourbon Distillers to market their variety of brands, which all probably come from → Heaven Hill distillery, which is also located in Bardstown.

Couvreur, Michel A Belgian wine dealer and → independent bottler of Scotch whiskies living in Burgundy. His bottlings used to be labelled → 'Meldrum House' but now bear his own name.

Cowie & Sons, George Scottish whisky company whose name first became known to a wider public when → DCL had to remove their best-selling→ Johnnie Walker from the market and replace it with → John Barr, produced by their subsidiary . They had previously been known to lovers of malt whisky because they held the licence for → Mortlach Distillery in → Dufftown, their name appearing on the bottles of this highly-regarded malt, brought out by → Gordon & MacPhail. Cowie had owned the distillery since 1854 and the name is still on the manager's office door, although the distillery now belongs to → UDV.

Crabbie's Until 1993 this name applied to a blended Scotch, but is now only to be found on bottles of 'Green Ginger Wine'. This is good for mixing cocktails and indispensable for the famous → Whisky Mac. John Crabbie founded the company in 1801, and for a time it also owned →

Balmenach distillery. In 1922 the family company merged with Macdonald Greenlees and came under the control of DCL and therefore later → UD, which sold it to → Macdonald Martin/→ Glenmorangie plc in 1994.

Cradle Mountain Australian malt whisky produced by the → Small Concern Whisky Co in Ulverstone on the island of → Tasmania.

Cragganmore Scottish malt distillery. Its name comes from the Gaelic for 'large rock'. It lies between Grantown-on-Spey and → Aberlour, between the A95 and the southern banks of the Spey. It therefore belongs to the → Speyside whisky region. The founder, John Smith, was able to make use of his great experience at → Macallan and → Glenlivet when building his own distillery in 1870. This malt became one of the most coveted of all – with the unfortunate result for malt lovers that it soon came to be used exclusively for blends. The malt is said to be 'aristocratic', and owes its opulence and its complexity to the unusual T-form of the → still heads. Although it now has four → stills, Cragganmore is still a small distillery. Via → White Horse Distillers and → DCL it passed to → UD, who transferred the licence from D & J → McCullum to → MacDonald Greenlees in 1992. Today it belongs to the UDV empire.

Cragganmore had previously only been available in very limited quantities as a single malt in a → distillery bottling, before it was deservedly selected as one of the six → 'Classic Malts' from → UD. Here, as a 12-year-old, it is a splendid representative of the Speyside region. At the end of 1997 the series 'The → Distillers Edition', bottled a malt distilled in 1984, which had received a second maturation in a port cask as an extra → finishing.

Craigduff Scotch single malt, whose name was unknown until it was found to be a component of the → Century from → Chivas Bros. Its home distillery is → Strathisla, where → Chivas Bros had some of its malts distilled in the 1970s in a manner that deviated from their → house-style and were much more heavily peated than usual. The distillery was to supply what the company didn't have: an → Islay-type malt. The experiment was soon discontinued. The whisky is not available as a single malt. either as a → proprietor's bottling or as an → independent bottling.

Craigellachie Scottish malt distillery. Its name, pronounced 'kreg-elláchie', emphasised on the second syllable, comes from the Gaelic for 'rocky hill'. It is situated not far from where the A95 crosses the road from → Rothes to → Dufftown, almost in sight of the River Spey, and it belongs to the → Speyside whisky region. One of the members of the founding syndicate was Peter Mackie, whose name, like that of the Craigellachie Distillery, is inseparable from → White Horse Distillers and their famous blend. They were still registered as licence-holders in 1998, and their name was written in large letters on the → stillhouse.

When in 1927, after Mackie's death, the takeover of his company by → DCL could no longer be prevented, the distillery, built in 1891, passed into their ownership. In 1987 it passed to → UD. Ten years later their successors UDV, parted with the distillery: along with → Aberfeldy, → Aultmore and → Royal Brackla, it found itself, together with the brand → Dewar's, sold to → Bacardi.

UD had made the malt, which was rarely obtainable from → independent bottlers, more accessible to a wider public as a 14-year-old single malt in a → proprietor's bottling in their → 'Flora & Fauna' series. The → 'Rare Malts Selection' included a 22-year-old Craigellachie from 1973 (60.2%). The lion's share is naturally used mainly for White Horse, as well as for → Logan. UDV have ensured fresh supplies by means of long-term contracts with the new owners. It is not certain what will happen to the single malt. It has occassionally been available from → independent bottlers.

Craiglodge One of six malts from the → Loch Lomond Distillery, of which only two, the → Inchmurrin and the → Old Rhosdhu, are available as single malts, whilst the other four, for the time being, are earmarked for blending. It is reported that only half of the malt used is peated.

Craignure, The Scotch single malt from →

Invergordon, one of five from its series brought out in the autumn of 1997, 'The → Malts of Scotland'. It distinguishes itself by having broken the rule that single malts carry the name of their distillery, although it is possible to guess where it comes from, as Invergordon then owned the → Isle of Jura Distillery which is located in Craighouse. Craignure is a village – on the island of Mull.

Cratur A Scots and Irish word for 'creature', often used in reference to whisk(e)y. On festive occasions, such as the annual Burns Supper celebrated on 25th January, or at the inauguration of the 'Keepers of the Quaich', the Scottish national dish, the haggis, is served 'wi' Champit Tatties an' Bashed Neeps wi' a Wee Drap o' the Cratur'.

Crawford's Scotch blend that is sold in two versions, as 3 Star and as 5 Star – the 3 Star label has remained virtually unchanged since the end of the 19th century. The brand, which used to be the most successful in Scotland, was established by the company A & A Crawford, founded in Leith in 1860. The firm was later absorbed by DCL, and was licensed to operate the → Benrinnes Distillery for them until 1992. → UD, the successors of DCL, sold the rights to the whisky in the UK to → Whyte & Mackay, but still hold the licence for the rest of the world. At present only the three star version is produced.

Crescent Japanese blend from → Kirin-Seagram, with Japanese as well as Scottish components, these have been readily available to the company via the former → Seagram subsidiary, The → Chivas & Glenlivet Group. Crescent is the leading product of the Japanese company and a → premium blend, a category which in Japan must contain more than a 40% malt whiskies. It is only available in Japan.

Crest Japanese blend from → Suntory which is available in two versions, though it is not made clear whether it is only the shape and volume of the bottle. Both bear the age 12 years. The 0.75 litre bottle is reminiscent of → Ballantine's.

Crested Ten Irish whiskey at 40%. Launched onto the Irish market in 1963 by → Jameson to compete with → Power's Gold Label and →

Crinan Water Canal

Paddy. It is in fact the oldest brand of this house (today's best-selling Jameson was only introduced in 1968). It contains whiskeys that are between 10 and 15 years old, with more → pot still whiskeys than grains, but is nevertheless light. Like all Irish whiskeys, except → Tullamore Dew and those from → Cooley, it is a part of IDG and therefore of → Groupe Pernod-Ricard.

Crinan Water Canal → Premium Scotch blend, from Cockburn & Co (Leith), who are nowadays called → Cockburn of Leith. It is named after the canal which separates Knapdale and Kintyre from the rest of Argyllshire, and which was created in the late 18th century to give ships direct access between the Firth of Clyde and the Atlantic, saving them a detour of more than seventy miles.

Croftengea Scotch malt. One of six different malts produced at the → Loch Lomond Distillery. It is not available as a single malt, but is used for blending.

Crown Royal Canadian whisky first sold in 1939. The occasion for the launch of this new whisky, which was created by Samuel → Bronfmann, was the visit of King George VI and Queen Elizabeth to Canada. The bottle was n the shape of a crown, and wrapped in purple cloth. A 10-year-old, it still counts as one of the most complex of Canadian whiskeys, and has been called the Canadian → 'Macallan'. In 1995, with the 12-year-old Crown Royal Special Reserve, which was made from a series of special 'Waterloo-814 Reserve' whiskeys that had been set to one side, and the 15-year-old Crown Royal Limited Edition (exclusively for America), two new exclusive versions were added from the house of → Seagram.

Cuba The island is better known for its rum (and of course for its cigars) than for whisky. In fact before Fidel Castro's time much whisk(e)y was drunk, but not produced there. There was, however, a whisky produced in Cuba called → Old Havanna, called itself a pure malt, and came from the Santa Cruz drinks combine.

Cumbrae Castle Scotch blend from → MacDuff International. It hasn't been on the market for long and is named after a sailing ship that got its name from the islands Great and Little Cumbrae, and from the castle that Oliver Cromwell razed to the ground, leaving just one tower standing. This → standard blend is mainly sold in South America and the Far East.

Custodian Scotch blend that is produced under the company name Denham by the London trading company → Red Lion Blending, and is mainly sold in South America.

Cut, Cutting Decisive stage in the production of malt whisky in → pot stills, the success of which can often only be judged years later, when the whisky has matured. Cutting is the task of the → stillman who, towards the end of the final distillation, has to watch very carefully for the right moment in the → spirit safe to separate the → foreshots from the → middlecut, the → heart of the run, and then later again separate these from the → feints (the alcohol that is unusable, partly poisonous and in part consists of indigestible fusel oils) from the usable, which then, as → baby whisky or → new spirit, is filled into casks to mature, with some water added.

Cutty Sark Scotch blend that isn't called 'Scotch' but 'Scots', and which bears a famous name with two sources. There was the witch with the 'cutty sark' who features in Robert-Burns' ballad *Tam O' Shanter. Cutty Sark* is the clipper ship, built in Scotland, which for a long time held the record for the quickest voyage from Australia to England. At the time when → Berry Bros & Rudd created a blend the ship was docked in London. This was in 1923, at the time of prohibition in the USA. The Cutty Sark's success originally owed much to the fact that the famous Captain Bill → McCoy was able to think up imaginative ways of smuggling it to the USA as one of the 'Real McCoy' products.

After prohibition had ended, Cutty Sark became the best-selling blended Scotch in America – and today it still occupies a leading position there, as well as worldwide. The pale colour of the whisky, to which no caramel is added, fitted the image of the light blend. The 'Scots Whisky' on the label designed by the Scottish artist James McBey, as well as its strong yellow colour, both allegedly the result of a printing error, are instantly recognisable. Cutty Sark, blended by → Robertson & Baxter for Berry's is available as a → standard blend, a 12-year-old Emerald, an 18-year-old Discovery and as a Golden Jubilee. This contains 50-year-old whiskies and is only available on flights of Cathay Pacific Airlines (and at Berry's shop in St. James's Street, London). The ship which lent its name to the whisky can also be admired in London where it is docked at Greenwich.

CWS UK company whose full name is the Co-operative Wholesale Society, which runs a large number of branch stores and is based in Manchester where it has a large bottling plant with an adjacent warehouse complex. It also bottles on behalf of other companies, but it no longer produces its own-label whiskies itself, having them blended and bottled by a prominent Scotch distiller. There are three → standard blends: → Heatherdale, → Highland Abbey and → Majority.

Czech Republic Some may find it surprising that whisky is produced in the Czech Republic. The Czechs are skilled at malting and peat is available, although nowadays it is mostly imported from Scotland. Czech malt is of such a fine quality that even the Japanese giant → Suntory imports malt from the Czech Republic. The → Stock company, who give their foundation date as 1920, own a distillery in a village near the company's base in Plzen, where during the Communist regime the Halberd distillery also produced malt whisky, which was mainly sold to eastern-bloc countries. Other distilleries had the same function. The only domestically-produced whisky which was obtainable in those days was Private Club. The brand was discontinued when the Dynbyl family, who had established their distillery before the war, had it returned to them again.

Nowadays only two Czech Whisky producers are active. The first is Stock, who for a short time produced a malt whisky named Halberd Whisky and a blend named Smoker Halberd Whisky, and now produce → Printer's. The second company is → Seliko, based in Olomouc (Olmütz) who have two distilleries →Testice and → Dolony. They concentrate on two brands, the blend → Gold Cock and → King Barley (this sometimes appears as a blend and sometimes as a malt whisky). Both companies have from time to time had to either stop production or reduce it, as they have to fight against the fact that, since the opening up to the West, many Czechs prefer Scotch to their home product, although some vouch that it can hold its own. This is probably a result of the Czech skill at beer brewing and because they use Scottish methods and casks made of Czech oak. The new food laws introduced in the country recognise any distillate from malted or unmalted grain, or corn and blends, as whisky. The rules regarding maturation are somewhat different to Scotland: the minimum period, which in Scotland is three years, is only valid in the Czech Republic for casks with a capacity of up to 700 litres, whilst casks with a capacity under 300 litres only have to mature for two years. The minimum strength is 40%.

D

D'Accord Spirits formerly from → Seagram. The Canadians use this name to produce and sell whisky, gin and vodka in China. The choice of a French name for these products, which aren't normally associated with France could be due to the fact that for a long time cognac was the only western spirit to find widespread acceptance in China. Seagram was the first of the big drinks companies to recognise the potential of this huge country once it had opened up economically. In 1988 they entered into a joint venture with Shanghai Distillers, the first result of which was a whisky named Seagram's 7 Star, although this is no longer included in the company's lists.

Dailuaine Scottish malt distillery. Its name, pronounced 'dall-yewan' and emphasised on the second syllable, comes from the Gaelic for 'green valley'. It lies on the southern banks of the Spey, near the disused railway station at Carron, and belongs to the → Speyside whisky region. The distillery isn't particularly well known because most of its whisky was only used for blends, and especially for → Johnnie Walker, with whose owners the Dailuaine proprietors had close connections after 1898 via the Dailuaine- → Talisker Distillers Co. In 1916 it became part of DCL and the distillery now belongs to → UDV; its licence has been held by → UMGD since 1992. The distillery, founded in 1854, has been rebuilt twice, once as the result of a fire and then to enlarge it to six → stills. Dailuaine has only been available as a single malt in a → proprietor's bottling since it was included as a 16-year-old in the → 'Flora & Fauna' series. There has been (at least) one bottling in the 'Rare Malts' series, a 24-year-old at 60.92%. The independents also occasionally bottle it. A Dailuaine 1962 from Signatory, brought out in 1998 at a cask strength of 57.6% in a cystal carafe, was outstanding.

Daks Scotch blend produced for Daks, the renowned gentlemen's outfitters, who along with their competitors → Burberry and → Dunhill, like to offer a whisky of their own. Theirs is a first-class 17-year-old blend presented in a glass decanter.

Dalaruan Scottish malt distillery that was founded in 1825 and closed down in 1922, shortly before its 100th anniversary. It belonged to David Colvill & Co and was located in → Campbeltown. Its name was chosen by the French champagne company Taittinger and the Scottish → Lang Brothers which up to now seems to have resulted in just one product, the Scotch → Defender.

Dallas Dhu Scottish malt distillery. Its name, pronounced 'dallas doo' comes from the Gaelic for 'black-water valley'. It is to be found on an unclassified road when driving from Forres on the A940 towards Grantown-on-Spey. It belongs to the → Highlands whisky region. The distillery was built in 1899 and a year later was sold to Wright & Greig, who at the time owned the blend → Roderick Dhu. Today the distillery is a museum. It ceased operating in 1983 when owned by → DCL, allegedly because the water source had dried up. The entire equipment, with its two → stills, remains just as it had been since it was installed after a fire in 1939. It is lovingly cared for and production could be started up again immediately, but → UD, the successors of → DCL, had the licence cancelled. The popular museum is managed by → Historic Scotland, the commission for ancient buildings and monuments.

There had not been a → proprietor's bottling of a single malt before 1995 when → UD brought out a 24-year-old → cask strength in a limited quantity in the → 'Rare Malt Selection'. It was followed by a second one aged 21 years at 61.9%. → Gordon & MacPhail still have stocks, which are rapidly decreasing, and at present offer a 14-year-old. They previously sold a 10-year-old and a 12-year-old. → Signatory have included it in their → 'Silent Stills' series. In April 1998 the last remaining cask from 1983 was bottled for Historic Scotland, bearing the number 327, having produced exactly 294 bottles at 48%. There were 438 more bottles for the 100th anniversary of the distillery, which Historic Scotland offered to its members in the spring of 1999, when a 15-year-old Centenary Dallas Dhu was brought out. For the millennium Historic Scotland released a 25-year-old from 1974, which was bottled at only 43%. Its buyers also receive a copy of a photograph taken in 1899 of the workforce.

Dalmeny Scotch blend. It is an old brand from J Townend & Sons of Hull, which they 'inherited' in 1930 when they took over J J Rippon. It used to be blended in the company's own cellars from Highland malts and grains from the → North British Distillery, but is now obtained from Scotland and is mainly to be found in Yorkshire. There are two versions, a → standard blend and a → de luxe blend.

Dalmore Scottish malt distillery. Its name comes from the Gaelic for 'large field'. It lies on the northern banks of the Cromarty Firth between Alness and Invergordon, and belongs to the whisky region of the northern → Highlands. It was founded in 1839 as a typical farmhouse distillery, and was connected with the → Mackenzie family for nearly a hundred years. Its owners merged with → Whyte & Mackay in 1960. The stagshead coat of arms of the Clan Mackenzie decorated the label for a long time, and is still on the bottle today. In 1966 Whyte & Mackay enlarged the distillery to eight → stills. At Dalmore whisky has been stored in sherry casks since 1870. A third of it is still → finished in them, which gives the smoky and rather dry malt a soft sweetness.

Dalmore was already an important ingredient of Whyte & Mackay blends before the merger, and there has long been a → distillery bottling of a 12-year-old single malt; in 1994 the bottle was redesigned. It is also available in some countries as a 21-year-old. There are also occasionally → vintages; in 1989 a 30-year-old Dalmore was brought out, and at present it is even possible to buy a 50-year-old – not for the £1,000 that it originally cost. A 26-year-old at 45% first appeared as a → 'Stillman's Dram', followed at the end of 1997 by a 29-year-old Dalmore. The growing interest in cigars was reflected by the Dalmore Cigar Malt, for which chief noser Richard Paterson chose whiskies which had largely been matured in Oloroso Sherry casks, because their greater viscosity is meant to harmonise particularly well with a cigar. The distillery now belongs to → Kyndal.

Dalvegan Scottish vatted malt, produced by → Glenmorangie plc, and exclusively sold in the → Casino supermarket chain in France.

Dalwhinnie Scottish malt distillery. It lies near the A9, where the A889 branches off to the A86 west to Spean Bridge and Fort William. The distillery's name is from the Gaelic *Dailchuinnidh* which means meeting point. The railway line between Perth and Inverness, which runs directly past it, compensated for the fact that Dalwhinnie was sometimes rather inaccessible. It is situated at a height of more then 1,000 ft. It is the highest distillery in Scotland, and is often snowed-in during the winter. It is the site of a year-round meteorological station and collecting the data for the weather service is one of the duties of the distillery manager.

It was originally founded as → Strathspey in 1897 (although it doesn't lie on the Spey), and was the first Scottish distillery to be in American hands for a short time. From 1926 it belonged to → DCL, who bought it from Macdonald Greenlees in 1819. It was subsequently licensed to James → Buchanan & Co, with whom the licence is still registered. Buchanan had a → proprietor's bottling of a single malt (8 years old), and → UD included it as a 15-year-old in the series of six → 'Classic Malts', originally classifying it as a representative of the northern → Highlands region. It is now more correctly classified as a → Highland malt. At the end of 1997 the new series 'The → Distillers Edition', was supplemented with a limited bottling of a malt distilled in 1980 with a → sherry cask → finishing. For the 100th anniversary of the distillery a special edition of the 15-year-old with a cask strength of 56.1% was brought out.

Daniel, Jack → Jack Daniel.

Dark Grains Term for the refuse left after distilling → grain whisk(e)y which is made into cattle feed. There are solid parts in the liquid which in Scotland is called → burnt or pot ale and in the USA → stillage. They are left over in the → wash still after the first run when the → low wines are produced. In America the liquid parts are processed for → backset or → sour mash. The solid parts can be turned into a profitable product by processing them into a dark brown syrup which is mixed with the remains of mashing known as → draff. The cubes or pellets thus produced have a very high protein content. The process, which was pioneered in Canada and the USA, is also often used in Scotland. The first dark grain plant was set up in 1964 in → Hiram Walker's → Dumbarton Distillery.

David Nicholson 1843 Kentucky straight bourbon that is available in two versions: at 90° (45%) and 100° (50%), both 7 years old. The brand comes from → Van Winkle and was originally intended for a company in St. Louis. The brand is also occasionally available in Europe.

Daviess County Kentucky straight bourbon sold by the David → Sherman Company of St. Louis. The brand originally belonged to → Medley, a family whose origins go back to the Englishman John Medley, who is said to have begun distilling in Kentucky in 1634. In 1901 one of his successors bought the Daviess County Distilling Co, which was built in 1873/4. Various members of the family owned distilleries in Owensboro, and their most important brand was → Ezra Brooks. Medley and the → Fleischmann Distilling Co were initially taken over by → Glenmore, who in their turn, were bought by → UDV in 1991. They soon parted with the distillery and most of the brands. Some went to → Barton, and Ezra Brooks and Daviess County went to Sherman. It is 80° (40%) and its label speaks of 'quality supreme' and of the → heritage, which also appeared on the labels of the bottles from Owensboro. They contained a blend whose share of 49% neutral grain distillates was, unusually, quoted on the label.

Dawson Ltd, Peter Scottish whisky company founded in 1882 in Glasgow, taken over by → DCL in 1925, and therefore today a subsidiary of → UDV, for whom they supplied the blend → Peter Dawson. The company held the licence for the → Glen Ord Distillery, at that time just called → Ord, for sixty years. They also used to supply a 12-year-old malt called Ord. For a short period (1923/4) they were owners of the → Balmenach Distillery.

DCL (Distillers Company Ltd.) Scottish whisky company that was officially founded on 24th April 1877 and played a key part in the Scottish whisky industry for more than a hundred years. They spent much time expanding their interests, whether through the rebuilding of distilleries or by means of acquisitions and takeovers. They began with the unification of six Lowland grain distilleries, and by the end of 1987 they had an impressive collection of 38 subsidiaries in their control – leaving aside the company's numerous interests in other spirits, chemicals, and the like. The Scottish list, from Ainslie to Begg and Haig to Walker and White Horse Distillers, reads like a 'Who's Who' of Scottish whisky.

The six DCL distilleries of 1877 were → Cambus, → Cameron Bridge, → Carsebridge, → Glenochil, → Kirkliston and → Port Dundas, and among their owners was: John Haig. Very soon after DCL's foundation the organisation began to expand. They erected their own buildings for bottling and exporting whiskies in Queensferry near Edinburgh. The first step abroad soon followed: they acquired the Chapelizod Distillery (later Phoenix Park) in Dublin.

In 1889 William H Ross became the leading partner. He was to determine the destiny of DCL for many decades, and was the driving force behind it and its insatiable appetitie. He was responsible for DCL beginning the cultivation and sale of baker's yeast. He formed the Scottish Malt Distillers, which consisted of five further distilleries, all in the Lowlands; Clydesdale, Glenkinchie, Grange, Rosebank and St. Magdalene. In 1916 they bought John Begg,

De luxe

shortly afterwards Andrew Usher & Co, and in 1919 the other branch of the Haig family Markinch, and the London gin company Gordon & Co. In 1925 John Walker & Sons, along with James Buchanan and Co and John Dewar & Sons, who had merged a decade previously, followed. Finally in 1927, with Peter Mackie's White Horse Distillers, the last of the → Big Five had been brought under the umbrella of DCL. The history of DCL from 1877 to 1939 has been described in detail by R B Weir in his study The History of the Distillers Company.

The amalgamations, rationalisations, closures and diversifications continued. DCL became increasingly active overseas; in Canada, in Australia and in Ireland. At one time this giant controlled 40% of all Scottish whisky companies. At the beginning of the 1980s they owned 45 of the existing malt distilleries. In 1983, the company had to close down 21 distilleries because their whisky stocks had become too large – although a year later the company acquired Stitzel-Weller in the USA. It was the year in which Philip Morrice's *The Schweppes Guide to Scotland*, with its impressive list of DCL subsidiaries, appeared. It looked as though the company (which by then had become a joint-stock company – no longer DCL but DC plc) was thoroughly sound and absolutely unassailable.

A short time later closures began. They were the first signs that heralded the end. For a long time DCL came out of each crisis restrengthened. They survived the → Pattison crisis, World War I and even prohibition. But in retrospect the victories were won at great expense. What appeared to be a victory, a splendid success, was often in reality a loss. DCL succeeded in representing their interests, but sometimes at the expense of others, and some problems that still exist today. Perhaps that is a result of the way they developed.

What became clear in the so-called 'What is whiskey?' case was that DCL were looking after the interests of grain distilleries, and later blending companies. Shortly after the beginning of the 20th century, consumers often got such poor quality whisky, that Parliament introduced an initiative whereby only real malt whisky could call itself whisky. DCL opposed this – and won. The problem was not solved. A Royal Commission was set up to scientifically and legally enquire whether blends and grains were really whiskies. Their research lasted several years and ended with a complete victory for DCL: since then every grain distillate, no matter from which mash it derives and no matter whether it has been distilled in continuous or in pot stills, may be called whisky. The decision affected England, Scotland and Ireland. It was a bitter defeat for malt whisky – and was a huge factor in malt disappearing for a while.

During the 1980s DCL seemd unaware of the newly awoken interest in malts, which was triggered off by the pioneering works of William Grant & Sons and their Glenfiddich. The company was also bound up in the painful aftermath of having been involved in the Thalidomide scandal, as one of its subsidiaries had sold the active substance for this medicine. And they had to suffer another blow: because they demanded different prices on different markets, Brussels ordered them to sell various brands. DCL chose to sell its classic Johnnie Walker – a further sign that they no longer knew how to react to the market. The time was ripe for a takeover. In 1987, after a fierce battle, DCL was taken over by Guinness, and continued under the name UD.

Debonair Cocktail Whisky drink invented by Gary Regan and Mardee Haidin Regan ('The Book of Bourbon'): take 1cl ginger liqueur, 2.5cl Oban or Springbank, shake with ice, pour into an iced cocktail glass and garnish with a slice of lemon.

De Danu Scotch blend formerly from → Seagram, with the name → Chivas appearing in the same-sized print on the label. The brand was introduced at the end of 1998, and was initially only available in the USA and Italy. The beautifully designed bottle is said to represent a Celtic mysticism. It shows the picture of the Celtic goddess after whom the whisky is named, crowned by the sun and surrounded by a garland of symbols.

De luxe Term used for whiskies belonging to the

upper market sector, above the → standard blends and the → premium blends, which are particularly expensive. The price should by no means be regarded as an automatic indication of superior quality. In the case of Scotch blends an age is often given for de luxe whiskies, and it can be assumed that they contain a particularly high share of malt whiskies. Examples of such luxury blends are → Chivas Regal, → Dimple and → Johnnie Walker Black Label.

De Vreng & Zn, H P Dutch company who, as → independent bottlers, offer a small series of Scotch single malts. The 'Whisky Merchant' considers its malts to be so precious that it sells them in 0.5 litre bottles with a very pretty design. They state the age, as well as the year of distillation and bottling. Amounts are very limited and the bottles quickly disappear among Dutch collectors. They include a → Bruichladdich, a → Laphroaig and a → Macallan.

Dean's Finest Scotch blend (40%) without an age statement, the label of which names the Dean Distilling Co in Edinburgh as producer, behind which is probably → Glen Catrine Bonded Warehouse Ltd of Loch Lomond Distillery.

Deanston Scottish malt distillery. It lies not far from the small town of Doune, known for its castle, on the southern banks of the River Teith and belongs to the → Highland region. The imposing grey buildings which date from 1784 originally housed a cotton mill, and were converted to a distillery in 1965/6. It was taken over by → Invergordon in 1972, but they shut it down 10 years later and sold it to → Burn Stewart in 1991. They put it and its four → stills back into operation. Since September 1998 they have been making gin and vodka at Deanston, using different equipment. There was a → proprietor's bottling of a single malt in → Invergordon's time, a light, unpeated whisky. The bottlings now on offer from the latest owners, aged 12, 17 and 25 years, derive from that time. The malt whisky is also used for the whisky liqueur → Wallace and for → Drumgray, the company's cream-liqueur.

Deerstalker Scotch 12-year-old single malt bottled by Aberfoyle & Knight in Glasgow, who do not state which distillery has supplied it. In Scotch Whisky Charles MacLean claims that it comes from → Balmenach. The brand was created in 1880 by J G → Thomson & Co, so that the rights to it fell to → DCL, and later → UD. In 1991 they allowed → Hedges & Butler to resurrect and sell it primarily oversees. It came to its present owners in 1994, they also have the blend → Black Top in their range.

Defender Scotch blend from → Dalaruan, a company in Glasgow which was established in the late 1980s, who named themselves after a former distillery in → Campbeltown. It is a joint venture with → Lang Brothers and the French champagne company Taittinger. France is also the principal market for the 3-year-old blend, which is mainly sold in night clubs. The 12-year-old Success is to be found in the Far East, in Japan and Taiwan, whilst the 5-year-old is marketed everywhere. They are all bottled at 40%.

Delany's Irish blended Whiskey. One of the many brands from → Cooley.

Derby Special Scotch blend from the → Kinross Whisky Company, which operates from Sussex and supplies it as a 3 and 5-year-old and as a 12-year-old → de luxe blend.

Destilerias y Crianza Spanish whisky company based in Segovia, which belongs to the → Allied Domecq PLC empire, and is mainly known for the blend named after it, → DYC. The company was also active in Scotland, running the → Lochside Distillery in Montrose, independent of its parent company from 1972. Lochside has been shut down since 1992, but its Spanish distillery is in operation. It is called → Molino del Arco and is located near Segovia. It was opened in 1959 and just like Lochside at one time, can produce both malt and → grain whiskies, a large share of which are intended for DYC.

Dew of Ben Nevis Scotch blend. The founder of the → Ben Nevis Distillery, → 'Long John' Macdonald, sold his malt whisky by this name. It was first marketed as a blend by the founding family, who then had to sell the brand Long

John as well as the distillery. Long John International, which took over the ownership of the distillery in 1981, also marketed the Dew. Today it is the Japanese company → Nikka, who own the distillery. There is a → standard version and a Special Reserve (also in a stoneware jar) aged 12 and 21 years. In 1995 the 250th anniversary edition Glenfinnan was brought out to commemorate Bonnie Prince Charlie.

Dew of the Western Isles Eight-year-old Scotch blend belonging to the range of the → Speyside Distillery Co.

Dewar & Sons, John Scottish whisky company, founded by John Dewar, who was born on a Perthshire farm in 1806. After John's death in 1880, both his sons, John Alexander and Thomas Robert, carried on the business, which exemplifies the evolution of modern Scotch whisky: it went from being a local product to achieving world recognition and importance – through hard work, skilful marketing, brilliant advertising ideas, and intensive political work. John Alexander, who was 24, assumed control, while Tommy joined the company in 1885 when he was 21 years old. After just 20 years they had turned their blend → Dewar's White Label into a world hit – and were knighted: they were the first → 'Whisky Barons'.

John Alexander stayed in Scotland and looked after production and administration, and in 1896 built the → Aberfeldy Distillery. Tommy went to London where he looked after sales. He was responsible for much of the success of the company. He had a good sense for advertising ideas, and set particular store on the attractions of Highland culture. The figure of a Highlander in traditional costume became the company symbol. In 1886 a bagpipe player attracted the attention of visitors to the Brewer's Show, a giant Highlander was lit up on an old tower on the bank of the River Thames in London, and before the turn of the century Tommy had discovered the new medium of film, and had dancing Highlanders appear in an advertising film on Time Square in New York (it wasn't the first of its kind, as cinema inventor Lumière had already made an advertisement for 'Cointreau' in 1896). For a long time elegant Highland regiment officers advertised the whisky, and a Highlander is still used in advertsing today.

Tommy travelled the world for two years – at the end of which he had visited 26 countries and appointed 32 agents, and written a book with the title *A Ramble Round the Globe*. Together with his friend, 'Tea Tommy' Lipton, 'Whisky Tommy' was a respected society figure, popular for his wit and his quick repartee. After they had been appointed court suppliers in 1893, the Dewars were knighted and later became barons. John Alexander became Baron Forteviot of Dupplin in 1916, and Tom became Baron Dewar of Homestall, Sussex in 1919. They were wealthy and had suitable hobbies to match; Tommy successfully bred racehorses and they were both early motoring enthusiasts. They also entered Parliament, Tommy for the Conservatives, and John for the Liberals.

In 1915 John Dewar and Sons had already united with James → Buchanan & Sons to form the Scotch Whisky Brands company, and in 1925 joined → DCL, without withdrawing from active business themselves. Another unrelated Dewar carried on their work between 1930 and 1946, before a member of the family became president again. Although mainly in the blends business, the company also owned, usually only for a short period, the following distilleries: → Aultmore, → Benrinnes, → Port Ellen, Pultney and → Royal Lochnagar, as well as the now defunct Glenfoyle/→ Glendarroch and → Parkmore distilleries. Its connections with Aberfeldy and Glen Ord lasted longest.

Dewar's headquarters remained in Perth, and in the early 1960s the company built a vast new blending and bottling plant at Inveralmond on the northern outskirts of the city. As a subsidiary of DCL the company came under the umbrella of → UD in the 1980s, and the imposing bottling plant was closed in 1995. In celebration of the 150th anniversary of their brand, Dewars organised a design competition and issued a small edition of 1846 Decanter, which unfortunately was only presented to business friends. The normal blend, sold as Dewar's Whisky, Dewar's White Label or just → White Label, is still one of the biggest brands of all – in the USA it stands unchallenged in first place. At the end of 1997, when UD's parent company → Guinness merged with → Grand Metropolitan to form the new drinks giant → Diageo, they were required to give up the Dewar brand by the trade regulatory bodies and control passed to Bacardi.

Diageo The largest drinks group in the world, arising in December 1997 from the – friendly – merger of two enterprises that were each already global players: → Grand Metropolitan with its spirits subsidiary → IDV, and → Guinness with its subsidiary → UD. Resistance to the merger came from outside: from Bernard Arnault, whose luxury goods group LVMH (Louis Vuitton Moet Hennessy) had various agreements and mutual interests with Guinness, but particularly from the Monopolies Commissions of the EU and the Antitrust Authority in the USA, who feared that the new enterprise would dominate certain markets and sectors. This suspicion was not unfounded as UD had the best-selling Scotch blend → Johnnie Walker Red and IDV the second best-seller in→ J & B. The new company was also represented by four other brands in the list of the top 12 Scotches, and were also strong in the gin and vodka sector.

The new partners could feel satisfied with the conditions imposed on their merger: their newly established spirits subsidiary, → UDV, had to part with several of its smaller brands, such as → Ainslie's. As such mergers lead to so-called synergy, and have repercussions in many countries, the sale and closure of subsidiaries which have become superfluous continues: in Germany World Brands were merged with UD Germany (Asbach), in Scotland Cherrybank, the former Bells headquarters in Perth, has been closed down, and apart from the brand Dewar's, the distilleries → Aberfeldy, → Aultmore, → Craigellachie and → Royal Brackla have been sold to → Bacardi. In Canada Diageo have parted with all their brands except → Gibson's, and sold the production plants → Palliser and → Valleyfield. In the USA they sold the → Bernheim Distillery and the brands → Old Charter, → Old Fitzgerald, → Rebel Yell and → W L Weller in March 1999 for 171 million dollars to a syndicate of → Heaven Hill, → Sazerac and the David → Sherman Company.

Diageo/UDV produce 109 million → cases per year, that is 20% of the world market, which is estimated at 600 million cases. The two keenest competitors, → Allied Domecq PLC and the former world leader → Seagram, together make up less than 15%, and taken together are even smaller than the new giant, which makes a combined turnover of an estimated £20 billion a year. The new name provoked some disapproval: originally the name GMG Brands (GrandMet Guinness Brands) was considered, but then Diageo was chosen .

Dickel & Co, George A American whisky company. The founder was born in Germany, in 1818, emigrated to America in 1844 and settled in Nashville, Tennessee nine years later. There he began to trade in whiskey, buying it from its producers and selling it under his own name. The date 1870, which appears on the label of the whisky named after him, could possibly be the year that he began to get his whisky exclusively from the → Cascade Distillery. In 1888 he and his brother-in-law bought the distillery, and acquired the exclusive rights to bottle and sell Cascade Whisky – a bottle still exists using the Scottish rather than American spelling of 'whisky', and extolling it as 'Mellow as Moonlight'.

In the same year Dickel fell from his horse and was badly injured, which forced him to retire. He died six years later as a result of the injury. His business remained in the safe hands of his brother-in-law and nephew. They made the distillery into the largest in the state, and were initially able to save the business and the brand from the effects of → prohibition, which had already begun in Tennessee in 1910, and forced them to move production to Kentucky, where its whisky was produced by → Stitzel. Even so Dickel & Co also became victims of the → Volstead Act. The rights to the name of the company and to the Cascade brand eventually passed to → Schenley, who in 1958 built a new Cascade Distillery in Tullahoma, scarcely half a mile away from the old one. In 1964 they gave their product the name of its founder, and in 1987 were bought by → Guinness and allied with its subsidiary → UD. Today they are owned by → Diageo, the spirits subsidiary → GuinnessUDV. George A Dickel & Co are responsible for running the distillery which has remained small, and for their whisky, of which four versions are bottled:

→ George Dickel Old No. 8 Brand, Superior No. 12 Brand, a 10-year-old and a Special Barrel Reserve.

Dimple Scotch blend, which has become famous through its unmistakable, characteristic bottle, which is triangular in shape with the dents that gave it its name: 'dimple' is used to describe the surface of a golfball, whose dimples improve its aerodynamic qualities. The brand has been in existence since the beginning of the 20th century, and was introduced by John → Haig & Sons (in the USA by → Haig & Haig with the name → Pinch), and soon was one of the biggest selling whiskies. The shape of the bottle became very popular and was often copied, which led the Haigs to protect it and officially register it as a trademark in 1919 – the second bottle to be registered after Coca Cola. The thin gold wire was originally meant to prevent the cork dropping out on stormy sea voyages. It is still put on by hand today. The quality of the blend, which is bottled at 12 and 15 years, is excellent. It contains more than 40 malts, with → Glenkinchie (considered to be its home) at its core along with → Dalwhinnie and → Royal Lochnagar. It is possible to find pewter bottles. In some countries there are Dimple Clubs for afficionados of this blend.

Diners A series of special bottlings from the Denham subsidiary of the London-based trading company → Red Lion Blending produced for the credit card company Diners Club. It is available as an 8, 12, and 21-year-old blend, an 8 and a 15-year-old vatted malt and an 8-year-old bourbon. Like the ports, cognacs and champagnes with club labels, they are only available to club members: by the glass in its lounges and by the bottle at the Clubhouse Cellar in London.

Diplomat Indian whisky from the → United Brewers of India, subsidiary McDowell & Co, mainly known for its single malt, which apart from → Kasauli is the only one in the country. They have a distillery near Goa on the west coast of India, which certainly contributes distillates to this blend. It is one of the reasonably priced kind available in → India and sells 1.4 million → cases.

Diplomatic Privilege Scotch blend from W → Brown & Sons in Glasgow: a 5-year-old → standard blend.

Director's Special Scotch blend from the → Premier Scotch Whisky Co and, like each of their numerous blends, available with five different ages of 3, 5, 8, 10 and 12 years. It is mainly to be found in Latin America and South East Asia, where it is often exported in → bulk and bottled locally. There is also a whisky of this name from the Indian company Shaw Wallace, which is bottled at the 42.8% customary in India. Sometimes the → Rampur Distillery & Chemical Company Ltd is given as its producer, and sometimes the → Benghal Distilleries in Calcutta. Like most Indian whiskies, it is a blend with a small amount of real whisky mixed with a molasses distillate.

Distillation Distillation follows fermentation, where yeast helps convert the sugar in the mash to alcohol. This liquid containing alcohol is called the → wash or the → beer. Distillation increases the alcohol content. It makes use of the fact that water and alcohol have different boiling points i.e. alcohol evaporates quicker than water. This means that alcohol vapours rise quicker than steam, and become liquid again in a condenser. The classical method is distillation in copper → pot stills, a process which is generally repeated twice, and in some Scottish distilleries and in most Irish distilleries, three times. The first distillation produces a raw distillate at about 22%, which is then distilled again in the → spirit still. Not everything from this final run can be used. The first run of the second distillation (the → foreshots) and the final run (the → feints) contains poisonous fusel oils. Only the → middle cut, with a strength of 70% to 72%, is taken and collected in a large vessel. The fresh distillate has some water added to it and goes into the casks for maturing at about 63% to 64%. There is a second, more modern form of distilling. It is based on the invention of Robert Stein and Aeneas Coffey, and allows continuous distillation in → patent stills. It is used for the production of → grain whisky in Scotland, and is in general use in Canada and the USA.

There is much debate regarding who discovered

Distillers Agency Ltd

and first used the art of distilling. Some historians attribute it to the Egyptians; China is also named. The Welsh believe that → chwisgi was already made in 3rd century Wales and the Irish, argue that the patron saint, Saint Patrick used a method of distillation. It is much more likely that it was first possible to distil a liquid with the use of stills and condensers in the middle of the 12th century and that it was Arabian scientists who brought this art to Europe, possibly to Salerno, the scientific centre of the day. It is conceivable that Irish monks learned about it there and took the knowledge home with them. Shortly after the invasion of King Henry II, English soldiers are said to have observed the Irish making and drinking whisky. It is the Scots who are in possession of the first documentary reference to whisky; the Exchequer Rolls of 1494 relate 'eight bolls of malt to Friar John Cox wherewith to make aquavitae'.

Distillers Agency Ltd Scottish whisky company, which was created in 1924 as a subsidiary of → DCL and was responsible for the production and (export) sales of its blends DCL, → Highland Club, → Highland Nectar and → King George IV. These blends were launched onto the market at the end of the 19th century. So as not to interfere with its dealings with the large Scottish companies, DCL thought it wiser not to carry on its activities in this field using its own name, but to hand them over to a subsidiary. The Agency was responsible for the → Knockdhu Distillery for a number of years, and after this distillery went to another subsidiary it became responsible for the → Rosebank Distillery in Falkirk, whose licence it held until 1992.

Distillers Edition, The Series of six malts which followed → 'Classic Malts of Scotland'. → UD, the creators of the successful series, therefore followed a trend that other companies such as → Glenmorangie plc and William → Grant & Sons with their → Balvenie had successfully initiated: maturing their malts in a second cask and thus giving them additional flavours and aromas with this → finishing. For each of the six distilleries represented by the 'Classic Malts', a special kind of cask was chosen that was optimally suited to the character of each whisky: for → Cragganmore from 1984 a portwine cask, for → Dalwhinnie from 1980 Oloroso Sherry Wood, for → Glenkinchie from 1986 an Amontillado cask, for → Lagavulin from 1979 casks from the heavy, sweet Pedro Ximenez Sherry, for → Oban from 1980 Montilla Fino and for → Talisker from 1986, with its traditional 45.8% (the others have 43%), Amoroso Sherry. The label states the year of distillation, that it is a limited edition. When it was first introduced the 'Friends of the Classic Malts' were able to take advantage of a special offer: they couldn't order the whole series, but were able to order for at least one bottle.

Distillers' Masterpiece A straight bourbon, although the legal prerequisites exclude it from being thus termed: they state that a whiskey bearing this name should only have been matured in brand new barrels. The Masterpiece belongs to the category of → finishings, that is whiskeys transferred to a second cask after the initial period of maturation. It comes from → Jim Beam and was the idea of their spiritus rector → Booker Noe, who blazed a new trail with it. He got together with the great man of cognac, the Frenchman Alain Royer, and placed his bourbon in a cognac cask. Its age (18 years) is also unusually high for a bourbon.

Distillery bottling Term for malt whiskies which are bottled by the distillery or their owners, and therefore mostly named → proprietor's bottling, in contrast to those named → independent bottling.

Distillery cat Found in almost every distillery pursuing the useful occupation of preventing the mice from eating too much of the grain or malt needed elsewhere. Their job is taken very seriously and the official job description is mouser. Some of them have left anonymity behind, such as Smoky, the → Bowmore cat, who was judged one of the seven most beautiful cats in the UK in a beauty contest run by the magazine *Country Living*, or Barley, the → Highland Park cat, who along with Smoky and other colleagues, has been interviewed by the specialist periodical → *Whisky Watch*. The most famous of all was → Towser, the mouser from → Glenturret, who not only reached the grand old age of 24 but also made it into the *Guinness*

Book of Records, as in her lifetime she caught the splendid number of 29,899 mice.

DJ Dougherty Irish blended Whiskey from the → Cooley Distillery who bottle it under the name of their subsidiary Andrew A → Watt. It is only sold in the USA, where it is labelled 'Imported Private Blend' and 'Special Reserve 1881 from Original Recipe'. The label on the back of the bottle states that this goes back to Daniel Joseph O'Doherty who brought it with him to America. It further states that his family still use the same recipe today to make Irish Whiskey: 'still Owned, Distilled, Matured and blended by the Irish People. May the Irish Spirit Live on!'

Doble V Spanish blend from Hiram → Walker, the subsidiary of the large enterprise → Allied Domecq PLC, who are active in Spain –a country where whisky is particularly popular. The Canadians had a distillery in Cuenca until 1991, and are behind the → Destilerias y Crianza who own the → Molino del Arco distillery near Segovia (and the → Lochside Distillery in Scotland), and who sell the successful blend → DYC. The Doble V isn't in the same class, but is nevertheless very popular and widely availble in Spain and in Latin America.

Dochan doris Term for the Scottish tradition of giving the guest another dram before they goes home – or, as the English say 'one for the road'. It is a phrase used by non-Gaelic speakers as well as Gaelic speakers.

Doctor's Special Scotch blend that nowadays comes from Hiram → Walker, and therefore from → Allied Domecq PLC. The brand was introduced in the 1920s by Robert Macnish & Co, who were mainly known for their → Grand Macnish.

Doig, Charles Chree Architect from Elgin who has now largely been forgotten although he was the inventor of the → pagodas that give the distilleries their distinctive appearance. They are very different to the former conical-shaped chimneys over the → kilns, and have become the distinctive feature of many distilleries and are used as a generic symbol on signs, maps or anywhere that points to where malt whisky is made.

Doig was born in 1855 and died in September 1918. The first distillery for which he built a pagoda was → Dailuaine. It was inaugurated in 1889 and was destroyed by fire 1917. Doig himself worked, amongst others, for: → Aberfeldy, → Coleburn, → Craigellachie, → Dalwhinnie and → Imperial. His sons carried on their father's work at → Ardbeg, → Caol Ila, → Highland Park, → Laphroaig and → Tamdhu (to mention but a few). In all they left more than 5,000 plans on 1,237 sheets and rolls, produced between 1870 and 1964, which are now kept in Elgin's Local Heritage Centre.

Dolany Czech distillery belonging to the → Seliko company that lies about six kilometres to the north-east in Olomouc (Olmütz). With its four stills it has a larger capacity than its sister distillery → Testice on the other side of Olomouc, but has not been in operation for some time. Since the end of the Communist regime it seems that the Czech people would rather buy imported Scotch. Of all the whisky - producing countries, the Czech Republic with its beer culture, malting skills, excellent water and efforts to adhere to Scottish methods (even importing peat from Scotland), is the best match for the Scottish role model.

Dominie, The Scotch blend, a → premium blend from → Cockburn & Company (Leith) who are best-known for their port. The name is an old Scots word for schoolmaster.

Don's Dram Scotch blend from The → Bennachie. Despite being 5-years-old and 40%, its label states that it is 'Superior'. The label is illustrated with a fooball player and is popular with supporters of the Aberdeen Football Club.

Double Dog Indian whisky described as a → de luxe blend. It comes from the → Haryana Distillery, a subsidiary of the large industrial combine Modi Enterprises.

Double wood Two different kinds of → cask for maturing whisky. It is not possible to use this method for bourbon in the USA, as new barrels which may only be used once. In Scotland, on the other hand, the only condition is that the casks must be made of oak. Casks which previously contained bourbon or sherry are mainly used, as are casks that have contained malt or a → grain whisky. Very few distilleries bottle their single malt from just one kind of cask: examples are → Macallan, where only Oloroso casks are used and → Glenmorangie, where the 10-year-old is matured in ex-bourbon barrels. Otherwise a carefully thought-out mixture of both kinds of cask is used. The term double wood was first used for the 12-year-old → Balvenie. Master Blender David Stewart had the idea of giving the malt a second maturing period of two years in a sherry butt, after spending 10 years in a bourbon cask. Since then there have been many similar → finishings. Glenmorangie plc, in particlaur, have used unusual cask types such as port, Madeira, red wine, Cognac, Malaga and, for their → Glen Moray, French white wine casks. Balvenie also has a 21-year-old port finish and the six → 'Classic Malts' have been supplemented with versions that have had a second maturation. A interesting comparison was provided by → Gordon & MacPhail at the end of 2000 when casks were brought to Elgin with malts from → Caol Ila, and → Imperial, were given a second period of maturation using cognac, calvados and claret casks.

Doubler Special form of still which is used in the production of some bourbons in the USA. It is a kind of → pot still and helps to increase alcohol strength, which can be achieved in the first run of the → wash through the → beer still (and which in contrast to the Scottish → patent still has only one column). The → low wines produced have a strength of about 55% to 60%. They run in liquid form into the copper doubler, where the strength of the distillate named → white dog is increased to about 65%. It then has water added to it before it is filled into barrels to mature.

Dougherty's Scotch blend which → Inver House Distillers Ltd had discontinued, but which is now in production again: a → standard blend with no age statement.

Douglas McNiven Scottish whisky company, also sometimes spelt MacNiven, which for a long time belonged to → Macdonald and Muir and therefore today belongs to → Glenmorangie plc. It was responsible for the blends Glen Niven, MacNiven Finest and MacNiven Royal Abbey. Today the name is used, for example, for blends in Africa, and a series of malts called → Glen Morven also bears the name McNiven as bottler. Glenmorangie made use of the name after a mishap in which, during the planned bottling of five casks of a 21-year-old → Glen Moray, a three-year-old cask was accidentially used. The product eventually came onto the market as → 80/20 and is now sought after by collectors.

Dowling Kentucky straight bourbon, with an 8-year-old version at 86° (43%) and a 12-year-old → Bottled in Bond at 100° (50%). The date 1869 appears on the bottle – the year that the family who had immigrated to Kentucky from Scotland began whisky distilling. Like most others, they became victims of → prohibition, but were able to survive in Mexico. When the dry period came to an end the brand was produced again, initially as a product of the Anderson County Distilling Co, and bottled by Dowling Distillers in Tyrone. Nowadays the whiskey comes from the Kentucky Deluxe Distilling Co in → Bardstown, behind which is → Heaven Hills.

Draff The solid part that is left behind from the grain after it has been ground to → grist when → mashing has ended, and the starch in the malt or other grains has been converted to fermenting sugar and washed out. The → wort is the end product of this process, but it also leaves dregs behind. Only grain distilleries use both the wort and the draff in the next process, → fermenting. In malt distilleries they are separated, but not treated as waste. It has long been known that they are a valuable animal foodstuff with a high protein content, which can either be fed straight to cattle or stored. Since the whisky industry has discovered that about 50% of the grain used can be recycled as animal foodstuffs, effective forms of processing have been developed, and modern plants have been constructed for the purpose. This by-product of distilling not only brings in additional money, but is also environmentally friendly.

Dram Term for a measure of spirits that is now almost universally used in connection with whisky, but which was originally Scottish, and frequently used together with the diminutive 'wee'. Although some authors assign a definite size to it, it isn't normally exactly defined. David Daiches considers the word to be of Greek derivation, coming from the word *drachma*, which is 'one-eighth of an ounce or sixty grains in apothecaries' weights'. On the other hand Neil Wilson talks of a third of a pint of whisky at 60% alcohol. The → Scotch Whisky Association define its size as being dependent on 'the generosity of the pourer'.

The word first seems to have appeared in 1752 in the *Scots Magazine*, and is also used together with other expressions: for example the whisky liqueur → Drambuie, which is usually translated as 'the drink that satisfies'.

In the 19th century there were dram-shops, the best-known of which were owned by William → Teacher. He opened the first one when he was just 19 years old, laying the foundations for one of the most successful whisky companies and brands in Scotland. In distilleries the word is also sometimes used as a verb. The workers used to be 'drammed' – not out of human kindness but to keep them from pilfering whisky. In → Talisker it is still possible to admire the dram that the workers used to be allowed to drink; a solid tankard that they received at the beginning and at the end of a shift, filled with baby-whisky! Those brave workers who climbed into the → pot stills to clean them were also rewarded with a dram. Although dramming ceased in 1970 (due to Health and Safety regulations), in 1997 Dr. Bill Lumsden was still giving the famous '16 Men of Tain' at the → Glenmorangie Distillery, but with matured malt, to demonstrate what they were supposed to produce everyday.

Drambuie The classic among whisky liqueurs, it was the first and is still the noblest. In 1745 Bonnie Prince Charlie returned from exile in France, attempted to seize the crown for the Stuarts and a year later finally met with defeat at the Battle of Culloden. Whilst fleeing he hid himself on the Isle of Skye with the MacKinnon family and comforted himself with a Drambuie. The word is Gaelic and means 'the drink that satisfies'. It is not clear whether it was his own recipe or that of his hosts.

It gives an idea of how the Highlanders used to drink their whisky: the best malt is mixed with heather honey and various herbs. It is still made that way today – by the descendants of the same MacKinnon family, who went to Edinburgh in 1906 and from small beginnings with just 12 cases a year, built up a brand of worldwide importance, probably also because Scottish regiments all over the world made Drambuie their digestif. The recipe for the herb mixture is traditionally guarded by the MacKinnon women, who have the finest stocks of malts at their disposal in Kirkliston. In 1997 they allowed a special edition of a 15-year-old liqueur named → Blue Ribbon to be made. It can be enjoyed pure or, particularly to be recommended, with ice, or it can be used for mixing. The classic Drambuie drink is the → Rusty Nail. Since the winter of 2000 there has also been a Drambuie Cream Liqueur.

Drop of the Irish Irish malt whiskey, brought out by the → independent bottler → Blackadder International. They are known for bottling their malts without → chill-filtering and without colouring and proudly confirm this on the labels, stating 'pure unfiltered Irish Malt Whiskies'. The use of the plural is significant, as this it is not a single malt but a vatted 'unique combination of Irish single malts'. Unfortunately it doesn't say where these malts come from. They are bottled at 45%.

Druichan Islay Scotch single malt produced by → Invergordon, one of five in the series 'The → Malts of Scotland', which were all named after great distilleries that have ceased to exist, or have been given made up names. Invergordon did own → Bruichladdich on Islay which shortly after its takeover by Invergordon was closed down by, so the 10-year-old malt could possibly be from there.

Drum maltings Maltings which provide most of the distilleries in Scotland (and Ireland) with their malt, and that have replaced the traditional → floor maltings. Modern, industrial maltings such as those at Burghead, → Glenesk, → Glen

Drumgray

Ord or Port Ellen, can produce large quantities of malt in a short period of time without the quality suffering. In order to satisfy the wish of each distillery to have its own malt with its a characteristic aroma, a special recipe is used for the amount of peat added to the fire under the drums that are used for airing and drying the barley. The biggest advantage of the drum maltings is that both germination and drying, take place in the same drum, thus saving space. Malting is now almost a fully-automised process and only requires one worker per shift. Today it is still possible to view a special form of drum maltings at → Speyburn Distillery.

Drumgray Scottish cream liqueur bottled at 17%. The full name is Mrs. Walker's Single Malt Drumgray Highland Cream. It comes from the → Wallace Malt Liqueur Company, a subsidiary of → Burn Stewart, who very likely use the malts from their → Deanston Distillery.

Drumguish Scotch single malt produced in the Christie family's → Speyside Distillery Co. Since the 1950s George Christie, an experienced whisky blender, worked on building a distillery where the Tromie flows into the Spey. In December 1990, after more than twenty years, the first distillate flowed. Exactly three years later Drumguish was launched onto the market, christened after a nearby village. They didn't use the name 'Speyside' because they didn't want any confusion with the series of malts that had already established the company name, and because they wanted to eventually market a single malt with a longer maturing period. So a subsidiary, the Drumguish Distillery Co, was formed to market the malt, which is also available in a special Christmas set.

Drury's Whisky produced in → Brazil by IDV. It is a local or *whisky nacionale*: that is a blend of malts that are imported in → bulk from Scotland, and grains that are distilled in Brazil.

Duart Castle Scotch whisky that was previously only available as a vatted malt, but which is now only obtainable as a blend. With the permission of Lord MacLean, it is named after his castle on Mull. It is made by Whighams of Ayr, who can trace their beginnings back to 1766. At that time a group of local traders from the town founded a business, initially with the name Alexander Oliphant & Co. In 1968 Whigham Fergusson broke away as an independent company and merged with the London wine merchants → Corney & Barrow in 1994.

Dublin Whiskey Distillery Company Irish company mainly known for a distillery named after the road on which it stood, → Jones Road Distillery.

Dubliner, The Irish cream liqueur brought onto the market by R & J Emmet and Co in 1980. It became so successful that the company, together with its second brand → Emmets and the production site in Bailieborough (County Cavan), were bought by their competitors → Bailey's in 1991. They sell the liqueur, at 17%, through their subsidiary, The Dubliner Liqueur & Spirit Company.

Dufftown Town in Scotland that despite its small population is the 'World Capital of Malt Whisky'. It belongs to the → Speyside region, and lies at the point, where the Dullan Water flows into the River Fiddich. At the end of the 19th-century there was a saying: 'Rome was built on seven hills, Dufftown stands on seven stills'. These distilleries were → Balvenie, → Convalmore, → Dufftown, → Glendullan, → Glenfiddich, → Mortlach and → Parkmore. The latter is no longer a working distillery but is used to store casks by owners UDV while Glendullan has expanded and has a second plant. In 1974 Arthur → Bell & Sons built → Pittyvaich, and at the end of the 1980s William → Grant & Sons built → Kininvie. If one counts → Allt A'Bhainne, which lies just a few miles away, then Dufftown has nine distilleries today, although Convalmore is used by Grants, who bought it from → UD, as warehousing. All the Grant distilleries lie attractively together on the left bank of the Fiddich. The other half of the village is the province of UD. Glendullan lies on the right bank of the Fiddich, the others along the Dullan, further down the valley are Dufftown and Pittyvaich, and further up is Mortlach. Mortlach Church lies in between and is one of the oldest in Scotland.

The Dufftown distillery was originally a mill. In 1933 Arthur Bell & Sons bought it, together with

→ Blair Athol, and enlarged it to six → stills in 1979, holding the licence until 1992 (since then → UMGD). They already had a single malt in a → proprietor's bottling: the 8-year-old had a label which made the connection with → Blair Athol clear. In contrast the 10-year-old had its own format. A 15-year-old Dufftown, from whose label Glenlivet has been removed, belongs to the → 'Flora & Fauna' series of UDV. In memory of the foundation of the distillery a hundred years previously there was a 10-year-old Centenary 1896 – 1996 (55.8%) and the → 'Rare Malts Selection' has, up to now, included one Dufftown (21 years old, distilled in 1975, 54.8%).

Dumbarton Mothballed distillery lying on the northern banks of the Clyde at the mouth of River Leven. It is situated opposite the Dumbarton Rock, from which it gets its name. The distilling complex was erected in 1938 by George → Ballantine & Son for its Canadian owner → Hiram Walker and now belongs to → Allied Distillers Ltd, a subsidiary of Allied Domecq PLC. Until recently it produced the → grain whiskies for the group's blends such as → Teacher's, → Highland Cream, → Long John, → Old Smuggler and also Ballantine's. Within the plant there was also a malt distillery which with its various → stills was able to produce two different single malts, the → Inverleven and the → Lomond. The Inverleven is available variously aged and is part of the → 'Allied' series from → Gordon & MacPhail. → Cadenhead had a 1969 Dumbarton-Inverleven which was bottled aged 26 years at 49.6%. The independent company The Bottlers also had a bottling. In contrast the Lomond is one of the greatest rarities among Scotch malts whiskies with, as far as its known, only one bottling up to now from the → Scotch Malt Whisky Society.

Dumbuck Scotch malt that in the 1960s was one of three produced by the → Littlemill Distillery in Bowling, using variously peated malts and a → rectifier on the → spirit still. Whilst the Littlemill was (and is) available as a single malt, and at least two → single cask bottlings of → Dunglass are known, the Dumbuck never seems to have been bottled, but was used for blending.

Dun Bheagan Collection Series of Single Malts from the → independent bottler Ian → MacLeod, brought out under the name of its subsidiary William Maxwell & Co. It is named after the clan whose ancestral seat is Dunvegan Castle on Skye. The labels give both the year of distillation and of bottling. Up till now, there has been an Allt-A-Bhainne (10 years), a Bowmore (21 years), and a Convalmore (16 years).

Dun Eideann Scottish whisky company who, under their own name, bring out a small series of Scotch single malts at → cask strength. It belongs to the independent bottlers → Signatory, based in Edinburgh. The company also has a sub-label in France called → 'Treasures from Scotland'.

Dunbar Whisky formerly produced by → Seagram in Latin America. As in all blends made there, Scotch malts are blended with locally produced grains. It is 6 years old. The brand is widely available in → Venezuela and → Uruguay.

Dundee, The Scotch blend from → Angus Dundee, a company founded in London, but which on the label names Glasgow as its base.

Dunglass Scotch single malt that was produced at the → Littlemill Distillery, which at the end of the 1960s fitted a → rectifier on the → still, and used variously peated malts to produce three different whiskies. The Dunglass seems to have been bottled only twice as a single malt: in 1990 Moon Import brought a malt distilled in 1967 onto the Italian market, from cask 3447-050, in its series 'The Animals'. In 1990, Signatory, the independent bottlers from Edinburgh, brought out a Dunglass from 1967, using the name of its subsidiary Dun Eideann. Like the Italian version, it was 46%. It is probable that Signatory divided its stocks into two bottlings with different labels.

Dungourney → Pure pot still whiskey. Encouraged by the attention aroused by its single cask bottling of a single malt from the old → Coleraine Distillery, → IDG decided not to let a precious single cask with → pot still whiskey from the old Midleton Distillery (now a museum) disappear into a blend, but bring it out for the lovers of such antiquities. In order to

97

Dunhill

avoid confusion, they strayed from the custom of naming a single malt after its distillery, and called it Dungourney, giving the information 'laid down in 1964'. Dungourney is the name of the little stream on which the old and the new Midleton plant stand.

Dunhill Since 1982 the English luxury goods company has not only had tobacco and cigars, pipes, smoking accessories and gentlemen's clothing in their range, but also a very luxurious, exclusive blend for their shops and duty-free outlets, especially those in the Far East. The company, part of the Vendome group, also own other Cartier, Montblanc and Vacheron. Old Master is produced by → IDV, whose → Strathmill Distillery in → Keith hung the sign 'Home of Dunhill' on its walls. In 1998 the responsibility for production, marketing and distribution of the blend passed to → Highland Distillers, whose sales department works together with → Rémy, and who concentrate on Asia. As this is an area where fine packaging and expensive bottles are very popular, the Dunhill is also available as Crystal Decanter, Celebration Edition and as the rare Centenary Cask Edition. There is also a → standard blend, the Gentlemen's Speyside Blend.

Dunkeld Atholl Brose Scotch whisky liqueur from → Gordon & MacPhail. The legend behind it is that the drink gave the Duke of Atholl strength to capture his enemy, the Lord of the Isles. He is meant to have done this by 'fortifying' the springwater with whisky, oatmeal and honey. In today's Dunkeld Atholl Brose the oatmeal has been replaced by herbs and mixed exclusively with malts. And that makes it a popular pick-me-up for exhausted 'field sportsmen', hunters and golfers.

Dunlow Irish whiskey, a blend at 40%, produced by → Cooley, taken in → bulk in road tankers to France, where it is bottled by the spirits company La Martiniquaise and sold with five different names by five different supermarket chains. It is called Dunlow by the Promodes company, Galoway by Leader Price, Highfield by Auchan's, Greenfield by Le Clerc and Ken Lough by Casino.

Dunn & Co, Alexander Whisky company based in Surrey who produce their blends and a vatted malt bearing the company name. They featured in the → Guinness Book of Records with the smallest whisky bottle in the world, containing about 1cl. They offered their customers the chance to have a name of their choice written on the bottles. This won them a lot of enthusiastic customers, particularly in Japan. The brand especially created for this idea is called → Slaintheva, a corruption of the Gaelic toast 'Slainté math'. The company were associated with → Tomatin Distillers, who were later taken over by a Japanese syndicate.

Dunphy's Irish whiskey described as Finest Old on its label, although it is a → standard blend at 40%. In the 1950s it was produced by the old → Midleton Distillery, mainly to provide Americans thirsty for → Irish Coffee with an inexpensive blend for mixing. Today it is only sold in Ireland, with another label, by the → IDG subsidiary → Fitzgerald & Co, as well as being available in a few shops on the Continent.

Dunville's Irish whiskey, a blend at 40%, that keeps alive the memory of the old Dunville company and their → Royal Irish Distillery in Belfast. The company ceased trading in the 1930s while the distillery continued to work, at least intermittently. The Belfast wine and spirits dealer Philip Russell attempted to resurrect the Dunville name with a whiskey that was spelt the Irish way, but was actually a Scotch (from → Invergordon). Cooley now provide their malts and grains. Russell supplies Cellars International, the UK distributors, directly, but Dunville's is also available in Northern Ireland.

Duthie, RW Scottish whisky company which brings out → independent bottlings. It is the second brand of → Cadenhead, and like them gives the old Aberdeen address. Both labels belong to J & A → Mitchell of the → Springbank Distillery in → Campbeltown. The single malts from Duthie's are somewhat cheaper than those from Cadenhead. There is an → Ardbeg from 1975, a → Highland Park from 1978, a → Lagavulin from 1978, a → Macallan from 1979 and a → Talisker from 1979. They are all bottled at the 46%. typical for Cadenhead.

DYC Spanish blend, an abbreviation for →

Destilerias y Crianza del Whisky, available in two versions, a → standard blend and an 8-year-old. The entire malt share came completely from Scotland, but now at least a part of its malt whiskies, and all its → grain whiskies, are distilled in → Spain itself, at the → Molino del Arco Distillery. They are run by the Destilerias y Crianza, who via Hiram → Walker belong to the → Allied Domecq PLC empire and formerly adminstered the → Lochside Distillery in Scotland, strangely enough, independent of the other Scottish interests of the company, which are grouped under the umbrella of → Allied Distillers Ltd. Malts from Lochside have no doubt been used in this Spanish blend that has been on the market since 1963, and which is not only popular in its home country, but also in Latin America, and is among the 30 most successful whiskies in the world.

Dynasty Decanter, The Scotch single malt in one of the most costly and attractive presentations that has ever been created for a Scottish whisky. The heptagonal crystal decanter is decorated with a silver stopper and its silver mantle has seven gold medallions set into it. They depict the portraits of seven regents from the house of Stewart or Stuart, who from James I (1406-1437) to Mary Queen of Scots (1542-1567), were Scotland's rulers. The edition commemorates these great monarchs and at the same time celebrates the fact that during the 200 years of their reigns, whisky, was 'born' and developed. → Hart Brothers have issued 850 examples of this noble piece, which comes in a sturdy wooden case with a certificate. The content of the decanter is more than worthy of its presentation, and perhaps even more valuable: it is, after all, a 31-year-old → Bowmore.

E

Eagle of Spey Trade name for a 10-year-old single malt that comes from the house of J & G → Grant, and from → Glenfarclas. It is somewhat drier than the malts bottled under the distillery's name, suggesting that the oak barrels used are either exclusively or mostly ex-bourbon barrels. Bourbon barrels are cheaper than others, which would help the company to reduce its excess stocks, assert itself in the marketplace and maintain its independence as one of the last companies in (Scottish) family ownership.

Eagle Rare Kentucky straight bourbon, which names the Old Prentice Company as its producer. The address on the label shows who is behind it: New Orleans is the ancestral seat of the → Sazerac Company who own the → Ancient Age Distilling Company in → Leestown. The brand is produced there today but originally came from the → Old Prentice Distillery in Lawrenceburg, which is nowadays called → Four Roses. The owners were → Seagram. The Canadians brought out Eagle Rare in the 1970s but sold the brand and the rights to the name Old Prentice to the present owners; a good example of how not only names, but also brands, can change hands in the USA, and of how a brand can suddenly be produced by a quite different distillery. There is a 10-year-old at 101° (50.5%0, and a 15-year-old (for export only) at 107° (53%). The 10-year-old's label points out that only one in 37 barrels is good enough for this whiskey in its striking square bottle.

Eaglesome Scottish whisky company which run a small shop in → Campbeltown, well-known for its good range of whiskies. The malts from the local → Springbank Distillery are particularly well represented, which is hardly surprising when one discovers that the shop and the distillery belong to the → Mitchell family. Eaglesome, like → Cadenhead, is a subsidiary of theirs. Apart from the single malts Springbank and → Longrow, the Mitchells have a wide range of brands bearing the names of both its subsidiaries: Eaglesome has the blends → Allan's, → Cairnbaan, → Campbeltown Loch and → Old Spencer as well as the single malt → Burnside. The Eaglesome is available as a → standard blend or as a 12-year-old → de luxe blend.

Early Times American distillery bearing the name of one of the two brands it produces; the other is → Old Forester. It has belonged to → Brown-Forman since they were founded, whilst Early Times was acquired during → prohibition by the only whiskey business in America in which members of the founding family still have a say to this day. The whisky, which like Old Forester is spelt without the 'e' customary in the USA, hasn't always been made at Shively to the north of Louisville. The first Early Times Distillery was established by John H Beam, the uncle of James → 'Jim' Beam in 1860, and was situated near → Bardstown; a picture of it with the date decorates one of the versions of the brand. There were several changes of ownership before the dry years of prohibition. Then the distillery had to be closed, and its stocks could only be sold for medicinal purposes with a doctor's prescription. Only 10 companies had a licence to do this, including Brown-Forman, who bought the existing casks and the rights to the brand. Today's distillery was established in 1935 and was originally called the Old Kentucky Distillery. It was acquired by Brown-Forman in 1940 and underwent a thorough reconstruction.

Master distiller Lincoln Henderson has two different → mash bills for his two brands. The 79% share of corn he uses for the Early Times is somewhat more than for the Old Forester, the rye content amounts to 11% and the malt barley share is 10% (sometimes he he also makes a rye that is needed for → Canadian Mist). Henderson also insists on using a special method of barrel maturation in his heated seven-storey → warehouses: a continual fluctuation between artificial heating and cooling allows the whisky to be absorbed deep into the wood and so mature faster. And there is something else unusual: since 1983 there has been an → Early Times Old Style Kentucky Whisky at 80° (40%) on the label of which the word bourbon is missing. Instead the following information is given: 'Matured at least 36 months in re-used oak barrels'. It could only be called a bourbon if it had been matured in new, unused barrels, like the Early Times Kentucky Straight Bourbon, that is only made for export at 80°(40%) or 86% (43%).

Eaton's Scotch blend from Douglas → Laing & Co in Glasgow, who are known for their good stock of very mature whiskies. This enables them to produce a whole series of relatively old blends. Eaton's Special Reserve is actually only a → standard blend, but there is also a 30-year-old → de luxe blend.

Eblana Irish whiskey liqueur that is labelled 'sweet'. At 40% it is produced by the → Cooley Distillery using an old Irish recipe and is marketed as a product of Adam → Millar, an old company whose name Cooley have bought.

Echo Spring Kentucky straight bourbon from → Heaven Hill. It is one of the many small brands from this large, independent family company, which are only sold in specific markets. It is not available outside Kentucky.

Edel Falcke German malt whisky whose producer calls it malt whisky but which does not adhere to the usual definition of that term. This stipulates that only malted barley may be used for its production. C W → Falckenthal Söhne is an old company founded in 1759 in Luckenwalde, and was initially able to maintain its independence in the days of the German Democratic Republic. In 1972, however, they were 'nationalised'. After reunification the Falckenthal family bought the company back again. They spoke of a product made of 'rye from Brandenburg and native malt' – which means that it doesn't contain 100% malt (which may be made from rye), but a grain distillate or possibly a blend of two distillates. But it was neither this confusion, nor the low age of 3 years, that caused the company problems. They had initially called their product Oldmaster, which brought the solicitors of the → Scotch Whisky Association into the arena. They are always on their guard to protect the status of Scotch whisky and will not tolerate English language names. That wasn't the only blow to the Falckenthals: due to large debts they had to sell out to the West German Berentzen company. They immediately closed down production in Luckenwalde, but continue to sell the remaining stocks.

Edinburgh Castle Scotch blend formerly produced by → Invergordon which was one of the many that the subsidiary of → JBB (Greater Europe) plc produced as so-called own-label-brands for other companies. It is now produced by → Kyndal. The blend is made exclusively for the supermarket chain → Tesco. The shape of the bottle is shared with that of the Tesco Premium Vodka and Greenwich Gin.

Edradour Scottish malt distillery. Its name, pronounced 'edra-dower', comes from the Gaelic for 'between two waters'. It lies to the west of Pitlochry, near Moulin, and belongs to the → Highlands whisky region. It is said to have been founded in 1825 and was at times also called → Glenforres. It is a real little doll's house of a distillery and looks just like the romantic image of a small distillery in the Highlands. In fact it is the only one in the whole of Scotland that has been maintained in the old farmyard style. Fortunately the present owners realise what a little gem they have and look after it lovingly: its gleaming white buildings with fire-red doors and window shutters are kept in good order: it is one of the most beautiful distilleries in Scotland and is the smallest as well. The staff of the visitor centre is larger than that of the distillery.

The two → stills produce just 12 barrels a week. In the days of the previous owner, William Whiteley, the total annual production was used for the company's many blends. Today only

Edrington Group, The

2,000 → cases, or 24,000 bottles, are produced as a single malt in a → proprietor's bottling, also available in a stoneware jug. The remainder is either used for the company's own blends, such as → House of Lords and → King's Ransom, or in the vatted malt → Glenforres. Both blends are brands and the company → Campbell Distillers' which has owned Edradour since 1982, running it (along with → Aberlour and → Glenallachie) for the French parent company → Groupe Pernod-Ricard. From time to time the independents also manage to bottle an Edradour.

Edrington Group, The Scottish company involved at all levels of the whisky business and interconnected with other related businesses. It is still in private ownership and its numerous subsidiaries and well-known brands tend to take the limelight. It was not until the autumn of 1999 that the name of Edrington became better known, when the family holding joined with the other privately-owned Scottish whisky company, → William Grant & Sons, to buy a joint-stock company and reprivatise it. The interesting fact about this was that Edrington already owned a 28% share in the company in question, → Highland Distillers. Since this time its official name has been The → 1887 Company; 30% of it belongs to Grant and the remaining 70% to Edrington.

The new name is a reminder of the year in which William Robertson from Glasgow founded Highland Distillers. At that time he was already the owner of another well-known company, → Robertson & Baxter. For a long time his three daughters were members of the board of directors, and the company was based at 106 Nile Street, Glasgow, which was also the address of Highland as well as → Lang Brothers (Glengoyne Distillery, → Lang's Supreme). These names alone demonstrate Edrington's extensive connections within the industry, but these are not their only partners; there are close connections with → Berry Bros & Rudd, for whom they produce → Cutty Sark, and even with → GuinnessUDV, with whom they had a half share in the → North British Grain Distillery. Edrington own the Clyde Cooperage and Clyde Bonding where Scotland's favourite blend → Famous Grouse is bottled. This is the central brand of the new group – alongside the malt → Macallan. When combined Edrington and William Grant are the second-largest distillery owners in Scotland, with two grain distilleries and no fewer than 11 malt distilleries. Edrington also cooperate with → JBB and → Rémy, with whom they have founded the joint venture → Maxxium.

1885 Special Reserve Canadian whiskey from → Brown-Forman, the company which is famous for its → Jack Daniel's and → Canadian Mist. In the mid-1990s bourbon companies also introduced → single barrel or → small batch bottlings, probably motivated by the remarkable successes achieved by special editions of Scottish single malts. The 1885 was the first Canadian of its kind, but it is backed by the expert marketing of the Jack Daniel staff. The 8-year-old whisky commemorates the 100th anniversary of the completion of the Canadian Pacific Railway, which had actually been in operation for 10 years before it was launched on the market!

1887 Group, The Scottish whisky company which, despite the date in its name, was founded in 1999. Nevertheless the expectations awoken by such a date are in this case justified: 1887 was the year in which William Robertson from Glasgow, and several partners, formed → Highland Distilleries, later Highland Distillers. He and his heirs, the three famous Robertson sisters, had a share in this company which for many years owned distilleries such as → Bunnahabhain, → Glenrothes, → Highland Park and → Tamdhu and later also bought → Glenturret. Above all it caused a stir by gaining control of → Macallan in a hostile takeover. It was also the owner of the → Famous Grouse. The → Edrington Group, as Robertson's successors called themselves, owned a 28% share in Highland, and part of their empire included → Lang Brothers with their → Glengoyne Distillery, Clyde Bonding and Clyde Cooperage, and a 50% share in the → North British Grain Distillery; furthermore there were close connections to → Berry Bros & Rudd. In the course of 1999 there were conflicts between Edrington and Highland about future strategy, about the management of Macallan and Famous Grouse and, above all, the question of whether

Highland should be reprivatised. In a sensational step the private Edrington Group joined forces with another privately owned Scottish whisky company, → Willam Grant & Sons. Together they made the shareholders of Highland an offer which was accepted. Since this time the shares have no longer been traded on the Stock Exchange; ownership is divided between Edrington with 70% and Grants with 30%.

80/20 Scotch malt whisky which is a curiosity because of a mishap during its production. → Glenmorangie plc wanted to bottle five casks of a 21-year-old → Glen Moray in Broxburn but mixed up one cask with a 3-year-old which, according to the Scottish law, would have determined its age. They had to resort to doing without both an age statement and the name of the distillery. The product was simply named after its proportions 80/20. The label design looks like an Art Deco bar code and does not name the parent company as producer but a subsidiary, → Douglas McNiven.

Eileandour 10-year-old Scotch vatted malt from the → Isle of Arran Distillers. Their modern distillery is at Lochranza on the Isle of Arran, which must have influenced the choice of name: the word, means 'island water'. Whisky from Lochranza is now sufficiently mature that it may be included in this vatted malt: distilling has taken place in Lochranza since 1995. All the malts included in it come exclusively from the Scottish → Islands.

Eldorado Whisky cocktail. Mix one part orange juice and one part Scotch with two parts punch and ice in a shaker and serve in a cocktail glass.

El Vino English wine merchants established at the end of the 19th century in London. They also run their own wine bars in London ('Old Wine Shades' in Martin Lane and 'El Vino' in Fleet Street). Like all other wine dealers of renown, El Vino has always been proud of being able to offer its customers their own bottlings of wines and spirits, of having its own house claret and its own whisky blend. The empty casks are then used to mature malt whisky from Scotland in a → sherry or port cask, thus following the fashion of → finishing. The company has an El Vino Islay Malt in its range, which, according to their own information, is a 13-year-old → Bunnahabhain. Their own blend is a 7-year-old → de luxe named El Vino Connoisseur's Blend. It isn't bottled straightaway but is married in sherry casks so that its individual components blend together.

Eldridge, Pope & Co English company whose history goes back to the founding of the Green Dragon Brewery in Dorchester, Dorset in 1837. It was one of the larger independent brewing companies until a managemant buyout in 1997, when the brewery operation was renamed The Thomas Hardy Brewery. This quickly gained a good reputation, mainly due to its real ales, whilst a second company bearing the old name concentrated on the lucrative pub business. They own no fewer than 200 pubs. The brewery had its own blends for its pubs such as → Chairman's and, since 1908, → Old Highland Blend. It is not certain whether they will continue to be produced following restructuring, but the pubs still have sufficient stocks for the foreseeable future.

Elijah Craig Kentucky straight bourbon from → Heaven Hill, the independent family company in Bardstown, which at the beginning of the 1960s began naming some of their brands after whisky pioneers. Craig was a Baptist preacher whose family had gone to Kentucky because they had been persecuted by the established (Anglican) church in Virginia. He settled in Lebanon, near Georgetown and it has been proved that he was making whiskey and even shipping it in 1795 – the same year in which he was sentenced for distilling without a licence. Whether, as is often claimed, he was the one to discover bourbon is doubtful (Craig never lived in Bourbon County). There is every reason to believe that the legend was invented as a religious bourbon pioneer was just what was needed to expose the bigotry of those who scorned whiskey. The label of the 12-year-old at 94°(47%) doesn't say a single word about the man, but speaks about a yeast recipe handed down from generation to generation. This is not a reference to the Craigs, but to the famous Beam family, who are third-generation master distillers at Heaven Hill. In 1995 an 18-year-old → single barrel was bottled at 90° (45%), which is generally regarded as the distillery's best straight bourbon.

Elmer T. Lee Kentucky straight bourbon, bearing the name of a man who assumed the same role at → Sazerac's → Ancient Age Distillery, that Booker Noe now has at → Jim Beam: both men are long since retired master distillers, both have lifelong experience of the whiskey business and possess an encyclopaedic knowledge of all the details of its production, both still keep an eye on their old workplaces, both are living legends – and both have helped change the world of bourbon by setting new quality standards: Noe with → small batch bottlings and Lee with → single barrel bourbons. Lee learned his craft with Colonel Albert B → Blanton and named the very first → single barrel (for which he still chooses the barrels today) after him. He does the same for the brand bearing his own name, bottled between 6 and 8 years old at 90° (45%). The barrels for this whiskey come from Sazerac in Leestown, despite the made up name on the label.

Emblem Japanese blend formerly produced by → Kirin-Seagram, the joint venture of the Japanese brewery giants and the Canadian spirits group. Together they ran a distillery producing malt and → grain whiskies which were not considered sufficient to produce a wholly Japanese blend. Emblem is a → premium blend, with a malt content between 35% and 40%. Some of the malts come from Scotland, probably the ones that lend a smokiness to the whisky.

Emmets Irish cream liqueur bottled at 17% described on the label as a 'Classic Cream'. R & J Emmet of Dublin are named as producers, having launched it on the market in 1980 from Bailieborough where they were located at the time. They had become so successful with both Emmets and The →Dubliner, that they were bought out by → Bailey's in 1991 and so via → IDV and → Grand Metropolitan became part of Diageo's → GuinnessUDV.

Erin Go Bragh Irish single malt whiskey from the → Midleton Distillery, which hasn't produced any malt for some time, but which still has stocks from earlier distillations. With the fighting name, which means 'Ireland Forever!', → IDG realised a longstanding wish to produce an additional single malt to stand alongside that produced by their → Bushmills Distillery. It is distilled in → pot stills, is 6-years-old and is matured in bourbon and Oloroso sherry casks that are up to 10 years old.

Erin's Isle Irish whiskey bearing the Gaelic name for Ireland. Although produced by → Cooley Distillery, it is not blended, bottled or distributed by them. Cooley, as a relatively small company, had to work with various partners in order to establish a firm footing outside Ireland. They have contracts with the American → Heaven Hill, with the supermarket giants → Sainsbury and with → UD, for whom Cooley also produced the now discontinued → Hackler. Erin's Isle was one of the blends that was developed with → Invergordon but this relationship has now been discontinued. The 40% blend can still be found in a few outlets.

Eternity Scotch blend from the Eternity Scotch Whisky Co. There is a → standard 5-year-old Finest Old, a Black Label – Very Special Old with no age statement, the 16-year-old Rare Aged and the 21-year-old Extra Old Special Reserve.

Evan Williams Kentucky straight bourbon from → Heaven Hill, who circa 1960 had the idea of promoting their products by naming them after whiskey pioneers. The impulse came from their competitors, who connected their whiskeys with a certain Evan Williams in one of their advertisements. Although he wasn't Kentucky's first distiller, he was the first to work commercially, having begun in 1783. He operated for 19 years before he was forced to give up by envious neighbours who felt disturbed by his work. However his appearance in the annals of Louisville is mainly due to the fact that, as a member of the board of trustees, he made their meetings more lively – which wasn't appreciated by all the members.

Since then Heaven Hill has saved from obscurity a whole series of other pioneers, such as Elijah Craig and Henry McKenna, but Evan Williams is their flagship and a very successful one, too.

The 7-year-old (90°/45%) with the black label is the second best-selling bourbon in the USA. There is also a standard version, probably about 4 years old, at 80° (40%). The 8-year-old is 86° (43%), the same as the 1783 with that significant historic date. There is a 12-year-old → Bottled in Bond at 101° (50.5%) and with a red label. The leading product is the Single Barrel which doesn't state its exact age but gives the year of distillation, and which was the first → vintage bourbon. The first bottling was a 1986 at 86.6° (43.3%). The 1987 and the 1988 had the same strength. The series will be continued, but it has not yet been established whether there will be a new one every year. The last bottling was from the year 1992.

The latest additions to this brand have been a Master Distiller Select, a creation from 7 to 10-year-old whiskeys in an earthenware jug (90°/45%) and a 23-year-old bourbon at 107° (53.5%).

Excellence Japanese blend from → Suntory. Bottled in a similar manner to the melon liqueur 'Midori'. Michael Jackson vouches for the whisky's clean, malty taste.

Excise, exciseman After the Union of Parliaments of Scotland and England in 1707, the Board Of Excise (the word describes a duty on domestic products) was established and the governement declared the making of whisky illegal. It is said that after a similar move in 1661, Ireland was turned into a nation of illicit distillers. Since that time the Irish have spoken of legal, taxed whiskey as 'Parliament whiskey', and still to some extent believe that being allowed to distil their → poitín is a civil right. In both countries strenuous attempts by the government to impose excise duty on distilled spirits were countered by the efforts of the distillers to avoid paying the duties at all costs. The government attempts at imposing taxes were nearly always associated with rises in illicit distilling and smuggling continued to increase.

The government employed excisemen to stamp out and police illicit distilling. Although they earned a bounty for hunting down and destroying equipment and liquid stocks, they also had to finance their posses out of their own pockets. The illicit distillers didn't treat them very respectfully, and quite a few paid for their zeal with serious injuries, or even with their lives. It would not be an exaggeration to claim that they were amongst the most hated people in the country. Their position wasn't improved by the fact that many people loyal to the government, such as landowners, judges and lawyers, didn't think twice about buying and drinking illicit spirits. Even King George IV asked for a → Glenlivet when visiting Edinburgh in the autumn of 1822. He knew perfectly well that the whisky wasn't produced legally.

On the other hand, the Irish and the Scots found a new identity in illegality and there are hundreds of stories relating to the cunning tricks played on the excisemen. The deeds of the smugglers, such as Magnus Eunson (a man of God on Orkney who used his pulpit to hide the stuff) have become a part of Irish and Scottish folklore and include the anecdotes about Helen, the ancestress of the Cummings who developed Cardhu. There are also some prominent names who worked on the other side. Robert Burns, for a time earned his living as an exciseman in Dumfries; he wrote the famous poem *The De'il's awa wi' th' Exiseman* and mourned the demise of duty-free status at the → Ferintosh Distillery (which had been exempt from the tax, thanks to the loyalty of its owner, Duncan Forbes, to the Crown during the Jacobite Rising of 1745-6). The author Neil Gunn found time during his work as an exciseman at Glen Mhor to write several novels and the classic book *Whisky and Scotland*. Steve Sillett, the author of *Illicit Scotch*, was also a revenue officer and worked in Keith. Under the pseudonym Keith Bond, Jimmy Brown related his *Memoirs of an Exciseman* in 1996, in which he tells how he caught out some of the poeple intent on defrauding the revenue service.

In the USA the government also felt the urge to regulate whiskey production. This resulted in a veritable 'Whiskey Rebellion', with which the name of George Washington is discreditably associated (he had been a whiskey distiller himself). In 1791 he imposed a tax that had been proposed by the Secretary of State for Finance,

Excise Officer's Dram

Alexander Hamilton. This met with instant resistance and the first altercations between government officials and the farmers, who saw it as their natural right to distil the grain which they didn't need for food. They set up 'liberty poles' and finally 12,000 soldiers were needed to put down the rebellion.

In Europe the laws in Scotland and Ireland were changed 30 times between 1707 and 1820, but it was the laws of 1822 and 1823 which managed to convert the lawbreakers in Scotland and Ireland. The new laws were deemed to be fair enough to warrant paying tax and going legal. The cost of a licence was lowered, as were the taxes per gallon of spirit produced and the minimum size of a still was set at 40 gallons. The distilleries were obliged to build a house for an exciseman on their grounds and to guarantee unhindered entry to any part of the distillery at any time. Resident officers remained a fact of distillery life until 1983, when a system of self-policing by distilleries rendered the 'man with the second key' redundant. The first person to acquire a licence under the 1823 laws was George Smith from Glenlivet. In that year 14,000 infringements of the law had been registered, but the number was reduced to 672 in 1834 and to only six 40 years later. The legal era of whisky distilling in Scotland was finally established.

Although there was now a secure base for production and export to England was regulated in a fair way, whisk(e)y was still expected to bolster the state coffers. Taxes rose annually from 1823 until the late 1990s. The only exception was 1973. In that year value added tax was introduced instead. Alan S Gray has gathered together the data in his *Scotch Whisky Industry Review*. In 1855 a litre of pure alcohol cost (in today's currency) 15p, in 1968 £7.26, and today £9.56, to which 17.5% VAT is added. These figures make it clear why a bottle of whisky costs more in the United Kingdom than it does in Germany or in France.

Excise Officer's Dram Scotch → Pure malt in a bottle of only 25cl, which the Cromdale Whisky Company in Inverness claims is a replica of the 'quality sample bottle' used by the excisemen. Just such a man decorates the label, wearing a uniform from 1823, the year in which legal distilling became widespread. The excise officers have always been the natural enemy of all whisky-makers and drinkers. It therefore takes a certain amount of chutzpah to commemorate them, of all people, with a bottle of whisky that also bears the provocate motto, 'My duty is my pleasure'. The company does not state where it comes from (it couldn't be illegal, could it?), but it is rumoured that it has something to do with → Macallan.

Extra Japanese blend with → Nikka Whisky printed in large letters on the label, and Extra in smaller print above. It is a special version of the house brand of the large Japanese group.

Ezra Brooks Kentucky straight bourbon now sold by the David → Sherman Company of St. Louis. Its label states that it is made in 'Kentucky's Finest Little Distillery'. It is no use looking for it, as it doesn't exist. It is certain that it comes from Kentucky, but Sherman keeps us in the dark about its exact source. The brand conveys a very solid, conservative and ancient impression, and extols itself as 'Sippin' Whiskey', which might point to George Dickel and Tennessee. However this is all misleading: the brand was established in the 1950s, in direct competition to → Jack Daniel's which was difficult to come by at the time. The name doesn't come from a whiskey pioneer, but it is a pure PR invention.

It was launched onto the market by the Hoffman Distilling Company, who soon sold it on to → Medley via Glenmore and → UD. Ezra Brooks passed it to its present owner. There are several versions: at 80° (40%) with golden or green labels, and at 90° (45%) with black labels. The → Old Ezra Rare Old Sippin' Whiskey is available as a 7 or a 12-year-old, both at 101° (50.5%). Finally there is the 15-year-old No.19 Special Reserve at 94° (47%) presented in a wooden box. New motif carafes are brought out from time to time which are similar in style to those of, for example, → Jim Beam. These are porcelain figures of items such as a jockey and horse, chess pieces or bells, and these are very popular with collectors. There is even an Ezra Brooks Collectors Club. The *Ezra Brooks Heritage China Ceramic Bottles* mostly contain a 12-year-old whiskey.

F

Fairlie's Scotch whisky liqueur from → Highland Distillers. Named after two men to whom this company and the Scotch whisky industry owe a lot: James Fairlie, who resurrected the silent → Glenturret Distillery, and his son Peter, who made the distillery and its malt well-known. Peter was the marketing director at Highland Distillers and was responsible for all their products. He has now founded his own business named → Morrison Fairlie Distillery, a company which is one of the many new → independent bottlers. The liqueur label shows the famous → Towser, the legendary → Glenturret distillery cat. The liqueur has been especially conceived as a 'Light Highland Liqueur' at only 24%, and it is very likely that Glenturret plays a dominant part in it.

Falckenthal Söhne, C W German spirits company dating back to 1759. It is said that Johann Christian Falckenthal, in the archives of the Zinna monastery, found a recipe for liqueur invented by the lovesick Friar Lukas. In nearby Luckenwalde Falckenthal founded his business which became known for this 'Zinnaer Klosterlikör'. After World War II the family-run company was initially able to maintain its independence produced a whisky named Der → Falckner. They were nationalised in 1972, and renamed VEB Edelbrände und Spirituosen, although Falckenthal remained manager. After reunification in 1989, the family were able to buy back their old business, but then sold it to the apple-schnapps giant Berentzen, who closed down operations in Luckenwalde and now make the liqueur themselves in Zinna.

Initially Falckenthal carried on selling Falckner and brought out another brand called → Oldmaster, which had to be renamed → Edel Falcke following a lawsuit initiated by the → Scotch Whisky Association. Problems also arose because it called itself 'Malt Whisky', which upon closer inspection proved to be incorrect. Neither whisky is produced any longer, but they are still on sale as there are large old stocks of it. Falckenthal once put a barrel at the disposal of the → Scotch Malt Embassy in Berlin. Just 10 bottles of Der alte Falckner, distilled in 1987, bottled in October 1994, resulted from this. Its handwritten label described it as 'Germany's only malt whisky', which is also inaccurate as Robert → Fleischmann has produced malts since 1984.

Falckner, Der German blend from Luckenwalde that was already in existence at the time of the German Democatic Republic. It was produced by the VEB Edelbrände und Spirituosen, as the company of C W → Falckenthal Söhne was called after nationalisation in 1972. In 1954 the government contracted the firm to produce a whisky, which after some experimentation they succeeded in doing. It became very popular in the GDR and other socialist countries (where it was sometimes relabelled 'Scottish whisky'). After reunification the Falckenthal family bought the company back and continued producing this popular whisky. However, it had to be sold to Berentzen. As there are still large stocks, the brand will continue to be available for a while.

Family Silver, The Series which presently only consists of two bottlings, leaving considerable scope for expansion. Highland Distillers brought it out in 1998, thus pleasing whisky lovers and collectors who had not experienced many special bottlings from the company's own distilleries. There was a vintage → Bunnahabhain 1968 in a limited edition of 4,728 bottles. Even more welcome was the vintage → Glenglassaugh 1973, as it comes from a distillery that has been closed since 1986 and from which there has just been one previous → proprietor bottling.

Famous Grouse, The Scotch blend named after a famous game bird. The blend was created in 1897 by the nephew of the company founder Matthew → Gloag. The new brand quickly became so successful and well-known that it was given its present name. 'The Grouse', as it is often called, achieved the ultimate breakthrough after it was sold, together with the company, to → Highland Distillers in 1970. Its malt whiskies from → Bunnahabhain, → Highland Park and → Tamdhu, are not hard to identify. Today, the Famous Grouse is the best-selling blend in Scotland, the seond-best in the UK and the seventh in the world. There is a → standard blend, a Prestige (in Asia only) in a bottle specially designed by Daniel Montgomery, and a china bottle in the shape of the bird. For its 100th anniversary the producers replaced the 15-year-old with a 12-year-old Gold Reserve that has a strong, rounded → sherry tone. In the autumn of 2000 Highland took advantage of the malt whisky trend to bring out the 12-year-old Famous Grouse Vintage Malt 1987, at whose heart are the malts → Macallan and Highland Park. In 2001 Highland Distillers followed the → finishings trend and brought out an Islay Cask and a Port Wood Finish. An 'alcopops' product called Grouse Rush has also appeared.

Feints Term used in Scotland and Ireland for the part of the final distillation run containing certain substances, such as fusel oils, that are undesirable and unusable. The feints, always in the plural and sometimes also called → tails, are separated from the 'good' alcohol, the → middle cut, by the → stillman in the → spirit safe and are subsequently redistilled.

Ferintosh Scottish distillery whose exact location is unknown, but which may probably have been near Dingwall on the Cromarty Firth. It belonged to the local laird, Duncan Forbes of Culloden. In 1689 the distillery was burned down by the followers of James II and Forbes was granted the privilege of building a new one, which he was allowed to operate tax free for a very small annual rent. Its whisky was renowned and held in very high esteem. When the tax privilege came to an end in 1784 and the distillery subsequently ceased working, it was lamented by no less a person than Robert → Burns: 'Thee, Ferintosh! O sadly lost! Scotland, lament frae coast to coast.'

There was another distillery by the name of Ferintosh at a later date, as → Ben Wyvis in Dingwall traded as Ferintosh for a while.

Fermentation The process by which a liquid containing sugar is converted to alcohol. The fermentation is an important stage in the production of whisky. Without it the conversion of starch-containing grain to alcohol couldn't take place, and it is at this stage that alcohol first appears. After malting or boiling has initiated the extraction of fermentation sugars in the barley, rye or corn, and after → mashing of the → grist has flushed the sugar out of the malted or boiled grain, the liquid which results, the → wort, has → yeast added to it in the → washbacks. This induces fermentation by splitting the sugar into carbon dioxide and alcohol. The process can be accelerated or decelerated by controlling the temperature, and as a rule lasts between 40 and 72 hours. At the end of it the resulting liquid, named the → wash, has about 7 to 9% alcohol. This is a kind of beer, which is why it is sometimes called → beer or → ale. Its alcohol content is increased in the next stage of the process, distillation, which makes whisky out of the beer.

Fettercairn Scotch malt distillery. Its name means 'field or wood in the corner'. It lies to the east of the Cairngorm Mountains, an area known for its fertile farmland, and belongs to the Eastern → Highland region. The distillery was one of the first in Scotland to apply for a licence after the new law of 1823 was passed. In 1887 it was rebuilt after a fire; the chairman of the company that owned it at the time was the father of the British Prime Minister, Gladstone. It was perhaps this relationship and the connections with the whisky industry that made the politician formulate the 'Spirits Act' in 1860, allowing the export of whisky in bottles and abolishing the tax on malt. After it was closed for a period, the distillery was run, via its Scottish subsidiary Train & MacIntyre, by National Distillers of America. In 1971 it came under the same control as → Tomintoul Distillery and a year later passed, via the new owner Scottish & Universal Investments, to → Whyte & Mackay, who decided to open the doors of their very pretty distillery to visitors and set up a visitor centre.

They brought out a whisky named → Old

Fettercairn, a 10-year-old single malt with a slight rubber taste and an unusual, well-balanced aroma, which is at present it is being produced for them by their subsidiary → Invergordon. At the end of 1997 it was complemented by a 30-year-old malt, and a 26-year-old in the → 'Stillman's Dram' series at the typical 45%. The → independent bottlers → Cadenhead and → Signatory have also had a Fettercairn (the 1980 version from → sherry casks is a sought after rarity) and they were also able to bring out a malt from 1970 at 57%. Today Fettercairn is owned by → Kyndal.

Fighting Cock Kentucky straight bourbon. It is 6 years old and is bottled at 103° (51.5%). It names the Fighting Cock Distilling Co in → Bardstown, Kentucky as its producer.

Fillings Term frequently used in Scotland for the freshly distilled liquid that is not yet called whisky, as the law prescribes a three year maturation period in the cask. That is why they resort to the names → new make, → new spirit or even → clearic spike (the term → baby whisky which one often hears is not strictly legal either). One mainly talks of fillings when the freshly filled casks are sold immediately. They are bought by other distilleries or companies who want to use the spirit later for blends. These fillings are either delivered to the buyer immediately or are warehoused at the buyer's cost in the distillery which produced them.

Filtering Before bottling practically all whiskies are filtered to remove certain particles which, for example, during maturation, have broken off from the wood of the cask. This process is used for single cask bottlings where the producers very often clearly point out that their whiskies are in their natural state and untreated. In this kind of filtering the whisk(e)y is simply drawn through a sieve made of stainless steel whereby no aromatic substances are removed. It is entirely different from the widely used chill-filtering process which can affect the smell and taste. Purists often reject that and it is not used by most independent bottlers. Another method is used mainly in Kentucky, where the fresh distillate is pressed through a layer of charcoal dust. This should not be confused with the method usual in Tennessee of → charcoal mellowing or → leaching, the famous → Lincoln County Process.

Findlater's Scotch blend of which only two versions in a normal bottle remain: the Finest is a → standard blend and the Legacy is a 21-year-old → de luxe blend. There are also motif carafes: the 15-year-old Findlater's First XV comes in a replica of a rugby ball, the 11-year-old First XI in a football, and the 25-year-old in precious Wedgewood porcelain, 15, 18, 21 years in special bottles for the 'Japanese Female Markers'. They all bear the name of Alexander Findlater, who as the son of an → excisemen, began dealing in whisky in Dublin, and then in 1850 established Findlater Mackie Todd & Co in London. They were among the first to print the name of its producer on the bottle. Charles →Mackinlay & Co was the original creator of the blend and then → Invergordon (on behalf of the parent company → Whyte & Mackay/JBB (Greater Europe) plc). → Kyndal still produce it at Salamander Place in Leith. Apart from the two blends, Findlater also has the → Jock Scott and the vatted malt → Mar Lodge in its range.

Fine Old Special Scotch blend. This is the own brand of Joseph Halt plc, a brewery based in Manchester since 1849, whis has managed to maintain its independence but which in recent years has been gaining more popularity. Like almost all breweries in the UK, the company also runs a chain of pubs, that are owned or contractually bound to them. They not only supply beer, but also often one or two whisky blends with their own label. Holt has 120 pubs where the whisky is served.

Finishing Term for a new trend that has arisen in recent years. A malt whisky that has matured for several years in a cask is refilled into a second cask, in order to make use of the spirit or the wine which the cask previously contained, thus giving the whisky more complexity, depth and, most certainly, further aromatic and taste nuances. After → Gordon & MacPhail had made the first attempt with → Speyside malts, which they matured in a port cask or even a brandy cask, other companies announced that they would not confine themselves to the usual ex-bourbon and ex-sherry casks and William → Grant & Sons brought out their new → Balvenie in 1992. Whilst the 10-year-old was a classic combination of Balvenies matured in bourbon and sherry casks and the 15-year-old was a → single barrel, the name of the 12-year-old, → Double Wood, showed that a new process had been used.

Since then → Glenmorangie plc in particular has been associated with the process and has brought out several single malts from its distillery with various finishings: apart from the sherry cask versions, there was a very unusual Madeira, and, in several different versions, one finished in a port wine cask. Even more unusual were the Tain and the Claret, for which red wine casks from the Rhone or Bordeaux were used. For three versions of the → Glen Moray, which the company also owns, they even used French white wine casks. Balvenie also has a port wine malt (21 years) and there is one from → Bushmills (16 years). At the end of 1997 → UD supplemented their six → 'Classic Malts of Scotland' with a whole series named 'The → Distillers Edition', for which very specially chosen casks were used for the six malts from → Glenkinchie, → Dalwhinnie, → Cragganmore, → Oban, → Talisker and → Lagavulin. The trend has been extended to blends with the → Famouse Grouse Islay and Port Wood Finishing and → Grants finished in ale and sherry casks. It has also reached America: the first example of non-Scottish whisky with a second maturation was provided by a → Canadian Club finished in a sherry cask. Even in the USA, where the definition of a bourbon really excludes the use of a second barrel, there has been at least one bottling. Jim Beam's → Booker Noe, together with the French cognac-master, Alain Royer, was responsible for the → Distiller's Masterpiece Straight Bourbon, which was allowed a second period of maturation in a cognac cask.

Finlaggan Scotch single malt from the → independent bottlers The → Vintage Malt Whisky Company in Glasgow. The whisky is named after Loch Finlaggan on Islay, where, on a small island, the Lords of the Isles had their seat. For centuries they ruled over the Hebrides and the north west of the country, as competitors of the Scottish kings. So the whisky, which is available as an Old Reserve with no age statement and as a 12 or 15-year-

old, comes from Islay. Some suppose it might be a → Bowmore, or a → Caol Ila or a → Bruichladdich (but really it is too smoky for that). However it is not possible to get more precise information. In any case it has been well chosen and quite justly won a silver medal at the International Wine & Spirit Competition in 1977.

Finnegan Irish whiskey produced by the → Cooley Distillery which, apart from its name, is identical with their Avoca – the label is also the same, with the brand name framed by the words 'Uisce Beatha'. It states that this → standard blend is 40%. Its Dutch importers were responsible for having the name changed to avoid confusion with the native 'Advocaat!'.

First Term used for Japanese whiskies that are bottled with a malt content of between 20-30%.

First fill Term used in Scotland for → casks that previously contained an alcoholic drink e.g. bourbon, → sherry, → port and more seldom, wine, and which are filled for the first time with whisky. The expression → new casks is also sometimes used.

First Tyrolean Single Malt Spirit whose producers avoid naming 'whisky', and simply (and more honestly) call 'spirit'. Although they use malted barley and → pot stills, they do not wish to wait for the three years which, in Scotland at least, are stipulated before a grain distillate may be called whisky. The name of the producer, Branger Bräu, is handwritten in gold letters on the front of the black designer bottle with a 20cm long neck. On the back of the bottle a printed label informs us that the 50cl contents are 40%, that the malt was matured in oak casks and is distributed by a company in Altach calling itself Whisky & m.o.r.e. It is expensive and as far as it is known, is the only Austrian malt. It has already achieved good results in blind tastings.

Fitzgerald & Co Irish whiskey company that is now a subsidiary of → IDG and thus belongs to the French company → Groupe Pernod-Ricard. They distribute, amongst others, → Dunphy's, the → pot still whiskey → Redbreast and the cheap spirit → Three Stills, and used to have →

Murphy's, which has since been discontinued, in their range.

Five Lords Scotch blend that is available in three versions, as a → standard blend, a 5-year-old and a 12-year-old. It used to belong to → Whyte & Mackay, and was marketed by A J Ponte.

Five Star Canadian whisky, which like all Canadians previously produced by Seagram was made in → Gimli. It is described as a rye, but is a blend at 40%. It was said to be the best-selling whisky of the Seagram range in its native country. There is also a Scotch of this name that used to be produced by → Haig & Haig, who although established in 1888 by one of the many members of the great Haig whisky family, have only been a subsidiary of John → Haig & Co since 1925. The blend, which nowadays comes from → UDV, is sometimes called Haig & Haig Five Star, sometimes Haig Five Star and sometimes just Five Star. The third whisky with five stars in its name is the → Crawford's 5 Star, which at present is not being produced.

500 Anniversary Blend Scotch blend with which → Whyte & Mackay won 'The → Spirit of Scotland' competition organised by the → International Wine & Spirit Competition in 1994, that the large whisky companies were invited to enter. The competition was organised to celebrate the fact that 500 years previously the monk John → Cor from Fife had obtained a certain quantity of malt in order to make whisky – a fact that is recorded in the royal account books. This was the first time that the drink had been mentioned in a document. The winner of the competition, which seven companies took part in, each submitting a specially-made blend, was the creation of Richard Paterson, the master blender from Whyte & Mackay, now known as →Kyndal.

Flavour, flavours Impressions on the senses from tasting and drinking of whisky. The flavours originate during the production process, but develop during maturation in the cask. Scientists have found up to 32 aroma groups in whisk(e)y, that include more than 300 aromas. There are scientific instruments to analsye them, but the human nose is still considered to be superior, especially when it belongs to a trained noser, a professional taster. They work according to a strict ritual, that not only involves the use of special glasses, but also the use of water. The aroma of the undiluted whisky is first tested with the nose. Then a sip will reveal its mouthfeel. This can be mouth-warming, mouth-coating, astringent or metallic, to name but a few impressions. It is then tasted, but the tongue can only differentiate between sweet, sour, salt and bitter. It is here that flavours can be identified. The palate also has a part to play as its detects flavours sending the information to the brain via olfactory channels. After this water is added (still water, if possible low in minerals), which releases most of the flavours contained in a whisk(e)y. Professional tasters always test whisky reduced to 20% to 25% alcohol. Water is nearly always good because it opens the whisk(e)y. It is difficult to put one's own impressions into words. A good approach to whisk(e)y for the layman is provided by the 'whisky wheel' developed in 1979 in the Pentland Scotch Whisky Research Institute and newly conceived for the consumer in 1996/7 by Charles MacLean. He has published two wheels in his book *Malt Whisky*. One shows nine expressions for the perception of taste and texture, the other assists the analysis of the flavours, that are initially divided into eight groups: grain, ester, floral tones, peat, tails (arising during production), sulphur, wood and wine tones (resulting from maturation in a wooden cask).

Flavourings Term for the addition of 'non-Canadian whiskies' that are permitted in Canada. 9.09% per bottle may be used. These are sometimes real whiskeys such as bourbons, but may also be distilled fruit juices, fortified wines such as sherry, or the particularly popular plum wine. The aromatic substances are said to lend the light Canadian whiskeys more taste and more colour.

Fleischmann, Robert German whisky producer in the Frankish Eggolsheim, between Nuremberg and Bamberg. In 1984 the Fleischmanns decided to try to make whisky. They still have two casks from this year, a genuine single malt made of malted barley, twice distilled and matured over a long period. But it has never been bottled and is intended for their own use. A single malt was

Fleischmann's Preferred

bottled in 1994. This was a whisky from 1986, which had matured for 8 years in an oak cask and was named → Piraten Whisky. The name of the whisky has changed and now the Fleischmanns have a → Glen Blue and a → Glen Mouse, made of two different kinds of malt. Their malt is now called → Krottentaler, Schwarzews Pirat or Spimnaker.

Fleischmann's Preferred American blended whiskey that was produced by the Owensboro-based family company, Fleischmann, who gave their address on the label as Dayton, New Jersey. The label tells us the following about the composition of the whiskey: it contains 27.5% → straight bourbon and 72.5% neutral spirit. In the 1980s Fleischmann was bought by → Glenmore, as were → Medley who were based at the same location. In 1991 Glenmore was taken over by → UD, who four years later sold the (closed down) distillery and several of its brands to → Barton. They have continued with these brands, so the name Fleischmann has, for the meantime, been saved from oblivion.

Floor Maltings Term for the building in which malting is traditionally carried out. At one time a distillery without its own floor maltings would have been unthinkable. Here the barley is soaked in large tanks (→ steeping) to encourage → germination, before being spread out on the malting floor. In order to maintain a constant temperature, which shouldn't exceed 16°, it is regularly turned by hand, so that over a period of five to 10 days, the original layer of about two to three feet is thinned out until it is only three or four inches deep.

Once the → 'green malt' is of a certain consistency, further → germination must be prevented. This is achieved by drying in the → kiln. This process not only needs a lot of room, but is also very labour-intensive and expensive, which is why measures were sought to rationalise it. → Glengoyne was the first distillery to close down its own maltings in 1910 and get its malt from another source. With the exception of just a few distilleries, all have followed suit; only → Balvenie, → Bowmore, → Glendronach, → Highland Park, → Laphroaig and → Springbank still have floor maltings and they only produce some of the malt required.

Most malt is now produced in modern, mechanised → drum maltings, which can make it far more efficiently.

Flora & Fauna Flora & Fauna Series of 22 Scotch single malts, whose appearance could be seen as a revolution in whisky history. For the first time → UD, the largest company in the Scottish whisky business, and the successors of → DCL, had not just used its malts for blends, but had made them available as → proprietor's bottlings. Counting the six → 'Classic Malts' and the individually marketed → Royal Lochnagar and → Cardhu, 30 → UD distilleries (out of 40) were represented. If the → 'Rare Malts' range are also included, the numbered had increased by even more by 1997 when merged with IDV to form UDV.

In 1992 Flora & Fauna was launched onto the market, the series name coming from the Scottish animals and plants that each whisky had been assigned. Along with the character of the whisky, the flora or fauna is described on the label. Initially the series was only available in the distilleries and at a few selected shops, although now it is more widely available, the costly wooden cases have also been replaced by cardboard boxes. However, the series, originally consisting of 22 malts, is no longer available in its entirety. The volume of alcohol is always 43%, but the age varies. The individual malts came from → Aberfeldy, → Aultmore, → Balmenach, → Benrinnes, → Bladnoch, → Blair Athol, → Clynelish, → Caol Ila, → Craigellachie, → Dailuaine, → Dufftown, → Glendullan, → Glenlossie; → Inchgower, → Linkwood, → Mannochmore, → Mortlach, → Pittyvaich, → Rosebank, → Royal Brackla, → Speyburn and → Teaninich. In 2001 four new bottlings were added: → Anchroisk, → Glan Elgin, → Glen Spey and → Strathmill.

Florian Whiskey cocktail. A version of whiskey sour. At the famous Schumann's Bar in Munich they take 4cl bourbon, add a dash of 'Chartreuse Verte', a dash of Angostura bitters, a bar-spoonful of caster sugar and 2cl of orange juice, shake it with ice, and then serve without the ice.

Foreshots Liquid that flows out of the → spirit

still right at the beginning of the last distillation (in Scotland normally the second, in Ireland the third). It is sometimes also called the → head. It is followed by the → heart of the run, the → middle cut, after which comes the → feints or the → tail. The → foreshots are strong and oily, containing esters, aldehyde and other toxic substances, which is why they are not run into the → spirit receiver but diverted by the → stillman. Like the → feints later, they go back into the vessel where the → low wines are contained awaiting the second distillation, and are then redistilled with them.

Forester Kentucky straight bourbon that is actually a modernised version of → Old Forester, the whiskey which George Garvin Brown and his half brother launched onto the market in 1872. It was the very first bourbon to be filled in bottles, and had a seal of approval and Brown's signature on the label. The fact that the word 'old' has been removed after so many years, is probably because they want to appeal to a new generation of consumers.

A Forester Barrel Reserve, a → premium at 96° (48%), was an Olympic Filling for the Atlanta games. The Forester 1870 may possibly completely replace the previous versions. 1870 refers to the year that the two Browns founded the company from which the → Brown-Forman Corporation developed. They have abandoned the old bottle style; the new one, with its rectangular form, is somewhat similar to that of → Jack Daniel's, which also belongs to the company. Perhaps one day it too will stand on the roof of the company headquarters in Louisville, but the break with tradition is not quite complete and the old water tower has retained its shape – that of a bottle of Old Forester.

Forfars Scotch blend that gets its name from the place in Angus, the area between Fife and the River Tay. The name of the producer, → Angus Dundee, also refers to this area.

Formidable Jock, The Scotch blend from The → Bennachie, who describe it as a 'Rare Blend of Strength and Character'. It is a 5-year-old and is available in large bottles for bars. Alongside this 'Superior' there is also an 8-year-old → de luxe blend.

Forth House A 5-year-old Scotch blend. It is one of the lesser-known brands of Brodie Crawford & Co, whose leading brand is → Brodie's Supreme.

Fortnum & Mason London company which since its foundation in 1707 has served '12 reigns of British monarchs' (Philip Morrice), not forgetting the innumerable subjects of her majesty, Queen Victoria who in the furthest reaches of the Empire did not have to go without the blessings of British civilisation in the form of pies, teas, Stilton, Gentlemen's Relish and, of course, wines and spirits, as they were supplied with all they needed from 181, Piccadilly. Nowadays the shop is a must for tourists but still also has an excellent food department, with its own products such as teas and jams – and an excellent wine department, with a whisky section which is well worth visiting. They have their own brands such as Fortnum & Mason 'Choice Old' Blend, as well as an 8-year-old blend and a 12 or 21-year-old Highland malt. Some distilleries also undertake exclusive bottlings for the company; in 1996 there was a 1961 → Linkwood. A cupboard which is only opened on special request contains such rarities as a 50-year-old Glenfiddich or a → Springbank from 1919 – the former sells for £10,000 the latter for £6,000.

Fortune 80 Japanese blend from → Nikka. It is the only whisky from this company that bears the signature of its founder Masataka → Taketsuru (on a shiny metalic label bent around the bottle). The actual brand name is to be found on an old-fashioned decanter label that hangs from a thin chain around the neck of the bottle – a reminder of the times when guests were served from a crystal decanter rather than from a bottle. The whisky comes in a container that is reminiscent of the classical old port decanters with three rings on the neck – a package that hints at something special: namely the 80th birthday of Taketsuru in 1974.

Fortune Brands Fortune Brands Group operating worldwide that was formerly known as → American Brands. It changed its name in 1997, shortly before this it had parted from its tobacco subsidiary Gallaher (top brand: Benson & Hedges), and the name-change indicates a wish to distance themselves from this image.

Forty Creek

The group owns the → bourbon brand → Jim Beam and in 1997 it restructured all its whisk(e)y interests under this name. Its Scottish subsidiary, → Whyte & Mackay, was party to this reorganisation and became → JBB (Greater Europe) plc in 1995. The rest of the world are served by JBB (The Americas) and JBB (Pacific).

Forty Creek Canadian whisky from the → Kittling Ridge Distillery. The label proudly describes it as 'Barrel Select' and 'Three Grain'.

Founders Scotch blend formerly from → Whyte & Mackay/ → JBB (Greater Europe) plc.

Four Roses In 1986 this American distillery was named after the bourbon that it has long supplied with individual whiskeys. It was owned by → Seagram, who also owned another distillery with the same name → Lawrenceburg

There is another distillery in the neighbourhood that bears the name of the bourbon it produces, → Wild Turkey. During the course of time Four Roses has sometimes been in shared ownership with → Wild Turkey – and they still share the → warehouses which, although they belong to Four Roses, are used for maturing Wild Turkey.

The present buildings date back to 1910, but the history of the distillery is older. It was founded by the Irishman → 'Old Joe' Peyton, who crossed the border to Kentucky in a canoe and started to distil whiskey – so successfully that it was simply called Old Joe (which made it one of the country's first whiskey brands). Peyton's business was bought by Gratz Hawkins and there followed a whole series of owners, including the → Medleys and the Ripy brothers, who owned the neighbouring distillery for a while, and proceeded to call it → Old Prentice. Frankfort Distilleries then became owners, and the brand Four Roses entered the equation, having belonged to the company since 1902.

Four Roses was made popular by Paul Jones, and there are several stories concerning the origins of its name: Seagram tells two on the whiskey labels. One tells of a whiskey-dealing Colonel Rose, who was said to have had four beautiful daughters (he actually had five), and the other says that Rose was the name of Jones's fiancée. What is certain is that Seagram bought the brand together with the distillery in 1943. They also used to produce → Benchmark and → Eagle Rare, but latterly they only made the whiskeys needed for Four Roses.

It is not obtainable as a straight in its native country; Seagram have only supplied a blended version in the USA. Nonetheless it is the most successful of its type in Europe and the third most popular worldwide.

Unusually, the distillery also produces differing straights, with 12 different → mash bills and different yeasts. They are then blended together for the individual versions, although they are not in the same place as they are been produced. The whiskeys which Jim Rutledge and his predecessor Ova Haney make don't mature in Lawrenceburg, but are taken in road tankers to Cox's Creek about 50 miles away to be matured in unheated → warehouses.

Afterwards the whiskey is taken to Scotland to be bottled at the Chivas Brothers' Paisley plant. The → standard blend is called Yellow Label and is 40%, the Black Label and the Platinum Label are both 43% and they are all meant for export. That is also true of the recently added → Single Barrel Reserve, which is at 43% and may possibly soon be available in the USA.

Four Roses Canadian whisky formerly from → Seagram, sold as a 'bar brand'. It has nothing to do with the great Kentucky straight bourbon that also came from Seagram, and now belongs to Kirin.

Four Seasons Australian blend, which is still possible to find. The bottles are already collectors' items, for the formerly successful brand from the Australian United Distillers (not to be confused with the former → Guinness subsidiary, → UD) is no longer produced, just like → Corio; in 1995 the company converted its stocks to gin.

France In France, sales of Scotch increased from 25 million litres per year in 1986, to a solid 37.04 million in 1997, overtaking the USA with 32.32 million litres and the UK with 32.28 million litres. The French are therefore the world's leading consumers of Scotch. Many French companies have secured distribution rights or by invested in whisk(e)y itself.

LVMH (Louis Vuitton Moet Hennessy) obtained a share in → Guinness, although the head of the company, Arnaud had at first been opposed to their planned merger with → Grand Metropolitan to form → Diageo. In Germany Moet Hennessy distributes the products of → Glenmorangie plc. → Remy Martin distributes whisky in a whole range of countries, and in Germany supplies the malts from → Highland Distillers. The → Groupe Pernod-Ricard are the most active of all. In Scotland they own → Campbell Distillers with their distilleries → Aberlour, → Edradour and → Glenallachie, and have a whole range of blends. In the USA the absinthe giants secured the → Wild Turkey Distillery with its bourbon, and at the end of the 1980s they fought a heated takeover battle in Ireland, which they won. They were then able to incorporate the Irish Distillers Group (IDG), and thereby initially even secure a monopoly in the country.

There had not been any whisky production in France before → Whisky Breton appeared in Britanny and the 'Artisan Liquoriste' Jacques Fusilier who, produces his → Glenroc (now (Gwenroc!) and → Whisky de Bretagne in Rennes. He describes the latter as a malt whisky. The → Armorik is a real Breton single malt.

The Belgian Michel → Couvreur, who lives in Burgundy is an → independent bottler, selling Scotch whiskies under his own name. The 'Maison du Whisky' in Paris operates in a similar way and is the most important whisky shop in the country.

Fraser McDonald Scotch → standard blend originally marketed by Barton and then later by their successors, Gibson International. It now comes from → Glen Catrine Bonded Warehouse Ltd.

Fraser's Scotch whiskies. There are several versions which are distributed by different companies. The blend Fraser's used to come from → Whyte & Mackay, but originally came from Donald Fraser & Co. Whiskies from Strathnairn Whisky in Inverness also bear the name Fraser. This is a subsidiary of → Gordon & MacPhail of Elgin. Fraser's Supreme is a blend, Fraser's Reserve is available as a Highland single malt and as an → Islay single malt, and on a recent label gave Glasgow as its address.

Friar John Cor Quincentenary Scotch blend with which → UD took part in the competition 'The → Spirit of Scotland' organised by the → International Wine & Spirit Competition in 1994. This was to commemorate the first time that whisky had been mentioned in a document, 500 years previously. Friar John Cor from Fife gained permission to receive 'eight bols of malt' for the production of 'aqua vitae'. The anniversary bottling consisted of an appropriate 1,494 bottles.

Frisco Sour Whiskey cocktail. A variation on Whiskey Sour, in which as well as bourbon, one part 'Benédictine' is used.

From the Barrel Japanese blend from → Nikka at 51.4%, an unusual strength for this country. It is also unusual for Japan that the whiskies used are blended before going back into the barrels, allowing a more successful 'marriage' after this second maturation.

Fuaran Isle Scottish single malt from Ian MacLeod & Co, the name meaning 'little island or Islay river'. The company describes it, without naming the distillery it comes from, as 'Reserve of Islay' and 'Classic Limited Islay Vintage Edition'. There are several single cask bottlings of it. The available bottle is from ex-Bourbon barrell no. IIII and contains a malt that was distilled in March 1991 and bottled in October 2000. There are 414 bottles of it.

Full House American blended at 40% (no °proof given), introducing itself on the label as 'Mc Intyre's Full House'. It is a standard supermarket whiskey.

G

G & G Japanese blend from → Nikka. The bottle is very similarly shaped to that of → Gold & Gold. However that bottle is transparent whilst the one for the 'mild & smooth' G & G is pitch-black.

Gairloch Scotch blend with 4-year-old and 5-year-old versions that is made for the small English brewery McMullen & Co in Hertford. The brand has existed since 1904 and is named after the town in Wester Ross, in the Scottish Highlands. It mainly serves as a house brand for the brewery's own pubs. It is made by → Robertson & Baxter, who use a whole range of malt whiskies for it, which they have access to as owners of → Glengoyne and through their connections with → Highland Distillers.

Gale's Scotch blend whose name is better known among lovers of real ale than those of whisky. George Gale & Co is one of the few remaining independent breweries in the UK and is still owned by the family who more than 250 years ago took over the 'Ship and Bell' pub in Horndean near Portsmouth. The Hampshire Brewery is still situated there. It not only supplies the 122 pubs owned by the company, but also more than 500 other hostelries and the members of its 'Gale's Club', with their ales 'Bitter', 'Mild', 'Winter Brew', 'Christmas Ale' and 'Prize Old Ale' as well as their own blend which proudly bears the name Gale's Blended Glenlivet. It is not made in the brewery but in London. Unusually its label names the distilleries providing the whiskies which make it up: the grains come from → Cameronbridge, → Dumbarton, → North British and → Strathclyde and the malts from → Ben Nevis, → Bunnahabhain, → Dalmore, → Dufftown, → Glen Grant, → Highland Park and Glenlivet.

Galoway Irish whiskey from → Cooley. They produce a → standard blend which is sold with five different names by various supermarkets in France. Leader Price sells it as Galoway. Another name used for it is → Dunlow.

Gamefair Vatted malt which is only of local importance, being marketed by → Hynard Hughes & Co in the Leicester area. It is a 10-year-old.

Gamekeeper Scotch blend from → Morrison Bowmore. It is a 5-year-old → standard blend.

Garnheath Now defunct Scottish distillery which is better known by the name → Moffat, which ran a grain distillery as well as two small plants for the production of malt whisky, → Glen Flagler/Glenflagler and → Killyloch. Andrew and Brian Symington, were all responsible for finding the only cask of Killyloch ever filled with single malt. For the '10th anniversary' edition, celebrating the foundation of their company → Signatory, they presented a Garnheath Grain, along with five malts. It was bottled in 1998 at 56.8%, and was distilled in 1973. Another Garnheath belonged to the fourth of their → 'Silent Stills' series, distilled in 1972 and bottled at 59.4% aged 27 years in 2000.

Gentleman Jack American whiskey, a Tennessee Sour Mash, which is named after → Jack Daniel. Gentleman Jack consists of distillates which come exclusively from the → Jack Daniel Distillery in Lynchburg.

Germany Only in recent years has Germany been found on a map of whisky producers: since Robert → Fleischmann and his wife produced a real malt whisky, Christian Gruel in Owen/Teck, made his single grain → 'Swabian Whisky' and the distillery Sonnenschein in Witten/Heven brought out a malt whisky, distilled in 1989 from Scottish malted barley, which has been matured in casks that had previously contained Scottish whisky.

There had been whisky producers prior to this, but they had only created blends from malt whiskies that they had bought in Scotland and mixed with grain distillates produced in Germany (as well as native water). The best-known, and the only survivor to this day, is → Racke rauchzart, whilst the attempt by the Stück AG in Hanau with their → Jacob Stück Whisky was very short-lived.

There were also whiskies in the German Democratic Republic: Goldener Stern came from the VEB Bärensiegel in Berlin, who also had an HC (for 'High Country') and an Old Joe Silver. Another East German whisky was → Der Falckner from the state company, formerly an old family firm, C W Falckenthal Söhne in Lübeck, who after reunification first brought out → Oldmaster and then → Edelfalcke. Even the Konsum Melde in Cottbus had a Ratsherrn Whisky, and the famous Nordhauseser Kornbrennerei had a whisky that was ordered by, and was exclusively produced for the government, named → Smoky Springs, which was also available after reunification when the company had been reprivatised.

In West Germany there may have been: Wilhelm Braun Erben in Heimersheim/Ahr, for example sold an Old Time Whisky. Robert Meisner GmbH in Heide called their blend Private Whisky. None of them was of much more than local importance.

The large hotels in Berlin, such as the Adlon, had their own brands. In 1939, the supreme court in Berlin determined that whisky produced in Germany was not to be called 'German Whisky' but just 'Whisky'. There was a 'Rauchmalt' produced in a plant named the Adler Destillerie within the Institute; in 1957 they filled a cognac cask which produced a few bottles, the last 20 in January 1997.

After the Second World War, whisky almost became the embodiment of the new values of democracy and freedom.

The commercial success of whisky was due to Racke rauchzart, which came onto the market in 1958 and was an instant success, not only because the public liked its taste, but because they could afford it. In 1969 it sold 3 million bottles and was the market leader in front of Johnnie Walker with 2.7 million, and → Black & White with 2 million bottles. It is still in the Top 10 at number 5. In East Germany whisky was popular, too, but the Scottish brands were only available, for a lot of money or against hard currency, in the Intershops.

Germany is now one of the countries with the highest consumption of whisky. Although bourbon has caught up, Scotch is still in the lead, and Germany occupies 6th place behind France, the USA, the UK, Spain and Japan. In 1996 Scotch had a share of 57% (worldwide 42%), of this 5.2% were malts, 31.7% American whiskey (world share 18%), German whisky 5%, Irish 2.6% and Canadian 1% with a world share of 12%, where Japanese whiskies are also represented with 12% and all others, including Irish and German, amount to 14%. In the past few years further intrepid distillers, who previously had mostly produced eau-de-vie, have had a go at distilling whisky: eg Walter Seeger (Black Wood) and Volker Theurer (Black Horse Original Ammertaler Whisky) – both from the Black Forest - and Reiner Möslein and E and R Brasch from Franconia.

George & J G Smith Glenlivet Single malt from → Gordon & MacPhail, who have long-standing connections with the distillery that these whiskies come from. In order to differentiate between these bottlings and those of the → proprietor, who use the name The → Glenlivet, the → independent bottlers from Elgin use the name of the person who founded the distillery. There is: a 12-year-old at 40%, a 15-year-old at 40%, 46% and 57%, and a 21-year-old at 40%, as well as many anniversary bottlings going as far back as the 1930s. The one from 1943 is a rarity, as hardly any whisky was being distilled in Scotland during the Second World War, because the barley was needed as food for the population.

George Dickel Tennessee sour mash named after → Dickel, George. There are four versions: the Old No. 8 Brand (previously 86.8° (43.4%), now 80° (40%)) with a black label and between 4 and 6 years old. The Superior No. 12 Brand (previously 90° (45%), now 86° (43%)) is a little older and has a beige label. On this the term Sour Mash has been omitted and replaced with 'Original Tennessee Finest Quality Sippin' Whisky'. Since the beginning of 1988 there has been a 10-year-old (with almost the same appearance) which also is 86° (43%). In 1994 → UD, who bought → Schenley in 1987 and now own the distillery and the brand, brought out a Special Barrel Reserve which is also a 10-year-old; these two must be the oldest Tennessee whiskeys (86°/43%).

The → single barrel belongs to the → 'Bourbon Heritage Collection', which may initially seem odd. George Dickel has already once been categorised as a bourbon in the course of its history, and although by definition a bourbon can never be a Tennessee, every Tennessee is also a → straight bourbon. Any whiskey produced in America may call itself bourbon as long as it has been distilled from a mash consisting of more than 51% corn and is not stronger than 160°, is filled into barrels at under 125°, matures for more than two years in a new oak barrel and is bottled at least 80°: criteria which apply equally toGeorge Dickel and to its famous neighbour → Jack Daniel's.

Georgia Moon Kentucky straight corn which is a curiosity It is one of the few whiskeys which, due to a corn share of over 80% in its → mash bill, is allowed to call itself 'corn', it also has an original appearance: it comes in containers that look like honey jars. It is almost clear in colour and everything about it is reminiscent of the legendary illicitly distilled spirits, which in the USA is called → moonshine. Many people like to drink it young, fresh from the → still and infernally sharp. Georgia Moon is used to be 'younger than 30 days', but nowadays it can be as old as 50 days. It originally came from Owensboro and today belongs to the Johnston Distilling Co, which means that it probably comes from → Heaven Hill. It contains 50% alcohol and is one of the few corn whiskeys that is relatively easy to obtain.

Germination One of the first stages in the production of malt whisky (and beer). This is the process during which the starch contained in the barley is released by soaking in water. The production of beer as well as malt whisky depends on the starch contained in the barley being converted into sugar. With the addition of → yeast it → ferments, which splits it into carbon dioxide and alcohol. The alcoholic liquid is then distilled several times to increase the alcohol content. The first stage of the process always consists of → steeping the barley in water. This induces germination in the barley and the starches contained within it are released. After a certain period germination must be stopped. Judging when that time has come is a matter of experience: it is said to have been reached when the → green malt is so soft that you could write your name on the wall with it.

Gibson International Whisk(e)y company arising from a management buy-out in 1989, when executives of → ADP, with the help of → Schenley (Canada), bought out their old company. At the time it owned the American → Barton Brands and the distillery of the same name in → Bardstown as well as the Scottish distilleries Littlemill and Glen Scotia. The company then went out of business. The Scottish part was taken over by → Glen Catrine Bonded Warehouse Ltd and the American part by → Canandaigua.

Gibson's Canadian whisky. The brand belonged to → UD who took it over when they bought → Schenley Canada. It was created by Master Blender Jacques Loiselle. The name has nothing to do with → Gibson International. There are two versions: the 12-year-old Gibson's Finest and Gibson's Sterling Edition. Both are 40%. → UDV, announced in 1999 that Gibson's would be the only Canadian that they would market in future.

Gilbey, W & A English company founded in 1857 in London by the brothers Walter and Alfred, who quickly became well-known as wine merchants and gin distillers. They entered into the whisky business before the end of the 19th century. They bought James → Catto & Co in Aberdeen and took over the distilleries → Glen Spey, → Strathmill and → Knockando. There were also branches in Ireland and Canada, where the important brand → Black Velvet has been produced since 1945. In India they make → Gilbey's and in Australia → Bond

7 and Milnes Gilt Edge (which no longer exist today) were produced in their own production plants. Although the blend → Glen Spey was made in Scotland, where they had their own bottling plants in Aberdeen, it wasn't bottled there, but exported in → bulk. In 1962 the company, whose 'Gilbey's Gin' was still very important, gave up its independence and merged with United Wine Traders to form the new group → IDV, one of the five international spirit giants, which then became a part of → Grand Metropolitan in 1972.

Gilbey's Indian whisky from → IDV, who were represented on the subcontinent via a joint venture with → Polychem and had their product made by International Distillers. It bears the name of the renowned old company → Gilbey, and is a blend which probably contains Indian as well as Scottish components. There are four versions, Green, Heritage, Gold and White. IDV also sold their → Spey Royal in India. After the company had merged with UD at the end of 1997, it was uncertain which products would continue to be offered in India.

Gillon's Scotch blend that commemorates the name of the former licence holder of the → Glenury Royal Distillery – a company whose history goes back to 1817, when it was founded in Linlithgow by John Gillon. It later became a subsidiary of → Ainslie & Heilbron, and with the parent company was absorbed by → DCL empire, whose brands are now owned by → UD/UDV. Gillon's is mainly available in Italy.

Gimli Canadian distillery built in 1969 in Manitoba, where the → Bronfmans, a family of Russian immigrants, first settled. Today it is the last remaining of all the → distilleries formerly owned by Seagram. Technically it is in a position to make any kind of whisky. Indeed the master blenders can claim to produce the various brands exactly as they were when their whiskeys still came from → LaSalle or Beaupré. Stocks from the old, closed-down and dismantled distilleries remained available, but whether they can still be reproduced is doubtful, as the character of whisky is very much influenced by the distillery from which it comes. Canada's blenders are masters of their trade, however, and can take liberties: add foreign → flavourings such as bourbons from the → Four Roses Distillery in Kentucky. Of course Everyone who has been able to taste samples of the individual Gimli whiskeys have confirmed their quality – and praise the beauty of the location between Lake Winnipeg and a vast grain producing area (the harvest from which is processed at Gimli).

Girvan Scottish grain distillery which lies in Ayrshire on the outskirts of the coastal town of the same name. Like most Scottish grain distilleries (→ Invergordon is in the Highland Region) it belongs to the → Lowlands whisky region. It was built in 1963 by the independent company → William Grant & Sons, who are mainly known for → Glenfiddich and their blends. The Girvan Distillery was constructed to provide them with the → grain whisky necessary for these blends (previously known as Standfast, now as → Grant's Family Reserve), thus securing some independence from their competitors. Girvan can produce 55 million litres of alcohol per year: apart from the → Coffey still needed for the grain, there are columns for neutral spirit, that make the production of gin and vodka possible. The residue from the distillery is processed on site as animal feed. From 1966 to 1975 the malt distillery → Ladyburn was also located on the same site.

Glamis Castle Scotch blend. The whisky comes from the → Speyside Distillery, and the fact that the Christie family is allowed to use this name results from a venture they started in the 1950s. With the → North of Scotland Distilling Co they built a small distillery called Strathmore near Glamis castle, where (with → patent stills) malt whisky was made – an experiment which they soon gave up. The → blend with the suffix Reserve is 12 years old. Of course the occasion of the 90th birthday of Her Majesty the Queen Mother in 1990 was celebrated – by a limited edition of a 25-year-old in a crystal decanter.

Glass A good glass is an important prerequisite for the proper enjoyment of a drink. An unsuitable glass can make this partly or wholly impossible, for example although it may encourage the development of the taste, it might hinder that of the aromas, or misdirect the flow to the tongue. It goes without saying that a good glass must be well designed. Many whisk(e)y connoisseurs and drinkers believe that the tumbler, often made of heavy (or cut) crystal is the best and most appropriate glass. All whiskies which are enjoyed with soda or ice, are best drunk from a tumbler. It is ideal for a Bourbon on the rocks, whose sweetness needs to be somewhat neutralised with ice or for a Scotch blend (which when drunk pure or with a lot of soda and ice, is drunk from a taller glass).

Using such a glass for malt whisky is wasting half its potential. The → nosing glass used by the industry and by master blenders is not necessarily to be recommended, neither is the malt glass from Riedel. Although its tulip shape directs and concentrates the aromas in the direction of the nose excellently, it is too narrow at the top and is thus difficult to drink from. Sherry glasses, which are often recommended, are also too narrow.

A good alternative is the INAO glass which has found general acceptance for wine tasting: it has a stem which can be held well, it stands solidly, offers enough room for a respectable measure, leaves enough space and air for the malt to develop, allows the addition of (still) springwater, is narrow enough for concentrated → nosing and wide enough to be able to drink from properly.

Glayva Scotch whisky liqueur that has been on the market since 1947. It is said to have been created by Ronald Morrison, (the owner of the company of the same name) who worked in the wine and spirits trade in Leith. He wanted to create a whisky liqueur modelled on → Drambuie and is reported to have spent months mixing and remixing malt and grains with honey and herbs. A Gaelic speaker sampled it and described it as *Gle Mhath* (pronounced 'glay-vaa') – in other words, very good. So the recipe was adopted, the product had a name, and it quickly became popular at home and abroad, especially among expatriot Scots. Nowadays it is produced by → Kyndal having formerly been a brand under the ownership of → JBB (Greater Europe) plc who acquired it through their subsidiary → Whyte & Mackay who from time to time produced special bottlings of it, for example. at Christmas.

Glen Albyn Scottish malt distillery. It was located on the outskirts of → Inverness, at the point where the old Great North Road crosses the Caledonian Canal. The → Glen Mhor Distillery was situated opposite. Both distilleries therefore belonged to the northern → Highland region. It had previously been a brewery and was probably established in 1846, after being used for a time as a flour mill during the 1850s, and totally rebuilt in 1884. It experienced its heyday under the ownership of a company belonging to members of the Mackinlay and Birnie families. In 1972 it was sold to → DCL, who closed it 11 years later and it was subsequently demolished. Today a shopping centre stands on the site.

The only known proprietor's bottling of a Glen Albyn Single Malt was a 10-year-old intended for sale in Italy. → Independent bottlings are still obtainable, but supplies are becoming scarce. A malt whisky from 1965 was included in the → 'Silent Stills' series from → Signatory. It was bottled as a 31-year-old in 1997 at 51.5%.

Glen Ardoch A 12-year-old malt that is described as a 'Single Vatted' by its producers.There is an 8-year-old and one without an age statement. As they all come from → Burn Stewart, it is possible they come from → Deanston and → Tobermory/Ledaigs. The company bottles a lot of blends, for which they require large stocks of malts from other distilleries, and one of them could also be Glen Ardoch.

Glen Argyll Scotch vatted malt from a company of the same name with an address in Largs. It is mainly sold in France as a 'Pure Highland Malt'.

Glen Avon Scotch single malt from the old-established trading firm → Gordon & MacPhail in Elgin. This company traditionally has good connections with the proprietors of many distilleries, and so has many excellent whisky stocks at its disposal. This brand, sold under the name of the subsidiary Avonside, is named after the valley of the small river that flows into the Spey near → Cragganmore. The → Tomintoul Distillery lies on the Avon (pronounced 'a-on').

→ Glenlivet is not far away either – and its founder, George Smith, once owned a distillery called Dalnabo which was also sometimes known as Glenavon. Thanks to their good connections G & M have their own series of Glenlivets. But their lips are sealed concerning the source of the Glen Avon and they will only divulge the fact that it is a → Speyside. It is available aged 8, 15, 21 and 25 years (all at 40%).

Glen Baren Scotch vatted malt available in two versions, aged 5 and 8 years, from the Surrey-based → Kinross Whisky Company.

Glen Blair Scotch vatted malt from → Burn Stewart whose predecessors also produced it, but called it Glenblair. They own both the → Deanston and the → Tobermory/Ledaig distilleries, so it may be assumed that their malt whiskies play a part in it, although an → Islay can also be tasted. It is not the company's only vatted malt, but it is their most successful one – with particularly good sales in France. There are two versions of it, one without an age statement and one aged 12 years. On some markets there are also a 5 and an 8-year-old.

Glen Blue German single malt from → Robert Fleischmann. Their whisky is either called → Glen Mouse or Glen Blue. The latter has been distilled from a rather more heavily peated type of malted barley, but like its 'brother' has been matured in an oak cask. Cask No. 2 was bottled in 1997, cask No. 3 in 1998, using three different bottle sizes, all at 40%.

Glen Cairn Scotch single malt available from the UK supermarket chain → Tesco in at least two versions: as a Single Highland Malt and as a Single → Speyside Malt. Both are 10 years old.

Glen Calder Scotch blend from → Gordon & MacPhail, that is named after Sir James Calder, who in the 17th century was member of parliament for Elgin, where the company is based.

Glen Carron/Carren Scotch blend. It is one of three brands belonging to the English company → Hall & Bramley Ltd, which has now lost its independence and become a subsidiary of → Halewood International Ltd.

Glen Catrine Standard Scotch blend. The brand comes from → Glen Catrine Bonded Warehouse Ltd.

Glen Catrine Bonded Warehouse Ltd Scottish company owned by A Bulloch Agencies Ltd, who are based in Catrine, Ayrshire. Its origins go back to the Bulloch family whose descendant is today's chairman. They originally only operated warehouses for maturing whisky, but then brought out their own blends such as → Glen Catrine, → High Commissioner and → Clansman. In 1984 they bought their first distillery, → Loch Lomond. In 1995 they took over → Glen Scotia and → Littlemill from the bankrupt company → Gibson International, which in contrast to Loch Lomond. Apart from the single malts from their distilleries, such as the → Inchmurrin, Old Rhosdhu and the 23-year-old Loch Lomond and the afore-mentioned blends, they have several vatted malts in their range → Royal Culross, → Glen Gyle, → Glen Nevis and → Glenshiel and the blends → Loch Lomond, → Old Troon and → Scots Earl as well as the brands taken over from Gibson, → Fraser McDonald, → Howard McLaren, → Scotia Royale, Royal Escort and → Glengarry. They also have other spirits such as a 'Grant's Gin' and a 'Grant's Blue Label': names which caused William Grant & Son to initiate legal action because of the danger of confusion. In 1999 the company produced the first → Single blended Scotch (called Loch Lomond; the name is also used for a single malt that is mainly sold in Germany) at its Loch Lomond Distillery, which can produce → grain whisky as well as various malts.

Glen Clova Scotch blend which like → Scots Club used to come from Ewen & Co but then belonged to the → Scottish & Newcastle subsidiary, → Waverley Vintners Ltd. As a result of the sale of most of the company's brands to → Invergordon Distillers, and the subsequent buy out of many of the assets of → JBB (Greater Europe) plc, the whisky is now one of the many → standard blends under the ownership of → Kyndal.

Glen Corrie Scotch blend from → QSI, a subsidiary of William → Grant & Sons. It is available as a 3-year-old blend and as a 5-year-old vatted malt in the UK, Italy, Spain and Germany.

Glen Crinan Scotch blend from Row & Co in Glasgow. The Crinan Canal joins the Atlantic Ocean to Loch Fyne, after which the vatted malt → Glenfyne from the same company is named. Both are mainly on sale in France at Intermarché outlets.

Glen Dee 5-year-old Scotch vatted malt. It is produced by the Glen Dee Distillery whose address in Keith identifies it as a former subsidiary of → Seagram. It is only obtainable in Italy.

Glen Deveron Scotch single malt, sometimes written as Glendeveron, from the → Macduff Distillery which lies near Banff on the River Deveron. William → Lawson Distillers, who ran the distillery until 1998, decided not to use the distillery's name for their → proprietor's bottling. This could be because it is very popular in Italy and France, where whiskies named 'Glen' tend to sell very well. It is available as a 12-year-old, as a 5-year-old in Italy, and as a 10 and 15-year-old in other markets. The limited edition in the elegant Baccarat decanter is also 15 years old. In 1998 Lawson's parent company, the Bacardi group, acquired four distilleries from UDV, as well as the top brand Dewar's, whose name is now used for all its whisky activities in Scotland, replacing the name Lawson.

Glen Dew Scotch vatted malt produced by Mitchell Bros in Glasgow. The company was a subsidiary of → DCL who transferred the licence of the North Port Distillery to them. Its malt whisky very likely played an important part in the 5-year-old Glen Dew. The distillery has been closed and DCL has been taken over by → UD, who no longer produce this brand, although it is still possible to find a few bottles of it.

Glen Douglas Scotch malt whisky produced at the → Loch Lomond Distillery. So far it has only been used for → blending.

Glen Dowan A → standard Scotch blend available as a 21-year-old. It comes from J & G → Grant and probably contains → Glenfarclas as a base malt.

Glen Drumm Scotch vatted malt. It is produced by Langside Distillers, behind which is Douglas → Laing & Co from Glasgow. It is bottled at 43%, in numbered bottles and is mainly for the French market.

Glen Drummond Scotch vatted malt, bottled at 8 years, whose label names the old established firm of → Hankey Bannister as its producer. The company was founded in London in the 19th century although the name only lives on in the form of a successful blend, which, like Glen Drummond has belonged to → Inver House Distillers Ltd since the 1980s.

Glen Eagle Scotch blend from Longman Distillers, a subsidiary of → Invergordon. It is available as a → standard blend with no age statement, as a 5-year-old and as a vatted malt, also 5 years old.

Glen Eason 10-year-old Scotch single malt. It comes from the → Speyside region. It is not sold by the → proprietor of its distillery but by → Isle of Arran Distillers.

Glen Elg Scotch vatted malt from → Burn Stewart who own the → Deanston and → Tobermory/Ledaig distilleries and who very likely use their malts, which are also sold as single malts, for this brand. Like the company's most successful vatted malt, → Glen Blair, Glen Elg is also meant for the French market. Glen Elg, which is palindromic, does exist.

Glen Elgin Scottish malt distillery. It gets its name from the Morayshire town which is located a few miles north of the distillery. It is on the A941 between Elgin and Rothes. It is the neighbour of → Longmorn and belongs to the → Speyside whisky region. → White Horse Distillers, whose name is prominently displayed on the label of its single malt, became licencees of the distillery when it was already a subsidiary of → DCL, belonging to → SMD. Today it belongs to GuinnessUDV. It was founded in 1898, at the time of the → whisky boom, and was completed two years later. For almost 60 years it remained the last distillery to have been built on Speyside. It was rebuilt in 1964 when its capacity was increased from two to six stills. Its water comes from the Millbuies Springs. Like the malt of its sisters, → Craigellachie and → Lagavulin, a large amount of its production used to go into the classic → White Horse, but it is also available as a 12 year-old single malt in a → proprietor's bottling. It bore the famous horse on its label. However, since → UDV have been in charge, the malt has officially only been bottled for the Japanese market, although it is also available elsewhere. In 2001 a 12-year-old Glen Elgin was launched as part of the → Flora & Fauna Series.

Glen Fern Scotch blend, produced by the → UD subsidiary → Macdonald Greenlees. It is hard to find; the last known bottling was for Chile in 1992.

Glen Flagler Scottish malt distillery. Sometimes known as Glenflagler. It lay near Airdrie and belonged to the → Lowlands → whisky region. Although it was only in existence from 1965 to 1985 and was located within the large → Moffat grain distillery complex, which → Inver House Distillers Ltd acquired on behalf of the American parent company Publicker Distillers Inc, converting a paper mill into a very large whisky plant. A second malt distillery named → Killyloch, a grain distillery, a maltings, a large bottling and blending complex and 32 → warehouses were all located on the site. Glen Flager had six → stills and its water was from the Lilly Loch. Its whisky was available as a single malt in a → proprietor's bottling (aged 5 and 8 years) and was mainly intended for the Italian market. The name was also used for vatted malts. At present Inver House Distillers Ltd, whose directors bought out the Publicker Distillers Inc in 1988, are again marketing an 8-year-old vatted malt called Glen Flagler. In 1994 → Signatory were able to bottle a cask each of Glenflagler from 1970 at → cask strength and a → Killyloch. A year later the Symingtons brought out one from 1972 at a cask strength of 52.3%. There is also a bottling in their series → 'Silent Stills' from the same year, this time written Glen Flagler.

Glen Fraser Scotch single malt from the → independent bottlers → Gordon & MacPhail in Elgin, who never give the exact source of their 'house brands' (→ Glen Avon, → Glen Gordon, → MacPhail's), but just the general region, in this case the → Highlands. As it is relatively smoky it could be a → Glen Garioch. It is available as an 8, 12, 15 and 21-year-old, all at the 40% typical for this firm.

Glen Fruin Scotch single malt with an age statement (10 years) and no stated source. It is one of the brands of the Glasgow company William → Lundie & Co.

Glen Garioch Scottish malt distillery, pronounced 'glen gerrie', means 'valley of the Garioch'. It lies in the village of Oldmeldrum to the north-west of Aberdeen and belongs to the eastern → Highlands. It was founded in 1785 and is one of the oldest distilleries in Scotland. Among its many owners were William → Sanderson and Booth's Distillers, via whom it finally passed to → SMD. In 1970 Stanley P→ Morrison bought the plant which had been closed down two years previously. He is to be thanked for the fact that, despite modernisation and expansion to four → stills and the installation of a pioneering energy-saving heat-recycling system with which a greenhouse is heated, its old character has been preserved. As at Morrison's → Bowmore Distillery, the → floor maltings are still in use. In 1995 Morrison's Suntory closed down Glen Garioch and put it up for sale. Having found no buyer, the Japanese owners invested in it themselves, and in autumn 1997 the distillery started up work again, much to the joy of the lovers of this whisky which, for a Highland, was very intensively peated. Since reopening there has been a less heavy degree of peating.

Single malts in a → proprietor's bottling have been available for a long time in several different age groups (e.g. 8, 10, 12, 15 and 21 years) and strengths, also as a → vintage from 1987. In 1997 → Morrison Bowmore opened their 'Official Distillery Archive' and, along with malts from its → Auchentoshan Distillery, brought out an 18-year-old Glen Garioch from 1978 (59.4%) as a 'selected cask vatting', i.e. a bottling of individually selected casks. The 21-year-old Glen Garioch (43%) is available in a ceramic bottle or in a numbered wooden box.

Glen Garry

The 29-year-old from 1968 (55.8%) and the 27-year-old malt from 1970 (48.8%) were single cask bottlings. The 200th anniversary of the foundation was remembered rather late when in 1998 a 37-year-old 200th Anniversary Edition was brought out with, appropriate to the occasion, 200 bottles.

Glen Garry Scotch blend that was first brought out by John → Hopkins in 1878, and which has survived the sale of its creator to → DCL and its takeover by → Guinness in 1987. Unlike the → Old Mull, which had to be sold to → Whyte & Mackay, this → standard blend is still produced by → GuinnessUDV, but is only on sale in Spain. There is also a → Glengarry, which is produced by → Glen Catrine Bonded Warehouse Ltd.

Glen Ghoil Scotch blend from → Hall & Bramley who were first established in Liverpool in 1860. Philip Morrice, in his *The Schweppes Guide to Scotch*, notes the analysis of the blend by the civic chemist Granville H Sharpe in 1890. He attests that it has 'great purity of composition and excellent qualities. It is particularly free from Amylic Alcohol or Fusel Oil ... and I consider it to be a throughly matured Whisky possessing important dietic properties, and well suited for ordinary and regular use.'

Glen Gordon Scotch single malt from Gordon Whisky, a subsidiary of → Gordon & MacPhail in Elgin. It is named after one of the two founders of the company. It is fuller and rounder than → Glen Avon and also comes from a → Speyside Distillery which, however, is not named on the label. It is mostly available as a 15-year-old and a 25-year-old (40%), and occasionally as a → vintage; the 1947 and the 1958 versions have most probably been drunk up by now.

Glen Grant Scottish malt distillery which lies in the whisky town of Rothes and belongs to the → Speyside whisky region. It produces one of the best-known and single malts, of which there are a large number of bottlings. There is a 5-year-old → proprietor's bottling that is the best-selling whisky in Italy, a 10-year-old and a (very young, probably only 3-year-old) malt with no age statement, which is marketed (particularly in Germany) with the help of a considerable advertising campaign. Glen Grant assumes second position worldwide behind → Glenfiddich. Its success is due to the fact that its owners launched it onto the market at a time when few other single malts were available.

The distillery was founded in 1840 by the brothers John and James Grant, who had previously owned a distillery at nearby Aberlour. The family firm, which built a second distillery (→ Caperdonich) opposite Glen Grant in 1898, remained independent until 1953 when they merged with → George and J G → Smith to form The Glenlivet & Glen Grant Distilleries. In 1972 → Longmorn became a further partner (and added another first class distillery). → Seagram, who had had interests in Scotland since acquiring → Chivas Brothers in 1949, could be sure that they had obtained a real jewel in 1977, when together with Glen Grant they also acquired the distilleries → The Glenlivet, Caperdonich, Longmorn and → Benriach. They were all joined under the umbrella of the Seagram subsidiary The → Chivas & Glenlivet Group, which opened the distillery to visitors at an early date. Its gardens are a special attraction where one can also admire the dram-safe, from which the two Grant brothers used to serve their guests and in which there is still a bottle and several glasses for guests of honour. Today Glen Grant is operated by the Diageo/Groupe Pernod-Ricard partnership which acquired Seagram's spirits interests in 2000.

Glen Grant produces on a large scale with 10 → stills, also supplying its parent company which has a high demand for its many → blends. Apart from its own bottlings, which traditionally nearly always come from bourbon barrels and are therefore very pale, there are also numerous bottlings of Glen Grant from → Gordon & MacPhail, which are often darker and represent a variety of age groups and strengths. The oldest of these date from the pre-war period, one is from 1936. They all bear the same Victorian label as the original bottlings, which is very unusual. The sensation among the many other → independent bottlings was a 1949 Glen Grant which Ian → MacLeod had found in its warehouse, which resulted in just 80 bottles.

Glen Gyle Scotch vatted malt whose youngest whiskies are 8 years old and which claims to be composed exclusively of → Highland malts. Previously with → Gibson International, it now belongs to → Glen Catrine Bonded Warehouse Ltd.

Glen Hamilton Scottish whiskies from → Inverarity Vaults. There is an 8-year-old malt (40%) from one of the most reputed distilleries in the Highlands, near the Spey river' which is aged in Bourbon barrels. The blend is available with two different labels, both of which inform us that it is 6 years old and consists of 67% grain and 33% malt.

Glen Hill Scotch vatted malt without an age statement which gives its place of origin as the → Highlands.

Glen Keith Scottish malt distillery. It is in the → Speyside region and lies in Keith, on the banks of the small river Isla, opposite → Strathisla which, via the → Chivas & Glenlivet Group, also belonged to the Canadian company → Seagram before the acquisition of its spirits interests in 2000 by a Diageo/Groupe Pernod-Ricard partnership. It was built in 1957 on the site of a former corn mill and was the first Scottish distillery to have been created since the turn of the century. Seagram also built huge → warehouses close to Glen Keith, in which the malts from its nine distilleries were stored and prepared for blending with grain. The distillery was closed until further notice in the autumn of 2000. The whisky had only been available as a single malt from → independent bottlers such as Gordon & MacPhail, until 1994 when Seagram made it available as a → proprietor's bottling within the scope of its → 'Heritage Selection'. It is without an age statement but carries the information that it was 'distilled before 1983'. It has now been replaced by a 10-year-old.

Glen Kella Distillery on the Isle of Man which produces a white spirit that is known as 'The → Manx Whiskey'. The → Scotch Whisky Association took the firm to court because they objected to the clear colour, and the process used to produces Glen Kella. The Scottish side won the case in 1997, and the court forbade the company belonging to Andrew Dixon from using the term 'whisk(e)y' for its product. Dixon initially declared the company bankrupt, although its existence has now been secured, as the bottles no longer bear the words Manx Whiskey or Glen Kella, but Manx Spirit. Dixon's problem was that his methods were explicitly sanctioned by the Tynewald, the island parliament, but the external policies of this body are represented by the UK.

The 8 and 12-year-old 'Natural White Whiskey' was a vatted malt. Now and then it is still possible to find stocks in the shops, including examples of the 5-year-old blend with the red seal. The new versions are called Manx red – distilled from Scotch Whisky and Manx blue – distilled from finest 12 years old malt whisky.

Glen Kindie Scotch blend from the → Montrose Whisky Company, founded in London in 1973. It is a → standard blend.

Glen Lyon Scotch blend that used to came from the Glen Lyon Blending Co. It was a subsidiary of MacLeay Duff, who had belonged to → DCL since 1933, and which on their behalf ran the → Millburn Distillery. After the takeover by → Guinness, DCL became UD and the owners of the brand, but they only continued to sell it in South Africa, selling a part of the rights to → Invergordon. Glen Lyon was a vatted malt and is now a blend.

Glen Martin Scotch blend. A small brand for export from → Glenmorangie plc.

Glen Mavis Scotch blend from → Inver House Distillers Ltd, a → standard blend without an age statement.

Glen Mhor Scottish malt distillery that used to lie on the old Great North Road opposite → Glen Albyn on the western outskirts of → Inverness, and belonged to the northern → Highland region. Glen Mhor, pronounced 'glen vor', is the → Gaelic term for the Great Glen where the Caledonian Canal joins the North Sea, via the River and Loch Ness and many other lochs, to the Atlantic. It was built by John Birnie (in 1892), who was also the manager of → Glen Albyn, which he and his partner John Mackinlay and their sleeping partner John →

Glen Moray

Walker later bought. In 1972 → DCL took charge and in 1983, along with many other distilleries, they closed it in order to reduce excess stocks.

It was only available as a single malt in a → proprietor's bottling for the Italian market before UDV included Glen Mhor (1979, 22-years-old, 61%) as part of the 'Rare Malt Selection'. There was also an 8-year-old at 40% or 57%, as well as a 12 and 15-year-old from → Gordon & MacPhail bearing the name of the licence holders, Mackinlay & Birnie; it is also sometimes included in their 'Connoisseurs Choice' series. The → Speyside Distillery Co brought out several casks from 1969 and 1970 under the name of → Campbell & Clark who they had taken over. → Signatory had a 1977 Glen Mhor (59.3%) in their → 'Silent Stills' series.

Glen Moray Scottish malt distillery. Its name comes from the Gaelic from 'valley of the settlement by the loch'. It lies on the western edge of Elgin, on the banks of the Lossie, and so just counts as a → Speyside. Like its 'sister' → Glenmorangie, it originated from the rebuilding of an old brewery. That was in 1897, shortly before the famous → 'Whisky Crash', which it survived without having to close. It was, however, silent from 1910 until 1923 when it was bought by → Macdonald & Muir who now trade as Glenmorangie plc. Nowadays it has four → stills. A visitor centre was opened in 1999.

It has been available as a single malt in a proprietors bottling since the late 1970s: as a 12, 15, 16 and 17 year old, and occasionally as a → vintage (e.g. 1962, 1963, 1964, 1966, 1967, 1971). They were all surpassed by the 1959 vintage, the oldest up to now from the company: in 1999 a total of 400 bottles were on sale for £600 each. The label is not only decorated with Elgin's motto, '*sic itur ad astra*' from Virgil's *Aeneid*, but also with the information that the fertile barley-growing area of the 'Laich of Moray' has 'forty days more summer than any other part of Scotland'.

For the 100th anniversary of the distillery there was not only a new edition of the tin box for the 12-year-old decorated with pictures of Highland regiments, but also a limited Centenary Edition, for which a cask each from 1976, 1977, 1978 and 1979 was chosen, which first matured for seven years in old bourbon barrels before being finished in port pipes. In March 1999 Glenmorangie plc, who set the trend for → finishings and are always willing to experiment with new → cask types, pulled off a surprise with three 'expressions' of Glen Moray that had been finished in French white wine casks. Whilst the youngest, presented without an age statement, had been finished in ex-Chardonnay casks, the 12 and 16 year old were finished in casks that had contained Chenin Blanc. There was a Manager's Choice 1981, 57.7%, 763 bottles, 57%.

Glen Morven Scotch malt whiskies whose bottler is named on the label as → Douglas McNiven, a subsidiary of → Glenmorangie plc. The series, in litre bottles, is mainly available at airports and in shops on ferries, where it offers a reasonably priced alternative to the brand-name whiskies. There is a 16-year-old → Speyside and a 14-year-old → Highland, both single malts, while a 12-year-old → Islay is a 'pure', i.e. a vatted malt.

Glen Mouse German single malt from Robert → Fleischmann. It has been matured in new oak casks whose character is clearly reflected in the whisky. Cask No. 2 is from 1988 and was bottled partly in 1997 and partly in 1998 – in three different sizes of bottle (all 40%).

Glen Nevis Scotch vatted malt that has nothing to do with the → Ben Nevis Distillery, although their malt whiskies may very well be included in it. The name comes from an old distillery on Kintyre. It is 12 years old and comes from → Glen Catrine Bonded Warehouse Ltd.

Glen Nicol 5-year-old Scotch vatted malt from Carmichael & Sons in Airdrie, a subsidiary of the successful → Inver House Distillers Ltd, who have had considerable attention in recent years with the purchase of distilleries such as Balblair and Pulteney. They now own five malt distilleries and therefore have a good range of whiskies for the production of vatted malts.

Glen Niven Scotch blend that now comes from

→ Glenmorangie plc but which used to be a brand from Douglas McNiven & Co. This company was taken over by → Macdonald & Muir and belonged to the → Macdonald Martin Distilleries holding, who in 1996 named themselves after their best-known product.

Glen Ogopolo Canadian → malt whisky (this fact alone makes it an absolute rarity). It is produced by Hiram → Walker's Okanagan Distillery and is only sold in Japan. It gets its name from the Ogopolo (a Canadian cousin the Loch Ness Monster) which wreaks havoc in Okanagan Lake.

Glen Ord Scottish malt distillery. Its name comes from the Gaelic for 'valley of the rounded hill'. It has also been known as → Ord and Glenordie. It lies to the south-west of the Black Isle and belongs to the northern → Highland region. It is in an area with a lot of water and lies in the middle of extensive fields of barley. Since 1838 it has operated under changing ownership, before being bought in 1923 by John → Dewar & Sons, who merged with → DCL the following year. They expanded it to six → stills, built a → Saladin plant and in 1968, the vast Glen Ord Maltings, which supply many distilleries with malt.

The distillery licencesee Peter Dawson Ltd brought out an → Ord as a single malt, but this was discontinued when DCL transferred the licence to Dewar's. It was followed by a 12-year-old → Glenordie, which named Dewar as proprietor. → UD, who took over DCL in 1987, called their 12-year-old → proprietor's bottling → Glen Ord. This was continued after the merger of UD with IDV to form UDV, although there have been rumours that the distillery and the brand are up for sale, which hasn't stopped the owners including a Glen Ord from 1974, bottled aged 23 years at 60.8%, in their 'Rare Malts Selection'.

Glen Osprey Scotch blend. It is one of those that didn't end up with → Whyte & Mackay as a result of mergers or takeovers, but has always been the second brand of the company which was swallowed up in 1990 and renamed → JBB (Greater Europe) plc in 1997 by its parent company → American Brands.

Glen Parker Scotch malt whisky, mostly sold in 1 litre bottles, mainly at airport shops. The company James Parker of Glasgow, which also has a reasonably-priced blend called → Parker's, is named as bottlers but the brand belongs to the portfolio of → Angus Dundee.

Glen Rosa Scotch blend without an age statement. It comes from the → Isle of Arran Distillers who used it and other brands to tide them over until they were able to use the whisky from their own distillery on the island to bring out a mature single malt. The Arran Malt – a ' single Island Malt Scotch Whisky'.

Glen Rowan Scotch blend from → Burn Stewart. It is 3 years old, the minimum age for a Scotch whisky: that being the legally required length of time that grain distillates must mature in a cask in Scotland.

Glen Scotia Scotch malt distillery. Its name means 'valley of Scotland'. It lies in the centre of → Campbeltown and thus belongs to the whisky region of the same name. The Kintyre peninsula, situated between the mainland and the Island of Islay, has with everything a distillery needs; there has even been coal for heating from the local Drumleble mine. The location made the export of whiskies to the USA easier. Kintyre used to have a lot of distilleries; there are said to have been more than 30, 20 of them in Campbeltown alone. Of these only → Springbank and Glen Scotia remain. The plant distills sporadically. It has been shut from 1928 to 1933 and then later from 1984 to 1990. Glen Scotia, was for a short time owned by Hiram → Walker and was sold by them to A Gillies in 1955, was bought by its managers, who already owned → Littlemill. But the new company, → Gibson International, went bankrupt in 1994. → Glen Catrine Bonded Warehouse Ltd bought the stocks of whisky and the distillery but did not put the two → stills back into production. Occcasional periods of distillation have, however, subsequently taken place using staff from Springbank distillery.

The single malt was sold as a → proprietor's bottling from Gibson aged 8 and then 12 years under the name of the licence holder, A Gillies, and is now on offer from the new owners as a

14-year-old (chiefly in Germany and North America). Its fresh and slight salty taste, which harmonises with the honey sweetness, is much appreciated. At the end of 1997 there was a small bottling (350) of a malt from 1973 aged 23 years. Three years later this was followed by a 26-year-old Glen Scotia from 1973. There were only 600 bottles and, unfortunately, the strength was only 40%. The malt whisky also plays an important part in the blends and especially the vatted malts of Glen Catrine. A whisky which Signatory sells without an age statement, the Vintage Campbeltown Malt, is also a Glen Scotia.

Glen Sloy Scotch vatted malt formerly from Longman Distillers, a subsidiary of → Invergordon, who were a subsidiary of → Whyte & Mackay / → JBB (Greater Europe) plc since 1994, until the → Kyndal buyout in 2001.

Glen Spey Scottish malt distillery situated in the 'whisky village' of Rothes and belongs to the → Speyside region. Of the five distilleries in Rothes it is probably the least known, especially as its malt has almost never been available in a → proprietor's bottling. It was established by James Stuart in 1878, and from 1887 was owned by the large firm of Gilbey's, and belonged via → IDV, to → Grand Metropolitan, who had it renovated and enlarged to four → stills in 1970. It is now owned by UDV, who indicate at the gate which famous blend is connected with Glen Spey: → J & B.

The previous owners sold an 8-year-old single malt as a kind of house brand via their off-licence chains Unwins and Peter Dominic. With the latter the distillery bottling of Glen Spey has also disappeared from the market and has become one of the most sought-after malts. It plays an important part in the company's J & B, and is sometimes obtainable from → independent bottlers, such as → MacArthur, who had a 21-year-old (55.4%), and from the → Scotch Malt Whisky Society. In 2001 a 12-year-old from the 'Flora & Fauna' series appeared on the market. There is also a blend called Glen Spey which, apart from the malts from Rothes, probably contains some from → Strathmill and the other IDV distilleries.

Glen Stuart Scotch blend from the Glasgow-based W → Brown & Sons. There are several versions, including a 5 or 8-year-old blend and three vatted malts aged 5, 8 and 12 years.

Glen Torran Scotch single malt without a statement of origin, from → London & Scottish Spirits. There are three versions: 3, 5 and 8 years old.

Glen Turner Scotch vatted malt with no information about its producer whatsoever. It is an 8-year-old which is mainly on sale in Italy, and is sometimes also available in Germany.

Glen Urquhart Scotch blend from → Gordon & MacPhail, where the first Urquhart, John, served his apprenticeship: in 1915 he took over the company which is still run by members of the family. It is a → standard (40%) blend.

Glen Vegan Scotch vatted malt produced by → Glenmorangie plc exclusively for sale in the French supermarket chain → Casino.

Glenallachie Scottish malt distillery quite near to its sister → Aberlour, belonging to the → Speyside whisky region. Together with → Isle of Jura and → Tullibardine, it belongs to the group of three new distilleries which W Delmé Evans built for Mackinlay McPherson, which at that time was a subsidiary of → Scottish & Newcastle Breweries. It began operating in 1968. In 1985 it changed ownership and was taken over by → Invergordon. Four years later it was resold to → Campbell Distillers who belonged to the French → Groupe Pernod-Ricard for whom they were already running Aberlour and → Edradour, thus almost doubling their capacity. It has four → stills. There was a 12-year-old → single malt in a distillery bottling from the previous owner → Invergordon, but this has become difficult to find. The present owners unfortunately use the entire production for their blends → Clan Campbell, → House of Lords and → White Heather.

Glenalmond Scotch vatted malt. It is made from whiskies from distilleries in the → Highlands which were distilled in different years (1986 and 1989) and bottled at 40% at 8 years of age. It comes from the → independent bottler → Vintage Malt Whisky Company in Glasgow.

Glenanrach Scotch single malt that is mainly sold in Spain and France. The producer of the 10-year-old whisky is R Carmichael & Sons of Airdrie which belongs to → Inver House Distillers Ltd.

Glenandrew Scotch single malt available in three versions as a 10, 15 and 20-year-old. They all come from the → Highlands, but its bottlers, the → Vintage Malt Whisky Company, do not disclose their exact source.

Glenbeg Scotch single malt without any information concerning its age or origin. The brand has only existed since 1996 and is marketed by → MacDuff International. The company's brands include, among others, a blend named → Strathbeag.

Glenburgie Scottish malt distillery. Its name comes from the Gaelic from 'valley of the Burgie' or 'the valley with the fortress'. It is situated at Alves, between Forres and Elgin, and is difficult to categorise: its full name is Glenburgie-Glenlivet, although of all the 'Glenlivet' distilleries, it is the furthest from Glenlivet and is more a → Highland than a → Speyside. It is said to have been founded in 1810, and was founded on present site in 1829. In 1829 it was called Kilnflat, the name which it bore until 1871. Ownership changed hands frequently and it was shut down between 1927 and 1935. The new owners, Hiram → Walker, entrusted its management to J & G → Stodart, who later also held the licence to Pulteney and are mainly known for their blend → Old Smuggler. Nowadays Glenburgie belongs to the → Allied Domecq PLC group. Like several other Allied distilleries it was able to produce two malt whiskies: in 1958 its two → stills were supplemented by two → Lomond stills. They produce a completely different malt whisky that for the sake of consistency bears its own name (→ Glencraig). Glenburgie has traditionally been a major component of the Ballantine's blends.

For some time there was a 5-year-old single malt in a → distillery bottling. Like other companies Allied is also trying to reduce its excess stocks (or 'dry out the → whisky loch'), and brings out new bottlings in limited quantities at high prices: an 18-year-old Glenburgie brought out in 1996 was mainly intended for duty-free outlets. A 15-year-old was included in the small series of six bottlings which Allied marketed with a uniform label in 2000; it was really only intended for company workers, but a small number made their way onto the market. → Gordon & MacPhail have various vintages of Glenburgie in their → 'Connoisseurs Choice' series as well as an 8-year-old in their → Allied series. In 1998 Signatory brought out a wooden box containing one from 1962 (50.8%) in a costly decanter with a sample miniature.

Glencadam Scottish malt distillery. Its name means 'valley of the wild goose'. It lies near the River Esk on the outskirts of Brechin and belongs to the eastern → Highland region. It is said to have been founded in 1825, and was closed in September 2000 by its owners → Allied Domecq PLC. From 1954 it belonged to Hiram → Walker, who had the name of the blending firm Stewart & Sons of Dundee, which they had also acquired, written on its grey walls. It is mainly known for its blend → Stewart's Cream of the Barley. Like Walker, Stewart and therefore the blend and the distillery are part of Allied Domecq PLC. Up to now the whisky from Glencadam has only once been available as a single malt in a → distillery bottling, as a limited edition in a decanter. A 15-year-old was then included in the small series of six bottlings which Allied brought out with a uniform label in 2000; it was really only intended for company workers, but a small number made their way onto the market. The → independent bottlers Gordon & MacPhail include it quite regularly in their → 'Connoisseurs Choice' series.

Glencoe Scotch vatted malt which bears the name of a place which in infamous in Scottish history. On 6 February 1692, in the spectacular landscape of Glencoe to the south-east of Fort William, the terrible massacre took place that remains unforgotten to this day.

The 8-year-old whisky (57%) was marketed by the successors of the branch of MacDonalds from which the famous → Long John also originates. Nowadays, following a merger, it no longer comes from R N MacDonald or from → Red Lion Blending, which also owned it for a few years, but from the → Ben Nevis Distillery, whose Japanese owners → Nikka bought the

Glencraig Scotch single malt. It was produced with → Lomond stills at the Glenburgie Distillery. These were installed in 1958 but were dismantled in 1980. The whisky from these specially formed stills is often described as being heavier, with more body than that from Glenburgie's → pot stills; it is actually more fruity and honey-sweet. In order to distinguish it from the malt whisky that had previously been made with the standard → stills at Glenburgie, it was named after Willie Craig, who at the time was the production manager of Hiram → Walker/→ Allied Distillers Ltd in northern Scotland. As far as it is known there has not yet been a single malt in a → proprietor's bottling. It has been occasionally available from → independent bottlers, especially → Gordon & MacPhail. A Glencraig, distilled in 1970, was included in the → 'Connoisseurs Choice' series. Stocks are small and the malt whiskies from Glenburgie's Lomond stills is becoming a sought-after rarity.

Glendarroch Scotch malt distillery on the Crinan Canal in Ardrishaig. Because of its position on Loch Fyne, in 1831 it was established as Glenfyne, but was later rechristened Glendarroch. It ceased distilling in 1937, after which its → warehouses continued to be used for a while. Glendarroch belonged to the Western → Highland region and was one of more than 20 distilleries in Argyll, of which nowadays only → Oban, Glen Scotia and Springbank remain. Until 1883 it was owned by William Gillies. A year later they bought Glenfyne but resold it again just three years later. There was a 10-year-old and now 12-year-old blend named Glendarroch, from William Gillies & Co in Glasgow (which should not be confused with A Gillies from → Glen Scotia). Richard Joynson and his wife Lyndsay have chosen a picture of Glendarroch for the label of their house brand, The → Loch Fyne.

Glendonnan Scotch blend formerly from → Whyte & Mackay, one of the older brands of the company that was bought by → American Brands in 1990 and later renamed → JBB (Greater Europe) plc. There is a → standard blend as well as an 8-year-old vatted malt.

Glendower, The Scotch vatted malt from John McLaren & Sons in Manchester.

Glendronach Scottish malt distillery. Its name, emphasised on the penultimate syllable, comes from the Gaelic for 'valley of the bramble bushes'. It is situated near Forgue, between Banff and Huntly to the east of the A97, and belongs to the eastern → Highland region. It was built in 1826 and from 1920 to 1960 belonged to the family of a son of William → Grant from → Glenfiddich. It was then acquired by Wm → Teacher & Sons, who at the time were the largest independent family-owned Scottish whisky company, and also owned the nearby → Ardmore Distillery. Whilst that is a modern (and large) plant, Glendronach is very traditional and still does everything itself (except bottling): the majority of the barley comes from the neighbouring arable fields of the fertile Forgue Valley and is processed in the distillery's own → floor maltings, the → wash backs are still made of wood and the four → stills continue to be partly fired with coal, whilst there are earth floors in the → warehouses. In the yard there is still an old delivery wagon which carries the slogan that made Glendronach known (and which unfortunately no longer appears on the label): 'most suitable for medicinal purposes'. Since 1976, the distillery and Wm Teacher, have belonged to → Allied Distillers Ltd, whose parent company, → Allied Domecq PLC, ordered its closure in 1996, but reopened it in the Spring of 2002.

Glendronach has been available as a single malt in a → distillery bottling for a relatively long time, but its 'recipe' has changed in the course of time: the 8-year-old was immediately followed by two 12-year-olds from → sherry casks and as an Original from → bourbon casks. They were replaced by the 12-year-old Traditional that still displayed a definite sherry tone. Along with this there was an 18-year-old from 1976, which was originally a pure sherry-cask malt, but was then just a 'marriage' of sherry and bourbon casks. When the confusion became too great, Allied Distillers Ltd decided to continue to bottle just a 15-year-old that had been exclusively matured in sherry casks. From time to time there are also several bottles with a 25-year-old malt from 1968 which was bottled in

1993 and orginally only intended for sale at the distillery. On the other hand the 'Millennium Malt', bottled in 1999 (48%) from one cask (no. 72), was only available to the 'Incorporation of the Maltmen'. The → independent bottlers, especially Cadenhead, are again making Glendronach available.

Glendrostan Scotch blend from Longman Distillers, a subsidiary of → Invergordon. It is available as a → standard blend without an age statement, as an 8-year-old and as a 12-year-old.

Glendullan Scottish malt distillery named after Dullan Water, which flows into the River Fiddich nearby. It lies in → Dufftown Glendullan was built in 1897 and a second distillery with six stills was built on the same site in 1972. The old plant was soon taken over by → Macdonald Greenlees who shortly afterwards were absorbed by → DCL, but were able to continue operating under the same name. Until 1985 the two distilleries operated as Glendullan A and B, and then the old distillery was closed down. The new building continues to operate whilst the pretty old distillery serves as a workshop for its owners UDV, in which repairs for all the distilleries in the district are carried out.

There was already a → distillery bottling of a single malt from → Macdonald Greenlees. UD then included it as a 12-year-old in their → 'Flora & Fauna' series. There are also several versions in the → 'Rare Malts' series, for example one from 1972 (62.2%), one from 1974 (61.1%) and another from the same year (63.1%). The 8-year-old is produced for France and is also available in a wooden container. The 100th anniversary of the distillery was celebrated in 1998 by a 16-year-old at an impressive 65.9%. → Betty Boothroyd, the former Speaker of the House of Commons, had the honour of having a Glendullan named after her. The independent bottlers also sometimes have it in their range.

Gleneagles Golf Scotch single malt from a company which give its address as Auchterarder, the home of the famous Gleneagles Hotel and its equally famous golf course. Pictures of the hotel and one of the courses decorate the label. As well as the bottle, the box also contains replicas of old golf balls. THe whisky is mainly sold at duty-free shops at UK airports.

Glenesk Scottish malt distillery. It lies a short distance from the River North Esk, to the west of Montrose and belongs to the eastern → Highland region. The → Glenesk Maltings are situated on the same site. It was converted from a flax mill and converted to a distillery, Highland Esk in 1897. Two years later it was rechristened North Esk. It was closed during World War I and first began producing again in 1938 under the ownership of a subsidiary of the National Distillers of America – as a grain distillery with the name Montrose. Via → DCL it passed to → SMD which again made a malt distillery of it, named → Hillside, which Wm → Sanderson & Son ran for them. This company, known mainly for its → VAT 69, closed the distillery in 1985 but launched its whisky on the market as a 12-year-old single malt in a → distillery bottling (available in Italy as a 5-year-old). → UD, which since 1987 has owned → DCL and therefore also Glenesk, unfortunately discontinued this bottling and finally shut down the distillery and sold the entire plant to Paul's Malting. Nevertheless they included a 1969 Hillside in their → 'Rare Malts' series with a cask strength of 61.9%. It was followed by further bottlings. The independents also sometimes have bottlings of it but use the name Glenesk. The licence was cancelled in 1992.

Glenesk Maltings Until it was sold to Paul's Malting, Glenesk was one of the four large maltings that → UD/UDV operated in Scotland – the others are → Port Ellen, Muir of → Ord, Burghead and Roseisle. It lies to the west of Montrose and bears the name of a malt distillery which has now been closed down, and which during the last years of its existence was known as → Glenesk, named after the nearby River North Esk. The capacity of the maltings is so large, that it not only served UD's own distilleries in the area, but other distilleries as well. In May 1993 the then owner celebrated the 25th anniversary of the maltings with a Glenesk, 1969 at 60%

Glenfairn Scotch vatted malt. It is one of → Invergordon's numerous brands.

Glenfarclas

Glenfarclas Scottish malt distillery. Its name means 'valley of the green grassland'. It lies in the heart of → Speyside near Ballindalloch Castle, close to the A95. It has a great name: its whisky belongs to the top category, the most sought-after by every blender. It is also one of the first to have been consistently available as a single malt, and, unusually, in various age categories and even as a → high proof. Glenfarclas also opened one of the first visitor centres in Scotland. The value of a policy of frankness and open-mindednes was recognised early on.

The fact that J & G → Grant took this path, and were able to do so, was a result of their independence. Like → Glenfiddich and → Springbank, Glenfarclas belongs to the very small group of distilleries that are independent and have for generations been in family ownership, and therefore totally in Scottish hands. In 1865 John Grant acquired the distillery built in 1844 by Robert Hay, but not originally with the intention of running it himself. He leased it to John Smith, who five years later gave in his notice in order to build → Cragganmore.

Since that time John Grant, his son George and their succesors, have managed the distillery. There was only one break, when in order to raise money for renovation, → Pattison was part-owner. The Grants survived the infamous bankruptcy of Pattison, Elder & Co which affected the whole of the Scottish whisky industry. In 1960 the number of → stills was increased to four, and in 1976 to six. Admission for visitors and the construction of a visitor centre, followed in 1973.

The company has had a single malt in a → proprietor's bottling for many years, the earlier age categories (15,17, 21, 25 and 30 years) used to be in square bottles and are now in round ones which are smaller and squatter than the normal whisky bottles, which are used for the the 10-year-old and 12-year-old and 8-year-old Glenfarclas 105 at → cask strength. The 15-year-old has a strength of 46% and the others just 43%. The preference of the Italians for younger malts is satisfied by a 6-year-old named John Grant's. The 'Heritage', which is without an age statement and has a strength of only 40%, is officially only on sale in France. From time to time there are → vintages, often expressly made for certain shops, but they appear in such small quantities and at such a frequency that it makes it difficult to maintain an overview. They are also often specially bottled for Germany. The 40-year-old Glenfarclas which was brought out for the Millennium was on general sale; It was a series of 30 different bottles, based around the selevted works of Robert Burns, Robert Louis Stevenson and Walter Scott. Three Scottish artists designed the labels.

The German importer, the Hanseatische Weinhandelsgesellschaft in Bremen, tries to encourage sales by offering special editions. There is therefore a series named after famous Scots, such as Bonnie Prince Charlie, Robert Burns, David Livingstone, Conan Doyle, Mary Stuart and James Watt. Every now and then a Family Reserve is also available, but there were 'limited stocks', for bottlings from 1954, 1968 and 1974. Another Glenfarclas from 1988 was called 'Limited Premium Edition'; this was an Oloroso Sherry Cask First Filling. Two casks from 1968 were presented in stoneware jars. The Grants of Glenfarclas also follow an unconventional course with regard to their bottlings. These do not bear the distillery name but rather in the style of blends they are called: → Eagle of Spey, → Highland Cattle or → Meadhan. They are all bottled in Broxburn near Edinburgh, where the Grants of Glenfarclas operate a plant together with J → Russell & Co.

Glenfern Scotch blend and one of the smaller brands from the huge range of → UDV.

Glenfiddich Scottish malt distillery. It lies in the whisky town of → Dufftown and belongs to the → Speyside region. Glenfiddich is the first malt that most get to know, and for many it is still the very essence of malt whisky. The owners of this distillery, founded in 1886/7 by William → Grant, were the first who to sell a malt whisky on the Scottish market, as well as 'exporting' it to England, and then to the rest of the world. Since that time the Glenfiddich Pure Single Malt has occupied the 'number one' position with a market share of about 20% in the UK and 26% on the world market.

Its success is also due to the consistent marketing strategy of William → Grant & Sons, which is today managed by the fifth generation of the founding family, who have been able to maintain their independence. Glenfiddich comes in a green, three-sided bottle which is decorated with a large label. This shows a stag, the 'Monarch of the Glen', which is also the heraldic animal of the Grants. Their marketing strategy included the recognition of the tourist value of the distillery and they built the first visitor centre in a Scottish distillery. Every year it attracts well over 100,000 visitors to Dufftown.

At Glenfiddich and at its sisters→ Balvenie and → Kininvie, its immediate neighbours on the same site, it would be possible to experience the production of malt whisky from the barley to the bottle – if its bottling operation were open to the public. A large proportion of the barley used comes from local fields and even from the immediate vicinity, and a part of the malt is processed in the → floor maltings and the → kiln of Balvenie. The water comes from the famous → Robbie Dubh springs. The fact that the single malt is bottled directly at the distillery is unique for the Highlands; the only other site of production where bottling also takes place is → Springbank. William → Grant bought two secondhand stills from → Cardhu, and now there are 10 → wash stills and 20 → spirit stills. They are unusually small and are coal-fired.

The light and pleasing, intensely malty whisky, which is an excellent introduction for newcomers, is available as a single malt in a → proprietor's bottling, mainly with the description Special Old Reserve in the standard version, which has an age statement (of 12 years), again since 2001. It used to bear the words 'over 8 years' and is probably still this age today. The Classic, also without an age statement, comes in numbered bottles and is from particularly slow maturing oak casks. It is about 12 years old and has now been discontinued, but is still available. The Excellence was 18 years old. They were described as 'pure', a term usually reserved for vatted malts. There have been bottlings in stoneware and china carafes in which malts of various ages have been 'married', as well as an Ancient Reserve and a Superior Reserve, also without ages. In 1965 a 15-year-old cask strength (51%) became available. The 100th anniversary of the distillery was celebrated with 12,000 examples of the Limited Centenary Edition. The Grants also have one of the most expensive malts of all, with their careful and costly presentation of a 50-year-old Glenfiddich; its original price was £3,500 and today it fetches more than £10,000.

In 1998 the family-run company extended their range with a Glenfiddich Malt Liqueur and comprehensively relaunched their malts: the 'normal' Glenfiddich is now just called 'single malt'. Alongside it since the summer of 2000 there is a 12-year-old Special Reserve, the 18-year-old Ancient Reserve and a completely new 15-year-old Solera Reserve. This represented a rather revolutionary innovation from 'chief nose' and Master Blender David Stewart, who with his Balvenie Double Wood started the → finishings trend. He was influenced by the old Scottish → Living Cask tradition that is used for sherry in Spain, based on the fact that the oldest wines are always in the bottom layer of casks and are topped up with younger wines from the casks above. Stewart introduced a well-thought out wood management policy that makes optimum use of the qualities of the casks used for the maturation of malts. All his Glenfiddichs are 15 years old and originate from former sherry or bourbon casks. A further part come from so-called refill casks, in which there was previously bourbon or even malt whisky. They are refilled in completely new, unused American oak casks whose wood has a quick and intensive impact on the malt. The individual casks of all three basis whiskies are separately 'married' before coming together in a large 'Solera' butt, where they are given more time to harmonise. At most only half of it at most is then bottled, the remainder being replaced, thus guaranteeing consistency and continuity.

The range has expanded considerably: initially with the addition of the 21-year-old Millennium Reserve, and then with a 30-year-old and even a Glenfiddich 40 Years, which furthermore includes even older distillates. It is a → marriage whose main ingredient is from 1960, but which also includes malts from 1939 and 1937 and even 1925; a malt from this year (49.2%) is only available at

Glenforres

the distillery itself. There are also numerous Vintages (1961, 1963, 1967, 1968, 1971) at cask strength.

Glenforres Former name of the → Edradour Distillery and also the name of a vatted malt, a good part of which comes from this distillery and is now sold as a 12-year-old. The present owners of the brand are → Campbell Distillers, whose parent company → Groupe Pernod-Ricard took it over together with → Edradour from William Whiteley.

Glenfoyle Scotch blend from Longman Distillers, a company belonging to → Invergordon. The blend bears the description 'Reserve' and is 12 years old.

Glenfyne Scotch vatted malt (40%) from a company named Row and Co in Glasgow, which is mainly sold at the French supermarket chain Intermarché. It is named after → Loch Fyne, which is joined to the Atlantic by the Crinan Canal. A blend from the same company is consequently called → Glen Crinan.

Glengannon 5-year-old Scotch vatted malt from the whisky company of the same name, who give Edinburgh as their base. That could be a hint that this reasonably priced supermarket whisky is made by → Invergordon.

Glengarry Scotch blend which should not be confused with → Glen Garry. Glengarry comes from → Glen Catrine Bonded Warehouse Ltd, who only sell it in Canada.

Glenglassaugh Scottish malt distillery. Its name, pronounced 'glen glasso', comes from the Gaelic for 'valley with the pasture'. It lies between the mouths of the River → Spey and the River Deveron, near the little coastal town of Portsoy, and belongs to the → Highland region. It is a lesser-known distillery and will probably soon be completely forgotten as it has been closed since 1986. In 1992 its licence was cancelled and its malt, only rarely available as a distillery bottling, will soon be used up. It is said to have been coveted by blenders. The distillery, founded in 1875 and taken over in 1892 by → Highland Distillers, is still owned by them. In the course of its history it was more often shut than open and working. The afore-mentioned bottling sometimes gave its age as 12 years, but there were also bottles which had no age on their labels. In 1998 Highland Distillers brought out a new (small) series which up to now has consisted of two bottlings with the name 'The → Family Silver', which greatly pleased lovers of the whisky. This Glenglassaugh was distilled in 1973. The independent bottlers have done more for it than its proprietors. → MacArthur had an 11-year-old, → Gordon & MacPhail included it from time to time in their → 'Connoisseurs Choice' series and had one from 1986 in their 'MacPhail's Collection'. → Signatory had a Glenglassaugh from 1967 (55.8%) in their 'Silent Stills' series.

Glengoyne Scottish malt distillery. Its name comes from the Gaelic for 'valley of the arrow' or perhaps also 'valley of the wound'. It lies a half an hour's drive to the north of Glasgow, outside the village of Killearn, at the foot of the Campsie Fells. It therefore finds itself just beyond the theoretical line which divides the → Highlands from the → Lowlands, and is the southernmost of the → Highland distilleries. It was founded in 1833 as Burnfoot. → Lang Bros, who acquired it in 1876, initially named it Glen Guin, and from 1905 Glengoyne. It is still licensed under the name of the brothers, although the company has been a subsidiary of → Robertson & Baxter for a long time, who in their turn are part of the → Edrington Group and closely associated with → Highland Distillers.

Thanks to its situation and its architecture, Glengoyne is one of the loveliest distilleries in Scotland: the whitewashed buildings are grouped round an inner courtyard that opens up to a small pond and a view of a spectacular waterfall. With just three → stills it is very similar to the old farmhouse distilleries. Because only unpeated malt is used and the water of the Campsie Fells never comes into contact with peat, the single malt is completely smoke-free, slightly sweet, clean, malty and very elegant.

It is available as a 10, 17 and 21-year-old, and there is a 12-year-old for export. The vintages from 1967, 1968, and 1969, each distilled on Christmas Day and bottled at 25 years, came in wooden boxes. In contrast the whisky from 1970, of which there are only 1200 bottles worldwide. It was produced on a 'normal' day, 27th March, whilst the Vintage 1971 was again produced around Christmas: on 27th December. There were 2100 bottles of it. It was followed by one from 1972 (51.7%). The information on two further → cask strength was even more precise: one from the autumn of 1969 (55.3%) and one from the spring of 1975 (55.0%).

There are only 100 examples of the 30-year-old → Middle Cut, which is packed in a solid copper vessel in the shape of a → spirit still. The same heavyweight container is used for the 1969 Single Cask, bottled in 1997 at 48.3%, of which only 50 were supplied to the American importer Disusa. Such marketing ideas come from Highland Distillers, who presented a 30-year-old in a little cupboard with a sliding shutter. The manager who was about to retire also had a special bottling dedicated to him, which was also presented in a safe. For some time a consistent niche-policy has been followed in which limited editions are issued serially: two sets of six Glengoynes from different years, each at cask strength, cost £500 per series. They are also presented in expensive packaging: both standard bottlings of the 10 and 17-year-old are also obtainable in decanters. The Glengoyne 2000 AD, which was brought out for the Millennium, came in quite normal bottles. However they were packed in an old-fashioned clock, which remains fully functional long after the whisky has been drunk. In 2001, 5,000 bottles of a 16-year-old Glengoyne were brought out. The whisky had been aged in a cask of Scottish oak; a rare occurence, as only 15 of these trees may be felled each year.

Glengyle Scottish malt distillery which, according to Michael Moss, was founded in Campbeltown in 1873 (other sources quote 1882), by William Mitchell and his brother, the family still own the → Springbank distillery. The present owner of Glengyle, Hedley Wright, acquired what was left of it at the end of 2000 and the beginning of 2001. He plans to rebuild the plant, which has been closed since 1925, and put it back into operation again in 2003.

Glenhaven Scottish company owned by William Y Thomson, based at Callander in the Trossachs, but operating from Glasgow. It deals with rum, cognacs, Scotch blends and single malts. Glenhaven is one of the newcomers among the ever-increasing number of → independent bottlers, and during the short time that they have been operating in this field, have made an excellent name for themselves. They mostly bottle → single casks, maintaining → cask strength, and do so without → colouring or → chill-filtering. On the label the age, month of bottling and usually also the date of distillation are given. The number of bottlings up to now has been quite amazing. They have only been available in the USA where the → *Malt Advocate* magazine has often given them very favourable ratings.

Glenisla Scotch single malt which until 1891 this was the name of the → Strathmill Distillery, which via → J & B and → IDV belonged to → Grand Metropolitan, and following their merger with Guinness now belongs to UDV. The former → Seagram subsidiary Chivas brothers owns nine distilleries, all of which are loctaed on Speyside. In order to be independent of 'foreign' → Islay distilleries, and to be able to obtain their own heavily peated malt, they experimented in the 1970s with recipes that deviated from the normal style by, for example, using more → peat for → malting. The whisky which was produced in that style, → Glen Keith distillery was never bottled as a single malt but was given the name Glenisla. Several casks seemed to have survived the experiments and are used for the → Century, which Chivas launched on the market as a vatted in 1996.

Glenkinchie Scottish malt distillery. It lies to the south-east of Edinburgh near Haddington, at the foot of the Lammermuir Hills that are better known for Walter Scott's and Donizetti's *Lucia* than for the distillery. It belongs to the → Lowland whisky region. The area is known for the quality of its barley. The distillery, which dates back to 1837, had its own large farm for a long time. Continuous production only really began after 1914 when the distillery was bought by → SMD and the business was taken over by John → Haig & Co. Its two stills were, unusually, also in operation during World War II. The old → floor maltings had already been

Glenleven

closed down by the previous owners, but it was → UD who really expanded the museum that had been built there. There is a 10-metre-long working model of a distillery which was built for the 1924 Empire Exhibition. The visitor centre was modernised in 1997 and is now an excellent and entertaining place to learn about whisky, its history, its production and its idiosyncracies, with the help of multimedia technology. The well-cared for bowling green, the only one to be found at a Scottish distillery, is reserved for the use of the distillery workers and the villagers.

→ UD included the whisky in its → 'Classic Malts' series to represent the Lowlands region, which this light, gently smoky and spicey 10-year-old does excellently. At the end of 1997 it was complemented by a limited bottling of a malt from 1986, which had been finished in an Amontillado → sherrry cask, in 'The → Distillers Edition' series. The 'blonde whisky', → Jackson Row, very likely contains Glenkinchie. The → Kincaple from Invergordon is also said to be a Glenkinchie. It is occasionally also available from independent bottlers. Signatory, for example, had a 60.8% cask strength 1996 bottling of a 1978 Glenkinchie.

Glenleven Scotch vatted malt, a very old brand that was introduced by John → Haig & Co. It was unusual that they also stated how many single malts had been used for it: six, all at least 12 years old, and among them very likely whiskies from → Glenlossie and → Glenkinchie. → UD, which later owned the firm, no longer produces it but it can still be found. It is very doubtful whether UDV will relaunch it.

Glenlivet Scottish malt distillery. It lies in the valley of the river after which it is named. It belongs to the → Speyside whisky region. A large number of other distilleries, some of them quite a distance away, used its name to identify with a particular qualitative group of malts. They attempted to profit from Glenlivet's fame by adding the suffix 'Glenlivet' to their names, for example → Longmorn, → Aberlour and even → Glenfarclas and → Macallan. In 1880, in order to make the distinction clear, the Smith family claimed the right to use the definite article and call its product 'The Glenlivet' .

Their fame is not only due to the quality of the product, but is mainly a result of their history. They can prove that their founder, George → Smith, was the first to gain a licence following the 1823 Excise Act, and so become the first to distil malt legally according to present-day standards. Even before this time he was very successful at his trade, having learned from his father who had been active since 1747. It is known that in 1822 King George IV, upon a visit to Edinburgh, insisted on a whisky from the valley of the Livet. A short verse recounts its fame:

'Glenlivet it has castles three,
Drumin, Blairfindy and Deskie,
And also one distillery,
More famous than the castles three.'

George Smith initially distilled in Drumin and then later also in Delnabo, before deciding on his farm at → Minmore in 1858, where Glenlivet still operates, after, of course, having frequently been renovated and extended. There are now eight → stills. Smith and his son proved their far-sightedness and pioneering spirit for a second time in 1870 when they had the name 'Glenlivet' protected as a trademark and claimed the right to the prefix 'The'. The distillery remained in family ownership until 1953 when they joined together with the → Grants from → Glen Grant to form the joint-stock company The Glenlivet & Glen Grant Distilleries, which later merged with → Longmorn and was bought by → Seagram in 1977. Glenlivet became one of a total of nine distilleries which their subsidiary, The → Chivas & Glenlivet Group ran and which are now owned by a Diageo/Ricard Pernod partnership.

Glenlivet single malt has been available for a long time in a → proprietor's bottling, but mostly only as a 12-year-old. There was a 21-year-old in Italy where it was packed in a silk-lined case. It was also available in the USA where it was presented in a wooden box containing a stocky black bottle. The 12,000 bottles were numbered by hand, lay in a bed of suede and cost $650. Apart from such special bottlings, an excellent 18-year-old has been available since 1995. In 1966 The Glenlivet Archive, a whisky composed of specially selected casks, became available; it is also available as a 15- and a 21-year-old. In 1998 the owners of this internationally successful brand finally acted to meet the growing demand: five → Vintages from 1967, 1968, 1969, 1970 and 1972 came onto the market, presented in decorative wooden boxes. However they only contained 0.2 litre bottles. Only the 1969 and the 1972 were available in normal bottles. Glenlivet also followed the → finishings trend and brought out a 12-year-old French Oak Finish and an American Oak Finish of the same age. At the end of 2000 there was a series of vintages bearing the name The Glenlivet Cellar, which was launched with one from 1967 (46%) in a limited edition of 500 → cases. The excellent relationship with the → independent bottlers → Gordon & MacPhail has resulted in a whole series of bottlings. Some of them are very old like the 1943 malt. The malt from Glenlivet is called George & J G Smith's Glenlivet and is 8, 12 or 15 years old, with 40%, 46% or 57%.

Glenlochy Scottish malt distillery. It is possible to visit the former distillery beside the A82 on northern outskirts of Fort William, and it is even possible to stay there. Glenlochy belonged to the western → Highlands whisky region and like so many others was shut down in 1983. In 1991 it was partly converted into holiday flats, with a great view of Ben Nevis. Directly after its foundation in 1898 the distillery was swept along by the whisky crisis caused by the → Pattison brothers' bankruptcy. For several years it was owned by the Canadian Joseph Hobbs who also owned → Ben Nevis, and Associated Scottish Distilleries, a subsidiary of the American company National Distillers, from whom → DCL took it over in 1953.

The whisky first became available in a → proprietor's bottling in 1996, when → UD, who had acquired the stocks upon purchasing → DCL, brought out a → cask strength (62.2%) from 1969 as a limited edition in their → 'Rare Malts Selection' (it was followed by a 26-year-old at 58.8%). There had previously only been → independent bottlings from firms such as → Gordon & MacPhail and from 'The → Select Hogshead'. → Signatory often bottled the malt, also including it in their → 'Silent Stills' series.

Glenlossie Scottish malt distillery. It lies to the south of Elgin near the railway, from which it profited considerably, and belongs to the → Speyside region. It was established in 1876 by John Duff and in 1919 was acquired by → SMD for whom it was run by their subsidiary John → Haig & Co, expanding it to six → stills in 1962. The modern distillery → Mannochmore was built on the same site in 1971. The whisky was always very much in demand with blenders and was only available as a single malt from → independent bottlers. → UD/UDV has been the owner since the takeover of → DCL and its subsidiary in 1987 and a 10-year-old was included in their → 'Flora & Fauna' series. It has also been available from the independent bottlers → Gordon & MacPhail in nearby Elgin, as well as from → Cadenhead and → Signatory with, for example, a Glenlossie from 1981 which has been matured in a sherry cask.

Glenluig Scottish distillery whose exact location is not known. Although it is known to have been run by a McFarlane in Dunbartonshire. → Invergordon revived this old name in autumn 1997 when they brought out a new series, 'The → Malts of Scotland'. Three of the five whiskies in the series bear the names of old distilleries, whilst two have made-up names. The company own → Tullibardine (on the border between the Lowlands and the Highlands) and → Tamnavulin (in the Highlands). Its American parent company → JBB, which bought it in 1993 (and proceeded to close both distilleries), also own → Fettercairn and → Dalmore.

Glenmorangie Scottish malt distillery. Its name, is emphasised on the second syllable and pronounced 'glenmóranjee', meaning 'glen of tranquillity'. It is situated near Tain between the A9 and the Dornoch Firth, from which it is separated by the Inverness-Wick railway line. It belongs to the northern → Highland region. In 1966 the joint-stock company → Macdonald Martin Distilleries, which has owned it via → Macdonald & Muir since 1921, was renamed Glenmorangie plc. The company also own → Glen Moray Distillery and, since the spring of 1997 → Ardbeg Distillery on Islay.

The consistent product philosophy, is carefully linked to the natural factors. The distillery's water comes from the company's own springs in the Tarlogie woods, and contains an unusual amount of minerals and is very hard. There are now eight → stills which are the tallest in Scotland and therefore suited for making a light malt. The location by the sea lends a gentle salty note to the fruity, delicate malt whisky, which is also the result of a consistent cask policy: the 10-year-old and the 18-year-old single malts are exclusively matured in bourbon barrels which the company buys in the USA, first having the bourbon bottled before shipping the barrels to Scotland.

A part of the rigid wood management policy involves experimenting with other types of cask and either maturing the malt completely in an unusual cask or, after its normal period of maturation, finishing it in a second cask – a process which has become something of a fashion, and is now used by many other distilleries. The upshot of these experiments were the highly regarded, sometimes very limited and thus expensive special bottlings of Glenmorangie from port, Madeira and red wine casks. Some came from Tain l'Hermitage in the Rhone Valley but there were also very small quantities of a Glenmorangie Côtes de Nuits and a Glenmorangie Claret finished in a 'Mouton Rothschild' cask which, although this was not expressly stated, could be deduce from the design of the label. There is also a 14-year-old Cognac Wood finishing and A 12-year-old Cote de Beaune.

Full barrels are exchanged with the producers of → Maker's Mark in order to find out how Scottish malt matures in the USA and how bourbon matures in Scotland. As unusual as these activities are, the decision that not a single drop of the production of the 'Sixteen Men of Tain' should be used outside the company itself, is even more so. Different opinions exist as to whether Glenmorangie is entirely used for bottling as a single malt or whether a part of it goes into the company's own blends such as → Highland Queen or → Bailie Nicol Jarvie. It is certainly true that the whisky has never appeared as an → independent bottling.

Glenmorangie has achieved number one position in Scotland, number two in the UK and number five worldwide. Nobody could have prophesied such success for this distillery which was converted from a brewery in 1843, especially not Alfred → Barnard who visited it in 1887 and described it as being 'the oldest and most primitive' of any that he had visited. Shortly afterwards it was renovated and modernised and was the first distillery to be fitted with internal heating. It was expanded several times, and eventually a new still-house was necessary.

Apart from the bottlings already mentioned it is also available at → cask strength, formerly as The Native Ross-shire Glenmorangie, and now as → High Proof. The special bottlings already mentioned which were originally thought to be just interesting experiments, became firmly established in 1996 with a series of finishings, which included malts finished in port, sherry and Madeira casks, whose age was not given. The 1979 vintage was meant exclusively for the supermarket chain → Sainsbury, but then became available generally, like the other vintages (1963, 1971 and 1972).

The lovers of this malt whisky were blessed with a whole series of novelties at the end of 1998 when five new products came onto the market simultaneously: a Special Reserve consisted of 'married' malts that had been distilled between 1980 and 1990. The 1977 Vintage came from oak casks and had matured for 21 years. The Glenmorangie Elegance is exactly the same age and is presented in an elegant mouth-blown decanter made in the Caithness Glass factory in Wick. There was a further finishing, a 15-year-old Fino Sherry which had spent 13 years in American ex-bourbon barrels and was finished in Fino Sherry casks. The Cellar 13 was the first single malt that had come from a single warehouse, namely no. 13.

In 1998 a further highlight was a special bottling chosen by the distillery manager of the time, Dr. Bill Lumsden, which he personally signed. He was the first academically qualified master distiller with a doctorate in Scotland and is now responsible for the production and control of maturation in all three of the company's distilleries. This was followed by a second cask with a new Distillery Manager's Choice (1st July 1983/4th May 2000) whose 300 bottles were signed by Bill's successor Graham Eunson and of a 1987 Port Pipe Finished. The new

Millennium was greeted with a Glenmorangie Millennium Malt, a 12-year-old whisky for which only first-fill casks were used, that is casks in which bourbon had matured and which are used for the first time for malt whisky and with a 24-year-old Millennium, only available in 0.5 litre bottles which were reproductuons of a shape from the 1920s. There was also a new Traditional, which was a → high proof whisky. Alongside these special bottlings the 15-year-old appears quite normal. Meanwhile the Malaga has taken a completely new direction, not only because of the unusual cask, but also because it is only available via the internet.

Glenmore American distillery and whiskey company of which nothing remains but a Kentucky straight bourbon named The Glenmore from → UD whose American subsidiary has, alos at times, been called UD-Glenmore since 1991. In the mid 1870s James Thompson, an Irish immigrant, joined forces with George Garvin Brown. Whilst the latter became one of the founding fathers of → Brown-Forman, Thompson bought the Glenmore Distillery in Louisville, Kentucky in 1910. The company's leading brand was → Kentucky Tavern. In 1944 they also bought → Yellowstone. At this time the company had another distillery in Owensboro and a grain distillery in Albany, Georgia. In 1970 they acquired Mr. Boston, named after the legendary barman and author of the 'Bartender's Guide', along with its range of liqueurs, mixed drinks and spirits

After Glenmore had acquired the locally-situated → Fleischmann and → Medley in the 1980s, they themselves were swallowed up by UD. A few years later the spirits subsidiary → Guinness, who at this point were using the Louisville an Owensboro plants for strorage only, parted with nearly everything that had borne the name Glenmore. Most of the brands and the buildings were sold to → Barton who now produce The Glenmore as well as → Old Thompson, whilst Yellowstone now comes from the David → Sherman Distilling Company of St. Louis and → Medley is exclusively made in → Heaven Hill for the German company Dethleffsen. The tall chimney that had advertised the Glenmore was demolished by Barton in 1995.

Glenmoriston Scotch vatted malt from → Burn Stewart. Although t longer produced, it is still possible to find a few bottles.

Glenmoy, The Scotch vatted malt. It contains 10-year-old malts and comes from Brodie Crawford & Co, who are best-known for the blend → Brodie's Supreme. Its name refers to the famous Whisky Trail on → Speyside which leads to the castles, gardens and, of course, distilleries around the river.

Glenochil Defunct Scottish grain distillery situated in Menstrie, Clackmannanshire. Reputed to have been established in 1746, it was converted from malt to grain distilling around a hundred years later. In 1877 it was one of the six grain distilleries which helped to create the production portfolio of the newly-formed → DCL. Distilling ceased in 1929 and the site was used as a yeast production factory and research facility for DCL until it was closed.

Glenora Canadian distillery that was founded in 1990 which has already had a troubled history. It has been closed twice. Although it is located in Canada it looks every part like a Scottish distillery.

It gets its water from the Scottish-sounding MacLellan's Brook, and has → pagodas like its Scottish 'sisters'. It was designed by a Scottish architect and equipped with a Scottish → mash tun and → pot stills from Forsyth of Rothes. The workers were trained by → Morrison Bowmore. The first whisky flowed in September 1990. In December of that year it was shut down, reopened in 1991 and closed again in 1993. Since 1995 it has been owned by Lauchie MacLean and seems to be out of danger.

The old whisky, has been redistilled and better casks are now being used. The future is said to be assured so that it will be able to give the world something that has not yet existed: Nova Scotia single malt, a real single malt from Canada. Although there are still stocks from 1990, there will nevertheless be some time to wait. For the time being the company is trying to establish its name with a rum, and with a spirit that looks like an illicit distillate called → Cape Breton Silver. → IDV has brought out → Breton's Hand and Seal a

Glenordie

blend of their own whisky from → Palliser and Glenora whisky. On the label the company calls itself 'The Glenora Distillers of the Cape Breton Highlands' and proudly claim to be the only malt distillery in the whole of North America.

Glenordie Scotch single malt from a distillery which has had a number of names in its history. Today it is called → Glen Ord and belongs to → UDV. For a time it was also called → Ord and, after the village where it is situated, Muir of Ord. In 1982, the name of the whisky to was change to Glenordie, which was generally available as a 12-year-old and in Italy as a 5-year-old.

Glenrob A → standard Sotch blend produced by the London-based H → Mayerson & Company.

Glenroc French → grain whisky made by the 'Artisane Liquoriste' Jacques Fislier in Rennes. The bottles are without an age statement, the whisky has a strength of 41% and is easily obtainable in specialist shops in northern France. Recently a whisky called → Gwenroc has also appeared.

Glenrothes Scottish malt distillery that lies in the 'whisky town' of → Rothes between → Elgin and → Craigellachie and therefore belongs to the → Speyside region. Sometimes its name is written as two words, Glen Rothes. It was founded in 1878 by William Grant & Co (not to be confused with the founder of → Glenfiddich). Its union with Islay Distillers, the owners of → Bunnahabhain, led to the foundation of → Highland Distilleries, now Highland Distillers to whom it belongs to this day. It is run by their subsidiary → Highland Malt Distilling. Scottish master blenders who have divided malts into categories have judged the whisky, which is now produced in 10 → stills, to be one of the best six. It is much sought-after and for a long time was difficult to obtain as a single malt. It plays a particularly important part in the company's → Famous Grouse and also in → Cutty Sark from → Berry Bros & Rudd.

They sell a 12-year-old single malt which is not strictly speaking a → proprietor's bottling but which, owing to the close connections between the two firms, can be described as such. More and more → vintages of the malt named The Glenrothes are being marketed: a 14-year-old distilled in 1979 and bottled in 1993, a 1984 bottled in 1995, a 1972 bottled in 1996, a 1982 bottled in 1997 and 1998, a 1985 which was bottled in 1998, a 1978 and a 1981, both bottled in 1999, a 1987 which was bottled in 2000, there were also a 1971, a 1973 and a 1983, all bottled in 2000. It was previously also regularly available as an 8-year-old from → Gordon & MacPhail who had one from 1978 in their → 'Centenary Reserve' series and another 8-year-old in their 'MacPhail's Collection'. → Independent bottlers such as → Signatory and → Cadenhead have also had Glenrothes from time to time.

Glenshiel Scotch vatted malt from the → Loch Lomond Distillery, a subsidiary of → Glen Catrine Bonded Warehouse Ltd. It is available as an 8-year-old in UK branches of the Spar Supermarket, and in France it is sold as an 8-year-old and as a 12-year-old.

Glenside Scotch blend that is only obtainable at branches of Thresher's, one of the large UK drinks-supermarket chains.

Glentauchers Scottish malt distillery. Its name, pronounced 'glen-tockers', comes from the Gaelic for 'valley of the wind'. It lies between Keith and Rothes at Mulben, and belongs to the → Speyside whisky region. James → Buchanan & Co, one of the → 'Big Five', built it together with two partners in 1898 and it became part of → DCL in 1925. They renovated the distillery and even expanded it to six → stills, but closed it down in the crisis year of 1983. It has been working again since 1989 when it was acquired by → Allied. The new owners brought out the whisky, which had previously only been available as a single malt (5 years old) in France, in the → Allied series; initially one from 1979 then another from 1984, both with no age statement. A 15-year-old was then included in the small series of six bottlings which Allied brought out in 2000 with uniform labels; it was really intended for company workers, but a small number found their way onto the market.

Glentress Scotch vatted malt from Peter J → Russell in Edinburgh.

Glentromie Scotch vatted malt which names the Glentromie Distillery Co of → Drumguish on its label but which comes from the → Speyside Distillery Co. It owns a distillery of the same name which after a very long construction period and considerable efforts by the Christie family, finally began operating in 1990. This distillery is situated on the River Tromie which flows into the Spey near Kingussie. On the one hand the family had been involved in the whisky business for a long time and already owned several brands, but they still had to bring out new ones to establish the name of Speyside and to raise urgently needed capital. Glentromie certainly contains malt whisky from the new distillery and is bottled at 12 and 17 years.

Glenturret Scottish malt distillery that lies on the western outskirts of Crieff and belongs to the southern → Highland region. Together with → Strathisla and → Littlemill it is one of the oldest distilleries in Scotland, and illicit distilling took place at the Hosh as early as 1717, and that its oldest building dates back to the year 1775. It was one of the first distilleries to open a visitor centre. It has several restaurants and attracts more visitors than any other distillery. All its employees are particularly proud of their famous → distillery cat → Towser.

The distillery has earned great respect because after having been shut for 30 years (from 1923 – 1959) it managed to build up the excellent reputation that it now enjoys. James Fairlie bought the distillery with the intention of reinstating malt whisky as a genuinely Scottish product which had, at that time, almost disappeared from the public consciousness. A small distillery like Glenturret, whose two → stills each process just 6,000 litres, was just what he needed to show world interest in the original, forgotten form of whisky could be revived. Cointreau and then → Highland Distillers came on board as partners. Even after his death his family initially still had great influence. His son, Peter → Fairlie, was responsible for running Glenturret for a long time and after it was taken over by Macallan he worked as Marketing Director of the company.

The whisky has been available as a single malt in a → proprietor's bottling, in many age categories and also as a → vintage aged 8, 12 and 18 years (40%), aged 15 years (43% or 50%), aged 21 years in a carafe and a 25-year-old in a somewhat remarkable china globe. There were several vintage malts from 1966 and one from 1972. The Glenturret MCMLXVI/MCMXCIII is 27 years old. Glenturret Original Malt Liqueur (35%) is a result of the connections with Cointreau, and was joined in 1966 by Fairlie's.

Glenugie Scottish malt distillery. Its name, pronounced 'glenyougie', means 'basin-shaped valley' or 'protected valley'. It lies near the sea, to the south of Peterhead near the A92, in Aberdeenshire. It belongs to the eastern → Highland region and has been closed since 1983, when some of the distillery buildings were demolished. Previously there had been a long chain of mergers and takeovers through which the distillery passed via Seager Evans and → Long John to → Whitbread, who sold it to a group of oil dealers in 1975. The distillery, which used to be the easternmost in Scotland, is still worth a visit because of the architectural interest of its main buildings. Its whisky was never available as a → proprietor's bottling but only as an → independent bottling from, for example, → Gordon & MacPhail and → Cadenhead. → Signatory included a 1966 Glenugie in their → 'Silent Stills' series with a cask strength of 53.9%.

Glenury Royal Scottish malt distillery. Its name means 'valley of the yews'. It is situated near the River Cowie and the town of Stonehaven, to the south of Aberdeen, and belongs to the eastern → Highland region. It was founded in 1825 and was associated with Captain Robert Barclay. King William IV is still commemorated with a blend that was brought out by John → Gillon & Co and that is now bottled by → UDV. UD took over the distillery which then belonged to → DCL in 1987. At the time it had already been shut for two years. The distillery has now been demolished to make way for a housing development.

The 12-year-old single malt bottled by John Gillon is now a rarity, along with the 1970, and 1971 → cask strength (57.0%/61.3%), which → UD included in its → 'Rare Malts Selection', and the → Signatory bottling in their → 'Silent Stills'

Glenwood

series. This Glenury Royal was from 1973 and had a strength of 53.7%. Other independent bottlers also still occasionally have it.

Glenwood Scotch malt whisky, selected and blended by a company named → Drumguish. That is also the name of a single malt produced by the → Speyside Distillery. Their owners also make the vatted version which is only sold in Spain.

Gloag & Son, Matthew Scottish company, which like so many other bearers of great whisky names, had modest beginnings as a grocer's, which was established in 1825 by Margaret Gloag. Unlike others, such as → Chivas, → Teacher or John → Walker, its name has not survived as a brand of Scotch, although its blend is a match for them all: their → Famous Grouse is number one in its native country. It was 'invented' by Gloag's nephew. The last Matthew Gloag sold the business to → Highland Distilleries in 1970. They not only gave up the old bottling plant in Perth, but also 'Bordeaux House', where the offices were situated and which housed the most wonderful wines. The label of the Grouse still carries a reminder of the name, as does 'Gloag's Gin' which Highland Distilleries launched on the market in 1996. For several years Matthew Gloag & Sons, as a subsidiary of Highland, were entirely responsible for the sales of the brands, i.e. in addition to the old blends also the new acquisitions → Black Bottle, the liqueurs → Glenturret Malt Liqueur and → Fairlie's and the single malts → Bunnahabhain, → Glenturret, → Highland Park, → Tamdhu and the Glengoyne of its 'sister' company → Robertson & Baxter. In 1998 Highland Distillers restructured their company and the name Gloag no longer appears in the new organisation. Highland Distillers are now entrusted with the sales of the various brands, but continue the Gloag association with Perth, now having a modern office complex at West Kinfauns, on the outskirts of the city.

Glorious 12th Scotch blend. It refers to the 12th of August, the date that the shooting season of the → Famous Grouse begins. The 12-year-old → de luxe blend is produced by the London-based company John Buckmaster & Sons.

Gold & Gold Scotch blend from → Nikka. One version is available in a bottle enveloped in splendid samurai armour. The 'Golds' stands for the → pot still, and he → coffey still which Nikka have operated in → Nishinomiya near Osaka since 1962. There is also a lighter version that is simply called → G & G

Gold Blend Scotch blend from the Sussex-based → Kinross Whisky Company.

Gold Classic Korean blend that is produced there originally for → Seagram, using, as is so often the case, locally distilled → grain whiskies blended with malt whiskies which are imported in → bulk from Scotland (and perhaps also from Japan or → New Zealand).

Gold Cock 3-year-old Czech blend with a strength of 40% from → Seliko in Olomouc (Olmütz) which owns two distilleries, → Testice and → Dolany, near this mediaeval town and is best known for its → King Barley.

Gold King Scotch blend that came from John Malay Ltd in London, but which is now supplied by a company called Gold King.

Gold Label Scotch blends from various companies. One is produced by the London trading firm → Red Lion Blending. It should not be confused with Haig Gold Label from John → Haig & Co or → BL Gold Label from → Bulloch Lade. What is now called → Bisset's also used to have the adjunct 'Gold Label'. Douglas → Laing & Co of Glasgow have several blends going by: → King of Scots Gold Label, → House of Peers Gold Label and → Sir Walter Raliegh Gold Label. → Lombard's Gold Label is the → standard blend of the company based on the Isle of Man. A further Gold Label comes from another British island, from → Bucktrout & Co on Guernsey. There is also a Gold Label version of the bourbon → I W Harper.

Gold Tassel Canadian whisky from → McGuinness.

Golden Age Scotch blend which, like other → DCL brands, was created at the end of the 1970s as a substitute for labels that had to be either sold or withdrawn from the UK market as the result of pressure from the Monopolies Commission; the best-known example is → Johnnie Walker, which at the time was replaced by → John Barr. Golden Age was the substitute for → Dimple from → Haig. → UDV still hold the rights to the brand, but do not actively market it.

Golden Anniversary Scotch vatted malt in a red ceramic decanter with a royal blue stopper, which → Gordon & MacPhail brought out on the occasion of the Golden Wedding Anniversary of Queen Elizabeth and Prince Philip, the Duke of Edinburgh, on 20th November 1997. This was in keeping with the company tradition of celebrating royal events, such as the wedding of Prince Charles and Lady Diana Spencer or the Queen's Silver Jubilee, by issuing precious old whiskies from its stocks. The vatted malt, which is numbered by hand and comes in a wooden box, contains whiskies from each of the 50 years of their marriage.

Golden Blend Scotch blend. This → standard blend was one of many small brands formerly from → Whyte & Mackay/→ JBB (Greater Europe) plc.

Golden Cap Scotch blend whose producer is unknown. All that is known is that it is produced soley for those pubs supplied by the brewery Palmers of Bridport in Dorset. This independent company, established at the end of the 19th century, has contracts with 120 pubs.

Golden Crib Kentucky straight corn Whiskey which is bottled by → Barton at 100°/50%. It is not possible to establish when it was made and whether it is still being made. In any case the German collector, Taubenheim, has a bottle of it. A 'crib' is a rack used for drying cobs of maize.

Golden Eagle Scotch blends from two different companies. One came from a subsidiary of H Stenham. One of these was the → Premier Scotch Whisky Co and when Stenham sold his business (due to old age) this name was adopted by the company. Like all blends of the firm it is bottled in five age categories 3, 5, 8, 10 and 12 years, and is exclusively intended for export, mainly to Central and South America and to South East Asia. The other blend is sold in a decanter, without an age statement, by → Kyndal.

Golden Irish Irish whiskey from → Cooley and made or the Irish chain Dunne's Stores. It is the successor of → Avoca, which is now sold everywhere. It is a blend bottled at 40%.

Golden Nail Whiskey cocktail. Four parts bourbon are mixed with two parts Southern Comfort and served in a long drink glass with ice.

Golden Piper Scotch blend from → Lombard Scotch Whisky, based on the Isle of Man.

Golden Sun Bourbon sold in the supermarket chain Lidl as their own brand. Its producer remains anonymous. The label only states that it is 6 years old and 'distilled and bottled under the supervision of the United States Government', but produced in Germany.

Golden Wedding Canadian whisky . → Schenley first brought it out, then → UD owned it after they purchased the Canadian company and its distillery → Valleyfield, until the merger of → Guinness and → Grand Met to form → UDV. In 1999 they sold the brand to → Canandaigua. Up to now it has been a → standard blend made of 4-year-old whiskeys with a strength of 40%.

Gooderham and Worts Canadian whisky company who provided the basis for the country's whisky industry. It was established in 1832 in Toronto by two English brothers-in-law, William Gooderham and James Worts, who had emigrated to Upper Canada (as Ontario was called in those days). The history of the firm, and of Canadian whisky, began with a mill. The distillery was added in 1837. Both were replaced with a new building in 1861 in which 150 people were employed and which, with an annual production of half a million gallons, was by far the largest in the country. A few years later it was already producing a third of all Canadian spirits and was successfully exporting to the USA, the UK and South America. In 1923 it was bought by Harry → Hutch, who a few years later joined together with Hiram → Walker to form Hiram Walker – Gooderham and

Worts, which soon began working in Scotland and after several further mergers is now to be found under the control of → Allied Domecq PLC. The respected old name appeared once again on the label of a whisky bottle, when Allied created its → Canadian Whisky Guild, which up to now has included three bottlings, one of which is called Gooderham & Worts. Its bottles are numbered and the label states that it is 'handcrafted' and 'Natural Small Batch'. It also quotes the year 1832, and the place of origin as the first distillery in Canada.

Gordon & MacPhail Scottish whisky company which is one of the oldest → independent bottlers and is now reputed to be the largest and most important whisky dealer (wholesale and retail) in the world. It was established in 1895 in Elgin by James Gordon and John Alexander MacPhail as 'Family Grocers, Tea, Wine & Spirits Merchants'. The original shop had a delicatessen department with a large selection of whisky. The co-founder James Gordon had a detailed knowledge of the whisky business and had good contacts with the neighbouring distilleries, which the prospering firm often helped out of financial difficulties in times of hardship. It is now operated by the → Urquhart family. John Urquhart began there as an apprentice, and in 1915 became the partner of Gordon's widow, after Mr. MacPhail had retired and Mr. Gordon had died of a heart attack.

The company has vast stocks of malt whisky at its disposal, some of which go back to before the Second World War. G & M have several blends of their own such as → Ben Alder, → Glen Calder, → Royal Findhorn, → Old Orkney, → Ubique and → Immortal Memory. → Dunkeld Atholl Brose is their own whisky liqueur. There is also a series of vatted malts such as → Old Elgin and → Strathavon and the → 'Pride of ...' series. The most prominent of its range are the single malts, several of which do not show their exact origin, such as Fraser's, and some of which are offered as a whole series such as → 'Connoisseurs Choice' and the → 'Cask Strength' series. In 1998 two new series were added, → 'MacPhail's Collection' and → 'Speymalt', which exclusively contains various old → Macallans. Two years later six bottles were brought out with the name → 'Private Collection', which included three different → Caol Ilas and three → Imperials which had received their → finishing in calvados, claret and cognac casks.

Good contacts with distillery proprietors has enabled the bottling of malts such as → Balblair, → Scapa, → Inverleven, → Glentauchers and Old → Pulteney, the → Allied Series, as well as → Linkwood and → Mortlach on behalf of their licence-holders. There is a particularly close relationship to Glenlivet, whose malts are marketed under the name of George & J G Smith's Glenlivet. Whiskies for Scottish regiments is a tradition which today is maintained by the → Highland Fusiliers malts. On the occasion of Queen Elizabeth II's silver jubilee, or for royal weddings, G & M have brought out special bottlings which fetch high prices today. The Golden Anniversary, produced in 1997 for the golden wedding of the Queen and Prince Philip, presented in a splendid decanter, is part of this tradition. In 1995 the 100th anniversary of the company was honoured with the → 'Centenary Reserve' series and a bottling which blended 100 malts. The Millennium was celebrated with a 2 litre jug. The MacPhails 2000 contained a vatted malt whose oldest whisky was 60 years old. Of the same age was a Mortlach (distilled in 1938, bottled in 1998) which was launched at the Vinexpo in Bordeaux in 2001.

Gordon Highlanders, The Scotch blend from William → Grant & Sons who have close connections to the regiment whose name the whisky bears: the company's founder was a major in the regiments voluntary batallion. Grant's master blender, David Stewart, created an 'official regimental whisky' for the 200th anniversary of the troop. It may no longer be used to celebrate acts of military heroism, but it keeps the tradition alive. The regiment has a museum in Aberdeen which receives a proportion of the profit from each bottle sold.

Grain whisk(e)y Although every whisk(e)y is distilled from a grain mash and is therefore a grain whisky in that sense, the term is reserved for a certain, clearly defined sort of whisky. A malt whisky is made of pure malted barley and is distilled twice or three times in copper → pot stills, an American straight bourbon must be made from a mash consisting of at least 51% corn, a straight rye from a mash of at least 51% rye, and a classical Irish whiskey consists of malted and unmalted barley which is distilled in pot stills. A grain whisk(e)y may be made from any type of grain. In fact the composition of the mash is not dictated by legal requirements, but by the market, and frequently by what happens to be cheapest at the time.

Grain does not become whisky in the classical pear or onion shaped stills, but by continuous distillation in → patent → stills, which are often called → Coffey stills after their inventor. → Aeneas Coffey, and before him, Robert Stein, developed a new process in the 1820s, in which the → wash, mainly consisting of water and alcohol, was not distilled by heating and condensing. Hot steam would rise from below in a column-shaped still to 'strip' the cold wash fed in from above of alcohol. Whilst the pot stills are operated batch-wise, the column or → continuous stills can work without interruption. It is obvious that in contrast to the traditional, original method considerable savings in costs can be made. It makes the grain whisky, which already profits from a cheaper raw material, even cheaper. It also allows a higher volume of alcohol and the distillate is very pure, although rather lacking in taste and aroma.

The invention of Coffey and Stein revolutionised the world of whisky. It enabled the production of good but cheap whisk(e)y in large quantities. Indeed grain was initially important in supplying England with a reasonably-priced whisky from Scotland. But the value of the invention of a new whisky type was proved just a few decades later when pioneers such as Andrew → Usher succeeded in creating yet another new sort of whisky, mixing malts and grains to form a blend. It has the advantage of being consistently reproducable, so that a fixed formula can be used again and again to mix it – the prerequisite for the establishment of an identifiable drink brand. From the mid 19th century Scotch began to conquer first England (helped by the *phylloxera vastatrix* catastrophe in France which robbed the English of their previously preferred brandy), and then the rest of the world. It lay the foundations for the establishment of an important industry, which provides the state with a large income in taxes. It was one of the most important factors in causing malt whisky to slip into oblivion and meant that until recently, blends, consisting mainly of grain, were a synonym for Scotch whisky.

Single grain was of very limited importance for a long time. The only one on the market was the Cameron Brig coming from the Cameronbridge Distillery, before Invergordon sold the → Invergordon single grain. William Grant & Sons were the first to attempt worldwide distribution of a grain with their → Black Barrel.

Grand Age Japanese blend from → Nikka that has been on the market since 1989. It appears to have replaced the Specialage (sic) that was the company's leading brand before the introduction of Nikka's single malts. Nikka offers many brands in glass carafes. Apart from the white porcelain of the → Tsuru, the angular decanter of Grand Age is the most elegant of the forms used by Nikka. It is a → super-premium blend, the highest category of Japanese whiskies.

Grand Castle 26-year-old Scotch blend which comes in a luxurious ceramic decanter: a → de luxe blend from → Morrison Bowmore, intended for the market in the Far East, where this company, which has a Japanese owner, is successfully represented, especially with extravagantly presented and very old whiskies.

Grand Dulky French whisky which is marketed as 'Noble' and 'Grand Whisky de luxe'. It is produced by La Marrinigeonise in Charente. It is made from malt whiskies imported from Scotland and → grain whisky distilled in France.

Grand Macnish Scotch blend that nowadays comes from → MacDuff International. It was introduced by Robert Macnish at the end of the 19th century and like → Doctor's Special, another creation of the Glaswegian whisky (and tea) merchant, was taken under the control of Hiram → Walker. Their present-day Scottish representative, → Allied Distillers Ltd, has kept the latter, but sold Grand Macnish in 1992 to the newly founded company MacDuff. It is available as a → standard blend without an age statement and also aged 12, 18, 21 and 25 years.

Grand Metropolitan International company which ceased to exist in its own right in December 1997: after several months of negotiations and following injunctions from the Monopolies Commissions in both the EU and the USA, it merged with → Guinness. The new company is by far the largest in the drinks sector, and with a combined turnover of more than £20 billion, leaves → the former whisky interests Seagram and → Allied Domecq PLC far behind it. GrandMet were the larger partner in the merger. It had slowly taken shape having operated in many different fields in the course of its history, for example at one time it was the largest hotel group in the world. At the time of its 'marriage' it had only retained the 'Food and Drink' interests with the strongest turnover (having chosen the right time to get rid of weaker interests). These included its subsidiaries Häagen Dazs (ice cream), Pillsbury (Baked Beans), Green Giant (frozen vegetables), Old El Paso (Mexican foods) and → IDV. This subsidiary was one of the five largest drinks companies in the world with production plants in Scotland (→ Auchroisk, → Glen Spey, → Knockando, → Strathmill as well as warehouses and bottling plants), Brazil, India and Australia and several very strong brands such as 'Gilbey's' gin, 'Smirnoff' vodka, 'Malibu' and, above all, the blend → J & B, which is number two worldwide and which Diageo was allowed to keep. The two best-selling Scotch blends, → Johnnie Walker Red and J & B, come from the new company which controls about 20% of the world market for spirits; it had to part with → Dewar's, but still has Johnnie Walker Black, → Bell's and → White Horse, and therefore five brands among the top 12 Scotch whiskies worldwide.

Grand Old Highland Scotch blend from → Morrison Bowmore, one of the company's → de luxe brands. It is 26 years old and presented in a ceramic container. It is aimed at the Far Eastern market.

Grand Scot Scotch blend from H → Stenham in London, who produce it exclusively for export, using the name of its subsidiary Highland Blending. It is available in five age categories of 3, 5, 8, 10 and 12 years.

Grande Canadian Canadian whisky imported by → Heaven Hill to the USA in → bulk and sold as their own brand there.

Grant & Sons, William Scottish whisky company established in → Dufftown in 1886 by William Grant. It is, after → Macdonald Martin and Arthur → Bell & Sons became joint-stock companies and the latter was taken over by → Guinness, the last remaining Scotch whisky company of worldwide importance that is still owned by its founding family. It is run from Scotland (only the export business is based in London, the headquarters are in Glasgow). William Grant learnt his trade in → Mortlach, the first distillery in the town that now has the largest concentration of distilleries in the world. Grant had two daughters and seven sons who, unusually for the times, were all allowed to study – and helped him build his first distillery with their own hands with just an architect to advise them.

The distillery was called → Glenfiddich and its first whisky flowed on Christmas Day 1887. It was followed in 1892 by a second distillery just a stone's throw away, named after → Balvenie Castle. William Grant later went blind but still carried on the management of the business which his family had resolutely built up. His signature still decorates each bottle to this day. Their greatest success was with a blend whose introduction onto the market was a result of the → Pattison collapse. It was called → William Grant's Standfast. The company wanted to remain independent and produce the majority of the → grain whisky needed for it themselves so that they would not have to rely on other firms, so they built a grain distillery in → Girvan in the → Lowlands in 1963.

At the same time they made a momentous decision: to market the single malt Glenfiddich – not only in Scotland, but also throughout the world. It was the first time that a whisky company had believed that customers could be won for a single malt – and that at a time when even in Scotland 'Scotch' was associated with blends rather than with the malt whiskies which had slipped into oblivion. Perhaps such a courageous step could only have been made by a family company. Today, nationally and internationally, Glenfiddich is the number one malt whisky by a wide margin. The success of the brand was assisted by consistent marketing, including the individually shaped bottle, as well as the revolutionary opening of the distillery to visitors. For many people Glenfiddich has been the first malt that they have encountered and in many countries it has come to represent the whole genre.

Shortly after the introduction of Glenfiddich on the market the Grants expanded further, by setting up a malt distillery called → Ladyburn within the distillery complex in Girvan, which ceased operating 10 years later. Neutral spirit as well as grain is produced at Girvan. In 1990/1 the company built a new malt distillery, → Kininvie, on their site in Dufftown and they bought the neighbouring → Convalmore from → UD which was completely empty and whose warehouses are now used for storing their own casks The strength of the company was displayed in 1999 when, together with the → Edrington Group, it bought → Highland Distillers, in which it now owns a 30% share.

Grants have now launched new varieties, such as the blend Grant's which is number four in the world rankings, the blends → Robbie Dhu, The → Gordon Highlanders or → Clan MacGregor, and gin, an unusual product for a whisky company, as well as the 'Virgin Vodka'. Alcopops, such as 'Mirage' and 'Taboo', have also been created. The 100th anniversary of Balvenie was the occasion of a relaunching. A 15-year-old → cask strength was added to the Glenfiddich series, and in 1998 it was complemented with Solera Reserve and Ancient Reserve. In addition there are Glenfiddich, Balvenie and Ladyburn Vintage Reserves. Another innovation came in 1995: → Black Barrel was promoted with the help of a massive campaign, again for the first time for this kind of whisky, not only nationally but also internationally, aimed at new consumer groups. William Grant & Sons also have a subsidiary, → QSI (Quality Spirits International) who have a range including more than 50 brands of spirit and above all offer value for money products.

Grant, J & G Scottish whisky company who own and run the → Glenfarclas Distillery which was bought by the company founder John Grant in 1865 and which he ran together with his son George from 1870. The company is now managed by members of the fifth generation of the family and is one of the very few to have maintained its independence and avoided a takeover by the giants in the business. J & G Grant have only looked for a partner once in their history, when they were trying to raise capital for the renovation of Glenfarclas and relinquished half of the company to → Pattison in 1895. They had difficulty surviving the 1898 Pattison bankruptcy which shocked the entire whisky industry. The malts from Glenfarclas were offered to blenders, and also sold as a single malt. The important marketing instrument of a visitor centre with guided tours of the distillery was recognised early on in 1973.

Apart from the single malts which are available in many versions, there is a → standard blend called → Glen Dowan, which is sold as a 21-year-old and as a 25-year-old. The → pure malt, The → John Grant was initially only available in Italy, where it was offered at six years old; in 1998 it was joined by a 17-year-old at 43%. In recent years malts have been marketed with trade names which clearly come from Glenfarclas, such as → Highland Cattle, → Eagle of Spey and → Meadhan, possibly following the example of the great Chateaux in Bordeaux with their second wines. The company owns a bottling plant in Broxburn near Edinburgh together with Peter J Russell & Co and can rightly claim to belong to the few distilleries who bottle their malt themselves – even if it isn't at the site of production.

Grant, J & J John and James Grant were the two brothers who founded Glen Grant. James followed many different career paths, including politics. He left a small memorial in the garden behind the Glen Grant Distillery, which resembles a small castle: he had a dram-safe installed. Its iron door guarded a bottle of his malt whisky which he offered to his guests. The company which he established maintained ownership of Glen Grant and → Caperdonich for more than a hundred years before they merged in 1953 with the → Smiths from →

Glenlivet and were transformed into a joint-stock company.

Great Glen Celtic Cream, The Scotch whisky liqueur based on cream, produced by the → Speyside Distillery Co.

Great Mac Scotch blend from the London-based → Montrose Whisky Company and mainly intended for export.

Great Macauley, The Scotch blend whose label names the → Ladyburn Distillery as its producer, but which actually comes from → QSI. This company is a subsidiary of William → Grant & Sons, who in their turn operated a distillery called Ladyburn on their large site at → Girvan. It has long since closed and its malt whiskies are among the most sought-after of all. It was, apart from a bottling for the USA, only available from the → independent bottler → Cadenhead. There are still a few casks of it which now and then awake the excitement of collectors. In May 1999 several dozen casks were still in existence and in 2000 one of them was bottled as Ladyburn Vintage Reserve 1973.

Great Outback Australian whisky, a few bottles of which turned up in Europe in 1999. The Great Outback Superior Blend Australian Whisky comes in a bottle with a swing stopper containing just half a litre. The Rare Old Australian single malt comes in a normal bottle but is packed in a wooden box. The label names a Sydney-based company Cawsey Menck as the producer and distributor.

Green Highlander Scotch blend that was distributed by G & J Greenalls, although it is doubtful whether they produced it. The company, which is a contract distiller and bottler is a subsidiary of Greenalls plc. This was originally a large UK brewing company which bought up a lot of smaller regional breweries, but completely withdrew from beer making in 1991 and limited itself to the management of its 1,400 pubs and its 'Stretton Leisure' chain of amusement arcades. In 1998 the company came under pressure and it is still not sure whether they will have to part with G & J Greenalls. They are mainly known for their 'Greenalls' and 'Richmond' gin. The Scotch is no longer included in their range.

Green Malt The expression used when → germination of the barley has been induced by → steeping it in water, thereby releasing the starches contained in it. In further stages it is converted to maltose, which by → fermentation and finally distilling, it is converted to alcohol. During germination the grain has to be constantly turned to control the temperature. After several days it has attained a certain consistency and the starch is white and chalky and is called green malt (although it is still yellow). Drying in the → kiln will then turn it into malt.

Green Plaid Scotch blend the full name of which indicates the owner of the brand: → Inver House Green Plaid. Inver House uses the full name to differentiate this blend from those (which are sold in the USA by → Canandaigua or its subsidiary → Barton Brands). They also use the name Inver House, which is made by → GuinnessUDV. In 1985 Barton had sold the → Loch Lomond Distillery to Inver House Distillers Ltd and in return received the distribution rights for the USA. The Green Plaid, is notably successful in southern Europe and South America. It is available as a → standard blend and aged 12, 21, 25 and 35 years.

Green Spot Irish → pure pot still whiskey. It is last of its kind which, until the introduction of blends, embodied traditional Irish whiskey and was very different from the whiskies/whiskeys of Scotland, the USA and Canada. → Red Breast, → Old Comber and, the single malts from → Cooley's for which, however, only malted barley is used. Some insist that it is not so much the triple distillation that determines the Irish → pot still whiskey, but the unmalted barley.

Green Spot is the last whiskey in the country to be produced and exclusively distributed by a wine merchant. Many wine merchants and grocers used to have their own brands and where in Scotland some of them became mighty companies such as → Haig, → Walker or → Dewar, in Ireland only Mitchell & Son remain with their shop in Kildare Street in Dublin. Green Spot was introduced in the early 1920s and because of its great popularity was complemented with versions that have long since disappeared, such as Blue (7 years old), Yellow (12 years old) and Red Spot (15 years old). The whiskey meant for Green Spot was initially matured for five years in various sherry casks, was then blended and after this 'marriage' allowed to mature for a further five years. It has always been produced by → Jameson, formerly in Dublin and nowadays in → Midleton. It has a strength of 40%, is now only seven or eight years old and the sherry share amounts to only about a quarter. There are no more than 6,000 bottles of it a year.

Green Stripe Scotch blend whose full name is Usher's Green Stripe, it was created by the company of Andrew → Usher. Usher senior and his son are generally accepted as being the two men who invented the art of blending malt and → grain whiskies. Green Stripe is something like the epitome of the original blend. → GuinnessUDV, to whom it now belongs, now mainly market it on the South American market. In Venezuela, which has the largest per capita consumption of Scotch, it is the leading brand.

Greenfield Irish whiskey from Cooley, identical to → Dunlow.

Greenmore Irish single grain aged 8 years (40%). It comes from the Cooley Distillery; the label states that the company is based in Dunalk, but their distillery is in Riverstown.

Greenwich Meridian 20° 0' 0" Scotch blend which was brought out onto the market for the Millennium. It comes from Balerno & Currie in Edinburgh.

Gregson's Whisky produced in Brazil. Like all *whiskies nacionale* it consists of → grain whiskies which are produced in the country and malt whiskies which are imported in → bulk from Scotland. It was produced by → IDV and is therefore now made by → GuinnessUDV. It is also on sale in neighbouring countries, chiefly in Uruguay.

Grierson's No. 1 Scotch vatted malt aged 12 years, which is made for Grierson, the respected London wine merchants. The company has other brands of its own such as the blend → Moorland.

Grist Term for the roughly milled grain that is used for making various types of whisky. In the case of malt whisky the → malt that has resulted from → germination and drying is milled to grist before being steeped in hot water in a → mash tun to extract the sugar, the maltose. The finer the grist the more alcohol can be obtained. It is believed that if it is too fine it will have a negative effect on the taste. Two types of mill are used: mills which use hammers and mills with a more gentle roller.

For the production of other whiskies the grain used, whether it is unmalted barley, rye or wheat, must be milled and turned into grist before it is boiled again to release the starches. Corn, which is used for both bourbon and → grain whisky, is not milled but boiled straight away. Malted grains must not be boiled as this destroys the enzyme that is needed for sweetening and for fermentation.

Guinness International drinks combine which grew from St. James's Brewery in Dublin when it as acquired in 1759 by Arthur Guinness. For 200 years Guinness was solely associated with their main product, the famous Irish stout. The brewery grew continually, thanks in part to its clever advertising with a toucan. In the early 1980s Ernest Saunders from Nestlé took over control at the London headquarters. Within two years he had landed two coups which turned Guinness into one of the world's largest spirits giants. The first was the hostile takeover of Arthur → Bell & Sons in 1985, one of the last independent Scotch whisky companies (even although it was already traded on the stock exchange). A year later it was the turn of the largest Scottish company → DCL, which was in a vulnerable position because of its almost Victorian business culture. A bitter fight resulted between Saunders and James Gulliver, the self-made man from → Campbeltown, who had built up the → Argyll Group (including → Safeway) and had also become involved in the whisky business. Gulliver lost the battle in December 1986. But because Saunders, assisted by Swiss and Austrian bank contacts, had employed unfair methods which were revealed when the American speculator Ivan Boesky, was prosecuted for insider trading, Saunders was convicted and jailed.

Guinness had possession of DCL and the headquarters were moved from Edinburgh to London, despite assurances to the contrary from Saunders. DCL became United Distillers (→ UD), which developed into one of the biggest players in the spirits business with gin brands such as Tanqueray and Gordon's, and five of the best-selling Scotch blends worldwide, → Johnnie Walker Red Label and Black Label, → Bell's, → Dewar's and → White Horse, as well as nearly a third of all Scottish malt distilleries. From that time Guinness was divided into two groups, GBW (Guinness Brewing Worldwide) and → UD (which also operated worldwide), with subsidiaries in more than 20 countries; besides this the company also owned the Gleneagles Hotel in Scotland and had joint ventures in, for example, India and China, as well as with the luxury goods company LVMH.

In the summer of 1997 merger plans between Guinness and → Grand Metropolitan to create a new organisation were made. The largest drinks concern in the world with a combined turnover of more than £20 billion was the result, and included, a world share in spirits of more than 20% and a turnover of 600 million → cases per annum. Amongst its opponents were not only the trade regulatory bodies in Brussels and the USA, but also Bernard Arnault, the boss of LVMH. Towards the end of the year their objections had been overcome, but the company had to part with several brands, notably → Dewar's, which was the best-selling blend in the USA (though the company has retained the number two position with → J & B). The merged company's name became → Diageo and in 2001 it was decided that the name of it's drinks subsidiary → UDV would change to → GuinnessUDV. → Diageo is still the world's largest drinks business.

GuinnessUDV The name of Diageo's drinks subsidiary from mid-2001. Formerly known as → UDV.

Gun Club Scotch blend from → Kyndal. The brand is sold under the name of Allan, Poyter & Co, whose manager Mr. Mackay brought the brand into his own company when he founded it in 1882.

Gwenroc French whisky previously known as → Glenroc. It is produced by Jacques Fisilier from Rennes,.

H

Hackler Irish spirit distilled from malted grain at 40%, invented by → UD and made for them by → Cooley in Ireland. It claimed to be → poitín and was something that by definition could not exist: an illegal whiskey, legally produced. According to information from its producers → UD, the company wanted to profit from the myth of the illicitly-distilled national drink among Irish sympathisers, especially in the USA and Australia, and at the same time appeal to a younger public who prefer 'white' spirits for mixing to the classical 'brown' ones. The product was therefore part of a concept to present whisk(e)y in a new form, such as the controversial → Loch Dhu or → Red Devil or ready-mixed drinks such as → Bell's with Coke, thereby targeting new consumer groups. In the case of Hackler, the experiment failed. In August 1998 the drink, which is said to have cost its inventors £2 million, was taken off the market owing to its lack of success, shortly after a Gold Label (50%) had been brought out and another company had launched → Knockeen, another 'poteen'. The → Bunratty, which spells its version 'potcheen', is still available.

Haddington House Scotch blend, a → standard blend from → QSI, a subsidiary of William → Grant & Sons. Haddington is a pleasant town to the east of Edinburgh.

Haig & Co, John Scottish whisky company established by one of the great distilling families. No other family has proof that it was involved in distilling from such an early date: there are reports from as early as 1655 that a Robert Haig was fined by the church for distilling whisky on a Sunday. Field-Marshal Douglas Haig had a distinguished military career during World War I, was made an earl and is commemorated by a statue of himself on a horse in front of Edinburgh Castle.

The family goes back to the Norman Petrus de Hage, who came over to England with William the Conqueror. Since 1162 the family seat has been Bemersyde, between Dryburgh Abbey and Scott's View, high above the River Tweed. The seer Tom the Rhymer prophesied that it would always remain so. But although → Glenkinchie Distillery, which for a time belonged to the family, is not far from Bemersyde, the whisky line of the family was mainly concentrated on the other side of the Firth of Forth, in Fife. Robert Haig settled there as a farmer and, like many of his colleagues, he liked to convert his surplus crop into liquid form. In 1751 John, one of his descendants, married Margaret Stein, whose family ran distilleries at Kilbagie and Kennetpans in nearby Clackmannanshire. This marriage was undoubtedly very significant in the history of whisky, not only because the Haigs went to Ireland and America to produce and sell whisky there, and because all five sons founded their own distilleries and one of the daughters married John → Jameson in Dublin. But above all a certain Robert → Stein invented the → patent still at Kilbagie in 1827, which made the production of → grain whisky vastly more efficient.

From this time on → Cameron Bridge, the distillery which another John Haig had built in 1813, only produced grain whisky – and today one of the few single grain whiskies on the market, comes from here.

John Haig, who had set up blending plants in Markinch three miles from the distillery, was also the driving force behind the amalgamation of several → Lowland distillers to form the → Distillers Co Ltd, the most powerful company in the Scotch whisky business. (This was bought by → Guinness in 1987 and turned into → UD.) In 1919 DCL acquired the entire shares of John Haig & Co, and in 1925 also acquired →

Haig & Haig, which had very successfully launched → Pinch in America, known as → Dimple in Europe. This → de luxe brand sold alongside the simpler but no less successful Haig Gold Label and → Haig & Haig Five Star and → Golden Age, which no longer exists. In order to promote their whisky the Haigs also created one of the most brilliant slogans: 'Don't be vague, ask for Haig'. Since 1994 the Haig Fine Old has been available again from → GuinnessUDV. A vatted malt, the → Glenleven, is also available. Under the umbrella of DCL Haig was responsible for Glenkinchie as well as → Glenlossie and the neigbouring → Mannochmore Distillery, built in 1971. The American NATO Commander-in-Chief, Alexander Haig, is also a descendant of the Bemersyde Haigs.

Haig & Haig Scottish whisky company founded in 1888 by a member of the great Haig whisky family, mainly for activities in the American market. There they had great success with → Pinch, the American version of → Dimple. Having been under the control of → Robertson & Baxter since 1906, and were sold to → DCL, before being taken over by John → Haig & Co in 1925. A blend named → Haig & Haig Five Star still bears their name.

Hair of the Dog A phrase meaning a cure for a hangover. It is said to derive from the English poet John Heywood, who recommended the hair from the dog that one had been bitten by on the previous evening. A generous shot of Scotch and a tablespoon of honey are shaken with ice. It is possible that one may feel worse than before.

Hakushu Japanese distillery 120 kilometres to the west of Tokyo, situated in a region that belongs to the 'Japanese Alps'. It is the most important wine-growing area in the country and → Suntory have wine vaults there. The huge plant, built in 1973, lies near to Japan's holy Mount Fujiyama, and would almost be swallowed up by the forest were it not for two pagodas joined by a footbridge. They resemble those which could formerly be seen at Suntory's older → Yamazaki Distillery, but here do not crown a maltings – Hakushu gets all the malt it needs from abroad. Instead, they adorn an excellent museum, in which valuable exhibits can be seen and where one can learn about the history of whisky in Japan and elsewhere.

The distillery has an annual production of 55 million litres of malt whisky, and it is without doubt the largest in the world. More precisely it is really three different distilleries, the third of which joined the two older ones in 1981. They are in one building but have different → mash tuns and → wash backs. Different yeasts and variously peated malts enable the 24 → pot stills to produce a variety of whiskies. The warehouses, which they call cellars, are also huge and can house 800,000 casks, most of which previously contained bourbon. They are prepared in the plant's own cooperage.

There is a → proprietor's bottling of a Hakushu malt whisky, which Suntory do not call single malt but → pure malt – so it could be that along with the malt whiskies from Hakushu there may be a shot of Scotch malt whisky; after all, Suntory also owns → Auchentoshan, → Bowmore and → Glen Garioch. As the company is fond of being vague and the label of the 12-year-old is by no means clear, drinkers will have to live with such speculation.

Halewood International Ltd English company. They are mainly importers of wine, but also have spirits in their range. The company is based in Huyton, near Liverpool. Apart from the bourbon → Kentucky Gold and the → Canadian Gold, they also have five Scotch blends, → Charly Richards named after a company subsidiary, → Highland Gold, → Highland Poacher, → Highland Prince and → Tartan Prince. Another subsidiary, the very old wine merchants → Hall & Bramley Ltd, has three other brands. There is a branch in Dublin which is responsible for the Irish cream whisky liqueur → Irish Meadow, which used to be called → Meadow Cream.

Hall & Bramley Ltd English wine merchants. The small enterprise, founded in 1860, remained independent for a long time but now belongs to → Halewood International Ltd, retaining its own address in Liverpool. Its most important brand was → Glen Ghoil, which no longer exists, but deserves a special mention as the whisky received an official certificate from a civic chemist recommending its 'regular use'. Other blends are → Clan Ardroch, → Glen Carron and → Highland Pearl.

Hallmark Scotch blend from → Morrison Bowmore. It is 8 years old and is said to be identical to → Islay Legend and to have a very high malt content of 50%.

Hamashkeh Scotch blend formerly produced by → JBB (Greater Europe) plc at the Invergordon Disillery. It was sold by EMA Kosher Foods, a company that guarantees that all it products are made strictly in accordance with Jewish dietary customs. This means that only certain raw materials may be used, that certain rules must be obeyed in their processing and that a rabbi guarantees that all the regulations have been observed. Only then can it be said to be → kosher.

Hammer German whisky. Its exact name is 'Club Whisky Extra Special'. It is produced by the company Hammer Brennerei Landau & Macholl in Heilbronn.

Hancock's Reserve Kentucky straight bourbon. Its full name is Hancock's President's Reserve and its producer is Hancock Distilling in Frankfort, but it actually comes from → Sazerac. Its name commemorates Hancock Taylor, one of the pioneers who went to Kentucky in 1774 and settled in the → Leestown area – where the → Ancient Age Distillery which produces this → single barrel bourbon is now situated. Master distiller Gary Gayheart selects the barrels for the whiskey which has been on the market since 1991. It has the unusual strength of 88.9° (44.5%) and comes in a square decanter.

Hankey Bannister Scotch blend from an old London company of the same name. Introduced at the end of the 19th century it passed via Saccone & Speed to → IDV. In 1988 they sold it at a 'friendly price' to → Inver House Distillers Ltd. The blend, which has always been popular, is available as a → standard blend aged 12, 15 and 21 years. Hankey Bannister are also producers of the vatted → Glen Drummond.

Happy Morning Whisky cocktail. Take equal measures of advocaat and Cordial Médoc, add a generous shot of Scotch and shake well with ice. Drain and serve in a wine glass.

Harrod's London's most famous department store. Its range is still breathtaking, but nowadays it is mainly tourists who flock to Knightsbridge – the 'top people', apparently shop there after closing time. The current owner, The wine department's range is no longer as great nor as exquisite as it was in the 1970s, when there was hardly a better address in London for malt whiskies. The number of their own brands, which, according to Philip Morrice in his *Schweppes Guide to Scotch* used to be made by → Whyte & Mackay, has also decreased. Of the three blends previously available only Harrod's VOH Special Blend remains. There is also a 15-year-old vatted, Harrod's Pure Malt. After a period in which, amazingly, they did not have an own-brand single malt of their own, they now have one again: a 12-year-old → Tamnavulin (40%).

Hart Brothers Scottish whisky company which for more than 30 years has mainly been involved in the blending and export business. Their house brand, with the name of the two brothers on the bottle, is → Harts. They also still have the blends → Scots Lion and → Old Glasgow. The other brands belonging to the company are not being bottled at present: Old Curlers, Old Fox, Old Keg and Speakers – possibly because the two brothers have been inspired by the success of other → independent bottlers and no longer use their stock of casks for blends, but for their own series of single malts which they market under their own name with the adjunct 'Finest Collection'. They are all bottled at 43%. A new collection appears about every six months, often with malt whiskies from distilleries which have long since closed down. A particularly costly single malt, a 31-year-old Bowmore, was chosen for their equally costly → Dynasty Decanter, with golden medallions set in silver displaying the pictures of seven monarchs of the House of Stuart.

Harts 8-year-old Scotch blend from Donald Hart & Co, one of the two → Hart Brothers, who have long been producers of blends in Glasgow, and more recently → independent bottlers of single malts.

Harvey's Special Scotch blend that nowadays is made by → GuinnessUDV and which is a reminder of one of the oldest firms in the Scotch whisky business. The origins of John & Robert Harvey go back to 1770. The company lost its independence as a result of the collapse in 1898 of the → Pattison brothers, and in 1902 found itself under the control of → DCL, who later registered the licence of the → Aultmore Distillery with Harvey. Since 1992 it has been in the name of→ UMGD/Wm → Sanderson & Sons, so that the → standard blend is all that remains of Harvey.

Harwood Canadian whisky, produced by → Seagram in Canada and sent in bulk by road tanker to → Heaven Hill in Kentucky, where it is bottled for the American market.

Haryana Indian distillery, situated in the far northern state of Punjab. It is one of the many businesses belonging to Modi Enterprises, one of the largest industrial groups in the country. In addition to the production and sale of whisky, they are also involved in chemicals, synthetic fibres, electrodes, electronic equipment, cement and textiles. The company is particularly proud of its social involvement in the fields of health and education. Apart from rum and gin, several whiskies are produced: → Benson, → Black Castle, → Champion, → Double Dog, → Knight King and → Old Barrel.

Hatch Canadian whiskey family who helped to form Hiram → Walker. Harry Hatch began his career with a hotel and bar and then became a sales representative for → Corby, and in 1923, with several partners, first bought → Gooderham and Worts, and then three years later Walker, forming the company Hiram Walker–Gooderham and Worts. He also had prohibition in the USA to thank for the ascent of his business. He believed in its imminent end and prepared for it by keeping large quantities of → Canadian Club at the ready. When the dry years were over in the USA he was able to conquer the US market; the American distilleries had been unable to produce anything for years and the public had long since grown accustomed to smuggled Canadian whiskey. A member of the Hatch family married into the French Courvoisier cognac dynasty, and another one later became boss of Hiram Walker.

Hazelburn Defunct Scottish malt distillery. It was one of the many distilleries in → Campbeltown which were forced to close following → prohibition in the USA. It was possibly founded as early as 1796, possibly in 1825, but was definitely in existence by 1836. It was bought by the whisky baron Peter → Mackie in 1920, who set up a scientific laboratory there. It was also the place where a young man named Masataka → Taketsuru gained experience, which upon his return to Japan helped him set up → Suntory and → Nikka. It therefore played a part in the establishment of the Japanese whisky industry.

Mackie's company, → White Horse Distillers closed the distillery in 1925, though its → warehouses continued to be used for a long time by → DCL. J & A Mitchell, the owners of two of the last three distilleries in Campbeltown (the others are Glen Gyle and Glen Scotia) have been using → multiple distillation in their → Springbank Distillery to make a second malt called → Longrow, which is also named after a Campbeltown distillery that has long since disappeared. The company, which has also kept the tradition of the region alive with a series of miniatures named after old local distilleries, announced in the autumn of 1997 that it had distilled a new malt, which was triple-distilled – unlike Springbank and Longrow, with a different separation of the → middle cut, and made from completely unpeated → malt. When it is ready in 10 or 12 years it will bear the name Hazelburn.

Head Term which has two meanings in the production of malt whisky: firstly it is the upper part of the → pot stills where the → lyne arm is attached, and secondly it is the initial liquid which runs out of the → spirit still during the distillation of the → low wines. It is usually called the → foreshots.

Heart of the run Term which is sometimes used instead of the customary → middle cut.

This means that during the final distillation (that is in Scotland usually the second one and in Ireland the third) that takes place in the → spirit still, the → stillman has the task of → cutting the unusable → foreshots, from the heart, the middle cut, and from the following, equally unusable, → feints towards the end of distillation. He has to keep an eye on the liquid running out of the still and through the → spirit safe in order to decide, based on the appearance, temperature and measurement of alcholic strength, when the heart of the run'good' begins and ends. This is collected and later filled into casks to mature. The → foreshots and → feints are redistilled.

Heather Cream Scotch whisky liqueur which is made by R Carmichael & Sons, a subsidiary of → Inver House Distillers Ltd. It attempts to provide a Scottish answer to → Bailey's, is also bottled at 17% and is based on a combination of whisky and cream. In contrast to Bailey's and all the others, it is said to be the first cream liqueur made from malt whisky. The producers used to claim that they used a single malt from the → Bladnoch Distillery, which belonged to them for 10 years. However they have not disclosed which whisky is currently being used. Following a relaunch, the brand now not only comes in a more modern botttle, but it is also considerably sweeter, with marked vanilla and chocolate flavours.

Heatherdale Scotch blend, a → standard blend from → CWS who are based in Manchester where they have a large bottling plant. They no longer produce it themselves, but it is supplied to them by a prominent Scotch distiller.

Heathwood Scotch blend, a small brand from → GuinnessUDV. C & J → Mc Donald are named as producers, having passed toJ → UD after its parent company, Arthur → Bell & Sons, was taken over by → Guinness in the 1980s.

Heaven Hill American distillery in Bardstown, which was built in 1935 with the participation of the Shapira family, who still own it. It is the only large whisky enterprise in the USA with its own distillery that remains independent. The large capacity of the distillery, the size of the warehouses (that store half a million barrels) and the rationalised method of production, are all factors which have helped maintain its independence. The fact that it owns a huge number of brands is a particular advantage: however there are so many that it is neither possible to give a complete overview here, nor is the company in a position to name an exact number. It is amazing that this has all been achieved in a relatively short time and without any company heritage or traditions.

The company began immediately after → prohibition, when the whole history of American whiskey really started anew and some old-established firms were forced to make a fresh start. The Shapiras recognised the chances that the end of the dry years would bring. They had the necessary money and a brand with which they could get through the early years. Moreover everything was on a large scale: 400 to 500 barrels could be produced a day, there were 31 fermenting vessels, several copper → beer stills and a doubler, 25 warehouses of their own and a further 19 in the old → T W Samuels Distillery in Deatsville and in another distillery in Bardstown – and despite all this they sometimes had to buy in extra supplies to satisfy the demand for their own brands, as Heaven Hill supplies a lot of whiskey to other bottlers. If a bottle bears an address in Bardstown and quotes an unknown name, it is very likely that the contents come from Heaven Hill.

The same → mash bill was used for all its own brands, with 75% corn, 13% rye and 12% malt barley for the straight bourbons and 65% rye, 23% corn and 12% malt for the straight ryes. The yeast goes back to a culture that Earl Beam, a member of the famous family of James → 'Jim' Beam, brought with him when he became the first master distiller in 1935; he was followed by his son Parker and his grandson Craig, who also holds a responsible position, is not sure when he will be able to take over the reins.

In November 1996 lightning struck warehouse J. The fire spread to warehouse No. 1 and from there the inferno raged on, burning barrels flew through the air, the escaping whisky burst into flames eventually consuming the whole distillery. 90,000 barrels fell victim to the flames. Nevertheless, it could have been worse. Production was moved to → Early Times. There are still enough barrels of maturing whisky and Max Shapira, the current vice-president, is working on reconstruction. The sale of the → Bernheim Distillery (together with the brand → Old Fitzgerald) in March 1999 will also have helped overcome the temporary difficulties; at that time → Heaven Hill was part of the consortium, also consisting of → Sazerac and David → Sherman, that paid $ 171 million to take over the distillery and three other bourbons from → GuinnessUDV.

At present it is uncertain whether, following the purchase of Bernheim, it is intended to rebuild the old distillery. If they do decide to do so, then it is planned to construct new buildings on the site where everything began in 1935, in the hollow by the river on the road to Loretto – on the site where William Heavenhill had his farm in the 19th century, and whose name the distillery should have borne if it had not been for a mistake made by the notary who wrote down Heaven Hill. This is the name of a blended whisky, but principally of the Kentucky straight bourbon. Paradoxically, Heaven Hill sometimes does not name its own distillery as producer but the Kentucky Deluxe Distilling Co. It is available as a 4-year-old (80°/40%), a 6 year-old (90°/45%) and a 10-year-old (86°/43%): a 28-year-old is to be bottled for Japan.

Old Heaven Hill is 7-years-old and → bottled in bond. But the most important brand of all is → Evan Williams, one version of which occupies second place among the top 10 bourbons in the USA. It was the first one to be named after a whiskey pioneer; → Elijah Craig followed. New purchases added other great names: → Henry McKenna, → J T S Brown (also available as a blended whisky), → J W Dant, → Mattingly & Moore, → T W Samuels and Old Fitzgerald. Other straights include → Old 1889, → Cabin Still, → Echo Springs and → W W Beam. The company also has the following ryes, → Pikesville and → Stephen Foster (but unfortunately no longer → Rittenhouse and → North Brook), the corn whiskeys → Georgia Moon and J W Corn and the blended American whiskeys → Paul Jones, → Philadelphia and → Wilson. And finally Heaven Hill produces → Medley and → Pennypacker which are only available in Germany.

Hebridean Whisky Liqueur Scotch whisky liqueur from a firm that has just added a 'Co' to the name of its product, is based in Glasgow and unfortunately gives no information as to which recipe it uses. At 20% it is one of the lighter representatives of its species.

Hedges & Butler Scottish company which for Glaswegians has the same ring to it as → Berry Brothers & Rudd has for Londoners: an old established wine merchants who can trace their origins back to 1667, meaning that they are even older than their colleagues in the south, who, however, are still independent. Both began as wine merchants and have made excellent names for themselves. Hedges & Butler were court suppliers to no less than nine monarchs, and if any firm has the right to call its products 'royal', then it has. Every bottle of whisky that leaves their premises displays the proud engraving of the date 1667. Like every self-respecting wine merchant the Glaswegians had their own whiskies, house blends which bore the name of their producer as a simple guarantee of quality. That is still the case, although the firm, which is also very successful in the export business, was bought out by the brewery giant Bass, which dealt in wines and spirits under the name of the old company (and who, of course, like their other subsidiary J G → Thomson, also supplied their own pubs). In the 1980s Bass, in the same ownership as their former competitor Charrington since 1967, also let Hedges & Butler take up the UK distribution rights to → Dewar's. They used to have five blends and the vatted malt → Royal Malt, which is still available. Of the blends only Royal, which is a → standard blend, and the 12-year-old Royal Finest de Luxe, which has received several awards (including a double gold medal at the Wine and Spirit Competition in Bristol) are still available.

The brand now belongs to Ian → Macleod which launched under the name of their subsidiary a series of 'Vintage Malts'.

Hedonism Scotch whisky from a company calling itself Compass Box. It was founded in London by the American John Glaser, who was formerly the manager at → GuinnessUDV responsible for → Johnnie Walker. In future he intends to bring out the new bottlings at about six-monthly intervals. The first, Hedonism, is a vatted → grain whisky. It combines a cask of each from two defunct grain distilleries, → Cambus and → Caledonian.

Henry Clay Kentucky straight bourbon belonging to the → 'Rare Bourbons' from → UD, a series which the company added to their Scottish → 'Rare Malts' which to the delight of whisk(e)y lovers (and historians) made whiskeys available from distilleries which had long since closed down. Whether the series will continue remains uncertain since the → UD successor, → GuinnessUDV, has parted with almost all its companies and brands in the USA. There really was a distillery named after the American politician Henry Clay, but it has not existed for a long time. It is a shame that, → GuinnessUDV do not say exactly where the bourbons come from; but fantasy names are traditional in Kentucky. Jim Murray has divulged where this one comes from: the old Astor Distillery, the remains of which lie right next to the → Bernheim Distillery, which also used to belong to → UD. It is 16 years old, has a strength of 90.6°/45.3% and with a total of 2,400 bottles it is very exclusive.

Henry McKenna Kentucky straight bourbon from → Heaven Hill. In 1960 it began to promote some of its products by naming them after whiskey pioneers – such as McKenna. But unlike the other brands this one was not originally created by Heaven Hill but was acquired from → Seagram in the early 1980s. Its origins go back to 1855 and the Irish immigrant who began to distil whiskey in the tradition of his home country, quickly earning himself a good reputation and becoming famous, chiefly because he allowed his whisky to mature for at least three years. Three years after his death in 1893 it was already available all over the country. The McKennas soon built their own distillery in Fairfield which shut down during → prohibition but afterwards recommenced production. In 1941 it was sold to Seagram who allowed the brand to die, followed by the distillery. At Heaven Hill it is not made according to the old formula but to that which is used for all the company's own bourbons (75% corn, 13% rye, 12% malt barley). 'Kentucky's Finest Table Whiskey Since 1855' is available at 80°/40%, without an age statement. For several years it has also been available as a 10-year-old → single barrel → bottled in bond at 100°/50%.

Heritage Scotch blend with which → Allied Distillers Ltd took part in 'The → Spirit of Scotland' organised by the International Wine & Spirit Competition in 1994. This was the year of the 500th anniversary of the first documentary mention of distilled spirits (John → Cor).

Heritage Selection, The Series of four Scottish → Highland single malts from → Seagram, in which the distilleries of → Longmorn and → Strathisla are represented as well as malts from → Glen Keith and → Benriach which had never previously been available as a → proprietor's bottlings. It is available as a 'Limited Edition' as well as in a gift pack of the four as miniatures with a normal-sized bottle of → Longmorn.

It is questionable whether this series will continue to be available. In the spring of 2001, Seagram's drinks portfolio was taken over by a consortium consisting of → Diageo and → Groupe Pernod-Ricard.

Hewitts Irish whiskey bottled at 40% vol. A blend whose label still bears the old address 'Cork Distilleries Co, North Mall, Cork', but which is nowadays produced in → Midleton and sold by → IDG in Dublin. Thomas Hewitt, who gave it his name, founded the Watercourse Distillery in Cork in 1782. From 1868 it was allied with Midleton as well as the three other distilleries in Cork, The Green, Daly's and North Mall, and later only used as a maltings and for the production of → grain. Until recently it was still possible to see its remains. Hewitts has been on the market since 1960 and describes itself as being a blend of 'old malt and light whiskies'. The malts are a lighter → Bushmills and an unusually oily Midleton.

Hi

Hi Japanese blend from → Nikka. The name indicates that it is trying to appeal to a young, western-oriented public. It is a → de luxe blend with the unusual strength of 39%. It is available in different sized bottles as well as in a white carton resembling a Tetrapak.

Hibiki Japanese blend which is on the borderline between the → premium and → super-premium sectors. The very high malt share is composed of about 30 different malts from → Suntory's → Yamazaki Distillery, all of which are about 20 years old. The name means 'choir' or 'harmony' in Japanese. Suntory promotes the brand as one of its top products and it is available internationally.

Hielanman Scotch blend from the renowned house of William → Cadenhead in Aberdeen. Its present owners, J & A → Mitchell, who also own → Springbank and → Eaglesome, have revived an old brand name with it.

High Commissioner Standard Scotch blend produced by A Bulloch & Co, part of the → Glen Catrine Bonded Warehouse Ltd. It is the company's most successful brand in the UK.

Highfield Irish whiskey from → Cooley, which in other markets (and in supermarket chains) is available by the name of → Dunlow.

Highland Abbey Scotch blend from → CWS which is made for them a prominent Scotch distiller.

Highland Bird Scotch blend from → QSI, a subsidiary of William → Grant & Sons.

Highland Black Scotch blend. The brand is produced exclusively for the UK ALDI and is obtainable at UK branches of the discounter chain. The 'Special Reserve' contains 8-year-old whiskies.

Highland Blend 15-year-old → premium Scotch blend. It comes from the renowned wine merchants → Avery's of Bristol, who are no longer independent and do not produce it as one of their own bottlings, obtaining it from an unidentified source. The company reports that they have particular success with this blend in Japan.

Highland Breeze Scotch blend. It is a brand from James → MacArthur Jr & Co, which is owned by → Inver House Distillers Ltd and is a → standard blend with no indication of age.

Highland Cattle Trade name for a 'Pure Highland Scotch Malt Whisky', which normally means a vatted malt, but which, owing to the description on the label stating 'Distilled and bottled by J & G Grant', is clearly a single malt from → Glenfarclas, as the company does not have any other distillery. They also produce other special bottlings such as Highland Cattle or → Eagle of Spey.

Highland Clan Scotch → standard blend formerly from → Seagram, produced by their Scottish subsidiary The → Chivas & Glenlivet Group, now part of → Groupe Pernod-Ricard.

Highland Club Scotch blend that used to belong to the portfolio of Distillers Agency Ltd, a subsidiary of → DCL, and is therefore now one of the many brands of its successor → GuinnessUDV.

Highland Collection Series of single malts produced and bottled in Scotland for the American company → All Saint's Brands in Minneapolis. The exact origin is not indicated, only its age: 12, 14 and 17 years. The labels are reproductions of pictures by the British artist Albany Wiseman and give the series its name.

Highland Cream Scotch blend that is better known by its full name → Teacher's Highland Cream.

Highland Dew Scotch blend from the Glen Lyon Blending Company in Glasgow, one of → UD's many subsidiaries.

Highland Distillers Glasgow-based whisky company that, until the autumn of 1999, was still independent. Unlike William → Grant & Sons or the Mitchells of → Springbank, it was not owned by a family but was a joint-stock company whose shares were traded on the London Stock Exchange. There had been takeover attempts (such as that in 1979 by Hiram → Walker) but they were successfully resisted. However 20 years later the →

Edrington Group, who already owned a large share in Highland, joined forces with William Grant & Sons, in order to take the company over completely and create The → 1887 Group.

The company has kept all the distilleries it has acquired. Even → Glenglassaugh, whose licence it cancelled in 1992, was not sold. Two distilleries have been in its hands for more than 100 years: → Bunnahabhain on → Islay and → Glenrothes; their builders amalgamated to incorporate Highland Distilleries in 1887. Glenglassaugh and → Tamdhu joined a few years later followed by → Highland Park in 1935. In all these years the company was solely involved in the distilling and sales of its malts to brokers and blenders. This changed in 1948 when it acquired a 35% share in → Robertson & Baxter, which via Lang Brothers also had a share in → Glengoyne Distillery and undertook the production of → Cutty Sark for → Berry Bros & Rudd. The latter are still located in London but the other three share an address in Glasgow.

In 1970 the firm acquired Matthew → Gloag & Son and their successful blend The → Famous Grouse, which is the bestselling blend in Scotland and number two in the UK. In the 1980s connections to another distillery were established via their association with the French company Rémy: at that time their subsidiary Cointreau had a share in the → Glenturret Distillery, which had in the meantime been completely taken over by Highland Distillers. In 1996, after the blend → Black Bottle had been acquired by → Allied, the company bought Rémy's 26% share in → Macallan – the beginning of a dramatic development. For a short time later, in July 1996, they made an alliance with → Suntory, who owned 25% of Macallan, and made a hostile takeover. A short time later the entire enterprise was restructured.

The common umbrella for all the company distilleries is now the subsidiary → Highland Malt Distilling with its headquarters in the old Macallan offices in Craigellachie. In 1996 Highland and Rémy entered into a joint venture with the Indian company DCM Shiram, so that they would be able to get a foothold in the promising Asian market. Rémy was also the partner responsible for the national distribution in various countries (for example in Germany). In 1999 it was announced that in future a new company, named → Maxxium, would be responsible for the distribution of all products and would unite Highland Distillers, Rémy and → JBB under its umbrella.

All the whiskies from the company's own distilleries, except those from Glenglassaugh, are also available as single malts in → distillery bottlings, although the Glenrothes is sold by → Berry Bros & Rudd. Since the good old name of Matthew Gloag & Son has been given up, the others are all sold by the subsidiary Highland Distillers Brands in Perth. Apart from The → Famous Grouse there is a second blend, Black Bottle. In 1997 → Dunhill decided to transfer its production of → Old Master from → IDV to Highland. There are also two → whisky liqueurs, → Glenturret Malt Liqueur and → Fairlie's. 'Gloag's Gin' was introduced in 1996.

Highland Earl Standard Scotch blend obtainable at UK branches of ALDI.

Highland Fusilier Scotch vatted malt from → Gordon & MacPhail in Elgin. The city plays a part in the history of the regiments of the Highland Light Infantry and the Royal Scots Fusiliers who were merged in 1959 to form the Royal Highland Fusiliers. The whisky was created for the establishment of the new regiment. It is available aged 5, 8, 15, 21 and 25 years. Its basis whiskies all come from the → Speyside region.

Highland Gathering Scotch blend from → Lombard Scotch Whisky based on the Isle of Man. It is available in various versions: as a → standard blend without an age statement, and aged 8, 12, 15, 18, 21 and 25 years.

Highland Gold Scotch blend. It comes from → Halewood International Ltd, based in Huyton on Merseyside.

Highland Legend Scotch blend from → Angus Dundee.

Highland Line Theoretical line dividing the → Lowlands from the → Highlands. On the map of

1799, which was included in the report of the Select Committee of the House of Commons, there was an 'intermediate area' between the two zones which encompassed large parts of the coastal strip of the Highlands. The purpose of such a division was the introduction and application of new taxes. The *Collins Encyclopaedia of Scotland* quotes Fullarton's *Gazeteer of Scotland*: 'The line commences at the mouth of the river Nairn; it then, with the exception of a slight north-eastward or outward curve, the central point of which is on the river Spey, runs due south-east until it strikes the river Dee at Tullach, ... then runs generally south ... (to the) North Esk; it thence, over a long stretch, runs almost due south-west, and with scarcely a deviation, till it falls upon the Clyde at Ardmore ... onward to the Atlantic Ocean'. The map mentioned has a second line which comes close to that used today to divide the → whisky regions. It begins in Greenock in the west of Glasgow and then runs to the north, past the city, and ends near Dundee.

Highland Line was meant to provide a clear division between the tax areas of the distillers to the north of it and those to the south. It was perceived as discriminatory in the Highlands, and as a provocation to distil illicitly and to smuggle.

Highland Malt Distilling Scottish whisky company. It is a subsidiary of → Highland Distillers and was first established in 1996, being formed after Highland and → Suntory together gained a majority share of → Macallan and then won complete control of the renowned family-owned distillery by means of a hostile takeover. In order to achieve synergy, Highland's marketing and distribution were initially concentrated at Matthew → Gloag & Son in Perth, which shortly after was rechristened Highland Distillers Brands. The entire production, including the running of the company's own distilleries, whose total had risen to eight as a result of the new acquisition, is in the hands of Highland Malt Distilling. The eight distilleries are → Bunnahabhain, → Glenglassaugh, → Glengoyne, → Glenrothes, → Glenturret, → Highland Park, Macallan and → Tamdhu.

Highland Mist Scotch blend that was formerly made by → Barton. The complicated history of this company explains why the present owner of Barton, → Canandaigua, as well as the Scottish → Glen Catrine Bonded Warehouse Ltd (and the → Argyll concern to whom → Safeway – among others – belong), asserted their rights to the brand. At present only the Americans are availing themselves of those rights, and bottle and sell the blend in the USA.

Highland Mountain Scotch blend from → Morrison Bowmore, made mainly for the USA and the Far East. It is available in two versions, aged 21 and 31 years.

Highland Nectar Scotch blend created at the end of the 19th century as one of the first brands of → DCL and which was solely intended for export. When DCL was negotiating with the large Scottish whisky houses around 1920, they parted with their own blending business and founded the Distillers Agency Ltd, which continued with this brand as well as → *King George IV* and → *DCL* (and initially ran → Knockdhu and then later → Rosebank Distillery). Today, like most former DCL companies and brands, it belongs to → GuinnessUDV.

Highland Park Scottish malt distillery on the southern outskirts of Kirkwall, the main town on Orkney, belonging to the Islands whisky region. It is the northernmost distillery in Scotland. Highland Park, which lies on a hillside, is one of the rare distilleries which still has traditional → floor maltings and two → kilns.

The distillery was founded in 1795 by David Robinson (although the present owners give the year 1798) and was taken over by James Grant in 1895. His father had been manager of → Glenlivet. The family, with whom the licence is still registered to this day, sold the distillery to → Highland Distillers in 1935. The whisky, which is one of the greatest malts, owes its rounded and harmonious character to the peat, the sea air and the sweet heather which is used during kilning. It has been available as a 12-year-old single malt in a → proprietor's bottling since the early 1970s. From time to time there is also a → vintage like that from 1967. The two new versions introduced at the end of 1997, aged 18 and 25 years, will be bottled regularly.

Highlands

In June 1998 the 200th anniversary of the distillery was celebrated with a limited and numbered bottling of the Bicentenary Vintage 1977. In the same year a tasting was organised via the internet, which was celebrated by a bottling of exactly 228 bottles of a 1974 Highland Park Online Tasting (52.6%). There are only 665 bottles of the Highland Park 1958, which was launched in summer 1999.

Highland Pearl Scotch blend. It comes from the old company of wine merchants → Hall & Bramley Ltd in Liverpool. It is a 12-year-old → de luxe blend.

Highland Poacher Scotch blend from → Halewood International, who are chiefly importers of wine.

Highland Prince Scotch blend from a company based in Huyton near Liverpool: → Halewood International Ltd.

Highland Queen Scotch blend from → Macdonald & Muir, a subsidiary of → Glenmorangie plc (until 1996 → Macdonald Martin Distilleries). The blend was created in the 1890s. Its name was inspired by the headquarters of the firm which for many years were located at Queen's Docks in Leith. The grey warehouses were decorated with the words 'Highland Queen' until 1998. Now that the company has moved near to Edinburgh Airport and the original buildings opposite the new Scottish Office have been converted to flats and small businesses, the name will soon disappear. But the whisky will remain the company's most important blend. It used to be available in numerous age categories and even as a whisky liqueur. Today it is bottled as a → standard blend without an age statement, as a → premium blend with the name Highland Queen Majesty, as a 15-year-old Grand Reserve, as a 21-year-old Supreme and a 15-year-old Highland Queen – Queen of Scots.

Highland Reserve A → standard blend produced by → QSI, a subsidiary of William → Grant & Sons.

Highland Rose Scotch blend from → Burn Stewart. The → standard blend is aged 3 years and a → de luxe blend at 12 years.

Highland Selection Sereis of single malts from → Inver House Distillers Ltd bottled at 46% apart from a single cask of 1975 → cask strength bottled for the German market. The series comprises → An Cnoc (1983, 18 years), → Balblair (1969, 31 yeras), → Balmenach (1972, 18 years), → Pulteney (1974, 26 years) and → Speyburn (1973, 23 years).

Highland Stag Scotch blend made by the UK company → Red Lion Blending, which resulted from the alliance in the 1970s of the Surrey-based Highland Stag Whiskies and R N → MacDonald, which in its turn was founded by one of the descendants of the great → Long John MacDonald. It is only available at English branches of the discount store ALDI.

Highland Star Scotch blend from → Premier Scotch Whisky Co, which produces it using the name of one of its many subsidiary labels. It is available in five age categories – 3, 5, 8, 10 and 12 years old – and is intended solely for export.

Highland Woodcock Scotch blend. It is produced for J T Davies & Sons located in Croydon, Surrey. Its distribution area is limited to London and the Home Counties as it is exclusively sold in the 30 or so pubs of the company and their wine shops, which are named 'Davison's'.

Highlander Scotch blend from H → Stenham, which is available in the age categories customary for this company of 3, 5, 8, 10 and 12 years old. There is also a vatted malt called Highlander Straight Malt, an unusual name for a Scotch whisky. The brand is produced solely for export, mainly to Latin America.

Highlands Scottish → whisky region, which broadly speaking encompasses the whole of the mainland north of Glasgow/Edinburgh. Because of the size of the area, the Highlands are divided into the Southern and Northern Highlands, and the Western and Eastern Highlands. There is also a core area which is named after the river flowing through it, → Speyside. Some authors are not satisfied with this and attempt an even more detailed division. For example Michael Jackson in his book *Whisky* endeavours to use other rivers such as the Findhorn, the Lossie and the Deveron. Problems arise when the subdivisions are also used to classify various whisky styles. These do not exist; it is not possible to reduce all malts to a common denominator with regards to character, either for the whole region or for individual parts of it. In fact it would be diametrically opposed to what makes malt whiskies so unique and special: that each one has its own, unmistakeable character.

High proof Term for whiskies which are bottled at higher than normal alcoholic strength so that the drinker can decide how much water is added. The term is often used as a synonym for → barrel °proof or → cask strength.

Highwood Canadian whiskey which is named after the company which produces it. It began in 1974 as Sunnyvale Distillers with a distillery in the town of High River, near Calgary in Alberta, which is probably the smallest in the country but belongs to the most rapidly growing independent whisky producers in Canada. The location was not chosen at random: the region at the foot of the Rocky Mountains and in the middle of the rich grain fields has also enticed other enterprises to build a distillery (→ Alberta, → Palliser). Highwood is the only distillery in the country which exclusively uses wheat for its standard whiskey, in order to make the purest – vodka. It has a wide range of different types of drink, including ready-made mixed drinks and Scotch. The latter is imported from Scotland and then diluted with water before bottling. The company's own two Canadian whiskies are the 4-year-old Highwood and → Centennial.

Hill & Hill Kentucky whiskey. It is one of the regional brands that were formerly produced by National Distillers in → Frankfort, but it is not known from exactly which of its three distilleries it came. Like their parent company, → Old Crow, → Old Taylor and → Old Grand-Dad passed into the hands of → American Brands in 1987. They now have the brand made by their subsidiary → JBB in their → Jim Beam Distilleries in Boston or Clermont, but, for some time now, only as a blended whisky. The straight bourbon is no longer produced.

Hill Thomson & Company Scottish whisky company whose origins go back to William Hill, who opened his shop in 1793 in Rose Street Lane, Edinburgh and later moved round the corner to Frederick Street, where the firm was situated until the 1980s. In 1857 the family-run business went into partnership with William Thomson and adopted its present name. Two decades later William Shaw joined the company and with → Queen Anne created the blend with which it has since been identified. It remained the flagship brand when they lost their independence and joined with → Glenlivet Distillers in 1970. From 1977 until the takeover of Seagram's spirit interests by a →Diageo/ →Groupe Pernod-Ricard partnership in 2000, Hill Thomson & Company was part of the → Seagram subsidiary The → Chivas & Glenlivet Group, which continues to offer several brands using the old name: apart from the Queen Anne, there was → Black Watch, → Prince Charlie, → St. Leger, → Something Special and → Treasury.

Hillside Scottish malt distillery which only bore this name between 1964 and 1980 and was then renamed → Glenesk. Whilst a single malt was available as a → distillery bottling from Wm → Sanderson, the former name of Hillside was preserved in several versions which →UD/ → GuinnessUDV, included in their → 'Rare Malts' collection. It is difficult to maintain an overview as differing versions are supplied to various markets. Three 25-year-olds are known, which were bottled at 61.9% (1969), 60.10% (1970) and 62.0% (1971). The 22-year-old was distilled in 1971 and bottled at 60.1%. In their → 'Silent Stills' series (No. 4) → Signatory had a 28-year-old Hillside, distilled in 1971 and bottled at 51.4% on 1 February 2000.

Hips Japanese blend that describes itself as 'The brightest Whiskey', a spelling which is unusual in Japan. This break with convention also represents a break with the Scottish tradition which is fostered in Japan. But → Kirim-Seagram, who produce it, and whose → News already plainly tasted of bourbon and was aimed at a young public, presumably wanted to cater for the interest in American-style whiskeys which can no longer be overlooked in Japan.

Hiram Walker's Premium Whisky from Hiram → Walker, which the Canadian firm exports in → bulk to Venezuela, where it is bottled.

Historic Scotland A Scottish quango which is responsible for many ancient buildings and monuments. On behalf of → GuinnessUDV Historic Scotland takes care of → Dallas Dhu Distillery, which has an excellently designed museum. It is well worth visiting and has retained the ability to restart production at any time. The museum shop also sells malt whisky from Dallas Dhu, bottled by → Gordon & MacPhail. In spring 1998 the last cask (number 327) distilled in the distillery (in 1983) was bottled, resulting in 294 bottles. The numbers 1, 294, 19 and 83 were put to one side, and the others sold at a price of £95 (with a 20% discount for the 'Friends'). The 100th anniversary of the distillery was celebrated with the bottling of cask no. 262 from 1983, the 438 bottles selling at a markedly higher price of £135 (£110 for the 'Friends'). For the Millennium Historic Scotland brought out a 25-year-old Dallas Dhu from 1974 which was bottled at 43%.

The names of some of Historic Scotland's greatest tourist attractions are also to be found on whisky bottles: a 15-year-old single malt bears the straightforward name The Castle, and shows a picture of Edinburgh Castle.

Stirling Castle is a 12-year-old single, whilst the 10-year-old St. Andrews Castle and the 8-year-old Urquhart Castle are → pure malts. The first three have been bottled at 46%, an indication that they have been bottled by → Cadenhead, whilst the latter is 40%. That is the customary strength of malts from → Gordon & MacPhail.

Hogshead The term used in Scotland to describe the most common type of cask used for the maturation of whisky. A hogshead is about 250 litres in capacity and made of American oak.

There is also a → vatted malt of the same name which comes from an Edinburgh-based firm called Inverheath Ltd. Their Hogshead contains a particularly high proportion of → Islay malts.

Hokkaido Japanese → pure malt from → Nikka. The distillery is situated on the Japanese island of the same name. It is usually called → Yoichi, or sometimes Hokkaido 'Yoichi' Distillery, and is the second oldest in the country. It was founded in 1934 by Masataka → Taketsuru. He gained his knowledge of whisky production as a student in Scotland and was first employed by the second Japanese pioneer, Shanjiro → Torii, before setting up on his own and building his distillery in Yoichi, where he distilled his own malt with a tiny → pot still. It took six years before he was able to sell his first whisky. In the meantime he earned money by producing fruit juices. During the war he was not allowed to make whisky, but afterwards his company rose to become the second largest whisky producer in the country, after Torii's → Suntory. In 1962 he opened a grain distillery in → Nishinomiya, and in 1979 a much larger malt distillery in → Sendai, where he intended to distil the lighter → Lowlands-style malts whilst Yoichi produced heavy, often very intensively peated malts. The single malts from there are called Yoichi, the Hokkaido is a 12-year-old Pure Malt, but it remains unclear why one is a single and the other simply a pure malt. In the case of the latter the distillery is not clearly indicated as the bottler, which is named as the Nikka Distilling Company.

Holle Single malt from Switzerland. Probably the first of its kind from this country where, until a few years ago, the distillation of spirits was against the law – a throwback to the times when hunger prevailed in Europe and grain was reserved for baking. The malt is produced by Ernst Bader, the owner of a farm called 'Holle' in Lauwil, near Basel. Although Bader had learnt about whisky making in Scotland, he forgot the fact that whisky has to mature there for a minimum of three years. However, he does at least mature what he has produced so far (15 barrels) in former white wine casks from Burgundy. The whisky comes in half-litre bottles with a label painted by Bader's daughter and in nornmal 0.7-litre bottles with a label showing his farm. The strength is a uniform 42%.

Holy Isle Scotch whisky liqueur from → Isle of Arran Distillers. Its takes its name from the small island which lies directly off the coast of Arran. This has recently become a spiritual retreat owned by the Buddhist community in Scotland. It is a cream liqueur at the customary strength of 17%.

Hopkins & Company, John Scottish whisky company founded by John Hopkins in 1874 in Glasgow, initially importing the cognac 'Otard', then bringing out their first blends → Glen Garry (1878) and → Old Mull (1880). In 1896, at the time of the whisky boom, they built the → Speyburn Distillery in Rothes, having previously bought → Tobermory on the island of Mull. From 1916 they were owned by → DCL and since 1930 John Hopkins & Co have been licencees of the → Oban Distillery. → GuinnessUDV have continued with the Hopkins' blend Glen Garry, but Old Mull was traded off in order to comply with a ruling of the Monopolies and Mergers Commission.

Horse's Neck Whiskey cocktail. A slight variation of the simple bourbon highball: add a few dashes of Angostura bitters to bourbon and ice, fill up with ginger ale and garnish with a twist of lemon.

Hot Buttered Whiskey Whiskey drink, popular in Canada, a kind of Canadian grog – with the surprising addition of butter. Pour a generous portion of whiskey over a teaspoon of sugar and heat it. Add hot water and sprinkle some flakes of cold butter on top. It is supposed to be a drink that revives those coming in from the cold.

Hot Whisky Skins Whisky cocktail. A variation of the toddy. Two or three teaspoons of sugar are dissolved in a shot of whisky. Add hot water and garnish with a twist of lemon. David Daiches recommends drinking it in bed.

Hot Whiskey American, Irish version of the → Toddy, which unlike the classical Scottish recipe is prepared with a slice of lemon and cloves.

House of Campbell Scotch blend from → Campbell Distillers who include it in their range as a → standard blend. It does not receive as much promotion as their top brand → Clan Campbell or the → House of Lords.

House of Commons Scotch blend made exclusively for the bar of the House of Commons. The exclusive right to supply the whisky was secured by James → Buchanan at the end of the 19th century. This was originally called → Buchanan's and was distinguished by a striking black bottle with a white label which the customers ordered as → Black & White, the name by which it was soon rechristened. The company also supplied the House with a blend, the House of Commons Number One Scotch Whisky. Today it comes from → GuinnessUDV The House of Commons now has a malt bottled at 8 years old. James → Martin (→ Glenmorangie plc) is the producer and it is distributed by Oddbins.

House of Lords Scotch blend brought onto the market in the 1920s by William Whiteley. Despite → prohibition it was intended for the USA and the legendary attempts to get it to its customers were a reminder of the great smuggling era of the 19th century: the saga speaks of hiding places in dustcarts, of torpedoes fired onto the beach of Long Island, and of a submarine that successfully outwitted the coastguards. It even came in particularly light yet stable bottles. Nowadays it is produced by → Campbell Distillers. The whiskies are aged 8 and 12 years. A 30-year-old comes in costly packaging and is limited in supply. It contains a large proportion of an → Edradour of the same age.

House of Peers Scotch whisky from Douglas → Laing & Co in Glasgow. There are four versions of the blend: a Black Label and Gold Label, and X O Extra Old and 12 years old in the → de luxe category. It is said to be put back in the casks to mature again after blending. There is also a 22-year-old vatted malt.

House of Stuart Scotch blend belonging to the range of → Barton Brands. The blend is created in Scotland but bottled and sold in the USA by Barton.

House style Term for something that officially doesn't exist in whisk(e)y production, but which nevertheless all producers pay attention to. This is the ideal of what their whisk(e)y should be like. In the case of blends this means that once a formula has been created it is maintained whenever a new batch is bottled. The recipe may have to be changed when, for example, a certain malt whisky is no longer available, but the style must be retained. Single malts or straight bourbons also have a house style. A house style can be described as 'Speyside' or 'Lowland', but there are more concrete descriptions. David Stewart, the master blender at William Grant & Sons, describes the house style of → Balvenie, for which he is responsible, as follows: 'It has a smoky but mild aroma, soft on the palate and mature with a hint of sherry. Very singular and delicate whisky with honey tones.' His description of Glenfiddich, for which he is also responsible is: 'Light, fresh, fragrant nose with a touch of dryness. It has a long lingering and round after-taste'. The owners of Glenfarclas expect their whisky to be 'a full flavoured typical Speyside malt, lots of character taken from the large percentage of sherry wood used in maturation'. Despite differences in the various bottlings and versions, the house style should still be evident. In *Single Malt Note Book* the individual house style of each Scottish distillery is described by the proprietors themselves.

Howard McLaren → Premium Scotch blend. Today the brand belongs to → Glen Catrine Bonded Warehouse Ltd, who inherited it from Gibson International.

100 Pipers Scotch blend formerly from → Seagram which was brought onto the market in the 1960s and enjoys particular popularity in Latin America, South-east Asia and the UK. It contains malts from → Glenlivet, → Glen Grant, → Glen Keith and → Strathisla, which also used to belong to Seagram. The headquarters of Chivas Brothers, who produce 100 pipers for Groupe Pernod-Ricard, are in Paisley near Glasgow, but they also own large plants in the → Keith area. 100 Pipers, named after a Scottish song, is produced there.

Huntingtower Standard Scotch blend from → Waverley Vintners, a subsidiary of Scottish Courage which is mainly sold in supermarkets.

Huntly Scotch blend named after the town in the eastern → Highlands, originally from the old firm of Slater, Rodger & Co in Glasgow, who later held the licence to → Banff Distillery. At the end of the 19th century they came under the influence of the → Walkers of Kilmarnock and soon found themselves part of → DCL, whose ultimate successor → GuinnessUDV continues to stock the blend as a bottling of Huntly Blending, the only one from the old firm apart from → Rodger's Old Scots.

Hynard's Scotch blend sold by Hynard Hughes & Co with the adjunct Finest and practically only obtainable in the Leicester area. Apart from this → standard blend there is also the vatted malt → Gamefair.

I

IDG (Irish Distillers Group) Formed in the early 1970s and less than 10 years later lost their independence. In this short period the entire Irish whisky industry was in the hands of IDG. Although there had once been hundreds Irish distilleries, many disappeared, unable survive the difficulties which both World Wars and → prohibition had brought upon an industry whose product was formerly particularly strong in export markets. The concentration of distilleries, bottlers and dealers had already begun in the 19th century and finally resulted in the fact that in 1966 only four distilleries remained: three in the Republic and one, → Bushmills, in Northern Ireland. In this same year → Jameson, → Power's and → Cork Distilleries joined to form the Irish Distillers Company. When Bushmills joined them a few years later the monopoly, now named IDG, was complete. The concentration of distilling interets did not result in the hoped-for economic strength. In the mid-1980s they were taken over by → Groupe Pernod-Ricard. Since then IDG has just been a subsidiary of the French company.

IDV (International Distillers and Vintners) Internationally operating drinks concern formed in 1962 as a result of the amalgamation of United Wine Traders, who were mainly active in the wine business, and W & A → Gilbey. As a result of the amalgamation of their activities they became one of the big players in the wine and spirits industry. The wine traders brought the renowned company → Justerini & Brooks into the new operation, and with their → J & B blend they owned one of the biggest brands of whisky. Gilbey, who had originally started up in the gin business but by the beginning of the 20th century had also become involved in whisky, bringing with them companies such as James → Catto & Co, and most notably → Glen Spey, → Knockando and → Strathmill distilleries, as well as the Canadian whisky → Black Velvet. The merger was immediately followed by restructuring; Justerini & Brooks became responsible for the Scottish activities, and the Canadian activities were grouped under the name of Gilbey. The company included old port firms such as Croft and large American wine companies such as Almadén and Inglenook and the two strong brands, 'Smirnoff' vodka and 'Gilbey's' gin. The scale of their success made it necessary to build a large complex including → warehouses and their own cooperage near Renfrew and a new bottling plant in → Dumbarton – and they attracted interested parties keen to buy the company.

In 1972 IDV was initially taken over by the beer brewers Watney, Mann & Co, and six months later by → Grand Metropolitan. Under the management of its new parent company IDV was able to expand further and become one of the five largest spirits enterprises. In 1974 they launched the first cream whiskey liqueur with → Bailey's. In the same year they built a fourth distillery, → Auchroisk, joined forces with Dunhill and created the blend → Old Master. In 1987 they bought the American company Heublein and participated with a 50% share in the grain distillery → North British (the other share was held by → Robertson & Baxter). In order to create new markets they engaged in business in → Brazil, → Australia (→ Bond 7) and above all in Asia, especially in → India where the blends → Gilbey's and → Spey Royal were produced, and where they co-operated with the Indian whisky producer → Polychem. However they dropped some brands, for example the Irish → Redbreast and → Catto's that since 1990 has been with → Inver House Distillers Ltd. The American wine companies were sold to → Canandaigua in 1993.

In the summer of 1997, with rumours circulating, it was officially confirmed that Guinness and GrandMet wanted to pool their resources and form the world's largest drinks combine. During negotiations further sales took place, which were justified by the concentration on the nucleus of the business; one result was that Dunhill parted from IDV. In December 1997 the new alliance was completed and named → Diageo. The Monopolies Commissions of the EU in Brussels and the USA demanded that they should part with other brands, most notably → Dewar's, which was number one in America. This was deemed to be painful but bearable in view of the fact that with → Johnnie Walker and J & B they still owned the world's two largest brands. Dewar's went to → Bacardi, who also got the distilleries → Aberfeldy, → Aultmore, → Craigellachie and → Royal Brackla. This business was completed by the newly-formed → UDV, which had resulted from the merger of IDV and the Guinness subsidiary UD. IDV's German subsidiary was given up and its products are now sold by UDV Germany. In Canada, former IDV businesses such as the → Palliser Distillery and all the brands except → Gibson's, were given up.

Ileach, The Scotch single malt that gets its name from the Gaelic term for an inhabitant of → Islay, and which for a long time was only obtainable on the island itself, for example in the two SPAR shops in Bowmore and Bridgend. Although the label warns that it is 'peaty', there is unfortunately no indication of its age, its exact origins or the firm which markets it. Only the fact that it has a strength of 40% vol is divulged. It names the Highlands and Islands Scotch Whisky Co on the label, but actually comes from the → Vintage Malt Whisky Company in Glasgow. It is a good example of its kind and is indeed so pleasantly smoky-peaty-medicinal, that it is probably correct to suppose that it comes from a distillery on the south coast of the island. Its German importer, Dudelsack in Aschaffenburg, asserts that it is a 5-year-old → Lagavulin.

Immortal Memory 8-year-old Scotch blend from → Gordon & MacPhail. In 1991 it received the 'Best blended Whisky in the World' prize, at the International Wine and Spirit Competition in London. The name refers to the speeches made on 25th January at → 'Burns Suppers', in celebration of Robert Burns.

Imperial Blue Whisky formerly from → Seagram that is produced in → India using malts imported in → bulk from Scotland, which are then blended with locally-distilled → grain whiskies.

Imperial Gold Medal Scotch blend from → Cockburn & Company (Leith), that was sold in 1981 by → Drambuie and now belongs to the Wine Emporium. It still bears the name of the old business, Cockburn's of Leith.

Imperial Scottish malt distillery. It belongs to → the Speyside region and lies beside the → Spey, next to Carron railway station, in the neighbourhood of the → Dailuaine Distillery with which it had business connections for many years. Built in 1897, the year of Queen Victoria's Diamond Jubilee, the name reflects this occasion. In the course of its history it was shut down periodically: from 1900 (following the → Pattison brothers' bankruptcy) to 1919, from 1925, when it was taken over by → DCL, to 1955 when it was rebuilt, and from 1985 to 1989. In that year it was bought by → Allied and reopened. Its whisky played an important part in the blend → Black Bottle, a fact which was displayed on a large sign at the entrance of the distillery; however the name was painted over after Allied sold the brand to → Highland Distillers who shortly afterwards also closed the distillery.

The whisky, which is so popular with blenders, was not available as a single malt in a → proprietor's bottling, but it is included by → Gordon & MacPhail in their → Allied series as a 1979 without an age statement. In the summer of 2000 there was also a Imperial in the series of six malts which Allied had orginally intended for its employees, but which then came onto the market in small numbers: 15 years old and diluted to 43%. Otherwise it is only available from other → independent bottlers such as Cadenhead (1979, 64.9%), Signatory (1976, 43%) or MacArthur (1979, 43%).

There is also an American blended called Imperial

from → Barton in → Bardstown. There is a Japanese blend from → Suntory called Imperial, and which on some markets is called → Signature. It is presented in a smart-looking crystal carafe which contains just 0.6 litres.

Inchgower Scottish malt distillery. Its name comes from the Gaelic for 'island of the goats'. It lies between Fochabers and Buckie on the A98, right on the border of → Speyside, the whisky region that it is classified as belonging to. The distillery opened in 1871, and in 1936 the civic dignitaries of Buckie paid a thousand pounds for the plant built by Alexander Wilson, and resold it two years later – at a profit – to Arthur → Bell & Sons. They still hold the licence for it, although they now belong to UDV.

Inchgower was sold by → Bells as a 12-year-old single malt in a → proprietor's bottling in two different versions. UD included a 14-year-old in their → 'Flora & Fauna' series and → UDV had a 22-year-old from 1974 (55.7%) in their → 'Rare Malts Selection'. It is more frequently available from the independents, for example Cadenhead have two 1977 sherry-cask matured bottlings (46% and 56%). Signatory also had several bottlings including malts from 1977, 1979 and 1986 (all 43%).

Inchmoan Scotch malt whisky that is one of six produced at the → Loch Lomond Distillery in Alexandria. Unfortunately it is not marketed as a single malt but solely used for blending. It has been reported that the same malt is used for it as for the → Croftengea, but that it is distilled like the light single malt version of → Inchmurrin.

Inchmurrin Scotch malt whisky. It comes from → Loch Lomond Distillery and is named after the largest, finger-shaped island of the loch. It was a vatted malt when its producer → Glan Catrine Bonded Warehouse only had small quantities of it available, but it is now a single malt. Along with → Old Rhosdhu, it is the second malt of the distillery to be sold as a single. The distillery produces six malt whiskies in all – each with slightly adapted equipment, various kinds of malt and a different → middle cut. It is available as a proprietor's bottling which is sometimes labelled 'Distilled 1975',

sometimes '10 years old' and also '12 years old'. At the end of 1997 there was a small edition of 350 bottles of a 30-year-old from 1966. It is occasionaly available from → independent bottlers, for example from → Cadenhead who once had it as one of a pair together with Old Rhosdhu.

Independence Scotch blend bottled at 40%. It was launched to celebrate the Scottish Parliament voted for in a referendum of 11th September 1997. The date was chosen with a considerable sense of historical consciousness: on this day 700 years previously 'Braveheart', William → Wallace, celebrated a great victory against the English. Its creator is unknown but the company calls itself Independence Scotland Limited.

Independent bottlers Companies that are not the proprietors of the distilleries whose single malts they bottle. These include → Cadenhead, Signatory, → Gordon & MacPhail, → MacArthur and → The Scotch Malt Whisky Society amongst others. Many of them obtain their casks exclusively from the distillers direct, others have for many years been active as blenders and brokers, such as the → Hart Brothers and the → Speyside Distillery (→ 'Scott's Selection') who they have their own stocks.

Apart from the independent bottlers already mentioned there are also the following (with no guarantee that the list is anything like complete): → Adelphi, → Blackadder, The → Bottlers, → Calchou, → Glenhaven, Douglas → Laing, → Kingsbury, → Mackillop's, The → Master of Malt, → Morrison Fairlie, Murray → McDavid, → Oddbins and → Wilson & Morgan. These are all based in Scotland but there are also independent bottlers in other countries such as the → Whisky Merchant in Holland or → Samaroli in Italy.

India In the case of whisky the amount of imported Scotch, amounting to just over a million litres a year, is very little for such a huge population, especially in comparison to small countries as → Venezuela. National production is increasing rapidly, and has even overtaken → Japan, achieving an annual growth rate of more than 50%. India has the largest number of distilleries of any whisky-producing country outside Scotland, with more than the USA, Canada and Japan, not to mention Ireland. There are 15 distilleries producing malt whisky alone, spread throughout the country.

In the very north of India, almost on the Tibetan border, lie → Kasauli and → Solan, whilst → Jagatjit and → Haryana Distillery, belonging to Modi Enterprises, lie in the Punjab. In neighbouring Uttar Pradesh the Narang company have a distillery and → Pampur and → Mohan Nagur are also situated there. Further south in Bophal → Some can be found, and in Maharashta there are Seven Seas and Sinclair. This lies in Aurangabad where → Shaw Wallace also have a plant. → United Brewers own the → McDowell's Distillery near Goa in Ponda, which bottles the only real single malt in the country, and still further south another distillery near → Kerala. A third one is in Bangalore, where → Khoday and → Amrut also operate.

Whisky produced in India sometimes carries notices about the dangers to health, the labels must show the date of bottling, and whisky may only be sold in the area designated on the label. More states are becoming dry and punish the possession of alcohol. In some places storage is confined to the distillery site (which limits capacity) and casks may not be used (instead large wooden vats, which greatly hinder maturation, are prescribed). A distillate of molasses, which elsewhere would be called rum, is called whisky, and is often used as it is cheaper to produce. 'Malt' or 'malted' appear on bottles which, as in the case of the popular → Aristocrat or the → Moghul Monarch, contain a small percentage, and many Indian whiskies use malt extract.

There an assortment of products produced domestically: apart from the single malt previously mentioned and a → pure malt named → Solan No 1, there are many blends, in many forms. They may be blended from Indian malt whiskies and → grain whiskies or consist of Indian distillates which are mixed with blends already composed in Scotland – and there are blends from Indian grains and Scottish malts. All of them have a strength of 42.8%. The most important companies in the country are, in alphabetical order: Amrut with the brands → Maqintosh (sic), Haryana with → Benson, → Black Castle, → Champion, → Double Dog, → Knight King and → Old Barrel, Jagajit with → Aristocrat, Khoday with → Peter Scot and → Red Knight, → Mohan Meakin with Solan No. 1, → Black Knight, → Colonel's Special, → Summer Hall and a further 12 brands, → Polychem with → Men's Club, → Royal Secret and → White House, Rampur with → Genesis and → White Hall, Shaw Wallace with → Antiquity, Moghul Monarch and → Director's Special and United Brewers with McDowell's, → Diplomat and the bestseller → Bagpiper.

The number of potential customers on the subcontinent has naturally meant that the international drinks companies have also become interested; the potential is calculated to be as high as in the USA. The former → JBB subsidiary → Whyte & Mackay took over 51% of the Rampur Distillery and → Glenmorangie plc have a joint venture with Mohan Meakin, → Allied Domecq PLC with Jagatjit, → Clan Morgan of Delhi and → Tiiliknagar. In 1999 → Groupe Pernod-Ricard acquired the majority share in United Agencies in order to export 'Indian Made Foreign Liqueurs'.

→ IDV, who were already represented with → Gilbey's, were associated with Polychem, and → UD, who had their own Indian subsidiary, also worked with United Breweries; it is not known how they, now operating as → UDV, will restructure their Indian interests. Seagram was represented on the market with the three brands → Imperial Blue, → Oaken Glow and → Royal Stag.

Inishowen Irish whiskey produced by the → Cooley Distillery in Riverstown, who do not sell it under their own name, but under that of Andrew A → Watt, an old whiskey company purchased by John J → Teeling, the driving force behind Cooley. Apart from Inishowen, Watt used to own → Tyrconnell, which is occasionally available as a single malt. Its label names Riverstown as Watt's address, and Inishowen's quotes Derry. The blend has a strength of 40% and is by no means light, but is, according to the Irish specialist Jim Murray,

Intermediate Still

'exceptionally deep' for an Irish blend, which he attributes to the → peated malt rarely used in Ireland. It gets its name from the peninsula with Malin Head at its point, the site of a spirit distillery which shares Cooley's Czech architect.

Intermediate Still Term for the second of two stills that come into use when three runs take place while making whisk(e)y in → pot stills. Irish whiskey (apart from those of → Cooley) is always triple distilled, Scotch whisky only rarely, and then mostly in the → Lowlands. The only Lowland distillery still working with an intermediate still is → Auchentoshan. But → Benrinnes also use a form of triple distillation. There are also three → stills in → Springbank which can produce completely different malt whiskies.

Inver House Distillers Ltd Scottish whisky company which has only existed in its present form, as a business in private ownership, since 1988, when its directors acquired it in a management buy-out from the American Publicker Industries Inc, which had run into difficulties. The Americans had been successful with → Old Hickory at home, and wanted to expand to Scotland. Instead of buying an interest in a company as others do, they established Inver House as a subsidiary, choosing Airdrie to the south of Glasgow as a base, acquiring the former paper mill → Garnheath and in 1964/5 converting it to a huge complex. Here → grain whisky as well as malt whisky could be distilled, blending and bottling took place and there were 23 → warehouses. The complex was named Moffat (not to be confused with the neraby Borders town). One malt distillery was called → Glen Flagler and the other → Killyloch. None of the distillery plants is still standing today. In 1973 the company acquired → Bladnoch Distillery, which they sold 10 years later to Arthur → Bell & Sons. In 1985 they bought Barton's → Loch Lomond Distillery in Alexandria, which now no longer belongs to them.

The first upswing really came once the Americans had departed: Inver House has become something of a shooting star in recent years in Scotland and an established force, especially after acquiring the two important brands → Hankey Bannister and → Catto's, and is the proud total of five distilleries from companies which no longer wanted or could afford them. → Knockdhu and → Speyburn were followed by → Pulteney and → Balblair, and in December 1997, → Balmenach. In autumn 2001 the company was sold to Pacific Spirits, which belongs to the Great Oracle Group, situated on the Virgin Islands and owned by the Thai entrepreneur, Charoen Sirivadhanabhakdi. Inver House has the single malt → An Cnoc which comes from Knockdhu, Speyburn and → Old Pulteney. Older whiskies from thses distilleries are available as → Highland Selection. It has several vatted malts in its range: → Blairmhor, → Glen Drummond, → Glen Flagler, → Glengalwan and → Glen Nicol. The most important brands, apart from the two already mentioned, are Inver House → Green Plaid (in contrast to the simple Inver House made by → UD and sold in America by → Barton) and → Pinwinnie. There are also → Coldstream Guard, → Glen Mavis, → Highland Breeze, → Kinsey, → MacArthur's and → Sir Terence and the whisky liqueur → Heather Cream. Inver House Distillers Ltd was represented at 'The → Spirit of Scotland' competition with the blend The → Quintessential.

Inverallan Scotch blend formerly from → Whyte & MacKay / → JBB (Greater Europe) plc who had stopped producing this 30-year-old → de luxe whisky before the → Kyndal takeover. It is still possible to find bottles of it.

Inverarity, The Scotch blend from Inverarity Vaults in Edinburgh. The company and the brand get their name from Ronnie Martin's mother's maiden name. For many years Martin was the director of production at → DCL and in 1991, after retiring, he and his son Hamish wanted to create their own individual blend. They also supply the → Glen Hamilton and the 8-year-old The Inverarity Single Speyside Malt matured in bourbon Casks, which was actually an → Aultmore, but now comes from → Balmenach. In 1998 it was joined by the 14-year-old malt → Ancestral. A further masterpiece created by the two Martins is the → Loch Fyne which they made for Loch Fyne Whiskies.

Invergordon Distillers Scottish whisky company founded in 1960 as a subsidiary of Hawker Siddeley. Although Invergordon Distillers included a small malt whisky making facility called Ben Wyvis, it was mainly equipped for making → grain whisky and later, neutral spirit. It lies on the northern shores of the Cromarty Firth and is the only one of its kind in the Highlands, now equipped with four → patent stills which can produce nearly 40 million litres of alcohol per annum. The → warehouses belonging to the complex can store almost double that amount. The company also owns the distilleries of → Tamnavulin, → and Tullibardine having sold off Deanston and Bruichladdich. In 1985 they acquired → Isle of Jura Distillery. The company, which was bought by its directors in 1988 and went on to the stock market, also had a large bottling plant in Leith.

Apart from the Ben Wyvis it sold all its single malts as → proprietor's bottlings and in 1990, with → The Invergordon, they launched one of the first single grains onto the market (aged 7 and 10 years. In 1995, after hostile takeover bid, they were taken over by → Whyte & Mackay, who were already owned by → American Brands. Immediately after the takeover three distilleries were closed, and only → Isle of Jura was able to continue in production. Invergordon now operates under ownership of → Kyndal and is still producing single malts from → Fettercairn, → Tamnavulin, and → Tullibardine. They bottle a lot of their own brands in Leith, as well as the whiskies from the parent company either using brand names or the customer's own label, including those for large UK supermarket chains. The contract with the Northern Irish distillery → Cooley has now lapsed, but a bourbon named → Smokey Jim and the → Canadian Rocks Falls are still bottled by → Kyndal.

Invergordon, The Scotch Single Grain launched onto the market in 1990 by the company of the same name. Both are named after the distillery on the Cromarty Firth where it is produced and matured. Before the launch of the Invergordon there had been few single grains available – only rare offerings from independent bottlers and → Cameron Brig. It is 10 years old, light, and can also be drunk with ice, and is aimed at young buyers unfamiliar with whisky.

Inverleven Scottish malt distillery which until 1991 was situated within the large → Dumbarton Distillery which had been built in 1938 and belonged to the → Lowlands. It was the first distillery where the two → stills had been supplemented by a third unusually shaped still, which its inventor, Fred Whiting, had named a → Lomond still. It was a combination of a → pot still and a → column still and was able to produce a very different sort of whisky. Modelled on the example of Inverleven, other → Allied distilleries were also equipped with Lomond stills (→ Glenburgie/→ Glencraig and Miltonduff/→ Mosstowie). The whisky produced in the conventional → stills was never made available as a single malt in a → proprietor's bottling, but one from 1979 became available in the → Allied series from → Gordon & MacPhail. It was followed by an Inverleven from 1984 and 1985. The independent bottlers have also had it, including , for example, → Cadenhead with a 26-year-old distilled in 1969 and bottled in 1995 at 49.6%.

Inverness Cream Scotch blend from → Invergordon, who sell the whisky under the name Longman Distillers.

Iona Royale Scotch blend with a venerable name. It is named after the island off Mull, where the Irish St. Columba set up his monastery in the 6th century, and which became the spiritual centre of Celtic Christianity for a long time. It was here that the famous 'Book of Kells' originated, and from here that monks first converted Scotland to Christianity, then spreading their beliefs as far as Germany and Switzerland and even to upper Italy. The whiskies in this creation from the firm J & G Grant, based at → Glenfarclas, are at least 25 years old.

Ireland Many believe that Ireland is the original home of whisky. However, the first written document that clearly refers to whisky was written in 1494 in Scotland. There is a supposition that it was Irish monks who brought back the knowledge from Italy of how to produce a strong alcoholic drink by means of heating and condensing.

The Irish can boast of having the oldest licensed distillery. → Bushmills, in County Antrim in

Ireland

Northern Ireland, an area for which King James I granted a licence to one Sir Thomas Phillipps in 1608. The present distillery uses this date on the labels of its whiskies, even though it was built much later. In 1556, and then again in 1620, the government felt forced to point out the risks to health of drinking whiskey; it was not *aqua vitae* but *aqua mortis*. On Christmas Day 1661s, the government passed a law which imposed → excise duty, on whiskey. Since that time the Irish have known two kinds of whiskey: the 'Parliament whiskey' and → poitín, the illegal, 'authentic' stuff. There followed 150 years of war with the excisemen. As in Scotland, it was only the laws of 1822 and 1823 which made the acquisition of a licence feasible.

At that time the drink was spelled quite arbitrarily with or without an 'e', which many people believe is the main difference between Irish and other whiskies. Only since the beginning of the 20th century was a uniform spelling decided upon. Like Scotch malt whisky, Irish whiskey is distilled in → pot stills (which are, however, much larger than those in the neighbouring country). It is triple distilled, making the distillate purer and lighter. Peat is not traditionally used in malting, meaning that Irish whiskey lacks any smoky aroma. The greatest difference is that the mash does not consist of malted barley, but of unmalted barley to which a small amount of malted barley is added. The result is → pure pot still. It is difficult to find nowadays. Many people find it tragic that this original form of Irish whiskey is now only obtainable in three versions, Redbreast, Green Spot and the new Jameson Pure Pot Still, apart from the Old Comber which is too old to be enjoyable.

It was → pure pot still whiskey that made the Irish whiskey companies great and their product more popular than Scotch in, for example, England, and the USA. John Power, John Jameson (a Scot), William Jameson and George Roe were the owners of the four largest distilleries in the country and their whiskies were so good that they were imitated, although the quality of these imitations often left a lot to be desired. In 1879 they joined together to publish the book 'Truths about Whisky' (sic) in which they warned against bad and adulterated whiskies. The following hundred years in the history of Irish whiskey are marked by defeats. They happened in rapid succession. Irish whiskey became a product that was only drunk in Ireland. More and more distilleries had to close or pool their resources with others. In the 1980s there were only two distilleries and one company, IDG, remaining, around which a mighty takeover battle soon flared up, this was finally won by a foreign enterprise, the French Groupe Pernod-Ricard.

There were four main reasons for the decline. The first was the existence of temperance groups in Ireland. Between 1838 and 1844, the number of pubs went down from 21,000 to 13,000. The invention of continuous distillation by Robert → Stein and Aeneas → Coffey (a Dublin exciseman) also left its mark. It enabled the production of → grain whisk(e)y and eventually of Scotch blends, which were cheaper than the Irish Pure Pot Stills. The decision in 1909, in the → 'What is Whiskey Case' (sic), whereby any grain distillate was recognised as whisk(e)y, was not only a terrible defeat for Scottish malt distillers, but also for the Irish. It resulted in the final breakthrough of the blends – and led the Irish to blend cheap grain whiskies with their Pot Still. Prohibition in the USA took away an important market for the Irish and, following the struggle for independence, the English imposed a trading embargo in 1916 cutting off the most lucrative market for Irish Whiskey.

The demise of distilleries continued into the 1950s and this was when → Tullamore decided to close. In 1960 Jameson, Powers and the Cork Distillers formed IDG, which a short time later was also joined by Bushmills. Since their decision to build a large modern distillery in → Midleton, there has no longer been a distillery in the capital. The new plant was cleverly constructed, making it possible to produce a variety of brands on one site by using various mashes and combining different distilling methods.

That was the position in 1987 when → IDG was taken over. An Irish businessman, who had written a thesis on the unexploited export potential of Irish whiskeys, was also involved in the takeover battle. John J Teeling was not successful in this fight, but built up a business of his own → Cooley Distillery, a new distillery that could produce → grain whisky as well as malt whisky according to Scottish methods. He introduced new brands, including single malts, The number of brands has almost doubled in the last few years and has now reached nearly 100.

Groupe Pernod-Ricard have taken the initiative. Only Jameson, which is one of the fastest growing spirits, is still heavily promoted, (Power's is number one in the country; Tullamore Dew is known only in Germany and Denmark). Many variations on old brands have been brought out, including the fantastic Jameson Gold. Bushmills is also being marketed well. In Midleton there is the Jameson Heritage Centre, Bushmills is open to visitors, and in Dublin an excellent museum has been opened in the buildings of the old Jameson Distillery. Things are looking up for Irish whiskey.

Irish Meadow Irish whiskey liqueur. It was formerly called → Meadow Cream and used to contain Dutch cream. → Halewood International have kept to the low volume of just 14.5%.

Irish Mist Irish whiskey liqueur. In contrast to → Bailey's, which was invented much later, and its numerous imitators, it is not based on a mixture of cream and whiskey. Like its Scottish equivalent, it combines whiskey with honey and herbs. It is said to come from a very old Irish recipe. Today neither the distillery that made it → Tullamore ,nor the producing company exist anymore. The Irish Mist Company has long since become a subsidiary of → Cantrell & Cochrane, and therefore belonged to → Allied Domecq PLC and → Guinness, then to → Allied alone for a short time. Since January 1999 it has belonged to BC Partners. The liqueur (35%) is still made in the town of Tullamore. It contains Irish and Scottish whiskies.

Irish Velvet Irish whiskey liqueur, from → IDG but bottled by the Dutch firm Koninklijke Cooymans. It is a mixture of coffee, sugar and whiskey, and is supposed to be made exclusively from → Jameson, which might even induce a whiskey lover to drink it. However it is also a suitable basis for instant → Irish coffee, which can be made by pouring hot water onto two parts of it and rounding off the result with cream.

Irish Whiskey The traditional Irish whiskey was a → pot still whiskey, that might have been distilled two or three times, but was always made from barley, the greater part of which was malted (possibly using peat), and the smaller part was unmalted. Today → pure pot still whiskey has become rare. Only → Green Spot, → Old Comber, → Redbreast, the new 15-year-old → Jameson Pure Pot Still and the malt whiskeys from → Cooley remain. Whether the latter can really be called 'pure pot still' is a matter for debate, as they are only double-distilled and made solely of malted barley. They were the first new single malts which joined those from → Bushmills which had up to that time been the only surviving ones. Nowadays the most widespread form of Irish whiskey is the blend, a mixture of → pot still whiskeys or malts with → grain whiskeys. Since the existence of blends Irish whiskey has almost lost its identity, which had differentiated it from all the other whiskeys in the world.

Irish Whiskey Corner A museum set up and run by → IDG in → Bow Street, the site of the old distillery of the → Jameson company. It displayed documents on the history of the company and Irish whiskey in general, a Jameson whiskey could be sampled and the senses sharpened in a → tasting competition. In 1998 a larger museum with a video presentation, shop and restaurant was opened in the old buildings of the Jameson Distillery opposite.

Island Prince Scotch blend from → Isle of Arran Distillers. Its founder, Harold Currie, was a successful and experienced master blender. There was a 12-year-old but now there are just two versions aged 15 and 21 years, the latter coming in a crystal carafe.

Islander Scotch blend with a particularly high share of malt whiskies from the Scottish islands which are especially smoky and peaty. It was introduced by → UD in the late 1980s and its full name is → Bell's Islander.

Islands Scottish whisky region including all the distilleries which are situated on the Hebrides

Islay

and the northern islands. Whisky is not distilled on the Outer Hebridean islands such as on Lewis, Harris (at least none that is legal). The most northerly whisky island is Orkney Mainland where there are two distilleries, → Highland Park and → Scapa. On the west coast of Scotland, going southwards, are the islands of → Skye, with → Talisker Distillery, and Mull with → Tobermory / → Ledaig. In the south is → Islay, which due to the large number of distilleries (eight), is sometimes counted as a separate region, and on the neighbouring island is → Isle of Jura distillery. Since the beginning of the 1990s, when Harold Currie built his distillery at Lochranza on the → Isle of Arran and 1995, when it was put into production, this island has also been put back on the whisky map after more than a hundred years. Between Arran and Islay is the Kintyre peninsula with → its 'capital' of Campbeltown, which gave a region its name, but which now has just two active distilleries remaining, → Springbank and → Glen Scotia. These are now sometimes either included in the → Lowlands or the Western → Highland region.

As is generally the case, it is also difficult to define a definite style as being typical of the Islands whisky region. Island malts are often identified with intensive smokiness, a strong peat aroma, hard phenol tones and a heavy body, which reflect a character influenced by the sea air and sea-weed, giving them a medicinal aroma. This may be true of the whiskies from → Ardbeg, → Laphroaig, → Lagavulin and Talisker, although not of → Bunnahabhain. There are few similarities between a → Highland Park and the smooth → Isle of Jura.

Islay The southernmost of the Scottish Hebrides is either included in the → whisky region of the → Islands or, more often, judged to be a separate region of its own, which is justified by the unusually high concentration of distilleries alone. At present there are seven working distilleries, though all the buildings of an eighth, → Port Ellen, are still standing and its malt whisky is also still obtainable, but of a ninth, named Port Charlotte or Loch Indaal, only a few → warehouses still remain. If one begins the count in the order that most visitors to the distilleries get to see them when they arrive with the ferry at Port Ellen and go round the island of Islay (pronounced 'Eye-la' and not the anglicised "Eye-lay", it is named after a Norse princess), then the order is as follows: → Ardbeg, → Lagavulin, → Laphroaig, Port Ellen, → Bowmore, → Bruichladdich, (Port Charlotte), → Bunnahabhain and finally, opposite the → Isle of Jura, → Caol Ila, which lies on the Sound of Islay.

It cannot be denied that the three distilleries on the south coast all produce heavy, powerful, meaty malts, with a distinct smoky and peaty aroma, and definite phenol and medicinal tones, showing the influence of the sea and seaweed. All the distilleries lie on the coast and they all use the peat that has been formed from the seaweed with which large parts of the island are covered. But not all of them use the peaty, yellow water that is so often found; Bruichladdich, for example, has light-coloured water coming from the hills. The three south coast whiskies are at the 'heavy end' and Bunnahabhain at the other 'light' end of the whisky scale. Experts mainly account for these differences with the amount of peat added at malting and use parts per million (ppm) as a measurement. According to Jim McEwan, master distiller of Bruichladdich distillery, Ardbeg has 50ppm and has the most intensive of the malts, followed by Lagavulin with 40 ppm, then Laphroaig with 35 ppm, followed by the middle group, all close together, of Caol Ila (30 ppm), Port Ellen (25ppm) and Bowmore (20 ppm), then the two 'B' malts, with between 5 and 8ppm each. The distinctive Islay whiskies do not find favour among all fans of malt whisky, but long practice and an open mind has been known to convert an opponent into an ally. They are popular in small quantities with the blenders, who covet them because of their character.

Islay Legend Scotch blend which should not be confused with the famous → Islay Mist. It comes from → Morrison Bowmore, and is therefore likely to contain a share of → Bowmore, whilst the Islay Mist contains → Laphroaig. The whisky, with a malt share of no less than 50%, is an 8-year-old and mainly available in France, where it is called → Hallmark.

Islay Mist Scotch blend created in the 1930s by the owner of → Laphroaig for Lord Margadale's coming of age, using their own malt whiskies and → Glenlivet. It became so popular that the proprietors of the distillery decided to launch it onto the general market. It belonged to → Allied Distillers Ltd, along with the distillery on → Islay, which they however sold. Today the brand belongs to → MacDuff International, formed in 1992, who include the blend aged 8 years, Master's aged 12 and 17 years and Islay Mist De Luxe without an age statement, in their range.

Isle of Arran Scottish malt distillery. It was opened in 995 and is therefore the youngest distillery in Scotland, but after → Speyside and → Kininvie, the third of the decade. It has fulfilled Harold Currie's dream. He had spent a lifetime in the whisky industry and was a sought-after master blender. Like George Christie from Speyside, he wanted a distillery of his own so that he could produce a malt whisky according to his own ideas. He found the location for it on the island between the Scottish mainland and Kintyre, where more than a century had gone by without legal distilling. In 1990 he began building at → Lochranza, on the north-western end of the island popularly known as 'Scotland in miniature'. The opening was planned for 1994, but a pair of nesting Golden eagles, delayed the opening for a year. In 1995 it was ready and the first distillate flowed from the five → stills.

Currie showed that he was not only skilled at whisky-making: he was able to gather together a lot of money by selling bonds that entitled the buyer to five cases of the blend, and in 2001, the single malt. After the opening he sold miniature bottles of new make spirit, which have been followed on each anniversary by further miniatures, which are much coveted by collectors. It was also possible to buy casks which remain in the distillery and can later be bottled when desired. There is a society whose members receive information and offers or, when there is something to celebrate, an invitation – as in the summer of 1997, when the Queen visited in the Royal Yacht *Brittannia* to open the visitor centre. And Currie also launched a whole range of whiskies onto the market, a further parallel with Speyside, in order to accustom the public to the products of his company: the blends → Glen Rosa, → Island Prince, → Loch Ranza and → Royal Island, the vatted malt → Eileandour and the single malt → Glen Eason.

A special limited edition of the malt was issued as soon as it had reached the legal minimum age of three years. Around the neck of the convex bottle there is a labe signed by Currie. In 1999 there was a malt which was only 4 years old, named Arran, followed by a series whose labels were designed by Scottish artists. The Golden Eagle, First Production 1995 appeared in 2001.

Isle of Jura Scottish malt distillery. It lies on the eastern side of the island of Jura, in the little village of Craighouse, the only settlement on the island. It belongs to the → whisky region of the → Islands. The name Jura derives from the Norse and means 'deer-island'. The red deer living on the island outnumber the 225 people living there almost 30-fold. The long and tapering island is only separated from the Scottish mainland by a narrow strip of water, but the dangerous Corrievrechan whirlpool makes it almost impassable. Jura can only be reached by ferry from neighbouring → Islay, from which it is separated by a narrow strip of water and a five-minute ferry trip.

The present distillery has only been in operation since 1963, but there were previous legal activities, as well as illicit distilling. These have been documented since 1810. In the 19th century James Ferguson and his son were distilling on the island; but the plant was dismantled when Ferguson could no longer reach an agreement with his landlord. Between World War I and 1958 there was no activity and then two island inhabitants decided to rebuild the plant, mainly to create jobs. They won over Charles → Mackinlay & Co/Scottish Brewers who appointed W Delmé Evans for the construction. He had already designed → Tullibardine and → Glenallachie. Five years later it was finished. The number of → stills has now been increased to four, the water comes from a loch called a'Bhaile Mhargaidh, and the malted barley is brought over from → Port Ellen. It is only slightly peated, which is why the slogan 'The Highland from the Island' is used. From 1985 Isle of Jura belonged to → Invergordon Distillers, who also made their whisky available as a 10-year-old single malt.

Isle of Skye

After the hostile takeover of Invergordon by → Whyte & Mackay/ → JBB(Greater Europe) plc in 1993, unlike others belonging to the company (→ Bruichladdich, → Tamnavulin and → Tullibardine) the distillery was not closed down. The malts included a 26-year-old (45%) in their → 'Stillman's Dram' series; a 15-year-old, a 16-year-old and a 21-year-old were also brought out. The 20-year-old Isle of Jura, bottled in 1993 (still in Invergordon's time), is a real rarity, with 261 bottles at 54% → cask strength; it was the first cask to have been bottled in the distillery itself and was chosen by a handful of journalists (who received a cask stave as a souvenir). Every single bottle is signed by former manager Willie Tait. In 1998 a new 10-year-old single barrel came out, with 304 bottles with a cask strength of 61.7%. It is officially only obtainable in France. The → Craignure in Invergordon's controversial 'The → Malts of Scotland' series, is also clearly a Jura. Of the → independents → Cadenhead, for example, offered bottlings and → Signatory had several versions, including the 1966 (50.6%), brought out for the 10th anniversary of the distillery. Jura is now a → Kyndal distillery.

Isle of Skye Scotch blend from Ian → MacLeod, a subsidiary of Peter J → Russell, available in several versions: as a → standard blend for the UK market aged 8 years, without an age statement for the export market, as a → premium blend aged 12 years and as a → de luxe blend aged 18 and 21 years. Whether the choice of name derives from the home of the MacLeod family or whether the blends contain a large proportion of → Talisker, the malt whisky from Skye, remains a company secret.

I W Harper Kentucky straight bourbon, whose label is decorated with the numerous gold medals that it has won, the oldest one being from 1895. The brand has been registered since 1879. Its creator, Isaac Wolfe → Bernheim, whose whiskey career in the United States began when he was a successful dealer, decided to sell his whiskey in bottles rather than in barrels or china jugs. He did not give the whiskey his own name, but that of a horse-breeder friend.

In 1897 Bernheim and his brother Bernhard were able to build their own distillery in Louisville and produce their brand themselves. During → prohibition it was sold as 'medicinal alcohol', and afterwards the brand changed hands several times. In 1937 it passed to → Schenley, who were taken over by → UD in 1987. Under their management the old distillery was closed to make way for a new building, which was opened in 1992. The formula used there is 86% corn to 6% rye and 8% malt barley. There are five versions: the → Bottled in Bond (101°/50.5%), the Gold Label (86°/43% – also without an age statement), the 12-year-old (86°/43%), the President's Reserve (86°/43% – intended solely for export) and the 15-year-old Gold Medal (80°/40%) which belongs to the → 'Bourbon Heritage Collection'. The brand is the only one, apart from the Tennessee whisky George Dickel, which the UD successor, UDV, kept when they practically withdrew from North America in 1999. At that time they also sold the Bernheim Distillery.

J

Jack & Jill Slovenian blend from the Dana company in Mirna, which began operating as a small brandy distillery in socialist times and now produces a whole range of spirits. The malt whiskies they need for their blend are imported from Scotland and are blended locally with the grain distillates that they produce themselves.

Jack Daniel American distillery that is probably the best-known of all American whiskeys. But it is not a bourbon; its label proudly states that it is a Tennessee Sour Mash. In 1941 the government officially recognised this term as a description of an individual type of whiskey, alongside that of bourbon. It is important to note that it is not the use of the → sour mash method that makes it different (the method is used in making all American whiskeys), but its origin, from the state of Tennessee, and, in particular, the process of → charcoal mellowing, in which the fresh distillate slowly trickles over charcoal before being filled into barrels.

This process, also known as → leaching or the → Lincoln County Process, is said to have been invented by a man named Alfred Eaton and was used for the first time on the spot that Jack Daniel chose for his first 'proper' distillery: The Hollow, near Cave Spring, a place well-known for its excellent water. The year was 1866 and Jack Daniel was just 20 years old, but he had already had considerable experience in the whiskey business. As his mother had died a year after he was born and he didn't get on with his step-mother, he left home and first decided to live with neighbours, and then with the Call family. Dan Call was a distiller as well as a Protestant lay preacher, and taught Jack Daniel his trade, selling the 14-year-old Jack his equipment when he decided that making alcohol wasn't compatible with his religious beliefs.

After Jack had gathered experience as a whiskey trader, he built his distillery and became a successful businessman – and an important figure in society. He called his first whiskey Bell of Lincoln. Daniel's nephew, → Lem Motlow, became manager and persuaded his uncle to stop selling his whiskey in barrels, but to bottle it. It is uncertain why he called it Old No. 7, and to this day the name still appears on the label as does 'No. 1 Distillery', an expression which the firm registered in Washington.

Success was quick in coming: their whiskey received a gold medal at the World Fair in St. Louis as early as 1904, and it was followed by six more. In 1905 Jack injured himself when he kicked a safe that wouldn't open; his broken toe wouldn't heal, and in 1911 the injury cost him his life. In that year prohibition began in Moore County, where the distillery was located. The new proprietor, Motlow, was first able to dodge it in Missouri and then in Alabama, but finally had to give up when the → Volstead Act made the whole country dry. Motlow returned to Tennessee and began breeding horses and mules; as he used the name 'Jack Daniel' for this enterprise, he was able to hold on to the rights to the name. prohibition ended in 1933, but Moore County remained dry. Nevertheless Motlow managed to get a new licence and in 1938 he set up production again at the old distillery. Although it was possible to produce whisky, it was not possible to buy, let alone open, a bottle of whiskey. It was 1995 before visitors could buy a bottle of Jack Daniel's on site, but they still weren't allowed to drink it, and instead drank the famous lemonade which the company served. Motlow died in 1947 and nine years after his death his four childless sons sold the business to → Brown-Forman, who since that time have made sure that their product has also prospered on the international market.

Jackson's Row

In all these years there were just two versions: Jack Daniel's Old Time Old No. 7 Brand with a black label (4 years old, previously 90°/45%, now 86°/43%) and the Jack Daniel's No. 7 Brand with a green label (about 6 years old, previously 86°/43%, now 80°/40%). Master distiller Jimmy Belford uses the same → mash bill for them both, 80% corn, 12% rye and 8% malt barley. A slightly different recipe is used for → Gentleman Jack, which was introduced in 1988 as the first new brand brought out by the firm in over a hundred years; before bottling it is charcoal-filtered once again. There was also a one-year-old → Lem Motlow, which was only sold locally for a short while. Since the beginning of the 1990s new bottlings have been launched in quick succession, some with the Old No. 7 in special bottles, and others as → small batch or → single barrel versions, which were Brown-Forman's contribution to the new trend. In 1995, the 1895 Replica Bottle appeared. It was a square-shaped bottle with a swing stopper, and in 1996 there was the Bicentennial Tennessee State for the 200th anniversary of the founding of the state (96°/46%).

One year later a series was launched to commemorate the seven gold medals which are illustrated on the bottles of the Old No. 7: the first 'Gold Medal Decanter' was dedicated to the St. Louis World Fair in 1905, the second to that in Liege in Belgium; others are to follow. They all contain the Old No. 7 (90°/45%) as does the Maxwell House Bottle, which however is bottled at 85°/43%. The Master Distiller has a strength of 90°/45%. The Jack Daniel's Single Barrel Tennessee Whiskey originally came from the top barrels in no.1 warehouse, and had a handwritten label, giving the barrel number and the shelf number. It appears to be identical to the Barrel House One, of which just a few barrels are bottled every year, making it a sought-after and expensive rarity. In contrast, a new → single barrel (90°/45%) in a cube-shaped bottle with a printed label, is on general sale. The Silver Select also comes from a single barrel but is at 100°/50%; the barrel number, shelf number and date of bottling are quoted. In addition to there are cans with Coke, as well as several beers such as 'Summer Brew' and 'Honey Brown Ale', which are produced using the name Jack Daniel and sold in the stores of the town. There it is also possible to buy other products bearing the name of Jack Daniel, premixed cocktails and 'Lynchburg Lemonade'.

Jackson's Row Scotch → malt with an unusual yellow colour, in an opaque bottle. Its contents are described as 'All Malt Blond Scotch Whisky', and bears the seal of the → Glenkinchie Distillery, who is also named. It gives Edinburgh as an address, although this is not where it is located. One of the six → 'Classic Malts' is a Glenkinchie, but Jackson's Row is a 'pure malt', which means it could be a vatted, from various distilleries, or a single malt from Glenkinchie. All the names, companies and brands however belonged to → UD, who in recent years have experimented with new whiskies (→ Hackler, → Alcopops).

Jacob Stück German whisky, made from Scotch malt whiskies and German grain distillates. Its producer, the Stück AG, which was based in Hanau and Berlin, made use of the success of → Racke rauchzart when launching its product. At its peak it managed to sell just 750,000 bottles, whilst its competitor Racke had a turnover of 3 million bottles in 1969. It disappeared from the market, but has not been forgotten, not least because of its presentation – a leather holster.

Jacob's Well Kentucky straight bourbon that proudly calls itself 'the world's first microbourbon', alluding to the many new 'microbreweries' that have arisen in recent years, and the traditional beers that they seek to preserve. It is the latest creation of → American Brands, and is produced in their distilleries in Boston and Clermont. This is where Booker Noe Jr, the grandson of James → 'Jim' Beam, created the first → small batch bourbon with → Booker's in 1989, one of a series of four different whiskeys. It has now been joined by this new creation, which gets its name from the spring that the founding father of the Beam dynasty, Jacob Beam (born Jakob Böhm) is said to have used when he began distilling on a commercial scale in 1795. A new method of maturing has been conceived for this new creation: it initially rests in charred oak barrels, and after 4 years is then 'married' to whiskeys from specially selected barrels, before being returned to the original barrel. In all the maturation period lasts up to 7 years, and bottling takes place at 85°/42%.

Jacobite, The Scotch blend launched onto the market in 1983, with the aim of providing UK supermarkets with a reasonably-priced blend. The speculation of Nurdin & Peacock, who have it produced by → Invergordon (naming Independent Cellars on the label), has been successful. The name of the blend, which is said to contain 47 malt whiskies, in tribute to supporters of Bonnie Prince Charlie.

Jagatjit Indian company that owns the country's largest malt distillery, situated in northern India, in the Punjab on the border with → Pakistan. It is called the Jagatjit Nagar Distillery and is located in the town of Hanira. The company's two best-known brands are → Aristocrat and → Bonnie Scot, which are both described as 'malted whisky', but which are quite definitely not single malts, containing just a small share at most (or possibly even just malt extract).

James B Beam Distilling Company → Jim Beam.

James E Pepper Kentucky straight bourbon, one of the great old names in American whiskey history, which has been saved from obscurity by → UD. It bears the name of a family that had been in business for so long that the bottles bear the date 1776, and the information: 'Born with the Republic'. It was in this year that Elijah Pepper settled in Old Pepper Springs in Kentucky County, Virginia. His son, Oscar, founded the Old Pepper Distillery in Glenn's Creek, to the south of Frankfort, where the famous Dr. Crow practised his craft, after whom the new distillery later built in the neighbourhood was named, → Old Crow. Oscar's son, James E , later sold the distillery to the equally famous E H Taylor of → Old Taylor Distillery, whilst he sold the original distillery to → Labrot & Graham in 1878, who in their turn sold it to → Brown-Forman in 1940. They closed it down, but started production again in 1996.

Pepper did not retire but founded a new business with the two brands James E Pepper and → Henry Clay (named after the famous senator). In 1890 Pepper applied for the licence to bottle his own whiskeys, because he (and his customers) wanted to protect themselves against inferior imitations. Pepper died in 1906, and five years later his company was bought by investors. In order to protect the whiskey from prohibition, they even sold it to Germany – in the same year, 1919, a soldier coming home from World War I suggested that the slogan 'Born with the Republic' should be supplemented with 'Died with Democracy'. Indeed Pepper did not survive prohibition, and the distillery and the brand were bought by → Schenley, who discontinued them. UD, who bought the company in 1987, produced the whiskey again (80°/40%), solely for export, and since 1992 production has taken place at the → Bernheim Distillery in Louisville which has undergone total reconstruction. It was one of the brands which UDV, resulting from the merger of IDV and UD, parted with in 1999.

James Foxe Canadian whisky formerly produced by → Seagram in Canada and exported in → bulk to the USA, where it is distributed by → Sazerac.

James Gordon's Blend Scotch blend bearing the name of one of the founders of the important company → Gordon & MacPhail. It is an 8-year-old and one of the best → premium blend whiskies.

James Martin Scotch blends and malt whiskies which now come from → Glenmorangie, previously simply called → Martin's. 'James' was introduced because of an agreement with the Italian Martini & Rossi, who allegedly feared confusion of the Scotch with their Vermouth.

Jameson Irish whiskey, and name of an Irish company of great tradition and reputation. The whiskey has only existed in its present form since 1968, and has become the top selling Irish whiskey in the world – in 1996 it was the fastest-growing of all. The date 1780, which a further Jameson brand bears and is given as the official date of foundation of the company. The founding father is said to have been the Scot John Jameson, who married a daughter of John → Haig and Margaret Stein, and emigrated to Ireland in 1770. His son, John, took over the →

Bow Street Distillery which belonged to John Stein (also related to Haig and a descendant of Robert → Stein, inventor of the → patent still). John's brother, William, took over the Marrowbone Distillery.

John's firm prospered and had a huge production (which was sold in barrels), becoming a joint-stock company in 1902. In 1966 it merged with → Power and → Cork Distilleries to form → IDG, and discontinued production. Its whiskey was made by its former competitors Powers, on the other side of the Liffey, before being transferred to → Midleton. A large part of the old premises had fallen into ruin and it was to be feared that they wouldn't survive much longer. They were renovated in 1998 and now house a museum (the → 'Irish Whiskey Corner' opposite was closed down).

Apart from the bottling already named there is → Crested Ten (the earliest form in which a Jameson was bottled), the → premium brand Jameson 1780 (also 40%), that contains 12-year-old whiskies. The Jameson 12 Years Old is very similar and is sold mainly in the Far East by World Brands Duty Free, which like IDG belong to the → Groupe Pernod-Ricard. Jameson Gold, originally Jameson XO is intended for the same market and is also bottled at 43%. The Jameson Distillery Reserve is only available in Midleton where the 'Jameson Heritage Centre' is located. There is also a Distillery Collection, and Jameson Marconi, which will probably soon become a sought-after curiosity. It commemorates the fact that the inventor of the radio was a great grandson of John Jameson on his mother's side. New barrels of American oak were used for it for the first time in Ireland. A very welcome addition to the portfolio came at the end of 1999: a 15-year-old Jameson, a → pure pot still, which at least inceased to four the number of these original Irish whiskies.

Jamie Stuart Scotch blend from J & G → Stewart. Since 1917 the company had belonged to → DCL, who were bought up by → Guinness in 1987 and restructured to form → UD. Because of laws relating to monopolies, the new proprietors had to part with various brands. The blend then belonged to → Whyte & Mackay / → JBB (Greater Europe) plc.

J & B Scotch blend. One of the leading brands, it is in second place worldwide and on the important US market, and in 17th place among spirits in general – positions which gave rise to speculations about its future, when at the end of 1997, → Grand Metropolitan merged with → Guinness to form the largest drinks combine in the world. However, the Monopolies Commission in Europe and the Antitrust Authority in the USA, decided that although the new giant had to part with → Dewar's (number one in America and Greece), and several other brands, they could keep J & B as a second flagship, along with → Johnnie Walker. The brand was established by → Justerini & Brooks and grew to its current importance after prohibition, a period for which the company was well prepared, when they stormed the American market with this pale-coloured blend, indicating lightness of character. It consists of more than 40 different malt whiskies, including those of the company's own → IDV distilleries, → Auchroisk, → Glen Spey, → Knockando and → Strathmill. There is a J & B Rare, a J & B Reserve, a J & B Jet and a J & B 1749. J & B Edwardian and J & B Victorian, which were formerly produced exclusively for Japan, have now been discontinued. In 1994, for the 500th anniversary of Scotch whisky, a J & B Ultima was created, a name which it earned as it contained, believe it or not, 128 whiskies (116 malts and 12 grains) whose casks are illustrated on an attractive panoramic poster, a special delight as many of the distilleries included longer exist.

Japan The country is now the fourth-largest whisky nation after the USA, Scotland and India in the latter half of the 20th century. This position is due to the initiative and passion of just two men. The Scottish influence has deeply affected everything to do with whisky in Japan.

It is not surprising that Scotland is the mould for Japanese whisky making as Shanjiro → Torii and Masataka → Taketsuru are the founding fathers. They were the founders of → Suntory, and → Nikka. The two companies share more than 80% of the national market. One man was a successful wine producer and had the necessary capital, whilst the other man had the technical knowledge. Taketsuru went to

Scotland at the age of 24, just after the Anglo-Japanese Treaty had been signed, to learn beer-brewing. He was even more fascinated by the whisky, however, whose production he learned about at, among other places, → Hazelburn and → Lagavulin.

He fell in love with the country and in 1923 he helped Torii build the → Yamazaki Distillery. In 1929 they brought out the first whisky to be produced in Japan. In 1934 he founded his own company and built his own distillery, Yoichi on → Hokkaido. Hokkaido had peat, coal to heat the → pot stills and barley even grew there. Nowadays hardly any malting takes place in Japan and barley and malt are imported, often from Scotland. In 1940 Taketsuru was able to launch his first whisky, but then the war stopped further production. After the war things really began to look up, and the rise of whisky as a Japanese cult drink was not just a result of interest in western culture and lifestyle, although it led to record imports of Scotch. Turnover was also increased by a clever campaign conducted by Torii, with his country-wide 'Tory Whisky Bars', which only sold his own brands.

The distillate tends to be light and flowery rather than heavy and full-bodied and although Japanese whisky is very popular foreign brands are also coveted, despite the high import levies; many luxury brands are exclusively made for Japan. Even though the recession in the Far East has had its effects on whisky consumption, Japan occupies fourth place behind France, the USA and Spain and still ahead of the UK (figures from 1999). Although the amount of Scotch malt whisky imported in → bulk has considerably decreased, Japan is still by far the largest buyer; it is needed to produce domestic brands together with grains and malts distilled in Japan.

The foreign whiskies are easily obtainable for the Japanese companies: Suntory owned a share in → Macallan and owns all of → Morrison Bowmore with the distilleries → Auchentoshan, → Bowmore and → Glen Garioch. Nikka has acquired → Ben Nevis, → Kirin-Seagram has had access, via its Canadian partner, to its nine Scottish distilleries. Only → Sanraku-Ocean has no partners. The consortium → Takara Shuzo & Okura (Okura went bankrupt in 1998 and was replaced by Marubeni) owns the → Tomatin Distillery and, in partnership with → Sazerac, → Ancient Age. One would think that Japanese production would be sufficient to meet demand: it doubled in the 1970s and yet again the following decade, achieving a splendid 375 million litres per year by the end of the 1980s. However the figures are now declining again while sales are decreasing. Japanese whiskies are also relatively expensive: nowhere has such high production costs as Japan.

The country has five malt distilleries and a number of grain distilleries. Suntory own the largest distillery in the world (→ Hakashu) and has another one that has not yet been completed in Noheji. Nikka has built a second malt distillery in the → Miyagikyo area near → Sendai, and has two plants in Toshigi and → Nishinomiya with old-fashioned → Coffey stills, true to the Scottish spirit of the company's founder. Kirin-Seagram own a distillery near Gotemba that produces malt whiskies as well as grain, and Sanraku-Ocean have a small malt distillery in the spa town → Karuizawa (which for some time now has been called → Mercian), and a grain distillery in Kawasaki.

In all these distilleries different whiskies can be distilled by using various types of yeast and varyingly peated malt. Production follows the Scottish pattern; bourbon and sherry casks are used for maturation, they also use new, charred oak casks far more often than in Scotland. As in Scotland, the law requires the distillate to mature for at least three years. Single malts have only been bottled relatively recently whilst so-called → 'pure malts' have been bottled since the 1960s. At that time the first experiments with blends were carried out, which were influenced by the American style and tasted more like bourbon. Blends now make up the major share of the whiskies on sale in Japan. The market for them is divided between the two giants Suntory and Nikka, the much smaller Sanraku-Ocean and Kirin-Seagram (each with approximately 4%) and about 20 other companies whose total share also amounts to approximately 4%. In contrast to Scotland, with three categories, → 'standard', → 'premium' and → 'de luxe', there are five categories defined by the amount of malt whisky used in them (and by tax class): → 'super-premium' has a malt content of over 40%, → 'premium' has 35– 40%, → 'special' over 30%, → 'first' over 20% and → 'second' over 10%.

Jazz Club A series of 12 Kentucky straight bourbons from → Kentucky Bourbon Distillers. Following a series named after figures in American history (→ 'Legends of the Wild West' and → 'Outlaws'), this one is dedicated to jazz. There is a Boogie Woogie, a Bee Bop, the Jazz Singer, Guitar, Drum and Trumpet. Each version of the Jazz Club has two expressions, a 12-year-old (101°) and a 15-year-old (114°).

JBB (Greater Europe) plc Whisky company which until 1997 bore one of the great names in Scotch whisky history: → Whyte & Mackay. From 1990 they were owned by → American Brands, and through them were involved in a three-year-long takeover battle for → Invergordon Distillers which lasted until 1994. The takeover was followed by the closure of three of the four Invergordon distilleries, a redistribution of the brands of both companies, and the rechristening of the company as JBB (Greater Europe) plc. JBB is an abbreviation of the most successful American whiskey and stands for Jim Beam Brands. In 1997, the parent company was renamed → Fortune Brands and in October 2001, → Kyndal was formed from the European assets of JBB (Greater Europe) plc after a £200m management buy out.

Jefferson's Reserve Kentucky straight bourbon whiskey which is similar in appearance to the → Woodford Reserve. The bottle is slightly more distinguished. It is not known by whom or where it was made. The small label, numbered by hand, shows that it is only available in very small quantities, and that it is a 'Very Small Batch Bourbon'. It is 15 years old and has a strength of 92°/45.1%. It is marketed by McLain & Kyne Distillery Co whose ancestors had been selling spirits eight generations previously in 1799. They see their product as a 'tribute to Thomas Jefferson's integrity and independence'.

Jesse James Kentucky straight bourbon, aged 8 years (40%), whose label gives no indication of its producer. It is produced solely for the Italian market.

Jim Beam American whiskey distilleries. Both are to be found close to the small town of Belmont. They bear the name of their most famous product, the bourbon Jim Beam, on whose bottles just one of the place names is mentioned: the smaller (and older) of the two is in Clermont, the larger, founded in 1953, is about 15 km away in Boston (both are much nearer to Bardstown than Frankfort, the state capital, which is also named).

The bottles are decorated with the portraits of six Beams, representing six generations of a family who have left their mark on the history of bourbon. Its members were dispersed among several distilleries in Kentucky, and the deepest impression has been left by the company that bears their name. Although it has not been in family ownership for a long time, but has belonged to → American Brands since 1967, it is still one of the very few in the USA to have direct connections with the descendants of the founding family. The Beam who gave the company his name, was Jim Beauregard, the great-grandson of Jacob Beam, the first of the dynasty, and grandfather of → Booker Noe Jr, who as 'Master Distiller Emeritus' remains a living legend and the company's best ambassador (and the generally accepted authority on all questions regarding whiskey production).

In 1989 Booker Noe decided that instead of just producing the standard whiskey in different versions they would select the best barrels, allow them to mature for a longer period and bottle them in small batches. Just as → Blanton's had represented a new stage in the history of bourbon, Noe's → small batch bottlings led bourbon into a new dimension. His invention has not simply resulted in a new trend, but has also proved that bourbons can be as characterful and individual as otherwise only malt whiskies can be; one of the new bourbons, → Booker's, therefore bears his name. Booker Noe's father worked at the → Ancient Age Distillery for a long time, and another Beam founded the → Early Times Distillery.

The old Jacob Beam emigrated as Jakob Böhm from Germany, settling in Kentucky in 1788. Like every other farmer he turned his surplus grain harvest into liquid form with the help of a → still, which he had brought with him. 1795 is the year that was when Jacob first distilled and sold his whiskey commercially. His great-grandson Jim took over the company in 1880 when it was still relatively small, although it already had a brand, Old Tub, which was sold all over the country. Jim was 55 when → prohibition forced him to stop production and close down the company. But he didn't give up: the modern history of the company began in 1933 when Jim Beam, then 70 years old, applied for a licence, and together with the businessman Harry Blum had enough money to survive the four years before they could sell their first whiskey. This was still Old Tub, → Jim Beam first appeared in 1942, three years before Blum bought out his partner Beam.

In 1953 the new distillery was built in Boston. Like Clermont it has 19 fermentation vessels and uses a → column still with a → doubler. Although no difference is made between them, both distilleries produce slightly differing whiskeys. The same → mash bills are used but the water comes from different sources. The recipes at Jim Beam are top secret, some people think there are two and others that there are three, with varyingly high proportions of rye. It is proudly pointed out that the yeast, which has hops added to it, is still from the same culture that Jim Beam used in the 1930s. straight rye is produced twice a year. The scale of production is enormous: 600 barrels are filled per day and 600 mature barrels are emptied.

In 1987 American Brands bought the company National Distillers who owned the brand → Old Overholt and the three distilleries → Old Crow, Old Taylor and → Old Grand-Dad. They were immediately closed down but their names have survived on the three brands which are now made by Jim Beam – allegedly using the original yeast. The Jim Beam bourbons, which contain half Boston and half Clermont whiskeys, have the lowest rye share, whilst Old Grand-Dad and the small batch brands → Knob Creek and → Basil Hayden have the highest. The 'normal' version is the straight Jim Beam with the white label, which is 4 years old (80°/40%) and by far the best-selling of its kind worldwide. In the USA it is also available as a 7-year-old (and pre-mixed with Coke in a can). Beam's Choice bore a green label (it is no longer produced) and was also 80°/40% (previously 85°/43%) and was supposed to hark back to the Old Number 8 Family Formula and to be 5 years old. Beam's Black Label (90°/45% in the USA and 80°/40% elsewhere) used to carry the age statement '101 months', but today it is just plain '8 years'. There is a Gold Label (100°/50%) which is only obtainable in Australia. The company also has a rye (80°/40%) with a yellow label and the unusual statement that it is 'copper distilled' and, like other versions, bears the signature of James B Beam, with the note, 'None genuine without my signature'. For the 200th anniversary in 1995 a Jim Beam Anniversary Label was issued, in a bottle with a swing stopper, aged 75 months (95°/47.5%).

A special 'Barrel Bonded' is bottled for → Nikka, the Japanese importer of Jim Beam. There is also the blend → Beam's 8 Stars. The company is also famous for their motif carafes, that is whiskey filled in every conceivable form of container. These may be in the shape of a Chevrolet or the bust of John Wayne; many collectors are fascinated by them. The spirits subsidiary of the large concern looks after the → Alberta Distillery in Canada and its bottling plant in Cincinatti, Ohio, and is responsible, apart from the previously mentioned brands, for the following: → Bellows, → Bourbon Deluxe, → Calvert, → Hill & Hill, → Kessler, → P M and → Sunny Brook, as well as the small batch bourbons Jacob's Well and → Knob Creek and the liqueur → Rock and Rye. Nowadays the rye whiskey → Old Overholt is also produced by Jim Beam.

J M & Co Superior Mountain Dew Scotch blend from Malpass Stallard in Worcester. This company can trace its history back to 1642, and could be even older than that. Their blend is the last with the synonym → 'Mountain Dew', that was used in Scotland and Ireland for whisky.

Jock → Scotch from The → Bennachie Whisky Co, a company named after the mountain near Inverurie. Its full name is → Formidable Jock

Jock Scott Scotch blend from → Invergordon who sell it using the name of the company that first marketed it in the 1930s: Findlater Mackie Todd & Co. It is available as a → standard blend aged 3 and 5 years, and as a 12-year-old → de luxe blend.

John Barr Scotch blend which owes its creation in 1978 to a decision by EU bureaucrats. In that year Brussels forbade → DCL to sell their whiskies in the UK at different prices to those for export – a measure adopted to protect their official importers from → parallel imports. As a reaction to the directives the company withdrew, of all things, its market leader → Johnnie Walker from the domestic market. They attempted to obviate their financial losses by launching a new blend, John Barr, which they registered in the name of their subsidiary George → Cowie & Sons (→ Mortlach). The classic Johnnie Walker has long since returned to the UK, but John Barr has also survived. After the takeover of DCL by → Guinness, it has been resold, again because of directives from the Monopolies Commission. Nowadays it comes as a → standard blend, as a 'Special Reserve' and as John Barr Black from → Kyndal.

John Begg's Blue Cap Scotch blend with the name of the early owner of the → Royal Lochnagar Distillery. The slogan 'Take a peg o' John Begg' was devised by the founding family, who were taken over by → DCL in 1916. It helped shape the image of the brand, and David → Daiches reports seeing a translation into Yiddish in a Jewish magazine in Glasgow, unfortunately undated: *Nem a schmeck fun Dzon Bek*. The once great and popular brand unfortunately now only plays a small part in the large range of → UDV. It was formerly also available as Gold Cup and De Luxe, but is now only available as Blue Cap in the lower price segment, mainly sold in Germany.

John Collins Whiskey cocktail. It is the American version of Collins, that is often called Colonel Collins. John may sometimes turn into a Jack or a George, when the drink is prepared with a Jack Daniel's or a George Dickel instead of a bourbon. However the recipe remains the same: take 3cl whiskey, 1cl fresh lemon juice, and a teaspoon of sugar and shake together with ice, add 3cl soda water and garnish with a maraschino cherry and a slice of orange.

John Finch American blended from → Kentucky Bourbon Distillers, a company in Bardstown.

John Grant, The Scotch → Pure Malt from J & G → Grant, who own the → Glenfarclas Distillery on → Speyside. There has been a 6-year-old version for Italy for quite some time now. It is very likely a single malt from Glenfarclas. The malt has made a good name for itself in Italy and was therefore joined by a new version in 1998, which is a splendid 17 years old. It tastes different to the Glenfarclas of the same age as it comes from different casks.

John Grant's Scotch single malt aged 6 years – an age which suggests that it is intended for the Italian market. It comes from J & G → Grant.

John Lee Kentucky straight bourbon (40%) without an age statement. The 'Personal Reserve' is sold exclusively in France by Bardinet, who unfortunately do not divulge which source the whiskey comes from.

John Player Special/JPS Scotch blend, available in four versions and named after the well-known brand of cigarettes. Their proprietors allowed the Glaswegian company → Laing & Co to use their name. The → standard blend is called Fine Old, whilst the Rare, the 12-year-old, and the 15-year-old JPS, belong to a higher category.

John's Lane Street in Dublin where the distillery named after it is situated. It was founded around 1796 by John Power. The famous → pot still whiskey from John Power & Son, as the company was called until 1809, came from here. In 1871 it was renovated in Victorian style and since that time has enriched the general aspect of Dublin. It lies near Father Mathew Bridge on the Liffey and near the 'Brazen Head', the oldest pub in the city. Since the merger with the rival company of → Jameson on the other side of the river, and since the decision of the new company to produce solely in → Midleton, the buildings have housed the National College for Art and Design. The → Cadenhead bottling of a

34-year-old cask, distilled in 1965 at a mighty 73.2%, commemorates the glorious past of a great whiskey name – as do the three great pot stills which were fortunately not dismantled, as in the case of the → patent still which had been installed in the 1950s.

Johnnie Walker Scotch blend (and vatted malt), which is perhaps the most famous brand of all, and certainly the most successful – not least of all because of its famous slogan, 'Born 1820 – still going strong'. Although this was coined in 1908 John → Walker opened his grocer's shop in Kilmarnock in 1820, where he also sold wine and whisky. 'Walker's Kilmarnock Whisky' was already being distributed worldwide (and was particularly successful in Australia) when the manager, James Stevenson, and John's grandson, Alec Walker, had the striking square bottle created for them in 1908, as well as the figure (designed by the artist and caricaturist Tom Browne), which has since become the distinctive mark of the whisky: the dandy in his riding clothes with a monacle. The bottle and the character have such a timeless quality that they have survived practically unchanged to this day, having been only slighty modified in 1997 and then, in 2000 with the new slogan 'Keep walking', and with a new direction: the striding man is now hurrying off towards to the right.

There can be no other Scotch that has been so shamelessly copied. In 1984 20,000 cases were found to be copies when it was noticed that the information 'Product of Scotland' was missing from the Bulgarian label; in Egypt a whisky called *Waker* was being sold to unsuspecting tourists.

Numerous versions of the brand are available. The *Red Label* is the classic and comes without an age statement. Just as it leads the world rankings in the → standard blend sector, the *Black Label*, which is mostly sold as a 12-year-old, is number one in the → premium blend sector. The *Swing* is the same age and was created in the 1920s for the great ocean liners, coming in a bottle which, thanks to its rounded base, doesn't fall over in a storm but swings; in some places it is called *Celebrity*, and in Taiwan is sold as *Swing Superior*.

The Asian market is important for *Johnnie Walker*. In Japan there is the *Premier* and the *Gold*, which is blended according to a recipe from Alexander Walker (and supposedly based on malt whiskies from → Clynelish). The *Gold 18 years old* is only available in duty-free shops in East Asia and the USA. The *Honour*, with numbered certificates, is also only available in the duty-free shops in the Pacific area (and at → Glenkinchie Distillery where it costs £200), as well as the *Quest* and the *Excelsior*, which were both launched in early 1998, aimed at a target group of 25-35-year-old (wealthy) travellers. → UDV, who as successors of → UD and → DCL, with whom John Walker & Sons merged in 1925, today own the brand and launched a *Blue Label*, whose malts are said to be up to 60 years old. Amongst these, as in the case of all their blends and the *Johnnie Walker Malt* (15 years old) introduced in 1997, there are certainly spirits from the distilleries of → Cardhu, with which they have special associations, and → Talisker. At the beginning of 1999 further versions were launched for the Asian market: a 21-year-old in a specially-created carafe is only available in Taiwan, and 'economical' half bottles, the *Deco*, are only available in Japan. There was a special bottling of *Black*, with a view to the Millennium, the *1998 Special Edition – First Production* and the *Johnnie Walker 18 years Centenary Blend*. There is also a *Johnnie Walker* liqueur and a ready-mixed *Johnny Walker Red and Cola*.

Johnny Drum Kentucky straight bourbon whose label names Johnny Drum Distiller as its producer, but which is actually made by → Kentucky Bourbon Distillers. They own the → Willett Distillery near Bardstown which closed down in the 1980s. This 15-year-old whiskey (101°/50.5%) is from their old stocks and really does derive from 'Private Stock' as it says on the label. It is one of their four → 'small batch – boutique bourbons'. Further versions which probably no longer come from the old distillery are the 8-year-old (86°/43%) and the 12-year-old with the same strength.

Jones Road Location of the → Dublin Whiskey Distillery Company (DWC), which began operating in 1873, exactly a year after the foundation of the company. It was located on a spectacular site: beside the ruins of a castle and an abbey on the river Tolka. Although the DWC merged with William Jameson and George Roe in 1891 to form the Dublin Distillers Company Ltd, all three continued production of → pot still whiskey under their own names. The business did not prosper and at the end of World War II finally came to an end. The name is comemmorated in a bottling of a cask from 1942, that after 49 years still had 65%, when → Cadenhead included it in their superb series of → pot still whiskeys from old, bygone Irish distilleries.

Joseph Finch Kentucky straight bourbon from → UD in the series → 'Rare Bourbons'. Like the Scottish counterpart → 'Rare Malts', the series was intended to represent bourbons from UD distilleries which have long since closed down, but on the American labels the exact origins are not given. It was distilled in spring 1981, and was bottled as a 15-year-old at a strength of 86.8°/43.4% in exactly 2,400 bottles. It gets its name from a man who, in pre-revolutionary days found a spring which then became the source of water for a distillery. The whiskey is sure to become a rarity as the UD successors UDV parted with nearly all its American brands at the beginning of 1999 and will certainly not continue this series.

J T S Brown Kentucky straight bourbon and blended Whiskey nowadays produced by → Heaven Hill, the last independent distillery in the American whiskey business, which not only unites an unusually large number of brands under its umbrella, but which has also saved some of them from extinction. The name is due to a spelling mistake but J T S Brown is an important name in the history of bourbon. He was one of the two Browns in the early days of another important family, the Brown-Formans. John Thompson Street and his half-brother George Garvin established their company in Louisville in 1870 and created a whiskey of great repute → Old Forester. J T S left the company soon after, allegedly because he didn't believe in the high quality standards that George set, but thought that they could make money faster with cheaper product. In the next 100 years the name J T S Brown kept cropping up, as the builder of the → Old Prentice Distillery, then in 1923 as the purchaser of the closed-down → Early Times Distillery (the rights to the brand were owned at that time by Brown-Forman) and in the 1950s as the owner of a distillery in → Lawrenceburg, Kentucky. At the end of the 1970s the rights to the name were acquired by Heaven Hill. The straight (80°/40%) is without an age statement.

Julian, Charles H Small firm in family ownership established by the former master blender of → Justerini & Brooks. The firm, which via a subsidiary is also engaged in storage and distribution, owned several brands of its own, of which only → Carlton remains, whilst the Excalibur and Camlan are no longer produced. They now have the → Royal Club, a brand that was formerly available from → ADP They are also responsible for the worldwide distribution of Sir Iain's Special → Moncreiffe, which nowadays belongs to Ian Lockwood.

Justerini & Brooks In the year 1749 the Italian Giacomo Justerini emigrated to London. He opened a grocer's store with George Johnson, in which he also sold liqueurs from Italy. In 1831 the businessman Alfred Brooks bought the flourishing business that since then has borne the name Justerini & Brooks. It not only consists of two wonderful wine shops in London's St. James's Street and Edinburgh's George Street, but was also a part of → Grand Metropolitan, which merged with → Guinness in 1997 to become the largest drinks combine in the world. GrandMet brought their spirits subsidiary → IDV with them into the marriage, which itself had resulted from a merger in 1962 between Justerini & Brooks and → Gilbey. Justerini & Brooks (Scotland), ran four distilleries on behalf of IDV, → Auchroisk, → Glen Spey, → Knockando and → Strathmill – and were responsible for the enterprise's best-known brand, the blend → J & B. Whilst this is a brand with worldwide distribution, the → Club is now only available in the two shops. But the fact that they allow themselves the luxury of cultivating such a small brand shows a great sense of tradition. The bosses of Diageo also showed a rare respect for tradition by leaving Justerini & Brooks untouched (although, of course, rationalisation took place with, for example, the closure of the old J & B bottling plant in Dumbarton, which cost 500 jobs), whilst almost all their other interests in the spirits trade are handled by their subsidiary UDV. The single malt Knockando also continues to bear the venerable name.

J W Corn Kentucky straight corn whiskey, behind whose producer J W Corn in Bardstown stands → Heaven Hill. The label shows a picture of corn, which must make up more than 80% of the mash so that it can be called 'corn'. It has a strength of 100°/50% and is → bottled in bond.

J W Dant Kentucky straight bourbon from → Heaven Hill. The initials stand for Joseph Washington. In 1836 he set up a small distillery in Marion County. His son Joseph Bernard founded the Cold Spring Distillery and created → Yellowstone. His second son, George, stayed with his father and became president of the company. During → prohibition stocks were also stored at → Stitzel-Weller and sold as 'medicinal alcohol'. According to reports there were still old barrels, at least before a big fire in 1996, but even if they have been destroyed or used up, the bourbon is to be continued. At present it is sold at 100°/50% and without an age statement.

J W Gottlieb American straight rye whiskey, bottled by the Commonwealth Distillery Co in Lawrenceburg in 1997. The company J P → Van Winkle and Son are behind this name. The Private Stock was actually intended exclusively for Johnathan W Gottlieb, but is now more generally available. It is 95.6°/47.8% and is 13 years old.

K

Kakubin Japanese → standard blend from → Suntory that has been on the market since 1937. Since 1989 there has been a new version containing a distinctly higher proportion of malt whiskies, which has made it even more popular. It is the number one by a wide margin in Japan. Its name means 'angular bottle'.

Karuizawa Japanese malt distillery which gets its name from the popular spa town which lies near Mount → Asama – on the route from Tokyo to Nagano, which the location for the 1998 Olympic Games and which the Japanese regard as a holy place. The tiny distillery which is open to visitors, was first built in the 1960s by a firm named after the successful sake brand → 'Sanraku', which they had produced in 1937. They chose the adjunct → Ocean. All stages of production from mashing to fermenting and distilling in the four → pot stills takes place in one single building. The water comes from Asama but the malt is imported from Scotland, as well as some of the casks. All distillates are first filled in newly-charred oak casks which have contained sherry or have been treated with wine – not surprising for a company that is also very successful at wine making and wine selling. Its wines are sold in Japan by the name of → Mercian and are so well thought of that the company decided in the mid 1990s to give the distillery this name. A malt, which is described as 100% malt, is already being sold with this name. The Karuizawa in the carafe with the porcelain label round its neck is described as 'Fine Aged straight Malt Whisky'.

Kasauli Indian malt distillery whose origins go back to 1855. Its history began, like many others, as a brewery, the first in → India, founded by the Scot Edward Dyer to provide the large British army with fresh beer. The distillery still uses old equipment, such as cast iron fermenting vessels, from the days of its foundation. Dyer chose a location high up in the Himalayas which can only be reached from Chandigarh, the capital of the Punjab, by crossing through Haryana. Kasauli looks like one of the illustrations of Scottish distilleries in the 19th century; there are chimneys on the maltings. The complex lies on a hill.

Whisky production first began after World War I. There are no documents recording ownership in those days but it is known that at some time Dyer joined forces with an Irishman named Meakin, to whom he had already sold his → Solan Brewery, to become Dyer, Meakin & Co. They were bought by N N Mohan in 1949, and they named the company → Mohan Meakin and made it into a mighty undertaking with several distilleries and 11 breweries. Everything was left as it was at Kasauli, and the old → floor maltings still exist in which only coal (and no peat) is used. The four → pot stills are now steam-fired and no longer coal-heated. Since 1955 there have also been two small → patent stills, completely made of copper, which do not produce → grain whisky but malt whisky. This is not matured in casks but in tanks. It only matures for a few weeks. The malt whiskies from the pot stills are matured in wood. Kasauli's malt whisky is so coveted that supply cannot keep pace with demand, partly because of the small size of the fermenting vessels. Strangely, although Mohan Meakin sell it as 'Pure Malt Whiskey' (sic) from the Kasauli Distillery, the description Solan No. 1 also appears on the label – this is its official name.

Keepers of the Quaich An association founded on 16th October 1988 with the aim of honouring and promoting the significance and prestige of Scotch whisky at home and throughout the world. Four large Scottish whisky companies were the original founders, but nearly all the others have since joined in. Members must have worked for the good of Scottish whisky for at

Kentucky

least five years. Membership is not by application, but by invitation and with the support of sponsors. Most members are important people from the industry and from politics, as well as whisky writers, connoisseurs or major collectors. They are all united by their passion for Scotland and whisky. There are about 1,200 members drawn from nearly every country in the world. There is a special tartan in the colours blue (for water), brown (for earth) and golden yellow (for barley and whisky), and a royally-approved coat of arms and the motto '*uisgebeatha gu brath*' (whisky forever). Meetings take place twice a year, at the beginning of spring and in the autumn, with a festive banquet in the wonderful rooms of Blair Castle, with a welcome by the private army of the Duke of Atholl. New members are inducted and an excellent dinner is served, including haggis, accompanied by exquisite whiskies. In the world of whisky there is no greater honour than to become a member of this exclusive association.

Kelly's Irish whiskey from → Invergordon which, as in the case of → Dunville's and → Erin's Isle, get their base whiskeys for it from → Cooley, blend it themselves and supply the 40% blend mainly to the Dutch supermarket chain Makro.

Kelt Scotch vatted malt from Kelt Whisky, who share the address in Leith with the company named as bottlers, → Invergordon Distillers. The second name on the label is '*Tour du Monde*'. Before being bottled the casks were loaded on board a ship and taken for a world trip. The ports of call, as well as the length of the journey (4th July 95 – 12th September 1995) and the shipping company (Evergreen), are recorded on the bottle. This resulted in the whisky being 'mellowed by the waves of the ocean', in accordance with an old custom from the times when whisky was shipped to the colonies in casks rather than in bottles and when the discovery was made that the journey suited some of them very well and helped maturation. Some sherries ('East India' from Lustau and '*Linje Akvavit*') still observe this custom.

Ken Lough Irish whiskey from Cooley, which is identical to the → Dunlow.

Kenloch Single malt Scotch whisky from – as the bottle states – Canada. It is only 'bottled' by → Glenora Distillers, not 'distilled' by them. Apparently the bottles contain → Bowmore, as the experts from Islay who helped to establish something previously unheard of in Canada: a malt distillery in classic Scottish style – in a region with strong Scottish connections, Nova Scotia. The bottle information is written in two languages and contains a malt whisky with a strength of 40% vol. and holds a generous 750 ml, as was formerly also customary in Europe. The Canadian newcomers hope to make some money with Bowmore, and make their name known, before they can earn money from their own whisky.

Kenmore Scotch blend produced by → Burn Stewart for the UK chain → Marks & Spencer.

Kentucky American state. From the middle of the 19th century it has enjoyed great importance. Apart from a few exceptions, nearly all US distilleries are to be found within its borders. There are several reasons for this. They are associated with the natural advantages that the settlers found in the state, as they passed through the Cumberland Gap in the Appalachian Mountains, in the footsteps of Daniel Boone, to settle in Bluegrass Country. Many of them were acquainted with the art of distilling, many had the necessary equipment for it in their baggage, and many were looking for a new life as farmers. This occupation naturally included distilling.

In the area later to become Kentucky they found good water, which owes its particular quality to the limestone there. They found soil on which they could plant grain. Maize also proved to grow particularly well, and they found large rivers which were ideal for transportation and made trading easier. The drink that they made should not be confused with what we nowadays know as bourbon, especially as they sold their distillate fresh, without any sort of maturing in a barrel, rather like the illegally made → moonshine.

The modern Bourbon County, after which the spirit is named, lies north east of Lexington and west of Frankfort, although there isn't a single

Kentucky Bourbon Distillers

distillery to be found here. 'Bourbon' is not a description of origin. Any whiskey produced in the USA may use this name as long as it has been made, according to the law of 1964, from a mash consisting of at least 51% corn, comes from the still with no more than 160°/80% and has matured for at least two years in unused barrels made of American oak which have been charred inside. The two whiskies made in Tennessee, Jack Daniel's and George Dickel, would also be allowed to call themselves bourbon if the companies didn't prefer to call the → Tennessee Mash (however, they use the Lincoln County Process that is they also filter their whisk(e)y over charcoal).

The following distilleries are to be found in the state of Kentucky: Ancient Age, Barton, Bernheim, Early Times, Four Roses, Heaven Hill, Jim Beam, Labrot & Graham, Maker's Mark and Wild Turkey. All the many hundreds of different bourbon brands come from this handful of distilleries (to which Willett will also possibly soon belong).

Kentucky Bourbon Distillers American whiskey company based in Bardstown which produce such a large range of brands and whole series such as → 'Outlaws' or → 'Jazz Club', that it is difficult to maintain an overview. They are distinguished by the fact that as producers they choose names which are purely imaginary and which can rarely be assigned to a distillery. The company however is really associated with a distillery, as the → Willett family, who have an interest in the company, own a distillery of the same name near Bardstown. The Willetts are working on reopening it, but most whiskeys are at present probably supplied by the → Heaven Hill Distillery which is just around the corner. One of the four whiskeys that they describe as → 'small batch – boutique bourbons' indeed comes from old Willett stocks: the → Noah's Mill aged 15 years. The → Johnny Drum of the same age also comes from the old plant, but not the younger version of it. The other → small batch bottlings are called → Kentucky Vintage, → Pure Kentucky and → Rowan's Creek. → Bourbontown Club, → Kentucky Crown, → Lone Oak, → Old Bardstown, → Old Distiller and → Red & Gold are all Kentucky straights. The → Very Old St. Nick versions are rare bourbon whiskeys (that is not Kentucky straights). The blended → John Finch also belongs to their range.

Kentucky Crown straight bourbon whose strength is not given in °proof and the word 'Kentucky' is omitted. It is available in two age categories: aged 8 years (47.5%) and aged 16 years (63.5%), described as 'very rare'. The label states 'distilled and aged in Kentucky' and names the Kentucky Crown Distillery in → Bardstown as bottlers, which leads to the supposition that the whiskies came from → Heaven Hill. The brand belongs to the → Kentucky bourbon Distillers, who are also located in Bardstown.

Kentucky Dale Kentucky straight bourbon from the → Sazerac Company in New Orleans which is produced in their → Ancient Age Distillery in → Leestown.

Kentucky Dry American blended whiskey from a company that does not name a distillery, and name the bottlers as Kentucky Custom Distillery. As the brand comes from → Bardstown it is probable that either the → Kentucky Bourbon Distillers or the → Heaven Hill Distillery are behind it.

Kentucky's Friend Kentucky straight bourbon from an unknown producer that is imported by the Distilleries Ryssen in Hesdin for distribution in France.

Kentucky Gentleman Kentucky straight bourbon that was created in the 1940s by the founder of today's Barton Distillery in → Bardstown. There are three versions, a standard (80°/40%) and a → bottled in bond (100°/50%), both with no age statement, and a 6-year-old (86°/43%). There is also a blended with a strength of 80°/40%.

Kentucky Gold Kentucky straight bourbon which T W Turnbull's Sour Mash Company, a subsidiary of Halewood Vintners based in Robertson Lane, Liversedge, West Yorkshire, gets from an unnamed American distillery. The whiskey (40%) is only on sale in the UK.

Kentucky Legend Kentucky straight bourbon

from → Austin, Texas. Nichols Distilling Company have launched it as one of the two → single barrel versions of their classic → Wild Turkey. It is 8 years old and has 101°/50.5%, a strength which master distiller Jimmy Russell believes to be ideal for the whiskeys produced at the → Boulevard Distillery in Lawrenceburg. He selects the barrels himself, the bottles are numbered and also sometimes bear the words 'Beyond Duplication'.

Kentucky Pride Kentucky straight bourbon at 90°/45% from a distilling company of the same name, who give their address as → Bardstown – a clear hint that this → small batch bourbon is one of the many products from → Kentucky Bourbon Distillers.

Kentucky Spirit Kentucky straight bourbon from Austin Nichols. This is a → single barrel version of → Wild Turkey. It looks like an expensive bottle of Cognac and a picture on the stopper shows where it comes from. The barrels from which it originates are chosen by the legendary Jimmy Russell, master distiller at the → Boulevard Distillery in Lawrenceburg. He was probably also responsible for the strength, which he believes shows his whiskey in its best form: 101°/50.5%.

Kentucky Tavern Bourbon produced by → Glenmore which for a long time was only available as a blended whiskey. In 1991, when → UD bought this company together with its distillery, it was decided to launch a Kentucky straight that was produced at → Bernheim in Louisville, but stored in the old Glenmore → warehouses in Owensboro. This whiskey is still being sold, but it is doubtful whether that will remain the case as UD/Glenmore parted with the brand in 1995 and sold it to → Barton, who don't disclose the → mash bills they use or whether they use whiskeys from other distilleries. There are two versions: one with a strength of 80°/40% and the other → Bottled in Bond (100°/50%), both without an age statement.

Kentucky Vintage Kentucky straight bourbon which names the Kentucky Vintage Distillery as its producer (this has never existed). The brand belongs to → Kentucky Bourbon Distillers in Bardstown who bottle a whole range of bourbons to which they give imaginary names. Four of them are → small batch whiskeys. It is bottled without an age statement at 90°/45% and comes in a pale linen bag. A → vintage from 1976 comes in an elegant black velvet bag.

Kessler American blended whiskey which seems to be a great success in the USA, where it is sold at a strength of 80°/40%. The brand is older but nowadays comes from → the American Brands subsidiary → JBB.

Khoday Indian company who own a malt distillery in Bangalore. Two of its brands are especially well-known: the → Red Knight and → Peter Scot, one of the best and most successful whiskies of the country.

Kilbeggan Irish distillery in County Westmeath to the west of Dublin. It competes with → Bushmills for the honour of being the oldest in the country. In fact Kilbeggan first began operating in 1757, when it was named → Brusna, after the river on which it lies. It was taken over in the middle of the 19th century by J → Locke and remained in the ownership of his family until after World War II. It was sold to a German who was also only interested in its casks and sold an → Old Galleon.

In 1953 production finally ceased and the distillery deteriorated. It was saved from final ruin by the villagers of Kilbeggan ('little church') who made a fine museum out of it. From then on things began to look up: John J → Teeling acquired it in order to use its warehouses for maturing the whiskey that he produced in the → Cooley Distillery in Riverstown. The Kilbeggan is a blend at 40% which sells very well and has become the number two Irish whiskey in Germany. It is the flagship of the company, created by the Scottish Master Blender Jimmy Lang (formerly of → Chivas). Over the years the whiskey has changed somewhat.

Killyloch Scottish malt distillery. It lay within the Moffat complex of → Inver House Distillers Ltd, near Airdrie, and therefore belonged to the → Lowlands. The distillery consisted of a single → still, and it shared everything else with its sister

Kiln

→ Glenflagler/Glen Flagler, operating in the same complex. It also shared the water, which came from Lillyloch. When the first barrels were inscribed, the first letter of the stencil was, mistakenly, a 'K'. As the whisky was not to be sold as a single malt in the first instance, but was to be used in blends, it was left it as Killyloch. Eventually, however, the name ended up on whisky bottles when Inver House Distillers Ltd sold a Killyloch as a vatted malt in the 1980s. Killyloch existed as a distillery for an even shorter period than Glen Flagler and was dismantled in the 1970s. In 1994 Andrew Symington of → Signatory was able to acquire a cask distilled in 1972 and bring it out as an → independent bottling at a → cask strength of 52.6% in a very small edition.

Kiln Both the oven in which the → green malt is dried after → germination, and the building in which these ovens are located. They are crowned by → pagodas, which have become a kind of Scottish whisky symbol. In Scotland and Ireland every distillery used to have its own kiln. Now there are only a few left.

The word itself comes from the English *cylene*, which derives from the Latin *culina*, meaning burning-place. After → germination the barley has to be dried without destroying the enzyme which will convert the starches into sugar. It is laid out on a perforated drying floor and a fire is lit beneath it. In earlier days this was done using peat alone, but nowadays coal, coke, anthracite or oil are used. In the large modern maltings such as → Port Ellen, germination and drying take place in the same large drums.

Peat still plays an important part: it ensures that the whisky gets a smoky, peaty note. Recently Ireland didn't use peat until → Cooley again brought out a peated malt whiskey called→ Connemara. In Scotland every distillery has its own special recipe, and if they get their malt from outside they prescribe exactly how much peat should be used in the kiln. This ranges from → Glengoyne, which remains totally smoke-free, to the heavy → Islay malts like → Lagavulin, → Laphroaig and → Ardbeg, which is considered to be the most heavily peated whisky of all.

The distilleries which at least in part still use malt that they have produced themselves include, → Balvenie, → Bowmore, → Glendronach , → Highland Park and → Laphroaig; Ardbeg is also supposed to begin malting again soon. Although the kilns in the other distilleries are no longer used, they most have been converted, often being used as Vistior Centres.

Before → pagoda roofs were invented, the kilns were topped with conical chimneys of the type seen on oast houses in Kent.

Kiln, De A magazine mainly devoted to malt whisky published by the Dutch → Usquebaugh Society containing information about new bottlings, portraits of distilleries, trips to Scotland etc. It is only available to club members.

Kincaple Scottish distillery on the outskirts of St. Andrews which has ceased to exist, but is remembered because it was run by Robert → Stein and John → Haig. It was these two names which → Invergordon chose for a 10-year-old single → Lowland malt in their 'The → Malts of Scotland' series launched in 1997.

Kinclaith Shortlived Scottish malt distillery. Its name means 'head of the (river) Clyde'. It was situated in the middle of Glasgow, belonging to the → Lowlands → whisky region, and was built in 1957 by the beer brewers Seager Evans. It was owned by the American company → Schenley, who not only → brought Long John International with them but also their large grain distillery → Strathclyde in Glasgow, which they had begun to expand in 1954. They invested heavily in the malt whisky business with American capital and built → Tormore Distillery on → Speyside, having previously built Kinclaith with two → stills on the Strathclyde site. The water came from Loch Katrine in the Trossachs, one of Glasgow's large water reservoirs. Kinclaith ceased production in 1975 when the Americans withdrew from Scotland, and the UK brewing company Whitbread took over the management; the malt distillery had to make way for an extension to the grain distillery and was dismantled in 1976. Whilst Strathclyde now belongs to → Allied Distillers Ltd and continues production, there is nothing more to be seen of Kinclaith. The same is also true of its malt whiskies. It had never been available as a → proprietor's bottling, but there was a bottling from → Cadenhead. → Gordon & MacPhail regularly included it in their → 'Connoisseurs Choice' series. The last available year after the 1966 and 1967, was a 1968. It is no longer obtainable and there is no prospect of a further vintage. There was a Kinclaith from → Signatory, distilled on 4th July 2001, at 54.3%.

King Arthur Scotch blend introduced by → Bulloch Lade & Co, who later lost their independence to → DCL and then belonged to the → UD empire.

King Barley Czech whisky which sometimes comes as a malt and sometimes as a blend, always accompanied by the same picture of a king decorated with ears of corn and which for a time was also called King Barleycorn. It is six years old and is available in bottles of several sizes (up to 4.5 litres). As there were apparently still some old casks available and there is considerable demand for 'exotic' whiskies, the German importer Jack Wievers in Berlin, was able to persuade the manager of the → Seliko company to fill some bottles for him. He first brought a 12-year-old version of King Barley onto the German market, in a glass carafe and a huge wooden box, which had a clear golden label and was defined as malt whisky. In Summer 1999 Wievers brought out a limited amount of a 20-year-old King Barley.

King Charles Scotch blend from → QSI, a subsidiary of William → Grant & Sons.

King Edward I Scotch blend from → Clan Munro Whisky, a subsidiary of William → Lawson Distillers, who run the → Macduff Distillery and who since 1995 have belonged to the → Bacardi empire.

King George IV Scotch blend. The brand was produced by → DCL at the end of the 19th century and was mainly intended for export. At the beginning of the 1920s, when DCL joined together with the large Scottish whisky companies, it continued under the name of a new subsidiary, → Distillers Agency Ltd. Like all DCL enterprises it then passed to → UD. It is particularly successful on the Danish market. The name commemorates the English king on a visit to Edinburgh in 1822 asked for a → Glenlivet, without being bothered that what he was asking for had been illicitly distilled.

King Henry VIII Scotch blend from the Highland Blending Co in Glasgow and London, a family firm backed by H → Stenham. It bottled more than 40 brands, mainly for export. In 1996 Stenham was sold to a Scottish company who had chosen the name of a former subsidiary: → Premier Scotch Whisky Co. This blend is one of its two main brands. It is obtainable in supermarkets in southern Europe and in Latin America, aged 3, 5, 8, 10 and 12 years.

King James VI Scotch blend. It is named after the king who was James VI of Scotland and James I of England. He was the son of Queen Mary, who was executed by her English rival Elizabeth I. James became the first king of both countries in 1603. The blend comes from Forth Wines, who also have → Strathfinnan in their range.

King John Scotch blend from Highland Shippers. Behind this name was the London-based family firm of H → Stenham who produced more than 40 brands mainly for export (partly in → bulk for local bottling) to Central and Latin America and South East Asia. Stenham sold his business in 1996; it has been continued under the name of a former subsidiary, → Premier Scotch Whisky Co. Like all the blends of the company it is produced aged 3, 5, 8, 10 and 12 years.

King of Kings Scotch blend from → UDV who inherited this brand upon the takeover of → DCL by → Guinness. It was introduced by James Munro & Son, a firm whose origins are unknown, but were temporary licence-holders of → Knockdhu, and → Dalwhinnie. It has been a subsidiary of → Macdonald Greenlees since 1925. The blend is available mainly in Japan.

King of Scots Scotch blends, that come in a range of formats, from the Glaswegian company Douglas → Laing. They bought this brand which had been created in the 19th century and established it in the market place. All versions are either in decanters made of china or crystal or in leather-bound pocket bottles, which make them particularly attractive to the east Asian market. Apart from the two → standard blends Gold Label and Numbered Edition, which are both without age statements, there are → de luxe versions aged 12, 17 and 25 years and, again without an age statement, Rare Extra Old, Proclamation and Flagship.

King Robert II Scotch whisky available in two versions, as a → standard blend and as a 12-year-old → de luxe blend. The label names Wm. Maxwell as producer, but it in fact comes from Peter → J Russell & Co. William Maxwell was an old-established Liverpool firm of whisky blenders and exporters which had been founded in 1796.

King William IV Scotch blend which now comes from → UDV, but which was first introduced by John Gillon & Co. This subsidiary of → Ainslie & Heilbron received the licence in 1953 to → Glenury Royal Distillery which had been founded by the famous long-distance runner Captain Robert Barclay. He was not only a farmer, but also a member of parliament for Kincardineshire and was especially friendly with the Prince of Wales, who became King William IV.

King's Crest Scotch blend which is presented in luxurious ceramic decanters and is available in several age categories. The brand belongs to the → Speyside Distillery Co, which also produces it. It is sold by Alexander Muir. Both companies have a common series, the → 'Scott's Selection', for which they bottle single malts at → cask strength. The blend is available aged 5, 12, 15, 21, 25 and 30 years.

King's Legend Scotch blend: a small brand which is only available locally, from → Ainslie & Heilbran.

King's Pride Scotch blend from → Morrison Bowmore who took it over together with T & A → McClelland who are now their subsidiary, and market it as a → standard blend without an age statement, and as → de luxe versions aged 12, 17, 21, 25 and 30 years.

King's Ransom Scotch blend with the reputation of having at one time been the most expensive blend of all and the favourite whisky of the American White House. It is said to have been on the conference table at Potsdam in 1945. It was created by William Whiteley (→ House of Lords). Unfortunately it was discontinued after → Groupe Pernod-Ricard took over the company.

King's Whisky Scotch blend from → Burn Stewart who, however, no longer produce the brand and are at present just selling off the remains.

Kings Scotch Scotch blend from the High Spirits Company, which is associated with the → Speyside Distillery Co are hidden. A → standard blend without an age statement.

Kingsbury Wine & Spirit Co One of the many companies that have recently expanded their activities and became → independent bottlers, taking advantage of the continued growth of enthusiasm for single malts. The use the terms 'Original', 'Celtic' and 'Valdespino' for their products – the latter refers to casks that previously contained sherry – and to a very famous Spanish firm. They bottle → single casks and neither use → chill-filtering nor colour additives. In addition to a 1965 → Glen Albyn (49.1%) and a 1971 → Glencadam (55.6%), there was also an → Islay from an unnamed distillery, distilled in 1973 and bottled, aged 27 years, at 47%.

Kingsland Japanese blend of the lighter kind. Its producer, → Nikka, call it 'Premier' and supply it in a smart glass decanter.

Kininvie Scottish malt distillery. It belongs to the → Speyside region and lies next to its sisters → Glenfiddich and → Balvenie on the outskirts of → Dufftown. Before the → Isle of Arran Distillery was built, it was the newest distillery in the country. It was founded by William → Grant & Sons in 1990/1.

Kinross Whisky Co Company based in Haywards Heath, Sussex, in southern England who, however, do not have their four brands produced there. Their range includes the vatted malt → Glen Baren, the blends → Derby Special and → Gold Blend and the blend of their subsidiary Scottish Albion Blending, → Albion's Finest Old. The company's most important markets are in South East Asia.

Kinsey Scotch blend. It has been in → Inver House Distillers Ltd's range for quite some time and is a → standard blend without an age statement.

Kirin-Seagram Former Japanese-Canadian enterprise whose shares were jointly held by → Seagram and the Japanese company Kirin. Kirin's name comes from a mythical being, half horse and half dragon, which is said to have appeared to the mother of Confucius before his birth. The company, which traces its origins back to a brewery founded in 1869 in Yokohama, has now become the largest beer brewery in the country (and the third largest producer of beer in the world behind Miller and Anheuser-Busch) and belongs to the Mitsubishi empire. → Suntory, the largest whisky producer in the country, went into the brewing business in 1963, and 10 years later Kirin took the opposite path when they diversified from their main business in the beer branch and began to produce whisky. This happened at an opportune moment, for the Canadian Seagram company had been systematically expanding its business on nearly every continent following World War II, and was eager to enter joint ventures. In Kirin they found a partner whowas already well established and had excellent distribution networks, and Seagram could bring with them all the malt whiskies that their nine Scottish distilleries produced. These could be shipped in → bulk to Japan and provided an excellent basis for locally produced blends.

They also built a new distillery in Japan, in which malt and → grain whiskies were to be produced in separate buildings. A site was chosen on the main Japanese island of Honshu, to the south west of Tokyo, near Gotemba. On some days it looks as though the mountain Fujiyama is directly behind the distillery and seems to crown it with its snow-covered peak. The water needed for the mash comes from three springs from the mountain. Malted barley with varying degrees of peating is imported from the UK and made into quite different malt whiskies by the four → pot stills. The → column stills can be used in various combinations to make → grain whiskies. Ageing takes place in the six high-shelf warehouses, which each have a capacity of up to 35,000 barrels. Former bourbon barrels are mainly used, but some maturation takes place in charred new-oak barrels and, infrequently, in ex → sherry butts. Despite the abundance of their own whiskies, all Kirin-Seagram brands also make use of additional Scottish imports. The company produces the following blends, which are only available in Japan: → Boston Club, → Crescent, → Emblem, → News, → Robert Brown and → Ten Distilleries, as well as → Hips, which is bourbon-like and is described as 'the brightest whiskey'. Kirin-Seagram is the only Japanese producer who have not yet brought a single malt from their distillery onto the market.

Kittling Ridge Small Canadian distillery not far from Niagara, in Grimsby, Ontario. It was built by the Rieder company which was founded in 1970 and whose name points to its Swiss-German origins. Its stills actually only produced eau de vie and brandies, but it established itself in the whisky business by distributing → Canadian Mist and their own blends → Pure Gold and → Canadian Company (two versions), which they made from whiskies bought from other distilleries. John Hall has been the owner since 1992. He began to use his → stills for rye and corn whiskies, apparently with success. It is already possible to buy a Kittling Ridge Rye, and a 'Barrel Select Three Grain', named → Forty Creek Premium. The Kittling Ridge Corn is still maturing (in → sherry casks). The financial backbone is still provided by the blends and other spirits such as rum, vodka and coffee liqueurs, as well as the wine trade.

Knappogue Castle Irish whiskey with three vintages on the market from 1951 and 1992 and 1993. Of course the older one is a rarity. It was produced by B Daly in a distillery which bears a very well-known name: → Tullamore Dew. When they had to close, a few ex → sherry casks were acquired by a whisky dealer. After 36 years the old casks were finally bottled by Waterford Liqueurs in 1987. In the USA they came on to the market together with the new whiskey, which is not so rare. This is a product of the → Cooley Distillery. The castle which gave both whiskeys their name lies in County Clare.

Knight King Indian whisky. The brand belongs to the → Haryana Distillery, part of the Modi combine, who also use this name for a gin and a rum.

Knob Creek Kentucky straight bourbon from the → small batch series from the → American Brands spirits subsidiary → JBB, distilled in their → Jim Beam Distilleries in Boston and Clermont. It is 9 years old (100°/50%) and many people think that its perfectly balanced sweetness and dryness make it the best of the 'band of four'. The front label bears its name set against a background showing a newspaper article, the label on the back states: 'Deep in Kentucky, tiny Knob Creek spills and riffles down through the hills. Like the bourbon bearing its name, there's not much of Knob Creek, but what there is rewards you finding it.'

Knockando Scottish malt distillery. It lies on the left bank of the → Spey, not far from → Tamdhu, and therefore belongs to → the Speyside region. Its name is usually translated from the Gaelic as 'the little black hillock' and is emphasised on the penultimate syllable – however there are also persuasive arguments for the meaning 'mountain ash hillock' from the Scots 'knowe of the Rowan Tree' and the Gaelic 'cnoc an caoruinn'. It is one of those distilleries built during the whisky boom of 1898. It survived this period and has experienced very few changes in ownership through the years. In 1904 it was taken over by → Gilbey, which merged with → Justerini & Brooks in 1962 to form → IDV. Via Watney Mann it subsequently became part of → Grand Metropolitan. Until 1997 Justerini & Brooks (Scotland) held the licence to the distillery, which was renovated in 1969 and now has four → stills. For the time being, even after the merger of its parent company with → Guinness, it still bears its old name, now as part of UDV. Its malt whiskies play a major part in the company's most important blend, → J & B, which is number two worldwide.

The demand for it is so great that Knockando is hardly available as a single malt from → independent bottlers, although there is no difficulty in obtaining it as a → proprietor's bottling. In contrast to most other single malts its age is not given, but the year of distillation and the year of bottling are stated, a sign that quality consciousness guides the time of bottling when optimal maturity has been achieved. This generally seems to be the case after about 12 years, and in the case of the 'Extra Old Reserve' after 25 years; however the 1979 Master Reserve bottled in 2000 is only 21 years old. Since 1997 (but unfortunately only in the USA) there have also been an 18-year-old and a 21-year-old from → single casks, which bear the date of distillation and bottling, as well as the number of the cask and the bottle. There was a Centenary bottling on the occasion of their 100th anniversary in 1998, selected by the manager Innes Shaw. The Knockando Pure Single Malt 1980 was made especially for the French market and the label states that it was 'slow matured in an oak hogshead cask'. Several years ago, before the great boom, there was a series of cigars bearing the name Knockando.

Knockdhu Scottish malt distillery. Its name, pronounced 'nock-doo', comes from the Gaelic for 'black hill'. It lies near Huntly and is therefore better categorised as belonging to the Eastern → Highlands rather than the → Speyside region. It is not open to the public, only has two → stills and has been able to maintain much of its Victorian style. It was built in 1893/4 by → DCL, who had only formed a few years earlier, mainly at the behest of John → Haig & Co, for whose blends its whisky was mainly intended. It was the first distillery built by DCL themselves and remained in their hands until 1987 when DCL was swallowed up by → Guinness. It had already been shut since 1983. In 1989 production recommenced, a year after → Inver House Distillers Ltd acquired it from the Guinness subsidiary → UD.

The new owners also brought out the whisky as a single malt, naturally bearing the name of the distillery, as is customary in the case of a 12-year-old → proprietor's bottling. But it had hardly appeared when it was rechristened. Since then it has had the Gaelic name for Knockdhu and is called → An Cnoc, a change requested by → Justerini & Brooks for fear confusion with their → Knockando. At least Inver House Distillers Ltd gave the 21-year-old → cask strength (57.5%) its old name back, as well as a 23-year-old at 57.7%. It is also available under its 'proper' name from → independents such as → Gordon & MacPhail.

Knockeen Irish spirit which shines crystal clear in the bottle, and is described as 'Irish Poteen' on the label. This is the third such attempt, following → Bunratty Potcheen (sic) and → Hackler, which has now been discontinued. It was made possible because, as is proudly stated on the bottle, the tax authorities withdrew their opposition to it on 7 March 1997. The 'Spirit Drink' is produced by the Canterbury-based Vins Francais, and comes in two versions: the 45% is obtainable at the usual shops, whilst the 'Gold Extra Strength' is only available at duty-free outlets (e.g. in the Eurotunnel). With a mighty 90% it is probably the strongest spirit there, but is praised for its mildness, a result of → triple distillation.

Kosher Whisk(e)y In order to earn this name whiskies must be made in accordance with the regulations of the Jewish religion. These stipulate that only certain food and drink is acceptable, for which only selected ingredients may be used, which must have been made according to strictly controlled processes. The observation of the rules must be supervised, confirmed and guaranteed by a rabbi. The Scotch → Hamashkeh and the bourbon → Old Williamsburg are expressly labelled and confirmed as being Kosher.

Krottentaler New name for the malt whiskies produced by Robert → Fleischmann and his wife. The name change was quite involuntary and arose after the → Scotch Whisky Association had objected to their production.

Kyndal International Ltd The Scotch whisky company formed in October 2001 after the £200 million management buy-out of the European whisky assets of → JBB (Greater Europe) plc. The company's now owns 24 trade brands including → Whyte & Mackay and Vladivar vodka. The buy-out constituted the single largest transaction of its type in Scottish commercial history. The malt whisky distilleries in the Kyndal portfolio are → Dalmore, → Tamnavulin, → Fettercairn, → Isle of Jura and → Tullibardine. There are also major suppliers of supermarket own-label bottlings in the UK. They maintain close links with Jim → Beam.

L

Labrot & Graham

American distillery to the south of Frankfort, the capital of Kentucky. This was the oldest of the three closed-down distilleries in Glenn's Creek, but unlike its neighbours, → Old Crow and → Old Taylor, it was reopened on the 17th October 1996. This was a great day for Kentucky and lovers of bourbon and its history, for this was the oldest distillery still in existence in the USA. Over a door is a millstone whose inscription reads: 'Old Oscar Pepper Distillery Est. 1838 Labrot & Graham Est. 1878'. Oscar Pepper's father, Elijah, was one of Kentucky's whiskey pioneers and had begun distilling in 1780 when he was a farmer; Pepper called his whiskey Old 1776 and used the slogan 'Born with the Republic'. Oscar also employed the famous Dr James Crow. After Oscar's death, his son → James E Pepper succeeded him and in 1878 sold the distillery to Labrot & Graham, who renamed it. In 1940 the business was sold to Brown-Forman who shut the distillery in 1971, but 25 years later decided to invest a lot of money, buy back land, set up a visitor centre – and to produce a very special kind of bourbon.

Three → pot stills were brought from Scotland making this the first production from such stills since the pioneering days by an American firm. They distil → beer obtained from a mixture of 72% corn, 18% rye and 10% malt. This is all proof that the original intention was to make a bourbon to compete with the new → small batch and → single barrel whiskeys of other companies. It will take some time before the first bottles are on the market. To reacquaint the public with the name Labrot & Graham, Brown-Forman have brought out → President's Choice and → Woodford Reserve. Although they come from → Early Times, they give us an idea of the joys to come as they are the creation of the master distiller Lincoln Henderson.

Ladyburn

Scottish malt distillery. It was located within the → Girvan complex in the coastal town of the same name in Ayrshire, and therefore belonged to the → Lowlands region. Its four → stills were only in operation for 10 years, from 1966 until 1975, and were then completely dismantled by William → Grant & Sons, so that today nothing whatsoever remains of the plant – except for a few casks which continue to arouse the interest of collectors. There has only ever been a single → proprietor's bottling of a Ladyburn as a single malt which was reserved for employees and other company members. The only known → independent bottlings were the 14 and the 20-year-old (46%) from Cadenhead. Ladyburn is one of the most sought-after malts of all, and the Cadenhead bottles, which rarely turn up for sale at auction, achieve record prices.

The name Ladyburn also appears on the label of a blend called The → Great Macauley, and the suspicion is that the remaining casks were used in the blend, thereby providing the Grants with an elegant solution to two problems: the dangerously high age for a Lowland and the covetousness of collectors. Grants became nervous when it became known that → QSI were not only selling the blend, but had also brought out a malt named Ladyburn in Spain. In April 1999 David Stewart, who is responsible for the casks at Grants and is their 'chief nose', gave the credible assurance that this Ladyburn is a vatted malt – and that several dozen old casks of Ladyburn are still in store at Girvan. In the year 2000 he at last fulfilled the wishes of collectors and presented them with a Ladyburn Vintage Reserve 1973. Up to now at least three casks of it (numbers 3188, 3201 and 4500) have been bottled (all 50.4%) for the European market. Shortly before → Gordon & MacPhail had brought out an Ayrshire Malt, quite obviously also a Ladyburn which, however, was not named as such in order to avoid problems with the owners of the distillery.

Lagavulin Scottish malt distillery. Its name, pronounced 'lag-a-vool-in', comes from the Gaelic for 'the mill in the valley'. It lies on the southern coast of the whisky island of → Islay, between → Port Ellen and Kildalton, and is the middle distillery between → Ardbeg and → Laphroaig. In the mid-18th century there were said to have been no less than 10 (illegal) distilleries crowded together in this valley with its mill. At the beginning of the 19th century there were two (legal) distilleries, one belonging to John Johnston and the other to Archibald Campbell. In the following years it seemed as if they were continually taking each other over.

Their story becomes a little bit clearer after 1837, when just one distillery remained. One of Lagavulin's partners was James Logan Mackie, the uncle of Peter → Mackie, who became an apprentice there and inherited it in 1889. Since that time it has belonged to the company which became White Horse Distillers. In 1908 Mackie built a second distillery on the Lagavulin site, → Malt Mill, which shared Lagavulin's → mash tun but had its own → stills and → floor maltings, so that he could produce a heavily peated and medicinal-tasting, phenolic, malt whisky. This is now the location of a wonderful hall which is used for receptions and seminars (but which is unfortunately not open to tourists). The ruins of Dunyveg Castle on the cliffs in front of the distillery are an attraction for visitors. This was the castle of the Lords of the Isles, who governed the islands from Islay and competed with the kings on the Scottish mainland.

At the time of → DCL, who took over the business after Mackie died, there was already a highly esteemed single malt from Lagavulin. It was not as powerful as the malt whiskies from Ardbeg and Laphroaig, but was praised for the balance and elegance which made it a typical Islay. Nowadays it is peated with 35 to 40ppm (parts per million phenols) and is thus distinctly more smoky-peaty than the Laphroaig. It was available as a 12-year-old and as a 15-year-old in a small edition of stone jugs. → UD, who were owners until becoming UDV in 1997, included it in their series 'The → Classic Malts of Scotland', where it was a splendid representative of the Islay region; aged 16 years it is the oldest in the series. At the end of 1997 a limited edition of a malt distilled in 1979 was added to it in the new series 'The → Distillers Edition'. This had been finished in a cask which had previously contained a heavy Pedro Ximenez sherry, admirably suited to the character of the whisky. The independent bottlers also regularly use this malt whisky. A very young and turbulent 5-year-old Vintage Islay Malt is particularly interesting. It is undoubtedly a Lagavulin, and is available reduced to 43% and at cask strength.

Laing & Co, Douglas Scottish whisky company. It was established in Glasgow in 1950, and is one of the few to remain completely independent and in family ownership. From the very beginning it has specialised in selling mature whiskies, and its stocks of them have enabled it to build up, or further develop, a successful series of their own brands. The two most important are → King of Scots and → House of Peers, but → John Player Special (→ JPS) and the → McGibbons series are also of significance. Other blends, some of which are bottled using the names of subsidiaries, are: → Sir Walter Raleigh, → Langside, The → Sovereign, → Royal Galleon, → Eaton's, → 77 and → Glen Drum. They also market the → SS Politician, and have business connections with the Indian company Kedir. In 1998 the 'Scotch Whisky Blenders and Bottlers' remembered the old casks of rare whiskies in their stores and joined in the single malt trend. Since then they have also appeared as → independent bottlers and have brought out several single cask bottlings named 'The → Old Malt Cask'. The name McGibbons is also used for single cask bottlings, mostly under the term Provenance, whereby the name of the distillery was not always stated to avoid conflict with the owners. This strategy is also behind bottlings with the label Tactical.

Laird's Reserve Scotch malt whisky which is exclusively available at branches of → Unwins, the UK wines and spirits company. It is 10 years old. Unfortunately its exact origins have not been disclosed.

Lambert Brothers Scottish wines and spirits company which was mainly known to the public for its well-stocked shop in Edinburgh's Frederick Street, which, even before the malt whisky boom, had a sensational selection. The company is known to collectors for its miniatures. There were various series such as the 'Ben' series, which was named after Scottish mountains. Lambert Brothers had a whole series of its own bottlings; the only one to be distributed internationally was the blend The → Monarch. High rents forced the shop to close in 1995.

Lammerlaw New Zealand single malt from → Wilson Distillers, a comparatively young business that first opened a distillery in 1968 in Dunedin, on the southern island of the country. From 1981 the company belonged to → Seagram, who not only invested a great deal of capital, but also saw to it that certain factors which stood in the way of producing a good whisky have been removed, and has used its worldwide distribution network to ensure widespread marketing. In 1991 the first 10-year-old Lammerlaw came out; those who have drunk it regularly since then will have noticed the changes in it. In recent times the taste of peat has become more marked, which is possibly because malted barley is now also imported from Australia. The water comes from Deep Creek and maturing takes place exclusively in American oak barrels. The distillery gets its name from the Lammerlaw mountains where the stream that provides the water has its source. Although the whisky won a lot of friends in England where → Oddbins, the chain belonging to Seagram, had it in their stock, and was also increasingly popular in Germany, the distillery had to close down in 1995 after a sales deal with South Korea fell through. The closure is supposed to be only temporary. The independent bottlers → Cadenhead also included a 10-year-old Lammerlaw (50.8%) in their range.

Lands of Scotland Series of Scotch malt whiskies which are produced for the → Maison du Whisky in Paris. This includes an → Islay, a → Speyside, a → Lowland, a → Campbeltown and a → Highland malt (all 40%). Their exact origins have not been made known.

Lang's Scotch blend named after the Lang Brothers who founded their business in 1861. In 1876 they bought the → Glengoyne Distillery, which at the time was known as Burnfoot, and whose licence is still registered in their name; they themselves have been owned by → Robertson & Baxter since 1965. Through this company they are linked with → Highland Distillers and via them with the → Edrington Group. Their subsidiary, Matthew → Gloag & Son (renamed Highland Distillers Brands in 1998), takes care of the distribution of the → standard blend Lang's Supreme whilst the 12-year-old Lang's Select is sold by Robertson & Baxter. The company also has a blend named → Auld Lang Syne.

Langside Scotch blend from the Glasgow-based company Douglas → Laing & Co's, subsidiary Langside, who were formerly also responsible for → John Player Special. The → standard blend is called Black Label, and the → de luxe version comes with the age statement '25 years old'.

Laphroaig Scottish malt distillery. Its name, pronounced 'la-froyg', comes from the Gaelic for ' beautiful hollow by the wide bay'. It is the most westerly of the three distilleries which lie between Port Ellen and Kildalton on the southern coast of → Islay. The whole area was famous for illicit distilling and even in legal times had five distilleries. In the mid-19th century, the Ardenstiel Distillery stood next to that of Laphroaig. The two brothers Donald and Alex Johnston, whose father took refuge on Islay after the Jacobite Rising of 1745, began supplementing their farming activities with distilling.

The distillery was established in 1815 and remained in the hands of the founding family, whose name still appears on the plain label, until the last member of the family died childless in 1954. He left it to his secretary Bessie Williamson. In 1967 she sold her firm to → Long John International, but remained director until 1972. The present owners are → Allied Domecq PLC. Laphroaig has seven → stills (three wash stills and four spirit stills), gets its water from Kilbride Dam, has its own peat banks and malts part of its barley itself in its own → floor maltings. The malt used is said to have 35 to 40ppm (parts per million phenols), the same as its arch-rival Lagavulin. The distillery bottlings make exclusive use of ex-bourbon casks, which are obtained from Maker's Mark. Part of the production is used for → Long John and for → Islay Mist, which also used to belong to Allied.

The whisky is much coveted because it is still one of the most distinctive Islay malts, with intensive medicinal phenol components and a heavy peaty smokiness. These characteristics are best expressed in the relatively recent bottling of a 10-year-old at → cask strength, whilst many admirers and connoisseurs consider that the normal 10-year-old single malt has become somewhat flatter. This may be the result of → chill-filtering, which is known to deprive malt whisky of important aromatic substances. It is not used for the → cask strength (57.3%). Nevertheless the 10-year-old is Allied's flagship malt and, before the 16-year-old malt of their neighbour Lagavulin became more widely available as one of the → 'Classic Malts', was the best known of the Islay whiskies. Opinion has always been divided – it either provokes absolute enthusiasm or total rejection. During → prohibition in America it was even prescribed as a medicine. The coat of arms of the Prince of Wales, who awarded laphroiag a Royal Warrant in 1994.

The coat of arms has also been displayed for some time now on the distillery itself which, like all other Islay distilleries, proudly has its name painted in large letters on the buildings facing the sea with the addition of an ® to show that Laphroaig is a registered trademark. Apart from the bottlings already mentioned, the proprietors also offer a 15-year-old, and in their new visitor centre sell (as long as stocks last) several → vintages (1976, 1977) and a 30-year-old. Laphroaig is also frequently available from → independent bottlers: → Cadenhead, as well as → Signatory, had several vintages of various strengths, which were always bottled at cask strength. Murray → McDavid has a Laphroaig in its range which was distilled in 1984 and bottled in 1996, whose 46% shows that the company must have something to do with either Cadenhead or → Springbank. Another of its bottlings was a → Leapfrog distilled in 1987 which caused some concern between the bottlers and the distillers, but which was later resolved.

LaSalle Canadian distillery. It was built by the → Bronfmans in Quebec in 1924 and four years later it was part of the 'dowry' when they took over → Seagram and their distillery in → Waterloo. Later it was joined by other distilleries, such as that of Reifel and Calvert (→ Lord Calvert) and Beaupré, also situated in Quebec. They were all unable to keep up with the demand and were also no longer up to modern standards of production. Latterly, Seagram only produced at → Gimli and not even pious respect for the fact that it was LaSalle that produced all the whisky that was smuggled into America when it suffered → prohibition, helping the company grow to become one of the largest drinks combines in the world, was able to prevent the demolition of the fine buildings.

Lauder's Scotch blend that was launched onto the market in the 19th century by the company of the same name. Later it was one of the brands belonging to Hiram → Walker. Their Scottish acquisitions are now under the control of → Allied Distillers Ltd, who sold the blend, which is particularly popular in Latin America, to the newly-established company → MacDuff International in 1992. It is available as a → standard blend without an age statement, and aged 12 years. In the USA it is sold by → Barton Brands.

Lawrenceburg American distilleries which are named after the towns in which they are located – and are always the cause of confusion as there are two completely different towns in two completely different states and two different distilleries. Also, they both belonged to the same company, → Seagram. One Lawrenceburg is situated in Kentucky, on the Kentucky River, and the other one is in Indiana, to the west of Cincinnati, on the Ohio River. Seagram made efforts to rename the Kentucky distillery and to give it the name of the bourbon which it produces: → Four Roses (on whose old bottles, incidentally, the town is spelt Laurenceburg, which might also help to tell them apart). The Indiana distillery nowadays looks a little like → Walkerville and → Dumbarton with its large buildings and gives no hint of the small plant that began operating here in 1865. Its producers mainly use it for making gin and vodka, and perhaps this was the reason why the production of whisky was suddenly stopped. Until that time a large number of whiskey sorts with various → mash bills were produced, which were never bottled as → straights, but were mainly used for the company's own blend, → 7 Crowns. After June 1996, when → beer from the 14 fermenting vessels was distilled for the last time, the end of the Indiana-made bourbon seemed to have arrived. But the management of the company considered the matter and the green light was given again in February 1997, at least temporarily – especially, according to reports, to produce the whiskeys which are needed for its new brand → Sam Cougar, which is, at present only sold in Australia.

Lawson, William Scottish company mainly known for its blends → William Lawson's Finest Blend and William Lawson's Scottish Gold (12 years old). The name goes back to a wine merchant who established his business in 1849 and soon expanded it to include whisky. At the end of the 19th century Lawson was supplying a Dublin company with his blend. The Dubliners kept the brand when they parted with Lawson, and during → prohibition did excellent business by shipping to the Bahamas, from where it was smuggled to the USA. The Scots recommenced exporting whisky after 1945 from Liverpool. In 1967 they built a blending and bottling plant in Coatbridge, to the east of Glasgow. They entered into a close partnership with the Italian vermouth company Martini & Rossi, who had in the meantime bought the rights to the Lawson's brand. From 1980 the Scots company belonged to General Beverages, a holding company based in Luxembourg, and the parent company of Martini, who were taken over by → Bacardi in 1995. Meanwhile William Lawson Distillers operated as a subsidiary of General Beverages and managed the → Macduff Distilery near Banff which was acquired in 1972. Their malt whisky is sold under the name of → Glen Deveron as a → proprietor's bottling. Apart from the blends named after the company, there are also → Clan Munro and → King Edward I. They also have connections with William → Lundie & Co. After they had acquired the brand → Dewar's (as well as four distilleries) from → Diageo in 1998, Bacardi decided to continue their Scottish activities under the name of the better known company John Dewar & Sons, and had the name Lawson removed from the commercial register.

Leaching Term for a special process that is only used in Tennessee by Jack → Daniel and George A → Dickel, with the result that since 1941 their whiskeys have been categorised as a separate kind of whisk(e)y, although they do not otherwise differ from those produced in neighbouring Kentucky. The process, which each company carries out slightly differently, is normally termed → charcoal mellowing or sometimes the → Lincoln County Process.

Leapfrog Scotch single malt which comes from → Laphroaig, whose Gaelic name is allegedly written in the way the → independent bottler Murray → McDavid has used for its bottlings. The fact that the usual name has not been used for this malt (distilled in March 1987, bottled in April 1999) is because for a long time now a conflict has been brewing between independent bottlers and distillery proprietors, who regard the names of their malts as brands and who do not like others to use them – especially when they have no control over the quality. Laphroaig's owners, → Allied Distillers Ltd, even took the matter to court and, after having lost the case in the first instance, made the name Laphroaig a trademark.

Ledaig Scottish malt distillery. Its name, sometimes pronounced 'le-dég' and sometimes 'léddig', means 'safe haven'. It lies on the island of Mull and is normally known by the name of → Tobermory. It was only called Ledaig temporarily but its present owners, → Burn Stewart, used the name again for several single malts which they brought out as → vintages. Two were distilled in 1974; when the distillery was actually called Ledaig. They were bottled in 1992 and so were then aged 18 years; one has a strength of 43% and the other 56%. At the end of 1997 there followed a Ledaig 1979, and two years later a 20 and a 15-

year-old Ledaig. In those years peated malt is said to have been used. In any case the company stress that in future Tobermory and Ledaig will be differentiated by the former being made with unpeated malt and the latter with peated malt. Ledaig, which sells particularly well in France, is special in another way: after the traditional maturation it is placed into a completely new oak cask to mature a second time – a very unusual use of the → double wood and → finishing practice; for some time now it has borne the information 'Peated Scotch Malt'. In France there is also a 15-year-old Ledaig, → Oddbins also once had a 20-year-old Ledaig, on whose label Douglas Murdoch & Co. in Glasgow were named as bottlers. Signatory sell a very young Vintage Mull Malt which is said to be a Ledaig. It is available reduced to 43% and at cask strength.

Leestown American whiskey distillery situated in Leestown, Frankfort, Kentucky. It was established in 1869 as O F C Distillery and was later called Stagg Distillery, → Schenley Distillery, → Blanton Distillery and, after its best-known brand, → Ancient Age Distillery. It is now known as → Buffalo Trace. The American → Sazerac Company and the Japanese consortium → Takara Shuzo & Okura (whose smaller partner Okura went bankrupt in 1998), own it in a joint venture. The blended whiskey bottled by Ancient Age at 80°/40% is also called Leestown.

Legacy De-luxe Scotch blend which was formerly available aged 12, 17 and 21 years. It was originally introduced by Charles → Mackinlay & Co, is now part of and therefore now belongs to → Kyndal.

Legendary, The Scotch single malt from → Blackadder International, who use this name to market → single cask bottlings of → Speyside malts without naming the distilleries. They are 10 years old, have a strength of 43% and present a reasonably-priced alternative to other whiskies from → independent bottlers. Legendary is also the name of an 18-year-old version of → Clan Campbell.

Legends of the Wild West Series of → Kentucky straight bourbons representing great figures from American history, each available in two versions. There is nothing to distinguish them from each other but for the different faces and the different names on the label. One version is 12 years old and 96°, the other is 15 years old and 114°. The 11 'legends' are: Levis & Clark, Davey Crockett, Geronimo, Abraham Lincoln, Daniel Boone, General Custer, Buffalo Bill, Kit Carson, Wyatt Earp, General George Washington and Doc Holliday. These 'goodies' have been supplemented by a series of 'baddies', the → 'Outlaws Series'. Both series come from the imaginative → Kentucky Bourbon Distillers, who are behind the name Legendary Distilling Co and make equal use of patriotism and the passion for collecting to maximise sales.

Lem Motlow's Tennessee sour mash whiskey from → Jack Daniel, a name found on the label of the famous Old Time Old No. 7: here Motlow is still named as 'proprietor' of the distillery. He was the nephew of Jack Daniel and began to work for his uncle in the early 1880s, taking over the business after his death. When → prohibition was introduced to Tennessee in 1910, he initially evaded it by moving to Missouri and then to Alabama. He managed to keep the business and the rights to the brand, by using the name Jack Daniel to run a horse and mule breeding business when the American production of whiskey was forbidden.

It was this ability to persevere which enabled him to get a licence to distil in 1938 – although Tennessee remained 'dry'. Motlow died in 1947, and nine years later his sons sold the company to → Brown-Forman. Lem Motlow surely deserves a more significant bottling than this young whiskey at 90°/45%, which, in addition, is only sold in Tennessee and, according to reports, will soon be withdrawn from the market. It will possibly make way for a → small batch or → single barrel whiskey, which at last will Lem Motlow's name on the label.

Licensed bottling Term for bottlings which do not come from the owners of a brand or from the → proprietors of a distillery themselves, but which are carried out with their permission. In the case of Scotch single malts where there are a large number of autonomously operating → independent bottlers, licensed bottlings are an intermediate form: they are marketed by an independent bottler, but along with their name and the name of the distillery, there is also the name of the company which owns the distillery. For many years → Gordon & MacPhail have had such malt whiskies from → Mortlach and → Linkwood in their range. They also have their own series of whiskies from → Glenlivet using the description → 'George & J G Smith's', as well as the so-called → Allied series by arrangement with → Allied Distillers Ltd.

Limited Editions Series of Scotch single malts. The → independent bottlers → Blackadder International chose this name for their whiskies which are not reduced to 43%, but bottled at → cask strength.

Lincoln American President who used whiskey as a source of tax revenue. Since his childhood in → Knob Creek he had been familiar with distilling, as his father worked in a distillery. His childhood home has been reconstructed and is now a place of national pilgrimage. A brand of bourbon also commemorates the place where Lincoln lived for several years. His earlier connections with whiskey didn't stop him sympathising with the temperance movement later on. Although he wasn't a member, he supported temperance in public speeches and by stating that he considered alcohol to be harmful and wouldn't drink it himself. In 1862 he signed a law to levy taxes on the production and sale of whiskey, designed to help to finance the Union army in the war against the southern states.

Lincoln County Process A process used by → Jack Daniel and their nearby competitors George A → Dickel. The process gets its name from the fact that the area to which Lynchburg and the Jack Daniel Distillery belong used to be a part of Lincoln County.

The whisk(e)y is not filled into barrels immediately after distillation, but for several days is first allowed to trickle over a very thick layer of charcoal that is stacked in vessels which are nearly four metres high. Although other distilleries also occasionally use filtering, this process, which is also known as → charcoal mellowing or → leaching, is only used in this form in Tennessee. Alfred Eaton is said to have developed the process at his distillery in Tullahoma in 1825.

Linkwood Scottish malt distillery. It lies just to the south of Elgin and therefore belongs to the → Speyside region. It was founded in 1820/21 and completely rebuilt in 1871. One hundred years later a second → stillhouse was added. The most important renovation work was done in 1962 by Roderick McKenzie, the manager for many years. From 1933 onwards the distillery was owned by → DCL, whose subsidiary John McEwan (known for its blends → Abbot's Choice and → Chequer's), was registered as licence holder until 1992, when the new owner → UD had it transferred to their own name. It is now a part of → GuinnessUDV.

McEwan had a single malt Linkwood in a proprietor's bottling which came in a six-sided box, but it was particularly associated with Gordon & MacPhail in nearby Elgin, who had 12, 15 and 21-year-old versions, as well as several vintage bottlings. Then UD included a 12-year-old in the → 'Flora & Fauna' series, as well as a cask strength from 1983 (59.8%). There were also several versions in the → 'Rare Malts' series, such as a 22-year-old from 1972 (59.3%) and a 23-year-old from 1974 (61.2%). The 25th anniversary of the nearby Burghead Maltings was celebrated with a special bottling. → Cadenhead, → Signatory and → MacArthur have also been able to offer a Linkwood from time to time. Incidentally, no bottling has distinguished between the whiskies from Linkwood B and the old Linkwood A; they flow, undifferentiated, into the casks.

Linlithgow Scottish town to the west of Edinburgh, the birthplace of Mary Queen of Scots. There used to be four distilleries in this small place, none of which still exist. All that remains are the listed buildings of the → St Magdalene Distillery, closed down in 1983. For a time they bore the name of the town, a name which the independent bottler → Cadenhead preferred for a bottling whose label had a different design to the usual one. It identifies the malt whisky as being from 1982, and apart from the strength (65.4%), it also shows the cask number (2839) and the number of the bottle. → Signatory also chose the name Linlithgow for a malt whisky from 1975 (51.7%) which they included in their 'Silent Stills' series.

Lismore Scotch whiskies which are available as blends, vatted malt and single malt. They are named after the little island just off the mainland in Loch Lhinne and come from William → Lundie & Co. in Glasgow. The Finest and Signature ar → standard blends without an age statement, the Select is 8 years old, the various Special Reserves are 12, 15 and 21 years old. Lismore is an 8-year-old vatted malt, and the single malt of the same name (with no statement of origin) is 12, 21 and even 25 years old.

Littlemill Scottish malt distillery. It lies in Bowling on the north bank of the Clyde, close to the Erskine Bridge and belongs to the → Lowlands region, although it gets its water from the Kilpatrick Hills which belong to the → Highlands. Together with → Glenturret and → Strathisla, it can claim to be one of the oldest distilleries in Scotland, with a founding date of 1772, or possibly even 1750. It has had an eventful history with an unusual number of closures and, until very recently, many changes in ownership. In 1931 it was acquired by the American Duncan G Thomas who, in 1959, sold shares to → Barton Brands (who built the → Loch Lomond Distillery in 1965/66). In 1982 it returned to Scottish hands but was closed down in 1984. In 1989 it was taken over by → Gibson International, who also owned → Glen Scotia, and was reopened after extensive renovation.

After their bankruptcy it was taken over by → Glen Catrine Bonded Warehouse Ltd in 1994, who run it under the name Loch Lomond Ltd., together with → Loch Lomond and → Glen Scotia. They even planned to demolish it and build houses on the site, but they had to give up the plan because several buildings are listed monuments, and they are now looking for a buyer. → Triple distillation was employed at Littlemill into the 1930s and they also had mechanical → maltings. In the 1960s and 70s a → rectifier was added to the → stills so that a variety of whiskies could be produced. A peated malt whisky named → Drumback was made (which has never been bottled as a single malt) as well as a lighter unpeated one named → Dunglass. At their → Loch Lomond Distillery the new owners Glen Catrine Bonded Warehouse Ltd had succeeded in producing a variety of whiskies by using various ingredients and adaptable equipment, and to some extent they also tried to do this at Littlemill. Littlemill appeared as a single malt in a → proprietor's bottling aged 5 years and is now sold in two different bottles aged 8 years. At the end of 1997 there was a small edition of 350 bottles of a 1964 32-year-old. In March 2000 600 bottles of Littlemill distilled in 1975 came onto the market, which were 24 years old and, unfortunately, reduced to 40%. → Signatory included a malt whisky distilled in 1965 with a cask strength of 49.1% in their → 'Silent Stills' series. There are also bottlings of Dunglass.

Living Cask, The Scotch vatted malt with which Richard and Lyndsay Joynson, the energetic owners of → 'Loch Fyne Whiskies' in Inveraray, have revived an old Scottish tradition. Perhaps they were inspired by the new → Glenfiddich Solera Reserve, and certainly by reading Professor George Saintsbury's classic *Notes on a Cellar Book* for they have installed an upright cask containing a good single malt. The tap is easily accessible, allowing it to be gradually emptied to the level of the tap. They replace the missing malt whisky with a slightly younger malt and allowed it to 'marry' with the older one already in the cask. Thus the new whisky gains from the character of the older malt as well as passing on its own character to it, or, as Saintsbury says, 'the constantly changing character of the old constituents doctors the new accessions, and in which these in turn freshen and strengthen the old.' In sherry production this process is called the solera system. Such a cask was once to be found in many Scottish households. The whisky is bottled at cask-strength, in 10cl bottles and state the 'pouring' date. In Spring 1999 it was the turn of Volume II, which had a much smokier character than Volume I.

Loch Dhu

Loch Dhu Scotch single malt from the → Mannochmore Distillery, launched on to the market at the end of 1996 by → UD. It is remarkable for its extremely dark, almost black colour, which on closer inspection has dark brown, orange-coloured reflections. UD denied that the colour had been achieved by the intensive use of caramel, and suggest the reason is the use of particularly intensively charred bourbon casks. As the whisky is 10 years old, it must have already been filled into the casks in 1986, at a time when the distillery still belonged to → DCL, who had a conservative reputation. It is unlikely that they would have taken such an experimental approach. It is more likely to be a product of UD marketing strategists who have made many attempts to attract new types of customer (further examples are the → Hackler, → Jackson Row, → Red Devil or the → alcopops from → Bell's). They seem to have succeeded in the case of Loch Dhu: despite all their protests to the contrary, the whisky has an intensive caramel (and liquorice) taste to it which the many lovers of malt whisky disapprove of, considering it to be a designer product, whilst newcomers voice their enthusiastic approval. For the sake of thoroughness and in honour of an old company, it should be mentioned that there had already been a Loch Dhu – a 'Fine Old Scotch' from McDiarmid & Co in Leith.

Loch Fyne, The → Premium house brand of Loch Fyne Whiskies in Inveraray. The blend bears the date 1884 because the rights to the old brand have been bought by the Joynsons. On the label there is a picture of → Glendarroch Distillery, which operated from 1831 to 1937. The blend is a highly successful creation of Ronnie Martin from → Inverarity Vaults. It was awarded a bronze medal at the 1996 International Wine and Spirit Competition.

Loch Indaal Scotch single malt that was launched onto the market in 1998. It comes from Bruichladdich which was closed by → JBB (Greater Europe) plc – which was rectified in December 2000 when Murray → McDavid bought the distillery and reopened it. The large '43' on the label and packaging refers to the alcoholic content. The malt whisky is marketed by an American company named Associated Distillers.

Loch Kindie Scotch vatted malt aged 8 years which is produced by → QSI, a subsidiary of William → Grant & Sons. The rights to the name, however, belong to another company.

Loch Lomond Scottish malt distiller based on the outskirts of Alexandria to the south of Loch Lomond, and north of the imaginary border between the → Lowlands and the → Highlands. It belongs to the latter region. The distillery on the River Leven, which connects the loch to the Clyde, used to be a factory and was built by an American company which also owned → Littlemill and had a share in → Barton Brands. The new owner, → ADP, closed it in 1984 and a year later sold it to → Glen Catrine Bonded Warehouse Ltd. It has three pairs of unusual → stills which can be adapted to produce completely different whiskies: → rectifiers, which can be used as required, are installed in the heads of two of the six stills. Various kinds of barley are also used and, above all, varyingly peated malt, including one from → Port Ellen which has a lot of phenols. Moreover the → middle cut of the second run is varyingly separated.

Loch Lomond produces many different malt whiskies. Only two of these are marketed as single malts, → Inchmurrin and → Old Rhosdhu. → Glen Douglas, the heavily peated → Croftengea, → Inchmoan and → Craiglodge are used by blenders. For a long time the name Loch Lomond could only be found on the → independent bottlings from → Cadenhead, followed in brackets by Inchmurrin and Old Rhosdhu. In 1998 the → proprietors finally brought out a Loch Lomond, presented in the same way as a previous → Glen Scotia and a → Littlemill, which had matured for 23 years. A Loch Lomond Pure Malt – Single Highland Malt, without an age statement, appears only to be available in Germany, where it is sold by the Borco company. In 1999 a limited edition 33-year-old → cask strength expression of Loch Lomond was produced in a copper-clad, still-shaped decanter with a brass stopper that resembled the head of a still. It retailed at about £500.

A grain distillery is also part of the complex at Alexandria. A 'normal' and a → single blend bear the name of the loch. Malt whiskies from Glen Scotia and Littlemill also mature in the warehouses here. Many of them were victims of the fire which swept through the → warehouses in the spring of 1997, destroying many casks.

Loch Morar Scotch single malt aged 8, 12 and 18 years available in the USA from the Minneapolis-based → All Saint's Brands. It does not name the distillery, but professes to be a 'classic → Speyside from the town of Elgin'. However the loch whose name it bears is on the west coast near Mallaig.

Loch Ness Water Scotch blend 'selected for the Loch Ness Monster', which the label shows rising from the loch. It is a → de luxe blend from → Signatory, bottled for the German importer Dieter Kirsch and only obtainable in Germany.

Loch Ness, The Scotch single malt of uncertain origin: a distillery is not mentioned, only the → Highland region. Up to now only one company, the Martinelli Group (who previously dealt in gin), has been clever enough to make use of this famous name. They founded their own subsidiary called The Loch Ness Whisky Company to market their product worldwide, especially in duty-free outlets. The bottles and tube packaging of these 40% malt whiskies naturally picture Nessie.

Loch Ranza Scotch blend without an age statement from → Isle of Arran Distillers whose founder, Harold Currie, had been a successful master blender until his retirement, It gets its name from the Arran village of Lochranza where the ferry to Kintyre docks and where the new distillery lies. Lochranza castle and the village are written as one word, whilst the whisky and the bay are called Loch Ranza.

Lochan Ora Scotch → whisky liqueur from → Chivas Brothers (with the old address in Aberdeen!). It has a strength of 35% but its ingredients, apart from whisky, not disclosed. However the label provides us with the translation of the Gaelic name – 'Golden Loch' – which is also a good description of the liqueur's honey tones.

Lochside Scottish grain and malt distillery which lies in Montrose and belongs to the eastern → Highland region. From the outside it is plain to see that the buildings were not erected with whisky production in mind. In fact they housed a brewery which latterly belonged to Deuchar's. Joseph Hobbs, who at the time also owned → Ben Nevis, bought it and, as in Ben Nevis, installed equipment which could be adapted for the production of malt whisky or → grain whisky which, after maturation, could be further processed on the same site to make blends. The company gave it the name Macnab Distilleries and the blend was called → Sandy Macnab's. In 1973 the Spanish company → DYC (Destilerias y Crianza) bought Lochside, which at the time caused just as much consternation as Japanese participation in the Scotch whisky industry had done. However the Spanish owners initially left everything as it was, allowing the four → pot stills to carry on production and only shutting down the grain distillery and shipping some of the malt in → bulk to Spain for use in their DYC. However the distillery was then closed in 1992. For some time the situation was rather confusing. It was known that Hiram → Walker, whose parent company is → Allied Domecq PLC, were behind the Spaniards, but their Scottish division, → Allied Distillers Ltd, did not feel responsible for Lochside. They were eager to get rid of it (and finally sold the buildings to Morrison Construction Development) and removed all the casks and no longer bottled the 10-year-old (previously 8 and 12-year-old) single malt. However from time to time it is available from → independent bottlers, for example → Gordon & MacPhail included versions from 1966 and 1982 in their → 'Connoisseurs Choice' series. → Signatory has had several bottlings, including a very old one from 1959 and one from 1966 (57.7%), which they included in their 'Silent Stills' series. → MacArthur even succeeded in unearthing a → grain whisky which they bottled at 27 years old and 60.5%.

Locke's Irish whiskey the name of which commemorates the former owner of the → Brusna Distillery, in the village of → Kilbeggan. In 1980 a bottling was made from the last known cask filled on the 1st of March, 1946. The brand now belongs to the → Cooley Distillery which bought it and its old buildings and now run a cooperage there. Above all they mature a large part of their stock there, distilling in → Riverstown and transporting it to Kilbeggan in road tankers. There are two versions of Locke's: a blend (40%) and a single malt (of which there was a bottling of a 1989 vintage in a limited edition of 5,000 bottles). These were bedded in a velvet-lined wooden box, whilst a new edition in 1997 came without packaging.

Logan Scotch blend that bears the name of James Logan Mackie, the man largely responsible for the → single malt from → Lagavulin. He became a partner in the distillery on → Islay in 1837 and gave his nephew Peter → Mackie the opportunity of learning the craft of distilling, bequeathing him the distillery in 1889. Mackie built up the distillery to become one of the → Big Five, and whose → White Horse became one of the most successful blends of all. Logan is akin to the → de luxe version and was formerly called Laird o' Logan. Nowadays it is a 12-year-old which still comes from White Horse Distillers who, however, now belong to the → GuinnessUDV empire.

Lombard Scotch Whisky Whisky company based on the Isle of Man who have a whole range of their own brands. The blend Lombard's is available as a → standard blend with the suffix → Gold Label, as well as stating that it is aged for 5 and 12 years. Lombard's Pure Malt is a 12-year-old vatted malt. The firm specialises in collectors' items: it has taken over the → Beneagles series in which the whisky is bottled in collectable ceramics; the birds of prey series is popular, as well as motifs such as a curling stone or Nessie. The 'Limited Edition' of single malts is also aimed at the collector and its labels illustrate 'Golfing Greats'. Other brands belonging to the company are: → Age of Sail, → Golden Piper and → Highland Gathering. The company brought out a special bottling for the Millennium. It had previously created its own series of → single cask bottlings bearing the name → 'Jewels of ... ' which emphasised the region rather than the distillery from which the malts came. → Islay was particularly strongly represented with, for example, a Bowmore, a Caol Ila and also a Port Ellen.

Lomond Scotch single malt once produced in the → Dumbarton Distillery. Within this complex, built in 1938, which was mainly devoted to the production of → grain whisky, there was a small plant for distilling malt whisky until 1991. It had three → stills, a → wash still and two different → spirit stills, one of which was a so-called → Lomond still. This produced a malt whisky which, logically, was given the name Lomond. It has never been available in a → proprietor's bottling. As far as it is known, only the → Scotch Malt Whisky Society has succeeded in bottling any of it.

Lomond still A special form of → still for the production of malt whisky, which was installed in several Scottish distilleries in the 1950s alongside the normal → pot stills. The reason for these new stills was that Hiram → Walker, the owner of the distilleries at that time, needed 42 malts for its blends but only owned six distilleries. In 1955 the young engineer Alistair Cunningham (later managing director of → Allied Distillers Ltd), was asked by his boss to find out how a distillery could produce several different malts. After experimenting with the → mash, he suggested a new form of still. They were not to be pot-bellied but cylindrical in shape and have moveable copper seive plates in their heads. The first pair were installed at → Dumbarton, where traditional pot stills produced → Inverleven. A pair was also installed alongside the stills at → Glenburgie and at → Miltonduff. At → Scapa the → wash still was replaced with the new equipment. In order to differentiate between the malt whiskies they received new names, excepting the whisky from Scapa. Lomond was made in Dumbarton, → Mosstowie in Miltonduff and → Glencraig (after the company's North of Scotland manager) in Glenburgie. However the method did not achieve the hoped-for success and were first removed in Dumbarton and then Scapa. The project was abandoned at the beginning of the 1980s, mainly because the demand for → Inverleven, → Glenburgie and → Miltonduff rose. The → Lomond stills were dismantled to make room for more → pot stills. For this reason the malt whiskies are rare and sought-after. Only the → Lomond still in Scapa can still be admired, but even there production has been suspended for several years, though spirit is occasionally distilled using staff from neighbouring Highland Park. Similar distilling apparatus to the → Lomond still can also be seen at → Loch Lomond Distillery.

Lomond malt whiskies are claimed to be 'oilier and heavier' than those made with the stills of the other four distilleries. It is easy to form one's own opinion by trying the malts. In the case of the Lomond few will be able to do so, as there has only ever been one cask of it which has been bottled. But Mosstowie is available and is lighter than Miltonduff. Glencraig is sweet and fruity and by no means heavy. Scapa is an exception, but it has been distilled a second time in a traditional → spirit still. When asked which opinion he considered to be correct, the Director of Brand Heritage at Allied, William F Bergius, anwered: 'The plan was to produce several whiskies with one still and they were to be richer than was previously possible in the distilleries concerned. Theoretically the same still should have produced very complex yet very light whiskies. However these hypotheses were not achieved in practise. The new stills did not produce richer whiskies, and the idea with the range also didn't work. All the Lomond stills, wherever they were, quite to the contrary made elegant and light whiskies. The secret of Scotch has won again!'

London & Scottish Spirits Export company established in 1994 with its headquarters in Bramley, Surrey. Along with other products, it has a range of Scotch whiskies which have been developed so successfully within such a short period, that in 1997 the company won the title 'Exporter of the Year' from the magazine *Export Times*. They supply the Far East, South East Asia, southern Europe and Latin America. Their range includes the blends → Old Bridge, → Old Crofter, → Rory and → Scottish Reel as well as a vatted malt named → Glen Torran.

Lone Oak Kentucky straight bourbon available in two versions: a 6-year-old (86 /43%) and a 12-year-old (101 /50.5%). It is made in Kentucky, probably at → Heaven Hill, and bottled by one Kentucky Hilltop Distillery in → Bardstown, one of the imaginary names used by the → Kentucky Bourbon Distillers.

Long John Scotch blend belonging to → Allied Domecq PLC which at present is only available as a → standard blend and as a 12-year-old → de luxe blend. It has a long and convoluted history.

In 1825 'Long' John MacDonald set up his distillery at the foot of the highest mountain in the UK, → Ben Nevis, and named his whisky → Dew of Ben Nevis. In 1911 the brand was sold to the London spirits dealer Chaplin, who 25 years later sold it to → Seager Evans, who had made their name through the production of gin and now wished to diversify. They ran their whisky business using the name Long John International, later also bought → Glenugie Distillery and in the 1950s acquired a large site on the Clyde to build the → Lowland distillery → Kinclaith. Before it was finished Seager Evans, and with it Long John International, were bought by → Schenley. This was followed by the building of → Tormore, the purchase of the brand → Black Bottle and the acquisition of → Laphroaig Distillery. Schenley sold its Scottish interests to the brewery giants Whitbread. In 1981 they also bought Ben Nevis for their subsidiary and so they were reunited after many years during which the blend, and the distillery from which it originally came, had been separated. But their luck did not last as, a short time later, the distillery was sold to the Japanese company → Nikka.

The blend Long John is said to contain over 30 different whiskies and is a Scottish classic. The → Real Mackay and → Scorsby Rare are relatives.

Longmorn Scottish malt distillery. It stands next to → Benriach, near the A941 road leading from Elgin to Rothes, and belongs to the → Speyside → whisky region. Its name is from the Gaelic for 'place of the holy man'. Its history is unsensational, although the fact that a Scottish distillery has been able to operate throughout its entire history without closure and with few changes in ownership is unusual. It was built in 1894/5 by John Duff on the spot where, many centuries ago, a holy man had erected a chapel and it was prophesied that its water source would spring eternally. Directly after the → Pattison brothers' bankruptcy and the resulting end of the whisky boom Duff and his associates gained possession of their neighbour Benriach. The merger with → Glenlivet and → Glen Grant in 1970 enabled a thorough renovation and the expansion to initially six → stills and then to eight, which until 1993 were coal-fired. Fans of its malt whisky feared that the change from coalwould have an effect on its character.

Longmorn has always been rather overshadowed, even in the eyes of its owners (from 1977 to 2000 → Seagram). Although there was a → 15-year-old proprietor's bottling in 1986, they did little to publicise it. From 1994 Longmorn (again aged 15 years) was part of the → 'Heritage Selection' of the Seagram subsidiary → Chivas & Glenlivet Group, to which → Chivas Brothers belonged and under whose name the distillery was licensed. It is now part of → Groupe Pernod-Ricard. Since 1994 the malt whisky has been more readily available, and hopefully will now gain the attention it deserves, especially since Jim Murray, in the *The Complete Guide to Whisky*, placed it among the 10 best whiskies in the world. It is certainly one of the greatest and most complex in Scotland. In 1995 the opening of the distillery was commemorated by a 25-year-old Centenary Bottling (45%). It is also regularly available from → independent bottlers, such as → Cadenhead and → Blackadder. → Gordon & MacPhail have a 12-year-old and various vintages in their → 'Connoisseurs Choice' series. Signatory brought out a Longmorn from 1969 for their 10th anniversary with a cask strength of 56.3%.

Longrow Defunct Scottish malt distillery in → Campbeltown on the site of what is now → Springbank Distillery's car park. A few remains are still in use. The Mitchells of Springbank have managed to preserve the name of their former (and somewhat older) competitors by calling their second malt Longrow. It is seldom produced and differs from Springbank as it uses heavily-peated malt and a different separation process in its → distillation. The descriptions of this in whisky literature vary considerably and are confusing. According to John McDougall, the former head of production, the whole of the second run is simply regarded as → feints and distilled a third time, giving a rawer result and, together with the peat, a heavy, phenolic character.

It is much sought-after and only ever comes on to the market in small quantities, which also increases demand. There was a 14-year-old malt in a → proprietor's bottling followed, one after another, by a 16-year-old, 18-year-old and 21-year-old, each stating 1974 as the year of production. A 19-year-old, a 1973 without an age statement, the First Distillation Last Cask Longrow 1973 and the Longrow Bond Reserve, costing about £400, and the 25-year-old also from 1974, were particular rarities. Even the 10-year-old from 1987 is sought after. The bottlings from the German importer Dieter Kirsch and → Signatory also both come from that same year. → Blackadder and the Italian companies Moon and → Samaroli also had a cask. And every now and then it is available from → Cadenhead, the → independent bottlers, who also belong to the same company as the distillery, J & A Mitchell. A Longrow from a sherry cask was announced for the summer of 1999. It was sold out within a few days.

Lord Calvert Canadian whisky which has kept alive the name of the small Calvert Distillery in Amherstburg in the south of Ontario. It was founded by the Reifels, a family of German origin, who first made their money in British Columbia with beer brewing and later founded the British Columbia Distillery Company. It was particularly successful during American → prohibition when it officially exported its whiskies to Tahiti. In 1942 Samuel → Bronfman bought Reifel's business together with Calvert. The 3-year-old whisky now comes from → Gimli and is produced solely for export.

Lord Connell Scotch blend from Duncan MacKinnon & Co in Glasgow who extol their product as 'specially selected for coffee drinkers', without saying whether they have a Scottish version of → Irish Coffee in mind, or a simple accompaniment to a cup of coffee.

Lord of Islay Scotch single malt. Its bilingual French-English label speaks of a Single Islay Malt. It shows a sailing ship, which reminds those who know their whisky history of the old bottles and packaging of the malt whisky from Bowmore, Sherriff's Bowmore, now sought after by collectors. Whether the similarity is a coincidence or a subtle hint that the malt whisky which came onto the French market in 1999 is really a Bowmore, must remain within the realms of speculation. It is a product from The Vintage Malt Whisky Co. in Bearsden and they are not telling.

Lot No. 40 Canadian whisky and a rarity of its kind. It is possibly the first → small batch bottling in the country. It is part of a series which → Corby launched under the name 'The → Canadian Whisky Guild' and to which → Gooderham & Worts and Pike Creek also belong. On the bottle there is an illustration taken from an old print of the distilling process, and the label describes how the whisky is distilled in a single copper → pot still by D Michael Booth, who uses a recipe from his predecessor of seven generations ago, Joshua Booth. It is said to be based on a → mash of grain and malted rye, and the result is 'a naturally, unrefined taste you won't forget'.

Lottas Home Kentucky → straight rye aged 13 years which comes from the Commonwealth Distillery and is described as 'Pappy van Winkle's Private Family Reserve', which make it clear that this is a product from J P → Van Winkle and Son.

Low wines Term for the distilled spirit which has a strength of about 22-25% and is produced in → pot stills after the → wash has been distilled in the → wash still (also known as the → low wines still (although confusingly this expression is also sometimes used for the → spirit still). The 'low' refers to the strength of the alcohol. It is likely that the expression was adopted from brandy distillation, where the term is customary in English. It has been used for whisky since 1790. The low wines mainly consist of alcohol and water and are re-distilled in the → intermediate still (in triple distillation) or the spirit still (in cistomary double distillation).

Lowlands Scottish → whisky region lying to the south of the → Highlands and demarcated from them by the → Highland Line which is an imaginary line drawn from from Greenock to Dundee. Nowadays this region includes the distilleries of → Auchentoshan, → Bladnoch, and → Glenkinchie. Closures have included → Glenflagler/→ Killyloch, → Kinclaith, → Littlemill, → Rosebank, → Lomond (in Dumbarton) and → St Magdalene/→ Linlithgow. Several distilleries, such as → Glengoyne, → Deanston, → Loch Lomond and → Tullibardine, lie just to the north of the line.

The Lowlands style is associated with lightly peated and delicate, smoky whiskies. They are generally regarded as poor cousins to thier Speyside and Highland neighbours and this may be the result of competing with the Scottish grain distilleries which were once very numerous and also with the practice of → triple distillation which they generally employed. The truth is that within the region there is a variety of depth and style which can surprise even the connoisseur. Expressions Rosebank, Bladnoch, St Magdalene and Glenkinchie are examples of this.

Lowrie's Scotch blend from → GuinnessUDV which bears one of the most significant names in the history of Scotch whisky. It is named after William Lowrie who in his youth worked at → Port Ellen and in 1869 became self-employed and was one of the first to take an interest in developing blends (although the 'official' story credits Andrew → Usher with this). The company also claims to have been the first to have bottled → in bond. In any case it was important in the blossoming whisky business and not only had its own blending and bottling plant but also made the cases and the bottles itself. There were particularly close connections with James → Buchanan whom it initially supplied and who, upon Lowrie's retirement, took over the company. With this company, with which it jointly owned → Glentauchers (whilst having sole ownership of → Convalmore), it passed to → DCL.

Lundie & Co, William Scottish whisky company still in family ownership and run by the third generation. The 'Co' in the firm's name was David → Sandeman, from the dynasty which had created → VAT 69. The company is based in Glasgow and used to work mainly as → brokers, that is as agents between those who produced whisky and those who needed it for their blends. In recent times the company, which co-operates with William →

Lowrie, have brought out their own blends and several vatted and single malts. The brand with the most expressions is → Lismore, and alongside this there are the the blends → Award, → Prestige d'Ecosse, → Royal Heritage and → Tribute, as well as the single malt → Glen Fruin.

Lyne arm The term in Scotland for the part of the → pot still which extends from the top of the head and connects this with the condensing equipment.

The lyne arm is much more than a connecting pipe. It is believed that its angle has quite a considerable influence on the character of the whisky and contributes to giving it a light or a heavy body. Various positions can therefore result in differing whiskies. If it is almost horizontal or even T-shaped as at → Cragganmore, reflux occurs and some of the distillate returns to the → still and is redistilled. Sometimes, as at → Ardbeg or → Talisker, purifiers are installed as pipes on the bottom of the arm leading back to the still body. Again this results in more reflux.

The Irish appear to define the lyne arm differently and E B McGuire, in his book *Irish Whiskey* (published in 1973) appears to be describing a purifier as he states that the lyne arm is a 'thin return pipe ... fitted to convey these liquids back to the still', and points out that it was then possible to see this in the large distilleries in Dublin and → Midleton. The word derives from the English 'lean'.

M

MacLeod and Co, Ian Scottish whisky company which is a subsidiary of Peter J → Russell & Co. The main brand is → Isle of Skye, but they also produce some → single cask bottlings such as the Chieftain's Choice range, Dun Bheagan collection, Hedges & Butler and Migillican Irish Single Malt.

Mac NaMara Scotch blend from → Pràban na Linne, lighter than their → Té Bheag and from the very beginning (1992) intended for export. The Gaelic name means 'son of the sea'. The company is based on the Isle of → Skye, which is best known for → Talisker.

Mac Pay A brand popular in Uruguay where it is produced. Like all *whiskies nacionales* produced in Latin America it is a blend of domestic → grain whiskies and malt whiskies which are imported in → bulk from Scotland. It is 6 years old.

Macallan Scottish malt distillery which lies opposite → Craigellachie, above Telford's famous arched bridge on the high ground overlooking the river Spey. The old manorhouse of Easter Elchies stands nearby. It houses offices and a unique visitor centre. Here there is a small round theatre in which a genuine cinema organ sets the mood for a highly original 'magic lantern' show about Scotland, its whisky and Macallan. The wit and professionalism of this presentation are not a coincidence as Allan Shiach, chairman until 1996, was responsible for it. Under the pseudonym Allan Scott he is a very successful Holywood scriptwriter who penned the screenplay of *Don't Look Now* starring Donald Sutherland and Julie Christie and many TV plays. The early death of his brother resulted in his leaving the business. Macallan-Glenlivet, the official name of the business, was a family firm and the Shiachs are direct successors of Roderick Kemp who sold his share in → Talisker in 1892 so that he could take over the distillery which had been built in 1824.

Macallan-Glenlivet would have been, along with the → Grants of → Glenfiddich, the other → Grants of Glenfarclas, the Bullochs of → Loch Lomond and the → Mitchells of → Springbank, one of the last remaining independent family-run firms, had they not lost their independence in 1996. On the 1st July, the day that the company had invited a handful of friends to drink a Macallan distilled in 1874 and presented as a limited edition with the appearance based on the original bottle, the newspapers carried the news of a hostile takeover bid by → Highland Distillers.

The fact that Macallan eventually had to concede defeat resulted from an earlier financial deal, when Macallan had sold a 25% stake to the Japanese giant → Suntory, and the fact that Rémy also owned a share of the company. This 26% was acquired by Highland who had made a pact with Suntory, thereby gaining a majority share. Highland hope that the greater resources at their disposal will enable them to improve turnover. Everything that has contributed to making this whisky famous and has given it the reputation of being the 'Rolls Royce' among malt whiskies, leading to its success in blind tastings and the record prices that old bottlings have achieved, increasing from auction to auction, is to remain unchanged.

There are now no fewer than 21 → stills, which are very small and exact copies of the originals. The → warehouses are among the most modern of all – but in the case of the casks, they rigidly maintain the quality that they have decided upon: everything that is bottled bearing the name Macallan is exclusively matured in casks which previously contained Oloroso sherry.

When it became difficult to get fresh supplies of such casks they began to buy wood in Spain, to have the casks made for them and then lend them to wine companies, so that they could use them for their own purposes afterwards. The influence of the heavy Oloroso is plainly recognisable in the malt whisky, but it has enough power of its own not be dominated by it, and to allow it to age.

There are a large number of versions of the single malt aged 7 years for Italy, 8 years for France, 10 years (at 40% and as a → high proof), 12 years, 18 years and 25 years. The 18-year-olds (in Italy it was occasionally available as a 17-year-old, such as the 1965 and the 1966), which always give the vintage, are particularly coveted by collectors.

At the end of 1998 a 30-year-old → vintage from 1946 with a relatively smoky taste was released at a cost of about £1,500. It was followed by bottlings from 1948, 1951 and 1961, each of precisely 365 bottles. The millennium was also celebrated with a Macallan 1949, which came in a glass decanter and was exactly 50 years old. In contrast the Macallan Grand Reserva from carefully selected Oloroso casks, was more affordable. The fact that the proprietors consider their whisky to be precious is shown by the half-litre bottles in which they now prefer to offer it. There has been a 'Vintage Travel Range' whose four versions represented a method of transport from a decade in the 20th century – a car for the 20s, an ocean liner for the 30s, a locomotive for the 40s and a plane for the 50s. A 1981 Macallan also came in small bottles. Their labels looked as if they had been written by hand, stated that the whisky was unfiltered and had a cask strength of 56% and praised its contents as 'smooth and strong'. This was followed by a second expression of Exceptional Single Cask (ESC), a 1980 at 59.3%.

There are also special bottlings such as the 1874 already mentioned. These celebrate various occasions, for example, the 35th anniversary of the magazine *Private Eye*. The sales record was achieved by the 12 bottles of a Macallan which had been distilled in 1926 and bottled in 1986, and were therefore 60 years old, with a label designed by an artist and a small shrine made out of brass and glass. One of the bottles achieved a price of £15,000 at a Christie's auction in 1993 which, due to the increased exchange rate, was still less than the £12,000 which the nightclub owner Lou Manzi had to pay in 1997. At Heathrow a Japanese tourist bought a Macallan from 1926, of which there were also only 12 bottles, for £10,000. A lot less is asked by the → independent bottlers such as → Cadenhead, Murray → McDavid and → Signatory, who also have access to the malts from Macallan; but they are often not those that have been matured in sherry wood. → Gordon & MacPhail brought out a whole series of Macallans from various years via its subsidiary → Speymalt. There was also an → As We Get It bottling from J G → Thomson.

MacAndrew's One of the many Scotch blends currently available from → Glenmorangie plc. The brand was established by Alistair Graham Ltd, who were later taken over by → Macdonald & Muir.

MacArthur & Co, James → Independent bottler that used to name Glasgow (or sometimes even London) as its base, but whose bottles today give Edinburgh as the address. They are managed by the company of Arthur H B Winning of High Wycombe, Buckinghamshire. It was long assumed that a dealer in casks was behind the company, whose good connections give it access to → single casks, and who first appeared on the scene at the beginning of the 1990s. Initially they bottled their single malts at 43%, but they have since also taken up the → cask strength trend and forego → chill filtering and → colouring. The malts with a strength of 43% are called 'Fine Malt Selection', the ones with a higher percentage are named → 'Old Masters'. Their range is constantly changing but the company regularly includes less common distilleries such as → Ledaig or → Glen Spey, and they were amongst the first to have a malt whisky from → Allt A'Bhainne. In 1994 they presented a small special series 'In Celebration 500 Years of Scotch Whisky', which included, among others, malts from → Glen Keith, → Springbank and → Teaninich. The bottling of three single grains was of particular interest, from → Ben Nevis (27 years), → Carsebridge (27 years) and →

Lochside (28 years). The 10-year-old single malt → Auld Acquaintance comes without any precise information as to its origins and shows a picture of Robert → Burns on its label.

MacArthur's Scotch blend that was introduced in 1877 by the Glaswegian James MacArthur Jr. & Co, who should not be confused with today's independent bottlers, although common roots may very well exist. The brand now belongs to → Inver House Distillers Ltd, who include it in their range as a → standard blend without an age statement and as a 12-year-old → de luxe blend.

MacDonald & Co, R N Scottish whisky company established in the 1970s by Major Andrew MacDonald, a great grandson of the well-known → Long John from the → Ben Nevis Distillery in Fort William. The company settled in nearby Glencoe and named their vatted malt after it, bottled at a strength of 57% and 8 years of age. The company no longer exists and for several years the brand belonged to → Red Lion Blending, but → Nikka, the Japanese owners of Ben Nevis, bought it back.

Macdonald & Muir Scottish whisky company established in 1893 by the two businessmen, Roderick Macdonald and Alexander Muir. Initially they were colleagues but then became competitors, before becoming partners as a result of the marriage of Muir's sister to Macdonald. Shortly after the turn of the century, after the shock caused by the → Pattison brothers' bankruptcy, they moved into buildings at Queen's Dock in Leith (which were only given up in 1996). The company's most important blend was → Highland Queen. Having already been shareholders in → Glenmorangie and → Glen Moray, Macdonald & Muir bought both distilleries outright in 1918 and 1923 respectively. Further acquisitions included James → Martin & Co. and in 1995 → Crabbie's, which is situated nearby. In 1996 they decided to adopt the name of their most famous product, and changed from → Macdonald Distilleries to → Glenmorangie plc, keeping Macdonald & Muir as a subsidiary company responsible for production and adminstration. In 1997 → Glenmorangie plc also acquired → Ardbeg Distillery on → Islay

from → Allied Distillers Ltd. Until the spring of 1999 a grandson of the founding Macdonald was part of the management of the company, which has belonged to a joint-stock company since 1949.

Macdonald Greenlees Scottish company which was established at the end of the 19th century, when the businessman John Calder brought the two companies, Alexander & Macdonald and James & Samuel Greenlees, under his control. The latter was the successful creator of the important brand → Old Parr. This was the beginning of a significant company conglomerate, to which William Williams & Sons belonged, together with their distillery → Glendullan, as well as other companies such as → Ainslie & Heilbron, John Gillon (→ Glenury) and James Munro & Son (→ King of Kings). In 1925 they all came under the umbrella of → DCL, who allowed many of them to remain active under the management of Macdonald Greenlees. Their names at least remained in the commercial register, from which → UD, since the takeover of DCL, had many old companies struck out. They are officially registered as owners of the brands Old Parr, → Gillon's, → President and → Sandy Macdonald.

Macdonald Martin Distilleries Scottish firm established in 1949 as a holding company for a series of family businesses including, and most importantly, → Macdonald Muir, James → Martin & Co. and the distilleries of → Glenmorangie and → Glen Moray, which were run as independent companies. Although it was a joint-stock company it belonged to the small group of independent and family-run businesses. David Macdonald continued as a director after the spring of 1999, having previously been chairman. 1996 was an important year in the history of the company because the old buildings in Leith were given up in favour of a new plant at Broxburn. The name was also changed to → Glenmorangie plc. The company, which exports to more than 120 countries and which is one of the few to have successfully exported to → China.

Macduff Defunct Scottish malt distillery situated on the outskirts of the coastal town of Banff, overlooking the River Deveron and belonging to the → Highland whisky region. It was built in 1962 and got its name from a small settlement nearby (and from Duff House on the other side of the river). Stanley P → Morrison was one of its owners for several years. Nowadays it belongs to the Bacardi empire, and its purchase marked their entry into the whisky business. Since 1972 the licence for the distillery, which had successively been enlarged to four → stills, has been registered with William Lawson Distillers, who sell the whisky as a single malt in a → proprietor's bottling using the trade name → Glen Deveron. It is only available under the distillery name from → independent bottlers.

MacDuff International Scottish whisky company that has nothing to do with the distillery named → Macduff, but which was established by a consortium managed by Stewart MacDuff. All it members had worked in the whisky business for a long time and wanted to become independent. They have managed to do so with remarkable success: in the short time since 1992 the enterprise has been able to establish itself with the help of several well-known brands, such as → Grand Macnish, → Islay Mist and → Lauder's, which they were able to buy and develop. The company's other blends are → Cumbrae Castle, The → Stewart MacDuff, → Regent and → Strathbeag. The latest, but definitely not the last addition to their range, is the single malt → Glenbeg.

MacGavins Scotch blend from the → Speyside Distillery Co which belongs to the Christie family. They bottle it using the name of Alexander MacGavin, who originally launched it. It is a → standard blend without an age statement.

Macgregor's Scotch blend named after Macgregor, Ross & Co., who originally produced it. It was taken over by → Whyte & Mackay / → JBB (Greater Europe) plc whose interests were bought out by → Kyndal in October 2001.

Mackie, Peter Scottish whisky pioneer whose company, (which was renamed White Horse Distillers after his death in 1924), belonged to the → 'Big Five'. Mackie was honoured in 1920 with a baronetcy, and he joined the illustrious group of → whisky barons. He was a particularly energetic and dynamic man, full of self-confidence; his nickname was 'restless Peter' and Sir Robert Bruce Lockhart, a member of another whisky family, called him 'one third genius, one third meglomaniac, one third eccentric'. Nevertheless these characteristics led to him having a company at the end of his life which produced a brand of worldwide importance and owned three distilleries. He inherited → Lagavulin, where he had learned distilling from his uncle, helped to build → Craigellachie on the Spey and later took it over entirely, and bought → Hazelburn in → Campbeltown. He was deeply involved in the dispute between the grain distillers of the → Lowlands and the malt distillers, who were involved in the vexed question as to what could be defined itself as → Scotch whisky. He also prevented his firm being swallowed by his opponents, → DCL, during his lifetime (it happened three years after his death). He was what is called a 'colourful character': politically he was a Tory, an imperialist where his country was concerned, a great country sportsman and something of a despot in running his own company.

Mackillop's Choice Series of single malts from an → independent bottler which appeared on the market at the end of 1999. Mackillop is said to be the chief of the clan himself. Only single casks at the original strength are available, and the number of the cask and the month of the distillation and bottling are stated. The first series constisted of a 1985 Ben Nevis (62.2%), a 1979 Blair Athol (57.2%, sherry cask), a 1977 Convalmore (61.7%), a 1977 Dallas Dhu 59.9%), a 1978 Dufftown (58.3%, sherry cask), a 1982 Linlithgow (62.7%) and a 1979 Mosstowie (59.4%, sherry cask). They were all bottled in October 1999.

Mackinlay & Co, Charles Scotch whisky company founded in 1815 in Leith by Charles Mackinlay and famous for the blend bearing the founder's name. For five generations it passed from father to son, and was very successful in blending, as well as in the distillery business, with various partners, such as the Birnies or the McPhersons, and with the distilleries → Glen Albyn, → Glenallachie and → Isle of Jura. The brand used to belong, via → Waverley Vintners, to the brewery giant → Scottish & Newcastle, who sold it to → Invergordon. The brand and all its associated assets are now owned by → Kyndal. The Original Mackinlay, to give it its full name, is available as a → standard blend, as well as aged 12 and 21 years. The history of the brand proudly notes that the Polar explorer Ernest Shackleton took 10 cases of Mackinlay's on his expedition (a fact which the late Gordon Brown in his *Classic Spirits of the World*, supplemented by reporting that, on his expeditions of 1914 and 1921, Shackleton took → VAT 69 with him).

Mackmyra Swedish malt distillery in Gävle, 200 km to the north of Stockholm, which was founded in 1999 by a group of whisky enthusiasts and named after the province in which it is located. It has two small → stills and is said to produce about 1,000 litres of alcohol per annum. According to reliable information the first distillates are already maturing in their casks.

MacLeay Duff Scotch blend that still bears the name of the old Glaswegian company which was established in 1863 and which lost its independence to → DCL in 1933. On DCL's behalf they held the licence to the → Millburn Distillery in Inverness, until it was finally closed and eventually partly demolished. Apart from this blend and → Glen Lyon, there was also a vatted malt called The Mill Burn.

MacLeod Scottish clan which has two branches; the MacLeods of Lewis and the MacLeods of Skye (whose seat is Dunvegan Castle). The company Ian MacLeod in Edinburgh, was founded by descendants of the Skye branch. They became best-known for their blend → Isle of Skye which is available in several versions: as a → standard blend and aged 8, 12, 18 and 21 years. Single malts have also recently borne this name: without an exact statement of origin, there are MacLeod's → Islay and MacLeod's Highland, each available aged 8 and 15 years. The name MacLeod is also used for the → Chieftan's Choice range and for the brands of → Hedges & Butler.

The 'De luxe Malt' MacLeod of MacLeod, has nothing to do with the company. Its label is signed by the clan chief, John MacLeod and can only be obtained by those who visit Dunvegan Castle. It is a vatted malt and it may be assumed that the → Talisker was used in creating this brand for MacLeod, the only malt whisky made on Skye.

Macnab Distilleries Scottish whisky company founded by the businessman Joseph Hobbs when he bought the → Lochside brewery from John Deuchar & Sons, part of → Scottish & Newcastle Breweries. He also acquired the → Ben Nevis Distillery as a working model and equipped Lochside so that it could produce both grain and malt whiskies. In 1973 he sold the company to the Spanish concern → Distilerias y Crianza (→ DYC) which continued to produce the blend → Sandy Macnab and later brought out a 10-year-old Lochside single malt. → DYC dismantled the grain plant and shut down the entire distillery in 1992. → Allied Domecq PLC bought → DYC and have liquidated Macnab and sold the buildings to a development company.

Macnair's Scotch blend. It is the last remaining brand of the Scottish firm Harvey Macnair & Co. It was one of the smaller businesses acquired by Hiram → Walker when they extended their Canadian interests to Scotland. Its history explains why the blend now comes from → Allied Distillers Ltd.

MacNaughton's Canadian whisky (40%). The standard 4-year-old whisky was the first brand that the Canadian branch of → Schenley, founded in 1945, brought out for export. It was exclusively intended for the American market. For a time the brand belonged to the American company → Glenmore, who were bought from → UD in 1991. They already owned Schenley and its distillery → Valleyfield, where MacNaughton's had always been produced, and kept it when they sold most of the other brands from Glenmore together with its old buildings. John MacNaughton Co, New York, are named as importers on the label. However in February 1999 the brand changed hands when its owners, who had merged with → IDV to form → UDV, decided to withdraw entirely from North America. It now belongs to → Canandaigua.

MacPhail's Scotch single malt from → Gordon & MacPhail. It could be regarded as the house brand of this company, which must have thought very carefully about which product they would lend the name of their co-founder to, knowing that the name stands for top quality. It is not stated from which distillery the malts in question come, it can differ from bottling to bottling, but it is always a → Speyside. It is also always a whisky from their own large, and often very old stocks. That is why there is a considerable choice of ages and packaging: aged 10, 15, 21, 25, 30 and 40 years, each at 40%, just as the → vintages from 1973 and 1965; malt whiskies distilled in 1937, 1938, 1939 and 1940 are only available as miniatures. A 50-year-old is presented in a cut crystal decanter. A → high proof comes with the adjunct 'Gold 106' and is bottled at 60.5%. The 1967 Port Cask has become rare. It was one of the first attempts at experimenting with various types of cask (see also → Glenmorangie plc, → Balvenie, → Bushmills, → finishings). In contrast to these, MacPhail's Port was not just finished in a port cask, but spent its whole life in one. On the 100th anniversary of the company in 1995, the company brought out a Centenary, a vatted malt consisting of exactly 100 different malts.

MacPhail's Collection Series of Scotch single malts brought out in 1998 at 40% by the → independent bottlers (and largest whisky dealers in Great Britain), → Gordon & MacPhail of Elgin. It joined the large → 'Connoisseurs Choice' series. Two → Speysides were the first of the series, an 8-year-old → Glenrothes and a → Tamdhu of the same age. These were followed (without an exact age but with the year of distillation) by a → Glenglassaugh from 1986, a → Glenturret from 1988, a → Bunnahabhain (also from 1988) and a → Highland Park as an 8-year-old. All these distilleries are owned by → Highland Distillers, with whom → Gordon & MacPhail have always had a good relationship. It remains to be seen whether the series will be limited to these malt whiskies.

Maison du Whisky French whisky shop in Paris, located near the famous Madeleine, at 20 Rue d'Anjou. Its founder and director is Thierry Bénitah, who has not only made it into one of the best whisky sources in France but has also created a European centre for whisky culture. He has a massive range of 'ordinary' whiskies and his own exclusive bottlings, mostly from → Signatory. Together with Andrew Symington's company Bénitah has created the → 'Lands of Scotland' series, and recently the → 'Stills of Scotland' series which aim to show the influence the shape of the → pot still has on a malt whisky. The series has a uniform strength of 45%. Bénitah has also founded a club which undertakes trips to Scotland and meets regularly to enjoy a special kind of cuisine: the combination of food with malt whisky. There is also a newsletter for the club members named 'The → Angels' Share'. Two books have been produced by Flammarion for the shop: *ABCdaire du Whisky* and the two-volumed *Le Whisky*.

Majesty Scotch blend with the description 'Rare Old'. Its name refers to Mary, Queen of Scots after whom → Glenmorangie plc's top blend, → Highland Queen, is also named.

Major Gunn's Scotch blend which now comes from → Glenmorangie and which originated at Andrew MacLaggan & Co.

Majority A → standard Scotch blend made for → CWS by a prominent Scotch distiller.

Maker's Mark American whiskey distillery which is sometimes also known as the Star Hill Distillery, but which usually bears the name of the → Kentucky straight bourbon which it produces and has made it famous. On the bottles there is a symbol, a circle broken by a five-pointed star, which stands for Star Hill. The 'S' inside it is for the → Samuels family who founded the business, and a Roman IV because at its founding T William Samuels said the family had been making whiskey for four generations. This is, unusually for the bourbon industry, an understatement: his son, Bill Samuels Jr, who now runs the company, represents the family's seventh generation. Several other things make this company and its product unusual. The whisky (sic) comes in a very striking bottle, each example of which is decorated with a handmade label and the stoppers are hand-sealed with red wax – their 'Maker's Mark'.

In 1780 Robert Samuels, a former officer from Pennsylvania, went to Kentucky to settle as a farmer and distiller. In 1844 his nephew Taylor William began distilling on a commercial scale in Deatsville, where the family still own and use warehouses. He was followed by William Isaac and Leslie, who after → prohibition started up again with a new building in Deatsville and reopened the old distillery. His son T Williams followed him, but sold the business and its distilleries so that he could retire in 1943. But he did not retire, and 10 years later he acquired a rundown distillery called Happy Hollow in Loretto, to the south of → Bardstown, and decided to make it unique. He succeeded and the distillery has been so lovingly restored that it was declared a National Historic Landmark.

The high share of almost one third → sour mash is unusual. The → mash bill is also unique: 70% corn and 16% malted barley, and the rest is wheat rather than rye. In the distilling process they are careful to limit themselves to a strength of about 125°/62.5%, so that certain aromatic substances are preserved and the distillate has more character. The casks are initially stored and dried in the open for a year before filling – a costly process (no wonder that → Glenmorangie plc, who are fanatic about the significance of wood, mainly obtain their casks from Star Hill). And just to underline how special they are, they have never spoken of whiskey but of whisky (as in the case of → Dickel and → Early Times).

They also decided to remain small. At the beginning they only produced 36 barrels a day, and even after being taken over by Hiram → Walker in 1981, Bill Samuels Jr was able to prevent too much expansion: the only concession he made was the installation of additional fermenting vessels, which were no longer made of wood but of stainless steel, but daily production remains at a maximum of 54 barrels. A further concession to → Allied Domecq PLC, the parent company of Hiram Walker, was the introduction onto the market of a premixed → Mint Julep. Otherwise everything remains as it was, and Bill Jr. is still President.

The best-known version is the Red Seal which is about 6 years old and is available at 86°/43% and 90°/45%. The white and the blue versions have the same strength, and the latter has a blue speckled label. The Limited Edition is sealed with golden wax and is 101°/50.5%. The Black Seal Maker's Mark Select (95°/47.5%) and the equally strong 1983 Vintage, which is to be followed by new → vintages each year, are even rarer. Whoever wishes to do so can have their name put on the label.

Malcolm Stuart Scotch blend marketed by Melrose Drover, which was founded in 1872. It was taken over in 1968 by Saccone & Speed, whose best-known blend was → Hankey Bannister, which they, however, did not 'invent' themselves. The company had a large bottling plant in Broxburn near Edinburgh Airport, which is now run by Peter J Russell & Co together with Glenfarclas. The brands were bought up by → IDV who no longer produce the blend, although it is still possible to find it.

Malt The term given to barley which has been steeped in water, allowed to germinate for a period to convert the starch contained in the endosperm to fermentable sugars and then had this process stopped by drying the grains so that the sugar content is preserved.

It is also used in beer brewing, as required by the 'Reinheitsgebot' in Germany, and is used in making other types of whisk(e)y.

After malted barley is dried it is milled to become → grist and hot water is added to separate the sugars from this → mash. The addition of → yeast results in a liquid containing → alcohol named the → wash or → beer, the alcohol content of which is increased by → distillation.

Malt Advocate A quarterly magazine established by John Hansell in 1992, which is published in Emmaus, Pennsylvania. Originally

Malt Club

it had an emphasis on articles about beer, but over the years the section devoted to malt whisky has continually grown. Hansell was initially interested in the small, independent beers from so-called 'microbrewers' – known as real ale in the UK. Hansell became increasingly enthusiastic about small European breweries and in this way discovered malt whisky.

Authors such as Michael Jackson (for beer and whisky), Jim Murray, Charles MacLean and Gary Regan, contribute to the magazine which regularly profiles distilleries and provides information about new products. Their website is at www.maltadvocate.com.

Malt Club Japanese malt whisky from → Nikka, which was introduced onto the market in 1995 as a new version of their famous → All Malt.

Malt Distillers Association of Scotland
Scottish association formed by the proprietors of malt distilleries to represent their economic and political interests. The MDAS was founded in 1874 as the North of Scotland Malt Distillers Association, from 1925 they were called The Pot Still Malt Distillers of Scotland, and since 1971 they have worked under their present name. Their headquarters are in Elgin, where several full-time workers are employed. The chairman has an honorary position. Until 1988 John McDonald, the manager for many years at Tomatin, headed the association. In the *Scotch Whisky Review* he described the MDAS as an 'organisation that deals with the sharp end of any production problems that the industry has. Environmental issues take up a lot of time, especially dealing with ... Brussels. Health and Safety is important and there are committees for animal feed products, Customs & Excise, wages – it is a good organisation.' The MDAS works together closely with the → SWA, but is independent of it.

Malt whisky The spirit distilled from the fermented → wort produced from a → mash created from purely malted barley.

In Scotland the differences between the individual malt whiskies stem from numerous factors. Among the most important are the water used in the distilling process (which must be abundant and cold), the quality of the → barley (which can come from anywhere), the manner in which the malt is kilned or dried (drying over peat increases the phenolic content of the grain), the quality of the yeast cultures, the clarity of the → wort and the speed of → fermentation, the shape of the → pot stills and the time that the distillate is in contact with the copper surface of the stills, the temperature at which the condensers are operated and the range of micro-climates in which the spirit matures and the wood type used for the casks. The spirit must be matured for a minimum of three years before it can be legally termed → Scotch whisky.

Irsih malt whiskey is rarely peated and is → triple distilled.

From the mashing stage onwards the distillery must carry out all production work itself. Every distillery also used to have its own → floor maltings. Because this process is very labour-intensive and therefore very expensive, only a few distilleries such as Balvenie, Bowmore, Highland Park and Laphroaig make a proportion of their own malt. Others distilleries get it from large industrial maltings, which are given exact specifications regarding the type of malt required. The shape of the stills can have an influence on the character of a malt whisky and particularly its body depending on how much → reflux occurs during distillation. When they have to be repaired or replaced, or if the distillery's capacity has to be increased, then exact parts and copies of the originals are made.

Although it is also made elsewhere, malt whisky is quite rightly identified with Scotland – in the two Irish malt distilleries of Bushmills and at Cooley in Riverstown, Scottish methods are used. In Scotland, over 100 distilleries now remain of which around 80 are active. Around 20 others are mothballed. A further 25, which have been partially or completely demolished, still have stocks of whisky maturing. The availability to the consumer of so many malts is a comparatively recent phenomenon. Nowadays 90% of Scotch whisky production is used for blends.

The resurgence in interest in malt whisky can be largely attributed to William Grant & Sons and their Glenfiddich, which they launched onto the market in 1963 as a single, bottled malt. Since then more and more distillery proprietors have offered their malt whiskies in a similar manner. In the mid-80s books like Wallace Milroy's *Malt Whisky Almanac* and Michael Jackson's *World Guide to Whisky* contributed to this as well and helped to spread awareness of the availability and range of malt whisky. The creation of the → Classic Malts from → UDV also represented a milestone.

Fifteen years ago it would have been almost impossible to obtain a malt whisky from every whisky region and from every Scottish distillery, but today it is relatively easy. Many of these are available as → proprietor's bottlings, and even more are available from the independent bottlers. In addition, not only single malts are available, but also single cask expression which are particularly popular with collectors. Vatted malts have become somewhat neglected, though they can be excellent. However they are no match for a single malt. This remains the first, the original, form of whisky.

Malt Whisky Association, The A business formed by a group of investors around Robin Tucek in Great Britain at the end of the 1980s, based in Tunbridge Wells, Kent, with a Scottish office in Largs. The Association offered membership, for a fee, to those interested in malt whisky, to provide them with information and, above all, with whisky. Their advisor was the wine and whisky expert John Lamond, who was awarded the title → Master of Malt in 1987. *The Malt Whisky File* from Tucek and Lamond, which has become a bestseller, was originally intended as a handbook for members. There was also a newsletter, but this was discontinued after a few editions, so that the main purpose of the organisation was the mail order business, conducted using the name The → Master of Malt, which it registered as a trademark. Apart from normal bottlings, there was a series of their own whiskies using this name, which the association had bottled for them. Anyone can buy from the company which is also an → independent bottler, but members receive a discount. Lamond and Tucek left the organisation and formed a new company, → Blackadder International.

Maltings Term for the buildings in which the → barley that is needed for brewing beer and distilling malt whisky is made into → malt. The word first came into use from 1840 onwards; previously the term malt-house was used. The most common type of maltings nowadays are the industrial → drum maltings as seen at → Port Ellen and → Muir of Ord, → Glenesk and Roseisle.

A maltings plant consists of the equipment in which barley is first soaked in water (→ steeping) to activate → germination. This helps to convert the starch contained in the grain into fermentable sugars. The grain (usually about 25 tonnes) is then either spread out evenly on the → floor maltings or poured into the rotating drums as at Port Ellen which effect the same changes. The temperature must not exceed 16°C and the barley must be regularly turned by hand, a process which is very labour-intensive. In this way the layer becomes thinner.

When maximum starch conversion has taken place (about six days in the drums and one week on the floor) → germination must be halted. This is done by drying over a fuel source in a → kiln. The → green malt, as it is now known, is converted into → malt by this process which conserves the fermentable sugars. Floor maltings incorporate a → kiln one the end of the floor (the steeps are at the other end). → Drum maltings utilise hot air to dry the grain in the drums.

The traditional form of malting is, however, only used in a few distilleries nowadays, such as → Balvenie, → Bowmore, → Glendronach, → Highland Park, → Laphroaig and recently again at → Springbank. The reasons are obvious: it is an expensive process which is very labour-intensive. Most distilleries obtain their finished malt from the large industrial maltings. The → Saladin boxes which are used at → Tamdhu are another mechanised form of malting.

Malts of Scotland, The Series of five Scotch

single malts brought out by → Invergordon in the autumn of 1997 which provoked reaction because of the names used for the five malts. They were called → Craignure, → Druichan Islay, → Ferintosh, → Glenluig and → Kincaple. The last three bear names that have played an important part in the history of Scotch whisky; the → *Scotch Whisky Review* calls them 'the most historical of all Scotch Whisky's heritage'. When the marketing strategists of Invergordon used these names they broke with a tradition that gave single malts the names of their distilleries (at least when they were → proprietor's bottlings). Invergordon used to own the → Isle of Jura Distillery in Craighouse and → Bruichladdich on → Islay, and Craignure and Druichan most likely came from these. But neither they nor their then parent company → Whyte & Mackay / → JBB (Greater Europe) plc – owned by → American Brands – owned a distillery in the Lowlands or one named Ferintosh or Glenluig. They described their Ferintosh as a → Speyside and their Glenluig as a → Highland.

Glenluig used to be in the Lowlands, probably in Dunbartonshire, and Ferintosh was on the Cromarty Firth. So where did these malt whiskies come from?

Manager's Dram, The Series of single malts that are not generally available to the public but are meant exclusively for the employees of → GuinnessUDV. The cask is chosen by the distillery manager whose signature on the botttle guarantees it. Nevertheless several bottles leaked out via auctions and charity events and led to the series becoming the object of keen interest to collectors. The author has been able to sample the following: Blair Athol 15 years (bottled in 1996, at 59.4%), Caol Ila 15 years (1990/63%), Clynelish 17 years (1997, 61.8%), Cragganmore 17 years (1997, 62%), Glen Elgin 16 years (1993, 60%), Linkwood 12 years (1999, 59.5%), Mannochmore 18 years (1997, 66%), Oban 16 years (bottled in 1994 for the 200th anniversary of the distillery, 64%) and Ord 16 years (1991, 66.2%).

Manchester United Scotch blend, the house brand of the football club of the same name. The standard→ blend used to come from → Whyte & Mackay, and is now included in the range from The → Bennachie Whisky Co.

Manhattan Classic whisk(e)y cocktail. Its discovery is surrounded by legend and there are many versions of it, the original ones being made with Canadian whisky (supporting the view that it originated during prohibition), but today bourbon is also used. For the Manhattan Perfect take four parts of Canadian whisky to one part of dry vermouth and one part of vermouth rosso. Stir vigorously with a few dashes of Angostura bitters and serve with a cherry. For a Manhattan Dry the vermouth rosso is replaced by a further part of dry vermouth. For a Manhattan Sweet all the dry vermouth is replaced by rosso.

Mannochmore Scottish malt distillery. Its name means 'large monk'. It is situated near → Elgin, next to the → Glenlossie Distillery. It was built for → DCL by John → Haig & Co. This was in 1971 and its six → stills were able to produce one million litres of alcohol per year. Although its whisky soon became popular with blenders, expectations were too high: it had to be closed down during the whisky recession of 1983, but began production again in 1989 with the DCL successor → UD when Glenlossie shut down for renovation. Although the same workers are employed in both distilleries Mannochmore had to close again in 1995, but was active again at the beginning of 1997. Previously it was only once bottled as a single malt by the → Scotch Malt Whisky Society, before → UD included it in their → 'Flora & Fauna' series and brought out a 12-year-old malt. The 10-year-old → Loch Dhu attracted a lot of attention. It was a very dark, almost black whisky and → UD stated that it originated from Mannochmore – but it did not sell well and was withdrawn from the market. There was a 22-year-old Mannochmore at 60.1% in the → 'Rare Malts' collection. The independent bottlers have also made several bottlings available. There was a Cadenhead from 1977 at a cask strength of 60.9%. Gordon & MacPhail included a 1984 Mannochmore in their 'Connoisseurs Choice' series.

Mansion House Indian spirit from → Tiliknagar, a company which has been involved in a joint venture with → Allied Domecq PLC since 1997 and distributes on their behalf, amongst others, → Teacher's and → Old Smuggler, which is imported in → bulk by another partner, → Clan Morgan of Delhi, and bottled in → India. The company also has several brands of its own including the Mansion House series which includes a brandy, a gin and an Indian blend.

Manx Whiskey Spirits which for several years came from the Isle of Man; apparently for that reason the Irish spelling was preferred. The 'Natural White Whiskey' from the → Glen Kella Distillery has not been allowed to use this description since the beginning of 1997, when the → Scotch Whisky Association went to court to forbid it doing so – a victory which almost led to the bankruptcy of the small business that produced a 5-year-old blend and an 8 and 12-year-old vatted malt. The objection of the SWA caused them to rename their product Manx Spirit. There are two versions of this, the Manx red and the Manx blue, one distilled from Scotch and the other from 12-year-old malt whiskies. They are obtained from Scotland and are distilled for a third time on the island, thereby losing their colour to become crystal clear.

Maqintosh Indian whisky. A blend of Indian malt whisky and 5-year-old Scotch, which in its turn is probably a blend of Scottish malts and → grain whisky. Neutral spirit distilled in → India, probably made from sugar syrup, is also added to the blend. The producers of the brand are → Amrut Distilleries in Bangalore.

Mar Lodge Scotch vatted malt created by → Findlater Mackie Todd & Co, which belonged via → Invergordon prior to the takeover of → JBB (Greater Europe) plc by → Kyndal. Production is discontinued, but bottles of it are still available in Scotland.

Mark Twain American whiskey liqueur imported by Borco, a company in Hamburg, Germany, who have the → Kentucky straight bourbon → Pennypacker made exclusively for them. That comes from → Heaven Hill so it is probable that this liqueur, whose appearance is reminiscent of the classic → Southern Comfort, is based on a bourbon from this distillery. A second ingredient of this spirit is fruit. The label speaks of the 'Old Tradition from the South of the United States', referring to the drink itself as well as to the American author Mark Twain.

Marks & Spencer UK chainstore that sells products with the St. Michael label, including various blends and malt whiskies. There are some exceptions to the name rule, such as the Irish whiskey → Cassidy's or the Scotch → Kenmore.

Marlfield Irish spirit described on its label as 'Old Irish Liqueur Whiskey', a description which leaves a lot of questions unanswered. It was marketed in the very small amount of 1,000 bottles, and that was not the only factor that justified its higher price. The contents of these bottles come from 1946 and were distilled at the → Tullamore Distillery, which used to belong to George Daly. His name appears on the label, although it was Daniel E Williams who was fighting to save the distillery that year. It is known that he was trying to create a liqueur, → Irish Mist, which first came on to the market in 1948. The drink contains 20% alcohol, typical for a liqueur. The source of the name is known: it was an old distillery operating 300 years ago, of which a few walls still remain.

Marriage Term for the bringing together of whiskies from different casks in a large vat made of wood or stainless steel in which they are 'married' before being bottled. The process serves to harmonise the various individual whiskies used for a blend or a vatted malt, so that a union is achieved. As the process is time-consuming and therefore expensive, it is seldom used nowadays. The fact that it was not always used in the past is made clear by the advertising of some companies, which emphasised that the whiskies for their blends had been 'married'. → Whyte & Mackay is a famous example. Another form of marrying is used for → Canadian Club, in which the whiskies are already mixed in the casks before bottling. In the case of some single malts, certain companies insist on first marrying the individual casks in order to smooth out their differences. A particularly elaborate system has been worked out by master blender David Stewart for his → Glenfiddich Solera Reserve. It consists of 15-year-old Glenfiddichs from ex-sherry casks, ex-bourbon casks and from refill casks. The contents of the refill cask are placed in brand new American oak casks. Following this all the whiskies are 'married' in a 40,000 litre Solera tun until bottling.

Marrying In English several terms are used to describe the bringing together of whisk(e)y from various individual casks. Marrying is the process whereby a blend remains for a longer period in casks before being bottled to optimise the harmonisation of its individual whiskies. Blending is the mixing of malt whiskies and → grain whiskies to create a blend. In Ireland vatting is a synonym for blending. In Scotland it is only used for vatted malts, ie for those which consist of malt whiskies from various distilleries.

Martin, James Scottish whisky company established by a merchant of the same name, who was also a boxer and philanthropist. The firm has belonged to → Macdonald & Muir since the 1920s. It was their → blends, Martin's VVO and Martin's De Luxe, which were aboard the → SS Politician in 1941 when she ran aground off the island of Eriskay. Compton Mackenzie described in his book → Whisky Galore, how the plunder consoled the islanders during the rigours of war.

Martini & Rossi feared confusion between their brands and Martin's, and instigated the changing of the name to include James. It is still occasionally available as Martin's VVO ('very very old' or 'vatted very old') as a → standard, and as a → premium 12 and 20-year-old Martin's Fine & Rare. The new names are James Martin's Premium, James Martin's Special, James Martin's 17 years old and Martin's 20 years old. They are all difficult to get in Europe, but popular in the USA. → Oddbins have the vatted James Martin Finest Pure Malt and a James Martin 20 years Lowland. In the case of the latter, it is not clear whether this is a vatted or a single malt. They also sell an 8-year-old malt called House of Commons.

Mary of Scotland Whisky cocktail. Take one part green chartreuse, one part Drambuie and one part Scotch, shake with ice, and serve in a cocktail glass with a cocktail cherry.

Mash The term for the porridge-like mixture of → grist and hot water which is created in the → mash tun. The resultant sweet liquor which is drained from the → mash tun is known as the → wort.

It is a similar process in the case of → grain whisky, when the unmalted cereal, or the ground maize, is milled mashed. A certain amount of malted barley must also be used in order to initiate the conversion of starch to sugar.

Mashing is a much more complicated process in the case of bourbon, which uses different kinds of grain. Mashing begins with the corn, for which the water temperature is increased from 50°C to almost 100°C. Rye is added when it has been cooled to 80°C. The malt barley is added later and the very last addition, if it is used at all, is wheat. It is therefore important to keep a strict watch on the temperature, as hotter water destroys certain enzymes and makes the → fermentation of sugar impossible. In America, and the majority of grain distilleries, the → wort as well as the remaining solids are used after mashing in → fermentation.

Mash bill Term used in American distilleries to describe which types of grain make up the → mash, and their relative proportions. The law prescribes, for example, that a → Kentucky straight bourbon must have at least 51% corn content and a straight rye at least 51% rye. The proportions are actually mostly higher. A proportion of rye and/or wheat is also added and there is always a certain amount of malted barley. Each distillery has a fixed recipe for its mash bill which used to be secret but since Gary and Mardee Haidin Regan published their *Book of Bourbon*, the mash bill for most distilleries has been made known.

Mash tuns Term for the large, circular vessels in which the process of → mashing takes place in breweries and distilleries.

In the production of malt whisky, the malted barley which has been ground to a → grist is steeped in hot water at 63-64°C. When the sugars – maltose and dextrin – are dissolved, the → mash, which initially looks like thin porridge, has become a liquid which is called → wort. Up to three further infusions of increasingly hot water (up to 93°C) take place to maximise extraction with the last 'water' being retained and added to the first 'water' of the next → mash. The resultant sweet liquor which is drained from the → mash tun is known as the → wort.

It runs through a perforated floor into the → underbacks. The remaining solids are known as → draff and are used for cattle feed. The mash tuns, which vary in capacity and size, are now mostly made of stainless steel (but there are still some made of iron or copper) and are often canopied to aid temperature control and moisture. In recent times increasing use has been made of → lauter tuns, first used in German breweries, which are more efficient.

Mason's Scotch blend from Peter J → Russell & Co in Edinburgh who, however, do not market it using their own name, but that of their subsidiary Wm Maxwell, also known for the blend → King Robert II.

Master Blend Blend from Thailand which → Seagram produced as the first 'real' whisky in a country where bottles can be found inscribed with the word 'whisky', but which contain a spirit that has been distilled from rice. In the past few years → Thailand has been one of the countries which have experienced an economic boom leading to a keen interest in western (luxury) goods; the consumption of Scotch has also risen disproportionately. Seagram, often a pioneer in the conquest of new whisky countries, reacted with a product made with locally produced → grain whiskies and malt whiskies imported from Scotland. The brand came on to the market in 1995.

Master blender Term for the employees at whisk(e)y companies responsible for choosing the casks which are ready for bottling after maturation, from which either a new batch for a particular bourbon, or a particular single malt is put together or a new bottling of a blend. In many companies they are also responsible for the control of all the stored casks, constantly checking their quality and deciding when they are mature enough to be bottled. For this reason they may be encountered in either the → warehouses or the → nosing rooms. These are laboratory-like areas with shelves containing row upon row of small sample bottles, each one drawn from a cask. In the middle of the room there is a stainless steel basin in which the spent samples are disposed. The whiskies are arranged on a work table in nosing glasses, which are often dark blue or black, so that the colour of the spirit is not visible. The whisky is never tested neat but diluted to about 20% to 30%. A glass lid prevents the alcohol from escaping too quickly. However master blenders never drink at work. They only nose whiskies, never taste and it takes a long time to become a master blender. Of all the workers he probably has the most responsible task: the satisfaction of the customers depends on the quality of his work, and they expect their blend, or even their single malt, to be of consistent quality, with the same aroma and the same taste. The master blender selects from hundreds of cask the samples that will guarantee this and must determine how many casks of which malt and which grain he needs to ensure consistency. UDV's Maureen Robinson, Richard Paterson of → Kyndal or David Stewart from William Grant & Sons are therefore extremely influential in the trade.

Master of Malt, The The title Master of Malt was first established in 1987 in a competition run jointly by the Scottish Licensed Trade News and → Tamnavulin-Glenlivet. One of the first to be awarded this title was John Lamond, an acknowledged wine expert who had also demonstrated his knowledge of malt whisky in blind tastings. Together with Robin Tucek, with whom he also wrote the bestseller *The Malt Whisky File*, he was active in the → Malt Whisky Association, which decided to use the title for their whisky mail order business and for the → single cask bottlings of malts which they brought out.

Master's Choice Whisky made from Scotch malt whisky and Canadian → grain whisky which is shipped in → bulk to → Venezuela, where it is bottled for the local market which once was the largest on the continent. The blend has a strength of 40% and is a brand from → GuinnessUDV.

Mattingly & Moore → Kentucky straight bourbon. The name is made up from those of Tom Moore and Ben Mattingly, who joined together in 1876 to buy a distillery and produce a whiskey called Belle of Nelson. Several years later Moore built a distillery named after him in Bardstown, which after → prohibition became the → Barton Distillery (which today still produces a → Tom Moore). The brand Mattingly & Moore changed ownership several times, ending up with → Seagram after → prohibition and finally at → Heaven Hill, the company in Bardstown which seems to specialise in saving old historic American whiskey names. They sell the whiskey (80°/40%) without an age statement.

Maturation See → maturing below.

Maturing Term for one of the last stages in the production of whisk(e)y. It follows distillation and lasts from the time that the fresh distillate is filled into the casks until the time they are emptied. The character of the whisk(e)y is influenced to such an extent during maturation that some people say it is the most decisive stage of all in whisk(e)y production. The length of maturation is important, as well as the type and the quality of the individual cask, and the micro-climate in and around the warehouse. Whisk(e)y does not continue to mature once it has been bottled.

Maturing has not always been practised, but is a relatively recent development in the history of whisk(e)y. Previously it was customary to drink alcohol young and to reduce its rawness by using herbs or by adding honey to make → cordials). Even today young distillates have admirers who consume → moonshine in the USA or → poitín in Ireland, fresh from the still.

It is undisputed that whisk(e)y benefits considerably from maturing. The practice of filling casks is hard to date but given that for centuries stave casks were the most common container for all sorts of goods, the use of them for maturing spirit was inevetiable. The lawmakers are also of the opinion that whisk(e)y has to mature. In most countries there are legal regulations regarding the minimum period for maturation. In Scotland and Ireland this is three years, and in the USA two years, or in the case of → Bottled in Bond bourbons, four years.

Maxxium International marketing operation company founded in 1999 by three of the world's most important wine and spirits enterprises in order to combine and optimise their market penetration. The new firm was backed by → Highland Distillers, → JBB (itself owned by → Fortune Brands) and the French company → Rémy Cointreau, which was already selling Highland's brands in many countries. Its → Famous Grouse is the largest brand of Scotch in this new combine whose portfolio also includes → Black Bottle and the malts → Macallan, → Highland Park and → Bunnahabhain – the bourbon → Jim Beam (and the cognac Rémy Martin, the liqueur Cointreau, and the champagnes Piper Heidsieck and Charles Heidsieck. Interestingly Highland itself was taken over a short time after the formation of Maxxium by a syndicate formed by the → Edrington Group and William → Grant & Sons.

Mayerson & Company, H London-based whisky → brokers founded in 1953. They buy new whisky or → fillings from the producers and resell them to companies for their blends, or they act as agents between distillers and blenders. Mayerson are engaged in the import business and also ship a large amount of whisky in → bulk abroad. In addition own-label blends are made for other companies. It produces the blends → Glenrob and → Scottish Envoy as well as → Strath-Roye with the label of the subsidiary company Glen-Roye (Blenders).

McCallum's Perfection Scotch blend which really lives up to the claims of its name, and also underlines its exclusivity by calling itself 'Scots Whisky'. The brothers Duncan and John McCallum set up in business in 1807 in Edinburgh with an inn that quickly became so popular that they were able to expand, and specialised in blends of a particularly high standard, but also invested in distilleries such as → Benromach. Their Perfection came onto the market in 1911, five years before all their production buildings were completely destroyed in a German air raid on Edinburgh. In the 1930s the company was acquired by → DCL, who transferred the licence of → Cragganmore to them. That malt plays a significant part in this blend and its quality. In contrast to → Auld Acquaintance it remained with → UD when they bought DCL in 1987. At present the brand belongs to → GuinnessUDV.

McCarthy's American single malt whiskey which calls itself 'Oregon Single Malt'. It comes from the Clear Creek Distillery in Portland which had previously only distilled Eau de Vie. Then the → pot still was used to make a real single malt from 'Peat Malted Scottish Barley'. The malt is mashed and fermented at Widmer Brothers' brewery, before being distilled in Clear Creek. The whiskey matures for three years in American → barrels and is bottled at 80°/40%. It is the second American single malt, following → Old Potrero, and preceeeding the → Peregrine Rock.

McCauley's Canadian whisky, one of many produced in Canada, transported in → bulk to the USA and sold by American companies on the domestic market. The brand belongs to → Sazerac.

McClelland, T & A Scottish whisky company whose origins can be traced back to 1818 when Bladnoch Distillery was built. Jimmy Barclay was their chairman for a long time and became well-known because he enabled Hiram → Walker to participate in the Scotch whisky industry by the sale of J & G → Stodart. The company and its brands now belong to → Morrison Bowmore. They also use the name for their blends → Clan Roy, → King's Pride and → Rob Roy, and for three malts: a single → Islay, a single → Lowland and a single → Highland. These come from the company's own distilleries, → Bowmore, → Auchentoshan and → Glen Garioch respectively. They are just as good, but considerably cheaper than normal bottlings, but at 5 years, are much younger.

McCormick American whiskey company with the full name Distilling Co., who own two distilleries and a whole series of brands. It is based in the small town of → Weston on the the western borders of Missouri which is also the location of one of the distilleries, sadly closed since 1985. It has been decided not to reopen the plant, which is still kept in good order. The other distillery is → Pekin, near Peoria in Illinois which, although it has not been closed down, has not produced any whiskey since 1991, but only industrial alcohol. McCormick sells rum, tequila, gin, vodka and brandy under the company's name and also has a Canadian whisky and a Scotch in its range. The company's name is also used for a straight bourbon (80°/40%) which bears the date 1856; this refers to the year in which the distillery began operating in Weston. Also belonging to the range are the straight bourbons → B J Holladay, → Plainsman and → Stillbrook, which is available as a straight bourbon and as a blended American, and → Platte Valley, a straight corn. Both the latter bear the information 'Distilled in Illinois', which will soon be replaced by 'Distilled in Kentucky', when the whiskeys made at Pekin have been used up and their successors come from → Heaven Hill.

McDavid, Murray Glasgow-based → independent bottlers and distillers who brought out their first series of → single malt bottlings in 1996. They named the the 'Vintage Selection' with precise information stated on each label giving the name of the distillery in large letters, the year of distillation, a short description of the distillery and then the cask number, the month of distillation and bottling and the exact kind of → cask. All are bottled at 46%, are not → chill-filtered and have no colour added.

The company was formed in 1995 in London by Gordon Wright (part of the family who own → Springbank Distillery), Simon Coughlin and Mark Reynier, who owns La → Réserve in London. The first malt whiskies from Murray McDavid were: → Bunnahabhain (1979), → Caol Ila (1974), → Glenturret (1986), → Laphroaig (1987), → Linkwood (1979), → Macallan (1974) and → Royal Brackla (1979). A bottling of → Leapfrog (→ Laphroaig) caused particular controversy.

In December 2000 the company bought for £4.3m → Bruichladdich Distillery on → Islay (which had been closed since 1994) from → JBB (Greater Europe) plc and relocated to Glasgow. James McEwan (previously at → Morrison Bowmore) was recruited as distiller and in the spring of 2001, production started again.

McDonald, C & J Scottish whisky company that belonged to Arthur → Bell & Sons and produced the blends → C & J Fine Old, → Heathwood, → McDonald's Special Blend and → Queen's Choice for them. The blends now belong to → GuinnessUDV.

McDonald's Special Blend Scotch blend from C & J → McDonald, a subsidiary of Arthur → Bell & Sons who were bought by → Guinness in the 1980s. Their spirits subsidiary → GuinnessUDV is now responsible for the brand which is mainly sold in South Africa.

McDowall Scotch blend from the Surrey-based Brodie Crawford & Co., whose best-known product is → Brodie's Supreme.

McDowell & Co Indian whisky company based in Madras, owned by → United Brewers of India, on whose behalf it runs the McDowell's Distillery in the south of → India, on the west coast in the village of Ponda, near Goa. In 1988 they extended a brewing plant to produce a distillate from molasses which is called 'whisky' in India. In fact this is a kind of rum, used for blending with real whisky. In the 1980s it was decided to use malt for production. There is a → mash tun of stainless steel, six fermenting vessels and two → pot stills for this purpose. For some time now they have even been using peat imported from Scotland and → maturation takes place in ex-bourbon casks, which is very unusual for India. They do not use caramel to colour the single malt.

Up to now McDowell's is the only real single malt distilled in India. The → Moghul Monarch, for example, is not a real → malt whisky and only the → Solan No 1, a → pure malt, approaches McDowell's (its quality is sometimes actually superior). It is bottled at the 42.8% customary in India and its label bears the date of bottling and, as also prescribed, the state in which it may be sold if it is not for export. There are also blends which bear the name of the distillery and come in various versions: No. 1, Travel, Vintage Classic, Premium and Centenary (which is said to consist of Scottish → grain whiskies and Indian malt whiskies). The → Diplomat also comes from Goa.

McGibbon's Scotch blend from Douglas → Laing & Co's Glasgow subsidiary Douglas McGibbon & Co. The various versions all come in packaging which has something to do with golf: a bag, a ball, a club. Sometimes they are called Golf Bag and Golf Club but contain either the → standard blend McGibbon's Special Reserve or the → premium blend McGibbon's Master's Reserve and McGibbon's Premium Reserve. In the USA they are sold with the name 'Scotch for Swingers'. The Master's Reserve is also available in the shape of a curling stone. They are popular souvenirs of golfing holidays and gifts for golfers. For this reason they are mainly available at airport duty-free shops. A competely different group of consumers is the target of the → Provenance series (sold under the name of McGibbons): single malts in single cask bottlings which, in contrast to Laing's The → Old Malt Casks at 50%, has been reduced to 43%.

McGuinness Canadian whiskies from → Corby. The name goes back to a company which had distilleries in Toronto and in Kelowna, British Columbia, but which also owned the Central Canadian Distillery in Weyburn, Saskatchewan and the Arcadian Distillery in Bridgetown, Nova Scotia. The company later belonged to Heublein and had an extensive range with the → premium brands → Captain's Table, NC Tower and several local brands, including a crystal-clear White Canadian, which was distilled four times and filtered three. Of these the McGuinness Old Canada and → Silk Tassel, which is available in two versions, 40% and as a 'light' with 27%, are left over today, whilst the → de luxe version and the Gold Tassel have been discontinued.

McIntyre's Malt Whisky Co Scottish whisky company which is one of the newcomers among the independent bottlers. They produce, amongst other bottlings, a Bruichladdich from 1986, a Dufftown from 1979, a Highland Park from 1978, a Macallan from 1989 and a Rosebank from 1990.

McKullnich American → straight bourbon whiskey without the customary 'Kentucky'. It is 8 years old and is only sold in France, by a company called Fayenne. They do not say where they get it from.

McMasters Canadian whisky that is only obtainable in the USA. It carries no information about its origins, but as it is distributed by Heublein it is likely that a large proportion of the whiskies used for the blend come from Gilbey's → Palliser Distillery. It is here that Smirnoff vodka, Heublein's best-known brand, is also produced. The company owner is → Canandaigua.

McNiven, Douglas Scottish whisky company, also spelt MacNiven, which for a long time belonged to → Macdonald & Muir and therefore today belongs to → Glenmorangie plc. It owns the brands Glen Niven, MacNiven Finest and MacNiven Royal Abbey. Today the name is used, for example, for blends in Africa, and a series of malts called → Glen Morven also bear the name McNiven as bottler. → Glenmorangie plc also made use of the name after a mishap in which, during the planned bottling of five casks of a 21-year-old → Glen Moray, a three-year-old cask was accidentally emptied. The product eventually came onto the market as → 80/20 and is now much sought after by collectors.

Meadhan 12-year-old Scotch single malt from J&G → Grant in Ballindalloch, who own the → Glenfarclas Distillery. Like → Eagle of Spey and → Highland Cattle, it is an attempt by this company, which is still independent, to win new markets and reduce surplus stocks by offering reasonably-priced second blends.

Meadow Cream Irish whiskey cream liqueur. It differed from its competitors in two respects: instead of the usual 17% it was 14.5%, and Dutch cream was used in its production instead of Irish cream. For this reason its label described it as a 'blend of Dutch Cream with White Wine and Irish Whiskey'. Some time ago the 'Dutch' was replaced by 'fresh', which is why its producer, → Halewood International Ltd, has renamed it. It is now called → Irish Meadow.

Meaghers 1878 Canadian whisky, a rye from → Corby, originally made for the Meaghers company who mainly dealt with fruit schnapps and liqueurs.

Medley → Kentucky straight bourbon which, until the appearance of → Wathen's, was all that remained of a formerly glorious old American whiskey family. They can trace their beginnings back to the English Catholic John Medley, who emigrated to Maryland in 1635. It is not certain whether the family began making whiskey there, but they certainly did so once they had moved to Kentucky. In the course of time they owned several distilleries and married into the Beam family. Both before and after → prohibition they had a distillery in Owensboro and produced, amongst other things, → Ezra Brooks and → Rittenhouse Rye. It was probably a late effect of the dry years which led to the company having to give up its independence. They ended up under the wing of → Glenmore, who discontinued production and only used the buildings for storage. They too ceased to exist when Glenmore was taken over by → UD in 1991. They parted with a whole series of the firms, or their production sites, which they had acquired and sold their brands partly to → Barton, partly to Sherman and to → Heaven Hill. This is where the whisky is made nowadays, but it is only available in Germany, where the Dethleffsen company in Flensburg imports it exclusively in → bulk and bottles it. The Medleys have not completely withdrawn from the business. Charles Medley and his son have brought out Wathen's, a → single barrel.

Meiklers Scotch blend (40%) sold by Meiklers of Scotland, from Newtonmore in Inverness-shire. The company also has a → whisky liqueur named → Stag's Breath in its range.

Melchers Canadian whisky from the Melchers Incorporation in Montreal. Although Jan Melcher didn't produce any whisky himself, he was a Dutch immigrant who settled in Quebec and made the distillate that he knew from his home country: genever, or Dutch gin. In the 1920s the company he had founded began, under a new proprietor, to make whisky. The → Melcher's Very Mild (40%) is four years old.

Melcher's Very Mild 4-year-old Canadian whisky which is now made in Gimli and comes from the Melchers Incorporation in Montreal.

Meldrum House Series of Scottish whiskies

which the Belgian → Michel Couvreur, who lives in Bouze-Les-Beaune in Burgundy, offers as an → independent bottler. The name refers to Oldmeldrum to the north-west of Aberdeen the home of → Glen Garioch Distillery although there is no connection with the series.

Mellow Corn American corn whiskey from → Medley in Owensboro, a brand which perished with the company, but which can still be found, especially in Kentucky. It was a → Bottled in Bond at 100°/50%.

Mena Dhu Scotch blend. The house brand of the St. Austell Brewery, which is best known in Cornwall. It is one of the dwindling number of independent breweries in the country and runs more than 150 pubs and hotels in the region in which it sells its own beers, and also its own Scotch (and rum).

Men's Club Indian whisky which the company → Polychem launched as a reasonably-priced brand in 1974 and which is available in two versions, Black Label and Red Label, both with the 42.8% customary in India. It is particularly popular in the south and the west of the country, in Bombay where the company is based and in Maharashta where they own a distillery. There they sell almost four million bottles of the blend per year. Like → White House, another brand of the company, it is a blend of Indian malt whisky and blended Scotch, which is imported ready-mixed.

Mercian Japanese malt distillery which has only had this name since the early 1990s and is otherwise known as the → Karuizawa Distillery of the Japanese company → Sanraku-Ocean. It is active in many fields, producing tinned foods as well as chemicals. Its main business is alcoholic drinks: since 1937 it has produced a sake called 'Sanraku', it is successful in wine-growing and in the 1960s decided not to leave the whisky business solely to the two pioneers → Suntory and → Nikka.

A small malt distillery was built in the popular spa town of Karuizawa at the foot of Mount → Asama. Whilst the company markets its whisky brands under the name → Ocean, the distillery is named after the place in which it is located.

Perhaps Sanraku-Ocean are planning a completely new presentation for their products and the rechristening of their distillery is part of it. In any case the name Mercian has, up to now, only been used for the very successful and respected wines of the company. A 17-year-old malt whisky is already being sold under this name; it is, however, not described as a → single malt, but as '100% Malt'. Mercian is also the Japanese distributor of William → Grant & Sons.

Merlyn Welsh whisky cream liqueur from the → Welsh Whisky Co who market the blend → Swn y' Mor and → Prince of Wales. They use whiskies which are bought in Scotland and processed in Brecon, Wales. Since 1992 they have been making malt whisky and the first casks are said to have been used for the liqueur. Production had to be discontinued to replace the stills but in the autumn of 2000 they were distilling again. The liqueur contains 17% alcohol and is named after the medieval magician and teacher of King Arthur.

Merry's Irish whiskey. First there was a blend, then there was an Irish cream liqueur and finally, in 1999, a bottle whose front label described the contents as 'single malt Irish Whiskey'. The name Merry's was written without an apostrophe. On the back label it was correctly written, however there was also the information that 'the best Malt and mild Grain' had been carefully mixed. On inquiry this is apparently the result of a printing error that after correction will make these original bottles collectors' items. The whiskey is supplied by → Cooley Distillery and sold by the small A Merry & Co in Clonmel, County Tipperary, who also have a pub there. Both the whiskeys have a strength of 40%, and the cream liqueur 17%.

Michel Couvreur Belgian → independent bottler who lives in Burgundy and markets a series of Scotch whiskies under his own name. He leaves it open to speculation as to whether the contents of his bottlings are vatted or single malts and emphasises the fact that he works without → chill-filtering. In the case of his Single Single, this is a single malt in a single cask bottling (45%), which does not state from which distillery it comes.

The information on the Special Vatting from three casks is better understood. However, in the case of the Unfiltered, which is also available in a large bottle of 2.27 litres, he calls the bottle 'semi-imperial'. None of this is necessary – the whiskies are good.

Michter's American distillery in Scheaferstown, a small place between Philadelphia and Harrisburg in Pennsylvania, a state which used to have a great whiskey tradition. The story of American whiskey production began in Pennsylvania, before becoming concentrated in Kentucky and Tennessee as rye whiskey named Monongahela, after the valley in which it was distilled. Michter's was the last distillery which recalled this great past. Its buildings, which have been declared a national monument, are still a reminder, but have not seen active whiskey production since 1988. The distillery used to have the only direct-fired → pot still in the whole of North America. It was installed in the 1950s when Louis Forman, owner since 1942, and Charles Everett Beam, a descendant of the great James → 'Jim' Beam, restarted production.

At that time it was almost exactly 200 years since whiskey had first been made on this site. In 1753 the Shanks family, Swiss Mennonites, added a small distillery to their farm. From 1861 the distillery was run commercially by Abe Bomberger. At the end of the 19th century, the distillery bore his name and was decorated with the witches' signs which can still be seen toda but it did not survive → prohibition. The distillery was reopened and christened Michter's in 1975, but closed in 1981, reopened in 1984 and final shut down in 1988.

In the 1950s a Michter's Pot Still was successful, with an unusual → mash bill of 38% rye, 50% corn and 12% malt barley. They were also able to survive by supplying rye whiskey to the owners of → Old Overholt and → Wild Turkey. The production of rye was not continued when they reopened in 1984 as it was considered old-fashioned, but perhaps this decision caused the final closure after four years in 1988. After 1988 there were still large maturing stocks in the → warehouses at the distillery and more than 1,000 casks are said to have been stolen. The American courts summarily demanded that all the remaining casks should be destroyed.

However, Adolf Hirsch, former manager of → Schenley, was able to buy some casks just before this. The contents were marketed as → A H Hirsch Straight Bourbon aged 16, 19 and 20 years. The remainder now belongs to the Hue family who run the spirits store Cork 'n' Bottle in Covington, Kentucky and who work together with the → Van Winkle family. To prevent it ageing any further they have refilled the Michter's whiskey into steel casks and continue to sell it as A H Hirsch, or as → Boone's Knoll, unfortunately with no indication of its origins. The stocks are not large and so bottles are correspondingly rare and expensive. Once they have been drunk there will be nothing left of a whiskey which could once proudly claim that it 'warmed the American Revolution'.

Middle cut Term used to describe the portion of the spirit run during the final distillation (in Scotland this is usually the second and in Ireland the third) which the → stillman diverts into the → spirit receiver. It is preceded by the → foreshots and followed by the → feints, which are retained in a separate vessel for redistillation. It is only the middle cut, also known as the → heart of the run which is then filled into casks to mature. The size of the proportion of alcohol declared as middle cut depends on the philosophy of the respective distilleries. At → Macallan it is said to be just 18% which is allowed into casks, whilst elsewhere it is about 60%.

Midleton Irish distilling complex near Cork. Founded in 1825 by the three Murphy brothers it has survived the process of rationalisation in the Irish whiskey trade along with the Northern Irish → Bushmills.

Its old buildings are still standing and its huge → pot stills can still be viewed. They were not only the largest in Ireland, but also in the whole world. Here, the distillery's owners, → IDG, have created a whiskey museum, the Jameson Heritage Centre. This name is a little surprising as Midleton had nothing to do with → Jameson, at least not until the Cork Distillery

Company, itself the result of a merger between Midleton and four other distilleries in → Cork, merged with → Power and → Jameson to form → IDG in 1966.

Since the firm decided to transfer its entire whiskey production to Midleton (in Dublin there was insufficient space), almost every Irish whiskey, with the exception of Bushmills and (since 1989) the brands from → Cooley, has come from Midleton: → Paddy, → Power's, Jameson, → Hewitts, → Dunphy's,→ Murphy's, → Redbreast, → Green Spot, → Tullamore Dew and Midleton Very Rare. The → Crested Ten has a proportion of Bushmills distillates added to it. They are all bottled in Dublin and consist of Midleton whiskies.

In July 1975 the new distilling complex was opened. Built in sight of the old buildings and hidden behind trees, it is a highly complex plant with → pot stills and → patent stills which can be used together in any combination desired so that malt whiskies, as well as → pure pot still whiskey and grains, can be produced. Malts have not been made here for a long time. Another feature is that the → wash backs (called → 'fermenters' here), made of stainless steel, also make up the outside walls of the plant. Two bottlings of whiskeys from the old distillery have recently been brought out: → Dungourney and → Old Midleton Whisky (without the 'e'). The Midleton Very Rare comes from the new distillery and was first bottled in 1984. Since then there has been a new limited edition every year. All the bottles (40%) are signed by Barry Crockett, the distillery manager. The owners can register themselves, along with the number of their bottle, in a book in → IDG's new whiskey heritage centre in → Bow Street, Dublin. The surprising single malt Irish whiskey → Erin Go Bragh also comes from Midleton. The 12-year-old Jameson Distillery Reserve, which has a strong sherry note, is exclusively available only at the heritage centres

The 175th anniversary of Midleton Distillery was commemorated with 1000 bottles of a 20-year-old → pure pot still whiskey which had been finished in port pipes.

Mike Collins Whiskey cocktail. It is the Irish variety of the Collins.

Mild Japanese blend from → Nikka, one of their many brands which can only be obtained in Japan and whose label describes it as being 'Matured in Wood'.

Millars An Irish whiskey brand revived by the → Cooley Distillery.

Millars was founded in the 19th century in Dublin by a cousin of John Jameson who emigrated from Scotland, to trade in tea and whiskey. Cooley initially named his product 'Black Label', but finally rechristened it 'Special Reserve', because they needed → UD to distribute their products and did not want the possibility of confusion with the famous Johnnie Walker Scotch. It is still possible to find the older bottles. There is also a Millar's Gold which, like → Three Stills is only bottled at 30%, and is therefore not allowed to call itself whiskey but is defined as 'Specially Selected Spirits'.

Millburn Defunct Scottish malt distillery which lay on the eastern outskirts of Inverness, and belonged to the → Highlands whisky region. In 1985 its owners DCL closed the distillery, and part of the site was cleared, with some distillery buildings being converted into a bar and restaurant. At the time of the closure its licence was registered with the old company of → Macleay Duff, founded in 1863, which since 1943 had belonged to → DCL.

Millburn goes back to the year 1807 and was one of the first legal distilleries. In 1825 a new owner took charge, but what happened next is not clear. From 1853 until 1876 it was used as a flour mill. It was then rebuilt and was taken over in 1892 by two members of the → Haig whisky family. The commander of the Cameron Highlanders, who built their barracks close to the distillery and helped to prevent the entire stock of whisky from being destroyed during a great fire in 1922, was a member of this family. At the time it belonged to the gin company, Booth, who resold it to → DCL. Macleay Duff sold a vatted malt on which the name was written as two words, The Mill Burn. A single malt from the distillery was only available from → independent bottlers such as → Cadenhead and → Gordon & MacPhail. The latter included a 1971, 1972 and 1974 in their → 'Connoisseurs

Choice' series. → MacArthur sold a 12-year-old from 1983. → Signatory also had a Millburn from 1974 (58.7%) in their → 'Silent Stills' series. The first → proprietor's bottling was the → cask strength in the → 'Rare Malt' collection from UD, aged 18 years, distilled in 1975 and bottled at 58.9%.

Millwood Whiskey Cream Liqueur which, although it contains Irish whiskey, cannot be termed an Irish Cream Liqueur. It is the successor of → Meadow Cream, which also comes, via Halewood International, from → Groupe Pernod-Ricard. It only has a strength of 14.5% and is based on a mixture of Irish whiskey (from → Midleton) and Dutch cream. Millwood is also produced in the Netherlands by Koninklijke Cooymans B V in Tillburg.

Milner's Brown Label Scotch blend which was originally produced by W H Milner & Co. In 1957 it was acquired by Marston, Thompson & Evershed, who, although their shares were dealt in on the Stock Exchange, were one of the few larger breweries who had succeeded in remaining independent, despite being based in the old brewing town of Burton-upon-Trent. In 1999 they lost their independence: Marston was taken over by Wolverhampton & Dudley Breweries. Like all breweries they supply the pubs belonging to them, or with whom they are contractually bound, not only with beers, but also with other products. This nearly always includes a Scotch. In 1910 the brewery already had three blends, including a Special Old (Brown Label). Milner's whisky revived this tradition. It is now available in all the nearly 900 pubs between Yorkshire and Hampshire that are supplied with Marston's Ales (including the well-known Pedigree).

Milord's Scotch blend which its producers → Glenmorangie plc mainly made for the Venezuelan market and which then became very popular in Denmark. Nowadays it is no longer marketed very intensively.

Milroy's of Soho London licensed retail and wholsale business (correctly named The Soho Wine Market) established by the Milroy brothers, Jack and Wallace. The small shop and wine bar is still situated in the ground floor of a narrow house in Greek Street, between Shaftesbury Avenue and Soho Square. It was established in 1964 primarily as a wine shop and in the early 70s, the brothers bought the Ship Wine Co in Beak Street to help expand their increasing sales of malt whiskies. From this base they were able to offer a vast selection of bottlings to the public and hotel trade alike. Their enthusiasm for the product enabled their customers to gain a valuable understanding of the world of whisk(e)y before the big producers had really begun to exploit their portfolios of malt whiskies. The Ship Wine Co was sold in the early 80s and in 1993 John Scott of Ingleton Wines bought the Milroys out entirely. In April 2002, the business was acquired by the → La Réserve chain of wine shops owned by Mark Reynier and Simon Coughlin.

Jack Milroy continues in the trade as an → independent bottler and Wallace is a consultant and well-known whisky author whose book, *The Original Malt Whisky Almanac*, won him the 1987 Glenfiddich Whisky Writer of the Year Award. It has sold over 280,000 copies in seven editions in many languages since it was first published in 1986.

Miltonduff Scottish malt distillery whose name means 'black mill'. It lies to the south-west of → Elgin, and belongs to the → Speyside rather than to the → Highland region. Nearby are the ruins of Pluscarden Abbey, which makes it tempting to believe that the medieval monks not only brewed beer here, but also distilled → *uisge beatha*. It was founded by the partners Pearey and Bain in 1824, one year after the British government had attempted to overcome illicit distilling by granting licences under the provisions of the Excise Act. Later Miltonduff was owned by Thomas Yool, who sold his firm together with the distillery to Hiram → Walker – Gooderham & Worts in 1936, and they transferred the licence to → Ballantine & Co, which they had also acquired shortly before. In 1974/5 it was completely renovated a decade after two → Lomond stills had been installed. The malt made by these was called → Mosstowie.

The name Ballantine still appears on the bottles of the 12-year-old → proprietor's bottling.

Every now and then one hears, however, that it will be discontinued as part of a pruning of brands which has led the present owners → Allied Domecq PLC to give up a whole series of brands (→ Black Bottle) and distilleries. However it is possible that the lack of character which the single malt is said to suffer from is the cause of its uncertain future. This does not alter the fact that it is very popular with blenders. A 15-year-old belonged to the small series of six bottlings which Allied issued in the year 2000 with uniform labels; it was actually only intended for the company's employees, but a small number came onto the market. The → independent bottlers like to write the name as two words Milton Duff, and → Cadenhead has bottled a 1964, bottled in 1994 (50.9%) and a 1978/1992 (59.4%). → Signatory has a 1961 (bottled in1996) at 53.4%.

Minmore A rarely used name for the Scottish distillery better known as → Glenlivet. The name derives from the locality around the distillery.

Mint Julep Whiskey cocktail. It has always been claimed that this is the classic drink of the American south. In fact it is found there much less frequently than supposed. However a 'true gentleman' would drink one at the Kentucky Derby. It was well-known at the beginning of the 19th century and at that time was mainly a morning drink. There are numerous recipes, many of which have been passed down from generation to generation. They are all based on a mixture of bourbon, sugar and mint (which should be absolutely fresh). At Charles Schumann's bar in Munich it is made in the following way: two lumps of sugar are crumbled into a glass, the mint is added and the leaves are lightly crushed. Add crushed ice and 4cl of whiskey and garnish with mint leaf.

Mississippi Sound American whiskey liqueur imported by the Lobuschkellerei in Hamburg and sold in Germany. This company also imports the Candian malt whisky → Blackstone, which is only obtainable at ALDI, and then only at Christmas.

Misty River Whisky liqueur formerly made in → New Zealand by → Seagram, very probably using the whiskies from their distillery in Dunedin, which can produce both grain and malt whisky, and which is the source of the single malt → Lammerlaw as well as the blend → Wilson's.

Mitchell & Co, J & A Scottish whisky company that belongs to the seventh generation of a family that has run → Springbank Distillery legally since 1837. It is now run by Hedley Wright. He is an exception in the business in so far as he belongs to one of the two companies which are still owned by their founding families. They also own → Cadenhead, one of the large → independent bottlers. A further subsidiary is → Duthie. The → Eaglesome shop, which also carries various brands, is in Campbeltown, not far from the distillery. The individual whiskies are to be found under the names of these subsidiaries. They can all be bought at the Cadenhead shops in the Royal Mile in Edinburgh and in Covent Garden, London. In 2001 the company resurrected the → Glengyle Distillery in → Campbeltown with plans to commence distilling again.

Miyagikyo Japanese single malt from → Nikka, a company which, like its domestic competitor → Suntory, leaves much unsaid, rather speaking of → 'Pure Malt' and not saying where the whisky in the bottles actually comes from. In the case of two whiskies there is, however, nothing to explain: the → Yoichi and the Miyagikyo without doubt come from Nikka's second malt distillery, founded in 1969, which is sometimes just called → Sendai, and sometimes Sendai 'Miyagikyo' Distillery. The whisky, bottled at 43% is 12 years old.

Moffat Scottish distillery built by Inver House Distillers Ltd in Airdrie in 1965 and better known as → Garnheath. It was principally a grain distillery, but six → pot stills for the production of malt whisky were included though these were dismantled in the 1970s. Now only the → warehouses remain. The single malts → Glenflagler and → Killyloch came from Moffat.

Moghul Monarch Indian whisky, which the owners of the brand → Shaw Wallace proclaim to be the 'Finest Malt Whisky'. In → India this by no means denotes the same thing as in Scotland. On the subcontinent it is permitted to use so-called molasses whisky, a distillate of sugar syrup, something akin to rum. Shaw Wallace have a distillery in the state of Maharashtra to the south of Delhi, and on some bottles they are also given as the producers. There are, however, also bottles with the address of the Delta Distilleries in Bombay. Jim Murray reports that a completely immature malt is used for it from the → Rampur Distillery, which Shaw Wallace also names as the producer of its → Director's Special.

Mohan Meakin Indian company which arose in 1949 from the purchase by N N Mohan of the company Dyer, Meakin & Co, which was founded by a Scot and an Irishman. Since that time it has grown to become a veritable empire that comprises four distilleries and 11 breweries, employs 15,000 workers, carries 14 whisky brands and also produces food, has a branch in Africa, and in 1994 established the joint venture Macdonald Meakin with → Glenmorangie plc. The Scots have thereby created an excellent base for themselves on the subcontinent, as well as a functioning distribution network to market their malts → Glenmorangie and → Glen Moray and the blends → Highland Queen and → James Martin in India; the latter is in future to be sent in → bulk to India, where it will then be bottled. The company's distilleries are → Kasauli, where the malt → Solan No. 1 is made, Solan, which however has not yet produced anything, Lucknow, which has not been in operation for several years and → Mohan Nagar, where the brands → Black Knight, → Colonel's Special and → Summer Hall are made. The brands made for Africa include → Adam's Choice and → African Safari.

Mohan Nagar Indian distillery. It lies in a place of the same name. It quite simply means 'Mohan town', and is named after N N Mohan who in 1949 built up the empire of → Mohan Meakin by purchasing Dyer, Meakin & Co, and in 1962 established the town. It lies to the east of Delhi within another town, Ghazibad, and includes a large industrial area as well as

housing for more than 5,000 employees. In the utilitarian buildings food, beer and whisky are produced. The fermenting vessels of the brewery are shared to make the whisky and there is also a common maltings with no fewer than three mechanical → Saladin boxes, which use coal for drying. Additional malt is bought in. The distillery has stills made of stainless steel which are used to distil molasses whisky. Four → pot stills distil malt whisky and → continuous stills also produce → grain whisky. The principal difference to the normal production process has been imposed by Indian officials, for reasons that are known only to them, whereby casks are not allowed and great oak vats are prescribed, which slow down maturation. The whisky from Mohan Nagar is mainly used for the three brands → Black Knight, → Colonel's Special and → Summer Hall.

Moidart Scotch vatted malts from → Cadenhead. They are named after the area between Loch Shiel and the west coast of Scotland. The brand is available in various age categories, aged 10, 12, 15, 21, 25 and 30 years (all at 46%).

Molino del Arco Spanish distillery near Palazuelos de Eresma, close to the old town of Segovia, at the foot of the Sierra de Guadarama and on the River Eresma – surroundings similar to Scotland, particularly → Tamdhu Distillery. The distillery has been in operation since 1959 and, in fact operates according to the Scottish model. Just as at Tamdhu, a winding road leads down to it and to the river, from where the pagodas can be seen, and as at Tamdhu, the malt is dried in a → Saladin box. Both malt and → grain whiskies are produced, and after several years of maturation, the single grain is better than the single malt. Both of them are (however) not bottled but are intended for blending, mainly for → DYC, which is not only popular in Spain. The abbreviation stands for the company → Destilerias y Crianza del Whisky, which via Hiram → Walker is owned by → Allied Domecq PLC and runs the distillery. The → pot stills for the malt whisky look just like Scottish ones but were made in Madrid; there are seven of them, but not all of them are always in operation. The → grain whiskies are distilled from corn, and sometimes from rye as well, in a → patent still. The distillates age in ex-bourbon casks in warehouses with earth floors which are a few hundred metres away from the distillery.

Monarch, The Scotch blend that is made on behalf of the Edinburgh wine merchants → Lambert Brothers. The label does not show the portrait of a king but the majestic head of a stag, a reproduction of the famous painting 'The Monarch of the Glen' by Sir Edwin Landseer. The blend, which used to be particularly popular with the soldiers of Scottish regiments, is still available, although the shop run by the Lamberts in Edinburgh has had to close.

Moncreiffe Scotch blend from Moncrieffe plc in Glasgow, which is produced in several versions; as a → standard blend and as an 8-year-old, the 15-year-old is not being produced at present but is still obtainable. The full name of the brand is Sir Iain's Special Moncreiffe, and Charles H → Julian are responsible for its worldwide distribution. Moncreiffe established the brand in 1983 and ensured that it was mainly served in the London night clubs and bars that Sir Iain visited. His name was Moncreiffe of that Ilk, 11th Baronet and 23rd Laird of Moncreiffe in Perthshire. He was described as 'one of the most colourful Scots of his generation'. The company of Charles H Julian belongs to Ian Lockwood.

Montgomerie's → Independent bottlers run by the family-run → Angus Dundee. Their 'Single Cask Collection' first appreared in autumn 2000 and include two sherry-casked expressions of → Tamdhu (1970) and 30-years-old, and a 1977 → Braes of Glenlivet finished in a madeira cask.

Monster's Choice Scotch blend from Strathnairn Whisky, a subsidiary of → Gordon & MacPhail.

Montrose Whisky Company English whisky company established in London in 1973. It mainly exports to countries in South East Asia and South America. The four brands → Glen Kindie, → Great Mac, → Old Montrose (also available as a vatted malt) and → Pipe Major are included in their range.

Moorland Scotch blend that used to come from the London wine merchants Grierson, who also sold → Grierson's No 1. The brand now belongs to the UK wine producing and wholesale group of Matthew Clark, which were bought by → Canandaigua at the end of 1998.

Morning Glory Whisky cocktail. A version of fizz based on Scotch. Take 4cl Scotch with 3 spoonfuls of lemon juice, one egg white, 2cl sugar syrup, a spoonful of caster sugar and a splash of Pernod. Shake well with ice, strain off and serve in a highball glass with a lot of soda.

Morrison Bowmore Distillers Ltd Scottish whisky company that developed from the firm of Stanley P Morrison Ltd when the successful whisky dealer and broker of the same name acquired the → Bowmore Distillery on → Islay in 1963. At this time the company also owned several other subsidiaries such as the Scottish Trading Co, which in turn owned the brand → Rob Roy and T & A → McClelland, whose name is still used today for malt whiskies such as McClelland Highland, which are not marketed under the distillery's name. In 1970 Morrison acquired → Glen Garioch, followed in 1984 by → Auchentoshan. In 1987 the company was renamed Morrison Bowmore Distillers Ltd. In 1994 → Suntory, which had had a 35% share in it, became the sole proprietors. Since 1997 the firm has been operating all three distilleries, and is very imaginative in marketing its single malts, which are regularly available in various versions and as special limited editions. The company was named Distiller of the Year in 1995 and 2000. Their range also includes the blends → Burn's Heritage, → Clan Roy, → Gamekeeper, → Hallmark, → Islay Legend, → King's Pride, → Premier, Rob Roy and → Sword's. For the market in the Far East, which is especially important to them, they have created several brands of very old blends in elaborate and luxurious ceramic decanters (→ Grand Castle, → Grand Old Highland, → Highland Mountain). Under the name of their subsidiary McClelland they have three single malts in their range, an → Islay, a → Lowland and a → Highland, which are without age statements. After three editions of Black Bowmore they have brought out a very attractively designed special edition of the Bowmore 40 years old, one of the most expensive whiskies in the world: anyone wishing to purchase it in the UK will pay at least £4,000.

Morrison Fairlie A recently-launched → independent bottling company established by Peter → Fairlie. He is the son of the man who revived the → Glenturret Distillery, and worked tirelessly to create much of Glenturret's success. After → Highland Distillers' hostile takeover of → Macallan he was appointed manager there until he set up on his own. His new business is at Woodend House in Craigmill, near Stirling and apart from whisky it also sells gin and vodka with the names Scotgin and Scotvod Silver. The company's new blend is named → Scotdram. Bottlings of single malts from various Scottish regions are labelled → Scotmalt. The first were a Bruichladdich and two Macallans (from 1988 at a cask strength of 55.1% and 1990 at 40%). A Scotdram Millennium Malt came from an unnamed Islay distillery.

Mortlach Scottish malt distillery. It belongs to the → Speyside region and lies on the outskirts of → Dufftown, the region's whisky capital which, depending on whether one counts those that have been shut down, has seven, eight, nine or even 10 distilleries. Mortlach was founded in 1832, or possibly 1824. Considering its age, it has had relatively few changes in ownership: it belonged for a short period to J & J Grant (not the William → Grant of → Glenfiddich but he learned his trade there and was certainly their most important apprentice). In 1854 it was acquired by George → Cowie, and this name is still on the office door, although the company was acquired by John Walker & Son in 1923, at became a subsidiary of → DCL, two years later, thereby first belonging to → UD and now to → GuinnessUDV. Mortlach even has two → kilns which are no longer used, but still look very traditional. One should not however be misled by the external appearance. Following extensive renovation Mortlach has become a distillery which can operate almost entirely automatically and only requires one worker per shift. Not far from here is the famous Mortlach Church, one of the oldest in Scotland, dating back to AD566.

In 1010 the Scottish King Malcolm II defeated the Danes here, which is why the name Mortlach is sometimes translated as 'massacre of the wild geese', comparing the Danes to birds. Others are content with 'dish-shaped valley', but 'great green hill' is also in circulation. The malt whisky from Mortlach has always been very popular, especially with blenders, to such an extent that its owners never thought of bringing out a single malt as a → proprietor's bottling. They nevertheless allow → Gordon & MacPhail from nearby Elgin to offer it from time to time, aged 12, 15, 21 and 25 years, and as vintage bottlings which are sometimes very old, going back to 1936. → UD then finally included the Mortlach in the → 'Flora & Fauna' series which, aged 16 years, was perhaps a little too old, but then brought out a 10-year-old on whose label George Cowie & Sons appeared again as producers. It was also to be found several times in the → Rare Malts' series (22 years 65.3%, 23 years 59.4% and 20 years 62.2%). Gordon & MacPhail, who brought out a → 'Centenary Reserve' for their 100th anniversary, have a version with a different label aged 15 and 21 years and 100 decanters of 60-year-old, released in 2001. Of the other → independent bottlers → Adelphi , → Cadenhead and → Signatory have also had it. The → Wine Society has sensational bottlings from casks which had previously contained Oloroso sherry.

Mosstowie Scotch malt whisky which was produced by two → Lomond stills, at → Miltonduff Distillery. Hiram → Walker installed these in order to repeat an experiment which they had already carried out at their large complex in → Dumbarton, and also at → Glenburgie. In 1964 they added the two new stills to the existing traditional → pot stills. After a renovation of the distillery in 1974/5, the → Lomond stills were dismantled in 1981. The malt had never been bottled by the → proprietors → Allied Domecq PLC. For the time being it is still available in the → 'Connoisseurs Choice' series from → Gordon & MacPhail. They bottled one from 1970 and then a 1975 and a 1979. → Signatory also brought out a Mosstowie in their 'Silent Stills' series; it was from 1976 at 54.8%.

Mount Royal Light Canadian whisky that would not be allowed this name in other countries because it has an alcoholic strength of less than 40%. Its label states that it is only 30% and also has 30% less calories. It is thus one of the new 'light' whiskies which is intended to satisfy the younger consumer's taste for lighter spirits.

Mountain Dew A synonym for whisk(e)y which appeals to the expatriate Scots, Irish, musicians, bards and poets. There was also a very famous blend named Real Mountain Dew from W & S → Strong, and its label showed a certificate from Doctor Ivison McAdam of Edinburgh confirming that it was an 'old and well-matured spirit, free from impurity, and possessing a fine aroma and taste. A clear and well-blended whisky of the best class'. At the end of the 19th century there was a Mountain Dew from Robertson Sanderson, who proudly called it 'the oldest Whisky-brand in Scotland'. Donald McGregor & Co, a subsidiary of William → Whiteley, also had a blend of this name. Nowadays there is the → J & M & Co. Superior Mountain Dew from Malpass Stallard in Worcester.

Mouthfeel Term for the way a whisk(e)y reacts with the palate and the impression it leaves on it.

In a tasting the mouthfeel is the third criteria used to determine the characteristics of a whisk(e)y after the appearance and aroma. The mouthfeel reveals something about the body, which may be light, medium or full, and about the intensity and texture. The impressions may be described as mouth-warming or mouth-coating. Whiskies/whiskeys can be creamy, soft, smooth, oily, burning, astringent or dry.

Muirhead's Scotch blend which is a reminder of the old company of Charles Muirhead & Son, founded in 1824, who launched it onto the market in the 1920s. It was taken over by → Macdonald & Muir and is now one of the many (but nevertheless widely available) brands of the group, which was rechristened → Glenmorangie plc in 1996.

Mulligan Irish whiskey liqueur from → IDG produced for W & E Mulligan & Co, Dublin. It is not a cream liqueur, but a mixture of whiskey and other products which are not specified, including an ingredient with a bitter orange taste. It can most easily be compared with → Irish Mist, with which it shares the strength of 35%.

Murdoch's Perfection Scotch blend that nowadays comes from the → Speyside Distillery Co, belonging to the Christie family who have also developed and run the distillery of the same name near Kingussie. The Christies have been in the whisky business for a long time and had, amongst other things, a share in → Campbell & Clark (who are associated with the American firm → Sazerac) and produced this blend mainly for export. It is available in several → standard blend versions, without an age statement, aged 5 and 8 years and 12, 15, 17 and 20 years as a → de luxe blend.

Murphy's Irish whiskey which is especially popular in the USA where it is used for → Irish Coffee. It originally came from → Cork, where a beer of the same name is produced, and later from → Midleton. Whereas → Dunphy's, which is of a similar concept and lightness, is available again after a break of several years, no relaunch plans are known for Murphy's.

Murrayfield, The Scotch blend which is named after the famous rugby Edinburgh stadium, home of the Scottish Rugby Union. A picture of a game is shown on the label of the 10 and 12-year-old blend from The → Bennachie Whisky Co.

Murree Pakistani distillery in Rawalpindi which is on the site of the Murree Brewery. Their owners, the Murree Brewery Company, founded their brewery in 1861, in the foothills of the Himalayas near Ghora Gali, and was mainly intended to provide the British soldiers with beer. The plant was built in terrace fashion, and the old buildings are shown covered in snow on the bottles of the 8-year-old Murree's Malt Whisky Classic. In 1947 fire almost completely destroyed them, and production was switched to a distillery built in 1899 next to the Rawalpindi Brewery, erected some 10 years earlier. The newer distillery took the name of the older one.

It has both → floor maltings and a → Saladin

box, which is probably unique in the world of whisky but has to import extra malt from the UK. The practically smoke-free malt is processed in one of 26 fermenting vessels, which are also used for brewing beer. Four → wash stills of stainless steel (they are outside) are used for distilling, as well as two copper → spirit stills. The biggest difference to Scottish methods is in the storage, which is not in → warehouses but in deep cellars which, due to the high summer temperatures, are also air-conditioned. Maturing takes place only partly in casks, the majority of the distillate ages in very large vats. Production methods give real malt whiskies but they hardly get the chance to develop body and are relatively light. There used to be a 12-year-old Murree's, but this is no longer bottled. Apart from the Classic already mentioned, there is the Special Reserve Malt Whisky which is 3 years old and 'oak matured'. Islamic Pakistanis are, of course, neither allowed to buy or drink it, and it is reserved for the religious minorities of → Pakistan.

Museum Blend Canadian whisky which was sold exclusively in the museum that → Seagram set up in the → Waterloo Distillery. In this building the story of the company began in 1857. The distillery was closed down, like all the other distilleries built or bought by the company, when production was transferred to → Gimli. All that remains are three warehouses, one of which houses the museum. The blend is a rarity as it only contains whiskies which were distilled, matured and blended in this distillery – and these are few.

N

Na-Geanna Irish pure malt whose name is printed on the black label and on the black packaging in much smaller letters than another famous one, which is usually seen on another kind of spirit: Hennessy. The world-famous French Cognac company has recently drawn attention to itself with several products which are quite obviously oriented to the activities of the successful Scottish and Irish whisk(e)y marketers, such as the 'Single Distillery Cognacs' and, above all, the 'Hennessy Pure White'. Of course the aim was to win back consumers as, particularly in its native country, Cognac has by far been outstripped in popularity by whisk(e)y. It was therefore only consistent to bring out a whiskey under its own noble name. However the company lacked the courage to market it in France or elsewhere in Europe; the back label in Japanese shows that it is intended for the Japanese market where the name Hennessy enjoys a high status. The whiskey, which despite being called → pure is clearly a single malt and comes from → Cooley. This choice has a certain logic as the ancestors of the present Hennessys came from Ireland and the company indeed wishes to celebrate its own history with this whiskey. The young Richard Hennessy was one of the many Irish known as 'wild geese' who had to leave their homeland to seek their fortune elsewhere. He served under Louis XVI before settling in the Charante and founding the House of Hennessy.

Natu Nobilis Whisky formerly produced in → Brazil by → Seagram, using malt whiskies imported from Scotland and local → grain whiskies. The brand is available in two versions: a simple one and a better one named Natu Nobilis Celebrity.

New Cask Term used in Scotland not, as might be supposed, for casks which are brand new, but for a cask which has previously contained, for example, sherry or bourbon, and which is being used for the first time for malt whisky, which is therefore, strictly speaking, a → first fill. Completely new casks made of European oak are only used extremely rarely, because fresh oak would give off undesirable, overbearing aromas. Normally second-hand casks are used. If fresh casks are actually used, it is only for a short period, and only for part of the whisky which is then 'married' with malts from other casks before being bottled. David Stewart, → master blender at William → Grant & Sons, used several such new casks for his → Glenfiddich Solera Reserve.

New Century Scotch single malt. The UK company of → Unwins succeeded in launching it as the first whisky for the new century. The company in southern England already had it on the market at Christmas 1998, a year before the big event, and therefore much earlier than all their competitors. To their credit they chose an impressive malt whisky, a 25-year-old → Tamnavulin (45%). It comes from → Invergordon Distillers, the owners of the distillery which has unfortunately closed down.

New make, new spirit Term for the freshly-distilled spirit that one would much rather call whisk(e)y. However this is not permitted by the law which prescribes that the spirit must have first matured in casks for a certain number of years. In Scotland and Ireland this period is three years. In the USA, where they mostly use the expresssion → white dog, they are not quite so fussy. There much younger whiskey may be sold, but its age must be indicated as, for example, in the case of → Georgia Moon, which is just a few days old. On the other hand, a bourbon without an age statement must be at least four years old.

New Zealand The only distillery is on the South

Island, the more Scottish of New Zealand's two islands. Almost everyone on the South Island who is not of Maori descent is a descendant of a Scottish immigrant. Dunedin is most Scottish of all; even the name of the town is from the Gaelic for Edinburgh (Dun Eideann). There is a distillery that has only been in existence since 1968, and there was only ever one other attempt to set up a distillery: in 1848 C R Howden and R M Robertson opened the New Zealand Distillery, but they only survived (as did a small competitor) until 1875, when they had to give up as a result of high taxation. For almost a hundred years, apart from imported Scotch, there were only illicit distillates. There was also a Clavisbrook which called itself a 'Matured Blend of Finest No. 2 Whiskies', but gave no indication of its producer.

It was the Wilson family who brought whisky production back to New Zealand. They first successfully set up the Wenn Park Brewery, and were even more successful with the production of a malt extract called 'Maltexo', before opening a distillery on the site of the former Willowbank Brewery. They waited for four years for a licence and began production in 1968. In New Zealand they had everything they needed for production: barley, water and peat. The only thing that was missing was the technical knowledge and they built their → stills of refined steel, which noticeably impaired the taste of the first distillates. They distilled both malt and → grain whiskies. The first product from Dunedin, the light blend South 45, was not particularly successful and nobody would have prophesied a great future for the → Wilson Distillers had the Canadian company → Seagram not stepped in, in 1981. They bought the business and replaced at least some of the stills with copper ones, and ensured that the blend Wilson's became so successful that it is now even said to be the number one brand in New Zealand. In 1991 they also brought out a single malt → Lammerlaw. Over the years it has changed and has become more peaty, which is probably due to the fact that the malt comes from Australia. It has, in any case, its fans. Because of surplus stocks resulting from a contract with South Korea that was cancelled, the distillery has been closed since 1995.

News Japanese blend from → Kirin-Seagram that tastes more like a bourbon. At 40% it is much lighter than other blends from the Japanese-Canadian joint venture, and the label suggests that the whisky is marketed to attract young people to whisky. Indeed, not only are the words 'Light & Smooth' to be found on this black and white label, but also 'Design – Taste – Life'. The large '1000' is supplemented with 'One litre per month'.

Nichols American blended whisky from → Austin, Texas. Nichols uses a large proportion of the Kentucky straight bourbon that this company is famous for, and which they make in their distillery of the same name, → Wild Turkey. It used to be called D L Moore and belonged to the Ripy brothers, but now mostly trades as the → Boulevard Distillery.

Nikka Japanese drinks giant founded in 1934 by the 40-year-old Masataka → Taketsuru. He went to Glasgow as a student in 1918, interested in beer brewing. Whisky distilling fascinated him even more, and he pursued his interest at → Hazelburn, → Craigellachie and → Lagavulin. He returned to Japan with his Scottish wife. His knowledge came just in time as the other pioneer of Japanese whisky, Shinjiro → Torii, who employed him as production manager in his → Yamazaki Distillery.

The two of them worked together for 10 years and in 1929 launched the first Japanese whisky. In 1934 they parted and Taketsuru set up on his own with a tiny → pot still. He chose the little town of → Yoichi for his distillery, on Japan's northern island of → Hokkaido, where he found conditions that reminded him of Scotland, as well as all the necessary ingredients; good water, cold winter weather, peat and locally-grown barley. During the time that his whisky was maturing he produced juices, including an apple juice named 'Kaju', which became the name of his company – Nippon Kaju – which in 1952 was shortened to 'Nikka'. In 1940 he was able to market his first whisky (as well as a brandy), but the war made further production impossible and Taketsuru was forced to make alchohol for war purposes. Afterwards things began to look up, and whilst → Suntory, the company of his former boss

Nikky

Torii, became the largest whisky producers in Japan, Nikka also prospered and is now in second place with a production share of 16% and a market share of 15%. Its wide span of activities includes wines and fruit spirits, as well as whisky production. The company is no longer independent and now belongs to Asahi, one of Japan's four large breweries.

Nikka also produces → grain whiskies, and at → Nishinomiya they even use a → Coffey still, which Taketsuru imported from Scotland for this purpose in 1962. In 1969 he built a second, much larger distillery, → Sendai, in the prefecture of → Miyagikyo. Both distilleries are able to make whiskies of differing characters so that Nikka has sufficient opportunity to produce numerous brands. In 1978, a year before the death of the company founder, a large technological centre was opened. Nikka is the importer of → J & B and → Jim Beam (there is a Jim Beam Barrel Bonded made exclusively for Nikka). In 1989 they expanded their whisky empire by purchasing the Scottish → Ben Nevis Distillery (in the same year they also bought the Dompierre distillery in Cognac). There is a second Coffey still distillery in Tochgi, where their blends are also matured in casks for a second time before being bottled in two large bottling plants.

Their bestselling blend is → Tsuru, named after the founder, who also created the → Super in memory of his Scottish wife Rita who died in 1961. Their house brand is The Nikka Whisky, which is available aged 17, 21 and 25 years and as → Choice, → Extra and → Prize. Other blends include: → Black Memorial, → Black Nikka, The → Blend of Nikka, → Connexion, → Fortune 80, → From the Barrel, → G & G, → Gold & Gold, → Grand Age, → Hi, → Kingsland, → Mild, → Super Session. → Corn Base is a kind of bourbon, whilst → Rye Base is something like a Canadian whiskey. There is a → new spirit (a fresh distillate) called → Nikky and a low alcohol Nikky Soft. The → Coffey Grain is unusual, as well as the → All Malt, with a second version called → Malt Club. A Black, a Red and a White are called 'Pure Malt', Nikka Pure Malt is a whisky from a sherry cask, and → Hokkaido and → Kitagenshu are also pure malts, whilst the → Miyaikyo → Sendai and the → Yoichi are clearly single malts.

Nikky Japanese spirit from → Nikka which is available in three versions: two are called Gold and White, which refer to the colour of the label, not the liquid. Nikky is a → new spirit, a fresh distillate which is too young to be called whisky. If it was absolutely fresh, and had not yet come into contact with the wood of a cask, it would normally be crystal clear. However, it might have some caramel added to it. Another honey-coloured Nikky is called Soft and is marketed at only 25%.

Nineteen-Hole-Cocktail Whisky cocktail for golfers. One third Scotch, one third Fino Sherry and one third Vermouth Dry are stirred with ice and served in a cocktail glass.

Nishinomiya Japanese grain distillery near the place of the same name in the Osaka area. It belongs to → Nikka. The → grain whiskies from it are added to a malt which together make Nikka's → All Malt, as well as the → Coffey Grain.

No Age Scotch vatted malt that is bottled in Italy. It was created by Silvano S → Samaroli, a pioneer of malt whisky who committed himself to the rediscovery of single malts and, by means of a large number of bottlings, ensured that his homeland for a long time remained the best address in Europe for all friends of the original Scotch whisky. The No Age was 'born' in 1992. It comes in bottles that are reminiscent of those of the 19th century, and single malts they contain are between 10 and 40 years old and each limited edition is carefully composed anew. It is an unusual fact that Samaroli allows them a year's time to 'marry' before filling them into numbered bottles.

Noah's Mill Kentucky straight bourbon from the → small batch series comprising four brands, from → Kentucky Bourbon Distillers. They belong to the Willett family, who also own the → Willett Distillery near Bardstown. At present they are preparing to reopen the distillery which has been closed since the 1980s. Although a Noah's Mill Distilling Co are named as producers, the whiskey is bottled from the stocks of this distillery. It is 15 years old, at 114.3°/57.15% and is really 'Handmade in the Hills of Kentucky', as the label decorated with a drawing of a little wooden mill claims.

North British Scottish grain distillery which was founded in Edinburgh in 1886 by several well-known men who wanted to maintain their independence from → DCL, which at that time was becoming increasingly strong and dominated the rest of the industry. Apart from Andrew → Usher, one of the pioneers of blending who is still known for his → Green Stripe, the members of the consortium included John → Crabbie & Co, William Sanderson & Son, James → Watson & Co and George Robertson from → Robertson & Baxter. The rather un-Scottish name comes from the North British Railway next to it and which played a significant part in the choice of location. The distillery is huge and can produce and store tremendous amounts. For a long time the old office buildings in Slateford Road served as headquarters for the independent → Pentland Institute, which carries out research into various matters concerning whisky and chemistry, and they are an example of the charm of many of the North British buildings. Although the North British were really a kind of co-operative (which DCL also later had a share in), it was able to maintain their independence. Since 1933 they have belonged to Lothian Distillers, a joint venture of → IDV (for their J & B they use a high proportion of → grain whiskies from North Port) and Robertson & Baxter, (one of the founding members) The current owners, with equal shares, are → Diageo and the → Edrington Group. North British's proprietors rarely bottled the whisky, and used an unusual composition of 20% malted barley and 80% maize, as a single grain. One bottling of just 64 bottles of a 1964 vintage celebrated the 'Forth Road Bridge Joint Board for the Period 1975 – 1996'. However → Signatory have had two casks, one from 1964, bottled in 1990 at a cask strength of 46%, and a sherry cask from 1979, bottled in 1995 at 43%. The American → independents → Whyte & Whyte also had a cask from 1964.

North of Scotland Distilling Co Scottish whisky company in which the Christie family, who later founded the → Speyside Distillery, had a share. In 1957 the company converted a former brewery in Cambus into the Strathmore Distillery, which undertook the unusual experiment of producing malt whisky with → patent stills. This didn't turn out to be very successful and so they continued with the production of → grain whisky, before giving up completely in the early 1980s. There is only one bottling of the whisky known: a single grain from 1963 which was included in the → 'Scott's Selection'.

North Port (Brechin) Scottish malt distillery which was closed down and subsequently demolished in 1983 to make way for a supermarket development. It lies in the little town of Brechin, which is mainly known for its Round Tower (and for a second distillery → Glenacadam which, unfortunately, is also no longer in operation), and it belongs to the → whisky region of the eastern → Highlands. It has been included in this book because its whisky is still bottled every now and then. It was founded in 1820 by a local family and was originally called Townhead. It was renamed Brechin three years later; but when exactly is not known. It was taken over in the 1920s by → DCL and closed down from 1928 to 1937, later passing to the DCL subsidiary Mitchell Bros from Glasgow, who never brought out the whisky as a single malt but sold a vatted, → Glen Dew. The distillery, had two → stills and got its water from Loch Lee. UD unexpectedly included a North Port as a single malt → proprietor's bottling in their → 'Rare Malts' series. They were vintages 1971 (54.7%) and 1979 (61.2%). It had previously only been available from the → independents like → Cadenhead and → Gordon & MacPhail, who had several vintages, such as a 1974 and a 1981.

Northern Light Canadian whisky whose label clearly shows it to be a product of Hiram → Walker, but which is sold exclusively on the American market by → Barton. In this case the 'light' has nothing to do with the fashionable trend for light spirits at 30% which in Canada are allowed to call themselves whisky. It is a solid 40%.

Northern Scot Scotch blend from Bruce & Co in Leith, who were a subsidiary of → Waverley Vintners and produced the brand in two versions: as a → standard blend without an age

Northern Scott

statement and as a 12-year-old. The simple version can still occasionally be found.

Northern Scott Scotch blend from → Invergordon who took over the brand, which was originally produced by Bruce & Co, from → Waverley Vintners, a subsidiary of Scottish Courage.

Nosing Term for a special approach to whisk(e)y. In this process it is not drunk, but the enjoyment is derived solely from the nose, by smelling it. For many lovers of good bourbons and above all single malts, nosing is an important element in tasting and drinking, as they appreciate the wealth and elegance of the aromas. Nosing is particularly important for the industry's experts. Their noses are trained to judge a whisk(e)y entirely by the impression it makes when smelling it. Although there is now equipment to analyse aroma, there is no substitute for the refinement of a talented and trained human nose. The → master blenders in particular depend on their noses. They use a special glass for their work which is high and tulip-shaped, being narrower at the top so that the fragrance is concentrated in the nostrils. The glass is marked so that exactly determined amounts of water can be added. It is important that a glass lid prevents the aromas escaping too quickly. Dark blue or black glasses are also often used so that the noser is not distracted by the colour of a whisk(e)y.

O

Oak The wood of this tree plays a vital part in the making of whisk(e)y, as the laws in the most important whisk(e)y countries insist that the casks used for maturing must be made exclusively of oak. In the USA all the straight whiskeys, that is Kentucky straight bourbon, rye or Tennessee Whisk(e)y, may only be matured in new, unused casks made of American white oak (quercus alba), which have been charred inside before use, and may not be reused. In Ireland and Scotland the oak doesn't have to be new. So these two countries are both grateful recipients of the casks that the Americans are not able to use. These ex-bourbon casks represent the majority share of the casks used in these two countries. However, they also use casks made of European oak (quercus robur), which mostly come from Spain and have previously contained sherry. In recent years, since → finishings have become very popular, more casks from European countries have been used, for example from Poland or France. Oak from Eastern Europe has also been tried out. Oak is ideal for whisk(e)y because it contains substances which have a positive influence on the fresh distillate and contribute a great deal to its range of aromas, such as hemi-cellulose or tannin. Oak also makes whisk(e)y softer and more complex.

Oak Cask Matured Scotch blend made exclusively for the UK supermarket chain → ASDA. It is sold with the information that 10 different malt whiskies and four → grain whiskies were used for it and that they had matured in three different kinds of oak → cask.

Oaken Glow Whisky formerly from → Seagram that is solely made for and sold in → India, using malt whiskies imported from Scotland blended with locally produced → grain whiskies.

Oban Scottish malt distillery, one of the few in the western → Highlands and one of even fewer to lie in the middle of a town. The driving force behind the distillery was the Stevenson family who established it in 1794. Oban is therefore one of the oldest distilleries in the country, although it has been shut down occasionally; at the beginning of the 19th century, in the 1930s and again from 1969 to 1972. It is also one of the smallest distilleries; there has been no addition to its two → stills. The location is unusual, the water comes from Loch Gleann à Bhearraidh some distance away, there is not enough room in its own → warehouses for all that it produces and the distillery and the old stone buildings of the distillery are squeezed up between the main road going around the harbour and steep cliffs.

Oban was taken over in 1923 by → Dewar & Sons and a short time after incoroprated into the → DCL empire, who transferred its licence to its subsidiary John → Hopkins & Co.

They brought out a 12-year-old single malt in a kind of perfume bottle as a → proprietor's bottling. They still hold the licence but have now become a subsidiary of → UDV, which included the Oban aged 14 years in their → 'Classic Malts of Scotland' series. The extra two years suit this round, intensive whisky, whose closeness to the Islands is just as distinct as its distance from them. In December 1997, a limited edition of a malt from 1980 was added alongside it in the new series → The Distillers Edition', which had been finished in a Montillo Fino sherry cask. Oban is occasionally available from the independent bottlers, but not very often, possibly because the proprietor's bottling is so popular and the malt is also used for many of UDV's blends.

O'Brien's Irish whiskey from the → Cooley Distillery, another → standard blend at 40%, which the company calls a 'Special Reserve' and which is sold by the wine and spirits chain P J O'Brien & Sons.

Ocean Japanese blends from → Sanraku-Ocean, a company which brought out a sake called 'Sanraku' in 1937, are also active as wine producers, and since the 1960s have made whisky at a malt distillery in → Karuizawa and a grain distillery in Kawasaki. The top Ocean Whisky blend is the → Asama, others are called → Route and → Status. Ocean has a smaller malt share; and is also known as 'Special Old'. There is also a 'Special Grade' in a carafe in the shape of a ship. The malt Karuizawa also bears the description Ocean Whisky on its porcelain label.

O'Connell's This won a gold medal at the International Wine and Spirit Competition in 1996, but there were only a few bottles of it. The success of this blend of malt, → pot still and → grain whiskeys came early and surprised its producers in the middle of marketing preparations.

O'Darby Irish cream liqueur (17% vol.). J J O'Darby are named as producers on the label. It actually comes from → Gilbey, the inventors of → Bailey's, and belonged to the portfolio of → IDV/→ Grand Metropolitan, and thus nowadays to → UDV.

O'Hara Irish whiskey. It is produced by the → Cooley Distillery, but distributed under the name of their brand → Millar Products, and mainly sold in the French supermarket chain Intermarché. The label of the blend (40%) not only describes it as having a 'Celtic Flavour', but also as 'The Greatest Flavour in Ireland'.

Oddbins UK chainstore which has expanded rapidly and whose branches are to be found in much of the UK. They have contributed much to popularising wine culture in the UK as they have been able to overcome the barriers that often exist in the more renowned stores: they are friendly and young, with competent service, they offer a fair deal for your money and the long opening hours are extremely customer-friendly. They have white wines, champagnes and beers in their range, also available chilled. The price lists, which are cheeky and lively, used to be designed by the caricaturist Ralph Steadman, and have become collectors' items. Oddbins has always distinguished itself by discovering new wines from the New World. There are also several branches with fine wines, offering very noble wines at reasonable prices. The London-based company got a bargain when they bought the branch of → Victoria Wine Cellars in Calais, France, in 1999, where UK customers make use of the considerably lower alcohol tax to shop cheaply.

Lovers of malt whisky will find a large selection, with whiskies which can only be obtained at Oddbins. They also undertake interesting experiments, including whiskies from unusual casks such as port or Madeira, which in contrast to the → finishings from, for example Glenmorangie, have spent the whole of their 15 years in the cask. A series of their own bottlings is always in their range, with a single malt from each of the five regions → Lowland, → Highland, → Speyside, → Islands and → Islay, whose distilleries remain unnamed.

Official bottling Used to describe single malts that are marketed by the proprietor of the distillerues, rather than independent bottlers.

Okanagan Canadian distillery in Winfield near Kelowna, British Columbia. It was built in 1971 by Hiram → Walker when the demand for → Canadian Club could no longer be met by production at → Walkerville. Some claim to be able to taste the difference between Okanagan Canadian and the 'normal' one – if they are able to get hold of an old bottle in Vancouver. The distillery had four → pot stills, which are very similar to those of → Inverleven in → Dumbarton, and in the 1980s even produced malt whisky. Their → Glen Ogopolo was sold in Japan. The distillery was closed in 1995 and put up for sale.

Old Japanese → Special Blend from → Suntory, which came onto the market in 1950 and remained a bestseller for many years. It still occupies third position among domestic whiskies. On the stocky, dark 0.75 litre bottles it is called Suntory Old Whisky, whilst on the new half-bottles the Old is in bigger type.

Old Angus Scotch blend, which along with → Robbie Burns and → Windsor Castle, is one of the three brands of the small R H → Thomson &

Co from Edinburgh. It belonged to → DCL and on their behalf held the licence of the → Teaninich Distillery, whose malt most certainly is used for this blend. Nowadays it comes from → UDV.

Old Argyll Scotch blend from → Burn Stewart. It is a → de luxe 12-year-old.

Old Bardstown Kentucky straight bourbon which is bottled by the → Kentucky Bourbon Distillers. It is from → Willett Distillery near Bardstown, which had this rather well-known brand in its range for a long time. The label speaks of it being made by the 'Fifth Generation of Distillers', although the distillery has been closed since the 1980s. Whilst stocks still remain, these bourbons aged 6 or 10 years are too young to have come from there. It is more likely that they have been bought from → Heaven Hill, which is also in Bardstown. The 6-year-old is 80°/40% and the 10-year-old with its 101°/50.5% is a → Bottled in Bond. The 15-year-old (also 101°/50.5%) could indeed come from the old Willett stocks.

Old Barrel Indian whisky, a blend from → Haryana Distillery, the subsidiary of Modi Enterprises. The label does not state the malt content, but describes the whisky as a → 'premium'. There is also a → 'standard' version.

Old Blacksmith American straight bourbon with 80°/40%. There is no information about which distillery it comes from. The label states that it is 'Distilled and Shipped for Willow Springs Distilling', a company based in San Francisco.

Old Bridge Scotch blend from a recently-formed company → London & Scottish Spirits, which is based in Bremley in Surrey. The blend is available as a → standard blend and as a 12-year-old.

Old Bushmills Distillery, The Irish malt distillery. It lies not far from the coast in County Antrim in Northern Ireland and has borne this name since 1896, but, like its whiskies, is often simply called → Bushmills. Its current owners, the Irish Distillers Group (→ IDG), proudly call it 'the oldest licensed distillery in the world' and quote 1608 as the year of foundation. They base this claim on the fact that the English King James I, through his Irish governor (one Thomas Phillipps), issued a licence allowing the production of whiskey. Historical research has shown that the licence did not refer to a particular distillery, but to a large area of County Antrim, to which Bushmills also belongs. Whilst Bushmills is not named → Coleraine, is mentioned, and this was indeed the site of a distillery which had long been in competition with Bushmills. Now a blend of this name is produced nowadays by Bushmills.

In the 19th century the date of Bushmills' foundation was quoted as 1784 on the bottles of the famous Old Glynn Bush. This date makes Bushmills the oldest distillery in Ireland still in operation. Its history is difficult to reconstruct: all the documents were twice destroyed on two occasions by fires: in 1885 the distillery itself went up in flames and in 1941 the administration building and the bottling plant in Belfast were destroyed. After the fire the distillery was rebuilt in the form seen by the visitor today. It is smaller than other Irish distilleries have been, and looks more like a Scottish plant.

Only since the rebuilding have they produced malt whiskey. Since the closure of Coleraine, Bushmills has been the only distillery in Northern Ireland. Following frequent changes in ownership (it belonged, amongst others, to → Seagram and the beer brewer Charrington), it came into the ownership of IDG. However, it is due to the new owners → Groupe Pernod-Ricard. The French owners are looking after Bushmills that the malt from Bushmills isbecoming more and more popular outside Ireland. They have also considerably expanded the range of brands available bearing the name → Bushmills.

Old Canada Canadian whisky (40%) which now comes from → Corby, belonging to the empire of Hiram → Walker/→ Allied Domecq PLC. Its full name is → Mc Guinness Old Canada, the company that the brand once came from.

Old Carnoustie Scotch blend, named after a famous golf course, from → Glenmorangie plc.

Old Charter

Old Charter Kentucky straight bourbon that has been around since 1874. It was the creation of the brothers Adam and Ben Chapeze, children of French and English immigrants who had founded their own distillery seven years previously. They named the brand after the Charter Oak in Connecticut, which is still illustrated on the labels of the brand. In 1900 a → Bottled in Bond called Old Charter Bourbon was brought out, but by a new proprietor. During → prohibition all the stocks of this whiskey were stored at the → Bernheim Distillery in Louisville, whose owners bought both the stocks and the rights to the brand at the end of the dry years and still make the whiskey (since 1992, however, in the new distillery and under the management of → UD). They had belonged to UD since the → Guinness subsidiary (at that time) had bought up → Schenley in 1987. In March 1999 the UD successors → UDV parted with Old Charter. It was part of a package consisting of four brands and the Bernheim Distillery which was sold to a consortium that eventually decided to pass Old Charter (and → W L Weller) to → Sazerac. Whether the present → mash bill is retained is not certain. It consists of 86% corn to 6% rye and 8% malted barley. There are six versions: the youngest comes without an age statement at 80°/40%. The 8-year-old is the same strength. The 10-year-old is 86°/43%. The Classic 90 is 12 years old and is 90°/45%. The → Bottled in Bond has the prescribed strength of 100°/50% and is 7 years old. The leading product is the Proprietor's Reserve aged 13 years at 90°/45%, whose label states 'distilled by the old time proven method'. It was included in UD's → 'Bourbon Heritage Collection' which following the sale will probably no longer be available in this form.

Old Club House Japanese blend from → Suntory, one of nearly 20 brands from the Japanese company, who call this one, which is only available in Japan, 'Classic Fine Whisky'.

Old Comber Irish → pure pot still whiskey that is extremely rare. The 'at least 30-year-old' whiskey was already thought to have been 'sold out' when several hundred bottles were discovered during the 1990s. They had been bottled by the Northern Irish wine and whiskey company James E McCabe, who in 1970 had bought the last stocks from the old Comber Distilleries Company which had been closed in 1953. There were two distilleries in the little town of Comber in Ulster, the Upper and the Lower Distillery, both founded in 1825 and merged twenty years later. They suffered the same problems as all Irish whiskey producers, but in the latter half of the 20th century, Comber's heavy → pot still whiskeys could no longer compete against the modern light blends. The number of distilleries in Northern Ireland was reduced from 70 to just two: Coleraine (grain only) and → Bushmills (malt only). There aren't any → pot still distilleries any more.

Old Commonwealth Kentucky straight bourbon. The label carries the name of the Commonwealth Distillery in → Lawrenceburg and points to 'three generations of distillers'. It appears to originate from J P → Van Winkle and Son who, however, don't have a distillery in Lawrenceburg, and are based in Louisville. They don't disclose from which distillery they actually get this whiskey which they have developed as a second brand alongside their → Old Rip Van Winkle, → Van Winkle Special Reserve and → Pappy Winkle's Family Reserve. It is available in normal bottles aged 10 years and at 107°/53.5% as → small batch and at 80°/40% in ceramic containers, so-called motif carafes. These have included 'Irish Potatoes', 'Post Stamps of Ireland', 'Firefighter', 'Fireman Hero' and 'Peace on Earth'.

Old Court Scotch blend that was originally launched on the market by A Gillies, who at that time was the owner of → Glen Scotia Distillery. Both the company and the distillery passed to → ADP in 1970 and therefore later to → Gibson International. Upon their bankruptcy in 1994, → Glen Catrine Bonded Warehouse Ltd acquired the Glen Scotia Distillery and → Littlemill and a whole range of brands, some of which, such as Old Court, are not being bottled at present.

Old Crofter 12-year-old Scotch blend from → London & Scottish Spirits, based in Surrey and founded in 1994.

Old Crow American whiskey distillery. It lies to the south of Frankfort, Kentucky on a small side road which runs along Glenn's Creek. Nearby are the → Old Taylor Distillery and the present-day → Labrot & Graham Distillery, with which it has close historical connections. It is named after James Crow, a great figure in the history of bourbon. He was a Scottish chemist who emigrated to America in 1820, settling a few years later in Kentucky. Crow is considered to have been the first whiskey maker to use the → sour mash method, a fact which is still mentioned on the bottles today.

It is known that he used his scientific knowledge to make use of instruments such as saccharometers and thermometers to check the fermenting and distilling processes and, above all, insisted on using a corn share of 75% and allowing his whiskey to mature – most probably in charred casks. In 1894 his whiskey was being praised as 'red liquor'. At that time he was already working at the Old Oscar Pepper Distillery (which after years of closure has recently started up operations again bearing the name Labrot & Graham). In 1872 the Peppers built a new distillery which was also named after Dr. Crow, although they sold it together with the brand to E H Taylor, who a few years later founded the Old Taylor Distillery.

Together it and Old Crow were owned during → prohibition by the American Medicinal Spirits Company and in 1947 passed to National Distillers. The old buildings of Old Crow are well preserved but there has been no production there since 1987, when it was taken over by → American Brands and immediately closed down. However, the brand lives on. The whiskey is now made by → Jim Beam, using a lot of → back set, which would certainly have pleased Dr. Crow. It is available in two versions: as a Kentucky aged 4 years (80°/40%) and as a → Bottled in Bond (100°/50%). Both are, of course, Kentucky straights.

Old Decanter De luxe Scotch blend aged 12 years. It is a brand from the old → Cockburn & Company (Leith).

Old Dispensary American corn Whiskey (100°/50%) from → Barton/→ Canandaigua.

Old Distiller Kentucky straight bourbon whiskey. The company for which it is bottled and who sell it, Fairfield Distillery & Co from → Bardstown, does not disclose which distillery produces it, but proudly calls it 'Custom Made Bourbon'. It is one of the brands from → Kentucky Bourbon Distillers, who also own the → Willett Distillery.

Old Dublin Irish whiskey (40%) which comes from the → IDG subsidiary The Old Dublin Distillery. Although it only came onto the market in 1995 it already has its second label. The old blue label has been replaced by an elegant looking label which states that the company also supplies the Lord Mayor of Dublin, and that the whiskey, a blend of distillates from → Bushmills and → Midleton, has been matured in oak casks.

Old Eight Whisky produced by → IDV in → Brazil where the → grain whiskies which have been produced locally are blended with malt whiskies from Scotland.

Old 1889 Kentucky straight bourbon, one of many brands from → Heaven Hill. This whiskey is 4 years old and 80°/40%.

Old Elgin Scotch vatted malt from Elgin. There are 30 distilleries in the vicinity (although there are none within the town itself). Of the many bottlers and warehousers only the → independent bottlers → Gordon & MacPhail remain, a company of particular importance which, apart from its shop with its almost museum-like atmosphere in South Street, also owns precious stocks of old malt whiskies and modern technical plants. Old Elgin comes from here, but apart from the information → Speyside and → Glenlivet, there is no exact indication as to its contents. It is available aged 8, 15 and 21 years. There are also old → vintages like that of 1949 (older ones may be found in some shops, but are not available from G & M itself).

Old Ezra Kentucky straight bourbon whose full name is Old Ezra Rare Old Sippin' Whiskey and whose simpler version is known as → Ezra Brooks. The brand, introduced in the 1950s by the Hoffman Distilling Co and shortly after taken over by → Medley, now belongs to the

David → Sherman Company of St. Louis. The Old Ezra is available aged 7 and 12 years (both 101°/50.5%).

Old-Fashioned Whiskey cocktail. One of the classics of the genre. In a tumbler crush a lump of sugar soaked in angostura together with a lemon quarter and an orange quarter, mix with a generous measure of whiskey and serve with lots of ice and soda.

Old Fettercairn Scotch single malt from the → Fettercairn Distillery, owned by → Kyndal. It is available aged 10 years and 30 years, and there is a 26-year-old included in the → 'Stillman's Dram' series (45%). Fettercairn is the company's only distillery to be open to visitors.

Old Fitzgerald Kentucky straight bourbon. Until 1993 it was made in the → Stitzel-Weller Distillery in Louisville, before its owners → UD shut the distillery and produced it, using the original → mash bill, at the new → Bernheim Distillery. In the following years all six of the company's whiskeys came from here, (except those first introduced in 1997, which come from the old stocks of the closed-down distillery, such as → Henry Clay and → Joseph Finch). They are divided into two groups. One group consists of those whose formula includes rye, corn and malt barley; the others are the wheat whiskeys where the rye is replaced by wheat. They all came from Stitzel-Weller. The Old Fitzgerald is also composed of 5% malt, 75% corn and 20% rye.

The brand has not always been produced in Louisville. It goes back to John E Fitzgerald, who produced it in his distillery in Frankfort and in the late 1880s initially only sold it to private clubs (and the Mississippi steamers), before making it generally available. After the turn of the century the brand quickly became popular and was even on sale in Europe. During → prohibition Julian 'Pappy' → Van Winkle, the head manager at Stitzel-Weller at that time, was able to acquire the brand for his company. From 1972, when the company Somerset bought the brand and the distillery, until 1999, the distillery bore the name of the Old Fitzgerald, and appears as the producer on the bottles. Whether this will remain so is uncertain. In March 1999 the UD successors → UDV sold their Bernheim Distillery and the Old Fitzgerald to → Heaven Hill (the brands, which first went to a consortium of Heaven Hill, → Sazerac and David → Sherman, also included → Old Charter, → W L Weller and → Rebel Yell). UD had five versions: the Prime was 80°/40% and 86°/43%. The 8-year-old 1848 Celebration Bourbon was 90°/45% and its bottles state 'We make Fine bourbon its Quality unchanged since 1848'. The → Bottled in Bond at 100°/50% and the 12-year-old Very Special at 90°/45%, which is also included in the → 'Bourbon Heritage Collection', are top quality products.

Old Forester Kentucky straight bourbon from → Brown-Forman. It is one of the oldest brands in the country, and is still owned by the company that first launched it in 1872. It is the very first bourbon to come on to the market in a → proprietor's bottling. Two years previously George Garvin Brown had established a company together with his half brother.

Gavin sold the distillate in bottles, sealed by hand and the labels, which he wrote himself, stated: 'This whisky is distilled by us only, and we are responsible for its richness and fine quality. Its elegant flavor is solely due to original fineness developed with care. There is nothing better in the market.'

The whisky is spelt without the customary 'e', as a reminder of Brown's Scottish heritage. The Old Forester, which was originally spelt Forrester, has been produced in various plants over the years, but has always come from Louisville, for a time from the splendid buildings on the Dixie Highway, 'Distillery Row', where the headquarters of Brown-Forman are now located and a large water tower decorated like a bottle of Old Forester can be seen from some distance.

Since 1979 it has been made in the → Early Times Distillery, several miles further north in Shivley, where it has its own → mash bill of 72% corn, 18% rye and 10% malt barley. It is subject to the same ageing process and the continual alternation between heating and cooling in the warehouses as its stable-mate Early Times. For a long time there were only two versions, one at 86°/43% and a → Bottled in Bond at 100°/50%. The Olympic Games in Atlanta provided the occasion for a → small batch bottling with the information 'Olympic Filling'; this Barrel Reserve 96 Premium is 96°/48% and does not include the 'Old' in its name – just like the → Forester 1870, whose date refers to the year the company was founded and whose bottle has a new angular design.

Old Galleon Irish whiskey that was a → Kilbeggan. The estate of the bankrupt distillery in Westmeath, which had been badly affected by → prohibition, war and wild speculation, and had been closed since 1953, was bought for £10,000 10 years later by the German Karl Heinz Mellow, who (mainly in Germany) sold the remaining stocks of whisky.

Old Glasgow Scotch blend with the city's coat of arms on its black stoneware bottles. Donald Hart & Co is named as producer of the 8-year-old blend, a subsidiary of → Hart Brothers, the Glaswegian company which has been producing its own blends for many years, and which is also known as an → independent bottler of single malts.

Old Glen Scotch malts that are exclusively produced by → Glenmorangie plc under the name of the subsidiary Douglas MacNiven & Co, for the UK supermarket chain → ASDA. There are four versions: a 12-year-old single → Highland, a 12-year-old single → Speyside, a 10-year-old single → Lowlands and a 10-year-old → Islay, which is a pure malt. They are reasonably priced.

Old Glomore Scotch blend from James Williams, a company which has been making blends for more than a hundred years, based in Narberth/Dyfed, in Wales.

Old Grand-Dad Kentucky straight bourbon which is made at one of the two → Jim Beam Distilleries in Clermont or Boston and which is has the highest proportion of rye among all American bourbons. The rights to the brand were acquired by Jim Beam's parent company, → American Brands, in 1987, when they took over National Distillers. At that time the whiskey came from the Old Grand-Dad Distillery. An Old Grand-Dad distillery was built in 1882 by Raymond B Hayden. He died with no heirs and the distillery and the brand were sold to the Wathen family, who continued production in another distillery and closed the old plant at the beginning of → prohibition in 1920. A → Wathen established the American Medicinal Spirits Company, which was taken over by National Distillers in 1940. They also bought a distillery in Frankfort, and Raymond named it after the brand in honour of the family's forefather → Basil Hayden, the Old Grand-Dad.

Hayden's portrait appears on the bottles today. This is the same Basil Hayden who → JBB named one of their → small batch bourbons after. It is now produced not far from the site where it first came into the world in 1882, and is still made according to the old formula. It contains the highest proportion of rye of any of JBB's brands (except, of course, the → straight rye → Old Overholt). It comes in four versions: at 80°/40% aged 4 years, with the same strength as a Special Reserve, as a → Bottled in Bond at 100°/50% and as a → barrel °proof at 114°/57%, which gives the lot number and is therefore a → small batch.

Old Hardy Kentucky straight bourbon (40%) which does not give any information about a distillery or producer. The anonymous whiskey is obtainable in supermarkets in Germany and France.

Old Havana Cuban whisky produced on the island; 'distilado y envasado en combinado de bebidas Santa Cruz Cuba'. It is not known what raw materials have been used or which method of distilling; the label describes it as 'Malto 100%'.

Old Highland Blend Scotch blend which the brewery → Eldridge, Pope & Co began producing in 1908 exclusively for their pubs. It contains a high proportion of malt whiskies, and its label lists the most significant ones, including such great names as → Glen Grant, → Glenfarclas, → Glenfiddich and → Glen Rothes. It is still being produced and can still be found in the company's pubs in Dorset, although it may soon be finished as the company has split into the Thomas Hardy

Brewery and a business operating under the old name, which no longer brews beer, but manages 200 pubs.

Old House Scotch blend. One of the many brands from → Burn Stewart, available, as is frequently the case for this company, aged 3 and 12 years.

Old Huckleberry Kentucky straight bourbon '4 summers' old and produced according to an 'Original 1788 Formula. The label does not state a producer, but it does come from Bardstown, so may be produced by → Heaven Hill. The volume of alcohol is not expressed in the → °proof customary in the USA, but in the European way at 40%. It is meant for the European market and is distributed by Island Distributors, behind which are → William Grant & Sons.

Old Inverness Scotch blend from J G → Thomson, Glasgow, a company which belonged to the brewing giant Bass, who sold the blend in its pubs as a kind of house brand. The company, who took over the brand from HD Wines in Inverness, also supplied → As We Get It.

Old Joe American distillery. Since 1986, and after many changes in ownership and name, it has been known as the → Four Roses Distillery. It formerly belonged to the Canadian combine → Seagram whose spirits interests were acquired in 2000 by the Diageo and Pernod-Ricard partnership. Seagram had bought it in the mid 1940s from a company called Frankfort Distilleries; at that time it was called → Old Prentice. Its was founded by an Irish immigrant, 'Old Joe' Peyton, who came by canoe from Pennsylvania to Kentucky in 1818, and settled 20km to the south of Frankfort in what is now → Lawrenceburg, and began distilling. His products soon gained a good reputation and were called Old Joe, becoming the first whiskey brand in the country. After → prohibition Peyton was honoured once more when the distillery again bore his name for a short time.

Old Keeper Scotch blend that was once made by Burn McKenzie & Co in Dumbarton. Nowadays it comes, aged 'over 3 years', as an own-brand product from ALDI. The company imports part of it → in bulk to Germany, where it is then bottled by the Silverstone Brandy & Liqueur Company GmbH in Rottenburg/Laaber. It is not available in the UK. Some of it is produced by → Invergordon and bottled at their plant in Salamander Place in Leith.

Old Kentucky Kentucky straight bourbon available in two versions. The 10-year-old Amber is 90°/45%, and the 13-year-old is 94°/47% and is called No. 88. The label states that it comes from the Old Kentucky Distillery in → Bardstown which means that it is most likely produced by → Heaven Hill.

Old Kentucky Rifle Kentucky straight bourbon. It is produced at → Heaven Hill in the USA for Weinhandelshaus Eggers & Franke in Bremen, Germany, who import the whiskey in → bulk and bottle it at 40% vol.

Old Kilkenny Irish whiskey (40%) which is made exclusively for the UK supermarket chain → ASDA with whiskies from → Bushmills and → Midleton. Both distilleries belong to → IDG.

Old Malt Cask, The Series of Scotch single malts brought out by Douglas → Laing & Co in the autumn of 1998. As successful blenders and bottlers, the family-run company from Glasgow has many fine casks at its disposal, some of them containing very old and precious malts. They were formerly mainly used for the company's blends. The labels give the exact age, the name of the distillery and the number of bottles. They are all bottled at 50%. The first bottling was a 17-year-old → Pittyvaich, followed by a 21-year-old → Tormore, and a 31-year-old → Banff. The second series included a 20-year-old → Aberfeldy, a → Benrinnes and a → Glendullan both also aged 20 years, and a → Glen Keith and a → Macduff which were both 30 years old. A second series of bottlings, which however have been reduced to 43%, are available from the company under the name → McGibbons → Provenance.

Old Man Winter Kentucky straight bourbons (94°/47%) aged 12 and 14 years, from the 'Old Man Winter Distilling Co.' It most probably comes from → Kentucky Bourbon Distillers.

Old Master De luxe Scotch blend, belonging to the → Dunhill range.

Old Master's Series of single malts from the → independent bottler James → MacArthur, who uses the name to differentiate them from his malts bottled at 43%. These are bottled at → cask strength, and forego → chill filtering and → colouring.

Old Matured Scotch blend that now comes from → UDV, although its previous owners are mentioned on the label: Daniel Crawford & Sons, established in Glasgow in 1850, and later owned by → DCL. On their behalf Crawfords held the licence for → Parkmore Distillery in → Dufftown.

Old Midleton Irish whisky, spelt the Scottish way. There were only 33 bottles, which all contained whisky which was distilled before 1960, and came from one of the former stone jars that an earlier manager from Midleton found in a pub. His son sold the jar to → Milroy's in London, who resold it to the Irish Pub 'The Toucan'. There it was possible to have a taste of this rarity at £25 per glass, whilst at Milroy's the bottle cost more than £400.

Old Monarch Scotch blend from the → Speyside Distillery Co belonging to the Christie family, who before the opening of their new distillery at the confluence of the Tromie and the Spey, had a share in the company → Campbell & Clark (→ Murdoch's Perfection), which now belongs to them and which had this blend in its range. It is 'over 3 years old'.

Old Montana Red Eye Kentucky straight bourbon bottled for Montana Distillers and initially only brought out in 1989 for the Montana Centennial. It sold out so quickly that they were sure of a big success. Aged 6 years (40%), it is currently available in its home state as well as in Idaho, Minnesota, Utah and Iowa, and may be available soon throughout the whole country.

Old Montrose Scotch whiskies that are produced as a → de luxe blend and as a vatted malt and come from the London → Montrose Whisky Company.

Old Moor Scotch blend, available in two versions, a 'Major' and a → de luxe. It bears the name of the Italian company which has it made for them as their house brand by → QSI. The Guernsey-based subsidiary of William → Grant & Sons now also sell it on other markets.

Old Mull Scotch blend, registered by John Hopkins of Glasgow in 1880. They had set up business importing 'Otard' Cognac, brought out → Glen Garry as their first blend and later built → Speyburn Distillery. From 1916 the company belonged to → DCL. When → Guinness bought DCL in 1987, they sold it to the → American Brands subsidiary → JBB (Greater Europe) plc. The licence for → Oban is still registered with Hopkins.

Old New Orleans Kentucky straight bourbon from → Kentucky Bourbon Distillers in → Bardstown, who mostly get their whiskeys from → Heaven Hill in the same town. There are three versions: at 80°/40%, 90°/45% and 107°/53.5%. They have Mississippi paddle steamers on the label, the high percentage version is decorated with the word 'Antebellum' below the name, whilst the other two both have the words 'Since 1811' printed in the same position.

Old Orkney Scotch blend which bears 'OO' in larger letters on its label and is sometimes refered to as 'Double O'. It is an 8-year-old blend from → Gordon & MacPhail. Its name, suggests that it contains a goodly proportion of malt whiskies from → Highland Park and → Scapa.

Old Overholt straight rye whiskey, which comes from → Jim Beam and is made in one of their two distilleries. A Overholt is still named as producer and the date 1810 is also quoted. It is one of the few real rye whiskeys still available. Its home was originally Pennsylvania, where the Monongahela whiskeys were made from rye, the local grain. The Old Overholt, together with the Old Potrero, are the only examples of this genre nowadays, and give an inkling of the original taste.

Old Parr

Abraham Overholt was a farmer and distiller. By 1860 the business he'd set up in Broad Ford, Pennsylvania had grown to a respectable size. During prohibition the company caused a scandal as the Secretary of the Treasury, of all people, had a share in it. He sold the whiskey stocks to → Schenley and the rights to the brand to National Distillers, who, in their turn, were acquired in 1987 by → American Brands. Luckily Old Overholt, which was produced at 93°/43.5%, didn't share the fate of so many other traditional brands, it is sold with a strength of 80°/40%. The → mash bill, as is always the case with Jim Beam, has not been disclosed, but the proportion of rye is said to be 61%.

Old Parr Scotch blend which originated in the 1870s. It was first brought onto the market by the → Greenlees brothers (→ Macdonald Greenlees), and is named after Thomas Parr. Parr is said to have lived to be 152 years old. He was divorced for being unfaithful when he was 100. The bottle is a replica of the old tavern bottles. It is said to be based on the malt whisky from → Cragganmore and is owned by UDV. It is marketed in many countries and is particularly successful in Japan, where it has been available for more than 100 years, and where Old Parr Superior is exclusively sold. The Old Parr (12 years old), Old Parr Tribute and Old Parr Elizabethan are in the upper price sector. In the spring of 1998 an Old Parr Seasons was brought out, which for the time being is mainly available in South East Asia, in a set with half-litre bottles, one for each season of the year.

Old Potrero American single malt rye whiskey, the only one of its kind in the world. It is produced in California and until → Peregrine Rock appeared on the scene, was the first and only whiskey from this state.

It is located in the Potrero district of San Francisco, which gave the product its name. It is bottled at just 13 months and 124°/62%. It is rare and practically impossible to obtain. A first batch of just 1,448 bottles went exclusively to restaurants in San Francisco, Maryland and Washington DC. There is a second bottling from which is also very rare.

Old Prentice American distillery in → Lawrenceburg, Kentucky, which shares its name with another distillery in Indiana which belonged to Seagram. It is better known by the name of → Four Roses, which it has borne since 1986. It was established in 1818 by the Irish immigrant → 'Old Joe' Peyton, and over the years belonged to, among others, the Ripy Brothers, who owned → Wild Turkey Distillery, and the → Medleys and Frankfort Distilleries. It also produced → Benchmark and → Eagle Rare, which were sold by Seagram to → Sazerac. The label of Eagle Rare gives the Old Prentice Company as its producer.

Old Pulteney Scotch single malt from the → Pulteney Distillery in Wick which was founded in 1826. For a long time it was only available from → independent bottlers, especially → Gordon & MacPhail. They had a 15-year-old, and one from 1961 without an age statement, the 8-year-old (40% and 57%). In 1997, when the new owners → Inver House Distillers Ltd brought out a → proprietor's bottling for the first time. The new bottling is 12 years old and the → cask strength (various editions with differing strengths of approx 60%) which came out in December 1997 is 15 years old. The range has been extended by a Sherry Cask, which was brought out in limited bottlings which also had strengths of around 60% (60.8%, 60.5%). In the Spring of 2001 an 18-year-old in a single cask bottling (at a cask strength of 58.4%) was brought out in a wooden box accompanied by a certificate. For the Millennium there were various single casks, 15 years old, 59%, 60.9% and 61.1%. Inver House Distillers Ltd also followed the trend for sweetness and launched an Old Pulteney Liqueur consisting of 'Highland ingredients' and with a label showing fisherwomen working in the harbour: Pulteney, the most northern distillery on the Scottish mainland, lies near Wick harbour.

Old Regal Scotch blend which → UDV produce for → Venezuela. The label names James Munro & Son as bottlers, a company which joined → DCL in 1925, where they were under the control of → Macdonald Greenlees. For a time they held the licence on behalf of the mutual parent company for → Dalwhinnie and → Knockdhu. The whisky is only bottled on arriving in Venezuela.

Old Rhosdhu Scotch single malt from the → Loch Lomond Distillery. The distillery is able to produce six different whiskies by adjusting the heads of the → stills, using different types of malt and varyingly separated → middle cuts. Two of these are marketed as single malts (the others are used for blending): → Inchmurrin and Old Rhosdhu, which is somewhat fuller and more oily than its 'brother'. In some cases the bottles are without an age statement and sometimes show an age of 5 years. In 1996 there was a small edition of a 28-year-old from 1967, at the end of 1997 there was a 27-year-old from 1969 (350 bottles) and in March 2000 exactly 600 bottles of a 32-year-old (40%) from 1967. The → independents sometimes use the spelling 'Rosdhu' and occasionally leave out the 'old'; → Cadenhead have had a pair using the name of the distillery called Loch Lomond (Inchmurrin) and Loch Lomond (Rhosdhu), the latter aged 9 years and at 60.5%.

Old Rip Kentucky straight bourbon from the independent family company → Van Winkle, who name Louisville as their headquarters. The father and the grandfather of Julian Van Winkle Jr and Van Winkle III was the famous 'Pappy', who became president of → Stitzel-Weller in Louisville. The company chooses to market their whiskeys using three very similar, yet different names. Apart from the Van Winkle or the Pappy Van Winkle Family Reserve, Old Rip is also used, and their producers are quoted as the Old Rip Van Winkle Distillery in Lawrenceburg. The 4-year-old in its square bottle with the dark green label is 86°/43%, the 12-year-old with the black label 105°/52.5%. Old Rip Van Winkle is the name used for the '10 summer old' Kentucky straight bourbon at 90°/45%, and 107°/53.5%, the 15-year-old at 107°/53.5% and the 12-year-old Old Time Rye, a straight rye whose bottles are numbered and which is 90°/45%. It is no longer the only rye of the company whose bourbons are wheated whiskeys, a speciality in which the rye share is replaced by wheat and for which the Stitzel-Weller Distillery, for example, is famous. Following the closure of the distillery in 1993, the whiskeys have been produced in the → Bernheim Distillery.

Old Royal Scotch blends bottled with the age statements 12, 15 and 21 years which come from → Burn Stewart.

Old St. Andrews Scottish whiskies from a company of the same name in London. The UK distributor is Matthew Clark. They use a half-gallon bottle, placed in a golf bag mounted on a trolley. It is based on malt whisky from → Tomatin, which belongs to a Japanese consortioum. They also have a share in Old St. Andrews, and the blends, which are available aged 5, 12 and 21 years and are now also available in normal sized bottles, are most successful in Japan. The bottle shaped like a golf ball, which is available as a miniature as well as normal-sized, is also very popular, as well as another version shaped like a barrel. There is also an ice bucket shaped like a golf ball containing a bottle. The company has another blend called → Clubhouse. The owners of this brand lauched a 'Pure Malt' (presumably a vatted), and also brought out an 11-year-old single malt (40%) for the Millennium.

Old Scotch Whisky Scotch blends. The name is used for two products, which are aimed at two such different target groups that there is no fear of confusion. One is produced by Duncan McKinnon & Co in Glasgow and and is reserved for the passengers of the 'Nostalgic Istanbul Orient Express'. The other, in contrast, is a → standard blend which is on sale at an extremely reasonable price in branches of the Britiish supermarket chain → ASDA. Its label names James MacCrae as its producer.

Old Smuggler Scotch blend. It is now marketed by → Allied Domecq PLC, but the brand was introduced in 1835 by James and George → Stodart as a vatted malt. The bottles are shaped like the lanterns smugglers used to send signals from their boats. The brand is particularly strong in the USA and Germany, and only available as a → standard blend.

Old Spencer Scotch blends from → Eaglesome, a subsidiary of J & A Mitchell who also run the → Springbank Distillery in Campbeltown, and who own the → independent bottlers → Cadenhead.

Old Taylor American whiskey distillery a mile

from the → Old Crow Distillery in Glenn's Creek, to the south of → Frankfort, Kentucky. It was built in 1877 by Colonel Edmund Haynes Taylor Jr, who began his career as a banker and went into the whiskey business in 1868/9. He had a share in a distillery in Frankfort which had been founded by the → Blanton family and was known as the O F C (Old Fire Copper) Distillery. Today it is known as → Ancient Age and → Buffalo Trace. Taylor sold it in 1865 to build the Castle Distillery, so called because of its appearance which today, with its fortified battlements, bears his name. Some years later he bought the well-established distillery Old Crow, together with the rights to the brand, from his neighbours at the Old Pepper Distillery (→ Labrot & Graham, → James E Pepper).

Taylor fought for better whiskey in particular straight Whiskey. He is credited for being among those who supported the → Bottled in Bond Act. Taylor's successors did not survive → prohibition. Their company was initially bought by the American Medicinal Spirits Company and then, in 1936, by National Distillers, who closed down the distillery in the 1970s. Since 1987 the distillery and the brands have belonged to → American Brands, whose subsidiary → JBB produces the whiskey in one of its two → Jim Beam Distilleries. It is available as a straight aged 6 years and at 86°/43% as well as Bottled in Bond at 100°/50%.

Old Thompson American blended from → Barton in → Bardstown. It was James Thompson who gave the whiskey its name. Together with George Garvin Brown he formed the company which is now known as → Brown-Forman, and in 1910 bought the → Glenmore Distillery in Louisville. Glenmore later brought out the brand. The company was bought by → UD, who in 1995 sold a whole range of brands to Barton, from whom the whiskey now comes.

Old Times Whisky produced in → Uruguay. It consists of → grain whiskies produced domestically, mixed with Scotch malt whiskies. Its producers, Carrau & Cia, state that the Uruguayan ingredients are matured in oak and the Scottish ones are four years old. In 1997 the company joined together with → UD to form United Distillers Carrau SA.

Old Troon Scotch blend. It is one of the many brands from → Glen Catrine Bonded Warehouse Ltd.

Old Virginia straight bourbon which is described on the label as 'authentic'. It is probable that this whisky is intended for export as the strength is shown in percent rather than degrees.

Old Weller Antique Kentucky straight bourbon from → UD. It was produced at the → Stitzel-Weller Distillery and now comes from the → Bernheim Distillery. It is one of three versions of this wheat bourbon, in which the customary rye is replaced in the → mash by wheat.

Old Williamsburg No. 20 Kentucky straight bourbon. It is the only American whiskey that may call itself → Kosher and can be consumed by those of the Jewish religion who adhere strictly to the rules governing food and drink. A rabbi must confirm that the rules have been followed in its production and a stamp in Hebrew to this effect is to be found on the back label. It has been on the market since 1994 and is sold by the Royal Wine Corporation in New York, who get it from an unnamed distillery in Kentucky, and have named it after the district in Brooklyn where they are based. It is 36 months (3 years) old and 101°/50.5%.

Oldmaster German whisky from the old family company C W → Falckenthal Söhne in Luckenwalde who were best-known for their 'Zinnaer Klosterlikör'. After the reunification of Germany they bought back their business which had been nationalised in East Germany, and in 1992 they brought a product on to the market which they sold as 'Malt Whisky'. It was not made of malt, but was distilled from rye. It has now been renamed → Edel Falcke.

Oldmoor Scotch vatted malt from Mackay & McDavitt, aged 8 years and mainly available in Italy. Previously there was a 5-year-old '100% pure malt' from an Oldmoor Whisky Company in London.

O'Neill's Irish whiskey (40%) made by →

Invergordon, which uses the whiskies from → Cooley. It is the house brand of the chain of Irish pubs, O'Neill's.

OO → Old Orkney.

Orach Dram Scotch single malt aged 8 years (40%) from → All Saint's Brands in Minneapolis, Minnesota.

Ord → Glen Ord.

Order of Merit Canadian whisky (40%) formerly aged 15 years, now a 12-year-old → premium blend, produced at the → Valleyfield Distillery, which after the sale of its owner → Schenley Canada, passed to the → UD empire. When they joined with IDV to form UDV, the owners also parted with this brand in the spring of 1999.

Original Cowboy, The Kentucky straight bourbon from the → Kentucky Bourbon Distillers in → Bardstown, but who mostly get their whisky from → Heaven Hill. The 'Genuine' (90°/45%) is 12 years old.

Original Lakeland Liqueur Whisky liqueur made with Scotch whiskies in England. The producers, The High Street Trading, are based in Middlethorp. At 20% it is very light.

Original Mackinlay, The Scotch blend created by Charles → Mackinlay and one of the very first blends of all. It now comes from → Kyndal, who secured the assets of Invergordon in 2001, via → Whyte & Mackay/→ JBB (Greater Europe) plc, a subsidiary of → Fortune Brands.

Oscar Getz Museum of Whiskey History A whisky museum based in Kentucky. It gives a detailed history of Bourbon and its great personalities, telling how various brands have developed. One display are lovely old tools, labels and bottles and original advertising and posters.

Oscar Getz founded a company and a distillery called → Barton. He created the brand → Kentucky Gentleman. In 1983, after nearly 40 years as chairman, he had to give up his position. His company was bought by the Scottish Argyll Group's subsidiary → ADP, and the museum, which had been housed in the confined space of the distillery, moved to the Spalding Hall in Bardstown, where it has become an important tourist attraction. Along with the three distilleries within the town itself and two others nearby, as well as the annual bourbon Festival each September, it has guaranteed the town's position as the whiskey capital of not only Kentucky, but the entire USA.

Outlaws Series of Kentucky straight bourbons from the ever-imaginative → Kentucky Bourbon Distillers of → Bardstown. They also have a series of → 'Legends of the Wild West'. The outlaws are Wild Billy, John Wesley Harding, Josquin Murieta, Kid Curry, Butch Cassidy, Harry Longbough, Frank and Jesse James, My Dave, Belle Starr, Billy the Kid and Harry Tracy. There is no difference between the individual whiskeys and each legend is available in two versions, aged 12 or 15 years, each at 101°.

P

Paddy Irish whiskey which in the 1920s was called → Cork Distilleries Company Old Irish Whiskey. It was renamed after Patrick Flaherty, who would get the public used to the taste of the whiskey with the aid of generous free rounds. Soon the pub landlord's began ordering Paddy's whiskey, and eventually the name stuck. It used to be a → pot still, but today it is a light blend (40%). It was the only Irish whiskey that wasn't rehomed when → IDG was formed: it has always come (except for a shot of → Bushmills single malt) from → Midleton. There is also a very obscure Paddy produced in Argentina, available in two versions, one with a brown label, the other with a black one.

Pagodas As much a part of Scottish distilleries as whisky is of Scotland. They haven't always been there, or at least not in their present form. It was the → Elgin-based architect Charles Chree → Doig who, whilst rebuilding → Dailuaine Distillery, had the idea of replacing the former cone-shaped chimney above the → kiln with the shape that has now become so familiar. The attractive new symmetrical triangular shape instantly became popular and many distillery proprietors wanted pagodas. Doig and his sons were responsible for their design at → Aberfeldy, → Coleburn, → Craigellachie, → Cragganmore, → Benromach, → Dalwhinnie, → Dallas Dhu, → Glen Elgin, → Glen Albyn, → Glen Mhor and → Imperial. At many of these distilleries they can still be seen, although unfortunately no longer at Dailuaine where a fire destroyed them in 1917.

Pakistan Although most poeple in Pakistan are Islamic, whisky is produced there, and even as malt whisky. A distillery was established in 1899, at the time of British rule. There was a brewery built in Ghora Gali in 1861, and another oneanother one in 1889 in Rawalpindi, which 10 years later had a whisky distillery added to it. Production is not on a large scale, but it is carried out according to Scottish methods (apart from maturation), a fact which is proudly confirmed on the boxes of the 8-year-old Murree's malt whisky: 'Every drop contained in this bottle is distilled from barley malt in traditional Scotch-type pot stills and matured for a minimum period of eight years in oak cask or vat. We claim this single malt whisky classic compares favourably with Scotch malts of equal age.' Apart from this version, Murree also has a 3-year-old, and a drink named 'Gymkhana', which is sold as a whisky but which is only partly a malt, most of it consisting of a rice and molasses distillate.

Palliser Canadian distillery built by → Gilbey when the UK company extended their activities to North America in the 1930s. The Old Palliser Distillery stood in Toronto and initially produced gin. In the latter half of the 20th century, Gilbey created the brand → Black Velvet, which became so successful that it was necessary to build a new distillery. Gilbey's owner → IDV became part of → UDV in 1997. In February 1999 the new strategists decided to part with nearly all their Canadian interests and sell all their Canadian whiskies except → Gibson's. The package, which went to → Canandaigua for $185 million, included the → Valleyfield Distillery and Palliser. Apart from Black Velvet they also produce several other Canadian whiskies (→ Triple Crown, → Red Feather) and export whiskies in → bulk, in tanks. Their best-known product is 'Smirnoff' vodka. This, however, was kept by UDV.

Pappy Van Winkle Nickname for the great Julian → Van Winkle who began his whiskey life at → W L Weller and ended up as president of the → Stitzel-Weller Distillery.

Parallel import Form of importing products

which is not carried out by the 'official' importers. Producers of whisk(e)y have contracts with individual countries (or establish their own subsidiaries) and give them the exclusive distribution rights for their brands. This is of advantage to both partners of the contract – but not automatically to the consumer. It may happen, for example, that a new brand is launched on to the market but that the producer or the importer decide not to supply it immediately. With the ever increasing number of Scotch single malts or American → small batch bottlings, the situation has arisen where they were not included in the range of the official importers as they were only available in small quantities. Independent importers made use of this situation. They recognised that the alleged market niche actually had considerable potential and promised good business. They are often the exclusive, 'official' importers of independent bottlers and tend not to present any competition to the contracted importers of the large companies. They don't limit themselves to independent bottlings, but also offer their own bottlings, and not just those that the 'official' importers don't want, but also products from their portfolios. Such parallel imports are not popular with the official importers, mainly because their competitors are often cheaper and faster, than they are. For the large importing companies the activities of parallel importers are a nuisance and annoying, for the lover of whisk(e)y they are a boon, as they make it possible to buy bottles that would otherwise be impossible to come by (or only with difficulty and at great expense). The development of a whisk(e)y culture in Germany, for example, has been greatly (perhaps decisively) influenced by parallel importers such as Dieter Kirsch.

Park & Tilford Canadian whisky company who had a distillery in Vancouver and were famous for their → Royal Command. They were later owned by Canadian → Schenley, which is why the brand was produced in → Valleyfield by → UD, which they got when they bought Schenley in 1987. A further brand, Three Lancers, is no longer produced.

Parker's Scotch blend from → Angus Dundee.

James Parker of Glasgow (which also has the single malt → Glen Parker in its range) is the company named on the label. The blend is also available in decanters.

Parkmore Scottish malt distillery that lay opposite the → Glenfiddich Distillery on the other side of the River Fiddich on the outskirts of → Dufftown. It belonged to the → Speyside whisky region and was one of the distilleries referred to in the saying 'Rome was built on seven hills, Dufftown stands on seven stills'. It was built during the great whisky boom before the end of the 19th century, but soon got into difficulties. It was acquired by John → Dewar & Sons in 1923 and two years later passed to → DCL, who closed it down in 1931. It has been beautifully maintained and is a wonderful sight with its mighty pagodas, and is still used by → Highland Distillers. It looks as though it could start up production again at any moment, although it is only the → warehouses that are in use. There isn't a single malt from Parkmore nowadays, but several years ago a bottle fetched a high sum when auctioned at Christie's in London.

Passport Scotch blend launched by → Seagram in 1968 which has since become one of the leading brands – in countries such as the USA, Brazil and southern Europe. Whilst it is produced in Scotland, it is shipped in → bulk to the USA, where it is bottled. The malt whiskies used for it come from the distilleries Chivas Brothers, the former Scottish subsidiary of Seagram. It is also available pre-mixed as Passport & Cola.

Patent still Invented in the 1820s this enabled the production of new types of whisky. As it also allows the use of unmalted grain and also, unlike the distillation of malt whisky in → pot stills which is done by the batch, allows → continuous distillation, the patent still makes production much cheaper and it is possible to make far larger amounts. It is also known as a → continuous still or, due to its shape, a → column still. It is not based on the idea of extracting the alcohol from the fermented → wash by boiling and steaming in the pot stills which had up to that time been in exclusive use, but instead on driving off the alcohol directly from the cold wash by the use of hot steam.

Robert → Stein, a member of the → Haig family, is credited as being the inventor of this method, having first tried it out in his → Kilbaggie distillery in 1826. A short time later the Irish exciseman Aeneas → Coffey introduced an improved method that was soon well-established. The new method allowed the production of a cheaper, but also (from a chemical point of view) a purer and better whisky, and is used nowadays in Scotland for → grain whisky. This method revolutionised the whisky world: without it blends could not have been created, and without blends Scotch would not have achieved worldwide success. In Ireland, Canada and the USA, with just a few exceptions, it is the only method of producing the whisk(e)y typical of each country, although there are characteristic differences in the structure of the stills. In Canada two pairs of columns are used, the → beer still and a similar column, whereas in the USA the beer still consists of just one column and the distillate is then run through a → doubler or → thumper.

In contrast to the pot stills, which are aesthetic in appearance, the patent stills are quite utilitarian looking. They usually consist of two copper or steel columns up to 15 metres high, which are connected to each other. The first column is the → analyser, the separating column, and the second is the →rectifier (or rectifyer). In their insides perforated copper (or steel) plates are layered on top of each other, each one acting like a small still. The cold wash is led in from above through the rectifier and there meets the steam which has first been sent down to the analyser where it rises and is led into the rectifier via a pipe. Here the wash runs downwards in copper pipes inside the plates and finally reaches the analyser, where it is mixed with the rising steam, reaching the rectifier again as a mixture of alcohol and steam, before condensing as a result of meeting the newly introduced cold wash. Unusable alcohol and fusel oils, which condense earlier, remain in the columns and are redistilled. Ethyl alcohol with a strength of about 95% is left over. This is collected and diluted with water before filling into casks. The whisk(e)y produced in this way has a light body and is relatively neutral in taste, is 'purer' than malt whisky, but lacks its character-forming aromatic substances.

Pattison Scottish whisky company that went out of business in since 1898. Its bankruptcy led to a great crisis in an industry which had previously only known progress, growth and success, and caused great difficulties for many companies and, especially, distilleries. The brothers Robert and Walter Pattison had begun as grocers in Leith, but soon began producing blends, having been inspired by the success of the Dewars, James Buchanan, and Peter Machie → Big Five. They called themselves Pattison, Elder & Co, and bought whisky on a large scale, building enormous → warehouses in Leith for duty-paid goods as well as those in bond, with offices there and in London, and buying themselves country estates.

Everything had to be of the very best: The famous Alfred → Barnard ('The Whisky Distilleries of the United Kingdom and Ireland') was commissioned to write their whisky brochure. In this elaborately designed and remarkably illustrated book, the plants in Edinburgh were presented, as well as the → Glenfarclas Distillery in which the brothers had a 50% share. For an advertising campaign they had hundreds of trained parrots call 'drink Pattison's!'. Their success led them to form a joint-stock company and sell shares. They attracted a lot of investors and got even more money from the banks. Production blossomed, new distilleries were built. Then production exceeded demand and collapse followed. Nobody was prepared to give them any more money and they had to stop payments. They lost everything, went to court and were sentenced to several months imprisonment for fraud. But they were not the only ones to be affected: many distilleries, some of which had just been built, had to close down. This first crisis was followed by others: the First World War and the ensuing period of → prohibition. There was also a winner: → DCL, which became stronger because of the collapse of its greatest competitor and was able to swallow up many smaller bankrupt companies.

Paul Jones American blended whiskey from →

Heaven Hill, the independent family-run company in Bardstown.

Peat Although peat is widely found in Ireland as well as Scotland, and is still used as fuel in many rural areas, it doesn't play a very important part in making Irish whiskey. Before the → Cooley Distillery decided to bring out a peated malt whiskey, the → Connemara, → IDG used to advertise the fact that the particular purity of its whiskey was not only the result of → triple distillation, but also because they did not use peat.

In Scotland peat is very important, at least for malt whisky. Peat influences two factors which help define the character of a malt whisky: its water and its malted barley. Water is used in → steeping to encourage germination, and it is added to the → grist in the mash tun. This water has often come into intensive contact with peat and may then be a soft, yellow colour. This is why malt whiskies which are made using unpeated malt may still have a smoky, peaty taste; → Scapa is an example of this.

The peat plays an important part in the drying of the germinated malt in the → kiln or in the → drum maltings. Each distillery places particular importance on determining the amount of peat used, even if they no longer produce the malt themselves. This is to ensure that a certain → house style is maintained, making its malt whisky identifiable by its characteristic smokiness/peatiness. The material which has gone to make up the peat over the centuries is a determining factor, whether it has been formed from heather or, as in the case of the islands, it contains seaweed. It is generally recognised that the island peat is heavier and more intensive, which contributes to the 'medicinal' character of these malt whiskies; → Laphroaig and → Ardbeg are the most striking examples. The depth of the peat bed also seems to have an effect on its character.

Peat is hardly ever cut by hand these days, but is 'harvested' mechanically. This brings up the question of disturbing the ecological balance. The fact that whisky-makers take environmental problems seriously was proved by → Bowmore, where they have developed a new process in which the same intensity is achieved by dividing the long pieces of peat and dampening them before burning.

Other countries that make malt whisky often import peat from Scotland. Although Japan has peat of its own, it either imports peat or peated malt from Scotland because its own raw material is not of the same quality and has not produced such good results.

Pekin American distillery near Peoria in Illinois which was built in the 1920s. Since 1991, it has produced industrial alcohol. It used to belong to the Mid West Grain Company and is now owned by → McCormick, a company which, along with a whole range of other spirits, produce several straight bourbons as well as the straight corn → Platte Valley. It and → Stillbrook (still) come from Pekin. As soon as the stocks are depleted the brands will be produced with whiskeys from → Heaven Hill. Pekin is said to produce the sweetest bourbon in all America with a → mash bill of 74.5% corn, 15% rye and 10.5% malted barley.

Pennypacker Kentucky straight bourbon which is made exclusively for the family-run Borco company in Hamburg, Germany. It comes from → Heaven Hill and is shipped in → bulk to Germany, where it is bottled and then sold throughout Europe.

Peregrine Rock Californian → Pure single malt whiskey. It is produced by the Saint James Spirits Distillery in Irwindale, which previously only produced spirits such as a pineapple brandy, pineapple rum, a Williams pear, a cherry and Tequila (made from the agave plant), before deciding to experiment with a malt whiskey. In 1996 James Susuttil bought Scotch malt and mashed it together with the 'purest mountain spring water'. He used casks of American oak for maturation which had previously contained bourbon. After two years he was allowed to sell his whiskey in most American states, but not in California; the laws there prescribed a three year period for maturation.

Pernod-Ricard, Groupe French drinks

combine which arose at the end of 1974 from the merger of the two companies Pernod and Ricard to form the Groupe Pernod-Ricard, to give it its correct title, which although it was a joint-stock company, was still managed by a member of one of the founding companies, Patrick Ricard. The group occupies sixth place among all drinks companies and its drink 'Ricard' is a brand which the company says occupies third place among the best-selling spirits. They also have a very successful brand with their Scotch → Clan Campbell which is said to be the third most popular of its kind in the world. This brand comes from the Scottish subsidiary → Campbell Distillers which Pernod acquired in 1974, bringing it with them awhen they merged with Ricard.

The Scottish whisky that Pernod-Ricard was first interested in was S Campbell & Sons and owned → Aberlour (→ Edradour and → Glenallachie were added later) as well as the blends → House of Campbell, → House of Lords, → White Heather and the vatted → Glenforres. In 1980 the → Austin Nichols Distilling Company was acquired with their → Wild Turkey Distillery in Lawrenceburg, Kentucky, together with the brands → Kentucky Spirit, → Wild Turkey and the Austin Nichols range. In 1987, following a takeover battle, the Irish Distillers Group with the distilleries → Bushmills and → Midleton was purchased. At that time IDG owned the entire whiskey industry in Ireland, which therefore passed into French hands – a situation which was only ended by the establishment of the → Cooley Distillery. Pernod-Ricard have also extended their interests on other continents: in 1999 74% of the Indian United Agencies was acquired, a majority which was sufficient to obtain the coveted licence for the import of foreign spirits to → India, a country with enormous growth potential. In 2000 Groupe Pernod-Ricard formed a partnership with Diageo to acquire the spirits interests of Seagram. This sale was completed in December 2001, and the group now owns the → Chivas and Glenlivet group and are the third largest Wine and Spirits company in the world.

From Bushmills come the distillery's single malts and the blends → Black Bush, Bushmills Original, Bushmills 1608, Bushmills Distillery Reserve and → Coleraine. From Midleton there are → Crested Ten, → Dunphy's, → Hewitt's, → Jameson, Midleton Rare, → Paddy, → Powers, → Three Stills and → Tullamore Dew which although distilled at Midleton now belongs to → Allied Domecq PLC. → Buena Vista is made exclusively for the Buena Vista café in San Francisco. Recently Midleton has also produced a single malt called → Erin Go Brath. And finally the French group's whisk(e)y portfolio also includes → Royal Canadian.

Peter Dawson Scotch blend that is now produced by → UDV, but which first came onto the market before 1900, from the Glasgow-based family firm that joined → DCL in 1925. They held the licence on DCL's behalf for → Glen Ord Distillery. The brand is mainly intended for South America but is also available, for example, at the → Glenkinchie visitor centre.

Peter Scot Indian whisky described as a malt. It label states that it has been 'blended with the choicest whiskies'. It is of high quality and its producers, → Khoday produce more than a million bottles of it a year.

Phenols The aromatic chemical substances that whisky absorbs from the → peat which is burnt when drying the malt in a traditional → kiln or in the modern → maltings. The → Islay malt whiskies in particular get their characteristic taste from phenols, a taste which some hate, but others adore. They are measured in ppm, parts per million, and range from the mildly-peated Bunnahabhain with 5ppm to Ardbeg with 50ppm. In between, according to James McEwan, for many years the manager of → Bowmore (20ppm), and now master distiller of → Bruichladdich (8ppm), → Caol Ila with 30ppm, → Port Ellen with 25ppm, → Laphroaig with 35 to 40ppm and → Lagavulin with 40ppm. The phenols are responsible for the flavours: iodine, seaweed and smoke. In chemical terms phenols are derivatives of hydrocarbons.

Philadelphia American blended whiskey, one of the many small brands from → Heaven Hill in Bardstown which are so numerous that it is difficult to retain an overview.

Pig's Nose Scotch blend that began life as the special brand of a pub in the village of Oldbury on Severn near Bristol. It was produced by the blenders George Morton in Montrose. The brand belonged to M J Dowdeswell & Co who had previously made the brand → Sheep Dip. The label describes the whisky as 'as soft and smooth as a pig's nose'. It now comes from the → JBB/→ Fortune Brands subsidiary → Invergordon and is sold internationally as a 5-year-old → standard blend.

Pike Creek Canadian whisky belonging to the small series which → Corby has brought out under the name 'The → Canadian Whisky Guild'. The Pike Creek is described as double barreled: after maturation in oak casks it received a → finishing in a port wine cask.

Pikesville Supreme American straight rye, named after a place in Baltimore County. This was once the centre of rye whiskey, but is no longer produced there. It now comes from Kentucky and is made at → Heaven Hill according to the formula 65% rye to 23% corn and 12% malted barley. Its label states: 'The aristocrat of straight Whiskies Pikesville was distilled under an old Maryland formula and stored in selected charred white oak casks in modern warehouses to age and mellow.' It is difficult to find and practically only obtainable in Maryland.

Pinch Scotch blend that is only sold by this name in the USA. In the rest of the world it is known as → Dimple and is one of the most successful → de luxe blends. It was introduced to America by → Haig & Haig, a company which was originally independent of John → Haig & Co, although its founder was a member of the same family.

Pinwinnie De Luxe Scotch blend with the suffix Royal Scotch. It is presented in a distinguished tin box, comes from → Inver House Distillers Ltd and is particularly successful in the → USA and in → France.

Pipe Major Scotch blend from the London-based → Montrose Whisky Company who produce it aged 5, 12 and 21 years.

Piper's Clan Scotch blend from → Angus Dundee.

Piper's Preferred, The Series of Scotch single malts bottled for the German company Scotchconnection: single cask bottlings at → cask strength, with the name of the distillery from which they came as well as their age and month of distillation. The date of bottling hasn't always been given, but the newer bottles had it engraved in the glass. The company was located in the Swabian town of Lichtenstein and was the German importer for independent bottlers such as → Adelphi, → Blackadder International, → Glenhaven, → Hart Brothers, James → MacArthur, → Michel → Couvreur, → Pràban na Linne and → Vintage Malt Whisky Company.

Pirate's poison Whisky cocktail. Three dashes of angostura, 1cl Campari, 1cl white rum, 2cl peach brandy, 2cl pineapple and a generous portion of Scotch are shaken together with ice and served with a cherry and a few pieces of pineapple.

Piraten Whisky →Fleischmann → Glen Blue and → Glen Mouse.

Pittyvaich Scottish malt distillery built by Arthur → Bell & Sons in 1974 on the site of the farm belonging to their → Dufftown Distillery. Its name, pronounced 'pit-ee-vay-ich', means 'place of the cow-shed'. It is ultra-modern and operates with a very small staff. It was built so that Bell's would have enough malt whisky to swap with other blenders, and never appeared as a single malt in a proprietor's bottling. It was → UD, who have run the distillery since Bell was taken over by → Guinness in 1985, who first included a 14-year-old in their → 'Flora & Fauna' series – shortly after closing down the distillery. At present it only operates for several months a year and is used for experiments with new distilling methods and new types of barley. Of the → independents it was first available from → MacArthur, followed by bottlings from → Cadenhead and → Signatory.

Plainsman Kentucky straight bourbon from the Plainsman Distilling Company, whose address in Weston, Missouri suggesting that it must be from → McCormick. It is 80°/40%.

Platte Valley American corn Whiskey from the → McCormick Distilling Co, who give → Weston, Missouri as their headquarters, but who also ran the → Pekin Distillery in Illinois until 1991. This is where the 3-year-old whiskey at 80°/40% is made, but the clay jugs labelled 'Distilled in Illinois' are running out and will then be replaced with a corn whiskey made at → Heaven Hill.

PM American blended whiskey that nowadays comes from → American Brands, subsidiary → JBB, and originally belonged to National Distillers, who were taken over by the present owners of the brand in 1987.

Poit Dubh Scotch vatted malt from → Pràban Na Linne. It is pronounced 'potsch guu' and means 'black pot', and is the Scottish-Gaelic version of the Irish → poitín, meaning illegal, illicitly-distilled whiskey. There are three versions of the successful vatted malt, a 12-year-old at 40% and a black label and one at 46% whose green label points out that it is 'unchillfiltered'. Although this process makes the liquid clear, it extracts many substances which are responsible for a rich aroma. Malt whiskies which have not been chill filtered can become cloudy when they are 'treated' with a little water. The 21-year-old is 43% Pràban Na Linne is based on Skye, the home of → Talisker.

Poitín Gaelic term for illicity-distilled spirits. It means 'a little pot' and in English is sometimes written → potcheen, poiteen or poteen. Illegal distilling has taken place everywhere. In the USA, where the result is called → moonshine. At Christmas in 1661 the English rulers imposed a tax upon distilling alcohol. From that time on the illegal production of whiskey became something of a national sport. Legally produced whiskey is called 'Parliament whiskey' to this day.

Production takes place in the most unlikely places. Traditionally the recipe for the mash consists of equal parts of water and barley to which sugar is added, but maize, potatoes or even molasses may be used. Poitín doesn't always have to be whiskey. Its drinkers are mostly only interested in the pure alcohol, which is why there is no ageing in a cask and the stuff remains crystal clear. As this process is not always carried out hygienically, its consumption can have dangerous consequences.

Polo Club Scotch blend sold by Hurlingham International which was first established in 1993. They also use the name for other spirits such as gin and vodka, and mainly concentrate their activities in the Far East, South America, Mexico and eastern Europe. There are two → de luxe versions of the blend, aged 12 and 15 years.

Polychem Indian company based in Bombay, where they also own a distillery. In 1984 Polychem brought out → Men's Club, which with nearly four million bottles sold has become one of → India's most successful brands. They also make → Royal Secret and their → White House is a succesful export brand. In 1993 the company entered into a joint venture with → IDV which has made it easier for them to obtain the Scotch blends that they need (their whiskies are blended from Indian malt whisky and ready-blended Scotch). IDV were already well represented with → Gilbey's and → Spey Royal.

Port Cask Scotch single malt from an unidentified distillery which, however, must be in the → Speyside region. When it was brought out by → Gordon & MacPhail in 1994, at the same time as a → Brandy Cask, malt whiskies matured in a port or cognac cask had never previously been sold. There are now many whiskies that go through a → finishing, an extra period of maturation. → Glenmorangie, → Balvenie, → Bushmills and most recently → Cragganmore from the → 'Distiller's Edition' of the → 'Classic Malts' are examples; → Oddbins, however, had a pure port wine cask malt. Gordon & MacPhail brought out the first bottling in 1993 followed by another in 1994. The first one had been distilled on 22nd December1967 and bottled on 9th March 1993 from casks no. 8921 and 8922, the second one had been distilled on the same day but bottled on 14th July 1994 and came from casks no. 8923, 8924 and 8925. It is at the 40% which is G&M's standard.

Port Dundas Scottish grain distillery in Glasgow. It lies in the northern part of the city, next to the Forth-Clyde Canal, which has helped the transport of grain to it and casks from it. It began as a malt distillery around 1817, but shortly after was equipped with → patent stills – Aeneas → Coffey himself is said to have demonstrated his newly-found knowledge there for the first time on Scottish soil. Later it belonged to Macfarlane & Co, who were among the founding members of → DCL. They became part of → UD 110 years later, and UDV now operate it, along with → Cameronbridge, as their only grain distillery (having shut down → Cambus and → Carsebridge). From the outside the buildings still look just as they must have looked in the 19th century, Port Dundas was the starting point for Alfred → Barnard's famous journey to the distilleries of the British Isles. There has neither been a bottling of a Single Grain from DCL nor from UD, and there is no evidence of any from the → independents.

Port Ellen Harbour town on the 'whisky island' of → Islay with a malt distillery of the same name. In 1983 it was shut down by → DCL although they had completely renovated it and increased the number of → stills from two to four just a few years previously, following a long closure from 1929 to 1966. The buildings are listed (they are protected from demolition). The stills have been transported to the mainland and melted down and also much equipment has been dismantled and gone to → Caol Ila or → Lagavulin, the other → GuinnessUDV (the present owners) distilleries on the island. The sea air, which is so good for the malts still maturing in the → warehouses, has not been so good for the remains of the equipment and it is to be feared that the Port Ellen Distillery may soon have to be struck off the map of Scotch whisky.

It produced an excellent malt whisky, which was not too extreme but nonetheless a typical Islay. It was established in 1825 and taken over by John Ramsay in 1836 and is said to have played a part in the history of whisky: David Daiches and Philip Morrice report that both Robert → Stein and Aeneas → Coffey were invited by Ramsay to demonstrate their early experiments with their new → patent or → Coffey stills. A → spirit safe is also said to have been installed by Ramsay for the first time in any distillery before becoming a legal requirement everywhere. Ramsay was one of the pioneers of whisky exports, sending ships to America from Port Ellen. His successors sold the distillery to the Port Ellen Distillery Company Ltd in 1920, a firm owned by John Dewar and James Buchanan. It was subsequently absorbed into the DCL empire in 1925. In 1973 the Port Ellen Maltings were built in the immediate vicinity and now supply all Islay's distilleries as well as the → Isle of Jura Distillery.

The single malt from Port Ellen had not been available as a → proprietor's bottling until UDV brought out two → 'Rare Malts' at the end of 1998. It was distilled in 1978, was bottled aged 20 years and at 60.9%. A second one was 22 years old (from 1978) with a strength of 60.5%. The 21-year-old (58%) Port Ellen is a collectors' item and was brought out in 1998 to celebrate the 25th anniversary of the 'Islay Concordate', the agreement reached by all Islay distilleries to get their malted barley from the new maltings. However there have been many bottlings from the → independents, especially from → Gordon & MacPhail and → Signatory, who also included two versions (from 1975 at 56.1% and from 1979 at 56.3%) in the → 'Silent Stills' series, as well as from → Cadenhead and from 'The → Select Hogshead'. Malt from Port Ellen has become scarce in recent times.

Pot Lid Scotch blend which comes from The → Benachie Whisky Co, the company based in Inverurie to the west of Aberdeen, near the mountain of the same name. It is a → standard blend.

Pot still Form of distillery equipment which nowadays is particularly used in Scottish distilleries producing pure malt whisky. It is a legal requirement that only malted barley may be used and this must be distilled in pot stills. In Ireland, on the other hand, they are allowed to use unmalted grain, although → Bushmills and → Cooley use only malted barley. Formerly Irish whiskey was only distilled in pot stills. Now the → pure pot still whiskey that was a synonym for Irish whiskey, has become rare;

Pot still whiskey

there are only a few sorts such as → Redbreast, → Green Spot or the new 15-year-old → Jameson.

The Irish pot stills were traditionally similar in shape to the Scottish ones, but were much bigger. It is possible to see the biggest in the world at the museum in → Midleton. In Scotland there are also different shapes and sizes. They may be onion- or pear-shaped, they can be small like those at → Edradour, fat and stocky like those at → Glenfiddich or → Macallan, and sometimes they are tall and thin like those at → Glenmorangie. Sometimes they have a second ring-shaped indentation like those at → Balvenie. The shapes and size influence the character of the distillate. Generally speaking, the bigger the still, the lighter the whisky. The smaller stills produce a whisky which has more body and is oilier. Master distillers have great belief in the shape of their stills, which may become worn out and need to be replaced.

They are almost always replaced by exact copies of the old ones and if a distillery wishes to increase its capacity the stills are not made bigger, but their number is increased. Pot stills are always made of copper, a metal which is especially well-suited to whisk(e)y and appears to influence its quality. It is possible to work with a single pot still, but they normally come in pairs. The first run occurs in the → wash or → low wines still, the second in the → spirit still. In Ireland there is always a third run, in Scotland only occasionally. This takes place in the → intermediate still.

Pot still whiskey The original Irish whiskey (except for → poitín). It is made in copper pot stills which are much larger than those found in Scotland. Whilst the Scotch malt whisky is only allowed to be made from malted barley, pot still whiskey consists of a mixture of malted and unmalted barley (the unmalted share being the larger). In earlier times rye and oats were also sometimes added. Irish whiskey is distilled three times. Both the ingredients and the method of distilling lend the pot still whiskey its characteristic combination of smoothness, purity and oiliness. Whereas this kind of whiskey used to be the only type in Ireland, it has now become rare: most Irish whiskeys are blends, which is why the term → pure pot still whiskey has recently been introduced, to emphasise the fact that it is a traditional Irish whiskey. Apart from → Cadenhead's single cask bottlings from the old distilleries of → Bow Street, → Jones Road, → John's Lane, → Royal Irish and the → Dungourney, there are only → Green Spot, → Old Comber, → Redbreast and the new 15-year-old → Jameson. The → Tyrconnell, → Connemara and → Locke's Single Malt from the → Cooley Distillery, which carry the same description, are in fact single malts made of malted barley which have been distilled twice.

Potcheen → poitín.

Potter's American blended whisky at 80°/40%. It comes from Potter Brands, a company based in San José, California.

Potter's Special Old Canadian whisky only available in Canada that has a strong sherry taste, which comes from the Spanish wine that has been added. The Potter Distilling Company, based in Vancouver, owns the → Cascadia Distillery in Kelowna, but mostly obtains the whiskies for its blends elsewhere.

Power's Gold Label Irish whiskey. It is the most popular brand in Ireland, and those who are able to get hold of it outside its home country sing its praises. It was founded by James Power & Son in 1791 and was later renamed by the son, John Power & Son. They built the famous distillery in → John's Lane, Dublin and gradually grew to become the most successful enterprise, alongside their competitors → Jameson on the other side of the Liffey.

Its success was as much due to the quality of its product as to their innovative spirit; it was the first Irish company to only sell its product solely in bottles, and were the first to introduce a miniature, named 'Baby Power'. The distillery was extended in 1871. Its attractive and architecturally valuable remains survived the end of the company with the merger of Jameson and → Cork Distilleries, and along with their three splendid stills these can still be admired today. The whiskey has of course changed. It now comes from → Midleton and is no longer a → Pot Still, but a very charactderful blend. This change has not affected its popularity.

Pràban Na Linne Scottish whisky company based on the Isle of Skye which adheres to the Gaelic tradition. Its whiskies have Gaelic names, and are advertised in Gaelic, because their founder Iain Noble initially targeted the products at the Gaelic-speaking community. The popularity of → Té Bheag, → MacNaMara and especially the malt whiskies → Poit Dhubh, is no longer only confined to the Western Isles. The company's liking for the original was demonstrated when several of their bottlings were not → chill-filtered, a fact which they were the first to advertise. The company was established in 1976 and also welcomes vistors to its 'little whisky centre on the Sound of Sleat'. They proudly call their products 'Gaelic Whiskies'.

Prairie Gold Canadian whisky which is sold in the UK branches of the discount shops ALDI as the 'Finest Canadian'.

Premier Scotch blend available in three very different versions from three very different companies. One is a → standard blend from the Premier Scotch Whisky company, which until 1996 was a subsidiary of the family-run business of H → Stenham in London. Like all products of the firm, it is available in five age categories, aged 3, 5, 8, 10 and 12 years, and is produced exclusively for export.

In 1995 → Morrison Bowmore launched a Premier onto the market. This is a 15-year-old → de luxe blend, and the 'Premiers' referred to are actually those at 10, Downing Street, and their portraits decorate the labels. So one is not only buying a very good blend, but also different labels.

The third version is a → Johnnie Walker with the suffix Premier.

Premier Scotch Whisky Company Scottish whisky company that was a subsidiary of the London-based H → Stenham. From 1953 to 1996 Stenham built up a small empire of several subsidiaries and more than 40 brands, most intended for export and sometimes bottled at its destination. At the age of 82 he decided to sell his company to Alistair R F Sinclair's Scottish Rossendale Blenders. It still carries a range of Stenham blends, but concentrates particularly on → King Henry VIII and → Queen Mary I.

Premium Term mainly used in Scotland for a middle category of blends. They fall between the basic → standard blends and the → de luxe blends which represent the upper section of the market. Like the standards, they tend not to carry nan age statement but have a higher proportion of malt whiskies, and are more expensive. In the annual Scotch Whisky Industry Review the whisky market analyst Alan S Gray names the following examples of premium blends: → Ballantine's, → Bell's, → Famous Grouse, → J & B, → Johnnie Walker Red Label and → Teacher's.

In Japan premium whiskies contain between 35-40% malt content.

President Scotch blend which began life as President Special Reserve De Luxe. It came from → Macdonald Greenlees who are best-known for their successful → Old Parr blend, → Sandy Macdonald and their → Glendullan Distillery. Its present owners → UDV continue to market the brand as a → premium blend and mainly sell it in South America.

President's Choice There are three whiskeys with this name. Firstly there is a Kentucky straight bourbon whose full name is The President's Choice for a Distinguished Gentleman. The president in question is that of the American company → Brown-Forman, which owns the → Early Times Distillery in Kentucky and the → Jack Daniel Distillery in Tennessee. There were exactly 24 casks of this rare whisky, which is bottled at 90.3°.

Brown-Forman found the name appropriate for a quite different whiskey, which is also a straight bourbon, and is a brand from their subsidiary → Labrot & Graham and was meant to complement their → Woodford Reserve. Brown-

Prestige

Forman wanted to draw attention to the fact that in 1996 they had reopened the oldest distillery in the USA, and had great plans for it. Of course this whiskey doesn't yet come from the → pot stills at Glenn's Creek, to the south of Kentucky's capital Frankfort, but from the → Early Times Distillery. It has 100.4°/50.2%.

A Japanese blend also bears this name 'in memory of the cooperation between the Schloß Vollrads Winery and the Yamanashi Winery'.

Prestige Japanese blend from the → super-premium sector. This brand from → Suntory is also composed of malt whiskies which are very old for a Japanese brand; the bottle gives an impression of solidity and quality and its label bears the age statement of 25 years.

Prestige d'Ecosse Scotch blend from William → Lundie & Co in Glasgow which is available in two versions. One is without an age statement and the other is 5 years old.

Prestonfield Scotch whiskies produced for the hotel situated at the foot of Arthur's Seat in Edinburgh. The brand belongs to Andrew Symington from → Signatory. There is a blend as well as single malts, which sometimes bear the name of the distillery from which they come.

Pride of ... Series of Scotch vatted malts from → Gordon & MacPhail. They demonstrate the characteristic nuances in taste of whiskies from the four Scottish areas → after which they are named: Pride of → Strathspey, Pride of → Islay, Pride of → Orkney and Pride of the → Lowlands. They contain malt whiskies which are at least 12 years old and the Strathspey is also available as a 25-year-old. Apart from the 40% typical for G&M, the Orkney is also available at 57%. From time to time → vintage bottlings are also brought out. No information is given about which malts are used.

Prince Charlie Scotch blend from Chivas Bros The name refers to Bonnie Prince Charlie, the 'Young Pretender.

Prince of Wales Malt whisky from The → Welsh Whisky Company Ltd in Brecon. It has been available in three versions. The first one was a 10-year-old bearing the description 'Single vatted malt'. The contradiction is explained when one examines the history of the company Welsh Whisky Ltd who in 1974 decided to make → Wales a whisky country yet again. At the time they didn't have a distillery of their own, so they bought a single malt in Scotland and processed it in the same way that, according to old sources, used to be customary in Wales (and, incidentally, in Scotland as well), before discovering the blessed effect of wooden casks. This means that they added herbs to the whisky and omitted the usual → chill-filtering. According to reports the malt whisky came from → Tomatin. The company went into liquidation in 1996, but in 2000 another Welsh Company started malt whisky production in a new distillery in the village of Penderyn in Brecon. The Prince of Wales 'Special Reserve' carried no age statement. On the bottles of the 12-year-old neither the words 'single' or 'vatted' appeared, but instead 'Oak Aged Malt Whisky'. On the packaging of the 10-year-old the history of whisky in Wales was explained, as well as the fact that it was not named after the present bearer of the title, but after the mighty Prince Owain Glyndwr who ruled from 1400 to 1412. In 1994 a special edition was brought out to commemorate the 50th anniversary of the Normandy landings; part of the proceedings went to the 'Airborne Forces' charity.

Printer's Czech whisky produced by the → Stock Distillery in Plzen (Pilsen) whose label (decorated with an old printing press) states 'Finest blended Whisky'. It is said to be a 'normal' blend at the 40% which is the minimum requirement in the → Czech Republic.

Private Collection Series of single malts offered by → Gordon & MacPhail in 2000 which brought this → independent bottler in line with the modern trend of → finishing. There are two editions with three bottlings each and malt whiskies from two distilleries which are each distilled at the same time and matured for the same period, but then filled into three different casks. The first malt is a → Speyside from the → Imperial Distillery (closed in 1998) which was distilled in 1990 and matured in ex-sherry casks which had been used once before and then recharred. It was refilled in the autumn of 1998 and bottled in August 2000. The second malt is from → Caol Ila and was distilled in October 1988 and placed in reconstructed hogsheads which were being reused for whisky a second time. They were stored on Islay until 1994 when they went to Gordon & MacPhail in Elgin where, in the autumn of 1998, the whisky was refilled and then followed the same procedure as the Imperial. The new casks previously contained claret, cognac or calvados. They were all bottled at the usual 40%. The Caol Ila only produced 2,100 bottles (the Imperial Cognac had the highest number with 4,500 bottles).

Prize Japanese blend in glass decanters that its producer → Nikka often uses for packaging. On the label the name 'Nikka Whisky' is in larger print than the word Prize, but the appearance of the bottle is an indication that it belongs to one of the higher categories that the Japanese use to classify their blends.

Producer's bottling A term used mainly in association with Scotch single malts which are not marketed by → independent bottlers, but by the distillery or its owner. The term → proprietor's bottling is more customary.

Prohibition Legal forbidding of the production and sale of alcohol usually associated with the 'dry years' in the USA, a period lasting from 17th January 1920 to 5th December 1933. Prohibition was by no means limited to either the USA or to this period. The Temperance Movement had begun gathering followers everywhere in the mid-19th century. The industrial revolution in Europe and the hard life of the 'Wild West' in the USA had led to people trying to ease their lives by drinking. This had the disastrous result that many families were ruined and became impoverished, forcing the children to go out to work.

In 1869 the prohibition Party was formed. In Ireland the sermons of the Capuchin Father Mathew resulted in the number of pubs dropping from 21,000 to 13,000 in the period between 1838 and 1844, which led to considerable losses for the whiskey industry. In England the churches organised lantern slide shows which told heart-wrenching tales of alcoholic fathers. In Scandinavia the sale of alcohol is state-controlled to this day.

In the USA 'dry states' already existed before the First World War. Prohibition was introduced in Tennessee in 1910; it forced the owners of the George Dickel Distillery to move production to Kentucky. In 1917 the war led to general prohibition and a year later the 'National Prohibition Law' was included in the Constitution. The 'Volstead Act' ruled that from midnight on 17th January 1920 America was dry. Stefan Gabányi rightly remarked in his book Whisk(e)y that the 13 years that followed 'changed the world of whisk(e)y to such an extent that its consequences can still be felt'.

Prohibition brought about the total collapse of the whiskey industry in America. Nearly every distillery was forced to close. The production of alcohol for medicinal purposes continued to be permitted, but only six distilleries received licences to do so. This led to a rapid increase in the number of illnesses which could only be treated with whiskey! The number of illicit distillers also increased accordingly: in 1921 the police discovered 96,000, and in 1930 the number was 282,000 – not to mention all those who remained undiscovered. Speakeasies sprang up everywhere. These were illegal bars which sold whiskey that was often highly suspicious or of inferior quality. Nightclubs sold fruit cocktails that the guests could fortify with the alcohol they had brought with them. Smugglers earned a fortune and many a gangster became rich and powerful.

Many of the competitors of the American whiskey producers in Canada and Scotland profited from America's thirst. The distilleries in Campbeltown were very badly effected, however, and many of them had to close down. Initially other Scottish companies seemed to be suffering severe damage, however in retrospect it must be said that they actually profited.
The Irish lost their main market was wiped out in one fell swoop, the industry collapsed and it took years for it to recover.

Proof

The Scots and Canadians began producing lighter blends to suit the American taste: brands such as → Cutty Sark and → J & B are examples. When prohibition came to an end in 1933 they found themselves in a strategic position to conquer the American market. Hiram Walker and Seagram acted in a similar manner, and basically owe their position on the world market to prohibition. Even today the Americans drink more Canadian whisky than bourbon.

The official end of prohibition proclaimed by President Roosevelt was not universal. In the southern states of the USA there are still 'dry' counties to this day. Visitors to the Jack Daniel Distillery in Lynchburg have only been allowed to buy a bottle of the product within recent years, but they are not allowed to drink from it. There was, incidentally, a prohibition period in Scotland which actually lasted longer than that on the other side of the Atlantic. Fortunately it did not apply to the entire country but was confined to Wick where, between 28th May 1922 and 28th May 1947, it was forbidden to sell whisky. It is not known whether this is what caused the closure of the local → Pulteney Distillery, but in any case it was closed from 1930 to 1951.

Proof Standardised measurement of the strength of alcoholic drinks which was customary in the UK until January 1980. It is still used in North America, although it is also being replaced by the modern measurement that is based on the methods introduced by Guy-Lussac and now used by the International Organisation of Legal Metrology, which measure alcoholic strength as a percentage of alcohol by volume at a temperature of 20°C. A set temperature was also established before determination. This amounted to 51°F in the UK and 60°F in America. For this reason British and American proofs are not identical.

The American measurement is easy to work out as it is always exactly double the percentage. Therefore 50% is exactly 100°. However, according to the British definition 100° is 57%. In 1952 it was determined that: 'Spirits shall be deemed to be at °proof if the volume of the ethyl alcohol contained therein made up to the volume of the spirits with distilled water has a weight equal to that of $^{12}/_{13}$ths of a volume of distilled water equal to the volume of the spirits, the volume of each liquid being computed at fifty-one degrees Fahrenheit'. This is a lot more exact than the earlier method of damping gunpowder with alcohol and lighting it to see if it still ignited. The hydrometer made more exact measurements possible, but tables were still necessary to determine how much water and how much alcohol a bottle contained. Complicated formulae explained why the British 70 °proof was equal to the American 80 °proof.

Proprietor's bottling A term used for malt whiskies which are bottled by their producer or by the company owning the distillery. They are also called → distillery, → producer or → official bottlings, in contrast to those that are marketed by → independent bottlers. In the UK they are also sometimes called → market house bottlings. A → licenced bottling, such as that of the old-established company Gordon & MacPhail in agreement with the producer, as in the case of → Glenlivet or → Linkwood or → Mortlach or in the → 'Allied' series, is a mixture of these forms.

Provenance Series of single malts in single cask bottlings whose labels name → McGibbons, a subsidiary of Douglas → Laing, as producer. Whilst their series 'The → Old Malt Cask' usually offers malts with a strength of 50%, the McGibbons collection is only 43%. The malts are also relatively young. Among the first bottlings was a 9-year-old Ardbeg, a → Glenlossie and a → Rosebank (each 10 years old), an 11-year-old → Macallan and, as the old man of the series, an 18-year-old → Port Ellen.

Pulteney Scottish malt distillery named an area of Wick which is right by the coast of the North Sea, to the south of the harbour. Sir William Pultney, was director of the British Fisheries Society. which built the fishing port in 1810. It belongs to the northern → Highlands and is the northernmost distillery on the Scottish mainland. The small town was once the herring capital of Scotland and played a special part in the history of whisky. In the period between 1922 and 1947 there was total → prohibition in the town and the sale of whisky was strictly forbidden. In recent years the distillery has twice become the focus of attention: firstly, because it was one of the distilleries which the large company → Allied Domecq PLC parted with, and secondly, because its new owner, → Inver House Distillers Ltd, brought out a single malt (aged 12 years) as a → proprietor's bottling for the first time in 60 years.

In 1826 James Henderson built the distillery and until the 1920s the distillery remained in the hands of the family, before running into a turbulent period with frequent changes in ownership. It first passed to James Watson & Co, and then via → Dewar to → DCL, who closed it down from 1930 to 1951 (this could have been because of prohibition). In 1955 it was sold to the Canadian company Hiram → Walker, who transferred its licence to their subsidiary James and George → Stodart. The product that the two → stills made using the water of Hempriggs Loch was mostly used for blends (especially → Ballantine's), but Allied, who by that time owned Hiram Walker, allowed → Gordon & MacPhail to undertake several bottlings under the name of the licence holder and called → Old Pulteney. The name was retained by Inver House Distillers Ltd. In 1997 they complemented the 12-year-old with a 15-year-old → cask strength (60%). Several 15-year-old Sherry Cask then joined these two, which are issued as limited editions and also have a strength of about 60% (one was 60.8%, a second 60.5%). For the Millennium there were various Single Casks (15-year-old, 59%, 60.9% and 61.1%). Finally Inver House Distillers Ltd paid tribute to the trend for sweetness and launched an Old Pulteney Liqueur.

Puncheon Term for the largest cask used in Scotland for whisky. It has a capacity of about 550 litres and is one of the five main types of cask along with the → quarter, → barrel, → hogshead and → butt.

Pure Gold Canadian whisky aged 3 years and only obtainable in Canada. The whiskies used for the blend do not come from the → Kittling Ridge Distillery named on the label, but are bought from other distilleries.

Pure Kentucky Kentucky straight bourbon from the → Kentucky Bourbon Distillers in Bardstown who also own the → Willett Distillery. → Johnny Drum and → Noah's Mill come from its old stocks, but this → small batch whiskey, which the company itself names a 'Boutique Bourbon', probably does not. On its seal it bears the letters 'XO' and its label shows an old map of Kentucky.

Pure Malt Type of whisky that cannot be exactly defined. The expressions 'single malt' and 'vatted malt' are used for a malt whisky that is either from a single distillery (which is usually named) or composed from malt whiskies from various distilleries (and is therefore 'vatted'), the term 'Pure Malt' can mean either. William → Grant & Sons first described their → Glenfiddich, the first single malt to be marketed outside Scotland, as a 'Pure Malt', and until recently both expressions were to be found on the bottles of this classic. However, since more and more malt whiskies are becoming available in → proprietor's bottlings, there is an attempt to make things clearer. Now if a bottle of Scotch whisky has the words 'Pure Malt' printed on it it is, as a rule, a vatted malt. In other countries it is less consistent. The Japanese often use the term 'Pure Malt', which suggests that their malt whiskies perhaps do not only contain whiskies distilled in Japan, but also sometimes a drop of Scotch whisky (which wouldn't be so surprising as both → Suntory and → Nikka own distilleries in Scotland and → Kirin has access via → Seagram). A further example is the German malt → Piraten Whisky from Robert Fleischmann, which is described as 'Pure Malt' although it is plainly a single malt.

Pure Malt Japanese brand from → Nikka. Apart from the Nikka Pure Malt with the subtitles → Kitagenshu and → Hokkaido, there is also a Nikka Pure Malt from a sherry cask. In addition there are three versions of Pure Malt where the company name is not so plainly emphasised, the Black, the Red and the White. The latter is obviously a vatted: the malt whiskies used for it are imported from Scotland and 'married' in Japan. → Islay whiskies are dominant, but in which there is probably also some → Ben Nevis in it, which also belongs to Nikka. The Red is

Pure pot still whiskey

light, which leads to the conclusion that it mainly consists of whiskies that are produced at Nikka's distillery in → Sendai. In contrast the Black has more body and is a heavier whisky, consisting mainly of whiskies from Nikka's first distillery, → Yoichi on the northern Japanese island of Hokkaido. All three come in half-litre bottles and the company encourages its customers to buy them as a set and to perform their own blending experiments. They were the first pure malt whiskies to have been brought onto the market by a Japanese company.

Pure pot still whiskey Modern term for the traditional Irish whiskey that used to be called → pot still whiskey. The adjunct 'pure' became necessary after Ireland began almost exclusively to produce blends. Today only → Green Spot, → Old Comber, → Redbreast and the new 15-year-old Jameson represent the old style. The → Tyrconnell, → Connemara and → Locke's Single Malt from → Cooley are also Pure Pot Stills, but are different from the other three because they are produced by the Scottish method, using only malted barley (purists insist that → pot still whiskey should chiefly contain unmalted barley) and is only distilled twice.

Putachieside Scotch blend with a pretty, old-fashioned label on which it is still called 'Liqueur Whisky'. It also shows the square in Aberdeen that gave it its name. The brand was brought out in the 19th century by William → Cadenhead, a local wine and spirits merchant whose name is known to every malt connoisseur because this company was one of the first → independent bottlers. Cadenhead now belongs to J & A → Mitchell in → Campbeltown and they market this blend aged 12 and 25 years following their usual principles. The whisky is not coloured. They would like to make it more widely available and hopefully the old label will be retained.

Q

QSI (Quality Spirits International) Subsidiary of William → Grant & Sons based in Guernsey which has more than 50 brand names in its portfolio and mainly deals in value for money blends, some on single markets only and others as own brands for other companies (for example, supermarket chains). Sometimes names are used that do not belong to the company itself, as in the case of → Loch Kindie. The most important brands, to which William Grant & Sons themselves hold the rights, are: → Consulate, → Glen Corrie, → The Great Macauley, → Haddington House, → Highland Bird, → Highland Reserve, → King Charles and → Scottish Collie. The company also markets Loch Kindie and → Old Moor.

Quaich Scottish drinking vessel in the form of a dish. It has two handles by which it can be passed on to a newly-arrived guest or from drinker to drinker in a companionable round. It is also known as the 'cup of friendship'. It may be made of a precious metal such as silver or even gold, or may be of pewter, wood or horn. The word derives from the Gaelic 'cuach', is related to the German 'Kelch', and is probably an adaptation of the Latin 'caucus'. Quaiches were often used in the officers' mess of the Highland regiments but had almost disappeared from daily life. In 1988 the → 'Keepers of the Quaich' was established and with their hands on a large quaich keepers vow 'to promote the image and prestige of Scotch whisky'. Quaiches continue to be produced and have become popular souvenirs.

Quarter Term for a cask with a capacity of approximately 125 to 130 litres, which is a quarter of a → butt.

Queen Anne Scotch blend, and one of the oldest brands. It came from → Hill Thomson & Company, whose beginnings go back to William Hill's grocer's shop, established in 1793 in Frederick Street, Edinburgh. The blend was created in the 1870s by William Shaw who had joined the company and named it after the Stuart queen. In 1970 Queen Anne was part of the 'dowry' when Hill Thompson merged with → Glen Grant- → Glenlivet, and it became the flagship blend of the new company, The → Glenlivet Distillers. The brand could proudly claim that it contained malt whiskies from all the company's distilleries, and principally from → Longmorn, → Glen Grant and → Glenlivet. This special role has been lost now in the face of other brands such as → Chivas Regal, → Passport and → Royal Salute, but it is still one of the → standard blends of the → Chivas Bros.

Queen Eleanor Scotch blend from Highland Shippers in Glasgow and London, one of the numerous subsidiaries of H → Stenham who also produced this blend, exclusively intended for export, in the company's usual age categories of 3, 5, 8, 10 and 12 years. In 1996 the company's owner, then aged 82, sold his company, which continued operating as the → Premier Scotch Whisky Co Queen Eleanor lived from 1223 – 1293 and was married to King Henry III.

Queen Elizabeth There are two Scotch blends of this name. One is a → standard blend which is still in → GuinnessUDV's range, having come to it after → Guinness had taken over Arthur → Bell & Sons in the 1980s. At Bell's it was a blend of the subsidiary Burn Brae Blenders. The second Queen Elizabeth is a → premium blend and comes from → Avery's of Bristol, one of the most important wine merchants in the UK, who have always insisted on bottling their own brands themselves. Avery's is now owned by the Hallgarten Group.

Queen Margot Scotch blend produced by the

Queen Mary I

Tower Blending Company. The → standard blend is obtainable at branches of Lidl in Germany.

Queen Mary I Scotch blend from the Premier Scotch Whisky Company in Glasgow and London, which was previously one of at least seven subsidiaries of the London family-run company founded and managed by H → Stenham. It had more than 40 brands in its range, and liked to use the names of English and Scottish kings and queens. Stenham sold his company when he became too old to continue running it to Alastair R F Sinclair's Scottish company Rossendale Blenders, which carried on running it under the name of Premier and brought out the blend as one of its two main labels. This blend is not available in the UK, but in the supermarkets of southern Europe, South America and South East Asia. The whisky is available in the age categories customary for this company of 3, 5, 8, 10 and 12 years.

Queen of Scots 15-year-old → premium Scotch blend. The company's most important blend is also named after Mary: → Highland Queen.

Queen's Choice Scotch blend from → UDV. It passed to its predecessors UD when Arthur → Bell & Sons, the parent company of the company named as producer, C & J → McDonald, was bought by → Guinness in the 1980s.

Queen's Own Scotch blend whose origins are not clear. It is included in the range of the UK wine, spirits and mineral water wholesaler Matthew Clark, which since 1998 has been a subsidiary of → Canandaigua.

Queen's Seal, The Scotch blend from Peter J → Russell. There used to be two versions sold by the subsidiary company Ian → MacLeod, a White and a Black Label, and today it is available as a → standard blend aged 12, 21 and 32 years.

Quintessential, The Scotch blend with which → Inver House Distillers Ltd took part in the competition 'The → Spirit of Scotland' within the 1994 'International Wine & Spirit Competition'. This was to mark the 500th anniverary of the receipt by the monk John → Cor from Fife of 'Eight Bolls of Malt' from the king in order to make 'aqua vitae' – whisky – the first documented reference of the word.

R

R & H Blenders Standard Scotch blend from the relatively new company → London & Scottish Spirits.

Racke Rauchzart German blend, brought onto the market in 1958 by A Racke, a company in Bingen. Racke is a family business which goes back to the Raquets who had settled in the Rheingau as wine merchants in the 17th century, and which was founded in 1855 by Adam Josef Racke, a dealer in wine and vinegar. His son Georg passed the business on to his son-in-law Heinrich Moller-Racke, and Harro Moller-Racke took over from him.

He decided to concentrate the variety of products on a few brands. He also recognised that the time had come for Germans to have a whisky that they could afford. He used very clever advertising strategies to market his brand, which was initially called Red Fox, and sold 850,000 bottles in the first year. The red fox still appears on the bottles, but since 1961 the whisky has been renamed Racke rauchzart ('smoke smooth'). On the German market the brand is in fifth place behind → Ballantine's, → Jim Beam, → Johnnie Walker and → Jack Daniel's. The company was so successful that it has been able to bring other well-known firms such as Pott and Dujardin under its umbrella and it distributed licences to Austria and Yugoslavia, marketed a Kentucky-made bourbon called Old Red Fox and sold a premixed drink; although it seems that this was launched too early.

Originally the blend was made from malt whiskies from Scotland which were blended with grain distillates which Racke had distilled for them in Rinteln on the Weser. This has been discontinued and now all the necessary whiskies come from Scotland, but are blended in Germany with the famous water mentioned on the back label. This comes from a depth of 240 metres and is carefully filtered. The blend contains up to 25 individual whiskies. Apart from the 'Special Blend' there was a 12-year-old, and a very rare 25-year-old in a glass carafe. Both have now become collectors' pieces. In November 2000 the brand celebrated its 40th anniversary by presenting a very small number of bottles to friends of the company. They received a 40-year-old blend that still consisted of Scotch malt whiskies and a German → grain whisky.

Rampur Indian distillery in the town of the same name which lies to the east of Delhi in Uttar Pradesh. It was built in its present form by the Rampur Distillery Company in 1993. Previously the company had only produced a molasses distillate there, which was more akin to rum. The distillery was equipped by Jolly Bhargava and his production manager R B Singh, who had first learned his skills at Heriot-Watt University in Edinburgh, before going to → Invergordon and → Tullibardine; Jimmy Lang came over from Scotland to help them. The result was so impressive that Invergordon's parent company → Whyte & Mackay, took over a 51% share. After a short interruption the distillery restarted production in 1997 – with Indian malt whisky from a Scottish company. The distillery is small, with six fermenting vessels made of stainless steel and two small → pot stills. They are not the only reminders of → Edradour. It is also said to have a similar taste. It has not yet been decided whether to bottle it as a single malt. For the time being some of it will go to → Genesis and → White Hall, as well as to → Moghul Monarch from → Shaw Wallace where, however, it is used in its immature form.

Rare Bourbons A series modelled on the Scottish → 'Rare Malts' introduced by → UD in

275

Rare Breed

1997. Its intention was to present whiskeys from American distilleries that have long since closed down and from which there had been little hope of ever tasting a drop. Just like the Scottish series, the bottlings are extremely limited in number and come at → barrel °proof. Unlike the Scottish model the exact distillery is not named. The first one is said to be a Kentucky straight from the Astor Distillery, which was situated next to the → Bernheim Distillery in Louisville. It was named → Henry Clay after a famous senator who had once owned a distillery. It was followed by → Joseph Finch. It is unlikely that the series will be continued as UDV, which resulted from the merger of UD and IDV, parted with nearly all its North American interests in the spring of 1999.

Rare Breed Kentucky straight bourbon from → Austin, Nichols Distilling Co. They, and their master distiller Jimmy Russell, have succeeded in creating the masterpiece of their → Wild Turkey series with this → barrel °proof. The bottle bears the date 1855, the year the company was founded, below a vignette showing a bird on the label. The label shows a picture of the → Boulevard Distillery in Lawrenceburg in the background, where Jimmy Russell has worked since 1955. For many years he has been responsible for production and distils all the whiskeys that are bottled as Wild Turkey. He personally selects the casks chosen for the Rare Breed. It is bottled aged 6, 8 and 12 years old. There is a number on the collar of the bottle which documents that this is a → small batch bourbon. It normally has a strength of around 108°/54% and on some markets is also available as 1855 Reserve.

Rare Malts collection Following the → 'Classic Malts' and → 'Flora & Fauna', this was the third series from → UD who, were attempting to compensate for the decreasing sales of their blends, the branded whiskies, were reacting to the increasing demand from lovers of malt whisky. This series offers sensational whiskies. Fortunately the series has been continued by UD's successor, → GuinnessUDV. By the spring of 2002 the malt whiskies of more than two dozen distilleries had been brought out, sometimes in several versions: → Aultmore, → Benrinnes, → Benromach, → Blair Athol, → Brora, → Caol Ila, → Cardhu, → Clynelish, → Coleburn, → Craigellachie, → Dailuaine , → Dallas Dhu, → Dufftown, → Glen Mhor → Glen Ord, → Glendullan, → Glenlochy, → Glenury Royal, → Hillside, → Inchgower, → Linkwood, → Mannochmore, → Millburn, → Mortlach, → North Port, → Port Ellen, → Rosebank, → Royal Brackla, → Royal Lochnagar, → St. Magdalene and → Teaninich. Many of these are from distilleries which have been closed down or even demolished, or from distilleries whose malts are difficult to find in a proprietor's bottling.

All are bottled at → cask strength and are not → chill-filtered, which has led GuinnessUDV to recommend diluting them with two-thirds water, with the warning that they could become 'dirty' and cloudy, which proves that they really have been left in their natural state and have not been artificially 'cleaned'. They are limited in number, and always sell out extremely quickly.

Rare Old Label Series of single malts with which → Gordon & MacPhail, the largest of the → independent bottlers, once again extended its portfolio. These are 'Rare Vintages' which are presented in mahogany boxes but which, unfortunately, have been reduced to 40%. The series began gloriously with an → Ayrshire Malt which was no less than a long-hoped for → Ladyburn. Further bottlings came from the distilleries Bunnahabhain (1967), Convalmore (1960), Glenlossie (1961), Glenrothes (1961), Glenugie (1968), Highland Park (1978), Ledaig (1974), Lochside (1981), Strathisla (1948), Tamdhu (1960), Tomintoul (1967). Further vintages, and also malts from other distilleries, are sure to follow.

Rattlesnake Whiskey cocktail. It is a variety of whiskey sour made with two parts bourbon and one part lemon juice which are shaken together vigorously with one part sugar syrup, one spoonful of caster sugar and a dash of anisette, and then strained and served in a cocktail glass.

Real Mackay Scotch blend that is produced for

the Guernsey-based Mackay & Co (who have nothing to do with → Whyte & Mackay), and which is only available on the Channel Islands. It is produced in Scotland by → Long John International, who belong to the → Allied Domecq PLC empire.

Real Mackenzie, The Scotch blend which originated with Peter Mackenzie & Co of Edinburgh who were founded in the 1820s. They were the owners of → Blair Atholl and → Dufftown distilleries when they were bought by Arthur → Bell & Sons in 1933, the first distilleries to be acquired by the Perth company. When, in the mid 1980s, → Guinness first bought Bell, and then two years later → DCL, the British Monopolies Commission demanded that the new company → UD, must part with several companies and brands (some such as → John Barr and → Claymore completely, and others only in some markets). The two blends (→ standard and 20 years old) and the vatted version of The Real Mackenzie were among the latter group. The rights for the UK are now held by → Kyndal, whilst in other markets they are still marketed by the → UD successor → GuinnessUDV.

Rebel Yell Kentucky straight bourbon. Launched on the market in 1936, it was made in the → Stitzel-Weller Distillery until 1993, and the distillery's owners had launched it on to the market in 1936. It was intended 'especially for the Deep South' as its label still informs us, and in fact for a long time it was only sold there. The label bears the date 1849 which refers to the origins of the the brand → W L Weller, with whom it shares its formula: Rebel Yell is one of the three so-called wheated whiskies from Stitzel-Weller, in which the customary share of rye has been replaced with wheat. At present the → mash bill is 75% corn, 20% wheat and 5% malted barley. The brand had been discontinued for a while before being reintroduced in 1961 to commemorate the 100th anniversary of the Civil War. In 1984 it was made available to those in the north.

This was the year that the Scottish → DCL took over the company and the brand. Their successors, → UD thought they would be able to appeal to a young public with Rebel Yell. The stocks which had originally been intended for Rebel Yell were later used for a new brand, the 'prohibition whiskey' Dickel's → RX. The distillery was closed down and the whiskeys for Rebel Yell, W L Weller and → Old Fitzgerald produced at the → Bernheim Distillery. In March 1999 the distillery and the brand were part of the package that the UD successors → UDV sold to the consortium consisting of → Heaven Hill, → Sazerac and David → Sherman. The latter took over the brand, whilst Heaven Hill took over the distillery. The whiskey is bottled at 80°/40%. There is also a Rebel Yell Double Cinnamon Spiced Liquor at 101°/50.5%.

Rectifier The second of two columns used in the production of whisk(e)y in → patent stills or → column stills. The first column is the → analyser. Here hot steam extracts the alcohol from the → wash before a mixture of water and alcohol steam is rectified in the second column, that is made into a chemically pure, relatively neutral tasting alcohol at about 95%.

Red & Gold Kentucky straight bourbon whose label describes it as 'smooth and mellow', names Red & Gold Distillery as bottlers and gives Bardstown as its headquarters. This is one of the many names under which the → Kentucky bourbon Distillers operate. It is probable that this 4-year-old whiskey (43% – the label does not give a °proof measurement) comes from the → Heaven Hill Distillery.

Red Devil Drink described as 'Red Hot Whisky'. According to the label it contained → Bells 8 years old with red Chili pepper and came from → UD with the information that its producer was Arthur → Bell & Sons. Bottles of it were only available on a trial market and in a few selected shops. Like → Hackler, or the premixed drinks such as → Bell's with Coke or 'Irn Bru', Red Devil was designed to appeal to a new group of consumers. It did not prove a commercial success, however, and is no longer available.

Red Extra Japanese blend from → Suntory which is among the most reasonably-priced standard brands of the company. It is not often seen in bars, although it is often found in households.

Red Feather

Red Feather Canadian whisky from → Gilbey Canada, tested on a small local market before being discontinued. For some time it remained uncertain whether it would be reintroduced, but since UDV, Gilbey's successors, have parted with all their Canadian interests (except for one single brand), it seems unlikely.

Red Hackle Scotch blend which is now made by → Robertson & Baxter, but which was originally launched on the market by Hepburn & Ross. The proprietor of this company, which passed to new owners in 1959, served in the Black Watch regiment, whose soldiers wore a red-feathered bonnet with a red hackle. The blend was available as Blue Hackle and as a red → premium blend aged 12 years but now only the → standard blend remains.

Red Knight Indian whisky from → Khoday bottled at the 42.8% customary in → India.

Red Lion Blending UK company based in London which grew from the merger of → Highland Stag Whiskies and R N MacDonald. They are brokers, but also bring out their own whiskies such as the blends → Custodian, → Gold Label and → Highland Stag. They also bottle for other companies, such as Diner's Club. They have sold the vatted malt → Glencoe to → Ben Nevis' Japanese owner → Nikka.

Red Rooster Scotch blend from Peter J → Russell & Co in Edinburgh, an independent family company which is mainly active in the blending and export business, has several subsidiaries and bottles for other companies under their own labels. This → standard blend is one of Russell's owns brands, like the → Black Rooster which is not being produced at present.

Red Rose Blend the label of which displays the red rose of the coat of arms of Lancashire (and which the famous Wars of the Roses are named after). The 40% → de luxe blend calls itself the 'Product of the Palatine of Lancaster'. Its producers, the Lancaster Whisky Producers in Wigan, are hoping to give the impression that they have revived the local whisky tradition; in the 19th century the Bankhall Distillery in Liverpool was one of the largest in the country and the label of the Red Rose refers to the distilleries belonging to the Preston company and Walker and Hill's of Bolton, which had a capacity of 3 million gallons. The product and the stories surrounding it are the creation of E J Hamson, who learnt the brewing trade and is the manager of a large malt extract production plant.

Redbreast Irish → pure pot still whiskey of which two versions are still available. They have different labels, and also taste very different. Both are 12 years old, and one gives → Fitzgerald as its producer, the other bears the name of John → Jameson & Son as well as that of → Gilbey. Gilbey later became a subsidiary of → IDV / → Grand Metropolitan, first introduced it on to the market in 1939. The whiskey came from → Jameson's → Bow Street Distillery, but matured in Gilbey's own casks (with two sherry casks to every bourbon cask). When the distillery was closed Gilbey was dependent on the remaining casks, many of which were already very old, when they bottled the last batch in 1985. The whiskey was particularly popular with the clergy, and the nickname 'The Priest's Bottle'. Several years ago → IDG revived the brand. It was its only → pot still whiskey and one of the very few in existence at all. The sherry character is less obvious in the new version (40%).

Refill Term used in Scotland for → casks which have already been used once to mature whisky and are used for a second time (first refill) or a third time (second refill) for a malt, or less often a → grain whisky. Genuine → new casks are hardly ever used for Scotch malt whisky as they would dominate its aromas in an undesirable way. Casks which have previously contained bourbon or sherry are imported second-hand from the USA or Spain and used to fill them (see → first fill).

Regency Whisky formerly produced by → Seagram which is exclusively for sale in → Venezuela. A further Regency comes as an 'Old Scotch Whisky Extra Special' from Tanzania where the Tanzania Distilleries in Dar-es-Salam fill it, not in bottles, but in plastic portion packs, similar to those for Ketchup, containing 30ml (40%). The German importer even sticks on the 'Green Point' label by hand.

Regent Scotch blend from → MacDuff International, Glasgow.

Reliance Scotch blend, a brand that belonged to Arthur → Bell & Sons via their subsidiary Forbes, Farquharson & Co, and then passed to → UD and finally to → UDV.

Reserve Japanese special blend from → Suntory with a relatively high share of malt whisky. It was first launched on to the market in 1969 when the company was 70 years old. They sell 2.5 million → cases of it per annum in Japan, making it the second strongest brand in the country after the → Kakubin, which also comes from Suntory. On the normal bottles the name of the producer is printed three times larger than the word 'Reserve' on the black label; although this is reversed on the new half-bottles.

Réserve, La Wine shop at 56, Walton Street, London, within walking distance of → Harrods. As well as an excellent selection of wines (especially French wines), it carries its own whisky and is therefore also an → independent bottler. The whisky always comes from single casks whose number is written on the bottles. Colouring is not used, nor is → chill-filtering, and the whisky is bottled at 46%, a sure indication that it is bottled in → Campbeltown by → Cadenhead. The owner of the London company is Mark Reynier who, together with Simon Coughlin and Gordon Wright, founded Murray → McDavid and bought → Bruichladdich Distillery. McDavid is the nephew of Hedley Wright, the owner of Springbank – and the malts from there form the core of their whiskies: in 1997 there was a cask each from 1978, 1972 and 1965, as well as a → Macallan from 1974, a → Caol Ila from 1974 and a → Glen Moray from 1962. La Réserve also offers its customers whole casks, again mainly from Springbank, which are excellent new fillings, that is fresh distillates which, for a fee, are kept in bond at the distillery until they have matured, at which time tax is due whilst the whisky itself has already been paid for at the time of ordering. A → hogshead Springbank, containing 256 litres, cost £1,000 in 1999, so that a bottle works out at under £4. Those who would like a cask of matured malt whisky for their cellars can get a 1979 Springbank from La Réserve for £1,295 or a 1974 Caol Ila for £1,575 at → cask strength – these are the small 30 litre → blood tubs which were once found in every gentleman's house.

Rittenhouse straight rye of which just a few bottles may still be found, although it is not being produced at present. It started life in Pennsylvania, where whiskey production in America began. It is identified with a genre of whiskey which has become increasingly rare. When the Pennsylvanian Rittenhouse distillery closed it was already being produced by → Medley in Owensboro, named the Continental Distilling Co as its producer and was → Bottled in Bond at 100°/50%. After Medley had first been bought by → Glenmore in 1991, they both passed to → UD and the only brands remaining were exclusively bottled for a German company, before → Heaven Hill acquired the rights to it. There they concentrate on → Pikesville and → Stephen Foster.

Riverstown Village near Dundalk in County Louth, near the border with Northern Ireland. In 1987 → Cooley Distillery bought Cimicei Teo, the state-owned distillery plant designed by a Czech architect, which produced industrial alcohol. The plant was rebuilt to make a distillery where → pot stills and → patent stills could produce malt whiskies as well as → grain whiskies. They are taken to the old Irish → Kilbeggan Distillery to mature.

Rob Roy Scotch blend. It is named after the 'Scottish Robin Hood', the outlaw and folk hero 'Rob Roy' McGregor (1671-1734). Walter Scott dedicated a book to him, Bérlioz wrote an opera and Hollywood has made a film about him. The blend comes from → Morrison Bowmore via their subsidiary → McClelland. It is extremely likely contains malt whiskies from all three of the company's distilleries, → Auchentoshan, → Bowmore and, especially, → Glen Garioch. It is available as a → standard blend aged 3 years and as a → de luxe blend aged 12, 17, 21, 25 and 30 years.

There is also a whisky cocktail of the same name, a variation on the Manhattan in which the usual bourbon is replaced by Scotch.

Robbie Burns Scotch blend named after the Scottish national bard Robert → Burns. Like → Old Angus and → Windsor Castle, it belonged to R H → Thomson & Co, Edinburgh, a subsidiary of → DCL, which therefore now belongs to → UDV.

Robbie Dubh Name of the famous spring that supplies the water for the → Glenfiddich and → Balvenie distilleries. A 12-year-old Scotch has also been named after it, which naturally comes from William → Grant & Sons, but which is not available everywhere. The simplified spelling on the bottles is Robbie Dhu.

Robert Brown Japanese blend from → Kirin-Seagram which, like all brands from this Canadian-Japanese joint venture, is composed of whiskies distilled in their Japanese distillery and those imported from Scotland. The company describes this whisky as a 'deluxe', a category which doesn't really exist in Japan, where their classifications are based on the proportion of malt whisky. In Scotland it would be categorised as a → standard blend. Michael Jackson attests that it has quite a lot of body.

Robertson & Baxter Scottish company that dates back to 1857 and that has played a major part in the history of the whisky industry in Scotland. It established early connections with → Highland Distilleries Co, for whose malt whiskies it held an early and long-lasting sales monopoly, and with whom it is still closely associated through mutual interests, sharing an address in Glasgow as well as the management of its whisky interests. Despite many takeover attempts, for example by → DCL, → Seagram and Hiram → Walker, it has been able to maintain its independence. It still belongs to the family of its founder, which has gathered together its businesses under the umbrella of the → Edrington Group. The company also owns Clyde Bonding, one of the largest companies involved with the warehousing and bottling of whiskies in Scotland, as well as one of the largest Scottish cooperages, the Clyde Cooperage. Robertson & Baxter have a 50% share in the grain distillery → North British (the other half was owned by IDV, which became → UDV in 1997). They have also acquired the famous blend → Red Hackle as well as → Glengoyne Distillery and therefore the Lang Brothers company, their Langs blends and → Auld Lang Syne. They have had a long and close association with → Berry Bros & Rudd, whose blend → Cutty Sark is produced and bottled by Robertson & Baxter.

Robertson & Son, John Scottish whisky company, best-known as the licence holder of → Coleburn and → Speyburn Distilleries and from which the blend → Yellow Label used to come.

Rock Hill Farm Kentucky straight bourbon from → Sazerac. Blanton laid the foundation stone of the distillery when he began to distil whiskey on his Rock Hill Farm in Leestown. The bottle is shaped like a carafe, and is decorated with horses and a very stylish label. Of the five single barrels which now all come from Ancient Age, it is the only → Bottled in Bond and has a strength of 100°/50%. The current master distiller, Gary Gayheart, chooses the barrels for it.

Rocky Falls Canadian whisky from → Alberta which is first bottled in Europe before being distributed. The brand belongs to → JBB (Greater Europe)plc.

Roderick Dhu Scotch blend brought on to the market in the 19th century by → Wright & Greig. The company, the brand and the distillery → Dallas Dhu later came under the influence of the → DCL subsidiary → Bulloch Lade & Co (→ Caol Ila). Today the blend is mainly sold to visitors of the distillery museum at Dallas Dhu.

Rodger's Old Scots Scotch blend whose name is a reminder of an old Glasgow company which was particularly successful in the export trade and had a large number of blends in their range. Their business was so successful that in 1898 John → Walker took over the entire company. They ran the → Banff Distillery on behalf of → DCL. The Old Scots, which in some countries is also sold as Rodger Special, is the only brand of the old company, along with → Huntly, which UDV/UD, has retained in its portfolio.

Rory A → standard Scotch blend from → London & Scottish Spirits.

Rory o'Moore Whiskey cocktail. This variation on the Manhattan does without the dry Vermouth and replaces the bourbon with an Irish.

Rosebank Scottish malt distillery which was closed down in 1993 by its new owners → UD. Some of its buildings were subsequently converted into a restaurant. Many drinkers believe that Rosebank is the best malt whisky of the → Lowlands. The distillery lies on the eastern outskirts of Falkirk, beside the Forth-Clyde-Canal. There was a distillery on the site in 1798, and in the mid 18th century James Rankine founded Rosebank, making use of the remains of the old Camelon Distillery. Fifty years later a joint-stock company was created which came, via → SMD, under the umbrella of → DCL, who charged their subsidiary → Distillers Agency Ltd with its management.

They bottled an 8-year-old single malt. The → 'Flora & Fauna' bottling of the DCL successor UD is, on the other hand, 12 years old. In the summer of 1999 a cask strength bottling came out in the → 'Rare Malts' series, with a 20-year-old Rosebank from 1979 (60.3%). The independent bottlers were also always keen to own a cask. Gordon & MacPhail have included it in their 'Connoisseurs Choice' series several times and Signatory has had, amongst others, one from 1989 and from 1990 (both 43%). The old → stills, in which → triple-distillation was carried out, are still standing, as well as the ancient mill with which the malt is converted to → grist and the venerable iron → mash tun. The water was supplied by the Carron Valley Water Reservoir in the Fintry Hills.

Route Japanese blend from → Sanraku-Ocean. It is a whisky light in colour and body.

Rowan's Creek Kentucky straight bourbon. It comes from the → Kentucky Bourbon Distillers who own the Willett distillery near Bardstown. The company carries several brands, including four which represent the trend in bourbon for → small batch bottlings, which are called 'Boutique Bourbons'. This one is 12 years old (100°/50%) and its label states that it is 'made and bottled by hand in small lots, one batch at a time.' It is named after the Justice of the Peace John Rowan, and the creek is said to run 'through our little distillery'. The whisky hasn't been distilled in Willett for more than 12 years.

Royal A → premium blend from → Suntory, created by the company founder Shinjiro → Torii. It was launched on to the market in the 1960s and soon became a successful brand. It is available in two versions, in a high multi-cornered bottle with a white label and in a distinguished looking almost square decanter whose golden label is decorated with the letters 'SR'. The 20 or so different malt whiskies ranging in age from 10 to 15 years which make it up have all matured in ex-bourbon casks.

Royal and Ancient, The Scotch blend which is named after the most famous golf club in the world, which although it has a clubhouse in Scotland's St. Andrews, strangely enough does not have a golf course of its own. The course is municipal property and is therefore a public course. The exclusive club is also responsible for formulating the rules which govern golf throughout the world. Considering all these elite associations it is surprising that a blend which is allowed to bear such an illustrious name isn't exclusively reserved for the clubhouse bar, but is in fact also available in the pubs of the London brewery Young & Co, which is where the whisky comes from. The blend was originally brought out in 1913 by → Cockburn & Campbell who were based in Edinburgh and who now belong to the brewery. It used to be sold as a 7-year-old and nowadays is a 10-year-old → de luxe blend. Recently a 28-year-old 'Millennium' blend has also become available.

Royal Brackla Scottish malt distillery. Brackla, pronounced with an open 'a' and emphasised on the first syllable, means 'place of the fallen trees'. The distillery lies to the south-east of Inverness and to the south of Nairn. It is sometimes said to come from the 'Findhorn' egion, rather than the northern → Highlands.

Its founder, Captain William Fraser, was granted the royal warrant in 1835; and it is one of only three distilleries to have this privilege. After several changes in ownership, and in 1926 it passed to John → Bisset & Co, which became part of → DCL in 1943 but continued to hold the licence for the distillery until 1992 when → UD transferred it to their new subsidiary UMGD (United Malt and Grain Distilleries). Those who believed this was a good sign, indicating long-term involvement, were to be disappointed in 1998. Although UD reopened Royal Brackla (which had had four → stills since 1970) after six years of closure, it didn't prevent them (having in the meantime joined with → IDV to become → UDV) from selling the distillery to → Bacardi.

Its malt whisky was certainly used by Bisset for their blends, but it first became available as a → proprietor's bottling from UD, who brought out a 10-year-old in the → 'Flora & Fauna' series. A short time later it was followed by a single malt without an age statement, apparently so that they could offer a reasonably-priced malt in their range. The plans of the new owners remain uncertain. For the time being UDV still have stocks and brought out a 20-year-old Royal Brackla from 1975 (59.8%) in their → 'Rare Malts' series. It is also available from the → independents, including → Gordon & MacPhail (with examples from 1972 and 1974), as well as → Cadenhead, → MacArthur and → Signatory, who also brought out several versions.

Royal Canadian Canadian whisky with a good measure of rye in it. It is mainly intended for the Taiwanese market, but is also obtainable in the USA from → Austin Nichols. Iit comes from the International Potter Distilling Company, which also owns the → Cascadia Distillery in British Columbia, who contribute very little to this blend.

Royal Chalice Scotch blend from the → independent bottler the → Vintage Malt Whisky Company, which was established in Glasgow in 1992. It is a → de luxe blend and is also available in Japan aged 12 and 15 years.

Royal Citation Scotch blend without an age statement from the upper price bracket which is from the abundant range of → Chivas Brothers. Its producers state that it owes its character to the use of five different types of cask; apart from sherry butts and bourbon barrels, casks were coopered from old Scotch and bourbon hogsheads and, most unusually, new oak casks were also used. The wood and vanilla tones are clearly noticeable.

Royal Clan Stewart Scotch blend named after the former Scottish royal family. It was one of the smaller brands formerly from → Whyte & Mackay / → JBB (Greater Europe) plc.

Royal Club Scotch blend from the small independent company of Charles H → Julian in London. The was in existence before and came from → ADP, associated with → Barton.

Royal Command Canadian whisky (40%). It was a brand from → UD and was produced at → Valleyfield, but always bore the name → Park & Tilford on its label, from whose distillery in Vancouver it once came. It is said to be the Canadian whisky with the most body, and has a reputation for being dangerous as it is so light when drunk. In February 1999 its owners, who had joined with → IDV to form → UDV, announced that the only Canadian whisky they would continue with would be → Gibson's.

Royal Culross Scotch vatted malt whose youngest whiskies are 8 years old. It has quite a long tradition. It was introduced on to the market by the previous owners of → Glen Scotia and therefore belongs to → Glen Catrine Bonded Warehouse Ltd.

Royal Decree Scotch blend aged 10 years. It was taken over by → Whyte & Mackay when they bought Jarvis Halliday & Co.

Royal Edinburgh A → standard Scotch blend from → GuinnessUDV.

Royal Escort Scotch blend. It is a 12-year-old → premium blend and was part of the bankruptcy estate of → Gibson International which was bought by → Glen Catrine Bonded Warehouse Ltd. It has been marketed by this company since 1994.

Royal Findhorn Scotch blend from → Gordon

& MacPhail with an unusually high share of malt whiskies. Its youngest whiskies are 5 years old. It is named after the river that flows into the North Sea near Forres, between Inverness and Elgin.

Royal Galleon Scotch blend from Douglas → Laing & Co, a relatively young brand with very old, mature whiskies: it bears the age statement '25 years old'.

Royal Game Scotch blend produced for the UK chain Winerite for sale in their own shops.

Royal Heather Scotch blend produced by the company Old Chelsea Distillers, which is distributed in Scotland by Joseph Dunn, the soft drinks producers.

Royal Heritage Scotch blend from William → Lundie & Co in Glasgow. It is a 21-year-old → de luxe blend.

Royal Household Scotch blend that is now difficult to find. Its producer was James → Buchanan & Co and it was only available in: in the royal household and in the little hotel in Rodel, on the southern point of the Isle of Harris, Outer Hebrides. The hotel's owner, Jock McCallum, was invited by Buchanan's to take part in a competition with his house brand. The aim of the competition was to find a blend that would be fit for the royal household. Jock's whisky won, and from then on bore the prestigious name. It is now made in small quantities by → UDV and is exported to Japan. Those who have to have a bottle can try at Strachan's shops in Aboyne, Ballater or Braemar, who as suppliers to the royal household at Balmoral occasionally have a bottle.

Royal Irish Distillery The correct name for → Dunville's Distillery in Grosvenor Street in Belfast. It was built in 1869 and was the first commercial distillery in the Ulster capital, and until the sudden death of Robert Dunville in the 1930s, remained in the hands of the founding family, who also owned → Bladnoch distillery in the Scottish → Lowlands. The firm, which was financially healthy ceased operations at the distillery with its three → pot stills and two → grain stills. They have been in operation again from time to time at a later date because → Cadenhead discovered a cask from 1951 in an Irish → warehouse, which they were able to bottle at 66% in 1991 and to include in a series of extinct Irish distilleries (→ Bow Street, → John's Lane, → Jones Road, → Tullamore), which they brought out for their own 150th anniversary. The name → Dunville has recently reappeared on whiskey bottles.

Royal Island Scotch blend from → Isle of Arran Distillers, who began operating their distillery in 1995 and had to wait a while before they could bring out their whisky as a single malt The founder Harold Currie had worked as a professional blender and was able to create some of his own brands. This first-rate blend comes in three versions aged 17, 21 and 30 years old. The Queen opened the new visitor centre at the distillery in the summer of 1997.

Royal Lochnagar Scottish malt distillery. It lies in the valley of the Dee between Ballater and Braemar, directly at the foot of Lochnagar, and belongs to the (eastern) → Highland region. It is the only distillery remaining in an area which once had many. The original Lochnagar distillery was founded in 1826, but 'New Lochnagar' was founded in 1845 by John → Begg.

Lochnagar has long been available as a 12-year-old single malt. It was one of the first to be extensively marketed and was always relatively reasonably-priced. The 'Selected Reserve', doesn't have an age statement and isin numbered bottles, is all the more expensive. Royal Lochnagar is included in the → 'Rare Malts' series aged 23 years (59.7%) and as a 24-year-old at 55.7%. It is seldom available from the → independent bottlers. The malt is a gentle, rounded, extremely pleasant whisky.

Royal Lord Series of spirits produced by Brodie Crawford & Co. Their leading brand is the blend → Brodie's Supreme. The name Royal Lord is also used for a Scotch blend and a Canadian rye, which is produced in → Canada and bottled in, and for, the UK by the company.

Royal Malt

Royal Malt Scotch vatted malt without an age statement from → Hedges & Butler, a company whose founding date of 1667 is proudly engraved on the bottle. Nowadays it is a subsidiary of Ian → MacLeod. It used to have a whole range of blends bearing its name, only two of which remain.

Royal Mile Whiskies One of the best whisky shops in Scotland, located on Edinburgh's Royal Mile. They have an excellent range of proprietary and independent bottlings to offer, including several rarities and collectors' pieces, and a good selection of Havanas, and Scottish beers from small, independent breweries. The shop has some casks specially bottled for them, such as one from Bladnoch (1980), Bruichladdich (1985), Dufftown (1970), Highland Park (1978) and Macallan (1974), or a 22-year-old single grain from → Invergordon Distillery. A new collection has appeared under the name 'The → Dormant Distillery Company'. It was launched with two bottlings, a Linlithgow (1974) and a North Port (Brechin).

Royal Reserve Canadian whisky, a rye (40%) produced by → Corby, a subsidiary of Hiram → Walker, which is said to be their best-selling brand.

Royal Salute Scotch blend which was brought out in 1952/3 by → Chivas Brothers on behalf of → Seagram to celebrate the coronation of Queen Elizabeth II. Chivas was founded at the end of the 19th century in Aberdeen and has long-standing connections with the royal family: when Queen Victoria acquired Balmoral Castle she appointed the old-established wine and spirits merchants in nearby Aberdeen to become court suppliers. The military custom of firing a twenty-one gun salute at ceremonial occasions is reflected in the age of this → de luxe blend: it contains malt whiskies from → Glenlivet, → Glen Grant, → Longmorn and → Strathisla, as well as others, all of which are at least 21 years old. There are now even older versions with a 40-year-old and the 'LXX'. They all share the same regal appearance: the porcelain bottles are velvet-wrapped.

Royal Secret Indian whisky from → Polychem which also has the two successful brands → Men's Club and → White House in its range, and which participated in a joint venture with → IDV.

Royal Silk Scotch blend which is decribed as a 'Reserve Rare Scotch'. It comes from the International Whisky Company and is its first product. It is the creation of Jim Milne, a well-known figure in the whisky industry who was responsible for, among others, → J & B and the → Antiquary.

Royal Stag Whisky formerly from → Seagram which is intended for sale in India and is also produced there, using Scotch malt whiskies and locally-distilled → grain whiskies. They might be distillates from → Shaw Wallace, with whom the Canadians want to participate in a joint venture.

Royal Strathythan Scotch blend. It comes from → Chivas Brothers.

Royal Tara Irish cream liqueur that bears the name of the old Celtic-Irish kingdom and is produced by a dairy in Cork. It is probable that they get the whiskey for it from the neighbouring distillery in → Midleton. It has a strength of 17% and is only on sale in Ireland.

Russell & Co, Peter J Scottish whisky company established in 1936 by Leonard Russell, who was originally a broker before recognising that his chances would be better if he produced and sold blends himself. His business also grew with the aid of takeovers such as that of William Maxwell, a Liverpool trading firm founded in 1796, under whose name several brands of the house continue to be bottled (→ King Robert II, → Mason's, → William Maxwell). The names Ian → MacLeod, (Isle of Skye), → Hedges & Butler and → Cockburn & Murray (The → Seven Stills), also belong to the portfolio. Russell is now one of the largest independent companies in the whisky business and is particularly strong in the export sector, with Italy as its main customer. The company has a large bottling plant in Broxburn, near Edinburgh airport, that they run together with J & G → Grant of Glenfarclas and where they also undertake bottlings for other companies, such as →

Sainsbury, under their own labels. Their own brands include the blends → Black Rooster and → Black Shield, the vatted malt → Glentress and the → 'Chieftan's Choice' series, which includes blends, vatted and single malts.

Rusty Nail Whisky cocktail. The classic recipe is with 2cl → Drambuie to 4cl Scotch, which is served in a tumbler, either neat or with ice. It is even better with a good malt whisky such as a Balvenie, which also plays a large part in the composition of the liqueur. The ice helps reduce the rich sweetness. Those who like it really sweet will mix Scotch and Drambuie in equal parts and forget the ice.

RX Bourbon brought out by → UD who name their producer as George → Dickel, whose → Cascade Hollow Distillery and the address in Tullahoma are also mentioned. The whiskey was actually distilled in Kentucky at the → Stitzel-Weller Distillery, which has now been closed and also belonged to UD. → Rebel Yell was made there until 1993, a straight which for a long time was identified with the southern states of the USA – where Dickel moved to in 1912 when the production of alcohol was forbidden in his home state (several years before → prohibition was generally enforced in 1919 and also affected Kentucky). At this time vats were installed at Stitzel-Weller for → leaching, a process which is typical for Tennessee whisk(e)y. These vats have long since disappeared. In creating RX, UD solved the problem of having falsely speculated on Rebel Yell, whose name they hoped would attract younger customers, and suddenly left them with surplus stocks. It is really a combination of a bourbon and a Tennessee: the distillate is a real bourbon whose casks received an additional rich caramel fragrance reminiscent of a Tennessee by adding small pieces of charcoal. It was bottled at 6 years and 40% and will probably not be available for much longer since UD's successors UDV decided in the spring of 1999 to part with all but one of their North American brands.

Rye Type of American whiskey. There are not many examples of it left nowadays although it is the oldest in the country and considered by many to be the best and most expressive of all American whiskeys. When the Irish and Scottish immigrants tried to make the drink that they had known at home in their new country, they had to make use of the grain available and which could best be cultivated. They didn't have the barley which they had used in Scotland and Ireland and had to make do with rye. Maryland and Pennsylvania are the two states where whiskey was distilled from rye in the 18th century, and the settlers who followed the tracks of Daniel Boone and other pioneers to Kentucky, mainly used corn.

Rye is different from bourbon (the most widespread type of whiskey in the USA) in the grain that is initially used, but otherwise there are no differences. American laws prescribe that a straight rye must be made from a mash consisting of at least 51% rye (in the case of bourbon it is 51% corn). In practice they use more, and the remaining percentage is made up of either corn or wheat and about 10% to 15% malted barley, which assists fermentation.

The high proportion of rye gives the whiskey a dry bitterness which is very marked. This is what has brought it devoted followers, but possibly, has caused it to lose its significance.

It is very likely that the Americans got out of the habit of drinking it during prohibition between 1920 and 1933. At that time all that was available, if at all, was smuggled Canadian and Scotch whisky – types which were definitely lighter than rye. A change in the American taste for whiskey resulted and rye almost slipped into oblivion. Just a few years ago the remaining ryes were minimal: there was a rye version from Jim Beam, and there was Old Overholt, Pikesville, Rittenhouse and a Wild Turkey Rye. Several new companies extended this small group, and the → Van Winkle family made a special contribution. In San Francisco Fritz Maytag surprised the world of whisk(e)y by creating a malt distilled from rye, → Old Potrero.

Rye Base Japanese blend which unlike its stable-mate → Corn Base, also from → Nikka, consists entirely of distillates which have been produced in Japan. The rye-based distillate is blended with other whiskies.

S

Safeway UK supermarket chain, formerly in Scottish ownership. Like its competitors → Sainsbury, Asda → Tesco and → Marks & Spencer, Safeway has a large selection of Scotch blends and malts, including a series of single malts with its own label, which name the → whisky region but not the distillery. A 'Blended Irish' also comes from → Cooley.

Sailing Ships Series of → single cask bottlings from the → independent bottlers → Signatory. It has included three malt whiskies which commemorate famous sailing ships: a 15-year-old → Balvenie, a 16-year-old → Caperdonich and a 20-year-old → Glendronach, each with a strength of 43%.

Sainsbury Like all the large UK supermarket chains (→ Marks & Spencer, → Safeway, → Asda, → Tesco) J Sainsbury not only has an excellent wine department and many branded whiskies, but it also has whiskies with its own label, some of which come from Peter J → Russell. The selection varies and apart from several → standard (and cheap) blends, there are also malts from → Speyside and from → Islay, whose exact origins are not stated. However → Sainsbury's Irish Malt is made by → Cooley and the origin of the 1979 → Glenmorangie Vintage is also clear. In the UK it is sold exclusively in branches of this chain.

Sainsbury's Irish Malt Irish whiskey, a single malt from the → Cooley Distillery and practically identical to → Tyrconnell.

St. Andrews Castle Scotch pure malt belonging to a series which the executive agency → Historic Scotland (responsible for ancient monuments) has produced for sale in the shops of the historic buildings which it manages. The whiskies are named after some of the most important buildings (and most popular tourist attractions) in Scotland. This ruined castle bearing the name of the patron saint of Scotland, is situated in the town on the north-east coast of Fife which is famous for the oldest university in Scotland and its golf links. The malt is 10 years old and is bottled at 46%.

Saint Brendan's Superior Irish cream liqueur from the company of the same name in Londonderry. It is therefore the Northern Irish version of the kind of drink that was initiated by → Bailey's in 1974, and which has been able to gain an astounding share of the market. Like its competitors it is bottled at 17%. The word 'Superior' is justified by the information that it contains 'aged Irish cream' (and we thought that cream should be as fresh as possible ...). The whiskey is said to come from → Bushmills.

St. James's Scotch blend that gets its name from its producer: the main shop of → Berry Bros & Rudd is at 3, St. James's Street, in the Piccadilly area of London. It is available as a → standard blend and as a 12-year-old → premium blend.

St. Leger Scotch blend from → Hill Thomson & Company, who lost their independence in 1970 and from 1977 to 2000 belonged to the → Chivas & Glenlivet Group, which co-ordinated the Scottish activities of the Canadian drinks giant → Seagram. It is mainly intended for the Canadian market as the adjunct 'Light Dry' indicates.

St. Magdalene Defunct Scottish malt distillery, closed since 1983. Part of it has been converted in to apartments in the old → floor maltings, which were protected buildings and could not be demolished. It is still possible, therefore, to see the old pagodas and the large white letters with the name of the distillery when passing by on the train, or when visiting the town of Linlithgow on the Union Canal.

St. Magdalene was a → Lowland distillery which, like → Glenkinchie, only distilled its → wash twice and used quite a lot of peat for malting. The → Scotch Malt Whisky Society used to have a bottling which at a blind tasting could easily have passed for a medium → Islay. The first recorded owner was Adam Dawson in 1797. At the time of its closure it belonged to → DCL, and its successor → GuinnessUDV still has malt whisky from the distillery; having first found a cask in their stocks from 1970, they included it in their → 'Rare Malts' collection at a → cask strength of 58.1%. They had a second one at 58.4%, and a third one from 1979 was bottled aged 19 years at 63.8%. → Gordon & MacPhail regularly include the malt whisky in their → 'Connoisseurs Choice' series and brought out a → 'Centenary Reserve' from 1980 for the 100th anniversary of the company. At least once → Cadenhead preferred the name → Linlithgow. This name was also used by Signatory for its 'Silent Stills' series: the malt whisky was from 1975 and was bottled in 1998 at 51.7%.

Saladin box Term for an early form of mechanised → maltings. It goes back to the French engineer Charles Saladin who first used it for the malting of brewer's barley at the end of the 19th century. It is far less labour-intensive than the traditional form of → floor maltings. The barley which has been soaked to encourage germination is no longer spread out on the malting floor where it must be constantly turned by hand over a period of days to control its temperature. Instead it is placed in long concrete trenches where revolving metal forks turn and aerate the grain. In Scotland this new form of malting was first used after the Second World War. It was soon replaced by the more modern → drum maltings. The one distillery which still uses them is → Tamdhu.

Sam Cougar American blended whiskey formerly made by → Seagram which for the time being is only sold in Australia. The whiskeys used for it are 6 years old and are reported to come from the → Lawrenceburg Distillery in Indiana, which should not be confused with the other ex-Seagram distillery which is also in a town called Lawrenceburg (but in Kentucky) and which has now been renamed → Four Roses to make it more easily distinguishable. In 2000 the brand was sold to the brewery giants Foster – one of the first indications that its owner, Sam → Edgar Bronfman Jr, wanted to part with Seagram.

Sam Houston Kentucky straight bourbon which – to quote its producer – is named after a 'great Texan', a former governor of the state. The whiskey is a 10-year-old → small batch and, 'in keeping with the robust nature of the man', has a strength of 90°/45%. It comes from the McLain & Kyne Distillery Company in Bardstown, which is also responsible for → Jefferson's Reserve.

Samaroli → Independent bottler with company headquarters in Brescia, Italy, which believes, probably rightly, that it is the only one outside Scotland. Silvano S Samaroli established his business as early as 1968, at a time when – even in Scotland – single malts were seldon found, whereas in Italy there was such great enthusiasm for them that every ice cream parlour offered a good range. Samaroli was amongst those who satisfied the passion of his countrymen, and has retained his reputation for top quality to this day. The → single casks selected by him nearly always fulfil their promise and provide unalloyed enjoyment. One creation that he is particularly proud of is a vatted malt called → No Age.

Sanderson & Son, Wm Scottish whisky company established by William Sanderson in 1863 in Leith as a whisky wholesalers which also dealt with bitters and eau de vie. Sanderson was not one of the → Big Five, but his company still played an important part in the history of whisky in Scotland, chiefly because he was among the very first (encouraged by his son) to discontinue selling whisky in barrels and to favour bottles, making adulteration by dealers and inn-keepers more difficult. Sanderson and his son first achieved real fame with their → Vat 69 which they brought out in 1882 after an elaborate process had discovered which of almost 100 different mixtures found most favour with the public. Sanderson & Son were co-founders of the → North British Grain distillery, and in 1935 merged with Booth Distillers, who were mainly engaged in the gin business. Two years later they passed to → DCL. For a short time the company also owned the → Glen Garioch Distillery, and on behalf of → DCL they held the licence for → Hillside/→ Glenesk, which → UD halted in 1992 when the distillery had already been closed for 10 years. Sanderson used to have a single malt from Glenesk in its range, which was aged 5 years for the Italian market and 12 years for other markets. Sanderson's subsidiary was J & W Hardie, whose best-known product was the → blend The → Antiquary. Until → GuinnessUDV sold it to Bacardi, they were the licence holders for → Aultmore Distillery and their name can also be found on the blend → Sanderson's Gold, which first became available in 1991 and is a → UD product.

Sanderson's Gold Scotch blend which bears the name of Wm → Sanderson & Son, who were mainly famous for their → Vat 69. It has only existed since 1991, as a light blend especially developed for the tropics by → UD/UDV, who nowadays are the owners of the firm's name and its brands.

Sandpiper Indian whisky bottled at the obligatory 42.8%, which describes itself as a blend of (premixed) Scotch with Indian malt whisky and neutral spirits. It is produced for the Ugar Sugar Works in Belgium; this name leads one to suppose that the malt mentioned is in fact a molasses distillate which is so often used in → India.

Sandy Collins Whiskey cocktail. A variation on the Collins in which an Irish whiskey is used.

Sandy Macdonald Scotch blend from the → GuinnessUDV subsidiary → Macdonald Greenlees, which arose from the merger of the business belonging to the Greenlees brothers with that of the Macdonald brothers arranged by the Scottish businessman James Calder. Both were very old companies, the latter was founded in 1871 and the former in 1840. Each of them had a major brand: the Greenlees Brothers had the → Old Parr and the Macdonalds had Sandy Macdonald, which was as old as their business. Nowadays it is just one of the many small brands which are mainly sold in South America.

Sandy Macnab Scotch blend which came from → Macnab Distilleries and consisted mainly of grains and malts which, unusually, were produced under the same roof; namely at the → Lochside Distillery in Montrose.

Sanraku-Ocean Japanese company belonging to the Suzuki family, who have nothing to do with the car manufacturers. It is active in many areas, producing agricultural and pharmaceutical chemicals, animal food, tinned foods and is particularly engaged in the alcoholic drinks sector. In its present form the company goes back to the 1930s. In 1937 it brought out a sake named 'Sanraku' which became part of the company name. In the 1960s the company decided that they would not only produce sake and wines, which they do very successfully using the name → Mercian, but also participate in the whisky boom which had been triggered off by → Suntory and → Nikka. They built a malt distillery in the popular spa town of → Karuizawa and a grain distillery in Kawasaki, and began to produce a range of blends with the brand name → Ocean Whisky.

The headquarters of the company are in Tokyo. The company produces on a much smaller scale than its giant competitors, and its distillery in Karuizawa, which since the mid-1990s has been rechristened Mercian, is also small. However its market share of around 4% is slightly more than that of → Kirin-Seagram, the fourth of the four companies which dominate the Japanese market, and as large as the other 20 firms together. Apart from Ocean the blends → Asama, → Route and → Status are also available. With the vagueness typical of all the Japanese producers, Sanraku-Ocean had a malt whisky whose porcelain label did not describe it as a single but as a 'Fine Aged straight Malt Whisky'. A 17-year-old which describes itself as '100% Malt' also comes in a decanter and uses the distillery's new name.

Savoy Scotch blend that bears the name of a world-famous hotel. Of course an establishment whose 'Cocktail Book' has inspired barmen, barmaids and laymen for decades must have its own blend. It was, significantly, brought out in the USA by the former owners of the hotel and was not only served in their own hotel, but also in other luxury establishments such as the Waldorf Astoria in New York, and in London at the Berkeley, Claridges and the Connaught, as well as Simpson's in the Strand. The first two hotels listed also had blends of their own. The whisky is now available in many of the better hotels in France and also at the Savoy Hotel in London.

Sazerac cocktail Whiskey cocktail. It is really a variation on the Old-Fashioned which is said to have been created in the coffee house of this name in New Orleans. Originally absinthe was used instead of Pernod and cognac instead of whiskey. Both forms also existed together.

Sazerac Company American spirits company based in New Orleans. This is also the location of a famous coffee house in which the well-known → Sazerac cocktail was said to have been created. It is not known whether the modern company has its roots in this coffee house. Michael Jackson reports that it was established by two businessmen who 'were experienced in the spirits trade', Ferdie Falk and Robert Baranaskas, and is engaged in the production, import and distribution of wines and stronger drinks. In 1982 Sazerac acquired the → Ancient Age Distilling Company and their distillery in → Leestown; in 1992 the distillery was bought by the Japanese consortium → Takara Shuzo & Okura, whilst the distillery stayed with Sazerac who then established the Leestown Distilling Company as a subsidiary.

In March 1999 two further brands joined their portfolio when Sazerac, in a consortium together with → Heaven Hill and the David → Sherman Company, bought the → Bernheim Distillery and four bourbons for $171 million from → GuinnessUDV. In this way Sazerac obtained → W L Weller and → Old Charter. 'Dr. Gillicuddy's Schnapps' is another brand belonging to the company. They are the American distributors of → Glenfarclas and in order to protect this brand they took → Whyte & Whyte to court in a spectacular trial. Their bourbons include → Ancient Age, → Benchmark, → Bulleit, → Buffalo Trace, → Eagle Rare, → Kentucky Dale and the → single barrels → Blanton's, → Elmer T Lee, →

Hancock's Reserve and → Rock Hill. Their blends are → Ancient Age, → Brookstone, → Canadian Age and → Carstair's White Seal. They import the Canadian whiskeys → James Foxe and → McCauley's and also have a premixed version of their cocktail. The company name is borne by a Kentucky straight bourbon and a straight rye.

Scapa Scottish malt distillery. It lies about two kilometres to the south of the other → Orkney distillery, → Highland Park, and is situated on the shore of Scapa Flow. It belongs to the → Islands whisky region. The name Scapa is probably more familiar to naval historians than to whisky drinkers, as it was here that after the First World War the German sailors who had been taken prisoner by the British scuttled their entire fleet, and during the Second World War a German submarine torpedoed the The Royal Oak having broken through the Flow's barriers which had been thought to be impenetrable.

Scapa was built in 1885 by Macfarlane and Townsend and has always been put in the shade by its neighbour. Compared to Highland Park with its → pagodas and traditional → floor maltings, Scapa is a utilitarian building that from 1954 was owned by Hiram → Walker (and therefore today belongs to → Allied Domecq PLC). Since rebuilding in 1959 its → wash still has been of the → Lomond type. The water from Lingro Burn is already so peaty that they use entirely unpeated malt. Since 1994 the distillery has been mothballed, like so many others belonging to the firm, however in contrast to → Ardbeg, → Balblair and → Pulteney it has at least not been sold. Occasional distillations take place under the auspices of staff from Highland Park.

As a single malt Scapa was for a long time only available from the → independent bottlers. → Gordon & MacPhail had an 8-year-old (40%) and several bottlings (1979, 1983, 1984, 1985, 1986, 1988) in the → Allied series under the name of → Taylor & Ferguson who, following the takeover of Hiram Walker, were the nominal licence holders. They were also named on the label of the litre bottle of the 10-year-old, which was brought out in 1995 as the first → proprietary bottling. It was only obtainable in duty-free shops whereas there is now a 12-year-old Scapa in a normal bottle which is generally available. The German importer Dieter Kirsch from Syke had two special bottlings made by → Signatory of a 15-year-old and a 9-year-old Scapa, showing Scapa Flow with warships on the label. Cadenhead had a bottling from 1988 at a cask strength of 62.4%.

Schenley American-Canadian whisk(e)y company named after a town in Pennsylvania. It was founded by Lewis Rosenstiel who had been in the whiskey business before → prohibition and had spent the dry years buying, selling and even producing whiskey for medicinal purposes. He not only bought the stocks of → Old Overholt, but also, in the late 1920s, acquired the → Leestown Distillery and the distillery in Frankfort, which had started life as the Old Oscar Pepper Distillery, later belonged to → Labrot & Graham, and has recently begun production again under the ownership of → Brown-Forman. In 1937 Schenley acquired → Bernheim in Louisville together with all its brands. Directly after the Second World War the company, which had bought the rights to the name Cascade began, not far from the site on which it had originally stood, to rebuild the → Cascade Hollow Distillery in Tullahoma, which had been founded by George → Dickel. At the same time a Canadian subsidiary was established and, after an attempt to merge with → Seagram had failed, a fight began with the Canadians for the leading position in North America. The Canadian part of Schenley was later bought by a group of pension funds and continued operating independently as Canadian Schenley. This company owned the → Valleyfield Distillery and in addition to numerous successful brands of their own also carried that of → Park & Tilford.

In 1956 they extended their activities to Europe, but these were only to continue until 1971. They began with the takeover of Seager Evans, who at that time were the owners of the brand → Long John as well as the distilleries → Strathclyde, → Kinclaith and → Tormore. Later they were joined by → Laphroaig Distillery. After having parted with their Scottish interests, Leestown was also sold in 1982, but Bernheim, Dickel and Schenley Canada, together with Valleyfield, were still left when, in 1987, Schenley was acquired by → Guinness and affiliated to → UD. The usual rationalisation of products was just as inevitable as the closure of distilleries. The Bernheim Distillery had to make way for a new building in which all of UD's bourbons were made: → Old Charter, → I W Harper, → James E Pepper and the 'Wheated Bourbons' (in which the usual share of rye in the mash is replaced by wheat) → W L Weller, → Old Fitzgerald and → Rebel Yell. In Canada several labels such as Schenley Award were discontinued. Only → Canadian O F C, two bottlings of → Gibson's, Schenley → Golden Wedding, → MacNaughton's and → Royal Command remained in the portfolio. The marriage of Guinness and → Grand Metropolitan to form → Diageo and their subsidiaries to form → GuinnessUDV led to further 'market clearances' and to the sale of nearly all the North Ameican activities of the new spirits giant, which only kept Gibson's in Canada, and George Dickel and I W Harper in the USA.

Schenley Golden Wedding Canadian whiskey which is usually simply called → Golden Wedding. A further consequence of the merger of → IDV and → UD was that the brand changed ownership, and since February 1999 has belonged to → Canandaigua.

Schenley O F C Canadian whiskey which is identical with → Canadian O F C.

Schwäbischer Whisky German single grain from Owen/Teck, between Stuttgart and Ulm, where C and I Gruel run a distillery which normally produces eau de vie. Christian Gruel was interested in Scotch whisky and took a look round Scotland, but then decided to try making a → grain whisky rather than a malt – the only one in Germany. He places particular importance on allowing the distillate to peacefully mature for a long time in its wooden cask. As a result the whisky has a wonderful honey colour. It is bottled at 43%, but unfortunately the bottle looks more like a sweet white wine or a fruity eau de vie than a Swabian whisky.

Scoff-Law Whisky cocktail. A variation on the Manhattan with Canadian whiskey, dry vermouth, lemon juice and a shot each of orange bitter and Grenadine.

Scoresby Rare Scotch blend that is produced in Scotland and shipped in tanks to the USA where it is bottled and sold (very successfully) on the home market. With more than 600,000 → cases sold it is said to be the fourth largest brand of Scotch in the USA. This explains why → UD, which had acquired it when they bought → Glenmore, kept it even when they later resold many of their products to → Barton. The newly-formed → UDV then parted with it in the spring of 1999.

Scotch Guard A → standard blend from the → Speyside Distillery Co.

Scotch House No. 12 Scotch blend whose label reads 'old' and yet is a supermarket brand of unknown origin which is mainly sold in Germany.

Scotch Malt Whisky Society, The A members-only enterprise which is an → independent bottler and a club which sells its whiskies exclusively to its members. There are over 10,000 of these in Scotland alone, which goes to show that what began modestly in 1981 has developed into a genuine Scottish success story, which could not have existed without the resurgence of malt as the authentic, original Scotch.

It was founded by Phillip 'Pip' Hills, who whilst on holiday on → Speyside was surprised by a whisky that a farmer had sold him near → Glenfarclas. He had never tasted anything like it and wanted to be able to sample it more often, and so he and some friends got together to buy a cask and bottle it themselves. The group became a syndicate and the syndicate became a business. More and more people wanted this kind of whisky, which was offered in a newsletter that was initially very short, but which increased in size as, in the course of time, the distillery owners lost their early mistrust and became more willing to sell casks. The club's policy has contributed a great deal to these good relations, as they never write the name of the distillery of origin on the labels but give it a code number and allow their members to guess from the descriptions, which are sometimes very flowery, where the malt whisky comes from. The committee's tasting notes are even more poetic, and are written by such prominent whisky noses as Prof. David Daiches and the author Charles MacLean.

This policy of anonymity, which is also a test of the individual's knowledge of whisky, has been maintained to this day and code number 1 still stands for Glenfarclas; 1.35 means that it is the 35th cask from there which has been on offer. From the very beginning the labels of the Society's bottles have given exact information on the date of distillation and bottling. The fact that bottling is always at → cask strength and that they forego → chill-filtering, has also contributed to the renaissance of malt whisky – nowadays this may be taken for granted but at the beginning of the 1980s it was quite revolutionary. A further factor contributing to their success was that Pip Hills was able to acquire an historical building as the Society's headquarters, which suits it admirably and not only offers good office space, but also has a wonderful club room: The Vaults in Leith, wine cellars that belonged to J & G → Thomson & Co and the oldest commercial building in Scotland that was still used for its original purpose.

The Society has bottled malts from over 100 distilleries, many of them for the first time. The Society has expanded considerably and now has branches in France, Spain, Japan, the USA, the Netherlands and Switzerland. Perhaps the rate of expansion has been too quick and vigorous. In 1995 trouble arose which led to its founder leaving. However the Society has re-established itself with Richard Gordon as Managing Director and Willie Philips (who was a director at → Macallan) as Chairman, and continues to send offer its malts quarterly.

Scotch Single Malt Circle, The When Bill Miller, a Scot living in Düsseldorf, and his wife Maggie were refused permission to form a German branch of the → Scotch Malt Whisky Society, they decided to form a club of their own. Thanks to good connections in his homeland the Millers gained access to some very good casks which they bottled without → chill-filtering, without → colouring and at → cask strength. They usually named the distillery of origin.

The Circle expanded during the 1990s and now has about 1,000 members, who receive new offers quarterly. These are always accompanied by personal letters from Bill Miller in which he not only writes about the characteristics of a good malt whisky and how healthy it is to drink, but also about general political and philosophical questions: as if one were sitting together with him over a good → dram. This shows that the Circle is much more than one of the many → independent bottlers or a mail order business.

Scotch Sour Whisky cocktail. Whiskey Sour is really made with bourbon, but this variation with Scotch has its fans, too. One recipe recommends two parts whisky to one part lemon juice and two teaspoons of sugar, which are all shaken well together. It is then served in a tumbler and cherries and slices of orange and lemon are placed on the rim of the glass.

Scotch whisky The term which describes all the types of whisky produced and matured in Scotland. Malt and → grain whiskies are distilled and produced in other countries and are called 'whisky', but the adjunct 'Scotch' is a legally protected description of origin, whose use is guarded worldwide by, among others, the Scotch Whisky Association.

The decision was made in 1909 after a court case in Islington, London. The 'What is Whiskey?' case arose because inferior blends with very small proportions of malt to grain were appearing in London pubs and the producers of Scotch malt whisky and of Irish → pure pot still whiskey wanted to protect themselves against these competitors who were ruining their business, by achieving a clear definition of their product. On the other side was the → DCL who had already become an important and economically powerful concern. The exultant advertisements for the grain whisky → Cambus which DCL had published became famous, and claimed that → grain whisky was possibly even better than malt whisky. At first it looked as though the verdict would go against DCL, but finally they emerged victorious. Since that time every grain distillate has been termed 'whisky'.

Several other factors must be observed as well, such as the kind of cask used for ageing and the minimum period of maturing. However, in principle the definition has not changed since 1909. It was adopted by legislators and recognised by the European Union in 1989 and most recently summarised in the Scotch Whisky Act of 1998/99. Accordingly the name Scotch Whisky may only be used for a product:

" – which has been produced at a distillery in Scotland from water and malted barley (to which only whole grains of other cereals may be added) all of which have been
– processed at the distillery to a mash,
– converted to a fermentable sustrate only by endogenous enzyme systems, and
– fermented only by the addition of yeast.
– which has been distilled at an alcoholic strength by volume of less than 94.8% so that the distillate has an aroma and taste derived from raw material used in, and the method of, its production.
– which has been matured in an excise warehouse in Scotland in oak casks of a capacity not exceeding 700 litres, the period of that maturation being not less than 3 years.
– which retains the colour, aroma and taste derived from the raw materials used in, and method of, its production and maturation, and
– to which no other substance than water and spirit caramel has been added."

The Act also prescribes that Scotch whisky which is bottled and/or sold, or intended for use in, or exported from, the European Union must have a minimum strength of 40%.

Scotch whisky has evolved from the spirituous liquors which have been distilled in Scotland since the 15th century. The Scots may not have invented it, but their → uisge beatha, or 'water of life', but they have the satisfaction of owning the first documentary reference to it. In 1494 John → Cor received 'eight bolls of malt ... wherewith to make aquavitae' He was from

Fife, an indication that monks were active in distilling, probably to create medicine which they may not have restricted to external use only. It was perhaps Irish monks who brought distilling back from Italy to their own country and so extended the knowledge of their Scottish brothers.

It cannot have been long before the practice of distilling left the monasteries, as in 1505 the king issued an edict allowing the Guild of Surgeon Barbers in Edinburgh the privilege of distilling. By the mid-16th century the making of aqua vitae had become widespread in the country, as well as in the towns. The Scottish Parliament eventually passed a law on 31st January 1644 which imposed a tax of 2s 8d on every pint of aquavitae or 'strong waters'. This created the precedent for successive increases in excise duty on distilled spirits, wine and ale.

In 1707 the united Parliaments of England and Scotland continued with this policy, much to the annoyanvce of crofter-distillers in the → Highlands and → Islands who regarded the right of home distilling as sacrosanct.

Illicit distilling and smuggling was still widespread and the distillers in the Lowlands were also subject to taxation, but they were in a stronger economic position and were closer to the powers that made the decisions.

In 1784 the → Highland Line was drawn and the Highlanders felt yet again that they were not being treated fairly. It was not until the Excise Act was passed in 1823 that more and more decided to apply for a licence; the first to do so was George Smith of → Glenlivet. The number of illicit stills decreased (but never disappeared completely), the legal ones became more widespread and for the first time it looked as though the modern evolution of Scotch whisky was finally under way.

Considerable change then took place but it is a matter of opinion whether this was for the better or for the worse.

In the mid 1820s Robert → Stein and Aeneas → Coffey introduced their revolutionary innovations which allowed a completely new type of whisky to be produced. It flowed continuously out of a → patent still and didn't depend on expensive malt barley, but could be made from any type of grain. → Grain whisky had been born. Chemically it was a very pure form of alcohol, completely lacking in character, but cheap and quick to produce.

Just 20 years later pioneers such as Andrew → Usher hit on the idea of combining malt and grain whiskies to create a new kind of whisky: the blend. This has since become a synonym for Scotch. It combined the advantages of both its predecessors, the cheap grain and the characterful malt, and made it possible to produce a whisky which was consistent in taste, smell, colour (with a small addition of caramel) and taste as well. Whisky production was no longer just in the hands of the master distillers, but now also in those of the new companies which made a name for themselves with their own blends. Names like Walker in Kilmarnock, Teacher in Glasgow, Dewar in Perth and the Chivas Brothers in Aberdeen began to become well-known. They had all been merchants and grocers whose whiskies became world famous brands.

They were also assisted commercially by the outbreak of the *phylloxera aphid* in Bordeaux which destroyed the wine crops and halted the flow of brandy, so beloved by the English. The Scots were all too happy to step into the breach. They expanded to London and conquered it with advertising campaigns which were sometimes quite brilliant, and from there they expanded to Australia, India and the USA. By the beginning of the First World War, the Scotch blend had become so well-established that not even the halt in production necessitated by the war was of long term consequence. Neither was prohibition in the USA. Scotch was smuggled on a large scale and when prohibition was over the Americans had lost the taste for their own whiskey and preferred the lighter Scotch (and Canadian whisky).

At a much earlier date these firms had joined together to become economically stronger. The most important of these new conglomerates was → DCL, which had been founded in 1877 and swallowed many smaller firms until in

1925, when Buchanan-Dewar, Walker and finally White Horse were affiliated. Almost half of all Scottish distilleries and half the entire industry belonged to it. The stability that DCL brought to the industry during the difficult years before, during and after the Second World War is largely responsible for its ability to withstand the cyclical commercial peaks and troughs which it frequently experiences.

In the end it was this company which triggered off one of the greatest changes to the trade since the Second World War. In 1987 a takeover battle took place, at the end of which → Guinness swallowed DCL, which had lain dormant for too long, and began the restructuring that would result in → UD. Then, in 1997 Guinness merged with Grand Metropolitan, and shortly before Highland Distillers had taken over Macallan. Even earlier American Brands had taken over → Whyte & Mackay and → Invergordon, and the Japanese were firmly established as owners of Tomatin, Ben Nevis and → Morrison Bowmore: Scotch whisky was no longer in Scottish hands, but had become a field for global players.

These developments were inevitable. Without them the renaissance of malt whisky would probably not have occurred. But it was one of the smaller independent firms which led the way. In 1963, in the face of a bemused DCL, William → Grant & Sons launched a single malt from their Glenfiddich Distillery on to the world market. It would be fair to describe this action as the start of a revolution. Nowadays single malts from virtually every distillery are available, many proprietors bring out their own bottlings and the → independent bottlers look after the rest and have managed to introduce → single cask and → cask strength bottlings. Distilleries, which used to be closed to visitors, have been revitalised as a way of attracting tourists.

Scotch Whisky Association Scottish trade association which represents the interests of the Scottch whisky industry at home and abroad. It was founded in 1917 as The Whisky Association, with its headquarters in London, and was renamed in 1943. The SWA has 66 members who in their turn represent 26 corporations. Producers, wholesalers and brokers are allowed to become members and 95% of them have joined the SWA. Its activities are financed solely by membership fees. There are now two branches, one in Edinburgh with 36 employees and a smaller one in London, which mainly has representative functions.

The SWA is a lobby for the industry as well as its watchdog. Its aim is to promote and protect the interests of the Scotch whisky industry. They have, for example, prevented → Glen Kella from the Isle of Man calling itself whisky. It is now only allowed to call itself 'Manx Spirit'. It also prevents whiskies which are produced abroad from using an English name. They also try to maintain certain quality standards, such as in the case of Australia, where they have ensured that the minimum alcohol content of the whisky must be 40%.

A major function of the SWA is the fight against what it considers to be unjustifiably high taxation. In Japan Scotch has not been discriminated against in relation to Japanese whisky since 1997, although it is still at a disadvantage in relation to the national drink 'Shochu'. In the UK the Association lobbies the government in order to argue the trade's interests. Some success has been forthcoming with no increases in duty for the past five budgets. However, UK consumers still have to pay tax on a bottle of whisky in the United Kingdom which amounts to £5.87.

Scotch Whisky Review Bi-annual subscription newsletter which was originally intended to help promote sales of → Loch Fyne Whiskies. This is the shop in Inveraray which was founded in 1992 by Richard Joynson and Lyndsay Sheare. The SWR has developed editorially by way of trade commentary, interviews with leading executives in the whisky industry and contributions from such authors as Charles MacLean, Michael Jackson, Gavin Smith and Neil Wilson. The publication has become an alternative and frequently irreverent source for friends of whisky. The company founders have their own house brand, the prize-winning The → Loch Fyne, and have revived an old Scottish tradition with their → Living Cask.

Scotdram Scotch blend from the → Morrison Fairlie Distillery, a company which operates as an → independent bottler. It also uses the name for single malts, such as the Scotdram Millennium Malt, an unidentified → Islay.

Scotia Royale Premium Scotch blend aged 12 years. It was originally launched on to the market by A. Gillies & Co who at that time owned → Glen Scotia Distillery. → Gibson International later brought it onto the market in Japan and Korea, and nowadays it is available in Europe from → Glen Catrine Bonded Warehouse Ltd, and is enjoying increasing success. The royal Scotia is said to have been an Egyptian princess who married a Greek and gave her name to the people that her husband had settled in Ireland.

Scotland The country which produces the world's most renowned distilled spirit → Scotch whisky.

Scotmalt Series of single malts from the → independent bottlers → Morrison Fairlie Distillery, founded by Peter→ Fairlie, formerly of → Glenturret Distillery. Using this name they have brought out, among others, malts from Macallan (1990/99, 40%) and a 1985 Bruichladdich (which is not actually named as such, but whose identity can be guessed from the description). The → Scotdram Millennium Malt was an unknown → Islay, '757 weeks old', of which exactly 100 bottles were filled on 31st December 1999/1st January 2000. There are tasting notes on the label.

Scots Club Scotch blend that used to come from Ewen & Co. It passed to → Waverley Vintners, a subsidiary of the brewery giant Scottish Courage. The brand is now owned by → Invergordon, which also owns → Glen Clova, another brand that used to be bottled by Ewen & Co.

Scots Earl Scotch → standard blend from → Glen Catrine Bonded Warehouse Ltd.

Scots Grey Scotch blend from → Kyndal. The → de luxe blend is available in two versions aged 12 and 15 years.

Scots Lion Scotch blend from Donald Hart & Co. The company is named after one of the → Hart Brothers and is a subsidiary of theirs. The two brothers are based in Glasgow where they produce blends. In the last few years they have also become known as → independent bottlers of single malts.

Scots Poet Scotch blend from → Kyndal.

Scott, Sir Walter It was 1822 before a king visited Scotland folowing the Jacobite Rising of 1745. He was greeted in Edinburgh with festive ceremonies that Sir Walter Scott had orchestrated. George IV saw no irony in asking for a → Glenlivet, even though he knew it had been illicitly distilled.

Scott saw no irony in serving it to him and receiving the glass as a present in return. He also used the occasion to rehabilitate the kilt and tartans. Critics will say that many of the clichés which are associated with Scotland were established at that time by Scott, and that the Highland dress which he thought up had not previously existed. But it is equally possible to postulate that Scott merely wanted to help his country regain a sense of national pride – which he had also achieved in his unbelievably productive poetic and fictional works. Some of the figures from his books have been honoured by having a blend named after them, such as Rob Roy. Years ago Wm Teacher and Sons had a Sir Walter.

Scott's Selection Series of Scotch single malts brought out by the → Speyside Distillery Co and their associated company Alexander Muir (→ King's Crest). In this case they appear as → independent bottlers. The labels only shows the year of distillation, but these are all → cask strength bottlings.

Scottish & Newcastle Breweries UK brewery giant formed in 1960 from a merger between Scottish Brewers Ltd and Newcastle Breweries Ltd, and which is now part of Scottish Courage. It owns other brewing comapanies such as McEwan and Younger. For a time they owned the → Glenallachie Distillery, and → Waverley Vintners were a subsidiary of theirs with numerous subdivisions such as Charles → Mackinlay & Co and their Isle of Jura Distillery. Both distilleries were taken over by → Invergordon, as well as the brands → Mackinlay's, → Glen Clova and → Scot's Club. They are now part of the → Kyndal portfolio. The beer giants now only have, via Waverley, the blends → Beneagles and → Huntingtower, which are mainly intended for their own chain of pubs.

Scottish Castle Scotch blend aged for the minimum of 3 years. It comes from → Burn Stewart.

Scottish Collie Scotch blend from → QSI, a subsidiary of William → Grant & Sons.

Scottish Dance Scotch blend from the → Premier Scotch Whisky Co in Glasgow, which like all the (numerous) blends of this company, is produced aged 3, 5, 8, 10 and 12 years, and is exclusively intended for export.

Scottish Envoy Standard Scotch blend from H → Mayerson & Company.

Scottish Island Scotch whisky liqueur which was brought on to the market by the company Spirit Of Argyll in 1996. The recipe is said to come from this region and, as in the case of its old-established role-model → Drambuie, to have been passed down from generation to generation. It is 40% and consists of → Speyside malt whisky, heather honey and wild herbs and comes in 50cl bottles. Its Gaelic name, Càleach an Lochan, appears on the label, which also bears the name of the Melldalloch Liqueur Company as bottlers with an address in Tighnabruaich, Argyll.

Scottish Leader Scotch blend. It is → Burn Stewart's most successful brand, the firm formed by a management buyout in 1988 of the former company of the same name. One of its subsidiaries, Ross Bros, already had this blend in its range, but it has only been resolutely and successfully promoted by its new owners in recent years. It is now on sale in more than 50 countries. It is available in every price and age category: as a → standard blend without an age statement and aged 12, 15, 17, 25 and 30 years and as Platinum Seal.

Scottish National Tartan, The Scotch blend. The leading brand of the → Bennachie Whisky Co from Inverurie. It is available aged 21 and 30 years and is presented in a glass decanter.

Scottish Parliament Scotch single malt which celebrates the decision on the 11th September 1997 to reconvene the Scottish Parliament in Edinburgh. The date was chosen carefully: it was the day in 1297 on which William Wallace was victorious against the English at Stirling Bridge. There are 5,000 bottles of the 12-year-old as well as some glass decanters. Unfortunately the company that produces it, Flavours of Scotland, does not name the distillery from which it comes. They have marketed the name in a big way and by the end of 1998 they had already sold the licence to 25 Scottish firms allowing them to use the label 'Scottish Parliament' to sell typically Scottish products.

Scottish Prince Scotch blend from Forbes, Ross & Co, a subsidiary of → Campbell & Clark. Both names now belong to the Christie family's → Speyside Distillery Co. They offer the blend aged 19, 21 and 30 years.

Scottish Queen Scotch blend, one of the smaller brands from → GuinnessUDV, which are only offered on individual markets.

Scottish Reel Scotch blend from → London & Scottish Spirits which was first established in 1994. It is an 8-year-old → standard blend without an age statement.

Scottish Royal Scotch blend from → Angus Dundee based in Glasgow.

Seager Evans UK company founded in 1805 as a partnership between Messrs Seager and Evans, who made their name mainly as producers of gin. In the 1920s they began to diversify and produce whisky, building the large grain distillery of Strathclyde on the banks of the Clyde in Glasgow. In 1936 they bought the London wine and spirits merchants Chaplin and thereby acquired the brand → Long John, which led to the establishment of the subsidiary Long John International; in 1937 it was joined by the → Glenugie Distillery on the north-east coast. A second expansion phase began in the 1960s following the large-scale expansion of Strathclyde to include → warehouses, a bottling plant and the malt distillery → Kinclaith, and the building of → Tormore Distillery on the Spey. By the time it opened in 1959 Seager Evans had already been in the hands of the American company → Schenley for three years. They allowed Long John to buy → Laphroaig but then in 1971 sold all their Scottish interests to Whitbread, the brewery giants. They, in their turn, sold their wine and spirits sector to Allied Breweries, which after several other mergers became → Allied Domecq PLC.

Seagram Canadian company which began with a small distillery in → Waterloo and which for a long time was one of the largest drinks companies in the world, with 21 distilleries and bottling plants in North America, Europe, South America and in the Asian-Pacific area, as well as innumerable brands. Until recently it was still the third-largest producer in the world and the only one remaining in Canadian hands (where nowadays they only produce whiskey in a single distillery, at → Gimli). However, in the year 2001 Seagram ceased to exist as a whisk(e)y producer.

The company's history began with Joseph Emm Seagram, whose parents had emigrated from England and ran two farms in Canada. He was soon orphaned and received his education in the USA. When he returned to Canada he became the manager of the Granite and the Waterloo Mills, where, as in all mills at that time, the surplus grain was distilled in order to produce alcohol. Seagram first bought a share in the business and then took it over completely in 1883, founded the Joseph E Seagram Flour Mill & Distillery Company and in the same year brought out → Seagram's '83', the first blend in the country and the first brand of Canadian whiskey. The company was successful and exported large quantities to the USA. In 1911 it was renamed Joseph E Seagram & Sons Ltd and a whiskey was launched called → V O. After Seagram's death in 1919 his sons sold the company to Samuel → Bronfman, who brought it together with his own business under the name Distillers Corporation – Seagram Limited (DC-SL).

n 1928 he entered into a partnership with the Scottish → DCL, for which the motives on both sides remain a matter of dispute. The supply of the American market, which was thirsty for Canadian and Scottish whiskies during → prohibition, surely played a part. Bronfman thought prohibition would soon come to an end and had enlarged his distilleries in Waterloo and → La Salle so that he was well prepared when it was abolished in 1933. In that same year the connection with DCL ended. Canadian whiskey had gained a good reputation as being clean, in contrast to the illicit distillates in America, and so the booming market in the USA also contributed to expansion. Seagram's → 7 Crown was soon launched in the USA. Three years later a new distillery was built in Louisville, Kentucky and in the course of the following years several others were taken over, including → Old Prentice in Lawrenceburg, Kentucky, where → Four Roses was already being produced. Another was in Indiana, confusingly in a place that was also called Lawrenceburg, where → Benchmark and → Eagle Rare were made. The company acquired a total of seven distilleries in the USA (of these only the two in both Lawrenceburgs are still in operation). They also bought brands such as → Mattingly & Moore and → Henry McKenna (and sold them again). The US business became so successful that they moved into an imposing administration building in New York's smart Park Avenue, built by the star architect Mies van der Rohe (the company headquarters are in Montreal). Bronfman created new brands such as → Crown Royal and bought other distilleries and business such as → Adams and Reifel (→ Lord Calvert).

After the Second World War they expanded their interests to Scotland, initially acquiring → Chivas Brothers, and had nine distilleries and several bottling plants under the name The → Chivas & Glenlivet Group. Seagram distilled whisky in New Zealand (→ Wilson), Argentina (for example → Blenders Pride), had joint ventures in → China and Thailand and, especially with → Kirin in → Japan. Whisky was not its only field of business: Seagram produced gin and vodka, owned champagne and sparkling wine cellars (such as Mumm in Germany), cognac brands such as Martell and the UK chainstore → Oddbins. The last chairman Edgar Bronfman was also a scriptwriter but Seagram's first excursion in to the film industry was a costly failure, which didn't prevent him from from buying Universal Studios and its parent company MCA. Some observers of the stock exchange were even said to have observed signs that indicated Seagram was preparing to part with its drinks activities in order to concentrate on the media business. In 2001, this materialised.

After a long period it was sold to the French media company → Vivendi who made it clear that it was not interested in the drinks portfolio. It was acquired, in a kind of auction, by a consortium of → Diageo and → Groupe Pernod-Ricard, who shared the brands between themselves.

Seagram's '83' Canadian whiskey, reputedly the oldest in the country. It first appeared in 1883, a year before → Canadian Club from the competitors Hiram → Walker. In the same year the Canadian pioneer Joseph Emm → Seagram had bought the → Waterloo Mill and Distillery and founded his own company from which grew the huge drinks company which for a time was the largest in the world, a development to which the export success of his '83' contributed. Seagram's first whiskey also played a pioneering role as it was the first blended whisky outside Scotland and therefore the first blend in Canada, a country which had previously only known → straight whiskies.

Seal of Fine Malt An award thought up by → GuinnessUDV to draw attention to shops and bars which have a particularly fine selection of malt whiskies. The plaque in the shape of the bottom of a barrel is also meant to be a way of attracting customers. It was first awarded in the spring of 1998. Among the first six shops to receive the honour were Milroy's and The Vintage House in London, the two branches of The Whisky Shop in Glasgow and Edinburgh, Royal Mile Whiskies in Edinburgh and the old-established wine merchant's Tanner's of Shrewsbury.

Second Term used for Japanese bottlings which include a malt content of between 10-20%.

Secret Korean blend formerly from → Seagram. It consists of whiskies that are imported in → bulk from Scotland and blended with locally-produced → grain whiskies. It is a cheap alternative to the foreign blends which have enjoyed considerable success in → Korea in recent years.

Select Hogshead, The Series of Scotch single malts which are bottled by → Burn Stewart for The Whisky Shop chain in Edinburgh (Waverley Market), Glasgow and a number of other Scottish towns and cities. It has included, for example, a 14-year-old → Glenlochy from a sherry cask and a 16-year-old → Port Ellen. Both were bottled at 50%.

Seliko Czech company based in Prague and Olomouc (Olmütz), which produces and sells food and drinks. Amongst other things it makes Slibowitz, as well as the whisky brands → Gold Cock and → King Barley. Whilst the first one is quite clearly and indisputably a blend, the other used to be a malt but then became a blend, whilst the malt temporarily bore the name King Barleycorn. It bore the same label as its predecessor, which didn't exactly make matters clearer. Thanks to the efforts of the German importer Jack Wievers in Berlin, a limited amount of a 12-year-old King Barley has become available. It is simply called 'Malt Whisky' and is elaborately presented in a glass decanter and a wooden box.

The attitude of the company to their two distilleries → Testice and → Dolany is equally confusing. Testice is the only one which is still in production (although not continuously) but it is not mentioned on any bottling. The name of Dolany can be found, but they are only active as bottlers nowadays; Josef Kvapil even calls himself 'Manager of Dolany distilleries', as if the other one didn't exist. In fact the company should be proud to promote it and name it clearly: Jim Murray, probably the only journalist to have seen both of them and have had the opportunity of sampling their whiskies from the cask before bottling, writes that 'of all the world whiskies, I place Testice's – and especially the

20-year-old – easily in the top dozen', a quality which he not only ascribes to the excellence of the ingredients, but especially to the casks of Czech oak which are used for maturation.

Sendai Japanese malt distillery which is named after the town which lies on latitude 38° on the east coast of Japan's main island Honshu. The distillery itself is not situated in the town, but half an hour further inland. As it belongs to the → Miyagikyo prefecture it is also known as Sendai → Miyagikyo's Distillery. It belongs to the second largest whisky company in Japan → Nikka, whose founder, Masataka → Taketsuru, had helped the other Japanese whisky pioneer and founder of → Suntory, Shinjiro → Torii, to produce the country's first whiskies at → Yamazaki in 1924, and 10 years later to build his own distillery at → Yoichi on → Hokkaido. The production of whisky in Japan really only got going after the Second World War, but by the end of the 1960s demand had become so great that Taketsuru built another, far larger plant. It was opened in 1969, in very rural surroundings in the middle of a forest of bamboo, nestling between two rivers. Its larger → pot stills, mounted on marble bases, were meant to produce a lighter whisky than Yoichi, and although it also sometimes uses intensely peated malt, the company likes to make the comparison with whiskies of the → Scottish Lowland type. There is a 12-year-old single malt named Miyagikyo and a 12-year-old single malt (45%) named Sendai.

Sennachie Scotch single malts. They are all bottled as 30-year-olds and originate from different distilleries which are located on → Speyside. The brand belongs to the Glaswegian firm W → Brown & Sons. A 'sennachie' was an official chronicler of the Irish and Scottish kings or of a clan chief.

7 Crowns American blended whiskey formerly from Seagram whose whiskeys come from the → Lawrenceburg Distillery in Indiana (not to be confused with the → Four Roses Distillery, also previously belonging to Seagram, in a place which is also called Lawrenceburg, but which is in Kentucky). There they make gin and vodka as well as many different kinds of whiskeys, straight bourbons and ryes (including one from 100% rye) each with a different → mash bill, and there is even an Irish-style → pure pot still whiskey. They all form the basis for the blended whiskey, which is said to have been the best-selling spirit in the world in the 1960s and which is still in the top 50 today.

Seven Stills, The Scotch vatted malt from Peter J → Russell & Co, which at present does not supply the brand which was originally brought out by → Cockburn & Murray who were taken over in 1953. It is 5 years old, which indicates which country it was intended for: Italy, where such young malts are popular and where it is possible to get several young single malts (such as → Glen Grant) which are only available elsewhere aged 12 years or more. Its name suggests that it mainly contains malts from Dufftown ('Rome was built on seven hills, Dufftown stands on seven stills'), but that is by no means certain.

77 Scotch blend from Douglas → Laing & Co, a → standard blend from the Glaswegian company whose best-known brands are → House of Peers, → King of Scots and → John Player Special.

Shanagarry Irish single malt. A new product from the → Cooley Distillery in Riverstown. There they make → pure pot still whiskey according to traditional methods, as well as The → Tyrconnell (amongst others) and the → Connemara, which, contrary to the modern Irish custom, is peated. David F Hynes explains that the use of peated or unpeated malt alone makes it possible to produce a variety of single malts. Further variations become possible with the use of different types of cask and by bottling whiskeys at various ages. In the spring of 1999 the company had seven different malts in their range, as well as almost a dozen blends.

Shaw Wallace Indian company based in Bombay which owns a distillery in Aurangabad in Maharashta and is chiefly known for its → Moghul Monarch. The company calls this 'Finest Malt Whisky', although it only has a small proportion of real malt whisky at the very most and consists mainly of a molasses distillate. The company's other brands include → Antiquity and → Director's Special.

The large Canadian drinks concern → Seagram, which has always been amongst the first to extend their activities to new continents and participate on promising markets, tried for some time to arrange a joint venture with this Indian company.

Sheep Dip Scotch vatted malt which was launched in 1974 and was originally intended as the special brand of a pub in Oldbury on Severn, near Bristol, whose customers were familiar with the disinfectant used for sheep. The brand has always been made in Scotland, and is now also sold by a Scottish company, → Kyndal. They bottle it at 8 years, and it is mainly intended for export. → Pig's Nose, which also originated in Oldbury, also comes from them.

Sherman Company, David American whiskey company based in St. Louis with a whole range of brands, the best-known of which have only been in their programme since 1993. These were acquired from → UD who themselves had bought the → Glenmore company based in Owensboro just two years previously, which had, in its turn, taken over two businesses in the same town, → Fleischmann and → Medley. Old Medley brands include → Davies County and → Ezra Brooks, and Glenmore had had → Yellowstone in their range since 1944. This is a Kentucky straight, just like → Bourbon Supreme. In addition the blended → County and → Town Club also belong to the company, as well as the two Canadian whiskeys → Canadian Deluxe and → Canadian Springs. In March 1999 there were able to enlarge their portfolio when, together with → Heaven Hill and → Sazerac, they took over the → Bernheim Distillery and four brands (of these → Rebel Yell ended up with Sherman) from the UD successors → GuinnessUDV.

Sherry The fortified wine produced in the region of Jerez de la Frontera in southern Spain and matured in Spanish oak casks. These have come to have a profound effect on the maturation of Scotch whisky.

In the second half of the 19th century several Scottish whisky dealers noticed that their whisky was improved after storage in sherry → butts. Sherried malt whisky soon gained a following and the producers also began to use sherry casks for storing and maturing their malts. Nowadays many Scotch single malt bottlings are either partly, or wholly, matured in Spanish ex-sherry → butts.

The sherry and the Spanish oak impart distinct characterisitcs to the maturing spirit which are immediately recognisable on the nose and palate. A fragrant Fino has a different effect to a dark, dry Oloroso or a heavy Pedro Ximénez.

One example is the → Macallan, whose → proprietary bottlings come exclusively from Oloroso casks. Other distilleries prefer a balanced composition based on various types of cask. In addition, in recent years the trend has been to allow the malt whisky to age for a number of years in one cask before → finishing in a second cask. In this case sherry casks are also popular. Sherry casks have become very expensive and this may be a contributing factor in this new process. A cask can cost up to £250, compared with about £25 for an ex-bourbon → barrel. They have also become rare and those who are in need of a large supply, such as Macallan, have begun having them specially made in Spain, lending them out to sherry producers and shipping them to Scotland, in order to ensure that they are are of the quality desired.

Signatory Scottish whisky company which was first established in 1988 with the bottling of a → Glenlivet from 1968 and which was run, practically single-handed, by the brothers Andrew and Brian Symington (the latter left in 1998). In this short time both brothers managed to lead the Signatory Vintage Scotch Whisky Co from very modest beginnings to become one of the most important → independent bottlers. They are now able to compete with others who have been in the business for much longer, such as → Gordon & MacPhail (perhaps not as far as quantity is concerned, but as far as quality is concerned they can certainly match G&M or, for example, → Cadenhead or the → Scotch Malt Whisky Society; in fact they have even set new standards by labelling their bottles with information about the exact date of distillation and bottling and, which nobody had previously done, giving the number of the cask and the type of → cask used. The bottles are individually numbered and also state the total number of bottles produced.

The Symingtons have had several real coups, which have also attracted the attention of collectors. They were not only the first to bottle a → Braes of Glenlivet from the distillery which has now been rechristened → Braeval, but they were also able to find a cask of → Killyloch, which they bottled together with a malt from its sister distillery → Glenflagler. Naturally such → single cask bottlings only produce a few hundred bottles and the price is correspondingly high – if one can get hold of a bottle at all. Collectors willingly pay more than £1,000 for a Killyloch. Perhaps an even greater surprise was the fact that Signatory succeeded in bringing out a → Ben Wyvis, when is was believed that there wasn't a single drop of this whisky left. Of the five casks of the malt distilled on in 1968 that Andrew Symingtion was able to acquire, two were empty and the others were bottled singly; cask no. 685 yielded 191 bottles (51%), no. 686 produced only 84 bottles (50.1%) and no. 687 151 bottles (50.6%).

Signatory's bottlings differentiate between those at 43% and those which are at → cask strength. For the former standard bottles are used with a little → chill-filtering, whilst the latter are left in their natural state and come in stocky bottles. These have recently been bedded in taffeta, their boxes covered with velvet and with a window through which the label can be read. Particularly old and rare malt whiskies are also accompanied by a certificate.

Signatory is also willing to sell whole or part casks to customers using their own names and labels. The Dutch series 'Ultima', for example, comes from Signatory and the most important independent bottler in Germany, Dieter Kirsch,

works together with the Edinburgh company for his bottlings. Signatory also bottles an exclusive range for the → Maison du Whisky in Paris. In addition to the label with the characteristic 'S' logo on a cask, Signatory also uses the names → Dun Eideann, → Prestonfield and → Sailing Ships. Newer series are named 'Rare Reserve' and 'unchill-filtered' and there was a special series for the Millennium, the '2000 Edition'. The name Supreme was used for a bottling which, like the → Century from → Seagram or the → Ultima from → Justerini & Brooks, is composed of a large number of malts: in the case of Signatory this amounted to 104. The creation of the new series → 'Silent Stills' in 1997 was a great achievement. It is carefully presented, even surpassing Signatory's usual high standards, and consists of malt whiskies from distilleries which no longer exist. The 10th birthday of the company was celebrated with the '10th Anniversary' series of five even more exclusive malts and one single grain. This latter, again an absolute rarity, originated from the → Garnheath Distillery where it had been distilled in 1973. When bottled in 1998 it was still at 56.8%. The malts were a Bruichladdich (1968/98, 49.6%), a Highland Park (1972/98, 57.7%), an → Isle of Jura (1966/98, 50.6%), a → Littlemill (1965/98, 49.1%) and a → Longmorn (1969/98, 56.3%).

Signature Japanese blend from → Suntory. This name is only used in certain export markets; at home the whisky is called → Imperial.

Silent Stills Series of very rare single malts brought out by the important → independent bottler → Signatory. The name signifies that the series consists exclusively of whiskies from distilleries which have been mothballed for a long time or no longer exist at all. The company, which is known not only for the care which goes into the presentation of the bottlings but also for the descriptions on the labels, has emphasised the exclusive nature of these malt whiskies by packing them even more lovingly than usual. They lie bedded in a wooden box with a transparent lid, and because Andrew Symington knows how difficult it is for a collector to consume such a bottle, he has included a miniature with each one as a sample – however these little bottles have now also become collectors' items. The box also contains a small round piece of wood which has been cut out of the bottom of the cask and shows the name of the distillery and the number of the cask. There are 24 bottlings in all, consisting of four editions of six bottles each. Series no. 1 included a → Glen Albyn (1965/97, 61.6%), a → Glen Flagler (1972/97, 52.0%), a → Glenlochy (1965/97, 47.9%), a → Glenugie (1978/97, 57.4%), a → Littlemill (1965/97, 46.5%) and a → Port Ellen (1974/97, 59.2%). The second series included a → Banff (1978/97, 58.8%), a → Dallas Dhu (1978/97, 59.8%), a Glen Mhor (1977/97, 59.3%), a → Glenury Royal (1973/97, 53.7%), a → Millburn (1974/97, 58.7%) and another Port Ellen (1979/97, 56.3%). The third series included a → Glenglassaugh (1967/98, 55.8%), a → Glenugie (1966/98, 53.9 %), a → Linlithgow/ → St. Magdalene (1975/98, 51.7%), a → Lochside (1966/98, 57.7%), a → Mosstowie (1976/98, 54.8%) and the almost obligatory Port Ellen (1975/98, 56.15%). The fourth series included a Bladnoch (1980/2000, 56.2%), a Coleburn (1983/2000, 57.3%), a Convalmore /1976/2000, 60.8%), a Hillside (1971/2000, 51.4%), a Rosebank (1989/2000, 56.2%) and a → grain whisky from Garnheath (1972/2000, 59.4%). Bladnoch is no longer silent.

Silk Tassel Canadian whisky produced in → Walkerville for → Corby. It was originally a brand from → McGuinness Distillers. It is available in two versions, a 'normal' one at 40% and a 'light' at only 27% which is supposed to have around a third less calories than the stronger bottling.

Single barrel Term used in the USA for what is called → single cask in Scotland. In the case of bourbons as well, more and more producers are following the trend and bottling single barrels rather than mixing several barrels in order to create their own characteristic style. Of course these only result in a small amount of bottles and are also distinguished by the fact that each bottling may taste different from the previous one or the following one. The difference may sometimes be slight, but in other cases may be more extreme. The handful of American producers can be trusted to always choose the very best quality for their single barrels, such as → Blanton's, → Benchmark, → Elmer T Lee and → Booker's, to name just a few examples. Critics point out that the standard bottlings of the companies' brands are liable to suffer as they also rely on good whiskeys. In contrast to Scotch single malts, whose single cask bottlings are nearly always at → cask strength, the American bourbons and Tennessees are diluted to drinking strength, about 80°/40%.

Single blend Technically this type of whisky combines the characteristics of a blend with those of a single malt. The latter is defined as consisting exclusively of malts from a single distillery, the former is a mixture of → grain whiskies and malt whiskies. A single blend must therefore a) consist of malts and grains and b) come from a single distillery. It is of course not easy to find such a distillery. There have been various Scottish distilleries, such as → Ben Nevis or → Lochside, which produced both types of whisky, but a blend made of just one malt and one grain whisky would not have been a very satisfactory product. The → Loch Lomond Distillery makes grain whiskies and, thanks to the variable heads on the stills and slightly altered ingredients, they can also produce six different malts, enough for an experienced master blender to be able to create a good, complex blend: the first single blend.

Single cask Term which indicates that a bottling of a single malt does not consist of a 'marriage' from several casks, but that the contents of one particular cask from one particular distillery has been used. In the USA the term → single barrel is used. Such bottlings result in relatively small amounts, depending on the size of the cask chosen and its age. In the case of an old and small cask this may mean that less than 150 bottles can be filled. The number is seldom more than 500. The → Scotch Malt Whisky Society were the pioneers of single cask bottlings, and most → independent bottlers have since followed their example and have also adopted the practice of bottling at → cask strength, without the use of → chill-filtering or → colouring.

Distillery proprietors were slow to follow suit and were able to make a good case for their reasons. They have to guarantee consistent quality and make sure that, a → Lagavulin, for example, always looks, smells and tastes the way that the consumer is used to. This cannot be done in the case of single casks, because no single cask is absolutely identical to another. They try to balance out these differences by the careful selection of the casks which are chosen for bottling. A malt whisky from a single cask is always a special experience. It may surpass a normal bottling, or may be quite different from it, or it may even be a bitter disappointment – but that is what makes malt whisky so exciting.

Single cask bottling They have become more and more popular in recent years because they demonstrate in a very special way that single malts are highly individual drinks, not only differing considerably from distillery to distillery, but also from cask to cask. These differences are the result of the microclimate in the → warehouses, of the exact location in which a cask is stored, and of the length of maturation. The pioneers of → single cask bottling were the → Scotch Malt Whisky Society, who are now being emulated by more and more → independent bottlers and also, recently, by distillery → proprietors. They were often opposed to single cask bottlings because they thought that expectations might be disappointed if a consumer suddenly got hold of a bottling which tasted different to the usual one; their consistency is guaranteed by the careful choice of cask, so that despite their individuality, a certain uniformity can be achieved.

However it must be admitted that some regular bottlings are much better than some single cask bottlings, despite → cask strength and the foregoing of → chill-filtering and colouring. But that is the exciting thing about a single malt; it is always a sensual adventure. For that reason the large companies have not ignored the new trend and are now offering more and more such bottlings. The excellent → 'Rare Malts' series from → GuinnessUDV is a good example – and only one of many. Anniversaries are the ideal occasion to come up with one, sometimes very old, cask. The trend has even reached America, which long remained conservative in this respect, and makes itself evident in a whole series of so-called → single barrel bottlings.

Single malt Term for a malt whisky which, in contrast to a vatted malt, comes from a single, specific distillery. In historical terms this is the oldest kind of Scotch whisky, but it lost its importance economically when blends became predominant. The pioneering work of William → Grant & Sons and their → Glenfiddich signalled the rediscovery of single malts in 1963. It was to be another two decades before more and more companies began to realise the potential of single malts and commence to sell them as single malts as well. This process was made easier by the greater marketing possibilities opened up by continual mergers and takeovers in the trade. Within the last 10 years single malts have become the fastest growing sector in the whisky trade – a trend which still continues, though they still represent only a very small percantage of the total whisky market.

A single malt may only contain whisky which is distilled, and as a rule also matured, by one distillery. If it bears an age statement then this always refers to the youngest malt contained in it, which means that the contents of many different casks are used for single malts. It is the skill of the master blender in choosing the casks which ensures that a uniform style emerges, a kind of → house style, which is reflected in the consistency of the colour, aroma and taste. Single malts come in two different forms: they may be → proprietary bottlings or → independent bottlings. The proprietors use the name of their distillery for their single malts but do not appreciate it when the independent bottlers do so. There have been court cases (→ Whyte & Whyte) in which the proprietors have prevented the use of the distillery name by defending the assertion that it is their property. The → Scotch Malt Whisky Society avoids the problem by using a number (which is easy to decode) instead of a name on their labels.

Occasionally distillery proprietors offer their single malts under another name; Glenfarclas is an example with Eagle of Spey and Meadhan. Invergordon caused a stir when they used the names of several historic distilleries for their → 'Malts of Scotland' series; it was the first time that a Scottish company had broken the unwritten rule that the names of distilleries should only be used for whiskies that actually come from them. There are, of course, many single malts with invented names, for example when a large whisky company such as → Gordon & MacPhail brings out part of its stocks under a brand name such as → Glen Avon, or when supermarket chains are not allowed to (or do not wish to) reveal the exact origins of a whisky and prefer to sell it as a house brand using their own name. Many small companies which wish to profit from the single malt trend also supply their whiskies with made-up names.

Singleton of Auchroisk Scotch single malt from the → Auchroisk Distillery, a → proprietary bottling from → IDV with a name that deviates from that of the distillery. The bottling is no longer available. There was no age statement but the year of bottling was given. In Japan there was also The Singleton Particular 1980. Following the merger of IDV and UD the brand belongs to → GuinnessUDV. Now available as a 10-year-old Auchroisk in their → 'Flora & Fauna' series.

Sir Iain Special Scotch blend which is produced for → Moncreiffe in Glasgow and is distributed worldwide by Charles H → Julian of London.

Sir John Hawkins Scotch blend produced exclusively for Astor Wines & Spirits. The company is one of the best sources for whisk(e)y in New York.

Sir Terence Scotch blend from Mason and Summers in Airdrie. The place of origin already gives a hint, and the label on the back of the bottle confirms that this is a company belonging to → Inverhouse (spelt this way in this case), which produces this 'Premium Selected' exclusively for export.

Sir Walter Raleigh Scotch blend from a subsidiary of Douglas → Laing in Glasgow. It is available as a → standard blend with the adjunct 'Gold Label' and as a → de luxe blend with an age statement '25 years old'.

Skye Scenic Scottish island popular with tourists which belongs to the → Islands whisky region. There is only one distillery: → Talisker. Two prominent visitors were able to sample Skye spirit over 200 years ago: Dr. Johnson and his companion → James Boswell were guests at Talisker House, and also stayed at Dunvegan Castle, the seat of the → MacLeods. Skye gave the world the original form of whisky liqueur with → Drambuie, which is still produced by the Mackinnons. Their ancestors got the recipe from Bonnie Prince Charlie, because they had looked after him following his defeat at Culloden when he was fleeing from Scotland to France (at least that is the company's official story). Skye is also the home of the company → Pràban Na Linne, a business which respects the Gaelic tradition, with various blends and vatted malts. One must not forget the series of blends that Peter J → Russell & Co produce for their subsidiary Ian MacLeod & Co under the label → Isle of Skye.

Slaintheva Scotch blend from Alexander → Dunn & Co, which broke new ground with this 12-year-old whisky in 1959; they offered to put the name of the buyer or the recipient on the label. In France and especially in Japan this idea was very successful – and was made easier by the spelling of the name. Behind the name is the toast 'slainté mtha', which is difficult to pronounce for those not well versed in Gaelic. In order to make the gift truly fitting, the bottles are not only available in the normal size, but also in so-called 'kingnums' containing 1.75 litres.

Slieve na gCloc Irish single malt. This near-unprounounceable Gaelic word (try 'shleef-na-clog') is the name of a mountain near the Cooley Distillery in Riverstown. The distillery is able to produce a variety of malt whiskeys, because they use both peated and unpeated malt, and also because they use different types of casks. This new product, which the active Irish company first brought out in 1999, is a peated malt. There are only two malt whiskeys of this kind in Ireland and they both come from Cooley. The other one is → Connemara.

Small batch Term for a completely new generation of American whiskeys. It does not signify → single cask bottlings, but bottlings of very small quantities for which only the very best casks are selected: in other words it represents the continuation of the success which, firstly the Scotch single malts and then the → single barrels in the USA, such as → Blanton's, had in other ways. If one disregards → Maker's Mark, which is always produced on a small-scale, then the first to follow this new trend were → Jim Beam with → Basil Hayden, → Baker's and → Knob Creek. Other companies then became the market leaders, such as → UD with their 'Bourbon Heritage Collection' (which no longer exists as UD's successor GuinnessUDV sold nearly all of the brands belonging to the series at the beginning of 1999) or the → Wild Turkey Distillery with their → Rare Breed.

Small Concern Whisky Co Australian company which probably runs the world's smallest malt distillery in Ulverstone on the island of Tasmania, which is even smaller than the → Tasmania Distillery on the same island. They are only able to produce about two or three barrels per month, use unpeated barley and work with → stills which are partly made of refined steel. The first cask was distilled in November 1993. The Tasmania Distillery made a later start and waited for the legally prescribed minimum age (in Australia) of two years before putting their → Sullivan's Cove on the market. Small Concern seem to be giving the malt whisky in Ulverstone more time. Several casks of it are ageing at → Cadenhead in the Scottish air of the → Springbank Distillery. The whisky is made with water from → Cradle Mountain and the 'Pure Tasmanian Malt' at 43% is now available, but difficult to find.

SMD (Scottish Malt Distillers Ltd.) Scottish whisky company which arose out of the merger of the five distilleries: Clydesdale, Glenkinchie, Grange, Rosebank and St. Magdalene (Linlithgow) in 1914, in an effort to make them more effective in competing against other companies. Although all five were situated in the Lowlands they soon expanded into the Highlands by taking over Glenlossie and North Port. Of course their main competitor was → DCL, which had become even stronger by acquiring Buchanan-Dewar and Johnnie Walker, were able to acquire a minority share in SMD and eventually took them over. In 1929 it was decided that SMD should be put in control of all DCL's malt distilleries. Forty-one Scottish distilleries (including some which had been closed down) were in their charge when DCL, and therefore also SMD, was bought by Guinness in 1987 and reformed as → UD.

Smith Bowman Distillery, A American company which nowadays runs a distillery in Fredericksburg, Virginia, where they mainly produce gin, rum and vodka. They don't make whiskey, or to be more precise, they don't make all of it any more. The company was founded by A Smith Bowman Sr, who was actually a farmer-distiller, but not one of the pioneers of the 19th century. He had earned a lot of money as a car dealer and in 1927 he bought himself the Star Hill Farm near Washington DC as a hobby, and after → prohibition set up a distillery there. It started production in 1935 and its whiskey was called → Virginia Gentleman after William Byrd II, the 'first Gentleman of Virginia' and founder of nearby Richmond. The brand soon became popular with politicians and the rest of the establishment in the capital which is also nearby, and now it is the only Virginia whiskey from that era which has survived to this day.

However it no longer comes from the old distillery which was given up in 1987 after the Bowmans had already sold most of the land in the 1960s to build the town of Reston. In 1988 the new distillery was opened. It is equipped with a copper → doubler that almost looks like a → pot still, but has a rather unusual shape. It serves to redistil a bourbon which has already been distilled once or twice (the information differs) at → Heaven Hill and is then transported in tanks by rail to Virginia. The → mash bill has remained the same with 65% corn, 20% rye and 15% malted barley, and the label still reads 'Virginia Whiskey'. The 'new' version made at Fredericksburg on the Rappaphannock River has been on sale since 1996, but with luck it is still possible to find the old one from Reston. A Bowman Smith is now managed by John 'Jay' Adams who can count no fewer than three American Presidents amongst his relations – Adams, Jefferson and Buchanan – and who married into a family that has had its share of prominent people: the present chairman Robert E Lee IV is a descendant of the Civil War general and the current head of marketing Al Durante is Jimmy

Durante's nephew. It is all very reminiscent of old Virginia whose most famous son, George Washington, also made whiskey, one of many in a part of the country which regards itself as the cradle of American whiskey. Only one brand is left from this great and proud tradition, and one distillery which – at least partly – produces this Virginia Whiskey.

Smith, George Legendary Scottish farmer and illicit distiller. Born in 1792 he learnt his craft from his father, and made history when he was the first distiller to apply for a licence for the legal production of malt whisky in 1823. One year later he opened his distillery, → Glenlivet. This whisky had already become so famous that King George IV had chosen to drink it on the occasion of his visit to Edinburgh in 1822. After distilling in two other places, he set up the beginnings of the present-day distillery on at Minmore in 1858. Its whisky soon became so famous that nearly all the distilleries in the area added the name 'Glenlivet' to their own. As a result George Smith then had the name 'Glenlivet' registered. He died in 1871, nine years before his son was granted the right to call their whisky The Glenlivet to differentiate it from its imitators.

Smokey & Co Japanese blend from → Suntory which is available in three versions, Natural Mellow, Fine Mint (bright green) and Super Smokey.

Smokey Jim Bourbon bottled at 40% from an unnamed distillery in Kentucky which is mainly sold in the UK by a company using the name Smokey Jim's Bourbon and giving an address in Salamander Place, Edinburgh. This is the address of → Invergordon Distillers now part of → Kyndal.

Smoky Martini Whisky cocktail that will particularly be enjoyed by fans of → Islay malts. The recipe for it is included in Gavin D Smith' book *Whisky Wit and Wisdom*. Take three parts gin to one part Islay whisky, shake with ice and serve in a Martini glass.

Smoky Springs German whisky which originally came from East Germany where it was produced as 'Finest Whisky' by the VEB Nordbrand in Nordhausen and cost 27 DM. After reunification the brand existed for a short time and it named Nordbrand Nordhausen as its producer, but this time with the adjunct GmbH ('Ltd.'). The village was already famous for distilling corn schnapps in 1507. The modern company described their product as a 'Light Whisky, Smooth and Mellow' and as a → 'Pure single malt'. It was bottled at 40%; the word 'light' cannot have referred to its strength. There was also a blended whisky.

Smuggling Whisk(e)y and smuggling have gone hand in hand since the natural right of people to distil their own alcohol was outlawed by governments after imposition of excise duty. On 17th January 1644, the Scottish Government imposed its first excise duty to raise funds for the army. In Ireland it was on Christmas Day 1661, of all days, that the English Government enforced such taxation and since that time legal whiskey has been derided as 'Parliament whiskey'. In the USA George Washington, who had himself been a distiller, realised the revenue raising power of whiskey. The outbreak of the 'Whiskey Rebellion', which was eventually put down by force, was the result. A further result was illicit distilling and smuggling of → poitín and → moonshine. The government reaction was to set → excisemen on the trail of the lawbreakers. It was only the introduction of a relatively fair taxation system in Ireland and Scotland in 1823 which encouraged more and more distillers to apply for a licence. This, however, did not stop smuggling. Even such draconian measures as the introduction of → prohibition failed. In fact they had the reverse effect and increased the activities (and the profits) of the smugglers.

Snug Irish spirit from → IDG for the quick production of a → Toddy. Its whiskey is already sweetened and contains lemon and cloves, so that all that remains is the addition of hot water. One should be economical with the water as the whiskey is only 30%.

Solan Indian distillery owned by Mohan Meakin, which they built in the 1970s on the site of a brewery which had been established there for a long time, but which could not be put into production because the government of Himichal

Pradesh suddenly decided to refuse a licence. The buildings lie alongside the railway lines of Chandirgarh, which go to the old colonial town of Shimla. Although not a single drop has ever been distilled there, its name appears on the bottles of India's best whiskey (sic), a → pure malt named Solan No. 1. It plainly comes from Mohan Meakin's → Kasauli Distillery, as its label clearly states, but is bottled in Solan at the Indian national obligatory 42.8%, and also carries the required statement from the Royal Institute of Public Health and Hygiene that whisky can damage the health. In contrast to normal Indian custom it is actually a real malt whisky, with possibly a little bit of malt from → Mohan Nagar, the company's other distillery (it does not call itself a single malt), but it certainly does not contain the cheap molasses distillate which is otherwise so popular.

Som Indian distillery which is located in Bhopal in Madhya Pradesh. Its most famous brand is → 21st Century.

Something Special Scotch blend launched on to the market by → Hill Thomson & Company in Edinburgh. It was its leading product along with → Queen Anne, which is made clear by the suffix → de luxe. In 1970 the company merged with → Glenlivet and → Glen Grant, and its brands later belonged to → Seagram, through its subsidiary the → Chivas & Glenlivet Group. They are now in the ownership of the Diageo/ Groupe Pernod-Ricard partnership which acquired Seagram's spirits interests in 2000.

Sonnenschein German single malt. It comes from a distillery located in Witten, in the Ruhr area – a region which is not usually associated with whisky. In fact, distilling does take place there, although not of the eau de vies that are found further south-west, but of schnapps and vodka. In 1988/89 it was decided to experiment – and to make it as Scottish as possible. Malt was obtained from Scotland, the distillery equipment was specially adapted and the distillate was matured in 'original Scottish wooden casks'. These, of course, may have been new casks of Scottish oak, but were probably used whisky casks. The whisky matured for 10 years before being bottled in September 1999.

Sour mash Term for a special process that is customary in the production of American whiskey. Many firms emphasise the use of this process on their labels to give the impression that the product is a speciality with a particular quality. The truth is that all American distilleries use sour mash, even those which do not state the fact. The method used for → Jack Daniel's and George → Dickel is legally prescribed in Tennessee.

The expression itself refers to the fact that the → mash is no longer sweet, and therefore no longer contains sugar. It consists of substances from the liquid which are left at the bottom of the → beer still following the first run. In the USA this is called → stillage and in Scotland → burnt or → pot ale. It consists of solid and liquid parts which are separated into → dark grains, which are mostly processed for cattle feed, and → thin stillage which is reused. Whisky books often contain a lot of confusing or simply false information about this re-use, particularly about the moment when the sour mash is re-fed into the production process.

This is why an authentic source is used here, Lincoln W Henderson, master distiller for → Brown-Forman and responsible for the → Early Times Distillery as well as for the → Woodford Reserve: 'The sour mash or spent stillage is what is left over from distilling the fermented mash or beer. The heavy grain particles are screened from the stillage and what is left from this screening is called thin stillage. Distilleries will add this thin stillage to the next fermenter being set with corn, rye, barley malt and yeast. The thin stillage (sour mash) lowers the pH of the next set fermenter to such a level that will inhibit most foreign organisms from growing except the yeast. This is actually a protective measure.'

Depending on the distillery the sour mash is either added to the mash or added at fermentation, or to the → wash, the → beer, or sometimes to all three. Henderson: 'Jimmy Bedford, master distiller at the Jack Daniel, explained that he adds the thin stillage to the cooker along with the other grains prior to pumping to the fermenter. At Early Times they add the thin stillage to the fermenter and at the Labrot & Graham to the cooker much like JD'.

The amount also differs. It can be up to 25% which is added at mashing or fermenting. There is, however, agreement about the effect of this → backset: apart from the fact that the fermenting process is more easily controllable and undesirable bacteria are killed, the whiskey also retains its character over a long production period.

South Africa The land at the Cape is particularly well-known for its wine, but they also distil spirits. There is a liqueur named 'Amarula'; it consists of cream and a spirit distilled from the fruit of the Marula tree, which, as monkeys and elephants also know, has a beneficial effect. Although grain is distilled, malt whisky is not produced. Like many other countries South Africa imports it in → bulk and then blends it with locally-produced → grain whiskies; two well-known brands are → Teal's and → Three Ships. South Africa is an important market for Scotch blends and malt whiskies and is in eleventh position among the 12 countries with the highest consumption, following a considerable decrease in recent years which might be the result of political changes.

South Korea No other country in the world has experienced such a breathtaking increase in the consumption of whisky over the past 10 years as this one with its booming economy. If the figures from the *Scotch Whisky Industry Review 1997* are correct, then the number has increased from 1.65 million litres of Scotch in 1986 to 11.44 million litres in 1996; only Thailand comes anywhere close to these figures. However they were both seriously affected by the financial crisis at the end of 1997, which resulted in many of the new rich suffering serious losses. Apart from the imported whiskies, there are also cheaper, locally produced blends. → Seagram, as so often the first foreign company to work in this market, had → Gold Classic and → Secret in its range.

Southern Comfort American liqueur which is said to have been invented around 1860 by the barman M W Heron in New Orleans – allegedly because Heron wanted to make a disastrous whiskey drinkable by adding ingredients that tasted and smelt good. However it is no longer based on whiskey, but on neutral alcohol that is chiefly blended with peach aroma (and a hint of lemon aroma) and a hundred other ingredients and is then stored in oak casks for eight months: the wood gives it a light bourbon-like vanilla fragrance, which has led to the widely-held opinion that it is still based on whiskey. Heron moved to Memphis in 1889 and ran a bar there before beginning to bottle his creation in St. Louis. The 'Grand old Drink of the South' became a hit, and with over two million → cases per year it occupies fourth position worldwide among liqueurs. It is drunk pure or with ice and is used as a basis for cocktails, including a variety of → Whiskey Sour. The brand now belongs to the → Brown-Forman Corporation in Louisville. They are holding on to the charming label showing an old sugar plantation on the Mississippi Delta, but are also interested in developing and building up the brand and therefore allow it to be made under licence in many countries, and not only sell a Southern Comfort and Cola in a can, but they have also recently brought out a Southern Comfort Reserve (also at 40%), which goes back to Heron's original recipe and is a mixture of the liqueur with a 6-year-old straight bourbon.

Southern Star Kentucky straight bourbon from an unknown distillery. The bottler named on the label is the Southern Star Distillery and gives its address as → Bardstown; it could therefore come from → Heaven Hill or from the → Kentucky Bourbon Distillers, both of which have many brands: the 'Spirit of Kentucky' is without an age statement and is 90°/45%, the 'Aged 10 years' is 101°/50.5%.

Sovereign, The Scotch blend. One of the many brands from Douglas → Laing & Co based in Glasgow, it is available in two versions aged 12 and 25 years, and belongs to the → de luxe sector.

Spain Ranks high among whisky consuming countries, although it is a lesser known fact that it also belongs to the whisky producing nations and malt whiskies as well as → grain whiskies are distilled here. Until 1991 there were two distilleries, but in that year Hiram → Walker shut down its plant in Cuenca to the south-east of Madrid. → Molino del Arco is still operating and lies to the north of Madrid near Segovia. It is run by a company called → Destilerias y Crianza and is also owned by Hiram Walker's parent company → Allied Domecq PLC. At Molino del Arco both malts and grains are produced and go into the popular blend → DYC. Hiram Walker has a second brand, the → Doble V, which probably contains some whisky made in Spain. On the other hand it is not known who makes the mysterious → W Turkey. The Spanish not only love their own whiskies but particularly love imported ones, which they drink at meal times as well as in the late afternoon, as an accompaniment to tapas. Unfortunately there are no figures to show the consumption of American, Canadian and Irish brands, but they do exist for Scotch whisky. In 1999 Spain was in fourth place behind France, the USA and the UK with 32.06 million litres of Scotch.

Special Scotch whisky term for bottlings which are superior to → standard ones, and not as exclusive as → premium bottlings. In Japan this category refers to bottlings with a malt content of between 30-35%.

Special Malt Scotch vatted malt which was launched onto the market by → Cockburn & Campbell in Edinburgh. It now belongs to Young & Co, who are among the larger independent breweries remaining in the UK. They own about 500 pubs in the Greater London area in which this brand is served.

Special Old Canadian whisky which is a mere 4 years old. Like its big brother → Canadian Club, it comes from Hiram → Walker and is produced for the Canadian market. However a Special Old, which is labelled as a rye whiskey, is also shipped in → bulk to Scotland and filled there in litre bottles made of plastic.

Spey Cast Scotch blend that was introduced at the turn of the 19th/20th century by → Gordon & MacPhail. The 12-year-old → de luxe blend contains only → Speyside malt whiskies. The name refers to a fishing technique: anglers on the River Spey have developed a complicated casting, to avoid overhanging trees, in order to get their flies to the salmon.

Spey Royal Scotch blend earlier produced by Glen Spey Ltd, then by → IDV/→ Grand Metropolitan. Today it belongs to the portfolio of → UDV. It is chiefly intended for export to South America and also the USA, where it is also available aged 8 years. It is shipped in → bulk to India where, since 1993, IDV has run a joint venture with → Polychem. It is then bottled in India.

Speyburn Scottish malt distillery. Its name means Spey stream. It lies to the north of Rothes close to the disused railway line and the main road to → Elgin and belongs to the → Speyside region. It was founded in 1897, Queen Victoria's Diamond Jubilee year, which is why its builders, a subsidiary of John → Hopkins and Co, insisted that its architect Charles Chree → Doig should have it finished before the end of the year. He just managed to do so, with the help of the distillery workers who had to wrap themselves up like mummies in order to be able to start production in the windowless and doorless building, and made just one barrel from the → stills. In 1916 Hopkins merged with → DCL who transferred the licence to John Robertson & Son, in whose blend → Yellow Label, the malt whisky from Speyburn played an important part. Despite its attractive location and its traditional appearance this distillery, which gets its water from the Granty Burn, has never attracted much attention. For those who enjoy whisky archaeology, Speyburn has a special feature: an early form of small → drum maltings, which while no longer in use, have at least not been dismantled.

However the fact that the DCL successor → UD sold the distillery to → Inver House Distillers Ltd just shortly after they had brought out a proprietary bottling of a 12-year-old single malt for the first time in their → 'Flora & Fauna' series, did cause a stir. The new owners sell their malt whisky aged 10 years. They took advantage of the 100th anniversary of the distillery to bring out a 21-year-old Centenary Celebration 1997 – 1997. It was presented in an elaborate decanter, which is only fitting for a birthday present. A further 21-year-old Speyburn came out in the spring of 1999, in a wooden basket. There were just 120 bottles of a 27-year-old Speyburn from 1973 (46%).

Speyburn is also occasionally available from the → independents such as → Gordon & MacPhail and → Cadenhead.

Speymalt Scotch single malts that all come from a single distillery, → Macallan. However they are not → proprietary bottlings but come from → Gordon & MacPhail, the largest whisky dealer and → independent bottler in the UK. The relationship between the distillery proprietors and the independent bottlers has not always been without its problems, as the former do not like it when the independents use the names of their distilleries, and there have even been court cases where they have tried to prevent this. In 1998 the Urquharts brought out a whole series of Macallans for which they had a special bottle created, with an embossed scene showing salmon being caught. The malts were all bottled at 40%. The first one was a Macallan from 1990 (there was also a miniature which, to the delight of collectors, used the un-Scottish spelling 'whiskey'). The whiskies which followed were increasingly old and expensive, with one from 1978 and another from 1966. This latter one, as well as one from 1950, came in a wooden box with a transparent lid. The crowning glory up to now has been a 50-year-old Macallan from 1940, which is a rarity because it was made during the war years. It cost around £1,500. G&M appear as wholesalers under the name of Speymalt and used the name in 1994 when they brought out the small series → 'Spirit of Scotland'. This was on the occasion of the 500th anniversary of the first documented reference to whisky. It included an → Ardbeg, a → Port Ellen and a → Tomatin. G&M have also used the name Speymalt for bottlings for the Hanseatische Weinhandelsgesellschaft in Bremen and for an Italian importer of whiskies.

Speyside Scottish → whisky region surrounding the River Spey. If one takes the number of distilleries as a measure, then this region is the most important: almost one third of all Scotland's distilleries lie between Kingussie and Grantown-on-Spey in the south-east and Spey Bay in the north, along the river and around Elgin, Rothes, → Dufftown and Keith. There are several reasons for this. For one thing the countryside in this area provides everything that is needed to make whisky: water, barley and peat. Whilst the isolation and inaccessibility of the area earlier encouraged the development of illicit distilling, at the end of the 19th century, in contrast, it was the development of a sound transport network that attracted investors. At that time the term Speyside was not yet in use, and the region was named after its most famous distillery, → Glenlivet. In 1823 George Smith, the owner of this distillery, had been the first to apply for a licence under the provisions of the Excise Act and his whisky gained such a good reputation that many others used the name as an adjunct for their own distilleries, for example → Macallan-Glenlivet, including distilleries that were quite a distance away from the river. This custom continued for many years and it is only in recent years that it has been abandoned by an increasing number of distillery owners.

Speyside Scottish malt distillery which belongs to the Speyside Distillery Co. It lies near Kingussie, where the River Tromie flows into the Spey, and can justifiably be included in the → Speyside → whisky region, and yet it is so far from the other distilleries (actually being nearer to → Dalwhinnie), that it is also possible to allocate it to the → Highlands. It first began operating in December 1990, almost 25 years after building had begun. The fact that it got that far is due to the passion and perseverance of George Christie, who had the idea of building a small and very traditional-style of distillery not far from the site where a Speyside Distillery had once stood. He was no newcomer to the whisky industry having had a share in blending and export companies, but he had caused a stir in the 1950s by setting up the → North of Scotland Distilling Co in Cambus, which produced malt whisky with → patent stills. The experiment had to be discontinued after a short time but the distillery continued to produce → grain whisky for a while.

Throughout this time Christie sold blends and vatted malts, some of which went by the name of Speyside and used the self-confident description: 'The best whisky in the world!'. And meanwhile he was building on the Tromie. In December 1990 the first spirit flowed from the stills. Christie was able to lay claim to having built the first distillery in ages, the first of three that were set up in the 1990s (→ Kininvie and the → Isle of Arran being the other two). Three years later, exactly upon expiry of the minimum maturation period, he brought out his whisky as a single malt in a limited edition, not intended for general sale, but as a thank you to all those who had helped him build Speyside.

→ Drumguish was intended for general sale. In 1999 they finally brought out an 8-year-old single malt bearing the name of the distillery; in 2001 is was succeeded by a 10-year-old. For the Millennium there were 2,000 bottles from the first distillation, which were on offer in packaging of original design for £350 each, and have now become collectors' items. Matters are not made any clearer by the fact that the company also continues to use the name for the blend which they offer, together with a range of other blends, some of which they had acquired when they took over their former partner → Campbell & Clark. In addition to the Speyside aged 8, 12, 15, 17, 21, 25 and 30 years, in various versions, there is: → Dew of the Western Isles, → Glamis Castle, → King's Scotch, → MacGavins, → Murdoch's Perfection, → Old Monarch, → Scotch Guard, → Scottish Prince, The → Strathmore and → Thistle Dhu. → Glentromie and → Glenwood are vatted malts and there is also a cream liqueur named The → Great Glen Celtic Cream. They are all bottled at the company's own plant, the Speyside → Bonding Co. Here they also make → King's Crest for the company of Alexander Muir. Together they have brought out their own series of cask strength single malts called → 'Scott's Selection'. The name Campbell & Clark is still used for their single malt bottlings. In the autumn of 2000 Christie, the founding family, sold its business to a group of investors headed by Sir James Aykroyd who, with his company Alexander Muir, had been among their customers.

Spirit of Scotland, The In 1994 the International Wine & Spirit Competition, which was 25 years old that year, organised a competition with the motto 'The Spirit of Scotland' to commemorate the first documented mention of Scottish whisky 500 years previously. The large whisky companies were invited to create a blend especially for this festive occasion. → Allied Distillers Ltd took part with → Heritage, → Burn Stewart with a 25-year-old → Burberry's, William → Grant & Sons with an 18-year-old blend, → Inver House Distillers Ltd with the 15-year-old The → Quintessential, → Morrison Bowmore with a 21-year-old Bowmore Blended, → UD with → Friar John → Cor Centenary with an edition of 1,494 bottles and finally, → Whyte & Mackay with the 500th Anniversary Blend. This last whisky, the creation of master blender Richard Paterson, won the prize. The company of → Gordon & MacPhail, based in Elgin, also used the official birthday of whisky to bring out a small series of single malts through their subsidiary Speymalt which was also called 'Spirit of Scotland'. It contained an → Ardbeg from 1974, a → Port Ellen from 1979 and a → Tomatin from 1964, all bottled at 40%.

Spirit of Today Kentucky straight bourbon at 40% (and no statement of proof) from an unknown producer. The bottlers call themselves the Modern Times Distillery and give an address in → Bardstown, so it may come from → Heaven Hill or from the → Kentucky Bourbon Distillers.

Spirit safe The spirit safe was invented by Septimus Fox around 1820 and has been in general use since 1825. Tests to ensure that it had no harmful effects on the quality of the whisky were carried out at → Port Ellen Distillery. It is a term for a piece of control equipment mainly used in Scotland for the production of malt whisky in → pot stills. A wide 'cupboard' which usually has a copper frame with solid glass windows. It has several glass vessels that are receptacles for the distillate, as well as instruments such as a thermometer and hydrometer. The distillate flows from the → low wines still, and the → spirit still, through a tap which can be turned from the outside so that it runs through the glass receptacles into either the low wines receiver or, in the final run, into the vat which collects the → foreshots or → feints for redistillation or the → new spirit for filling into the casks. The spirit safe therefore helps the → stillman in the difficult process of → cutting, ie deciding on the right time to separate the unusuable alcohol from the usable alcohol. He uses the above-mentioned instruments but also adds water so that the clouding and the colour of the liquid indicate when the → heart of the run begins and ends. The whole process is made more difficult by the fact that it must take place in a closed space which is secured with a heavy metal bar, at each end of which there are solid locks. Until a few years ago these could only be opened by two keys, one of which was kept by the distillery manager and the other by the exciseman stationed at each distillery. Since the early eighties, things have become less bureaucratic in the whisky industry and the manager is now able to open the safe alone, but has to give an exact account of doing so and reckon with random spot checks by excise officials.

Spirit still Term for the still in which the → low wines from the → wash still and (in triple distillation) the → intermediate still are brought to the desired strength. The result is often called → 'baby whisky' in Scotland, although the law says that the distillate must have matured for at least three years in oak casks before it can be called whisky. The correct terminology in Scotland is → spirit, or when it is for human consumption potable spirit. It is also often called → new make or → fillings. In the USA the expression → white dog is used.

The spirit stills are usually somewhat smaller than the → wash stills in which the first run occurs and may be of a different shape. They are filled with the low wines which are brought to the boil, turn to steam and become liquid again in the cooled → condenser. Not everything becomes usable alcohol: at the beginning and at the end of a run the liquid contains undesirable substances which on no account must get in to the cask. It is the duty of the → stillman to wait for the moment when the spirit is good and usable so that it can be separated.

Despite the instruments the stillman must also rely on his experience and intuition. They are artists and bear a heavy responsibility; it will be many years until the taste of the whisky shows whether they have done a good job. The liquid instead into the → spirit safe where water is added, and observation of this and the temperature and strength of the alcohol will indicate when the → foreshots are finished. Depending on the size of the still this may take between a quarter of an hour and 45 minutes. After this comes the good stuff, the → middle cut, the → heart of the run. At the beginning this is about 70% – 75% and decreases within the following hours to about 65%.

This phase can last up to four hours, again dependant on the still, but also the instructions of the master distiller which, depending on the distillery, may be stricter or more generous; at → Macallan only about 18% of the run is declared to be of use and is taken as the → middle cut. The remainder are the → feints which contain undesirable substances. These are not destroyed. Just as the spirit goes into the spirit receiver, the feints go back into a the low wines and feints charger where the → low wines are waiting for the next distillation along with the → foreshots and in which the foreshots have already run back. However the spirit is now ready for the cask.

Springbank Scottish malt distillery and a special example of its kind. This begins with the → whisky region to which it belongs, includes its history and pattern of ownership and ends with the unique techniques which are used there. It is situated in → Campbeltown, on the southern end of the long Kintyre peninsula. Until the 1920s there used to be more than twenty distilleries in this area, but most of which were forced to close down as a result of → prohibition in the USA. Only → Glen Scotia and Springbank survived. Springbank stands on a site where the → Mitchell family had engaged in illicit distilling. In 1828 there was a legal distillery and by 1837 the Mitchells had become involved. Since that time Springbank has been in family ownership and is now managed by Hedley Wright who represents the seventh generation. It is one of the few distilleries, along with → Glenfarclas, which is still in family ownership, and with → Glenfiddich it is the only one which has remained in the hands of the founding family.

Some of the buildings still originate from its earliest years and in other ways things have remained much the same. The way that the →

wash still and both the → spirit stills have been used for → triple distillation is unique to Springbank, and is always described in very different ways. It enables the production of several malt whiskies of differing character. Springbank had been producing two different single malts for a long time and since 1997 it has been producing three different kinds, which in order to differentiate between them bear different names: apart from the Springbank named after the distillery, there is → Longrow, and most recently → Hazelburn. John McDougall, the director of production for many years, described the difference between them in this way: first completely different kinds of malt are used. For Hazelburn it is not peated at all, for Longrow it is intensively peated and Springbank lies in the middle. The first run of the distillation is the same for all three. The → low wines are then redistilled; whilst the → middle cut usually goes straight into the cask, it is distilled a third time in the case of Springbank and Hazelburn. In the case of Longrow the entire second run is distilled a third time.

Nobody has yet sampled Hazelburn but the differences between the other two are marked and make Longrow, which is at most made once a year, into one of the most sought-after of all malt whiskies, with a character that is a match for the most intensive of the → Islays: smoky, peaty and salty. The salt character is also very noticeable in Springbank, which in competitions has put many of the other participants in the shade (and which for a long time was the most popular malt whisky in Japan): a dry, oily, salty and extremely complex malt whisky. The fact that such differing methods are used proves that the Mitchells and Hedley Wright realise how important it is to observe old traditions – and how profitable this may be.

This is shown by the choice of name for the second and third malt whiskies: they are named after old Campbeltown distilleries which no longer exist. Longrow used to be situated where Springbank's car park now stands. They are proud that the entire production process is in the same hands: the peat is local, and the malt required for the various whiskies is produced in their own → floor maltings. This has been reflected in various bottlings; there have been several 'West Highland Editions' distilled in 1966 and 1967 (but bottled in different years), for which everything (except the sherry cask) has come from Campbeltown. There was also a 'Local Barley Edition' from 1966. In 1992 John Onstwedder, one of the founders of the UK organic food movement, had the idea of producing an organic malt whisky and he chose Springbank for this project. Several casks were aged there and were mature by the Millennium. A further special feature is that the bottling is also done at the distillery (unlike anywhere else in Scotland except Glenfiddich), in the same plant as Springbank's subsidiary the independent bottlers → Cadenhead, who bottle at 46%. They forego → chill-filtering or any sort of → colouring.

The Mitchells not only know a lot about producing whisky, they are also very clever at sales and marketing, as is shown by the number of special editions which are especially coveted by collectors. It is almost impossible to keep track of the numerous versions of their whisky. There is a no age C V (mostly understood to mean 'Chairman's Vat, although interpreted by Michael Jackson as 'Curriculum Vitae') and there are expressions aged 8, 10, 12, 15, 21, 25 and 33 years (whereby it must be asked how old the 12-year-old – which is also available at 57%. – really is as Springbank was not in operation between 1982 and 1988). The distillery presented itself in a sensational way with a very limited edition of the 'Millennium Series' which, long before the great event, was heralded by a 25-year-old malt. This was followed at six-monthly intervals, by malts whose age increased by five years with each new edition. The climax was achieved in the spring of 2001 with a 50-year-old. The → vintages are available in different strengths, usually as single cask bottlings. The two Cadenhead bottlings from a rum cask caused quite a stir because of their light green colour, which took a bit of getting used to. The → Triple S with a fresh distillate is just a curiosity. Of course Cadenhead regularly has Springbanks and of the other independents → MacArthur and → Signatory, for example, have also had bottlings. The → Oddbins bottling with the original name → Against the grain was a nice idea. The most expensive malt whisky from the distillery must be that from 1919 which can be bought at the company's own Cadenhead shop in the Royal Mile in Edinburgh, or at → 'Loch Fyne Whiskies' – for £6,000.

SS Politician Scotch blend that is named after the famous ship that in 1941 became stranded off the coast of the small island of Eriskay in the Western Isles with a large number of cases on board bound for the USA containing the Scottish national drink. Whisky became so rare during the war years, that the thirsty villagers, who otherwise were not suffering much from the effects of war removed much of the whisky from the ship under the cover of darkness – before the ship sank and the excisemen could intervene. One of these bottles is on display at the museum of local history on the neighbouring island of South Uist, with the legend: 'One of the bottles which made 1941 the best year of the war'. The story has been told in fiction by Compton Mackenzie in the bestseller → *Whisky Galore*.

It was believed that there must still be bottles on board the sunken ship and in 1990 preparations were made to search for them, with an eye on collectors and their wallets. The divers were only able to retrieve a few bottles, but these were still drinkable. In order to compensate for the money that had been invested a blend was created, *Whisky Galore Atlantic Reserve* with the participation of Douglas → Laing bearing the name of the ship, each bottle containing just a few drops of the truly historical whisky. They were presented in a kind of red shrine and it was soon possible to sellevery bottle at a price of more than £150 each.

Stag's Breath Scotch whisky liqueur at 19.8% from → Meiklers of Scotland. As well as whisky it also contains, as stated on its label, 'Fermented Comb Honey'.

Standard blend Term used for most straightforward Scotch blends. The standard blends represent the largest group. These whiskies are mostly without an age statement, and are relatively young, often not much older than the legal minimum of 3 years. The category often also reflects the proportion of malt whisky used and the relatively low price. However the age and the price shouldn't be taken to mean that they are of inferior quality. Many of them are a match for their competitors in the higher → premium blend category, or even the → de luxe class. Alan S Gray, a leading financial and corporate expert on Scotch whisky, gives the following examples of standards in his annual *Scotch Whisky Industry Review*: → Black & White, → Cutty Sark, → Dewar's, → Grant's, → VAT 69, → White Horse and → Whyte & Mackay. These categories are also often used in other countries. They are used in Japan but there they also have a 'special' category. This is used for blends with a malt content of about 30%.

Standfast Scotch blend from William → Grant & Sons which is no longer on sale with its old name but has been renamed → William Grant's Family Reserve. The name is a reminder that the company was in a difficult position after the → Pattison collapse and was only able to pull through because the family stuck together.

Star Hill American distillery which is better known by the name of its product: → Maker's Mark Distillery. The distillery was founded in 1953 by the father of the current president, T William → Samuels Sr. Loving restoration of the former Happy Hollow Distillery on the Star Hill Farm near Loretto has not only made it a real gem that is a protected monument, but also the home of a Kentucky straight bourbon which is almost unique – even using the Scottish spelling of 'whisky'.

Stars Scotch blend formerly from → Whyte & Mackay/→ JBB (Greater Europe) plc. It had ceased being produced but can still be found in some shops.

Status Japanese blend from → Sanraku-Ocean which the company describes as 'High Quality Whisky' and which has a full malty taste.

Steeping Term for the very first step in the conversion of a grain of barley into an alcoholic liquid called malt whisky or beer. It is made possible because the barley contains starch which is transformed into a sugar known as maltose which is fermented (in the case of beer and whisky) and distilled (whisky only) to make alcohol. The first step is to release the starches in the barley. Steeping takes place in large vessels in which the barley is soaked in water.

Stein, Robert Scottish inventor who came from a family which left its mark on the history of whisky, the deepest being made by Robert himself. The Steins operated distilleries at Kilbagie and Kennetpans in Clackmannanshire, and it was at → Kilbagie in 1826 that Robert invented a completely new method of whisky production, which neither depended on malted → barley nor on traditional → pot stills. Other types of grain could be processed and continuously-distilled in his → patent still. The result was a kind of whisky: → grain whisky. It was cheaper to produce, and from that time on was used principally to blend with malt whisky, thereby creating the type of whisky that has since become a synonym for Scotch and, thanks to the marketing skills of the pioneers who rose to become → whisky barons experienced an unequalled triumphant progression from being a small local drink to become one of the most successful drinks in the world. In 1751 Margaret Stein married a Haig. They had five sons, all of whom entered the distillery business, and one of their daughters married John → Jameson. A grandson another John, learned the craft of distilling at Kilbagie with his cousin Robert Stein and became one of the first to put his uncle's methods into practice, introducing the → patent stills at nearby → Cameronbridge.

Stenham, H Whisky company based in London which has numerous subsidiaries such as Highland Blending, Highland Shippers and the → Premier Scotch Whisky Co. What looks like a large concern is actually a family firm founded by Henry H Stenham in 1953. Over the years he has developed more than 40 brands, selling them without advertising or agents. They are all intended for export with the main markets being in southern Europe, Central and Latin America and South East Asia. Some whiskies are bottled in the UK before shipment whilst others are blended in Scotland and then shipped in → bulk by containers and bottled at destination, where they can be sold very cheaply as costs have been saved. All the company's brands, except its very few malts,

are produced in five age groups of 3, 5, 8, 10 and 12 years. In 1996 Rossendale Blenders in Glasgow bought the company from the 82-year-old Stenham and have since then run it using the name of its former subsidiary, Premier Scotch Whisky. They have mainly concentrated on two blends, → King Henry VIII and → Queen Mary I, but retain the others in their range. The most important of these are: → Black Barrel, → Director's Special, → Golden Eagle, → Highlander (also available as a 'straight Malt'), → Highland Star, → King John, → Premier, → Queen Eleanor and → Scottish Dance.

Stephen Foster Straight rye from → Heaven Hill which is identical to the → Pikesville Supreme which today is also produced there. Named after the composer of such American songs as *My Old Kentucky Home* which is about a house in → Bardstown, the state capital and home of the Heaven Hill Distillery. Foster died of alcohol poisoning aged only 38 years.

Stewart MacDuff, The Scotch blend whose name reveals where it comes from: → MacDuff International, who sell it as a → standard blend without an age statement aged 12 or 18 years.

Stewart's Cream of the Barley Scotch blend from → Allied Domecq PLC, whose predecessor Allied-Lyons brought the former owner and 'creator' of the brand, Stewart & Sons of Dundee, under its control in 1969 thus procured a distillery of its own, its first (→ Glencadam). The company, which was established in 1831, is mainly engaged in the export trade and has a range of subsidiaries under its umbrella with which it exports numerous blends to 75 different markets. Cream of the Barley is the best-known.

Stewart's Finest Old Scotch blend, named after the founding company J & G Stewart. It originated in 1779 in Edinburgh and soon became particularly successful in the export trade. In 1917 it acquired the important brand The → Antiquary and in the same year merged with → DCL, for whom it acquired and ran the company of Andrew → Usher (of particular significance in the history of whisky) shortly after the First World War. They also held the licence for → Coleburn Distillery, which was shut down by the DCL successors → UD. After DCL was taken over by → Guinness the rights to the blend Stewart's Finest had to be given up because of requirements from the Monopolies and Mergers Commission and it passed to → Whyte & Mackay/→ JBB (Greater Europe) plc.

Still, stills Term for the distilling vessels, mostly made out of copper, in which alcohol is created. The word derives from the Latin *stillare* and means to drop or drip. Stills come in differing forms and various methods of distilling can produce entirely different whiskies. However they all operate according to the same principle and have the same purpose.

Alcohol, when heated, vapourises quicker than water, so a stills will convert a liquid containing a low percentage of alcohol into a high percentage distillate. This liquid, called the → wash or sometimes the → beer, is made by converting the starch in the corns of grain to sugar and then adding yeast to induce → fermentation. The wash in the stills is subjected to high temperatures, which separates the alcohol from the water, which later evaporates. The rising steam or alcohol is then cooled and becomes liquid again. This process can be repeated several times until the desired strength of alcohol is obtained.

Although certain forms of distilling had already existed, the techniques used today were first discovered around the beginning of the second millennium. The most important invention was the alembic, a curved neck set upon the vessel in which the liquid is heated. It collected the alcohol vapour and conveyed it to the → condenser where it was cooled.

The → pot stills, which are still used for the production of malt whisky in Scotland, are larger but otherwise not very different from the original form. They can only be used to distil in batches. A more economical form, the → patent still, was developed in the 1820s and 1830s by Robert → Stein and Aeneas → Coffey. Still used today, the columns process the wash continuously. They are sometimes called Coffey stills after their inventor or → column stills after their appearance, but most usually they are known as → continuous stills. They are used for the production of → grain whisky and a very pure, high percentage alcohol used as a base for gin and vodka. It is also customary to combine the two forms. At → Midleton, Ireland's largest distillery, a whole range of whiskeys are produced for which various combinations of apparatus are used. In the USA the first distillation is normally carried out in a → continuous still and the second in a → doubler, a kind of → pot still.

Stillage Term used in the USA for what the Scots call → burnt or pot ale. This is what remains in the → wash still or → beer still after the first distillation. It consists of two components: the solid remains of the grain, which are mostly processed for cattle fodder and the → thin stillage, which is better known as → sour mash. In America it is re-used as → backset, when the → mash for the next distillation is prepared. It is sometimes first added at → fermentation. It has the purpose of reducing the acidity, thereby killing undesirable bacteria and ensuring the consistency of the whisky.

Stillbrook American straight bourbon and blended whiskeys from the McCormick Distilling Co, which owns two distilleries, one in → Weston, Missouri and the → Pekin Distillery in Illinois. Pekin no longer makes whiskey and Weston is no longer in operation. Both versions are still produced in Illinois but stocks are limited and when they are exhausted, will be replaced by whiskey from → Heaven Hill. The straight is 36 months old and is bottled at 80°/40%.

Stillhouse Term for the building where distilling takes place; the → stills are situated and the → stillman works.

Stillman Each and every distillery worker is important and believes that their job is the most significant of all. There are various opinions as to whether the → malting or the brewing including overseeing → fermentation, most influences the character of whisk(e)y. The → warehouse man and the → master blender put forward their claims. But they would all agree that the stillman has the most responsible job. They control the → stills and the distillation process itself, and are responsible for choosing the right time in the final run to separate the → foreshots from the → middle cut and this from the → feints in the → spirit safe, and ensuring that the spirit which goes into the cask contains no poisonous fusel-oils. It is often only possible to establish whether they have worked well years later, when the contents of the casks have matured and are ready for bottling. The job is made more difficult by the fact that they have no access to the liquid, as the → spirit safe is kept locked under excise regulations.

Stillman's Dram, The A limited edition brought on to the market by → Invergordon of its four malt whiskies → Bruichladdich, → Isle of Jura, → Tamnavulin (three versions) and → Tullibardine (two versions). They were all at 45% and were therefore markedly stronger than normal bottlings, and all over 20 years old. After the company had been taken over by → Whyte & Mackay and renamed → JBB (Greater Europe) plc, Dalmore, also bottled at 45%, was added to the series. There was also a single grain from → Invergordon Distillery. These bottlings are now produced by → Kyndal.

Stills of Scotland Series of single malts, bottled by → Signatory for the → 'Maison du Whisky' in Paris, which is intended to demonstrate the influence of → pot stills on whisky. Up to now it has included a 1995 Vintage Islay, a 1980 Dalmore, a 1976 Glenlivet, a 1989 Springbank and a 1988 Strathmill. They all have a uniform strength of 45%.

Stirling Castle Scotch single malt from the small series offered for sale by → Historic Scotland in the shops of their historic buildings and sites. The whiskies are named after some of its most popular tourist attractions. The castle overlooking Stirling in the Forth valley has lent its name to a 12-year-old whisky bottled at 46% which infers that it comes from → Cadenhead, and → Springbank Distillery.

Stitzel-Weller American distillery in Louisville, Kentucky which combines the names of two important whiskey companies. William LaRue Weller founded his business in 1849, and the brothers Philip and Frederick Stitzel began distilling in either 1870 or 1872. Both enjoyed success, the Wellers with trading and the Stitzels with distilling, and before the First World War they signed a contract together with a third, strong force, the legendary Julian 'Pappy' → Van Winkle. From that time on the Wellers obtained their whiskeys from the Stitzels, whose distillery was one of only six allowed to produce whiskey for medicinal purposes during → prohibition. By the time the dry years were over, Van Winkle had become president and the two firms were joined together. They built the distillery in Shively/Louisville in its present form, with its brick buildings, the sign 'No Chemists Allowed' on its gate and its tall chimney which is decorated with the name of the brand, → Old Fitzgerald.

It still stands today, although its stablemates → W L Weller and → Rebel Yell are no longer produced there, and come from the → Bernheim distillery, just six kilometres away. These three are different to all other bourbons: they are wheated whiskeys, in which the usual share of rye has been replaced by wheat. In 1972 Stitzel-Weller were initially taken over by Somerset (who renamed the distillery Old Fitzgerald). In 1984 they were taken over by the Scottish → DCL who in their turn were bought by → Guinness in 1987 and were reformed as → UD. The new bosses in London decided to make the Bernheim Distillery, which they had also purchased, into the centre of their activities and in 1992 completely rebuilt it, closed Stitzel-Weller and (having themselves become → UDV) in March 1999 also sold Bernheim. The Stitzel-Weller Distillery once had 28 fermenting vessels. These are no longer used. Their old stocks of Rebel Yell are being used for Dickel's → RX. The wheated whiskeys are now made by master distiller Edwin S Foote, who uses a special yeast for them and a → mash bill with 75% corn, 20% wheat and 5% malted barley.

Stock Czech spirit producer based in Plzen (Pilsen) which has its own distillery in the village of Pradlo near the town world-famous for its beer. The Stock Distillery was founded in 1920 and remained in production during the years when it was first occupied by the Germans and then ruled by the Communists. It was later reprivatised and now produces malt and → grain whiskies, taking care to follow the Scottish methods. The malt is lightly peated and comes from a maltings which also supplies → Suntory and imports its peat from Scotland. Mashing takes place in brewing tubs and fermentation and distillation in old kettles with a capacity of 25 hectolitres. The whisky is matured in charred casks made of Czech oak, whose size determines the length of ageing: new laws in the Czech Republic prescribe two years for casks containing up to 300 litres and three years for those up to 700 litres. For a short time Stock bottled a malt whisky called Halberd Whisky at 43% and a blend named Smoker Halberd Whisky. They were both replaced by → Printer's, which is a blend even although its label speaks of 'Blended Malt Whisky'.

Stodart, J & G Scottish whisky company which no longer exists but has contributed to the history of whisky because it not only discovered vatted malts, but is also said to have been the first to have 'married' its whiskies for a time in sherry casks, giving them an additional maturing period and extra nuances in taste. Their best-known creation is → Old Smuggler, which they brought out in 1835 and which is still on the market as a blend. The company was also involved in changing the course of the history of whisky a second time when they sold a share to the Canadian Hiram → Walker, thereby opening the way for them to do business in Scotland. At that time Stodart was under the management of James Barclay. Hiram Walker also bought → Ballantine and soon were playing a leading part in the Scottish whisky business. They bought many distilleries and put Stodart in charge of running → Glenburgie and then later → Pulteney.

Stonebrook Kentucky straight bourbon at 86°/43% which is bottled and produced by the Stonebrook Distilling Co. As they give an address in → Bardstown, it must be concluded that this is one of the many names used by → Heaven Hill.

Straight whiskey Term for American whiskeys which are not blended. They must be distilled from a mash which consists solely of grain, which in the case of bourbon must contain at least 51% corn and in the case of rye, at least 51% rye, and they may not be blended with a second distillate. Both the whiskeys from Tennessee, Jack Daniel's and → George Dickel, are straights. All American straights are also nowadays produced using the → sour mash method. Some bourbons are available as both straight and blended whiskeys; examples are Barton and Four Roses.

Strath-Roye Scotch blend from Glen Roye (Blenders), a subsidiary of the London-based H → Mayerson & Company, who are important → brokers, and have a several brands of their own.

Strathavon Scotch vatted malt from Avonside, a subsidiary of → Gordon & MacPhail. It is vatted with whiskies from distilleries in and around → Glen Avon, the valley of the river that flows past → Tomintoul and joins the Spey near → Cragganmore. → Glenlivet, is also nearby.

Strathbeag Scotch blend from CES Whisky, a subsidiary of → MacDuff International which was first established in 1992. The name means small, wide valley and is pronounced 'Strath-vic'. The company also has a whisky whose name means 'small, narrow valley', the single malt → Glenbeg.

Strathclyde Scottish grain distillery in the heart of Glasgow in the Gorbals on the southern bank of the Clyde, which, like the rest of the city, gets its water from Loch Katrine in the Trossachs. It was built when the London company Seager Evans, who were already known for making gin, became interested in Scotch whisky. This was their first activity in the area. They later bought → Long John, the Glasgow distillery is better known by this name. The changes in ownership went from Seager Evans and Long John International through → Schenley and Whitbread to → Allied Distillers Ltd, who run it as their only grain distillery after the closure of → Dumbarton. Because of the lack of space in the city, which also led to the closure of the small malt distillery → Kinclaith on the same site, the whisky is stored in Dumbarton. They also produce gin (for 'Beefeater'). A Single Grain has not yet been produced by Strathclyde, neither from the → proprietors nor from the → independents.

318

Strathconan Scotch vatted malt aged 12 years which formerly came from James → Buchanan and certainly contains malt whiskies from its distilleries, → Dalwhinnie and → Glentauchers. Although Buchanan, as a subsidiary of → DCL (since 1925) had belonged to → UD, and now to UDV, they are still designated as being responsible for the whisky.

Strathfinnan Scotch blend which is only available locally from Forth Wines, who also produce → King James VI.

Strathglen Scotch vatted malt aged 12 years which is described as a → Highland and was bottled by → Burn Stewart when the company was still based in → Dumbarton. They are now based in East Kilbride and no longer produce the brand, though it can still be found.

Strathisla Scottish malt distillery. It belongs to the → Speyside → whisky region and lies on the outskirts of → Keith on the banks of the river Isla, and its current name means 'broad valley of the Isla'. The earlier changes of name correspond to the numerous changes in ownership. However, these and the unusually high number of catastrophes which have happened to the distillery, have made it into what it is today: a picture-book distillery, perhaps the prettiest in Scotland. There is a generously-sized inner courtyard around which stand the pagoda roofs, and an old waterwheel. It is the flagship distillery for → Seagrams largest brand → Chivas Regal.

It is also one of the oldest distilleries in Scotland and certainly the oldest on Speyside. It was established in 1786 as Milltown, later changing its name to Milton. In 1876 it was damaged by fire and in 1887 by an explosion. At that time its name was Strathisla, but changed name again. In 1949 it was threatened with ruin when its owner, a speculator from London, was imprisoned for tax evasion. James Barclay was employed at the ensuing auction. He had made a name for himself during prohibition as a smuggler, and via his firm James and George → Stodard of the Canadian company Hiram → Walker, made it possible for the second giant → Seagram to start up business in Scotland. On their behalf he acquired this little distillery for → Chivas Brothers. Since that time the distillery, called Strathisla has been cared for, works with its old equipment (although its capacity has been extended from two to four → stills) and takes its water from the Fons Bullien Well. Since 2001 it has been owned by a Diageo / Groupe Pernod-Ricard partnership, in common with the rest of Seagram's Scottish spirits brands and distilleries.

The Canadians, through their Scottish subsidiary → Chivas & Glenlivet, produced a 12-year-old (a sought-after malt), but left it to → Gordon & MacPhail to market, in the same way as other distilleries they owned: → Longmorn, → Glenlivet and → Glen Grant. In all these cases the → independent bottlers from Elgin made the most of the potential of the malt whiskies with whole series whilst their → proprietors limited themselves to just one or two versions, when they didn't keep everything for their many blends, as in the case of → Benriach or → Glen Keith. Gordon & MacPhail include it aged 8 and 15 years (40% and 57%), 21, 25, 30 and 35 years, as well as many vintages, the oldest of which was from 1937. When Strathisla began to play an important part in Seagram's marketing concept with their visitor centre, it was only logical that they promoted their malt whisky (and let the wider public know that it is a classic). A 12-year-old is one of four in the → 'Heritage Selection' which was brought out in 1994. A year later the completion of renovations was celebrated with a special bottling of a 25-year-old which was reserved for the guests of the occasion in May 1995.

Strathmill Scottish distillery on the outskirts of → Keith. It belongs to the → Speyside region. It is one of the least-known distilleries, with equally little-known whisky. It was founded in 1891 as Glenisla (named after the river on which it lies which also gave → Strathisla its name) and renamed four years later by its new owners → Gilbey. The licence is held by → Justerini & Brooks, with whom Gilbey merged in 1962 to form → IDV, which later became a subsidiary of → Grand Metropolitan (the distillery is therefore now part of the UDV empire). Gilbey's had a → proprietary bottling of Strathmill's malt whisky, but that was a long time ago, which is a shame because the →

Strathmore

independent bottlings (such as → Signatory in their 'Wildlife' series as well as one from 1985 and an 11-year-old from → MacArthur) along with the tasting notes from the few who have had a chance of sampling it, have proved that the four → stills produce a delicate, sweet, only slightly smoky, but malty whisky. In 2001 a 12-year-old Strathmill became part of the 'Flora & Fauna' series. There was a sign at the distillery's entrance reading 'Home of Dunhill's' which told us what its whisky had been mostly used for (as well as for a blend named → Glen Spey): as the basis for → Dunhill Old Master. In future a different malt will probably be used, because in 1997 the owners sold the rights to this expensive blend to → Highland Distillers. However for the time being 100 casks of Strathmill are still stored at the distillery which Dunhill reserved in 1993 for its 100th anniversary; half of them are still for sale – at about £50,000, which would make the casks the most expensive in the world.

Strathmore Scottish distillery which was only in operation from 1957 to the early 1980s. It was located in Cambus and was run by the → North of Scotland Distilling Co in which the Christie family, known for their → Speyside Distillery, had a large share. Their → patent still initially produced, astonishingly enough, a malt whisky before changing the production of → grain whisky. The name is still familiar to whisky drinkers today because there is a Scottish mineral water of this name which is widely available. It comes from a spring near → Glamis Castle which does not belong to the estate but since 1992 to Matthew Clark.

Strathmore, The Scotch blend whose name is better known to drinkers of mineral water than whisky. They are both named after the Earl of Strathmore, whose home is → Glamis Castle in Fife. He allowed the → Speyside Distillery Co to use his name, and the Christies thanked him with a 15-year-old blend. Since 1992 the mineral water has belonged to the UK wine producers and drinks wholesalers Matthew Clark, who were taken over by → Canandaigua at the end of 1998.

Strong's Scotch blend. It is the last reminder of the once important and renowned W & S Strong & Co, established in 1820 in Dundee, one of the first to export whisky to Australia and New Zealand. They created the legendary Real → Mountain Dew and were co-owners of → Tomintoul and → Fettercairn. Strong and the distilleries were taken over by Scottish and Universal Investments in 1973 and then by → Whyte & Mackay.

Stump Lifter Whiskey cocktail from the Book of Bourbon by Gary and Mardee Haidin Regan. There is a version with three parts strong cider, and five parts apple juice. The basis for both are two parts bourbon. The Regans prefer the version with the cider, but recommend that with the juice as a very refreshing summer drink.

Sugarbuttie Whiskey cocktail created by Mardee Haidin Regan and christened by Gary Regan, both writers on bourbon. They courageously mix whiskey and wine, thus breaking the old rule that you should never mix grape with grain. The result is delicious. Take three parts of bourbon to two parts Tawny or Ruby Port and pour into a glass containing a lot of ice.

Sullivans Cove Australian single malt, which has only recently become available thanks to the Australian laws which prescribe a minimum → maturation period of two years for whisky (in contrast to the three years in Ireland and Scotland). The contents of the bottle from the → Tasmania Distillery in Hobart are the same age. They have therefore put Australia back on the map of whisky-producing countries. Their former name was, rather unromantically, the Gasworks Distillery. The malt whisky, which comes in a square bottle and in a glass decanter, is bottled at 40% which is also now prescribed in Australia, and has been distilled from Franklin barley in a → pot still. The distillery has been in operation since 1995 but claims on its lilac-blue label to be continuing the 'tradition from 1822'.

Summer Hall Indian whisky from → Mohan Meakin which first appeared on the market in the autumn of 1997, and is intended to become one of the leading products of this company, which employs 15,000 people in → India and owns 11 breweries, as well as the → Kasauli, Lucknow and

→ Mohan Nagar distilleries and another one in → Solan, which has never been able to go into production. However it was the site of the summer residence of General Mohan, the company's boss, which provided the name for this new brand. It does not include the customary portion of molasses distillate allowed in India and which makes Indian whiskies so cheap. They have used malt whiskies from Kasauli and Lucknow and malt whiskies and → grain whiskies from Mohan Nagar.

Sunflower Chinese whisky from → China National Cereals, Oils & Foodstuffs Import and Export in Tsinglao, which goes to show that whisky is not only drunk but also produced in the People's Republic. It is not known what the ingredients are or how it was produced; it is probably a grain distillate.

Sunny Brook Kentucky Whiskey which is available as a straight bourbon and as a blend. The brand belongs to the portfolio of National Distillers which, along with its three distilleries in → Frankfort (→ Old Crow, → Old Taylor and → Old Grand-Dad) was bought in 1987 by → American Brands. In the old days it was known exactly where the whiskeys for the brand came from, now only the two → Jim Beam distilleries in Boston and Clermont come into question.

Suntory Japanese drinks company, ranked fifth in the world. From humble beginnings in 1899 it has grown to a leading position yet remains Japanese in character. The top executive is a direct successor of the man who in 1899 had the courage to set up a business in his hometown of Osaka which was still unusual for his country, importing Spanish wine as well as growing vines in Japan. In 1907 he launched his wine, named 'Akadama', onto the market.

The company's headquarters are still in Osaka, but the adminstrative section is in Tokyo: it includes an art museum, which shows the breadth of Suntory's interests and demonstrates the company's tradition as a generous sponsor of the arts and music. The company's founder, Shinjiro → Torii, named his business after the national symbol of the rising sun and his own name, which in Japanese means the gate to a temple shrine. The fact that he anglicised the name shows his broad horizons which were again demonstrated when he decided to bring Scottish malt whisky to Japan. In 1923 he employed a young chemist, Masataka → Taketsuru, who had studied in Scotland to set up the first distillery in the country in the → Yamazaki valley near his hometown and produce malt whisky in the Scottish style.

In 1929 he launched his first brand Shirofuda, which soon became known as → White, after its label. It was not successful, unlike → Kakubin which came out in 1937 and is still Japan's number one. By that time Taketsuru had already left the company in order to set up his own business, → Nikka. Suntory only really became successful after the Second World War, considerably helped by a chain called 'Torys Whisky Bars', which sold only the company's products and helped to make whisky really popular. Suntory now has 71% of the country's domestic production of whisky in its hands and has a market share of 67% including imported brands, well ahead of Nikka.

In 1973 the company built a second distillery → Hakushu near Fujiyama. Its production of 55 million litres a year make it the largest malt distillery in the world, but it had to be enlarged by building a further plant in 1989. Noheji, another malt distillery on the northern tip of Japan's main island Honshu, is not yet finished. The distilleries are able to produce several different types of malt whisky and at any one time the company has 1.6 million casks in storage, 200,000 in Yamazaki, 800,000 in Hakushu and 600,000 in their 'Ageing Cellar' near Kyoto. They also operate grain distilleries. In 1963 it was decided to use the profits from the wine and whisky business to start up beer brewing; Suntory is now one of the four large beer brewers in the country with a further brewery in China. They have important chemistry laboratories and an institute for biotechnology, as well as being significant manufacturers of pharmaceutical products and active in many areas of food and drinks, ranging from production through distribution to their own restaurant and fast-food chains, from mineral water to ice cream. They also own a chain of Japanese restaurants operating in more than 10 countries. They own a share in the *Encylopaedia Britannica* and manage golf courses and other sports centres. They market a very successful melon liqueur called 'Midori'. In Germany they bought Robert Weil and made its wines into the best in the region: they had previously been involved with Schloß Vollrads, a connection which was celebrated by the whisky → President's Choice. In France the company's portfolio includes the Chateaux Beycheville, Lagrange and Beaumont. The company's programme encompasses more than 300 products and the list of its subsidiaries and international businesses takes up seven pages of its business report.

Suntory is also active in foreign whisky companies. They initially had a share in → Allied Distillers Ltd whose brands → Ballantine's, → Long John, → Old Smuggler and → Teacher's (to name but a few) were imported by Suntory, as well as the single malt from → Laphroaig. Since 1994 they have been in sole ownership of → Morrison Bowmore, including the distilleries → Auchentoshan, → Bowmore and → Glen Garioch. The single malt from → Macallan enjoys cult status in Japan and Japanese bar owners have paid record prices at auctions for its older bottlings. It is not just a brand that Suntory imports. The company owns a 25% share of the distillery and it was this share which led to Macallan losing its independence in 1996 when the Japanese joined with → Highland Distillers in a strategic alliance which gained them a 51% share.

Suntory produces many brands in Japan prominently featuring its name such as the blends Suntory Whisky (which is available in two versions), Suntory → Imperial (also sometimes called → Signature), Suntory→ Old, Suntory → Reserve, Suntory 30-year-old and White. The name of the company is also featured on the malt whiskies, and if the names of the distilleries appear at all on the labels then they are in very small print and in inverted commas; they are not described as Singles but as Suntory → Pure Malt. Other blends include → Ageing, → Crest, → Excellence, → Hibiki, → Kakubin, → Old Club House, → Prestige, → Red Extra, → Royal, → Smokey & Co and → Torys.

Super Japanese brand from → Nikka and now the company's most successful product. It was launched as a blend in 1996, and it is said that the company's founder Masataka → Taketsuru created Super in memory of his Scottish wife. It was important to him to create a fine blend and the descriptions 'rare' and 'old', between which the name Super appears on the label, are justified. There are two versions of the blend, the original and a → premium. The latter's bottle is a little slimmer and taller than the bottle of the → standard blend Super, which is rather like an Armagnac bottle. In 1995 it was joined by a vatted pure malt.

Super-premium Japanese category of bottled blended whisky which contains over 40% malt content.

Super Session Japanese blend from Nikka launched on to the market in 1989, especially in supermarkets, and which is one of the country's standard whiskies.

SWA Scottish trade association with the full name → Scotch Whisky Association.

Sweet Science Whisky cocktail. Take two parts Scotch to one part Drambuie, mix with two parts orange juice and serve in a cocktail glass.

Swn y' Mor A blend formerly produced in Wales by the → Welsh Whisky Company consisting of Scottish whiskies. The company formed in 1974 and launched the blend in 1976. The name means 'sound of the sea' and is pronounced 'sun i mor'. It is a Welsh name, → Chwisgi means whisky and Welsh whisky is *Chwisgi Cymreig*. There is more Welsh on the bottle including *Bragdy Aberhonddu Cym* (ru), meaning Brecon, Aberhonddu, Wales. The blend was also available in a container shaped like a rugby ball.

Sword's Scotch, a standard blend from → Morrison Bowmore, the old firm James Sword

& Company. It was founded in 1814 and since 1983 has belonged to the Bowmore. Sword's is the only band still sold of the old company's original eight.

Syndicate Scotch blend formerly from → JBB (Greater Europe) plc. It is a 30-year-old belonging to the → de luxe sector.

T

Tail Term often used in Ireland and Scotland instead of the otherwise customary → feints. It is the liquid that flows from the → spirit still after the final run (the third in Ireland and usually the second in Scotland). As it contains poisonous fusel oils it is unusable and it is the task of the → stillman to make sure that it does not taint the → heart of the run, the good, usable alcohol. After careful separation it is redistilled.

Takara Shuzo Co Japanese company based in Kyoto. They formed a consortium together with Okura (based in Tokyo) to participate in the whisk(e)y business in both Scotland and the USA. They had a share, together with → Sazerac, in → Leestown Distilling in Kentucky. In 1986 the company acquired the → Tomatin Distillery, the largest in Scotland, and the blending company J & W Hardie in Glasgow. In 1998 Okura sold their share of 20% to the larger partner who were then joined by another Japanese group, Marubeni.

Taketsuru, Masataka Japanese whisky pioneer, one of the two 'fathers' of the Japanese whisky industry. The other was Shinjiro → Torii, a former wine importer and grower who used his profits to build the → Yamazaki Distillery in 1923. The knowledge required to build a distillery and produce malt whisky came from Taketsuru. Together they succeeded in making Japan one of the largest whisky producers in the world. Takestsuru was born in 1894 and came from a family who had for a long time been involved with making sake. A beer brewer sent him to Scotland to study the craft of brewing, but he soon became more interested in whisky and continued his studies in distilleries. The company he founded, Nikka has a written company history that mentions Rothes and the → White Horse Distillery, however they did not have a business in Rothes, but in nearby → Craigellachie. Taketsuru was also at → Lagavulin and at → Hazelburn in Campbeltown.

After two years Taketsuru returned to Japan, accompanied by Rita, his Scottish fiancée. He worked for Torii for 10 years before leaving in 1934, allegedly because Taketsuru wanted to build a new distillery at a more suitable location, in → Yoichi on the northern island of → Hokkaido, on a site which reminded him of → Campbeltown and where there was good water, peat and even barley. Whilst the whisky from the first small → pot still was maturing he produced fruit juices, and the apple juice → Kaju gave his company the name Nippon Kaju, which in 1952 was abbreviated to Nikka. In 1940 he was able to launch his first whisky (and brandy), but then the Second World War stopped production and forced him to produce industrial alcohol for military purposes. His company really became successful after the war. Over the years it grew to become the second largest in Japan (after Torii's → Suntory) and in 1969 Taketsuru was able to build two much larger distilleries in → Miyagikyo near → Sendai, after having seven years previously installed a real old-fashioned → Coffey still (at → Nishinomiya). He died in 1979 and left his business, which now belongs to the brewing giant Asahi, to a nephew who is still a director of the company.

Talisker Scottish malt distillery. Its name, emphasised on the penultimate syllable, is sometimes translated from the Gaelic as 'water-hole'. It belongs to the → whisky region of the Scottish → Islands and is the only distillery on the Isle of Skye. Its malt whisky may be called exceptional, even unique. Not just because of its lovely location by the salt-water Loch Harport with a view of the snow-covered peaks of the Cuillins, but rather because it has an odd number of → stills (five) with which triple distillation was carried out (until 1928) and because the water from the spring at Cnoc-nan-Speireag is intensively peated and red-brown in colour. Its name comes from the farm whose owner founded the distillery in 1830, and where Dr. Johnson and → Boswell were once guests. For several years it also belonged to Roderick Kemp, more usually associated with the → Macallan Distillery, and formed a joint company with → Dailuaine from 1898 – 1925, which was then taken over by → DCL. In the 1960s it was almost completely destroyed by fire but fortunately was rebuilt again.

Its malt has been praised in the highest tones: Robert Louis Stevenson called it, together with → Islay and → Glenlivet: 'The king o' drinks …'. Jim Murray includes it in the list of his 10 'all time favourites' (which only includes five Scotch malt whiskies). 'The pungent, slightly oily, peaty ruggedness of the bouquet mounts into my nostrils. The corpus of the drink advances like the lava of the Cuillins down my throat. Then vroom! Steam rises from the temples, a seismic shock rocks the building, my eyes are seen to water, cheeks aflame I steady myself against the chair. Talisker is not a drink, it is an interior explosion, distilled central heating; it depth-charges the parts, bangs doors and slams windows. There's nothing genteel about Talisker.'

John → Walker & Sons, a subsidiary of DCL brought out the whisky as a single malt (aged 8 and 12 years) in the 1980s instead of using it exclusively for their → Johnnie Walker. The strength of the 8-year-old was a unique 45.8%. This has not changed under the DCL successors → UD, who have included the Talisker (now aged 10 years) in their → 'Classic Malts of Scotland' series. In 1997 the series 'The → Distillers Edition' included a limited edition of a malt from 1986 which had been 'finished' in a cask which had previously contained a special Oloroso → sherry from the Amoroso vineyard. The 'Friends of the Classic Malts' received a special Christmas present in 1999: a 10-year-old Talisker at the cask strength of 59.3%, of which there were exactly 7,000 bottles. There is another special edition in cask strength (60%, no age statement, which is only available at the distillery itself. In 2001, there were 6,000 bottles of a 25-yearold, signed by the manager, Alastair Robertson. Talisker is also sometimes available from the → independents, such as → Cadenhead and their subsidiary → Duthie. The → cask strength from 1955 from → Gordon & MacPhail was particularly remarkable.

Tam's Dram Scotch blend named after the famous one o'clock gun fired each day at Edinburgh Castle.

Tambowie Scotch vatted malt from the → Vintage Malt Whisky Company based in Glasgow. It is available without an age statement in the USA, and otherwise it contains malt whiskies which are all at least 8 years old.

Tamdhu Scottish malt distillery. Its name, pronounced 'tam-doo', is from the Gaelic for 'black knoll'. It lies in the heart of the → Speyside region and is only separated from the river by a dismantled railway line. This was certainly a reason for choosing the site in 1897, and for many years the railway station served as a vistor centre, but had to be closed down.

Tamdhu was built during the whisky boom which ended in 1898 as the result of the → Pattsion bankruptcy and a year later the distillery was taken over by the → Highland Distilleries Co, now Highland Distillers, who retain ownership to this day. It increased the number of → stills to six in 1975, and continues to work more traditionally than elsewhere at the plant built around its own spring, using only local barley and peat. It is the only distillery in Scotland that still produces all its malt itself, and it does so in → Saladin boxes, a mechanical process that replaces the → floor maltings.

Most of its malt whisky goes into the popular blend The → Famous Grouse, but it is also available as a single malt. Unfortunately the 15-year-old in its characteristic bottle and the 10-year-old are no longer available. At present the whisky comes without an age statement. → Gordon & MacPhail have one from 1960 and regularly include an 8-year-old in their range. This is the same age as the Tamdhu in their 'MacPhail's Collection'. → Cadenhead had two versions from 1980 from sherry casks at 46%

Tamnavulin

and 58.7%. Signatory also had a sherry cask Tamdhu from 1970 at 49.5%.

Tamnavulin Scottish malt distillery situated in Tomnavoulin. Both are pronounced 'tamna-voo-lin'. It belongs to the → Speyside → whisky region. Tamnavulin gets its water from subterranean springs in the surrounding hills. Its name means 'mill on the hill' and it was built in 1966 by Invergordon Distillers on the site of a wonderful watermill and has eight → stills. It was closed down shortly after Invergordon was taken over by → Whyte & Mackay. Today it belongs to →Kyndal. After its closure it served to store the whiskies from → Tomintoul for several years. The old mill continues to be run by a co-operative of villagers as a visitor centre, which at least provides a few jobs, and it is one of the loveliest picnic sites in the whole of Scotland.

The single malt from Tamnavulin was available as an 8-year-old in a square bottle, as well as a 10-year-old. This is also the age of the malt in a glass decanter which is shaped like a → pot still. A 22-year-old was presented in a wooden box. In 1997 the design of the labels and packing was changed and a new version came out aged 12 years. This was joined by a 22-year-old on whose label Invergordon emphasised its 'natural lightness'. There was a 25-year-old in the → 'Stillman's Dram' series, which was joined at the end of 1997 by a 27-year-old, and later by a 29-year-old. They both had the 45% generally used for this series. It is occasionally available from the → independents such as → Cadenhead and → Signatory (1978, 59.8%, matured in a sherry cask). The → New Century from Unwins was also a Tamnavulin.

Tangle Ridge Canadian whisky. It is a 10-year-old from → Alberta Distillers, the Canadian subsidiary of → Jim Beam Brands, the spirits branch of → American Brands. Its sweetness is not very typical of the distillates from Alberta, where they exclusively distil rye, and is the result of an additive. There is also a 10-year-old 'Double Casked blended Canandian' which comes in a bottle with a swing stopper.

Tasmania Distillery Australian malt distillery which was originally named the Gasworks Distillery, but then given its present name. They produce vodka, brandy and gin, as well as a blend named Sullivans Cove which was brought out to bridge the gap until it could sell its own single malt. Australian laws prescribe a minimum period of two years in the cask, and the distillery began operating in 1995 with a classical French-style still that was only fired every two weeks. In 1997 the whisky was bottled. Hobart is the site of a charming museum and the island is also the home of another distillery, run by the → Small Concern Whisky Co, whose even smaller production has not yet been bottled. In Hobart they use Franklin barley and rely on traditional methods 'going back to 1822'. As the history of whisky making in Australia only officially began in 1866, this can only be a reference to illicit distlling. Whatever the case may be, now that all the whisky distilleries have become extinct on the Australian mainland, the two small operations in Tasmania have at least put it back on the map of whisky producing countries.

Tantallan Scotch single malt bottled by the → Vintage Malt Whisky Company in Glasgow. It is said to come from → Speyside. It is available as a 10-year-old and as a → vintage from 1980 and 1984.

Tartan Prince Scotch blend. It belongs to the five brands in the range of the Liverpool-based → Halewood International Ltd.

Tasting Term for the sampling of whisk(e)y. In contrast to the method of → nosing and almost exclusively practised by professionals such as master blenders, the whisk(e)y is also taken into the mouth and swallowed. There are several stages to a tasting: the colour of the drink is inspected. It may be artificially influenced by colouring, but it should be able to give information about the age of the whisk(e)y and the type of cask in which it has matured. Its body is also inspected by gently rotating the glass and observing how the liquid runs back down the sides, noticing whether the → legs form thin tracks, or long broad ones like a church window. This is followed by nosing to absorb the aromas. A good mouthful is then taken and allowed to circle in the mouth to get an idea of the feeling and the subtleties of taste which the whisk(e)y leaves on the palate and the tongue. The finish is then ascertained. Experienced tasters recommend that this first sample be followed by a second with the whisk(e)y diluted with water. This changes its character and 'opens' it up, uncovering new aromas. The colour and body will now have become lighter but the impressions left in the nose and the mouth are of the most importance. Of course a well-conducted tasting must include glasses which are suitable for the purpose.

Taylor & Ferguson Scottish whisky company that is mainly known for its blend → Ambassador. It was one of the smaller companies which the Canadian Hiram → Walker – Gooderham & Worts bought in Scotland in the 1930s. After having acquired the → Scapa Distillery in 1954, they transferred the licence of this distillery on the → Orkneys to their Scottish subsidiary.

Té Bheag Scotch blend from → Pràban na Linne on the Isle of Skye who use a little boat as the company's trademark. The name Té Bheag nan Eilean (pronounced 'chay veck') appeared on the label of the first blend brought out by Iain Noble's company. It means 'little lady of the islands', but is also used to mean a wee → dram. The whisky contains a high proportion of malt whiskies which very likely also include the island's → Talisker. It is available in two versions, the original and a new one where the process of → chill-filtering has been omitted to retain more aromas.

Teacher & Sons, Wm. Scottish company which, until its takeover by → Allied Breweries in 1976, was the largest independent whisky company in the country still owned by its founding family. In the mid-19th century William Teacher set up as a wine and spirits merchant in Glasgow, establishing a chain of → 'Dram Shops', famous for their cleanliness, and in which it was possible to drink but not smoke. He became the city's biggest publican with 18 pubs in all. He then went into the wholesale trade, specialising in blends, which he mixed according to the wishes of his customers. One of these became the large brand that is still successful → Teacher's Highland Cream, which was entered in the commercial register in 1884. William Teacher & Sons were also pioneers in the export trade and successfully built up a widespread network which supplied a large number of foreign markets, many with their own branches. In 1898 the company built → Ardmore Distillery and in 1960 they bought → Glendronach. They are now a subsidiary of → Allied Domecq PLC. Apart from the → standard blend there is also the 12-year-old Teacher's Royal Highland, but unfortunately the Teacher's 60, whose name referred to the unusually high malt share of at least 60%, is no longer produced.

Teacher's Highland Cream Scotch blend from Wm. → Teacher, which since 1976 has belonged to → Allied Domecq PLC (who at that time were still → Allied Breweries). Shortly before the First World War it became the first brand for which a cork with a wooden top was used. It began to be exported to many countries and during → prohibition the exports to Canada enabled it to be smuggled into the USA, which later helped it achieve a good position in the market. About two million → cases are sold per year and in the UK it is in third position. It is available as a → standard blend and as a 12-year-old Teacher's Royal Highland. The Teacher's 60, consisting of 60% malt whiskies, is unfortunately no longer available. Instead Allied Domecq PLC brought out a limited addition of a Teacher's 50 in India, where the blend is imported in → bulk and bottled by a subsidiary, for the 50th anniversary of Indian independence in 1997.

Teal's South African blend made from Scotch malt whiskies and locally-distilled → grain whiskies. Although the words 'Special Old' appear on the bottle, the contents are only three years old. The brand was launched by → Robertson & Baxter in 1990.

Teaninich Scotch malt distillery which lies in the Northern → Highland region, not far from → Dalmore, near the Cromarty Firth and the River Alness. It was founded as early as 1817 by Captain Munro. Its malt whiskies were used exclusively for blends, especially for those from R H → Thompson who held the licence for it on behalf of → DCL who had owned it since 1905.

The distillery was rebuilt several times and in 1971 the number of → stills was increased to 10. Like → Glenlossie it has two → stillhouses called 'A side' and 'B side'. Both were closed down in 1985, however the 'A side' has been in production again since 1990 with a team including Cathy Earnshaw. DCL's successors → UD were the first to bring out their single malt as a → proprietary bottling when they included a 10-year-old in their → 'Flora & Fauna' series. There were also at least three versions in their → 'Rare Malts Selection': two were from 1972 (23 years old, 64.95% and 27 years old, 64.2%) and one from 1973 (23 years old, 57.1%). The → independents occasionally have bottlings, for example → Cadenhead and → MacArthur. → Gordon & MacPhail have included it in their → 'Connoisseurs Choice' series, most recently with bottlings from 1975, 1976 and 1982 (all at 40%). In 1992 → Signatory bottled a 1975 Teaninich and in 1998 one from 1981, both at 43%.

Teeling, John J Irish businessman who wrote his thesis at Harvard on the situation in the Irish whiskey industry. He concluded that the whiskey of his homeland was the best in the world, with the worst marketing. In the mid 1980s the → IDG crisis had reached the point where it could no longer survive alone and Teeling, who had by that time become a successful businessman, along with other investors, put in an offer for it but lost the takeover battle to → Groupe Pernod-Ricard. In 1987 he established the → Cooley Distillery and not only bought the Cimicei Teo Distillery in → Riverstown from the government, but also the remains of the old → Kilbeggan Distillery of John Locke and the rights to a whole series of old firms and brandnames such as A A → Watt, Adam → Millar and → Dunville.

In 1989 the first grain and malt whiskies flowed in Riverstown and in 1992 they came onto the market. Since then Teeling has signed contracts with → UD/UDV and → Heaven Hill. Apart from the malt whiskies The → Tyrconnell, → Connemara, → Locke's, → Shanagarry and → Slieve na sCloc, there are the blends → Kilbeggan (which is now the second most popular Irish whiskey in Germany), → Avoca, → Ballygeary, → Cassidy's, → Celtic, → Delaney's, → Erin's Isle, → Finnegan, → Golden Irish, → Inishowen, → Millars Special Reserve, → O'Briens, → O'Hara and → O'Neill's as well as the liqueur → Eblana. Cooley undertake many own-label bottlings for supermarkets such as Safeway and Tesco. → Clontarf, → Knappogue Castle and → Merry's also come from Riverstown.

Ten Distilleries Japanese blend formerly from → Kirin-Seagram which, like all their other brands contains Japanese whiskies as well as Scottish and possibly other whiskies. The Canadian-Japanese joint venture owned a distillery in Japan and → Seagram has nine in Scotland alone.

Ten High Kentucky straight bourbon which nowadays comes from → Barton and is produced in → Bardstown. The brand belonged to → Hiram Walker and it is still possible to find the old bottle with a majestic eagle and the motto 'American Native Spirit'. The newer label bears the date 1879, the year that → Tom Moore brought out his first whiskey. Ten years later he founded the Barton distillery. The label of this bottling shows a gentleman with a glass of whiskey in his hand, one foot on a barrel and a dog at his side. Both bottles contain the same whiskey (80°/40%). It is served as the house brand in many American bars.

Tennessee Southern state of the USA where the special kind of whisk(e)y process used has been recognised since 1941.

Tennessee Sour Mash Whilst bourbon may be produced in any American state, Tennessee Sour Mash indeed only comes from this southern state which used to be the home of hundreds of distilleries. Only two of these, the → Jack Daniel Distillery in Lynchburg and the → Cascade (Hollow) Distillery of → George Dickel in Tullahoma, survived the period of → prohibition which hit Tennessee in 1910. Jack Daniels belongs to the → Brown-Forman Corporation and George Dickel to → UDV. At the Dickel Distillery they have long used the spelling 'whisky', whilst at Jack Daniel they have stuck to the spelling of 'whiskey' typical in the USA.

Like all bourbon distilleries they both use a recipe consisting of more than 51% corn, rye and malted barley, and both use the continuous distilling method. What is so special about Tennessee Whisk(e)y is not the → sour mash method where part of the liquid remaining after the first distillation is added as → backset to the mash or the fermenting vats. What makes bourbon and Tennessee Whisk(e)y different is the → Lincoln County Process (named after the place where a man named Alfred Eaton is said to have used it for the first time). The process is also known as → leaching or → charcoal mellowing.

In this process great wooden tubs, about three metres high, are filled with charcoal made from maple wood. At Jack Daniel the whiskey flows through holes in copper pipes and at George Dickel the whisky runs through a perforated sheet of steel, before slowly trickling onto the charcoal, taking days to reach the bottom of the great tubs and dripping onto a woollen blanket before being collected and filled into barrels. It is an elaborate process, and strips the alcohol of certain substances whilst adding others to it from the charcoal. The people in Tennessee swear that it is this process that gives their whisk(e)y its unusual mildness and purity.

Tesco UK supermarket chain which like its competitors, → Safeway, → Sainsbury, Asda and → Marks & Spencer, sells a large range of whiskies, including some with its own label. Apart from reasonably priced blends they also offer single malts such as → Glen Cairn, which do not name the distillery of their origin, but give the area from which they come. The 8-year-old blend → Edinburgh Castle comes from → Invergordon. Their Tesco Special Reserve is an Irish whiskey at 40% from → Cooley and is signed by Cooley's blender Noel Sweeney.

Testice Czech distillery near the medieval town of Oloumouc (Olmütz). It was a brewery but was already producing malt whisky before 1989. It now belongs to the food and drinks company → Seliko, which also produces slibowitz there and owns the → Dolany distillery to the north east of Oloumouc. This is no longer in production but is used for bottling. The water comes from a well which previously supplied the brewery. The peat used for malting comes partly from Scotland and partly from the → Czech Republic itself. Testice has two → pot stills which are reminiscent of → Lomond stills. They produce a distillate which is matured in casks made of Czech oak. One can get an idea of what it is like from → King Barley, on whose label the name of Dolany appears, but which contains malt whisky from Testice, like the company's own blend → Gold Cock.

Thailand This country had the second highest increase in whisky consumption between 1986 and 1996 after → Korea. According to the *Scotch Whisky Industry Review 1997*, consumption rose from 1.21 to 9.0 million bottles per year. Some bottles are labelled 'whisky' but which in fact contain a spirit distilled from rice ('Singharay' or 'V O Royal Thai Whisky'). Both come from the United Products Co, the former being a 'Special Old Premium' and the latter a 'Unique Blend'. The label states 'Aged in Specially Imported Oak Casks', it is the casks and not the whisky which is imported. Other rice whiskies include 'Royal Thai Liqueur Sang Thip' from the Surathip Sawan Vichitir Company, 'Gunn' and 'Shina Chao Praya'. Since 1995 there has also been a 'real' whisky the → Master Blend, which was made for → Seagram from locally-distilled → grain whiskies and malt whiskies imported from Scotland.

Thin stillage Term for → sour mash and → backset that stands for a customary process (and legally prescribed) in the production of Kentucky bourbon and Tennessee Whisk(e)y. The remains left in the → beer still after distilling the → low wines which, after the solid remains of the grain have been extracted, are re-used in the next distillation either in the → mash or during → fermentation. This guarantees that the whisk(e)y maintains a certain consistency and the reduction in acidity also kills off undesirable bacteria.

Thistle Cocktail Whisky cocktail. Stir equal parts of Vermouth Rosso and Scotch with a dash of angostura and serve in a cocktail glass.

Thistle Dhu Scotch blend. The 'black thistle' is a product from the → Speyside Distillery Co.

Thomson & Co, R H Scottish whisky company that held the licence of the → Teaninich Distillery on behalf of → DCL and carried the blends → Old Angus, → Robbie Burns and → Windsor Castle. It is now a subsidiary of → UDV.

Thomson, J G Only two products are left over from this company which in 1709 was founded in Leith. It left its mark on the history of Scotch whisky as a partner of Andrew → Usher, as the owner of → Littlemill and → Glen Garioch, and as the owner of the venerable building The Vaults near Leith harbour where wine was traded in the 12th century and which now houses the → Scotch Malt Whisky Society. Thomson was part of → DCL when the brewery giant Bass Charrington acquired the rights to the name. The two surviving products are the blend → Old Inverness and the single malt → As We Get It.

Three Ships South African blend of 'Matured Scotch Whisky and Select South African Whisky': malt whiskies from Scotland and locally distilled → grain whisky that are blended and bottled in South Africa. The brand was launched in 1977 with a 3-year-old whisky and soon became the most successful in the country. Since 1992 the blend has also been available aged 5 years and is said to contain a particularly high proportion of malt whiskies.

3 Star Scotch blend whose full name is → Crawford's 3 Star. It is a → standard blend from A & A Crawford which is owned by → Kyndal in the UK and in other countries from → GuinnessUDV, who sold the UK rights in 1994.

Three Stills Irish spirit that is only 30%. It was brought on to the market by the → IDG subsidiary → Fitzgerald & Co to compete with the cheap supermarket schnapps. The alcohol is produced at → Midleton.

Threewood Term for several whiskies that have been matured in three different oak casks. As far as it is known the method and term was used for the first time by → IDG for a version of their → Bushmills Single Malt. When it was presented three coopers from three different countries were invited to demonstrate their craft. The demonstration also served to emphasise the importance of the wood to the maturing process. There was a cooper from the USA showing how casks are made out of American oak, a specialist from Spain responsible for making sherry → butts and a craftsman from Portugal to demonstrate the making of port pipes. The 16-year-old Bushmills is a composition of malt whiskeys which first spent about 14 years in bourbon and sherry casks before being 'married' and spending a further two years together in a large port cask. The → Auchentoshan Threewood was 'constructed' in a similar way, except that it was finished in a cask that had contained heavy Pedro Ximénez Sherry.

Thresher Chain of UK off-licences that, until 1998 belonged to the brewery giants Whitbread. Including its subsidiaries Wine Rack and Bottoms Up they had more than 1,400 branches in the country. Whitbread and → Allied Domecq PLC decided to bring their subsidiaries Thresher and → Victoria Wine (with almost 1,500 shops) under the umbrella of a new company called First Quench which has subsequently been acquired for £225 million by the Japanese bank Nomura, who are also the largest pub-owner in the UK.

Thumper Term for a still that is sometimes used in America for the second distillation. In the first run the → wash is distilled in a → beer still, which in contrast to the Scottish → patent stills only consists of one single column and produces → low wines with a strength of about 55% to 60%. If they continue to be processed in their liquid form then the next still is called a → doubler, but if they are processed in the form of steam then this is done in a thumper. Both produce a distillate of about 65% which the Americans name → white dog.

Tiliknagar Indian company producing several brands such as → Mansion House and since November 1997 has been participating in a joint venture with → Allied Domecq PLC's Scottish subsidiary → Allied Distillers Ltd. The company distributes the blends → Teacher's and → Old Smuggler which are shipped in → bulk to India and bottled there by another partner, → Clan Morgan of Delhi.

Tipperary Whiskey cocktail. A variation on the Manhattan using Irish whiskey, Vermouth Bianco and green Chartreuse.

Tobermory Scottish malt distillery on the Isle of → Mull. It lies at the entrance to the island's main town, next to an impressive waterfall. The distillery was established in 1795, at about the same time as → Oban, and although its founders contributed to the development of the little town, they had nothing to do with the distillery. For a time it belonged to the same John → Hopkins & Co as Oban. But whilst Oban remained almost continually in production, the only legal distillery on Mull was more often closed than not. From 1916 it was owned by → DCL and from 1930 to 1972 it was silent. It was then renovated, enlarged to four → stills and renamed → Ledaig. Bankruptcy, closure, reopening, renaming, closure, sale, conversion of the → warehouses to holiday accomodation, opening of a visitor centre and a cheese stall in the → stillhouse followed: it was one long melodrama that only came to an end in 1993 when the distillery was taken over by → Burn Stewart.

Only two → stills are used for production and either very slightly peated malt or completely unpeated malt is used, but they also plan to use peated malt from time to time in the future. There is now a Tobermory single malt from Tobermory and it is made from unpeated malt. The name Ledaig was used between 1972 and 1976 and appears on two bottlings of a malt whisky from 1974, one from 1979 and one distilled in 1980, which are all peated. They plan to make heavier whiskies again: there will be two names for two different whiskies. In 1998 Burn Stewart celebrated the 100th anniversary of their distillery (although there is no proof of its age) with a bottling of Tobermory which only differed from the normal one in its packing. The malt is seldom available from → independent bottlers. → Signatory has a Vintage Isle of Mull, which comes from Tobermory.

Toddy Popular drink, especially for fighting a cold or preventing the onset of illness. According to the classic Scottish recipe only hot water and sugar is added to Scotch, using measures which reflect the likely danger of catching a cold or the severity of the flu. It should preferably be drunk from a silver mug. Those who are not such purists may add a slice of lemon, possibly spiced with cloves. This → hot whiskey is preferred in Ireland and the USA. In Ireland the → Snug is a premixed version which only needs hot water added to it.

Tom Cobb Australian spirit. The label names the producers as the Tom Cobb Distilling Co in Forest Glen, Queensland with an address in 'Moonshine Valley'. It also states: 'This spirit is based on an old style saddlebag whisky which was originally distilled in the outback of → Australia. The distillation of this traditional dark liquor has basically remained unchanged since the late 1800s.' The strength is 80°/40%.

Tom Moore Kentucky straight bourbon, named after the man who established a distillery on the site of the present day → Barton Distillery in 1889. Moore's first whisky had already appeared 10 years before that date, when he established his business with a partner. Mattingly and today the brand → Mattingly & Moore is a reminder of them both. This comes from the neighbouring → Heaven Hill Distillery. Moore's distillery, like so many others, fell victim to → prohibition. The distillery was reopened by Henry Teur and 10 years later was taken over by → Oscar Getz, who renamed it. The Tom Moore is available at 80°/40% and without an age statement. There is a new product called 'The Clear Favorite' which is crystal clear and has a strength of 40%.

Tomatin Scottish distillery. Its name comes from the Gaelic for 'hill of the bushes' and is pronounced 'tom-átn'. It lies near the A9 on the northern edge of the Grampian Mountains. It was founded in 1897 during the boom years, although it was closed during the whisky crisis. In 1909 it was reopened and during the period between 1956 and 1962 it was considerably improved and enlarged. In 1974 12 new → stills were added to the 11 already existing, making it the largest distillery in the country with a capacity of more than 12 million litres of alcohol per year. The size had no influence on

Tomintoul

the production methods which remained traditional, but did lead to another collapse. The Japanese syndicate → Takara Shuzo & Okura (which later also bought the bourbon distillery → Leestown) saved the distillery in what was the first Japanese involvement in whisky production in Scotland. They consolidated the business, that still continues to be run as the Tomatin Distillery Co Ltd, but it doesn't produce even a sixth of what it could (or what could be stored in its → warehouses which have a capacity of 40 million litres of alcohol). In 1998 Okura sold its 20% share to its larger partner. A new Japanese group, Marubeni, then stepped in as the new partner.

The majority of the whisky is shipped in → bulk to Japan, where it is blended with Japanese → grain whisky. The company also own two blends, → Big T and The → Antiquary which contain a large proportion of malt whisky from Tomatin. It is also known that the → Welsh Whisky → Prince of Wales was a Tomatin. The company bottles its whisky as a single malt for the USA aged 12 years, and for the rest of the world aged 10 years. The 5-year-old, which used to be available in Italy, is already becoming a rarity. The 25-year-old is bedded on velvet in a wooden box. The 100th anniversary of the distillery was celebrated with a 30-year-old in an elegant glass decanter in a limited edition of 800 bottles. There have been → independent bottlings from → Gordon & MacPhail with a 1964 whisky in the small series the 'Spirit of Scotland', as well as several vintages (such as. 1964 and 1968) in the series 'Connoisseurs Choice'. There is a Tomatin from 1976 from → Cadenhead which was matured in a sherry cask and is 56.7%.

Tomintoul Scottish malt distillery. Its name translates from Gaelic as 'small hill like a barn'. The distillery is not to be found in the village of the same name, which is the highest in Scotland, but it is the home of the → 'Whisky Castle' and a nearby small brewery. From the village one must drive towards Grantown-on-Spey, turn right at the Bridge of Avon and then the distillery is situated by the river in a wild, romantic spot. It gets its water from the Ballantruan Spring. The very modern distillery, belonging to the → Speyside region, was built in 1964 by the → brokers W & S Strong and Hay & MacLeod, who were bought by Scottish & Universal Investments in 1972, which in the same year had also acquired → Whyte & Mackay. In 1974, the year of its 10th anniversary, the number of → stills was doubled from two to four. When Whyte & Mackay took over → Invergordon Distillers, it added another four distilleries to the three that it already owned (→ Dalmore, → Fettercairn and Tomintoul) and immediately closed three of the new ones. As long as they owned the distillery, Invergordon sold the single malt for them. In 2000 they sold Tomintoul to the family-owned company → Angus Dundee. Invergordon had an 8-year-old and a 12-year-old in their portfolio. A 10-year-old in a normal bottle was then first brought out for → Victoria Wines, before becoming generally available. It was joined by a 12-year-old and then at the end of 1997 by a 14-year-old. It is seldom available from the → independent bottlers. In 1996 Signatory was able to bottle a cask from 1966 at 52.7%.

Torii, Shinjiro Pioneer of Japanese whisky, founder of → Suntory, one of the largest (drinks) companies in the world and founder of the Japanese whisky industry. Together with the younger → Masataka → Taketsuru he built the first distillery in the country, with the result that Japan is now one of the world's largest whisky producers. He was born in 1879 and in 1900 he began importing Spanish wine. In 1907 he brought out a Japanese wine named 'Akadama' and became one of the foremost wine connoisseurs in the country. He made so much money that he was able to fulfil his dream of not just importing Scottish whisky, but of imitating it and producing it in his own country.

Whilst looking for a place which was reminiscent of Scotland he found the → Yamazaki valley in the Kyoto area, to the north of Osaka. Three rivers run together into the Yodogawa in this hilly, wooded area, and the differences in temperature provide the necessary damp, foggy climate. The distillery was built in 1923/24 and Taketsuru was its production manager. In 1929 Torii brought out his first whisky named Shirofuda, but which was soon renamed White

(Label). It wasn't particularly successful and it was only in 1937, with → Kakubin, that a really satisfactory brand was developed. After the war he began to accustom the Japanese to their country's own whisky in a chain with the name 'Tory Whisky Bars' spread throughout the country which exclusively sold the company's own whiskies. The profits from these bars were used to go into the brewing business, and lay a further foundation stone for the expansion that has helped Suntory to its present position in the global market. The chairman of the board is still a Torii.

Tormore Scottish malt distillery. Its name comes from the Gaelic for 'large hill'. It lies on the A95 between Grantown-on-Spey and Aberlour and therefore belongs to the → Speyside region. Aesthetes consider it to be one of the loveliest distilleries in Scotland. It looks like a lovingly-restored plant from the 19th century but is in fact hardly 40 years old. Its architect, Sir Albert Richardson, received the commission from → Long John International who at that time, via → Seager Evans, were owned by → Schenley. It was completed in 1959 and since then has attracted tourists with its white buildings, bell-tower and artificial lake complete with swans.

The whisky is still an important component of → Long John. There was a → proprietary bottling of a 5 and 10-year-old Tormore in a ribbed and angular bottle. In 1991 it was brought out in a new classical design and received the definite article 'The' in front of its name. Since 1997 it has also been available as a 12-year-old. In the summer of 2000 a Tormore was included in the series of six malts, which Allied had originally only intended for its employees, but which then became generally available in small numbers (15 years old and unfortunately diluted to 43%). It is seldom available from the → independents, but the → Scotch Malt Whisky Society occasionally has a cask and Douglas → Laing also had one in his series The → 'Old Malt Cask'.

Torys Japanese blend from → Suntory which is only important on the domestic market, where it is one of the most reasonably priced. Its name derives from the surname of Shinjiro → Torii.

Town Club American blended whiskey from the David → Sherman Company of St. Louis.

Treasures from Scotland Collection Series of Scotch single malts which the → independent bottler → Signatory markets under the name of its subsidiary Dun Eideann in France. The name of the distillery from which each malt comes appears in small print, as well as the year of distillation and bottling and the number of the cask and the bottle.

Treasury Scotch blend from → Hill Thomson & Co formerly a subsidiary of the → Chivas & Glenlivet Group, which in turn was owned by → Seagram. It is now owned by a partnership formed between Diageo and Groupe Pernod-Ricard.

Tribute Scotch blend from William → Lundie & Co in Glasgow. It is available as a → blend without an age statement and in the → de luxe category aged 15, 20, 25 and 30 years.

Triple Crown Canadian whisky. For a long time it came from → Gilbey Canada, a subsidiary of → IDV/→ Grand Metropolitan, whose leading Canadian brand was → Black Velvet. Both came from the → Palliser Distillery in Lethbridge, Alberta, but the Triple Crown was superior in taste. Whether this will remain so and whether the site of production and the taste will stay the same is uncertain as since February 1999 the brand has belonged to: → Canandaigua who acquired it along with several others as → UDV, have almost totally withdrawn from Canada.

Triple distillation A special form of distillation mainly identified with Ireland. During the production of malt whisky in Scotland (and elsewhere) the wash is distilled in just two runs to about 22% and then brought to just over 70% in the spirit safe, a third still comes into use in triple distillation, often called the intermediate still. Apart from Cooley, all whiskeys are traditionally triple distilled in Ireland. Their alcohol content is therefore somewhat higher than in Scotland, and the whisk(e)y is purer and lighter in body, but somewhat more spirity and the aromas are less defined. Triple distillation used to be customary in the Scottish Lowlands as well, but is now only practised at → Auchentoshan. There the first distillate leaves the wash still at 18–19% and is then distilled a second time, together with the → foreshots and the → feints from the third run in the second still, that is called a low wines still there. The → low wines leave this still at 55% and are then distilled again in the spirit still, reaching an alcohol volume of 82%.

Triple S Scottish spirit described as 'Single Scottish Spirit'. It has a strength of 60%, comes in small 50cl. bottles and names Wm. → Cadenhead as bottler. A band over the top states that it is an 'attitude free alcohol', and one label is fluorescent green whilst the other is blue. It is a fresh distillate that has never seen the inside of a cask, a → baby whisky. The different coloured labels show that one is a → Springbank and the other a → Longrow. For the former a kind of triple distillation is used, which might explain the name, or it may derive from the three 'S's in 'Single Scottish Spirit'.

Tsuru Japanese blend from → Nikka and the company's flagship. It is of course a → super-premium blend, belonging to the highest of the five categories used for blends in Japan. Blends in this category must contain more than 40% malt whiskies. 'Tsuru' is Japanese for 'crane'. The blend comes in two types of container. The first is a glass decanter with a white label and an additional decanter label around its neck with the name of the brand. The other is more elegant and is made of snow-white porcelain, decorated with cranes, with a gold-coloured decanter label.

Tullamore Dew Irish whiskey, once famous in Ireland but is now difficult to obtain there. Although there are plans to reintroduce the brand. A Heritage Centre has been built in Tullamore. Whilst it is now practically unknown in its country of origin, it is almost a synonym for Irish whiskey in Germany, France and Denmark, where it occupies the undisputed first position among its genre. The name originated from the distillery in Offally, and used the slogan: 'Give Every Man his Dew'. Like many other Irish distilleries, the company got into financial difficulties after the Second World War, which even the invention of the liqueur → Irish Mist could not overcome, and it had to close down in 1954. The brand passed via → Power to → IDG, who sold it in 1993 to → Cantrell & Cochrane, who at the time were a subsidiary of → Guinness and → Allied Domecq PLC. As well as the normal blend at 40%, whose clay jugs are particularly popular, they brought out a 12-year-old whose 43% indicates that it is mainly intended for sale abroad and in duty-free shops as it is a Heritage at 70%. → Cadenhead managed to obtain some whiskies from the old distillery and bottle them (some as miniatures only) – 1948/64.5%, 1949/65.6% and 1952/68.9% – using the name of the original owner, Daly. The → Knappogue Castle 1951 is in fact an old Tullamore.

Tullibardine Scottish malt distillery. It lies between the source of the famous water 'Highland Spring', and Gleneagles Hotel. The distillery belongs to the southern → Highland region and lies just to the north of the line which separates it from the → Lowlands. In 1949 the renowned architect W Delmé Evans, who was also responsible for → Isle of Jura and → Glenallachie, began construction work on the distillery. Its owners sold it in 1971 to → Invergordon Distillers, who enlarged it from two to four → stills. After the very hostile takeover battle lasting from 1991-1994, Tullibardine passed to → Whyte & Mackay who ran it on behalf of their American parent company → American Brands, who immediately shut it down, like the other Invergordon distilleries → Bruichladdich and → Tamnavulin. The single malt from Tullibardine was already available as a 10-year-old in the Invergordon era. At the end of 1997 the design of its label and packaging was changed. After the management buyout it now belongs to → Kyndal. There was a 21-year-old in a wooden box. It has also been represented in the → 'Stillman's Dram' series, for example aged 25 and 27 years, both at 45%. It is not often available from the → independents, but → Cadenhead occasionally has it and → Signatory bottled a cask from 1972 (53.5%).

Turkey In terms of its population Turkey does not have a very high consumption of whisky. With 3.3 million litres of Scotch sold in 1997, the country lies just ahead of such small countries as → Uruguay and Belgium and Luxembourg.

However, in 1985 the figure didn't even amount to 700,000 litres. Whisky is produced in Turkey itself, albeit in very tiny quantities. The country's own brand is called → Ankara and owes its existence to a group of agricultural students, who, according to some sources began distilling malt and → grain whiskies for research purposes in 1956. The same date appears on the bottles as the date when production at the 'alcohol factory in Ankara' began, 1963. Since that time the state-run business Tekel has had small amounts of 'Türk Visiki' in its portfolio. For several years now there has also been a *Malt Viski*, which according to its label is matured in special casks for 5 years before being sold.

T W Samuels Kentucky straight bourbon with a name that one would normally associate with the → Maker's Mark Distillery in Loretto rather than with → Heaven Hill in → Bardstown where it comes from. Maker's Mark was first opened in the 1950s by T William Samuels who was named after his forefather Taylor William. He had established the family's first distillery in Deatsville in 1844, which remained in the hands of the family until it had to shut down in 1920 because of → prohibition. Leslie Samuels then built a new plant and reopened the old T W Samuels Distillery. When his son T William retired in 1943, the old distillery and the rights to the name were sold. Ten years later he started again from scratch, establishing a new business. Heaven Hill only sells the → Bottled in Bond brand at 100° locally.

Twelve Stone Flagons American company based in Pittsburgh, Pennsylvania with a range of blends and a vatted malt named → Usquaebach and a bourbon named → American Biker. The commercial breakthrough apparently came with the assistance of the Prince of Monaco and Hollywood queen Liz Taylor.

21st Century Indian whisky from the → Som Distillery in Bhopal, Madhya Pradesh, to the south of Delhi.

Tyrconnell, The Irish whiskey which was a blend until the 1970s and has been a single malt since 1992. Its producers, the → Cooley Distillery, describe it as a → pure pot still whiskey and associate it with the company of A A → Watt. He not only owned a distillery in Derry (which had to close down in 1920 and was acquired by the Scottish → DCL), but also a famous racehorse which got its name from the Tyrconnell area, and which won the Irish Classic, the Queen Victoria plate, at odds of 100-1 in 1876. Watt immortalised the victory in the name of his whiskey and the family, who had long since discontinued distilling themselves, had it in their portfolio until 1970.

John J → Teeling took this name for the first single malt of his young company as well as using the old label decorated with a horse. It was launched it on to the market in 1992, at the tender age of three years. For a short time the name disappeared, but has now beem successfully re-established. Unlike most other Irish whiskies, but like most Scotch malts, it is only twice distilled. Whilst heavily peated malt is used for the → Connemara (which Cooley has subsequently launched on to the market), the Tyrconnell is unpeated. The three stars which originally appeared on the label have now become five, which according to the makers has nothing to do with the increased age of the whiskey, but simply looks nicer. There is a limited edition (as in the case of the → Locke's) from specially selected casks from 1989.

U

Ubique Scotch blend from → Gordon & MacPhail which is hard to obtain and really only available in Scotland. The name comes from the motto of the Royal Regiment of Artillery and the whisky is specially produced for them.

UD (United Distillers) Spirits giant which operated worldwide. It was formed in 1987 after a bitterly fought takeover battle when Guinness gained control of→ DCL, the company with a long tradition and interests in both Scotland and the USA. In some respects UD was the successor of the company formed in 1877, which at the time of the takeover owned nearly a third of all Scotch malt and several grain distilleries, as well as numerous subsidiaries and a large number of brands. DCL's complexity is reflected by its history, which began with the amalgamation of several Lowland distilleries and resulted in names such as → Buchanan, → Dewar, → Haig, and → Walker, continuing to exist as mere subsidiaries of the DCL conglomerate.

Arthur → Bell & Sons were amongst the few who were able to escape their sphere of influence, but it was with the takeover of this venerable old company that Guinness began spreading its wines and launched the expansion from being a brewery to a universal drinks giant. The American distillery → Stitzel-Weller fell into Guinness's control when they took over DCL, as it had been taken over by the Scots in 1984. Guinness continued with its acquisitions: in 1987 the purchase of → Schenley also brought with it the Canadian → Valleyfield Distillery with all its brands, as well as the → Bernheim Distillery in Kentucky and the gem of → George Dickel in → Tennessee. They did not confine themselves to acquisitions, they also engaged in thorough restructuring under the overall charge of the newly formed UD, whose headquarters were in Hammersmith, London, from where they controlled their activities in various countries. In Scotland several distilleries were shut down or sold, and those remaining continued to be managed under the name 'United Malt and Grain Distilleries' (UMGD). UD also owned five → maltings and several bottling plants.

UD participated fully in the blossoming business with single malts and whiskies from nearly all their distilleries were bottled, many of them for the first time. The creation of the series → 'Classic Malts of Scotland', → 'Flora & Fauna' and → 'Rare Malts' was of particular importance. On the other side of the Atlantic they closed down Stitzel-Weller and Bernheim in order to erect a new Bernheim Distillery. In 1991 they aquired → Glenmore, which had contolled → Fleischmann and → Medley. The name Glenmore was kept but many brands such as → Ezra Brooks and → Old Thompson were sold together with several closed-down distilleries to → Barton Brands. Apart from the Tennessee Whisky (sic) George Dickel they concentrated on the bourbon brands → W L Weller, → Old Fitzgerald, → I W Harper, → Old Charter, → Rebel Yell and → James E Pepper and created the → 'Bourbon Heritage Collection', based on the model of the six Scottish Classic Malts.

They also made a clean sweep with various Canadian brands. In Germany they bought Asbach in Rüdesheim and changed the company name to UD Germany. By 1997 UD had succeeded, by means of takeovers or joint-ventures, in being represented almost worldwide, with subsidiaries in 26 countries and interests in many more resulting from participation in distilleries or trading companies, partly also under the name UD. The mutual shareholding with Moët Hennessy, Bundaberg in Australia and a company named

Riche Monde operating in Thailand, Singapore and Malaysia, were of particular importance.

At the end of 1997 it was all over for UD: on 17th December the shares of a new company were offered on the Stock Exchange. UD's parent company Guinness had merged with the food multinational → Grand Metropolitan to form → Diageo, the largest drinks combine in the world. → IDV, which had previously been responsible for the wine and spirits business of Grand Met, and UD were joined together to form → UDV. This new creation is now in the middle of worldwide restructuring of all its sectors, from production through marketing to distribution, and in future will carry on the previous activities of both companies worldwide (making use of the effects of synergy and the possibilities for rationalisation). By March 1999 both Hammersmith and the Scottish marketing headquarters at Cherrybank, Perth had been given up, bottling and packing had been concentrated on three sites (Leven, Kilmarnock and Glasgow), Laindon in Essex and Strathleven had been closed down, gin production had been transferred to → Cameronbridge and in Germany Weltmarken had joined Asbach to form UDV Germany.

This was all small fry in comparison with the sale of the brand Dewar's to → Bacardi, who also received the distilleries → Aberfeldy, → Aultmore, → Craigellachie and → Royal Brackla (for £1.15 billion). In comparison the $185 million they received for the → Bernheim Distillery and the brands Old Charter, Old Fitzgerald, Rebel Yell and W L Weller seemed quite modest. In Canada → Valleyfield was sold to → Canandaigua, but there it was mostly former IDV possessions that came under the hammer. The only Canadian brand remaining is → Gibson's. In America they have kept Dickel (together with the → Cascade Distillery) and the brand I W Harper (together with the stocks still stored at Bernheim).

UDV (United Distillers and Vintners)

Internationally-operating combine which controls a large part of the world spirits market, but which itself is only part of the far larger multinational giant → Diageo. This new company, clearly the largest of its kind in the world and larger than both the two next largest, the former → Seagram and → Allied Domecq PLC, was formed at the end of 1997 as a result of the merger of → Guinness and → Grand Metropolitan. Both brought strong spirits and wine portfolios with them into the alliance: Guinness brought → UD and Grand Met brought → IDV. These two subsidiaries joined to form UDV (United Distillers and Vintners) but were not able to keep all their brands and processing or sites of production. The respective bodies controlling monopolies in both the USA and Europe imposed injunctions ordering the sale of the brand → Ainslie's, and more painfully → Dewar's, to prevent UDV dominating the market, particularly in America, where UD's Dewar's was the top-selling whisky and IDV's → J & B was the number two. They soon found buyers: → Ainslie's, which was particularly strong in Greece, went to the Belgian company Bruggeman and Dewar's went to → Bacardi, which in addition acquired four malt whisky distilleries, for a total of £1.15 billion.

This deal was not the final one and further sales followed in order to assimilate and rearrange their product ranges and, in particular, to realise the effects of the synergy which ensues after such large mergers and which the shareholders had been promised. In Scotland, where they particularly feared the loss of jobs, the sceptics' forecasts initially proved to be correct: UD's marketing headquarters at Cherrybank, Perth and head office in Hammersmith, London were both closed, bottling and packing was only continued at Leven, Kilmarnock and Shieldhall, Glasgow whilst Strathleven was closed down; however a new administrative building was built to the west of Edinburgh. The gin that was formerly produced at Laindon in Essex is now distilled at the → Cameronbridge Distillery.

In February and March 1999, it was first announced that → Canandaigua had taken over the Canadian distilleries at → Palliser (formerly IDV) and → Valleyfield (formerly UD), with all their brands except the Canadian whisky → Gibson's, for $185 million. A month later rationalisation followed in the USA: a syndicate consisting of → Heaven Hill, → Sazerac and the David → Sherman Company acquired four brands and a distillery (and several non-whisky brands) for $171 million. The → Bernheim Distillery and → Old Fitzgerald passed to Heaven Hill, → Rebel Yell to Sherman and → Old Charter and → W L Weller to Sazerac. This only left George A → Dickel's → Cascade Hollow Distillery and their Tennessee Whisky (sic) as well as just one bourbon, → I W Harper.

In mid-2001 the name of UDV was changed to → GuinnessUDV.

Uisge beatha The Scots Gaelic for 'Water of Life'; the Irish Gaelic is slightly differently spelt, uisce beatha. They both appear to be translations of the Latin 'aqua vitae' that is mentioned in the first documentary reference to whisky in the 'Exchequer Rolls of Scotland' from 1494. Both are pronounced 'isch'ke-bah'. The modern word whisk(e)y is a corruption of the Gaelic original. The IDG (Irish Distillers Group) explains that when the soldiers of King Henry II came across uisce beatha they never learnt how to pronounce it correctly. The Irish deliberately forget to mention that this aqua vitae was not a grain distillate but a brandy. There is also the interim form 'usquebaugh' in Gaelic, as the forerunner of 'whisk(e)y' (which actually only means water!), whose modern spelling without the Irish 'e' first appeared in 1746 and then also in Dr. Johnson's 'Dictionary', following the earlier use of 'uiskie' and 'usky'. Ironically the division of the Gaelic original has re-established itself: the Irish (and the Americans) write whiskey and the Scots (and Canadians) whisky. That is pure convention as it can be proved that in the early 20th century most Irish distilleries left out the 'e', and in America the Dickel, for example, also spells whisky without an 'e'.

Ulle bé Naomh Scotch single malt aged 8 years but of unknown origin, it is in the range of the Minneapolis-based company → All Saint's Brands and is available in the USA.

Ultimate Selection, The Series of single malts in → single cask bottlings which → Signatory produces for the Dutch firm van Wees in Ammersfoort. The contents of the bottle are precisely described, with the date of distillation and bottling, cask type and number and the name of the distillery. As a rule they come with a strength of 43%.

Underback The vessel into which the → worts flow at the end of → mashing. In all malt distilleries and some grain distilleries the liquid is separated from the solid substances named → draff when they pass though a perforated floor in the → mash tuns. The worts are then cooled before flowing to the → washbacks where they are fermented with yeast.

Union Glen Scotch blend from The → Bennachie Whisky Co, a young → standard blend with the minimum age of 3 years. The producer claims that it was available as long as 175 years ago when it came from the Union Glen Distillery.

United Brewers of India Indian company which is successful in the brewing sector, and is also involved in the whisky business. It has three distilleries of its own, one in Kerala, a second one named → McDowell's Distillery near Goa and a third in Bangalore. The company owns the → Bagpiper which is by far the most successful brand in India selling 40 million bottles per year. It also produces McDowell's, the first and still the only true single malt in → India (which is also available in a series of blends). Another of its brands is → Diplomat.

Unwins UK wine and spirits company with headquarters in Dartford, Kent. They are a typical High Street chain, and the company belongs to Phillips Newman & Co. It is targeted at customers with more modest requirements. Apart from a large number of blends and single malts in → proprietary bottlings, they also have a range of brands specially produced for them, such as the blend → Ben Roland and the malt whisky → Laird's Reserve. They brought out the → New Century Single Malt at Christmas 1998. This is a 25-year-old → Tamnavulin at 45% supplied by → Invergordon, the owners of this distillery.

Urquhart Castle Scotch → Pure Malt, belonging to a small series of malt whiskies which bear the names of important Scottish historical sites. The once mighty and imposing castle is situated to the south of Inverness on the banks of Loch Ness. The bottlings from J & A Mitchell's → Springbank Distillery, named after the castles at Edinburgh, St. Andrews and

Stirling are all at 46%, but this one is only 40%, the strength that the → independent bottler → Gordon & MacPhail is known for. The company from Elgin is managed by members of the Urquhart family.

Uruguay This Latin American country is one of the smallest on the continent but matches its large neighbours → Argentina and → Brazil in whisky consumption and whisky culture. They also produce whiskies, but these are blends for which the necessary grain distillates are made in Uruguay, whilst the malt whiskies are imported in → bulk from Scotland. The leading brands are → Old Times and → MacPay. One particularly successful blend is → Ye Monks, which sells so much that its market share in the → premium blend sector amounts to 50%.

USA Despite many adversities, the USA is one of the great whisky-producing nations and its Jim Beam and Jack Daniel's belong to the leading brands worldwide.

As more and more Irish and Scottish immigrants joined the English and the Dutch, the raw material used for distilling shifted to grain. Many of the new arrivals had also brought a small still with them and many were used to using surplus grain to distil an alcoholic liquid which could be easily stored and was excellent for trading, rather than using it for baking bread or making porridge. They either used the grain that they found in their new homeland or which they had brought with them, especially rye. Rye represented the beginnings of the history of whiskey in the USA and its distillation was particularly concentrated in Maryland and Pennsylvania, which makes it regrettable that these states hardly produce any whiskey anymore and that rye has also lost its importance.

Corn began to be planted during the latter part of the 18th century when the the first settlers moved westwards, crossing the Appalachian Mountains through the Cumberland Gap and making their homes on the banks of the great rivers in the area which is now known as Kentucky.

It is not known exactly who made the first bourbon, but → Elijah Craig and → Evan Williams were certainly among the first. Distilling became widespread. In 1838 there were 3,500 stills to be found in Pennsylvania and more than 2,000 in Kentucky. Just as in the case of malt whisky in Scotland, the spirits were raw and wild, maturation was unknown and everyone was allowed to sell their products in the form that it left the still. The expression 'firewater' was probably quite accurate.

It was a long time before men such as Dr. James Crow (→ Old Crow) and E H Taylor (→ Old Taylor) managed to establish quality standards and even legal requirements, such as the → Bottled in Bond Act of 1897. By this time whisky was already taxed. In 1794 Washington needed 12,000 soldiers to break up the → Whiskey Rebellion and Lincoln filled the coffers for the Civil War with taxes imposed on whiskey. A temperance movement had also been formed which not only wanted to prevent alcohol abuse, but also absolutely any consumption of whiskey. In some states such as Tennessee they were successful as early as 1910 and a prohibition law was passed 10 years later.

Prohibition ruined the American whiskey industry. Only six distilleries were allowed to carry on production for medicinal purposes. All the rest were closed down. Many remain closed today, others only recovered slowly and it was years before they could compete with the Canadian and Scottish producers. Great amounts of whiskey had been smuggled into the country and great amounts of → moonshine had been made. → Seagram and Hiram → Walker were able to achieve positions that resulted in them becoming great concerns operating worldwide. The Scots were successful, too. All this was the result of prohibition, but it did not manage to surpress the consumption of whisk(e)y. However tastes changed, so that the lighter Canadians and the light-coloured blends from Scotland were preferred. Even today more Canadian whisky is drunk in the USA than the bourbon which almost totally replaced rye. The fact that there are now hardly any distilleries left is certainly a result of the modern concentration of companies, but also of prohibition.

The law prescribes that any whiskey may call itself straight bourbon if its mash consists of at least 51% corn. It must also mature or at least two years in new oak casks (and if it does not bear an age statement the period is four years). Rye, in as far as it is still made, must contain 51% rye. Corn must contain at least 80% corn. There are also blended whiskies and 'lights', which are allowed to have less than 80°/40% alcohol. After prohibition a totally new type arose, the → Tennessee Whiskeys, which are made and matured in exactly the same way as the bourbons, but which undergo the → Lincoln County Process. Jack Daniel's (to a greater extent than George Dickel) is an example of an American success story following prohibition.

There are others, including the success of the small, fine distillery → Maker's Mark and that of → Blanton's who introduced a totally new chapter with → small batch and → single barrel bottlings according to the Scottish role model with their malt whiskies. Fritz Maytag and his → Anchor Distillery deserve a particular mention.

Usher, Andrew Both Andrew Sr and Jr, are credited with inventing the successful blending processa – a process that changed the course of Scotch whisky. They discovered the art of blending which created a totally new type of whisky, the blend. Others certainly experimented along these lines: W P Lowrie (who supplied James → Buchanan with his first whiskies) and Charles → Mackinlay & Co. The older Usher began his career as a spirits merchant in 1813, and it is no longer known what made him mix the contents of various casks (although this was already being practised with Cognac in France). Usher understood that storing the whisky in casks was much better than leaving them white and immature and in glass vessels or stone jugs before drinking. He completed his first blend in 1835, and it is really a vatted whisky as he had mixed it exclusively from malt whiskies from → Glenlivet, for whom he was an agent. The new creation was called 'Old Vatted Glenlivet'.

His son was said to have had the idea of mixing malt whiskies with → grain whiskies which could be produced by the → patent stills which had been invented in 1826. This new, light and above all consistent-tasting whisky was soon successful, particularly 'abroad' in the cities of England, where it quickly filled the gap left by the lack of brandy caused by the *phylloxera* catastrophe in France. Usher's company flourished and was active in the production of grain whiskies: with others they built the → North British Distillery in Edinburgh in 1886, the largest of its time. The Ushers also played an important part in the formation of → DCL, without losing their own independence. This finally happened in 1919 when J & G → Stewart acquired the company for DCL. The name Stewart still appears on the bottles of Usher's → Green Stripe and Usher's O V S, although they of course now come from → UDV, the successors of DCL. It really is a shame that these whiskies, that represent the original blends, are not available in Scotland, their home country. Anyone wishing to purchase them will have to take a trip to South America.

Usquaebach Scotch whiskies whose name comes from → uisge beatha, pronounced 'isch'ke-baah', to the corrupted English form 'whisky', via → 'usquebaugh', 'uiskie' etc. The producing company is → Twelve Stone Flagons and they are based in Pittsburgh, USA but also have a branch in Glasgow. At blind tastings of blends these whiskies have time and again got top marks. There is also a vatted malt aged 15 years and the blends are called Original Flagon, Special, Reserve and Ultra, all with the suffix → Premium. The → De Luxe is 8 years old and the Elite Silver and the Elite Gold are 25 and 50 years old. There is no age statement on the Crystal Decanter. They have brought out an Usquaebach Millennium, a blend of 21 Scotch whiskies which are up to 21 years old. In Japan there is a Scotch on the market which bewilderingly bears the same name, but which is not the same as the American Scotch; the Usquaebach Special is 12 years old and is made specially for → Nikka for sale in Japan by the → Ben Nevis Distillery.

Usquebaugh Society Dutch whisky club that calls itself 'Nederlandse Scotch Malt Whisky Vereniging'. It offers its own bottlings to its members and issues a club newsletter *De Kiln* about whisky, its history, distilleries and new bottlings, and organises trips and tastings.

V

Valleyfield Canadian distillery. It lies near Montreal, → Quebec and was bought in 1987 by → UD (whose name there is *Les destillateurs unis*), aged 30 years old, having been founded in 1945 by → Schenley as a Canadian subsidiary. It is the only survivor of eight distilleries which existed in the French-speaking part of the country at that time, which included such famous names as → La Salle and → Waterloo. Valleyfield produced all the Canadian UD brands as well as rum, vodka and gin. Their whiskies are reckoned to be among the best, strongest and most characteristic Canadian whiskies, accounted for by the copper → still and the fact that for a Canadian whisky, a relatively large proportion of corn and malt barley are used. Apart from the Schenley whiskies, Valleyfield also produces → Golden Wedding, → Canadian O F C, → Gibson's, → MacNaughton, → Order of Merit and → Royal Command. Of these Gibson's is the only brand that the UD successor still makes in Canada, having parted with all the others, selling them, along with Valleyfield and the → Palliser Distillery in Lethbridge, Alberta, to → Canandaigua.

Van Winkle and Son, J P American independent whiskey company based in Louisville, which was founded by the son and the grandson of one of the grand old men in the history of bourbon. Julian → 'Pappy' Van Winkle began his whiskey career in 1893 as a salesman at → W L Weller & Son. He soon became the driving force and leading figure of the company. Because the company did not have a distillery of its own, he secured its position by concluding a contract with the → Stitzel Distillery in Louisville and accomodated George → Dickel when he was no longer able to produce in → Tennessee because of → prohibition, which had begun there as early as 1910. During the dry years the distillery, which Van Winkle had by that time rented, was one of only six still allowed to produce alcohol. During this period he acquired the important brand → Old Fitzgerald. The final alliance of Stitzel-Weller occurred after prohibition and Van Winkle became president of the company, decorating the entrance of the new building with a sign reading: 'No chemists allowed ... This is a distillery, not a whiskey factory.'

The distillery today produces the whiskeys which Van Winkle Jr and Van Winkle III sell as their own brands. These are 'wheated whiskeys' in which the usual share of rye is substituted for wheat in the → mash bill. Rather confusingly the family-run company names one Old Rip van Winkle Distillery in Lawrenceburg on the bottles, which has never existed. The older bourbons surely come from the old distillery, whose production was discontinued in 1993 by → UD. Production was transferred to the nearby → Bernheim Distillery. The youngest version of the series must come from here; → Old Rip in a square bottle with a dark green label at 86°/43%. Another Old Rip is 12 years old and has a black label and is 105°/52.5%. The 10-year-old – '10 summers old', is called Old Rip van Winkle and is either 90°/45% or 107°/53.5% with a pretty label showing a long-bearded dwarf and the words 'asleep many years in wood'. Another Old Rip is 15 years old and is 197°/53.5%. The Van Winkle Special Reserve is 12 years old, comes from 'Lot B' and is 90.4°/45.2%.

The 13-year-old Van Winkle Family Reserve (95.6°/47.8%) and the 20-year-old version which is called Pappy Van Winkle Family Reserve (90.4°/45.2%), are even older and the latter shows a picture of 'Pappy' and, on the back label, him playing golf with a caddy and a dog pulling the golf-cart. The very limited edition of a further Pappy Van Winkle Family Reserve is even older, aged 23 years and is 95.6°/47.8%.

There is also an Old Rip Van Winkle Old Time Rye, a straight rye in numbered bottles at 90°/45%. This was followed by a further rye aged 12 years and at 95.6°/47.8%. A second brand from Van Winkle is → Old Commonwealth, which names the Commonwealth Distillery Co as its producer, this time based in Lawrenceburg. This company is also named on the → Lottas Home and → J W Gottlieb. Occasionally there are other special bottlings such as those for the Corlie Brothers from Sacramento. They also work together with the company that sell the last stocks from → Michter's under the name → A H Hirsch.

Vat 69 Scotch blend. It was chosen by the serious whisky merchant William → Sanderson and his son William Mark in 1882. Before it could be launched on the market there had been much activity that could be likened to one of the first systematic market research tests in the history of whisky. Both the Sandersons and a friend who was a master blender are said to have prepared about 100 blends and asked a large number of friends and acquaintances to sample them. They all chose the mixture contained in vat number 69. The choice of a striking bottle was also important for the marketing of the whisky and the form and black colour of the port bottles of the time was decided on. In the 1950s this whisky enjoyed cult status in West Germany; every young intellectual had an empty bottle of VAT 69 serving as a candle-holder on their desk. The brand survived the change of ownership first to → DCL and then to → UD/UDV and finally to → GuinnessUDV. Only the → standard blend version now exists in their range and they no longer stock the earlier varieties VAT 69 Gold and VAT 69 Reserve De Luxe. The VAT 69 Extra is still available, but unfortunately only in Korea.

Vatted malt Type of Scotch whisky that, in contrast to single malt (the product of a single distillery), contains the malt whiskies from at least two, and usually several, distilleries. It is therefore a special form of blending, the mixing of various whiskies. Apart from the special form of single cask bottling, all whiskies are mixed before bottling when the various casks are emptied and their contents are brought together. The single malts are no exception, as several casks are always required for them; the art of the master blender lies in selecting the casks so that their whiskies harmonise with each other and form a recognisable → house style, which is consistent in colour, aroma and taste. This process is usually called → marrying. In Scotland the combination of malt whiskies and → grain whiskies is called a → blend.

The word vatted comes from the vessel vat and in Scotland is used exclusively for vatted malt, whereas in Ireland it is used for blending in general. However vatted malts are hardly ever described as such on the bottle. More usually the term → Pure Malt will be found (which, however, is also sometimes used for single malts). From an historical point of view the vatting of malt whiskies is older than the blends, which were first created by Andrew → Usher and other pioneers. In contrast the distillates from various distilleries, which were sometimes extreme in character, were often mixed to try and balance out their differences and make them more attractive, more harmonious and more consistent and reliable in taste for the consumer.

It is wrong to assume that vatted malts are inferior to, for example, single malts. If the whiskies have been well chosen, then very good results may be achieved. Richard Joynson from → 'Loch Fyne Whiskies' recently revived an old form of vatted malt with his → 'living cask'. Several vatted malts can still be acquired. One very old brand is the Glenleven from Haig. The independent bottlers → Gordon & MacPhail have some vatteds in their range including the series → 'Pride of . . .', with an Islay, an Orkney and a Speyside. The vatteds Centenary from G&M and → Century from Chivas, each made of 100 separate malt whiskies are very special, and the → Signatory Supreme even contains 104 malts.

Venezuela Although it is not a whisky producer, for one of the smallest countries in Latin America, Venezuela has long occupied a leading position in Scotch consumption. From 1992 to 1994 it was even ahead of Brazil. The large international concerns not only sell their major brands, but also produce special ones exclusively for Venezuela, mostly in the country itself. → Seagram used to export a Scotch named

Glenson's in → bulk to Venezuela and later supplied the → Regency. → GuinnessUDV supply → Master's Choice, a blend of Scotch malt whiskies and Canadian → grain whiskies, and → Old Regal. → Allied Domecq PLC sell a → Hiram Walker's Premium.

Very Old Barton Kentucky straight bourbon from → Barton, akin to the company's 'house brand', which cannot be said to be more than an average whiskey. It is available in four versions: three aged 6 years and at 80°/40%, 86°/43% and 90°/45%. The → Bottled in Bond is 4 years old and has the obligatory 100°/50%.

Very Old St. Nick Bourbon calling itself 'Rare Bourbon Whiskey' and only using the word Kentucky in connection with its producer. This is said to be the Old St Nick Distillery in → Bardstown, which does not exist; this is another product from the company → Kentucky Bourbon Distillers. There are at least five versions of it: a 12-year-old with a brown wax stopper, a 15-year-old at 107°/53.5% and a black wax cap, an 18-year-old 'Antique Barrel' at 115.3%/57.65% with a black wax stopper. The stopper is blue in the case of the 20-year-old, which is 116.4°/58.2%. There is also a 9-year-old at 101°/50.5% and white wax, which is distilled using winter rye.

Victoria Wine UK chain of off-licences. Until 1998 its 1,400 branches (including those of subsidiaries such as Haddow) belonged to the → Allied Domecq PLC empire and were then united with the shops of their competitor → Thresher to form a new company called First Quench, which with 3,500 shops is almost a monopoly (and which has subsequently been acquired for £225 million by the Japanese bank Nomura, who are also the largest pub owners in the UK). The Victoria Wine Cellars, whose flagship shop in Calais, France was acquired by → Oddbins, did not belong to the chain. Victoria Wine mainly offers wines and spirits in the middle price category, but its range is less than that of its greatest competitor Oddbins. The whisky section has a fair range. There are occasionally bottlings such as the 10-year-old → Tomintoul which was supposed to have been selected especially for the company, but which only differed from the normal version in having a label to this effect. → Braemar is specially produced for the company.

Vidiz, Claive Brazilian whisky collector and founder of the influential *Associação Brasileira dos Colecionadores de Whisky* who, in his function as president, receives representatives of the Scotch and American whisk(e)y industry at his house. He is also a → Keeper of the Quaich. He proudly shows his visitors small bottles containing samples of earth from distilleries – Scottish soil. Whisky is his hobby and not his job (he worked in the pharmaceutical trade), and he has built up a collection that is so extensive that it is included in the *Guinness Book of Records*. The edition for 2000 quotes exactly 2,571 bottles, all Scotch whisky, but in the meantime he has added about 600 more to this figure. He has built a special house for his collection, which also includes an authentically-styled pub for his guests.

Vintage Term which used to be only customary for wine, but is now used for whisk(e)y. In this case it also refers to the harvest of one particular year. In the case of wine the harvest may indeed be totally different from year to year. The thought that this may also be true of whiskies at first seems bewildering. The distillery proprietors actually try to limit any such differences by selecting an increasingly large number of casks in order to 'marry' them so that a uniform → house style is maintained. But differences do exist, because of factors such as the grain used, the water, the use of peat, the shape of the still, and the temperature.

This can be observed in the case of → Macallan who for a long time had a bottling each year of an 18-year-old (and sometimes a 17-year-old) stating the vintage. Other distilleries such as → Aberlour, → Glenfarclas, → Glenmorangie, → Highland Park and → Springbank have also from time to time bottled particularly good casks as vintages. The breakthrough however occurred as a result of the activities of the → independent bottlers, especially the → Scotch Malt Whisky Society. They quote the date of distillation on their bottles (often to the exact day) and only offer vintages. The word, however, makes more sense when it is applied to really exceptional malt whiskies (or bourbons). It is used in this way by, for example, William → Grant & Sons for the rare (and expensive) → single casks of their → Balvenie and also for the → Glenfiddich Vintage Reserve. A particular form of vintage whiskey is the American → Bottled in Bond; it is legally stipulated that it may only consist of whiskeys from a single year.

Vintage Hallmark of St. James Whisky shop in central London which offers an excellent selection of whiskies. The successor to the legendary → Milroy's, it has secured the co-operation and advice of the two brothers, as well as of Doug McIvor who worked there latterly. The range not only includes whiskies from all the various companies, but also offers its own bottlings. The company has launched itself as an → independent bottler with malts from, for example, Aberfeldy, Banff, Glen Grant, Glendullan, Longmorn and Mannochmore, some of which have been diluted to 43% whilst others are available at cask strength. A 25-year-old vatted malt and a blend of the same age also belong to the portfolio.

Vintage Malt Whisky Company, The Scottish whisky company established in 1992 by Brian Crook in Glasgow, which as an → independent bottler offers several vatted malts without a statement of origin under their own label: → Finlaggan, → Glenalmond, → Glenandrew, → Lord of Islay, → Tambowie and → Tantallan. The name 'The → Cooper's Choice' is used to bottle single casks from various distilleries, and the range varies as bottlings which sell out are replaced by new ones. There is also a 'series within a series' of special bottlings from → sherry casks as well as a blend named → Royal Chalice. At present the main markets are in France, Italy and the USA.

Virginia Gentleman straight bourbon whose label calls it 'Virginia Whiskey', and with luck it is still possible to find a bottle which fully deserves this description. It comes from the stocks of the old Sunset Hill Distillery in Reston, Virginia, which was closed down in 1987. The production of the brand was then transferred to Fredericksburg, situated between Washington DC and Richmond. Here A → Smith Bowman produce all sorts of spirits in their distillery of the same name, and distil a whiskey that they get from → Heaven Hill in a → doubler resembling a → pot still, giving it a final distillation. It is not clear whether it has already been distilled once or twice at Heaven Hill, but it is known that the → low wines from Heaven Hill are brought by rail in tanks to Virginia, where they are redistilled.

Thus they can justifiably be named after Virginia, which was one of the first states to produce alcohol from grain (that is whiskey) and where George Washington was a distiller. Virginia Gentleman is the only one of its kind left from the many brands that Virginia used to produce. Although it presents itself in a traditional way, embodying old Virginia, it has only existed since the 1930s, when the hobby farmer and distiller Bowman Sr launched it on to the market. It soon won the hearts of the Establishment, especially particular of politicians in the neighbouring state. Today it is served, with a special label, in the National Press Club and is also represented in the bar of the President's yacht; General MacArthur was also keen on it. These traditions help it survive.

Vivendi French company which for a very short time owned the wine and spirits sector of → Seagram. It was originally engaged in the provision of water to French towns, and later with telecommunications and TV. As the owner of various channels it was also interested in acquiring a production company. This became possible when Seagram's owner, Edgar → Bronfman Jr, wanted to sell his business (part of which was Universal Studios in Hollywood and its extensive film library). So Bronfman sold to Vivendi. In a kind of auction, → Diageo and → Groupe Pernod-Ricard acquired what was left of the wine and spirits sector, including the Scottish companies, brands and distilleries, and activities in the USA and Canada (Foster in Australia had already taken over various parts and brands, and → Allied Domecq PLC had bought the Champagne houses Mumm and Jouët-Perrier). They obtained their share for $8.8 billion.

V O Canadian whisky formerly from → Seagram, brought on to the market in 1911, the same year that the company's founder Joseph Emm Seagram took his two sons into the company and gave it the name that this drinks concern, latterly carried: Joseph E Seagram & Sons. The new blend was brought out on the occasion of

V O 8

the marriage of his son Thomas, and the letters do not stand for 'Very Old' but for 'Very Own', because the whisky was originally only intended for his family. The bottles were decorated with the red-gold band of the racing colours of the horse-racing fan Joseph Seagram. Nowadays it is available in two versions: one at 40% and a V O light at a calorie-saving 30%.

V O 8 Scotch blend whose full name is Cockburn's V O 8. It comes from → Cockburn & Company (Leith) and means 'Very Old 8 Years'.

Volstead Act American law that was the final stone paving the way to prohibition, which made the United States dry from 17th January 1920 to 5th December 1933, ruined the American (and the Irish) whiskey industry, but created advantages for the Scottish and Canadian producers, from which they still profit. Of course the radical measures did not eradicate the consumption of alcohol; quite the reverse, they increased it, encouraged smuggling on a greater scale than ever known before and led to widespread crime and the strengthening of the position of gangsters, such as Al Capone.

Volume Term used nowadays to express the strength of alcohol contained in whisky. It has largely replaced the expression → °proof formerly used in the UK and still customary in North America, which presented difficulties in any case as both countries used different measurements. In the USA 100° were (and are) exactly 50%, but in the UK they were 57%; and 70° in Europe were 80° in the USA. Today the definition of the International Organisation of Legal Metrology (OILM) is used, based on measurement at 20°C and defining the proportion of water and alcohol. It is based on the methods of Gay-Laussac. The legal regulations are closely watched over by the → Scotch Whisky Association and prescribe a minimum of 40% alcohol for Scotch whisky. On some markets 43% is also customary. This is achieved by diluting the whisky, blend or single malt, with water to the required level upon bottling. In the case of bourbon, however, the water is added before the casks are filled. Scotch loses strength during storage, whilst in the USA this → angels' share often makes the bourbon even stronger. In recent years there has been an increasing tendency to leave the whisk(e)y as it is and not dilute it, and to bottle it at the strength which it has achieved naturally. The malt whiskies of the → Scotch Malt Whisky Society provided the model. They pointed out that whisky loses aroma when it is thus reduced, especially if it has first been → chill-filtered. Cask strength or → barrel °proof whiskies allow each consumer to dilute his whisky in the way that he wishes. The drinker should also realise that the whiskies will become slightly opaque and cloudy when water is added.

W

Waitrose UK supermarket chain with an excellent range of drinks, including whisky brands and a whole series of bottlings with their own label.

Wales When Alfred → Barnard travelled through the British Isles in 1887, there was not a single distillery in Wales that he could write about. It was not until the year that his book was published that the Frangooch Distillery in Bala at Lake Bala was built. It is said to have been very large and to have been in production until 1907. It supposedly had to close down because of the Temperance Movement in Wales. The history of whisky in Wales is much older than this, and it is said that distilling began even earlier in Wales than in Ireland, where they claim that one of their two national drinks (the other is Guinness) was first introduced by the Irish patron saint, St. Patrick.

In Wales it is believed that monks on Bardsey Island, off the Lleyn peninsula, began to practise the art which they had been taught by Greek traders. The name of the great pioneer is said to have been Reault Hir. Wales has everything needed to make whisky; barley, water and peat, as well as enough isolated spots to do so without being disturbed by estate owners, the police, excisemen or other government representatives.

There are documented sources which show that at the beginning of the 18th century two families were engaged in the making of whisky although they soon left the country to emigrate to America, where they settled in Kentucky. One of these men was → Evan Williams and the other was a forefather of the famous → Jack Daniel. A long time passed before Wales again became a country where whisky was drunk, and made. However initially only to the extent that whisky was brought from Scotland and processed in Wales. In 1974 Mal Morgan, Dafydd Gittins and his wife Gillian, founded the → Welsh Whisky Co Ltd in Brecon, with the far lovelier Welsh name of *Cwmni → Chwisgi Cymreig Cyf*. Two years later they brought out a blend named → Swn y' Mor and in 1986 → Prince of Wales, which they called a Single vatted malt because they had filtered the Scotch malt whisky from → Tomatin together with herbs, just as Reault Hir was supposed to have done on Bardsey. The company went into liquidation in 1996, but in 2000 a new Welsh Whisky Company started malt whisky production in a purpose built distillery in the Brecon village of Penderyn.

Walker & Sons, John Scottish whisky company that should not be confused with the enterprise which Hiram → Walker built up in Canada and which is now part of → Allied Domecq PLC. The company are famous for just one brand, although this is more successful than any other, → Johnnie Walker, which as the → standard blend Red Label and the → premium blend Black Label is number one worldwide. The spritely figure with his red hunting jacket, white breeches and riding boots helped make the brand famous with the slogan 'Born 1820 – still going strong'. This was the year in which the foundations of the company were set down when John Walker opened a small grocer's shop in his home town of Kilmarnock.

It took 30 more years for the business to develop and it was his son Alexander who really began working on a larger scale as a wholesaler in the whisky business. He opened an office in London and was able to sell his whisky on the many ships that set sail from Glasgow. It was Alexander's youngest son Alec who made the firm great, increasing its annual turnover to 100,000 gallons, acquiring → Cardhu Distillery and sending his older brother John to Australia where his whisky won one competition after another (as attested by the medals still shown on the bottles today). James Stevenson, who joined the firm in 1890, played an important part in its growth to become the largest blender and bottler in Scotland. It was he who commissioned the artist Tom Browne to create the advertising figure which, apart from occasional slight modifications, basically remained unchanged until 2000. He was also responsible for creating the slogan, and in 1908 for renaming the whisky, which until then had been simply called 'Walker's Kilmarnock Whisky', in its striking, instantly recognisable rectangular bottle.

Stevenson's organisational talent came to the notice of the government, and during WWI he was employed to administer the production of munitions, being appointed Surveyor-General of Supply at the War Office from 1919 to 1921. (In 1924 he was made a → 'whisky baron'). Together with Alec Walker he was responsible for the alliance with others from the → 'Big Five'; in 1925 Walker, → Buchanan and → Dewar found themselves together under the umbrella of → DCL. Walker was able to retain a certain degree of independence and occupied something of a special position shown, for example, by the fact that in some countries today Johnnie Walker is not distributed by the DCL successors → UD/UDV but by other companies (for example by → Bacardi in Germany until the end of 1999). There were already two single malts from Walker in DCL times: from their own Cardhu Distillery and from → Talisker, whose whisky also plays an important part in the Red Label and Black Label, but which was never under the control of the Walkers.

Walker, Hiram Canadian company named after the businessman who began as a small grocer and producer of vinegar in the USA and became the founder of one of the two great whisky companies in Canada. He was also a grain merchant and this took him to Canada where he became interested in whisky, recognising the potential of the British colony Upper Canada (now Ontario) with its railway network. In 1858 he founded the Windsor Distillery and Flouring Mill, but continued to trade in grain in Detroit. His Canadian business blossomed and soon developed into a town with a school, church and post office, which was named → Walkerville after its founder. Walker was a pioneer in several respects: he introduced distilling in → patent stills, recognised that the future did not lie with raw spirits but with whisky brands of a consistent quality, engaged in quality control by no longer supplying his whisky in casks and jugs but in bottles which he had filled himself, created a very successful classic with his → Canadian Club and had a share in making Canadian a whisky type in its own right, a blend of a basic whisky and straight whiskies.

At the time of his death in 1910 his company had become the second largest after → Seagram. In 1928 Harry Hutch allied it to his company to form Hiram Walker – Gooderham and Worts. They profited considerably from → prohibition in the USA, particularly towards the end when the American public was clamouring for the clean drink that they had grown to appreciate during the long dry years. Since this period more Canadian whisky has been drunk in the USA than bourbon. Hiram Walker was able to expand further, and built a distillery in Illinois, bringing out → Ten High and → Walker's De Luxe Bourbon, bought first J & G → Stodart and then in the mid-1930s → Ballantine. He then built the huge distillery complex on the Clyde at → Dumbarton, the technology in which was also a model for Walkerville. The company continued to grow in the latter half of the 20th century with further distilleries and brands being added in Scotland as well as the addition of new markets and the establishment of new partnerships to enable the production in, for example, → Spain and → Argentina. In America the → Maker's Mark Distillery in Loretto had been an important acquisition in 1881. As a result of various mergers Hiram first became a subsidiary of Allied Lyons and finally of → Allied Domecq PLC. The old name now stands for the concern's whisky interests in North America, and for its activities in Canada.

Walker's De Luxe Kentucky straight bourbon, which the Canadian company Hiram → Walker (owned by → Allied Domecq PLC) has sold in the USA since the 1940s. → Prohibition placed it in a favourable position and helped make it so successful that they built their own distillery in Illinois. When they then produced a bourbon it imitated the light style of Canadian whiskies so popular in America. The whisky is no longer produced by the company itself and they probably get it from → Heaven Hill in Bardstown. It is bottled at 80°/40% and its label always bears the date 1858, the year that Hiram Walker set up in business.

Walkerville Canadian distillery whose history goes back to 1858 and the construction of Hiram → Walker's Windsor Distillery and Flouring Mill. It stood on the Canadian side of Lake Erie but within view of Detroit, which at that time was still small. The business prospered to such an extent that Walker soon not only built houses for his employees, but also a church and a school. In 1869 a post office was opened and the little town was officially christened Walkerville. It is the only Canadian distillery that has survived from the pioneering years, is still in operation and looks just as it used to (from the outside at least). Inside the equipment is from the 1930s and is very similar to that used when the large plant at → Dumbarton in Scotland was set up. Since 1884 Walkerville's main product has been → Canadian Club.

Wallace Scotch whisky liqueur whose name is a reminder of the great William Wallace, who scored an important victory over the English army at Stirling Bridge on 11th September 1297. The Wallace Tower near Stirling was built to commemorate him and from here there is a view of → Deanston, where the single malt used for the liqueur (35%) is distilled. A picture of Wallace with the slogan 'The Spirit of Freedom' decorates the bottle, which was brought out to commemorate the 700th anniversary of the battle and was also inspired by the success of the film. The producer named is one Wallace Malt Liqueur Company in Deanston, behind which is the company → Burn Stewart.

W & M Barrel Scotch blend, behind whose name is Whyte & Mackay, the old Scottish company which in 1997 was renamed → JBB (Greater Europe) plc.

Ward Eight Whiskey cocktail; a kind of whiskey sour. Vigorously shake together 5cl bourbon, 2cl lemon juice and a spoonful of caster sugar with a splash of Grenadine and serve in a tumbler.

Warehouse Term used for the storage halls in which whisk(e)y matures: in the USA the term rackhouse is also sometimes used. In recent years it has been established that the warehouse and the cask are the two factors which probably influence the whisky to an even greater extent than the water, the yeast or even the shape of the → stills, and greater attention has been paid to their design. Each distillery has its own philosophy dictating the ideal warehousing conditions for its whisky. There has also been intensive research supported by scientific studies about the modern form of storage, for example in air-conditioned warehouses. Such buildings remain the exception. → Macallan has erected such modern buildings where the casks are stacked in so many layers that they can only be moved with the help of fork-lift trucks. In Dufftown they hold on to the old buildings which are only one storey high and in which the casks lie in just three layers on top of each other.

Most distilleries use such a form with one-storey buildings, few rows of casks, few windows and a mostly bare earth floor, which is thought to be more favourable than a stone floor. All these characteristics are important for the development of the whisk(e)y because they contribute to the microclimate and, together with temperature and humidity, are decisive in determining for example, slower or faster maturation. The geographic location is also important: a cask matures differently in the → Highlands than on an island which is exposed to long winter storms or which, as in the case of Bowmore, may be below sea-level. Inside the warehouses mould often develops which together with the alcohol in the air gives them a characteristic smell. This is something which few vistors are able to experience as the casks are stored in → bond. From the outside the warehouses usually look rather unattractive with their grey-black colours contrasting with the shining whiteness of the distilleries. However they are also part of many Scottish landscapes. In America the warehouses are mostly very high and often covered with sheets of corrugated iron, resulting in high temperatures inside. They leave their mark on the bourbon and make it necessary to keep a watchful eye on the barrels, whose position must often be changed so that they mature more uniformly.

Wash Liquid containing alcohol which is formed when the sugary → wort is fermented with yeast in the → washbacks. The sugar is thereby broken down into alcohol and carbon dioxide, both responsible for the process of fermentation being rather stormy. In Scottish malt distilleries the reaction may be so strong that washbacks have to be covered and their lids weighted down and the resulting froth inhibited by rotating blades. The length of fermentation, which normally lasts between 40 and 72 hours, can be either reduced or increased by lowering the temperature. The finished wash no longer contains any sugar and is therefore not sweet, but sour and bitter. It is often termed weak beer or → ale, although it is 7% – 9%. It is collected in a wash charger and is ready for distillation.

Wash still The still where the → wash is distilled, where the first of two or sometimes three runs take place, and the conversion of a weak alcoholic liquid into a high percentage spirit takes place. The wash is between 7% and 9%, and the wash still increases this to about 22% – 23%, in some distilleries to as much as 25%. Because the result of this process is called → low wines, the still can sometimes be called the low wines still; although this term is also occasionally used for the → spirit still. The low wines are carefully observed by the → stillman as they run through the → spirit safe into the low wines receiver. If the spirit is distilled only twice, the spirits then goes into the → spirit still, if it is distilled for third time it will run into the → intermediate still.

Washback Term used in Scotland; elsewhere → fermenters is used. Both terms refer to large vats where the conversion of the → wort containing sugar into an alcoholic liquid takes place. This fermentation results from the addition of yeast, and depending on the temperature can last between 40 and 72 hours.

In Scottish distilleries that only use malted barley the process is so turbulent that the washbacks are covered and the froth is inhibited by rotating blades.

In America the vessels used are also much larger. They were traditionally made of larch, oak or very often of Oregon Pine but recently stainless steel has been used as it is easier to clean, although it is thought by many that wood gives better results. The → wash remains at the end of the process, a sour, bitter liquid often known as beer or → ale, and which is between 7% and 9%. It is often described as a kind of weak beer.

Washington, George American President. Before he was elected head of the young state he was a farmer and distiller. In the 1750s he had stills on his farm at Mount Vernon, although they were used to distil rum, and not whiskey. The farm manager James Anderson, a Scotsman, persuaded him to plant rye and make whiskey from it. His distillery was profitable and when he died in 1799 a considerable amount of whiskey was maturing in his storehouse.

Washington knew a great deal about the production and consumption of alcohol, and had a positive attitude towards it. It is said that in 1777, when the newly-formed United States of America adopted the 'Stars and Stripes' as its flag, he was anxious that his soldiers were not getting enough whisky. He wrote to the President of the Continental Congress on August 16: 'The benefits arising from the moderate use of strong Liquor, have been experienced in all Armies and are not to be disputed'. He did, however, impose a tax on whiskey, and when the farmers showed their resistance to it in the → 'Whiskey Rebellion', he imposed it with force.

Water Considered by many to be the ingredient which is most decisive in forming the character of whisky. In Kentucky and Tennessee, for example, it is said to be the water, which runs over limestone and is therefore low in minerals, which contributes so much to the whiskey. Every visitor to the Jack → Daniel Distillery sees the imposing cave with its precious source of water. Some Scottish distilleries swear by the particular softness of the water and believe that the most suitable water is that which flows over → peat and granite. Others believe the exact opposite and claim that hard water gives whisky a special zest; examples of this are → Glenmorangie with its Tarlogie springs, → Glenkinchie and → Highland Park. Whatever their beliefs, they all take great care of their source of water and, like old William → Grant, buy land to guarantee their water supply and participate in the conservation of the area.

Recent research has shown that water doesn't play as an important a part as was previously thought and that it need not be particularly soft or particularly peaty. Of course its purity is very important and every distillery manager must see to it that the water flows. In Scotland many distilleries close during the summer months because they do not have enough water of good quality. Temperature is another important factor; the water should be cold. Water is needed at several different stages of production; in those places which still make their own malt it is needed to steep the → barley in the → kiln. It is also needed for the → mash. The alcoholic vapours from the → stills can only become liquid alcohol with the aid of condensers cooled by cold water (here the water can ust be river water). Water is also necessary directly after the final run to add to the whisk(e)y before the → new spirit, the → white dog, goes into the casks to mature.

Waterloo Canadian distillery in Ontario, located between London and Toronto, which was built as a mill in 1857. Like so many other mills at that time, the surplus grain was distilled. In 1883 it was bought by Joseph Emm → Seagram and considerably enlarged. It was the flagship of the growing company, with its mighty brick buildings and a chimney-stack that could be seen for miles. Nowadays it is only possible to get an idea of its size (and beauty) from old pictures, for after Seagram had decided to transfer the entire production of their Canadian whisky to → Gimli, Waterloo was closed down and everything, except for three warehouses, was demolished. One of these now houses the Seagram Museum, which is well worth a visit, showing the history of the company and of Canadian whisky. The → Museum Blend can also be bought there and the museum has published Lorraine Brown's book *The Story of Canadian Whisky*.

Wathen's Kentucky straight bourbon: the Wathens, the inheritors of → 'Old Grand Dad' Raymond B Hayden and the founders of the American Medicinal Spirits Company, and Charles → Medley. He and his son Samuel were members of the famous family who originated from English Catholics and emigrated to Maryland in 1635. The Medleys are related to the → Beams by marriage. Over the course of the years they have owned several distilleries, including one in Owensboro, but most recently have been working for other distilleries. Their most famous brand was → Ezra Brooks. In the 1980s their company lost its independence when it was taken over by its competitor → Glenmore, which was also based in the same town. It in turn was swallowed up by → UD in 1991, and they subsequently sold all the Medley brands. The only Medley that still bears the name of the family and the company is bottled in Germany by Dethleffsen in Flensburg. The → single barrel Wathen's, at 47%, may very possibly still contain stocks from the old Owensboro distillery, however it does not give its age, just the cask number and the date of bottling, 27th March 1997.

Watt, Andrew A Irish distillery owner who once owned the Derry Distillery which remained in family ownership until the early 1920s before being bought by → DCL and then several years later finally shut down. The family remained in the whiskey business until 1970 and sold, among other things, a blend named The → Tyrconnell. This was originally a → pure pot still whiskey and was particularly successful in the USA. It was named after a racehorse which belonged to Watt and which won the coveted Irish Classic, the Queen Victoria plate, in 1876. Now bottles again carry this name. The → Cooley Distillery acquired the rights to the brand and to the name Watt and in 1992 brought out The Tyrconnell, their first single malt. Another old whiskey from Watt has also been revived: the → Inishowen which Watt, however, spelt 'Innishhoven'.

Waverley Vintners Ltd UK subsidiary of the

Scottish Courage brewing concern. It has had various names in the recent past, and used to be based in Edinburgh, but now operates from Perth. It is mainly involved in the wine trade but has an interest in the whisky business, although not to such a large extent as before. Once several companies, with their own distilleries and a whole series of successful brands, had been joined together under the auspices of the group. Charles → Mackinlay & Co was an important subsidiary, with its → Isle of Jura Distillery and the blend → Mackinlay's. Another subsidiary was Bruce & Co in Leith with its brand → Northern Scot, and a further distillery belonging to the concern was → Glenallachie. At the beginning of the 1980s the beer brewers bought the small Scottish company of Peter Thomson in Perth with its two brands → Beneagles and → Huntingtower. These are the only two brands which Waverley still has made for it and which it distributes. In 1985 everything else, including the distilleries, was sold to → Invergordon, which brought out the Mackinlay's once again, and also has both the Ewan brands → Glen Clova and → Scots Club in its portfolio and which bottles both the Thomson blends for Waverley. The company now mainly concentrates on wholesaling and, for example, in 1997 took over the distribution of whiskeys from the Irish → Cooley Distillery. Until 1999 it was also responsible for the sale of → Glenfarclas in the UK.

Welsh Whisky Co, The See → Chwisgi Cymreig.

Western Club Kentucky straight bourbon, aged 8 years and bottled at 40%. Produced by an unknown distillery and sold exclusively in France by the company S L A U R in Le Havre.

Weston American distillery in the small town of Weston in the → Platte Valley, located in the west of Missouri, near the Kansas border. The place is named after its founder Tom Weston. The site on which the distillery stands is said to have been bought from its Native American owners for a single barrel of whiskey. It has existed since 1856 and has borne several names, including Blue Springs, Old Weston and McCormick Distillery. This company, which also owns the → Pekin Distillery in Illinois, shut down the plant in Weston in 1985, but remained in the whiskey business and made sure that all the equipment was well looked after so that a reopening may still be possible. However McCormick has recently signed a contract with → Heaven Hill which will allow them to continue to offer their various bourbons and corn whiskeys when the stocks from Weston and Pekin are exhausted. Before Fritz Maytag opened his → Anchor Distillery in San Francisco, the Weston Distillery was the most westerly in the country.

'What is Whisky?' Case A dispute that played an important part in the history of Scotch and Irish whisk(e)y, the effects of which can still be felt today: it ended with a definition of what may be described as 'whisk(e)y'. It was triggered off by complaints about blends of an inferior quality that were being offered for sale in many pubs. The case came to court in Islington, London in November 1905, and the two sides were represented by the producers of → malt whisky on one side and the producers of → grain whisky on the other. On 26th February 1906 the court decided in favour of malt whisky, with the result that the grain distillers immediately appealed. DCL was audacious enough to place an advertisement in the Daily Mail challenging people to try their → Cambus Grain 'to give the public the possibility of judging for themselves what a pure patent-still grain whisky was like'. This campaign continued for the length of the court case. The court made great efforts to arrive at a decision, which was announced in 1909. The Royal Commission issued a final report stating that they had had 37 meetings, had listened to the evidence of 116 witnesses and checked numerous documents. The verdict stated that they had found no evidence to prove that 'the form of still has any necessary relation to the wholesomeness of the spirit produced'. In other words, malts, blends and even grains were all whisk(e)y. Since that time this definition has been used in the English, Scottish and Irish laws, with a few additional details regarding the minimum maturation period and the use of oak casks. These definitions have also been adopted by the European Union and have certainly been a factor that has long hindered malt whisky in Scotland and led to the almost total extinction of Irish → pure pot still whiskey.

Wheated Whisk(e)y Term for a small group of bourbons that are not made according to the usual → mash bill of 51% corn, a share of rye and malted barley. In this case the rye is replaced by wheat. The process was mainly used for the brands produced by → Stitzel-Weller (later at the → Bernheim Distillery). These include → Old Fitzgerald, → Rebel Yell and → W L Weller. → Maker's Mark is also a wheated whisky (in this case without an 'e').

Whisk(e)y The word was first used in English-speaking countries to describe a spirit distilled from a barley mash. Today the word is used everywhere that this spirit from Scotland, Ireland, Canada or the USA is drunk or produced (sometimes using imported ingredients). 'Whisk(e)y' is not a protected description of origin unlike, for example, champagne. Whisk(e)y is also produced in countries such as Australia, Brazil, the Czech Republic, Germany, India, Japan, New Zealand and Switzerland, among others. The terms bourbon, Irish or Scotch on the other hand are protected and may only be used for whiskies/whiskeys produced in those places.

These whiskies differ greatly but all originate historically from distilled spirit, which was probably first made in Ireland, although the first documented source is Scottish and states: 'eight bolls of malt to Friar John Cor wherewith to make aquavitae'. New types of whisk(ey) have developed throughout history because the basic ingredient, malted barley, was not available everywhere and the search for cheaper alternatives led to the discovery that other types of grain may be distilled and other methods of distilling may be used. In Scotland they also soon began to use unmalted barley, because only malted barley was taxed. In the USA and Canada the new settlers worked with the grain that they found there or which they had brought with them. They used rye and later corn as well. Completely new possibilities were opened up by the invention of the → patent still in the 1820s, which allowed continuous distillation and was much more economic than distillation in → pot stills.

Most types of whisk(e)y are defined by the composition of the mash, which serves as the basis for fermenting and distilling. The stills, which are also important, no longer play a part since the decision of a London court in Islington in 1909 in the famous → 'What is whisky?' case stated that both malt whisky which had been distilled in → pot stills, and → grain whisky from → patent stills, were allowed to be named 'whisk(e)y'. Since that time malt whisky must be made of 100% malt, grain whisky may be made of all sorts of grain (mostly dependent on the market price) and Scotch blends are a mixture of both. The situation is similar in Ireland. In the USA bourbon may be produced everywhere, not only in Kentucky, but must be made from a mash consisting of at least 51% corn, whilst rye must consist of at least 51% rye. The term corn is used when more than 80% corn is distilled and Tennessee whisk(e)y must in addition undergo the → Lincoln County Process. There are also blended whiskeys in America, but fewer than in Scotland. All countries have additional legal requirements governing the period of maturation.

The word is an English corruption of the original → 'uisge beatha' from the Scottish Gaelic or 'uisce beatha' from the Irish Gaelic demonstrating that the difference in the two spellings has a long tradition. Ironically in English the first part of the word, simply meaning 'water', has been taken over, whilst the Gaelic stands for 'water of life' and is a translation of the Latin 'aqua vitae'. Via the Gaelic form 'usquebaugh', it became 'uisge', 'usky' and then 'whisky', and was included in this last form in *Dr. Johnson's Dictionary*. This was also the spelling used in Ireland at the beginning of the century, but several Dublin distillers had already begun to spell their product with an 'e' in order to distinguish themselves from their rural competitors. Both spellings also exist in the USA: on both sides of the Atlantic they were conventions which became rules. Nowadays the Scots and the Canadians write whisky, the Irish and most Americans prefer whiskey, and the rest of the world orientates itself depending on the kind of whisk(e)y it is trying to imitate.

Whisk(e)y cocktails

Whisk(e)y cocktails Whilst many whisky lovers consider even the addition of a few drops of water to be an inadmissable and unforgivable pollution of their beloved drink, many barkeepers and cocktail experts are of the opinion that whisk(e)y is not the ideal basis for a mixed drink. They consider bourbon to be more suited than Scotch or even Irish, and point out that there are only three real whiskey cocktails: the Manhattan, the Mint Julep and the Old Fashioned (which can be prepared in a variety of ways). Of course Whiskey Sour should also be mentioned, and it must be admitted that whisk(e)y is an ideal basis for various hot drinks, such as the famous Irish Coffee or the Toddy, which can also be made in several ways.

The following whisk(e)y cocktails are included in this book: Affinity, Apology, Bagpiper's Melody, Beatlestone, Beltline Cocktail, Blood and Sand, Bloody Macallan, Bobby Burns, Bourbon Crusta, Bourbon Highball, Bourbon Milk Punch, Bourbon Slushie, Braemar Cocktail, Brooklyn, Brown Fox, Bully, Bunny Hug, Captain Collins, Collins, Debonair Cocktail, Eldorado, Florian, Frisco Sour, Golden Nail, Hair of the Dog, Happy Morning, Horse's Neck, Hot Buttered Whisky, Hot Whiskey, Hot Whisky Skins, Irish Coffee, John Collins, Manhattan, Mary of Scotland, Mike Collins, Mint Julep, Morning Glory Fizz, Nineteen-Hole-Cocktail, Old Fashioned, Pirate's Poison, Rattlesnake, Rob Roy, Rory O'Moore, Rusty Nail, Sandy Collins, Sazerac, Scotch Sour, Smoky Martini, Stump Lifter, Sugar Buttie, Sweet Science, Thistle Cocktail, Tipperary, Toddy, Ward Eight, Whiskey Hot Toddy, Whiskey Sour and Whisky Mac.

Whiskey Hot Toddy A variation on the classic Toddy and Whiskey Sour. Take a good shot of bourbon with 2cl lemon juice and sugar syrup as desired and heat, add hot water and serve with cloves and a slice of lemon.

Whiskey Rebellion The Whiskey Rebellion deserves more than the footnote in American history which it usually receives. It first broke out in 1794 but the lead-up to it goes back to 1786. It demonstrates the spirit which inspired those who had left their old homes in Europe to settle in America's 'Wild West'. It also shows how quickly the newly-founded government discovered whiskey as a source of revenue, in this case not so much to finance an army, but rather to make the country into a trading nation. Alexander Hamilton, the Secretary for the Treasury, suggested imposing a tax on whiskey-making to George Washington, regardless of whether it was for commercial or for private purposes. It was the tax on alcohol which had caused many of the settlers in Pennsylvania to leave Scotland and Ireland, and they now thought that the government should be protecting them from their enemies instead of taking away their money, and so they refused payment. Their first victim was a tax official who they tarred and feathered after taking his gun away from him.

The actual rebellion itself began in 1794 when enraged settlers attacked the house of an exciseman and a distiller was killed. Soldiers were brought in and arrested 500 farmers. One of these was killed and a march to Pittsburgh was organised in which 7,000 people took part. So-called 'liberty poles' were erected. Hamilton requested the President (who had made whiskey himself!) to send troops, and finally 12,000 soldiers (more than in the struggle against the British) were brought in to quell the rebellion. Even in America, whose watchword was liberty, the natural right of a person to make his own whiskey without being taxed for doing so, had been abrogated.

Whiskey Sour Whiskey cocktail – perhaps the greatest classic of all. There are many recipes, including variations with Irish whiskey and with Scotch, but the traditional one uses bourbon. Take two parts bourbon to one part lemon juice, add a teaspoon of icing sugar and half a part of sugar syrup, shake with ice and serve in a champagne glass or tumbler.

Whisky Barons Nickname for the members of the → Big Five, the large Scottish whisky companies James → Buchanan & Co, John → Dewar & Sons, John → Haig & Co, John → Walker & Sons and → White Horse Distillers. Their successful businesses not only brought great wealth, but knighthoods as well. However the titles were not equally distributed to everyone: Douglas Haig was not honoured for his services to whisky or its export, but because of his part in a crushing victory over the Germans. There is a statue of him mounted on a horse in front of Edinburgh Castle. He was made an Earl, a title which he used to his advantage in promoting his family business. James Buchanan was 70 before he became Lord Woolavington in 1922. In contrast the brothers John Alexander and Thomas 'Tommy' Dewar had been knighted in 1901 and 1907. The older Dewar became Baron Forteviot of Dupplin in 1916, whilst 'Whisky Tommy' became Baron Dewar of Homestall three years later.

Peter Mackie, the driving force behind White Horse Distillers, never received one of the higher honours but was made a baron in 1920. Sir Alexander Walker received the KBE and James Stevenson, who had come from outside the Walker family, was made Baron Stevenson in 1924 but mainly for his outstanding services as Surveyor-General of Supply at the War Office from 1919 to 1921. In his book *The Whisky Barons* (1977), Allen Andrews also counts Walter Berry from → Berry Bros & Rudd as belonging to this group, although he was not honoured during his lifetime. He also helped make whisky a success in this period which lay between Strauss waltzes and the Charleston of the Twenties and between two 'American catastrophes', → prohibition and the *phylloxera* disaster, caused by the American vine louse, which destroyed the main competitor, brandy. It was David Lloyd George, a great supporter of prohibition, who as Prime Minister was responsible for putting forward the suggestions for the whisky barons' honours (apart from Stevenson's which came later).

Whisky Breton French whisky 'élaboré en Bretagne'. There are two known versions, one of which names Warenghem as producer and the other the Destillerie Menez-Bré, both at the same address in Lannion on the 'banks of the River Léguer'. Menez-Bré calls its whisky a blend, without mentioning where its ingredients come from.

Whisky crash It brought the years of the whisky boom in the 1890s to a quick and violent end and was personified by the →

Pattison brothers, Robert and Walter. These grocers from Leith had been tempted by the boom and the fabulous success achieved by Scotch blends, leading to the establishment of many famous brands and numerous new distilleries in the Highlands. The Pattisons established a business in Edinburgh with branches in Glasgow and London, employed more than 150 salesmen, Alfred → Barnard to write a brochure for their company, bought → Glenfarclas and lived in luxurious style. In 1898 Pattison, Elder & Co collapsed, with debts totalling £743,000. The two owners were taken to court and sentenced to several months imprisonment for fraud. However they were not the only ones to suffer serious consequences. The bankruptcy triggered a great crisis in the Scottish whisky industry and affected many others. Some were ruined, and many other companies lost their independence. Many distilleries, including those that had just been opened, had to be closed down. Many brands disappeared entirely. Not all had the strength or opportunity to develop a brand of their own like William → Grant & Sons and their Standfast, to compensate for the amounts that had been lost to → Pattison. It took years for the industry to recover from the crash.

Whisky de Bretagne French whisky which comes in numbered bottles, without an age statement and is bottled at 41%. It bears the signature of Jacques Fusilier, an 'Artisan Liquoriste' from Rennes, Britanny. He produces several alcoholic drinks and also has a whisky named → Glenroc which is not clearly defined (and whose name was recently changed to → Gwenroc). This is easy to obtain in the north of → France, but the Whisky de Bretagne is hard to find and little information exists about its content and production.

Whisky Galore A Scotch, a book, a film, a legend and a true story. The story is that: in 1941 the population of the Western Isles, like all British people, were subjected to whisky rationing. The little that was produced went to the USA as payment for war materials. One night a ship (which, as the islanders quickly found out, was carrying tens of thousands of cases of the best blends) ran aground just off the coast of Eriskay. Before the excisemen and

Whisky liqueur

the commander of the Home Guard could intervene, the precious freight had been unloaded, just before the → S S Politician sank. The commander of the Home Guard was the author Compton Mackenzie who, after the war, told the story in his book *Whisky Galore*.

The book became a bestseller and was made into a film. Alexander Mackendrick was the director of the film. Joan Greenwood starred as the postmaster's daughter, a leading role, for her wedding could not have taken place without sufficient whisky, and as the telephone operator, she listened in to everything the officer wanted to whisper to the custom service.

The rumour circulated that there must still have been bottles on board the ship. In 1990 enough investors had been found to equip an expedition, hoping that the bottles found would fetch a lot of money at auction. Only a few bottles were found and a blend named S S Politician was created which, although it was very expensive, was soon sold out. This success encouraged the creation of a successor, the Whisky Galore Atlantic Reserve, although there is doubt as to how much of the original whisky it contains. The name was also used by a company called Brands Development in Aberdeen.

Whisky liqueur A traditional whisk(e)y drink as old as whisk(e)y itself, for those who prefer something sweeter. This used to be drunk in its immature state, as a fresh distillate, it was often raw and sharp and the addition of herbs, honey or milk helped to make it milder. The 'Welsh Whisky' → Prince of Wales is a modern example of refinement with herbs, and → Drambuie, the classic among the liqueurs, is made with herbs and honey.

Such liqueurs, not only based on whisk(e)y, were widespread in the Middle Ages. On the other hand the liqueurs which are based on cream are a modern invention. The first of these, created in 1974, was → Bailey's, and it became so successful that a whole series of successors followed, especially in its home country, Ireland. The creams contain far less alcohol than the herb liqueurs, some of which are bottled at as much as 40%, whilst the cream variety seldom are stronger than 17%. A third kind are the liqueurs which are flavoured with lemon peel. There is such a liqueur from → Wild Turkey and → 'Rock and Rye' is available from several companies. On the other hand the very successful → Southern Comfort is not, as it is often assumed, a whiskey liqueur.

The number of liqueurs on the market constantly increases. Examples are the Glenfiddich Liqueur, the light Fairlie's, the Wallace and Cock o' the North, to name but a few. They are in addition to the herb liqueurs which have been on the market much longer, such as Dunkeld Atholl Brose (also a classic), Glayva, Irish Mist, Lochan Ora and Stag's Breath. Cream liqueurs include Carolans, Columba Cream, Dubliner, Emmets, Heather Cream, Meadows and Merry's.

Whisky loch This expression is used to describe over-production in Scotland's whisky industry. From the industry's point of view this endangers price stability, puts jobs at risk and causes an increasing number of distilleries to be mothballed, or even close down altogether. The problem the producers face is that whisky takes time to mature and no-one can predict exactly how much malt whisky from one distillery will be required in, let's say 12 years, for bottling as a single malt, for blending or for sale to other companies. The result of this uncertainty has always been the problem of over- or under-supply.

Whisky Mac Traditional whisky cocktail. It is a mixture of Scotch and an alcoholic liquid which is possibly not known elsewhere, ginger wine. An English person will most likely take Stone's, whilst a true Scot will only use that from Crabbie, an old company which had its production plant in Leith and was bought by Glenmorangie plc a few years ago. The correct proportion of Scotch to ginger wine is best found by experimenting.

Whisky magazine British magazine, first published in 1998, which filled a long inexplicable gap in the market. It was surprising that in the UK of all places there had been no regular publication aimed at the general public. Its founder and managing director was publisher Damian Riley-Smith, and the editor and publisher is Marcin Miller. They have gathered an illustrious team around themselves, which includes Charles MacLean as 'Editor-at-Large' and Michael Jackson.The themes covered range from distillery portraits and interviews with industry personalities (including innovative dealers), to such specific subjects as 'Women and Whisky', 'Whisky & Rock' or the relationship between the taste of a whisky and the location of its distillery.

Whisky Newsletter A monthly publication brought out by whisky expert Allan S Gray for Charterhouse Securities (ING Barings) in Edinburgh, which previously came from Campbell, Neill & Co, from 1990 to 1992 from Charterhouse Tilney and from then to 2000 from Sutherlands Limited. It is read by those who want to know all about Scotch whisky: Background history, analyses, personal histories, turnover and prospects, purchases and sales, products – and stock exchange ratings. The monthly newsletter is supplemented by the annual *Scotch Whisky Industry Review* with comprehensive reports, statistics, company information and the sponsoring activities of various companies. The subscriptive rate for both is currently £600 pa and is sold mostly to stockbrokers and investors.

Whisky regions While in the USA only two regions, → Kentucky and → Tennessee, are used as terms to describe origin, in Scotland several whisky regions aredefined. The differentiation between the → Highlands and the → Lowlands originates from old disputes between the proprietors of the large distilleries in the south and the smaller distilleries in the north, which often operated with an underdeveloped transport network. The division was also reflected in the different taxes imposed by the government in London. The disadvantages incurred by the smaller distilleries encouraged illicit distiilling and suggest the political difficulties and battles faced: the struggle for independence and freedom on one side and the control of rebels on the other. The introduction of the famous → Highland Line, a demarcation between the Highlands and the Lowlands introduced by the Select Committee of the House of Commons shown on maps published in 1793 and 1799, was an attempt to create a clearer legal situation. It was not absolutely identical used today.

The current dividing line between the Highlands and the Lowlands begins to the west of Glasgow, at Gourock, and runs to Dundee. The Highlands themselves are mostly subdivided into the Northern, Western, Eastern and Southern Highlands, with the separately defined area of → Speyside. Only a few plead for more detailed divisions. → Campbeltown on the Kintyre peninsula is a special region where there used to be a very large number of distilleries. Of these only two are still in operation, which is why this area is often included in either the Lowlands or the Western Highlands. The → Islands are without doubt a region in their own right, and → Islay is often mentioned separately because of its many distilleries. The other islands are the Orkneys, Skye, Mull, Jura and Arran. An attempt is often made to characterise each region's style with the aim of capturing for example, a typical Speyside or Islay whisky, but one only needs to compare the Islay whiskies → Laphroaig and → Bunnahabhain: to show how hard this definition sometimes is.

Whisky Trail A special route passing distilleries especially attractive to tourists. It was established many years ago by the British Automobile Association, and is promoted by the Scottish Tourist Board in a leaflet updates annually. The route includes Glenlivet, Glenfiddich, Strathisla, Glen Grant, Glenfarclas and Cardhu. Almost in the middle, on the outskirts of Craigellachie, is the Speyside Cooperage where it is possible to watch whisky casks being made.

Whisky Watch Quarterly newsletter that aims to give information about all the new whiskies and describes some of them more closely in tasting notes. It reports on new developments within the whisk(e)y industry and draws attention to related events, books and CDs. The illustrator is Alfred Prenzlow and the editor is Walter Schobert.

White Japanese blend which can claim to be the country's oldest brand, having been launched by Shinjiro → Torii, the founder of → Suntory and a pioneer of Japanese whisky, in 1929. The label states that the whisky 'originated in 1923', which refers to the year that Torii's → Yamazaki Distillery, the first in Japan, was opened. Shinfouda was its original name and it contained malt whiskies from Scotland, and its own distillery. Its was popularly known as 'White Label', and for a long time this was also its official name. Today the label shows only the name White. The blend which was said to have tasted 'very Scottish' early on is now much milder.

White and Gold Scotch blend that now comes from → Glenmorangie plc and formerly, like → MacAndrew's, was produced by Alistair Graham Ltd.

White Bush Former name of the blend from → Bushmills that was also once called 'Old Bushmills' and is now officially named Bushmills Original. It is usually ordered by its old name which comes from the colour of the label, differentiating it from its stablemate → Black Bush, and signalling that it is light whereas the other is more full in character.

White dog Term used in the USA for the freshly distilled spirit which has not yet matured in a cask. The word, an equivalent of the Scottish expressions → clearic spike, → baby whisky or → new spirit, is used by legal distillers but is also, along with → moonshine, a synonym for illicitly-distilled whiskey.

White Hall Indian whisky which deserves the name as it only contains grain distillates, which is something of an exception in India, with malt whiskies from Scotland and Indian → grain whiskies and, in addition, a small amount of malt whisky from the → Rampur Distillery.

White Heather Scotch blend from → Campbell Distillers and therefore → Groupe Pernod-Ricard, who sell it with particular success in France. It used to be available in various age categories but is now only sold as a → standard blend.

White Horse Scotch blend. It is one of the leading brands, currently number 12 in the rankings of world bestsellers, and is one of the rare examples of a product which later gave its name to its producer. White Horse Distillers have been thus named since 1924 and were previously named after Peter Mackie, the founder of the company. Peter Mackie came from an Edinburgh family who lived near the famous 'White Horse Cellar' in the Canongate on the Royal Mile. This never belonged to the family as Mackie's company once claimed in its advertising.

Mackie learnt his craft at → Lagavulin Distillery which belonged to his uncle James → Logan. In 1883 he established Mackie & Co (Distillers) but only registered his brand, named 'Mackie's White Horse Cellar Scotch Whisky', in 1891. He inherited Lagavulin in 1889. In 1892 he and a partner built the → Craigellachie Distillery and in 1915 he took it over completely. In 1920 he bought → Hazelburn in → Campbeltown, where he set up a laboratory. (It was here that Masataka → Taketsuru learned enough to set up → Suntory and → Nikka in Japan.) Mackie was deeply involved in the dispute about what could be called whisky, in which the → grain whisky producers supported by → DCL won against the malt whisky distillers. Mackie stopped → DCL from buying his company, but three year after his death in 1924, → DCL bought it and renamed it White Horse Distillers. In 1926 they were the first to replace corks with screwtops, thereby considerably increasing their turnover within the space of a few months. White Horse, then a subsidiary of the DCL successor → UD and now a subsidiary of UDV, also holds the licence for → Glen Elgin, whose single malt still shows the white horse, although it has disappeared from the entrance to Lagavulin.

The blend contains malt whisky from Craigellachie distillery (sold by → GuinnessUDV to → Bacardi) and other two of Mackie's distilleries. It is blended in Leven, but used to be blended next to the Port Dundas Grain Distillery, Glasgow, but now it is blended in Leven. It is available as a → standard blend as Fine Old and in Japan as a → premium blend; there is also a Mild version in Japan. In the USA it is possible to buy a 12-year-old Extra Fine. There is also a 12-year-old → Logan's, which may be described as the older version of White Horse.

White House Indian whisky from → Polychem. Its label states that it is a blend of Indian malt whisky and pre-blended whisky imported from Scotland. It has been available bottled at the 42.8% customary in India, since 1984. Since 1993 the company has had a joint venture with → IDV (therefore now with UDV) which is certainly responsible for the Scottish share in this whisky, which is now being successfully exported to eastern Europe.

White Label Scotch blend often also known by its full name Dewar's White Label. The brothers John Alexander and Thomas 'Tommy' Dewar, created it, after taking over their father's business in Perth on his death in 1880. Their father had success with Dewar's Whisky blends, but it was the brothers who made White Label a brand known throughout the world, receiving the royal warrant in 1896. White Label was marketed with imagination and by using new media (such as film which had only been discovered in 1895), as well as some Scottish clichés: the main character in adverts was often an elegant Highland Regiment officer or, more frequently, a Highlander in the outfit which had first been developed in this form for George IV and Queen Victoria.

The whisky, whose major ingredient has traditionally been malt whisky from Dewar's own → Aberfeldy Distillery and of which Ancestor is a → de luxe version, is one of the best-selling worldwide in some markets such as Greece, and above all in the USA, it is the number one. UDV, the successors of → UD and → DCL (in which the firm was amalgamated in 1925), held the rights to the company name and the brand. In 1997 the European and the American Monopolies Commissions compelled them to give them up when → Guinness and → Grand Metropolitan merged to become the largest drinks concern in the world and dominated the market in the USA with the two strongest brands Dewar's White Label and → J & B. → Bacardi are the new owners, and they also acquired the Aberfeldy Distillery as well as → Aultmore, → Craigellachie and → Royal Brackla distilleries.

White Whisk(e)y A term for crystal-clear, colourless whisk(e)y. In the USA the new distillate is called → white dog. In Scotland it is also called → baby whisky, or → clearic spike. Some legal distillers also try and give the impression that they are offering young, white whisk(e)y for sale. This has been distilled perfectly legally and examples of this include → Georgia Moon in the USA, → Bunratty Potcheen, → Hackler which → UD quickly dropped → Knockeen which is also produced in Ireland and → Cape Breton Silver from → Glenora. However many whisky lovers consider the first white whisk(e)y to have been → Glen Kella from the Isle of Man, which is no longer allowed to call itself whiskey and has been rechristened → Manx spirit. However this spirit, which had become white after a further distillation of cask-matured Scottish whiskies, was not the first of its kind. In Canada there had been a white version of → McGuinness, the blends The White and Carnaby Street used to come from Scotland and in the USA there had been a white → Tom Moore.

Whyte & Mackay Scottish whisky company which has also given its name to one of the leading brands. It no longer exists as a company name since → American Brands, latterly → Fortune Brands, decided to rechristen its Scottish subsidiary JBB (Greater Europe) plc, naming it after their most successful product, the bourbon → Jim Beam. Since October 2001, the brand has been owned by → Kyndal.

The brand history begins in 1844. This is not the actual year in which Whyte & Mackay was founded (that was 1882). It refers to the establishment of Allan & Poytner. Charles Mackay had worked for them for a long time before he went into partnership as a whisky merchant with James Whyte and a short time later created the blend. Throughout the course of the years it became very successful in the USA, South Africa and → New Zealand, and following the war, in the UK. In Glasgow it is one of the most popular blends.

Whyte & Whyte

In 1960 the prospering company bought → Dalmore Distillery from the Mackenzie Brothers. Further distilleries were added in the 1970s when Whyte & Mackay lost its independence and was bought by Scottish & Universal Investment; which also acquired → Fettercairn and → Tomintoul. In 1987 it was able to enlarge its portfolio considerably when → Guinness, after having taken over → DCL, was forced to part with a range of its brands. Whyte & Mackay acquired the worldwide rights to The → Claymore, → John Barr, → Stewart's Finest Old, → Jamie Stuart and → Old Mull and the rights in the UK to → Buchanan's, → Crawford's 3 (and 5) Star and The → Real Mackenzie. The blend → Haig's, which it also took over at the time, was resold to → UD.

In 1990 there was a further change of ownership when → American Brands, via its UK subsidiary the cigarette concern Gallaher, bought Whyte & Mackay. They immediately found themselves in another takeover battle to purchase the distilleries of → Bruichladdich, → Invergordon, → Isle of Jura, → Tamnavulin and → Tullibardine, which they succeeded in doing in 1994. Immediately afterwards the new parent company closed down three of the four malt distilleries and only kept the Isle of Jura distillery in production.

In 1997, the American parent company undertook a restructuring and as JBB (Greater Europe) plc concentrated on the large brands. They kept the single malts from Bruichladdich, Dalmore and Isle of Jura for themselves, and left the others and a large number of smaller brands to Invergordon, who undertook the entire blending and bottling operations in Leith. The old blend remained their flagship brand, and was famous for the procedure in which the individual malt whiskies were first married in → sherry casks; the → grain whiskies underwent the same procedure. They were then blended before spending another long period in oak casks and finally bottled.

Before the → Kyndal takeover, the blend was available in many versions. There is a → standard blend without an age statement, which was launched with a new 'blue' look and the slogan 'New distinctive look – same distinctive whisky', in the spring of 1998. The older versions were aged 12, 15, 18, 21 and 30 years. The 30-year-old was also available in a crystal decanter. The → High Strength was 52.5%, and the others, including the Tribute Decanter, have the usual 43%.

Whyte & Whyte → Independent bottlers based in Elk-Grove Village, Chicago, USA. They set up in the early 1990s and imported malt whiskies from Scotland an sold them in the USA. Success was rapid but came to an abrupt end in 1996 when → Sazerac, the official importer of → Glenfarclas, went to court in order to prevent Whyte & Whyte from using the name of the distillery on the bottle as it was a protected trademark. Sazerac, and therefore J & G Grant, the owners of Glenfarclas, won the case. Whyte & Whyte were given a six-figure fine which resulted in them having to discontinue part of their operations. The verdict has important implications: other distillery proprietors could go to court to prevent an independent from labelling their bottlings with the exact origin of the whisky.

Wild Turkey American whiskey which is available as a Kentucky straight bourbon in several versions and as a straight rye. The brand is relatively young, but is one of the most successful in the USA, and ownership, has now passed to the French concern → Groupe Pernod-Ricard, all over the world. It was introduced in 1942 by Thomas McCarthy, president of → Austin, Nichols & Company, a firm which was established in 1855 and whose activities included the sale of wine and spirits. Under McCarthy's management it also began to produce gin, blended and straight bourbons, but was still getting the whiskeys from other distilleries. The company history relates that one day McCarthy was out hunting turkeys with three friends, and the whiskey he had taken with him was so much appreciated that a year later his friends asked McCarthy to bring along the same sort. He found out which bottle he had packed that first time and immediately christened it Wild Turkey.

In 1970 the company acquired a distillery itself for the bourbons (the rye was obtained from → Michter's Distillery). They chose a distillery near Lawrenceburg which had been founded by D L Moore and was bought by the Ripy brothers in 1905. Nowadays it is either known as the → Boulevard Distillery, the Austin Nichols Distilling Company or as the Wild Turkey Distillery. In the mid 1980s the distillery and its brand were bought by Pernod (→ Heublein, later a subsidiary of Grand Metropolitan, acquired a share and still holds the distribution rights for the USA). However the strongest and most constant influence on the company has been its master distiller of many years, Jimmy Russell. He began working there in 1955, when the company was still being run by the Ripy brothers, and plays a similar role to → Booker Noe at → Jim Beam, → Elmer T Lee in → Leestown and Bill Samuels at → Maker's Mark. Production increased under his direction, but is still relatively small with about 60,000 barrels a year. Russell works with a → sour mash share of 33% and his formula for bourbon is 75% corn, 13% rye and 12% malted barley; for the rye, which is now also made at the Boulevard Distillery, he takes 65% rye, 23% corn and 12% malted barley. He also swears by a special yeast and stores his whiskey in unheated → warehouses and makes sure that the barrels are moved regularly so that they all have approximately the same conditions.

Russell believes that Wild Turkey is at its best bottled at 100°/50%, the classic → Bottled in Bond strength which is why the Russell's Reserve named after him is this strength. The 4-year-old is not as strong with one bottled at 80°/40% and another 86.8°/43.5%. The classic is the Old No. 8 Brand bottled at 86.8°/43.4% whilst an 8-year-old and a 12-year-old come at a bottled strength of 101°/50.5% as does the Wild Turkey 101. This is also the strength of the 8-year-old Wild Turkey 1855 Reserve and the Tradition Straight. There are also two → single barrels, the → Kentucky Legend and the → Kentucky Spirit, and the → barrel °proof → Rare Breed which is the leading product of the series. Only for the Japanese market there is a 17-year-old bottled at 101°. There is a Wild Turkey Liqueur whose label says it contains honey but it also smells strongly of lemon. From 1971 until the end of the 1980s the Wild Turkey in ceramic containers shaped like a turkey was very popular with collectors.

Willett American distillery near Bardstown which is dwarfed by its neighbour, the → Heaven Hill Distillery. It has been shut since the 1980s, but the Willett family have been working slowly towards reopening it. They have already had trial runs, and a traditional Kentucky-style → beer still and a → pot still have been installed with full priduction no far off. The bourbons → Johnny Drum and → Noah's Mill, which the company → Kentucky Bourbon Distillers have in their programme and in which the Willetts have a share, come from the stocks from the old distillery.

William Grant's Scotch blend from William → Grant & Sons, which appeared on the market at the end of the 19th century. It used to be called → Standfast, a name chosen for several reasons, one being that the Grant clan's battle cry was 'Stand fast Craigellachie!' It is also possible that the Grants used the name to encourage themselves after the collapse of →Pattison, which had been the main buyer of its malt whiskies from → Glenfiddich and → Balvenie, when they were in a difficult situation and forced to create a new blend of their own. That was 100 years ago. They have not only kept going, but also established themselves with the → standard blend which is now called Family Reserve and occupies fourth position in the world rankings for both the UK and internationally, and is extremely popular in South America. In Italy there used to be a BP, which stood for 'Best Procurable'. It was a 12-year-old as are nowadays the Royal and Old Gold. The Classic Reserve is 18 years old and the Rare Gold 25 years old. There is also a → high proof named Superior Strength at 50%. In 2001 the company followed and launched and Ale Cask Reserve and a Sherry Cask Reserve.

William Lawson's Scotch whisky that is available in two versions: as a → standard blend with the adjunct 'Finest Blend' and as a 12-year-old Scottish Gold. The brand has a long history. During → prohibition it was owned by an Irish company and large amounts of it were shipped to the Bahamas, from where it could easily be smuggled into the USA. At that time the whisky was simply called Lawson's, but the name was changed so that it would not be confused with → Peter Dawson. The brand then belonged again to a company with the same name, William → Lawson Distillers. Via the Vermouth giants Martini & Rossi, it was a subsidiary of → Bacardi, and on their behalf it ran the → Macduff Distillery, whose single malt → Glen Deveron, surely plays an important part in both blends. After Bacardi had bought John → Dewar & Sons from → Diageo in 1998, they consolidated their Scottish activities and struck the name Lawson from the commercial register. It is not yet certain whether the brand will also be discontinued.

William Low's Finest Scotch blend made for William Low, a supermarket chain which was to be found in most parts of Scotland. It was established in the 19th century and was able to maintain its independence until 1994 when it was taken over by → Tesco, who discontinued the brand.

William Maxwell Standard Scotch blend that is named after the subsidiary of Peter J → Russell & Co.

Wilson American blended whiskey that is easily confused with Wilson's from the New Zealand → Wilson Distillery. The American brand is from → Heaven Hill.

Wilson & Morgan Scottish whisky company, one of the countless newcomers since 1995 working as → independent bottlers, who are expanding a series of single malts under the name 'Barrel Selection'. They give an address in Edinburgh but as the bottlings are at 46% this points to a possible connection with → Cadenhead. The labels name the age of the malt whiskies and the year of distillation and bottling.

Wilson Distillers New Zealand distillery in Dunedin on the South Island. It was first opened in 1968 when the Wilson family, who had been doing good business with beer and especially with malt extracts, decided to convert the Willowbank Brewery. As they did not find an adviser in Scotland and were left to their own devices when equipping the old building, the → stills were made of stainless steel, which apparently had catastrophic results. In any case the first product, a blend named South 45, was not successful. In 1981 the Canadian drinks multinational → Seagram, always on the look out for new production sites and new markets, invested not only money in the project, but also know-how: since that time at least some parts of the stills are made of copper.

The second blend named Wilson's was more successful, and is now as strong as Scottish imports (but not in alcohol volume – it is just 37.5%). The decision to produce a single malt at the distillery (it can make grain and malt whiskies as well as gin and vodka) would not have been possible without the parent company's international connections and knowledge of markets and marketing. This single malt has been on the market since 1991 as a 10-year-old and is called → Lammerlaw. It is relatively successful in South East Asia and is also obtainable in England and Germany. However production had to be stopped in 1995 as Seagram's South Korean partner was not able to fulfil its purchasing contract, and this means that they have been left sitting on surplus stocks. As soon as the surplus stocks have been reduced they plan to begin production again.

Windsor The name of two quite different brands, and although one is a Canadian whisky it i named after the royal castle in England, and has nothing to do with the → Hiram Walker distillery of the same name. It is produced by → Alberta Distillers, the Canadian subsidiary of → Jim Beam, and is available in two versions, the → De luxe and the Supreme, (which is 4 years old and very successful). They are of different strengths in different countries. The other one also comes from a Canadian company, but is a Scotch blend. Its full name is Windsor Premier. It is a 12-year-old, formerly produced by → Seagram.

Windsor Castle Scotch blend, one of three brands from R H → Thomson & Co in Edinburgh, who belonged to the → DCL empire and are therefore now part of→ UDV.

Wine Society 1874 Society established in 1874 with the participation of the architect of the Royal Albert Hall, whose purpose was to supply its members with good and reasonably priced wines. These were stored beneath the Albert Hall. The Society soon became successful, its membership grew steadily and included many politicians, authors and poets.

The current membership numbers are around 160,000 and the cellars under the Albert Hall (and others used in the meantime) have had to be given up. Nowadays the 'International Exhibition Co-operative Wine Society Ltd', as it is officially registered, has huge storage rooms in Stevenage to the north of London, with excellent temperature-control in which members can lay down their precious wines until they are ready to be drunk.

The company sells fresh distillates of malt and → grain whiskies and allows them to mature in their cellars. The Society's Scotch Whisky is a light blend, whereas The Society's Highland Blend has more body. The Society has also traditionally always had malt whiskies from → Mortlach in its range, one bottled at 43% and 'over 10 years old' and a → cask strength whose alcohol content varies from cask to cask, but is usually bottled at around 55%. The bottlings are about 15 years old and are from Oloroso → sherry casks which previously contained the Society's own sherries.

Wiser's Canadian whisky that originally came from the distillery of the same name in Prescott, Ontario. Its founder, J P (John Philip) Wiser, was the son of Dutch immigrants and had success as a cattle breeder as well as with his distillery which was well situated for transport on the St. Lawrence River. He had taken over the distillery from a business partner, and in 1864, after a fire, had completely renovated it using modern techniques. He was probably the first to use the term 'Canadian Whisky' (in 1893 at the World Fair in Chicago). The company now has several versions of it made for them by their parent company Hiram → Walker in → Walkerville. There is a 6-year-old Wiser's Special Blend which is a rye Whisky, a 10-year-old Wiser's De Luxe and an 18-year-old Wiser's Very Old.

W L Weller Kentucky straight bourbon that bears a great name: that of William LaRue

Wolfe's Glen

Weller who began trading in whiskey in 1849 and was the son of whiskey pioneer Daniel Weller. Weller's business quickly prospered and he created several very successful brands, but never owned a distillery of his own. In 1893 Julian → 'Pappy' Van Winkle, came to work for him, and began his career as a company representative and later with a partner was later able to take over his employer's business. He had been the driving force behind a contract with the Stitzels, the successful distillers. After → prohibition the two companies joined together and in 1935 opened a new distillery at → Louisville to make their own whiskeys and → Old Fitzgerald, which Van Winkle had secured during the dry years, as well as creating → Rebel Yell. They all represent a separate type of whiskey known as → 'wheated whiskey', in which the normal share of rye is replaced by wheat.

All three were produced at the → Stitzel-Weller Distillery until 1993, when it was closed by its new owners → UD. The three brands were then produced at → Bernheim, which also belonged to UD and which had been rebuilt a year before. However this situation did not last long. The distillery and the bourbon W L Weller belonged to the package which the UD successor → UDV sold in March 1999 to a syndicate consisting of → Heaven Hill, → Sazerac and the David → Sherman Company; these brands and → Old Charter ended up in Sazerac's portfolio. Whether master distiller Edwin S Foote will be able to continue using his formula under the new owners remains to be seen. His → mash bill consisted of 75% corn, 20% wheat and 5% malt barley. The whiskey was available in four versions: as a Special Reserve aged 7 years and at 90°/45%, as → Old Weller Antique – The Original 107 Bourbon, 7 Summers Old and Genuine Old Line Sour Mash bottled at 107°/53.5%. Their leading product is the 10-year-old Centennial bottled at 100°/50%, which also belonged to UD's → 'Bourbon Heritage Collection'. The new owners have a 12 and a 19-year-old whisky.

Wolfe's Glen Scotch Single Grain whose label mentions its origin in the → Highlands. It comes from the → Invergordon Distillery, is 10 years old and matures in oak casks. It was brought on

363

to the market in 1996 and is at present only available in the USA.

Woodford Reserve Kentucky straight bourbon which has only existed since 1997 but which has revived one of the oldest and respected names in the history of American whiskey: → Labrot & Graham. It was reopened in October 1996, a good day for Kentucky and bourbon. Around the neck of the bottle hangs a map which includes the date 1812 as the distillery's year of foundation. The date on the distillery at Glenn's Creek near Frankfort is 1878 – and 1838, so the year 1812 may seem exaggerated → Old Oscar Pepper Distillery started production in 1938, but it is probably correct that Elijah, Pepper's father, was one of the first to begin distilling in Woodford County, possibly in 1812. Master distiller Lincoln Henderson has kept a very careful eye on his barrels at the → Early Times Distillery where he is responsible for → Brown-Forman's production. Only the very best are selected for this whiskey called 'Distiller's Select'. The numbered bottles of the → small batch bottling are signed by Henderson and are bottled at 90.4%/45.2%.

Worm Term for an old form of → condenser that was customary in the production of whisky in (though they can still be seen at, for example, → Mortlach or → Speyburn). It enables the alcoholic vapours resulting from heating in distillation to return to a liquid state. The vapours are collected at the head of the → stills in the → lyne arm and then led downwards through a coiled copper tube, the 'worm'. The worm runs through a tub filled with cold water and the vapours condense to alcohol, which then runs to the spirit safe where the stillman decides what can be used and what will be redistilled.

Wort Term for a dirty-coloured, almost opaque and heavily sugared liquid which remains after → mashing. After the solid remains of the grain have been separated the liquid is collected in the → underback, cooled and then pumped into the → washbacks where yeast is added to it in order to begin → fermentation. At some grain distilleries the wort and the → draff are not separated. The plural worts is also used.

Wright & Greig Scotch blend from → UDV which keeps alive the name of an old whisky company which was once the owner of the → Dallas Dhu Distillery and was famous for its → blend → Roderick Dhu. It later became a subsidiary of → Bulloch Lade and therefore of → DCL, through whom UD received the rights to the name.

W Turkey Spanish whisky whose label merely states that the spirit is 5 years old and is 'elaborado en Espana'.

W W Beam Kentucky straight bourbon that does not come from one of the two distilleries of James → 'Jim' Beam, but from → Heaven Hill. This is not as illogical as it seems, as this distillery has always employed members of the Beam family since it was opened in the 1930s: at present Parker Beam is master distiller and it looks as though his son Craig will one day take over from him. Parker's father was their first master distiller and brought the yeast from the Jim Beam Distillery which is still used in Bardstown today.

X, Y, Z

Yamazaki Japanese distillery established in 1923 by Shinjiro → Torii, a wine producer, who used the profits from the wine trade to become the first whisky producer in the country. He employed another visionary, Masataka → Taketsuru who had gained his knowledge of whisky production in Scotland. He worked for Torii for 10 years before setting up his own company.

Torii chose a site to the north of Osaka for his distillery, on the outskirts of Japan's old capital Kyoto, a wooded valley which gave the plant its name, with excellent water. Three rivers, two from Kyoto and one from Nara, converge in the Yodowaga and its fluctuating temperatures ensure that there is always a cool, damp fog – ideal conditions for whisky.

Work is carried out traditionally but modern equipment is used. The use of variously peated malted barley and of differing yeasts makes it possible for the 12 → pot stills to produce a whole series of different malt whiskies. Yamazaki is described as 'a versatile and flexible distillery that can produce three different types of malt whisky: 1. full-bodied with a full taste 2. medium-bodied with a taste of ester 3. mild with a hint of cooked mash'. The whiskies are often matured in new oak casks, ex-bourbon casks are also used. Ex → sherry casks are very rarely used. Suntory has huge cellars elsewhere, but also stores casks at Yamazaki.

Japanese whisky producers call the → proprietary bottling a → Pure Malt, and not a single malt. The bottles may contain a share of Scotch malts (after all Suntory owns several distilleries in Scotland), but the company itself give no precise information on the matter. There are several versions of Yamazaki: the 12-year-old is the most easily obtainable (also internationally) and the 15-year-old at 57% and the very expensive 18-year-old in numbered bottles are also permanently included in their range. In addition there are special bottlings, often in very small quantities, such as a Pure Malt from 1990 at 56% from sherry casks, whose numbered bottles are signed by Master Blender Keizp Saji. His signature is also on the numbered bottles with no age statement but which show a strength of 58%.

Yeast Used when the → wort is to become → wash, it is important because without it the sugar gained from the starch of the corns of grain could not ferment. It is a matter of dispute as to whether it influences the character of the final distillate; sometimes the opinion is voiced that the yeast has more effect than the water. In many distilleries it is looked after just as carefully as the water source. Every distillery has its special yeast, and whilst one swears by brewer's yeast, the other has a special recipe for its culture. In American distilleries they are very proud of having a yeast chain that has often not been broken for years, or even generations.

Ye Monks Scotch blend that is particularly popular in Latin America. In Paraguay it is the best-selling blend of all and in Uruguay it has a 60% share of the market for → premium blends. It is sold in antique-looking stone jars. It is the creation of Donald Fisher, from Perthshire and set up a successful whisky business in Edinburgh in 1836. He laid particular emphasis on quality and he allowed his whiskies to mature, and for this purpose mainly used → sherry casks. He may in part be credited with the discovery of the blessed effect on Scotch whisky of good casks. The company lost its independence exactly 100 years after its foundation to → DCL, from whom → UDV have inherited it. They now only produce the → standard blend. Unfortunately the → de luxe

Yellow Label

blend called Ye Whisky of Ye Monks has been discontinued.

Yellow Label Scotch blend that now comes from → UDV but which was called 'Robertson's Yellow Label' and came from John Roberston & Son. The company was founded in 1827 in Dundee, and later moved to Edinburgh as a subsidiary of → DCL. Until 1991, when DCL's successor → UD sold the company to → Inver House Distillers Ltd, it officially held the licence for the → Speyburn Distillery and at the end of the 19th century also owned → Coleburn.

Yellowstone Kentucky straight bourbon which comes from an important name in the history of whiskey: Joseph Bernard Dant, the son of J W Dant and founder of the Cold Spring Distillery in Gethsemane, Kentucky. His whiskey was popular and was sold throughout the entire west of the country. In 1872 one of his salesmen came back from a trip and told him about his visit to the newly-opened Yellowstone National Park, and suggested using the name for a whiskey. Later he built the Taylor and Williams Distillery in Gethsemane and after → prohibition (during which the whiskey was allowed to be sold for medicinal purposes) he built the Yellowstone Distillery in Louisville. The distillery and the brand were acquired by → Glenmore in 1944. In 1994 → UD bought this company, but resold the brand two years later to the David → Sherman Company of St. Louis, who do not reveal where they get the whiskey from. There are two versions, both without an age statement, one at 86°/43% and the other at 90°/45%.

Yoichi Japanese malt distillery situated in the west of the northern island of → Hokkaido, a one hour train journey away from Sapporo. It is named after a small town and is sometimes also known as Hokkaido 'Yoichi' Distillery. Even from a distance it looks very Scottish, with grey stone buildings crowned by red roofs. The location was chosen by Masataka → Taketsuru, who established it in 1934 as he believed it combined the ideal conditions to enable him to apply the knowledge that he had learned in Scotland. There was good water, cold winters, peat was available nearby and barley grows on Hokkaido. At that time he had already been working at → Suntory for 10 years but left the company to set up on his own. He began with a business that later developed into → Nikka, and initially produced fruit juices to bridge the time until his own malt whisky was ready. He brought this out in 1940, exactly 20 years after his return from Scotland. The small → pot still which he installed can still be seen today.

The distillery has not altered much in other ways, although they hardly do any malting themselves any more and have increased the number of stills to 6. These are still heated with coal. The use of different yeasts and variously peated malt makes it possible to produce several types of whisky, some of which have a very intensive smoky, phenolic character. This is hardly surprising as two of the places where Taketsuru served his apprenticeship were → Campbeltown and → Lagavulin. The warehouses are also modelled on the Scottish prototype, and are unheated with the casks lying on earth floors. Ex-bourbon casks are mainly used, as well as charred new casks. Sherry wood is hardly used at all. Nikka has a 12-year-old → Nikka Pure Malt Whisky whose label also shows 'Hokkaido' as the place of origin, which points to it coming from this distillery, the second-oldest in the country. This is quite clearly the case with the single malt named Yoichi, which is available in four versions aged 8 years (only obtainable at the distillery), 10 years (only in Japan), 12 years old (all three 45%), 20 years old (52%) and also in various single cask bottlings, which were also all 10 years old and naturally were of differing strengths.

Yukon Jack Canadian whisky which states that it comes from a distillery of the same name, but actually comes from Heublein. It is bottled at 50% and proudly calls itself 'the black sheep of Canadian Liquor'. It is also available as a 'Permafrost' with a mint taste and 'a touch of cinnamon', and as a lemon-flavoured 'Snakebite'.

A Whisk(e)y Bibliography

With special thanks to John Thorne:

Malt Advocate, Quarterly since 1992, Published by John Hansell
Scotch Whisky Review, Biannual since 1994, Published by Richard Joynson
Whisky Magazine, Bimonthly since 1999, Editor: Charles MacLean, Published by Marcin Miller
Whisky Watch, Quarterly since 1997, Editor: Walter Schobert, Published by Werner Jannek
Allen, H. Warner: *Number Three 3 St. James's Street* London. Chatto & Windus 1950. 269pp.
    (about Berry Bros & Rudd)
Amis, Kingsley: *On Drink*. London. Jonathan Cape. 1972. New York. Harcourt Brace Jananovich 1973. 109pp.
Andrews, Allen: *The Whisky Barons*. London. Jupiter Books 1977. 148pp.
Angeloni, Umberto: *Single Malt Whisky. An Italian Passion*. New York. Brioni 2001, 138pp
(Introduction by Charles MacLean)
An Old Scotch House. Arthur Bell & Sons Ltd. Distillers Perth Scotland. 22pp.
Arthur, Helen: *The Single Malt Whisky Companion, A Connoisseur´s Guide*. London. Quintet
    Publishing & The Apple Press 1997, 256pp
Arthur, Helen: *Whisky, Uisge Beatha, Water of Life*. London, Apple Press 2000, 224pp.
    (with a foreword by Charles MacLean)
Baird, Bryce: *The International Whisky Connoisseurs Quiz Book*. Doncaster, Privately published 1995, 112pp.
Barnard, Alfred: *The Whisky Distilleries of the United Kingdom*. London, Harper's Weekly Gazette 1887, 457pp.
    Reprint with new introduction by I.A. Glen: Newton Abbot, David & Charles 1969, VII + 457pp. The
    Centenary Edition. With a foreword by David Daiches and an introduction by Michael Moss): Edinburgh,
    Mainstream in assocation with Lochar 1987, 457pp. Reprint with German and English foreword by
    Gunnar Kwisinski and Jens Sagemann: Osnabrück, 2000 Rasch edition 2000. 457pp.
Barnard, Alfred: *Royal Gordon Whisky. A Visit to the Scotch Whisky Stores of Messrs. Pattison, Elder & Co., and
    Glenfarclas Distillery, Glenlivet*. London, Joseph Causton & Sons 1893, 46pp.
Begg, Donald: *The Bottled Malt Whiskies of Scotland*. Edinburgh, Gyler Press 1972. 14pp.
    Extended edition 1979, 20pp.
Bell, Colin: *Scotch Whisky: Colin Bell's Famous Drambusters Guide*. Newtongrange, Langsyne 1985. 107pp.
Bénitah, Thierry: *L´ABCdaire du Whisky*. Paris, Flammarion 1996, 120pp.
Bénitah, Thierry (in cooperation with Jean-Marc Bellier & Emmanuel Dron):
    Le Whisky. Histoires et Fabrication. 96pp. *Le Whisky. Itineraireset Degustations*. 96pp. Paris, Flammarion 1999.
Bergius, Adam: *Make your own Scotch Whisky*. Wm. Teachers 1972 (?) Reprint: Glendaruel,
    Argyll Publishing 1995, 32pp. (Illustrations by Rowland Emett)
Bielenberg, Andrew: *Locke's Distillery. A History*. Dublin, The Lilliput Press 1993, 122pp.
Birnie, William, C.A.: *Notes on The Distillation of Highland Malt Whisky*. Compiled in 1937 and retyped in 1963.
    Auchterarder, A.D.Gardie & Son. Second Edition 20th June, 1964, 29pp.
Bond, Keith (i.e. Jimmy Brown): *Still Life. Memoirs of An Exciseman*. Inverurie,
    Published by author 1996. 47pp.
Booth, John: *A Toast to Ireland. A Celebration of Traditional Irish Drinks*. Belfast, Blackstaff Press 1995,
    Boulder (Colorado), Roberts Rinehart Publ. 1996. 119pp.
Bosanko, Abigail: *The Scotch Malt Whisky Society. An Honest Tale*. Edinburgh,
    The Scotch Malt Whisky Society, 2001, 16pp.
Brander, Michael: *The Original Scotch. A History of Scotch Whisky from the Earliest Days*.
    London, Hutchinson, 1974. 150pp. Revised edition: *The Original Guide to Scotch Whisky*.
    Over 20 years old still going strong. Whittingehame Haddington, Gleneil Press, 1995. 174pp.
Brander, Michael: *A Guide to Scotch Whisky*. Edinburgh und London, Johnston & Bacon,
    1975 (1977, 1978 repr.). 96pp.
Brander, Michael: *The Essential Guide to Scotch Whisky*. Edinburgh, Canongate, 1990. 173pp. 21992, 176pp.
The Brewery Manual and Who's Who in British Brewing and Scotch Whisky Distilling 1992.
    Hampton: Hampton Publishing Ltd. 1992. 248 and 31pp.

Brooks, Brian: *Whisky Dispensers & Measures.* Privately published, 2000, 33pp.
Broom, Dave: *Whisky. A Connoisseur´s Guide.*Carlton Books, 1998, 96pp.
Broom, Dave: *Handbook of Whisky. A Complete Guide to the World´s Best Malts, Blends and Brands.* London, Hamlyn, 2000, 160pp.
Brown, Gordon: *The Whisky Trails. A geographical guide to Scotch whisky.* London, Prion, 1993, 224pp. Revised 1997, 224pp. (with a foreword by Kingsley Amis)
Brown, Gordon: *Classic Spirits of the World. A comprehensive Guide.* London, Prion, 1995, 264pp.
Brown, Lorraine: *200 Years of Tradition: The Story of Canadian Whisky.* Markham, Ontario, Fitzhenry & Whiteside, 1994, 148pp. (published by Seagram Museum)
Brunschwig, Hieronymus: *Das distilierbuch. Das Buch der rechten kunst zu Distilieren unnd die wasser zu brennen.* Straßburg, J. Grüninger, 1515, CXXX sheets, 239 wood engravings.
(4th of book). *The Vertuose Boke of Distyllacyon of all manner of Waters from the Herbes etc.* London 1527. Reprint with a new introduction by Harold J. Abrahams: New York, London, Johnson Reprint Corp, 1971. cxx and 276pp. (The Sources of Science, No. 79)
Buchanan, John, Norman Case, Emery Gellert: *Scotch Whisky. The Single Malts.* Syndey, Project Publishing, 1981, 158pp.
Burke, Gerry: *Scotch on the Rocks. Illustrated True Story of Whisky Galore.* Glasgow, Lang Syne, 1988, 52pp.
Burns, Edward: *It´s a bad thing whisky, especially BAD WHISKY.* Glasgow, Balvag Books, 1995, 176pp.
Cantini, Patricia: *Whisky. The Connoisseur´s Companion.* London, Pavillon Books, 1999, 116pp.
Caol Ila Distillery 1846 - 1996. A Photographic Celebration. Port Askaig, Caol Ila Distillery, 1996, 56pp.
Capt. W. S. Smith - Grant: *Glenlivet. Where Romance and Business meet being the Annals of The Glenlivet Distillery founded by George Smith in 1824.* Glenlivet, 1924, 32pp. _1959, 41pp. (with illustrationens by George Mackie, for the centenary of production at the same site). 41966, 41pp (extra plate).
Casamayor, Pierre, Marie-Josee Colombani: *Le livre de l´amateur de Whisky.* Toulouse, Éditions Daniel Briand, Robert Laffont, 1984, 192pp.
Checkland, Olive: *Japanese Whisky, Scotch Blend. The Story of Masataka Taketsuru, his Scottish Wife, and the Japanese Whisky Industry.* Edinburgh, Scottish Cultural Press, 1998, 148pp.
Classic Malts & Gastronomie. Paris 1997. 72pp.
Collison, Francis: *The Life & Times of William Grant.* Dufftown, William Grant & Sons, 1979, 102pp. _1984._1987.
Cooper, Derek: *Guide to the Whiskies of Scotland.* London, Pitman, 1978, 121pp. Continued as *The Century Companion to Whiskies.* London, Century Publishing, 1983. 169pp.
Cooper, Derek: *A Taste of Scotch.* London, André Deutsch, 1989,. 128pp.
Cooper, Derek, Fay Godwin (Phot.): *The Whisky Roads of Scotland.* London, Jill Norman & Hobhouse, 1982, 160pp.
Cooper, Derek: *The Little Book of Malt Whiskies.* Belfast, Appletree Books, 1992, 60pp.
Cooper, Derek: *The Balvenie. A Centenary Celebration 1893-1993.* Dufftown, William Grant & Sons 1993, 52pp.
Cousins, Geoffrey E.: *A Family of Spirit. William Teacher and his descendants in the Scotch whisky trade 1830-1975.* Glasgow, Wm. Teacher & Sons 1975, 174pp.
Craig, H. Charles: *The Scotch Whisky Industry Record.* Dumbarton, Index Publishing Limited 1994. XVI + 659pp. (with contributions from R. E. B. Duncan, John R. Hume, R.K. Martin and Michael Moss)
Craig, H. Charles: *Glenpatrick House Elderslie. The Story of An Unsuccessful Distillery.* Glasgow, Ambrosia Books Ltd., 1982, 39pp. (Typescript)
Cribb, Stephen & Julie: *Whisky on the Rocks. Origins of the "Water of Life".* Keyworth, British Geological Survey, 1998, 72pp.
Crombie, James: *Her Majesty´s Custom and Excise.* London and New York, George Allen & Unwin and Oxford Press, 1962, 224pp. (The New Whitehall Series No. 10)
Crowley, Roz: *The Story of Irish Whiskey. Die Geschichte des Irischen Whiskey. L´Histoire de Whiskey Irlandais.* Clogroe, Blarney, On Stream Publications, 1993, 20pp.
Daiches, David: *Scotch Whisky - Its Past and Present.* London, André Deutsch,1969, 168pp. _rev. edition, 1978, 170pp. Paperback with a new foreword: Edinburgh, Birlinn, 1995, 192pp.
Daiches, David: *Lets Collect Scotch Whisky.* Norwich, Jarrold, 1986. Reprint 1994, 32pp.
Daiches, David: *A Wee Dram. Drinking Scenes from Scottish Literature.* London, André Deutsch, 1990, 200pp.
Darven, James: *La Grande Histoire du Whisky.* Paris, Flammarion, 1992, 216pp. English: *The Illustrated History of Whisky.* Suffolk, Harold Starke, 1993, 215pp.
Delos, Gilbert: *Les Whiskies du Monde.* Paris, 1998, 160pp.
Dewar, Peter Beauclerk: *The House of Dewar 1296-1991. The Fortunes of Clan Dewar.* London, Published by Author, 1991, 137pp.
Donat, Jacques: *1e Répertoire international de Mignonettes d´alcool.* Le Mée-sur-Seine, Éditions Amatteis, 1998, 192pp.
Dunnett, Alastair: *The Land of Scotch.* Edinburgh, The Scotch Whisky Association, 1953, 179pp.

Elder, Andrew: *The Whisky Map of Scotland.* Edinburgh, John Bartholomew & Son, 1976.
Euler, Barbara E.: *Whisky. Kleines Lexikon von A -Z.* München, Compact Verlag, 1999, 256pp.
Fielden, Christopher: *A Dynasty in Drink: The Suntory Story.* Holt, Trowbridge, Wine Source, 1991, 193pp.
Fleming, Susan: *The Little Whisky Book.* London, Judy Piatkus, 1988, reprint 1992, 60pp.
Forbes, George: *Scotch Whisky.* Glasgow, Lang Syne, 995, 92pp.
Forbes, R.J.: *Short History of the Art of Distilling.* Leiden, E. J. Brill, 1948, 405pp.
Frankham, Jill: *William Grant & Sons 1887 - 1987. 100 years of achievment.* William Grant & Sons, [1987], 12pp.
Gabányi, Stefan: *Schumann's Whisk(e)y Lexikon.* München: Heyne 1996. 368 S. (with illustrations by Günter Mattei). English: Whisk(e)y. New York, London, Paris, Abbeville, 1997, 367pp.
Gardiner, Leslie: *The North British: The First Hundred Years.* Edinburgh, The North British Distillery Company, 1985, 64pp.
Graham, Duncan & Wendy: *Visiting Distilleries.* Glasgow: Angels´ Share 2001. 121pp.
Grant, Elizabeth: *Memoirs of a Highland Lady. The Autobiography of Elizabeth Grant of Rothiemurchus afterwards Mrs. Smith of Baltiboys. 1797-1830.* Edited by Lady Strachey. 1898, London, John Murray, 1928, 427pp.(Various reprints)
Gray, Alan S.: 2001 *The Scotch Whisky Industry Review.* Annual report. Edinburgh, Ing Barings Charterhouse Securities, 2001, 224pp.(Unti1989: Campbell, Neill & Co, Glasgow, 1990-1992: Charterhouse Tilney, Glasgow, 1993-1999: Sutherland & Partners, Edinburgh, 2000: Charterhouse Securities Sutherlands).
Greenwood, Malcolm: *A Nip Around the World. Diary of a Whisky Salesman.* Glendaruel, ArgyllPublishing, 1995, 112pp.
Greenwood, Malcolm: *Another Nip Around the World.* Glasgow, NWP, 1997, 92pp.
Greenwood, Malcolm: A *Ramble round the Globe Revisited.* In the Footsteps of Tommy Dewar. Glasgow, NWP, 1999, 94pp. (Illustrations by Erik Foseid)
Greenwood, Malcolm: *Unique Distilleries of Scotland & Ireland. In the Footsteps of Alfred Barnard.* Greenwood Publishing, 2001, 148pp.
Grindal, Richard: *Return to the Glen. Adventures on the Whisky Trail.* Chevy Chase, Alvin Rosenbaum, 1989, 159pp.
Grindal, Richard: *The Spirit of Whisky. An Affectionate Account of the Water of Life.* London, Warner Books, 1992, 256pp.
Grinling, Jasper: *Spey Royal.* London, W & A Gilbey Ltd., 1960.
Gunn, Neil: *Whisky and Scotland.* London, George Routledge, 1935, 198pp.Reprints: London, Souvenir Press, 1977, 198pp. 1998, 192pp.
Gutzke, David W.: *Alcohol in the British Isles from Roman Times to 1996. An Annotated Bibliography.* Westport, Connecticut and London, Greenwood Press, 1996, 266pp. (Nr. 44 Bibliographies and Indices in World History)
Hanley, Clifford: *A Skinful of Scotch.* London, Hutchinson & Co., 1965, 174pp.
Harris, James F., Mark H. Waymack: *Single-Malt Whiskies of Scotland for the Discriminating Imbiber.* La Salle, Illinois, Open Court, 1992, 194pp.
Harris, Paul (ed.): *The Rhythm of the Glass. Drinking: Contemporary Writing.* Edinburgh, Paul Harris Publishing,1977. 88pp. (with contributions by Bill Tait, Alan Bold, George MacKay Brown, Jeremy Bruce-Watt, Duncan McAra, Stanley Roger Green, Ronald Shaw, Norman MacCaig, Cliff Hanley, John Broom, Donald Campbell. Etchings by Donald Mackenzie, photos by Barry Jones)
Harrison, Brian: *Drink and the Victorians: The Temperance Question in England, 1815 - 72.* London, Faber & Faber, 1971, 510pp. _Keele, Keele Univerity Press, 1994.
Hastie, S.H.: *From Burn to Bottle. How Scotch Whisky s made.* Edinburgh, Philip Gee for The Scotch Whisky Association _1956, 24pp.
Helenius-Seppälä, Matti: *Über das Alkoholverbot in den Vereinigten Staaten von Nordamerika.* Jena, Gustav Fischer 1919. 131pp.
Henderson, Richard: *Chasing Charlie.* Black Raven Publishers,1996, 424pp. (Story of dug up treasure of 1,000 bottles of whisky).
Hills, Phillip (ed.): *Scots on Scotch. The Scotch Malt Whisky Society Book of Whisky.* Edinburgh and London, Mainstream, 1991, 192pp. (with contributions by George Rosie, Trevor Royle, Colin McArthur, David Daiches, Alan Bold, Ruth Wishart, Derek Cooper, Russell Sharp, Hamish Henderson, Norman MacCaig, Phillip Hills).
Hills, Phillip: *Appreciating Whisky. The connoisseur's guide to nosing, tasting and enjoying Scotch.* Glasgow, HarperCollins, 2000, 191pp.
Hobley, L.F. *Customs and Excise Men.* London, Allman & Son, 1974, 80pp.
House, Jack: *The Spirit of White Horse.* Glasgow, White Horse Distilleries, 1971.
House, Jack: *Pride of Perth. The Story of Arthur Bell & Sons Ltd. Scotch Whisky Distillers.* London, Hutchinson Benham, 1976, 135pp.
House, Jack: *The Romance of Long John.* Privately published, 1982, 32pp.

Howard, Kathleen, Norman Gibat: *The Lore of Still Building. A primer on the production of alcohol for food and fuel.* (1st printing 1973) Fostoria, Ohio, Noguska, 1994, 194pp.

Hume, John R.: *Dallas Dhu Distillery.* Edinburgh, Her Majesty's Stationary Office 1988, 16pp.

Islay Malt Whisky Trail Passport. Bowmore, Ileach Teleservices, [1994].

Jackson, Michael: *The World Guide to Whisky.* London, Dorling Kindersley, 1987, 224pp.

Jackson, Michael: *Malt Whisky Companion. A Connoisseur´s Guide to the Malt Whiskies of Scotland.* London, Dorling Kindersley, 1989, 220pp. _1991, 240pp. _1994, 272pp. 4th revised edition 1999, 336pp.

Jackson, Michael and Harry Cory Wright (Photography): *Scotland and its Whiskies* London, Duncan Baird Publishers, 2001, 144pp.

Johnson, Tom: *The Story of Berry Bros. & Rudd Wine and Spirit Merchants.* Privately published, 32pp.

Jones, Andrew: *Whisky Talk.* London, Judy Piatkus, 1997, 152pp.

Keegan, Alan: *Scotch in Miniature. A Collector's Guide to Whisky Miniatures.* Gartocharn, Northern Book/Famedram, 1982. Revised editions 1986, 80pp. 2001, 91pp.

Kenna, Rudolph und Ian Sutherland: *The Bevvy. The Story of Glasgow and Drink.* Glasgow, Clutha Books, 2000, 126pp.

Kobler, John: *Ardent Spirits. The Rise and Fall of Prohibition.* New York, Putnam, 1973, London, Michael Joseph, 1974, 386pp.

Kochan, Nick and Hugh Pym: *The Guinness Affair. Anatomy of a Scandal.* London, Christopher Helm, 1987, 198pp.

Kroll, Harry Harrison: *Bluegrass, Belles, and Bourbon. A Pictorial History of Whisky in Kentucky.* South Brunswick and New York, A. S. Barnes and Company, London, Thomas Yoscloff, 1967, 224pp.

La Dolce Vita: *Whisky.* London, Cape Town, Sydney, Auckland, New Holland Publishers, 1999, 64pp.

Laing, Robin: *The Whisky Muse. Scotch Whisky in Poem and Song.* Illustrated by Bob Dewar. Edinburgh, Luath Press, 2002, 207pp.

Lamond, John D., Robin Tucek: *The Malt File.* London, Benedict Books, 1989, 136pp. 21993, 160pp.

Lamond, John: *The Whisky Connoisseur´s Book of Days. Facts, Fables and Folklore.* Whittingehame, The Edinburgh Publishing Company, 1992, 140pp.

Lamond, John: *The Whisky Connoisseurs´s Companion. Facts, Fables and Folklore from the World of Whisky.* Leith, The Edinburgh Publishing Company, 1993, 136pp.

Laurin, Urban: *Whisky fran hela världen.* Västeras, ICA Förlaget, 1998, 168pp.

Laurin, Urban: *Whisky fra hele verden.* Oslo, Landsbruksforlaget, 1998, 168pp.

Laver, James: *The House of Haig.* Markinch, John Haig & Co., 1958, 75pp.

Lerner, Daniel: *Single Malt & Scotch Whisky.* Köln, Könemann, 1998, VII + 184pp.

Lockhart, Sir Robert Bruce: *Scotch. The Whisky of Scotland in Fact and Story.* London, Putnam, 1951, 184pp. 7th edition: Glasgow, NWP, 1995, 192pp. (with a foreword by Robin Bruce Lockhart).

Lord, Tony: *The World Guide to Spirits.* London, Macdonald and Jane´s, 1979, 256pp.

Macdonald, Aeneas: *Whisky.* Edinburgh, The Purpoise Press, 1930, 135pp.

MacDonald, Ian: *Smuggling in the Highlands.* Stirling, Eneas Mackay, 1914, 124pp.

Mackenzie, Compton: *Whisky Galore.* London, Chatto and Windus, 1947, 264pp. Edinburgh, Canongate, 1999, 405pp. (in assocaion with John Dewar & Sons Ltd.

Mackie, Albert D.: *The Scotch Whisky Drinker's Companion.* Edinburgh, Ramsay Head, 1973,124pp.

MacLean, Charles: *The Mitchell Beazley Pocket Whisky Book. A guide to malt, grain, liqueur and leading blended whiskies.* London, Mitchell Beazley, 1993, 192pp. _revised edition: *Scotch Whisky.* London, Mitchell Beazley, 1998, 223pp.

MacLean, Charles: *Sainsbury´s Guide to Malt Whisky.* London, Sainsbury plc, 1995, 96pp.

MacLean, Charles: *Discovering Scotch Whisky.* Christchurch, Dorset and London, New LifeStyle Publishing Ltd., 1996, 96pp.

MacLean, Charles: *Scotch Whisky.* Andover, Pitkin Guides, 1996, 29pp.

MacLean, Charles: *Malt Whisky.* London, Mitchell Beazley, 1997, 176pp.

Maggee, Malachy: *1000 Years of Irish Whiskey.* Dublin, O'Brien Press, 1980, 144pp. Reprint: *Irish Whiskey. A 1000 Year Tradition.* 1998.

Mahé, Patrick: *La Magie du Whisky.* Paris, Éditions du Chêne, 1997, 184pp.

Maltmap, The. *A Full Colour Map of Scotland's Most Famous Malt Whiskies.* Edinburgh, Cheldon Press, 1991.

Mantle, Jonathan: *The Ballantine´s Story.* London, James & James, 1991, 65pp.

Martine, Roddy: *Scotland. The Land and the Whisky.* London, John Murray in association with The Keepers of the Quaich, 1994, 224pp.(Photographs by Patrick Douglas-Hamilton).

Martine, Roddy (text) and Bill Milne (photos): *Single Malt Scotch.* New York, Friedman/Fairfax Publishers, 1997, 164pp.

Maxwell, Sir Herbert: *Half-A-Century of Successful Trade. Beeing a Sketch of the Rise and Development of the Business of W & A Gilbey, 1857-1907.* London, Pantheon Press for W & A Gilbey, 1907, 85pp.

McBain, Stewart: *200 Years of Distilling Tradition*. Strathisla Distillery Keith 1786 - 1986. Keith, Privately published, 1986, 68pp.

McCall, Robert: *500 Years of Scotch Whisky. Scotch Whisky - The Quincentary 1494-1994*. Glasgow, Arts & Entertainment Publishing Limited, 1994, 106pp.

McCreary, Alf: *Spirit of the Age. The story of "Old Bushmills"*. "Old Bushmill" Distillery Company, 1983, 232pp.

McDonald, John: *Secrets of the Great Whiskey Ring*. Chicago, Belford, Clarke & Co., 1880, 308pp.

McDougall, John and Gavin D. Smith: *Wort, Worms & Washbacks. Memoirs from the Stillhouse*. Glasgow, NWP, 1999, 215pp.

McDowall, R.J.S.: *The Whiskies of Scotland*. London, John Murray, 1967, 164pp. 4th edition revised by William Waugh: 1986, 184pp.

McGuffin, John: *In Praise of Poteen*. Belfast, Appletree Press, 1978, 1988, 167pp. Reprint: 1999.

McGuire, E.B.: *Irish Whiskey. A history of distilling in Ireland*. Dublin, Gill and Macmillan, New York, Barnes & Noble, 1973. 462pp.

McHardy, Stuart: *Tales of Whisky and Smuggling*. Moffat, Lochar Publishing, 1991, 160pp.

McIvor, Doug: *Scotch Whisky. Top Single Malts*. London, PRC Publishing, 1998, 96pp.

McNeill, F. Marian: *The Scots Cellar - Its Traditions and Lore*. Edinburgh, Richard Paterson, 1956, 290pp. (various reprints).

Mehrlich, Klaus: *Whisk(e)y von den britischen Inseln. Eine Untersuchung der Industrien und der wirtschaftlichen Bedeutung des Whisk(e)y für Schottland und Irland*. Frankfurt a.o.: Peter Lang, 1997, 374pp. (PhD. Erlangen 1997)

Milroy, Wallace: *Malt Whisky Almanac*. Moffat, Lochar, 1986, 94pp. _1987, 120pp. (foreword by Kingsley Amis). _1989, 144pp. (foreword by John AR MacPhail). 5th edition: Glasgow, Neil Wilson, 1992, 144pp. (foreword by Sir Iain Tennant), 6th: 1995, 160pp. (foreword by Earl of Mansfield), 7th revised edition: *The Original Malt Whisky Almanac. A Taster´s Guide*. Glasgow, NWP, 1998, 160pp.

Milsted, David: *Bluff your way in Whisky*. Horsham, Ravette Books, 1991, 62pp. (various reprints). _London, Oval Books, 1999, 64pp.

Minnekeer, Bob, Stefaan Van Laere: *Whisky*. Tielt, Lanno & Haarlem: Schuyt & Co., 1998, 96pp.

Minnekeer, Bob, Stefaan Van Laere: *Mijn favoriete whisky´s*. Oostkamp, Stichting Kunstboek, 2000, 208pp.

Mitchell, Ewan: *A Wee Guide to Whisky*. Musselburgh, Goblinshead, 1999, 86pp.

Monzert, Leonrad: *Practical Distiller*. New York, Dick & Fitzgerald, London, Trubner & Co., 1889. Reprint: Bradly, IL, Lindsay Publications, 1987, 156pp.

Moore, Graham: *Malt Whisky. A Contemporary Guide*. Shrewsbury, Swan Hill Press, 1998, 160pp.

Morrice, Philip: *The Schweppes Guide to Scotch*. Sherbone, Alphabooks 1983, 413pp.

Morrice, Philip: *The Whisky Distilleries of Scotland and Ireland*. London, Harper Publishing, 1987, 369p. (with drawings by Peter Haillay. Limited edition of 1000 copies, printed for the centenary Barnard´s book).

Morrice, Philip: *Strathisla*. Decanter, October 1986.

Morrice, Philip: *Elixir of Edradour*. Decanter, January 1987.

Morrice, Philip: *Still Making Whisky*. Decanter, April 1987. (Glen Grant)

Morrice. Philip: *Glenfiddich: 100 and still going strong*. Decanter, May 1987.

Morrice, Philip: *The Oldest Dram*. Decanter, June 1987. (Glenturret)

Morrice, Philip: *Glenfiddich Centenary*. Decanter, August 1987.

Morrice, Philip: *Island of Charme*. Decanter, August 1987. (Isle of Jura)

Morrice, Philip: *Highland Maltsters*. Decanter, September 1987. (Glendronach)

Morrice, Philip: *Aladdin's Cave*. Decanter, November 1987. (Gordon & MacPhail)

Morrice, Philip: *Glenlivet Greatness*. Decanter, December 1987.

Morrice, Philip: *Inchgower's Measure*. Decanter, February 1988.

Morrice, Philip: *Take the High Road*. Decanter, April 1988. (Highland Park)

Morrice, Philipp: *The Missing Link*. Decanter, May 1988. (Linkwood)

Morrice. Philip: *Bonny Bowmore*. Decanter, June 1988.

Morrice, Philip: *Cardhu's Clever Package*. Decanter, September 1988.

Morrice, Philip: *Knockando*. Decanter, November 1988.

Morrice, Philip: *Speyside's new malt*. Decanter March 1989. (Tamnavulin)

Morton, Tom: *Spirit of Adventure. A Journey Beyond the Whisky Trail*. Edinburgh and London, Mainstream Publishing, 1992, 188p.

Morton, Tom: *Dropping in on Highland Park*. In: *Orkney Stories. A specially commissioned collection*. Perth, Matthew Gloag & Son Ltd., 1998.

Moss, Michael S., John R. Hume: *The Making of Scotch Whisky. A History of the Scotch Whisky Distilling Industry*. Edinburgh, James & James, 1981, 304p. Revised: Edinburgh, Canongate, 2000, 368p.

Moss, Michael: *Scotch Whisky*. Edinburgh, W & R Chambers, 1991, 91p.

Mr. Seager & Mr. Evans. *The Story of a Great Partnership*. London, Seager & Evans Co., 1963.

Murphy, Brian: *The World Book of Whisky*. Glasgow, London, Collins, 1978, 192p.
Murray, Jim: Irish Whiskey Almanac. Glasgow, NWP, 1994, 159p.
Murray, Jim: *Complete Book of Whisky. The Definitive Guide to the Whiskies of the World*. [London], Carlton, 1997. 224p. (various reprints).
Murray, Jim: *The Complete Guide to Whisky. Selecting, Comparing and Drinking the World´s Great Whiskies*. [London], Carlton, 1997, 256p.
Murray, Jim: *Classic Irish Whiskey*. London, Prion Books, 1997, 256p. (revised edition of Irish Whiskey Almanac).
Murray, Jim: *The Art of Whisky. A Deluxe Blend of Historic Posters from the Public Record Office*. Kew, PRO Publications, 1998. 80p.
Murray, Jim: *Classic Bourbon, Tennessee & Rye Whiskey*. London, Prion Books, 1998, 272p.
Murray, Jim: *Classic Blended Scotch*. London, Prion Books, 1999, 256p.
Murray, Jim: *History of Black Bottle*. Perth: Highland Distillers 2001. 22p.
Neish, Alexander B.: *The art of Peat cutting*. Bowmore, Ileach Teleservices Ltd., _1966, 17p.
Nettleton, J.A.: The Manufacture of Spirits as conducted at the Various Distilleries of the United Kingdom. Belfast, Marcus Ward, 1893 431p. Nettleton, J.A.: The Manufacture of Whisky and Plain Spirit. Aberdeen, G. Cornwall & Sons, 1913, XXIV + 606p.
Newman, Peter C.: *King of the Castle. The Making of a Dynasty: Seagram´s and the Bronfman Empire*. New York, Atheneum, 1959, 304p.
The North British. Edinburgh, Pillans & Wilson, 1960, 43p.
North British. *The North British Distillery Co. Ltd.* Wheatfield Road Edinburgh 1885-1935. 47pp. M. Nouet and Jean-Jacques Magis).
Nown, Graham: *Edradour. The Smallest Distillery in Scottland*. Whitley, Melksham, Good Books, 1988, 48p.
Nown, Graham: *Malt Whisky. A Comprehensive Guide for both the Novice and Connoisseur*. London, Salamander Books, 1997, 128p.
´Ole Bottleman, The: *Pub-Jugs and other Advertising Jugs with Price Guide. Book 1*.Barnsley, B.B.R. Publishing, 122p.
Pacy, Joseph: *The Reminiscences of a Gauger. Imperial Taxation, Past and Present, Compared*. Newark, 1873, 127p.
Parish, Woodbine: Two Reports of W.P., Esquire, Chairman of the Board of Commissioners in Scotland, on the subject of ILLICIT DISTILLATION in Scotland; - dated London 25th April and 26th April 1816 (ordered, by the House of Commons, to be printed 7th June 1816)
Pattullo, Diane, Derek Cooper: *Enjoying Scotch*. London, Johnston & Bacon, 1980, 112p.
Perry, Stuart: *The New Zealand Whisky Book*. Auckland, Sydney, London, Collins, 1980, 141p.
Philipson, John: *Whisky Smuggling on the Borders*. Newcastle upon Tyne, The Society of Antiquaries, 1991, 46p.
Piggott, J.R. [John Raymond], R.[Russell] Sharp, R.E.B.[Robert Erskine Burt] Duncan (ed.): The Science and Technology of Whiskies. Harlow, Longman Scientific & Technical, 1989, 410p.
Pyke, Magnus: *Science and Scotch Whisky*. Edinburgh, The Distillers Company, 1966.
Quigley, John: *King´s Royal*. London, Hamish Hamilton, 1975, 442p.
Ramsay, Stuart Maclean: *Single Sensation. So many Single-Malt Scotches but which dram do we drink*. Cigar Aficionado Vol. 7, Nr. 1, December 1998.
Ravier, Michel: *Whisky. Wissenswertes für Genießer*. München, Ballentine´s / Nathan International, 1984, 79p.
Reeve-Jones, Alan: *A Dram like this... The Gourmet's Guide to Scotch Whisky*. London, Elm Tree Books, Hamish Hamilton for William Grant & Sons, 1974, 122p.
Regan, Gary und Mardee Haidin: T*he Book of Bourbon And Other Fine American Whiskeys*. Shelburne, Chapters Publishing Ltd., 1995 364p.
Regan, Gary und Mardee Haidin: *The Bourbon Companion. A Connoisseur´s Guide*. Philadelphia, London, Running Press, 1998, 191p.
Report respecting the Distilleries in Scotland. Ordered to be printed 12th July 1799.
Report respecting the Scotch Distillery Duties. Ordered to be printed 11th June 1798.
Report from the Select Committee on British and Foreign Spirits. Ordered by the House of Commons, to be printed, 30th April 1891. London, His Majesty's Stationary Office, 1891, 151p._1908.
Riddell, J.B.: *Observations on the Scotch WhiskyProduction Cycle*. The Invergordon Distillers, 1976.
Robb, J. Marshall: *Scotch Whisky. A Guide*. London and Edinburgh, W. & R. Chambers, New York, E.P. Dutton [1950], 80p.
Ross, James: *Whisky*. London, Routledge & Kegan, 1970, 158p.
Rousies, Jean-Bastien: *L´univers du Whisky*. Paris, Solar, 143p.
Rudolf, Karl. *Malt, Scotch, Bourbon & Co*. Düsseldorf, Econ TB, 1989, 116pp. (Econ Gourmet Bibliothek)
Ryan, John Clement: *Irish Whiskey*. Dublin, Eason & Son, 1992, 24p.(The Irish Heritage Series: 71)
Scarisbrick, J.: *Spirit Manual*. (Historical & Technical). Burton-on-Trent, 1891, 152p. (Revenue Series No. 2)
Saintsbury, George: *Notes on a Cellar Book*. London, Macmillan, 1920, 228p.
    (Various reprints and editions 1920-1978)
Schobert, Walter: *Malt Whisky Guide*. Führer zu den Quellen. Weil der Stadt, Walter Hädecke, 1992, 161p. _1994. 175p. _1996. 184pp. 4th revised edition 2000, 197p.